The Critical Theory of Religion
The Frankfurt School

Religion and Reason 29

Method and Theory
in the Study and Interpretation of Religion

Mouton Publishers · Berlin · New York · Amsterdam

The Critical Theory of Religion
The Frankfurt School

From Universal Pragmatic
to Political Theology

Rudolf J. Siebert
Western Michigan University

Mouton Publishers · Berlin · New York · Amsterdam

BL
51
.S 5255
1985

Library of Congress Cataloging in Publication Data

Siebert, Rudolf J., 1927–
The Critical Theory of Religion, the Frankfurt School.
(Religion and reason ; 29)
Bibliography: p.
Includes index.
1. Religion – Philosophy – History – 20th century.
2. Sociology – Philosophy – History – 20th century.
3. Communication – Philosophy – History – 20th century.
4. Habermas, Juergen.
5. Frankfurt school of sociology. I. Title. II. Series.
BL51.S5255   1985   200'.1   85-21561
ISBN 0-89925-119-6 (alk. paper)

CIP-Kurztitelaufnahme der Deutschen Bibliothek

Siebert, Rudolf J.:
The critical theory of religion: the Frankfurt School : from the
universal pragmatic to polit. theology / Rudolf J. Siebert. – Ber-
lin ; New York ; Amsterdam : Mouton, 1985.
(Religion and reason ; 29)
ISBN 3-11-010729-5
NE: GT

Printed on acid free paper.

Dedication

In eschatological anamnesis of my beloved wife, Margaret
(†October 20, 1978), who being most competent in communicative
praxis never gave up hope in absolute justice. In interaction
with others Margaret achieved the highest: non-possessive
devotion. In loving recognition and mimesis of others Margaret
lived toward universal and ultimate reconciliation and
liberation.

Acknowledgement

First of all, I would like to thank Professor J. Habermas. He gave me the initial stimulation and incitation to think about a possible paradigm change in the Humanities and Social Sciences from work and tools, instrumental or functional rationality to the struggle for recognition, inter- action, intersubjectivity, practical, moral, communicative rationality, during our discourses at the Meeting of the Hegel Society of America at Villa Nova Uni- versity, Villa Nova, in November 1976 and in my international course on The Future of Religion in the Inter-University Centre for Post Graduate Studies, Dubrovnik, Yugoslavia, in April 1978. Our discourses provided me with new insights not only into Hegel's early critical philosophy and theology, but also in M. Horkheimer's, Theodor W. Adorno's and W. Benjamin's critical theory of subject, society, history and religion. I found in Habermas's theory of communicative praxis a legitimate continuation of the critical theory of the Institute for Social Research at the University of Frankfurt, Frankfurt a.M., Germany, on the basis of the new paradigm of mutual recognition, interaction and intersub jectivity.

I am very grateful to Professor J. B. Metz, Dr. H. Peukert, and Dr. E. Arens. They pointed out to me the aporetical aspects of the theory of communicative praxis and showed me a way to resolve them during our meetings and dis- courses in the University of Munster, Munster, Germany, the IUC, the University of Frankfurt, Frankfurt, Germany, Kalamazoo College, Western Michigan University, Nazareth College, Kalamazoo, Michigan, USA in 1981, 1982 and 1983. The resolution of the aporias of the theory of communicative action enabled me to strengthen it and to render it more invulnerable to genuine religious-metaphysical objections and thus to increase its impact upon the humanities, the social sciences, the science of religion, fundamental theology and critical political theology.

I would like to thank Reverend Michael Ott and his wife, Marie Louise, for working out with great diligence, industry and assiduity the bibliography and the index of authors. They also helped to edit the entire manuscript and to correct the English style and to free it as much as possible from all traces of the Germanic cultural heritage and thus make it most readable to American and British readers.

I am grateful to Ms. G. West, Secretary in the Departments of Philosophy and Religion, Ms. A. Browning, Secretary in the Department of Languages and Linguistics, and Ms. K. Billingsley, Secretary in the Department of Communication Arts and Sciences at Western Michigan University for the excellent work they did in typing the manuscript. I thank especially Ms. West not only for doing the lion's share of the project, but also for editing and correcting it. I would like to give my special thanks to the Faculty Research and Creative Activities Fund, Western Michigan University for supporting this work by a Fellowship for the 1980-81 academic year. It made it possible for me to spend the spring and summer semester of 1981 on this study.

I would like to thank the Maryknoll Fathers and Brothers Mission Research and Planning Department, Maryknoll, New York, for giving me the Walsh-Price Fellowship Grant. It made it possible for me to continue work on this project in the spring and summer of 1982 and to complete it in the spring and summer of 1983.

Finally, I am very grateful to Professor H. Kung, University of Tubingen, Tubingen, Germany, Professor J. B. Metz, University of Munster, Munster, Germany, and Professor G. Baum, University of Toronto, Toronto, Ontario, Canada, for recommending this study to the Maryknoll Fathers and Brothers Mission Research and Planning Department. They also assisted me with their excellent advice and encouraged me to complete this project.

Table of Contents

Introduction

The purpose of this study is to explore and critically
evaluate J. Habermas's theory of communicative praxis as the
most advanced stage in the development of the critical theory
of subject, society, history and religion, initiated and first
explicated and promoted by M. Horkheimer, Th. W. Adorno,
W. Benjamin, H. Marcuse, E. Fromm, A. Sohn-Rethel and others
in the Institute for Social Research at the University of
Frankfurt a.M., Germany, the so-called Frankfurt School. In
doing so, I pay attention particularly to Habermas's critical
theory of religion, which constitutes an integral part of his
theory of communicative praxis and of religion out of G.W.F.
Hegel's early critical philosophy and theology, M. Weber's and
E. Durkheim's sociology of religion, G.H. Mead's philosophy
and sociology of action and T. Parsons's structural-functional
system theory. I show that Habermas's theory of religion is
not conclusive. I challenge his thesis that traditional
mythical and religious- metaphysical worldviews have become
entirely obsolete, since they can no longer provide support
for social and personal identity in highly differentiated
modern action systems, characterized by increase in
contingency experiences and of future orientation.

It is my thesis that more is to be rescued from the
traditional religious-metaphysical and mystical systems of
interpretation and orientation than the practical communicative rationality underlying them and a corresponding universal
communicative ethics, expressed, e.g., in the golden rule,
intrinsic to all presently alive world religions. Habermas is
fully aware of the fact that the enlightenment tradition, in
which he stands like all other critical theorists, has failed
to console people in the face of the terror and horror of
nature and particularly of society, state and history. This is
equally true for the bourgeois, Marxian and Freudian
enlightenment. At the same time, Habermas knows that the
enlighteners were also not able to remove people's need for
consolation. That is indeed the dilemma of all enlighteners.
It is also the dilemma of Habermas's theory of communicative
praxis. It includes the demand for the enlightened to live
disconsolately. Unlike Hegel, the Hegelian on the Left,
Habermas, can no longer console the people who at the same
time are not willing or able to live in an inconsolable
condition.

In this study I do not only point to this dilemma in

Habermas's theory of communicative praxis, but also try to
overcome it. I penetrate to the very aporia underlying this
dilemma and try to resolve it in the framework of a critical
fundamental theology with practical intent, a critical
political theology. What precisely is this aporia? Habermas
is, of course, fully aware of the fact that all human
intersubjectivity is continually in danger of the one or the
other dying and being destroyed. Even the most undamaged
interaction or intersubjectivity is nevertheless continually
open to the absolute damage of the annihilation of the one or
the other. Even the most unconditional mutual recognition
between the one and the other can in any minute be rendered
utterly conditional by the destruction of either of them. Even
the greatest and most intimate non-possessive devotion between
the one and the other can suddenly end in the catastrophe
which strikes one of them. The rest is ideology! That
precisely is the aporia of Habermas's theory of communicative
action. Its central value is universal solidarity. But it can
be truly universal only if it includes also the innocent
victims which have been destroyed in the past without ever
having had their day in court: anamnestic solidarity. But such
solidarity with the innocent other who has been annihilated is
not possible, if history is closed: if really nobody can help
the dead man or woman. This aporia makes the theory of
communicative action disconsolate. It is to be overcome, if
the theory of communicative praxis should be saved from
turning back into instrumental rationality and from falling
victim to positivism and finally nihilism.

It is at this point where I relate the theory of communicative action to critical practical theology. I understand
such critical fundamental theology as hope of absolute justice
or as the longing that the murderer will ultimately not
triumph over the innocent victim. It is a theology of
communicative praxis, which is not hermetically closed up
against the horror and terror of nature and history. It does
not limit its discourse internally in such a way that the
problem consciousness of everyday life can not penetrate. It
does not hide behind fixed liturgical formulas, which repress
such problem consciousness and can precisely therefore console
the people as little any longer as the enlighteners. It does
not proceed with its back toward the innocent victims who have
been destroyed and with its face toward the always new future
into which scientific technological progress drives us with
great force and speed as we forget equally fast the innocent

other who has died. This critical political theology does,
rather, move with its face toward the innocent victims who
have been slaughtered on the terrible Golgotha which is
history, and with its back toward the future. In the context
of this prophetic and messianic theology I refer to experiences in the great oriental and occidental religious-metaphysical and mystical worldviews, which make possible the
assertion of a Reality, which can rescue the innocent victim
who has been destroyed. Such reference alone can render
invulnerable intersubjectivity, mutual unconditional recognition between the one and the other, mutual non-possessive
devotion in the face of the otherwise overwhelming negativity
of nature and particularly of history. In terms of this
theological reference communicative praxis must not end in
death, guilt and meaninglessness. It can transcend the
annihilation of the other. It can enable the survivor to live
meaningfully in the hope of absolute justice for the innocent
other who has been slaughtered and for himself: in the longing
that the murderer shall ultimately not triumph over the
innocent victim. He can continue to act meaningfully in this
memoria of the innocent other and in this hope. History is
open: the messiah can connect the innocent other who has been
destroyed with the kingdom of perfect justice. The survivor
can live with his face toward the innocent other who has died,
but who has also been resurrected and with his back toward the
future and thereby toward his own death, toward which he moves
unavoidably. The survivor can live meaningfully in anamnestic
solidarity with the innocent other who has been destroyed, but
who has also been rescued, and thus as his own annihilation
approaches can also hope for his own delivery. As the survivor
has thus come to terms with the death of the innocent other
and his own death to come, he can continue to live and act in
truly universal solidarity, which will not only be anamnestic,
but also anticipatory, including the victims of the past as
well as the children to come. In anamnestic solidarity he may
work to diminish human suffering for the future.

In this study I shall show that besides practical
rationality and universal communicative ethics and solidarity
there are other elements which can be rescued into a universal
pragmatic: Creation as self-negation, original sin, second
commandment, messiah, resurrection, redemption, eschatological
anamnesis, messianic mimesis, messianic impulse, messianic
realm, etc. In this study I try to make a contribution to the
resolution of the modern dichotomy which continues in the

theory of communicative praxis: The split between faith and
reason, redemption and happiness. I would like to contribute
to a new coincidentia oppositorum, a new coincidence, a new
conjugation of grace and communicative freedom.

The aporetical aspect of Habermas's theory of action
consists in the contradiction between the mutual unconditional
recognition between the one and the other on one hand and the
death of the other on the other hand. This aporia of not only
Habermas's universal pragmatic but the theory of action in
general has, of course, not been discovered first by
contemporary theology or philosophy. It has long been a
prescientific intuition in the every day life world. An
example may illustrate this: On December 27th, 1892, a simple
office clerk, Marie Elisabeth Kraus from Baltimore, Maryland,
USA, typed in a moment of leisure a poem which expresses quite
adequately the aporia of any theory of action. She may have
clipped out the poem from one of the daily newspapers
available at the time in Baltimore: The World or The New York
Herald or some other paper. Since Marie Elisabeth Kraus was
very much into composing poetry herself as well as into music,
she may very well have created the poem herself. In any case,
the poem has no title. But it could very well be entitled:
"The Death of the Other." The poem reads:

> The day will dawn when one of us two will harken
> In vain to hear a voice that has grown dumb;
> And morns will fade, noons pale, and shadows darken
> While, sad eyes watch for feet that never come.
>
> One of us two must some time face existence
> Alone, with memories that but sharpen pain;
> And these sweet days shall shine back in the distance
> Like dreams of summer dawns in nights of rain.
>
> One of us two, with tortured heart half broken,
> Shall read long-treasured letters thro salt tears;
> Shall kiss with anguished lips each cherished token
> That speaks of these love-crowned delicious years.
>
> One of us two shall find all light, all beauty,
> All joy in earth, a tale forever done;
> Shall know henceforth that life means only duty--
> O God! O God! Have pity on that one.

Of course, the fundamental theology, which discovers the _aporia_ of the theory of action — the death of the other — has itself its own _aporia_: the theodicy — understood as the justification of God in the face of the horror and terror of nature and particularly of human life. Also this _aporia_ of theology has long been anticipated in everyday experience and intuition. Every day life has long tried to find a resolution, if not theoretical then at least practical, to this theological _aporia_ in order to ward off despair particularly in the face of the death of the other. An example may demonstrate this point: the secretary Marie Elisabeth Kraus of Baltimore typed on December 27, 1892, not only the poem we entitled "The Death of the Other," but on the other side of the page also a story called "The Rain." This story is the attempt of an answer to the _aporia_ of the poem on the death of the other. The story is on divine providence and as such expresses the _aporia_ of fundamental theology and tries to resolve it at the same time. The story reads:

The Rain

A merchant, riding home from a fair, had a portmanteau with a large sum of money behind him. It was raining heavily, and the good man became wet through. He was annoyed at this, and complained very much that God had given him such bad weather for his journey.

His way led through a thick forest. The fierce winds, the black clouds, the sad sighings of the swaying trees, the snapping and clatter of dead limbs, the roll of the thunder, the gleam of the lightening, and the hissing and roar of the tempest filled him with fear.

As he approached a tuft of small trees for shelter from the storm, to his great terror he saw a robber standing there, who aimed his gun at him and drew the trigger.

He would certainly have been killed, but the powder had become damp with the rain, and the gun would not go off. He immediately gave spur to his horse, and happily escaped the danger.

When the merchant was in safety, he said to himself: "What a fool I was to complain about the

weather, instead of taking it patiently as a
providence of God! If the sky had been bright and the
air pure and dry, I should now be lying dead in my
blood, and my children would wait in vain for their
father's return. The rain at which I murmured saved
my property and life. In future I will not forget
what the proverb says: "What God sends is always
well, though why, 'tis often hard to tell."

What Marie Elisabeth Kraus tried to explicate poetically and,
to be sure, in a most childlike form, in her poem on the death
of the other and in the story about the rain we will try to
resolve more reflectively in the context of universal
pragmatic and theology of communicative praxis: The
contradiction between mutual unconditional recognition and the
annihilation of the other. Marie Elisabeth Kraus became the
grandmother of Margaret, to whom this book is dedicated, and
thus may very well be included into this dedication.
    I shall develop my study of Habermas's theory of
communicative praxis as reconstructive continuation of the
critical theory of subject, society, history and religion in
three chapters. Chapter I is concerned with the origin,
genesis, structure and consequences of the theory of
communicative action. The second chapter explores critically
the origin, structure, and consequences of the theory of
religion which is intrinsic to the theory of communicative
praxis. In the third chapter I shall try to resolve the
aporetical aspects of the theory of communicative praxis,
discovered in the previous chapters, in the framework of a
fundamental theology with practical intent, a theology of
communicative action, a critical political theology.

Chapter I
Theory of Communicative Praxis

In 1982 the critical journal, Der Spiegel, called Jurgen
Habermas the most powerful thinker in the Federal Republic of
West Germany(1). Other journals in West Germany have certified
that it is "carrying owls to Athens" to speak about Habermas's
significance for present discussion in the social sciences.
Habermas's real field is social philosophy. But he has
promoted rational discourse not only in social philosophy and
in the social sciences, but also in psychoanalysis, philosophy
of language, theory of evolution, education and even in the
science of religion and in theology. It is obviously very hard
to put such a very manifold and productive thinker under any
of the traditional labels.

To the people on the far Right, Habermas is a Marxist
suspect of class-struggle thinking. To people on the far Left,
Habermas is a late bourgeois intellectual engaged in the task
of ideological subversion. As senseless as these determinations of Habermas's position may be, they also show very
clearly the utter insecurity and uncertainty with which many
people on the Right and on the Left stand before the enormous
productivity of Habermas.

Without doubt, Habermas's highly differentiated mode of
thinking has something to do with this insecurity and uncertainty. It needs clarification. This is particularly true for
Habermas's attitude toward religious worldviews and systems of
interpretation of reality and orientation of action. The
particular aim of this book is to clarify and critically
evaluate Habermas's more recent position on religious
worldviews. This task can not be satisfactorily fulfilled
without taking into consideration the genesis of Habermas's
thought on religion. This again is an integral part of the
whole development of Habermas's theory of communicative
praxis, which has reached its full maturity in his most recent

book carrying this very title(2). We shall discuss Habermas's theory of religion as integral part of his philosophy of communicative action. It is Habermas's version of the critical theory of society, initiated half a century ago and further developed by the social philosophers M. Horkheimer and Th. W. Adorno in the Institute for Social Research at the Johann Wolfgang Goethe Universitat in Frankfurt, Germany, the later Frankfurt School of philosophy and sociology(3).

Philosophy and Politics

Habermas studied philosophy since 1949, first in Gottingen, Germany(4). For Habermas originally, philosophy was something completely different and independent from politics. Only later Habermas became one of the great German and European representatives of social philosophy. But, still in 1954, Habermas completed his philosophical dissertation about Schelling, completely in the spirit of the old apolitical philosophical tradition. A key experience was for Habermas the appearance of M. Heidegger's Introduction to Metaphysics(5). Then Habermas saw that Heidegger, in whose philosophy he had lived for some time, had given this lecture in 1935, two years after Hitler came into power, and that he had republished it again, unchanged, after World War II without the slightest word of explanation. This lack of explanation was what shocked Habermas fundamentally. This made Habermas aware of the fact that philosophy can not really be separated from political intentions. It can not and must not be hermetically closed up from the horror and terror of political history. Otherwise, like Heidegger's philosophy, it completely passes by the contemporary historical events which concern people most deeply in their relationship to society and state, and to their own immediate life world.

After this experience Habermas let himself be inspired by Lukacs's History and Mass Consciousness and by Horkheimer/ Adorno's Dialectics of Enlightenment, which indeed tried to do justice to social-philosophical attitudes as well as to the negativity of bourgeois society and history(6). Habermas's own first great book, Change of the Structure of the Public Sphere, intended to throw light on the political situation of the Federal Republic of Germany in terms of a social= philosophical mode of thought(7). Habermas analyzed the bad side of the German political system, the advantages of which seemed only too obvious to him. But Habermas recognized very

early and particularly in this, his first book, that there
were serious mistakes built into this system which in time
could become dangerous. In this, as in later books, Habermas
starts from the fact that the bourgeois society has indeed
high ethical ideals - freedom, equality, brotherhood, public
discourse - but that it itself does not realize them. And this
is so in spite of the fact that these ideals are legitimations
for the smooth functioning of the German social order. This is
a contradiction between values and social reality which
irritates Habermas until today: that this German society
guarantees ethical achievements which are written firmly into
its political constitution, but that this society, on the
other hand, constitutes a purely capitalistic society with all
its mistakes and weaknesses. Later on Habermas had the
opportunity to discover the same contradiction in other
capitalistic societies, particularly in the USA. In Hegelian
terms, Habermas is aware of the enormous discrepancy between
bourgeois society as mechanical state of necessity and
understanding and an organic state of reason and freedom, a
free political state(8).

Modes of Thought

The analysis of Sohn-Rethel and Muller have shown that Marx
characterized the thought achievements of people living and
working in the capitalistic system as "purpose-rational," in
the Weberian sense of the word(9). These thought achievements
make the capitalistic mode of production safe and secure. They
are formed through the abstractions which come about with the
development of capitalistic production and exchange.
Habermas states against this all too simplified Marxian
base-superstructure theory, that even in capitalism these
purpose-rational thought achievements are not the only mode of
thought and that also not all social relationships can be
reduced to them. Everything subjective, which shoots - in
terms of Bloch - beyond the capitalistic mode of production
and thought, the "more" of subjectivity, which has
nevertheless remained also in capitalism, falls necessarily
through the Marxian analytical network. Marx is right insofar
as he was interested in establishing the abstract social
average in order to point out how much men under capitalistic
conditions are objectivated, reified, alienated, instrumentalized, functionalized and commodified. Habermas sees all
this the same way Marx does: modern societies have paid the

undeniable successes in the development of the forces of production and in the realization of legal domination by pressing step by step all areas of life into the forms of economical and administrative functional rationality and by repressing forms of practical rationality. Habermas's whole social philosophy turns around this dialectics of instrumental and communicative rationality. Precisely because Habermas emphasizes practical rationality so much more than Marx, religious worldviews and their morality become so important for his social philosophy.

In any case, in Habermas's view practical rationality is still part of the capitalistic system. On this is based much of the relative optimism of Habermas's social philosophy. Of course, since communicative rationality is indeed repressed in capitalism, it must be activated. Precisely, therefore, Habermas can say rightly against Marx that he neglects the fact that even in capitalism people are still more than mere factors of production. The normative structures form themselves relatively independently from the economic production. Only that way the revolutionary processes, which Marx intended to initiate, are at all possible and explainable. They do explode the captivity also of consciousness by capital. This peculiar contradiction in Marx proves Habermas right, when he sees in the Marxian method an instrumentarium, which can grasp human consciousness merely according to the pattern of economic production. That is why Habermas is a Marxist who must necessarily go beyond Marx, without losing his roots in him. Habermas stands for a reconstructed historical materialism, which appreciates the revolutionary power of practical reason versus instrumental reason(10). Thus Habermas opens up new social possibilities for ethics and indirectly also for religion, which for him as for Kant and Hegel before, is a matter of practical reason. He opens up a new social chance for religion and theology even if this might not be his intent or may even run against his intent. After all, he wants to be a "real atheist - like Adorno."

Basis and Superstructure

Habermas was never able to accept the totality conception of the Neo-Marxists(11). Cognitively all cows, as Hegel already remarked against Schelling, are black in the night of totality. Habermas himself researches the two cognitive realms

of superstructure and basis, life world and system or
normative realm of freedom and technical realm of production
in a separate way. In this he stands completely in the Kantian
tradition. For Habermas the realm of the normative is of
greatest importance. This is shown particularly in Habermas's
reality analysis of the crisis phenomena in late capitalism,
in his book on legitimation problems of advanced
capitalism(12). Here the elements, which produce a crisis,
move up to the level of the so-called superstructure
phenomena, which then receive an inadmissible overestimation.
But always when a methodological conception should be
criticized, the opposite is exaggerated. This is also true for
Habermas's overestimation of the cultural superstructure
against Marx's overemphasis on the economic basis(13). But
against Habermas we must say, particularly in the light of the
just recently past economic convulsion of 1981-1983 which
affected all capitalist countries, that the economic problems
which produce a crisis are so evident that they can not simply
be deemphasized or even discussed or interpreted away. In
general the economic basis realm has greater relevance for
social processes than Habermas may sometimes want to have it
true(14).

But this "deficiency" in Habermas's social philosophy
opens, nevertheless, his eyes for the importance of the
cultural superstructure, not only for art, philosophy and
science, but also for religion. While Adorno and Marcuse,
whom Habermas greatly admires and rightly so, concentrated
their attention mainly on art, Habermas pays, like Horkheimer,
Benjamin and Fromm, much attention to religious systems of
interpretation and orientation. Particularly in his latest
book on the theory of communicative praxis, Habermas can
understand the evolution of modernity only against the
background of the great premodern religious worldviews(15).
But this appreciation of the importance of religious history
particularly for the problem of social and personal identity
goes back to Habermas's early Hegel studies(16).

Positivism

Since for Habermas the Marxian method was not entirely useful
and satisfactory for a social analysis of late capitalistic
society, he had to test, like Adorno before, the bourgeois
social-scientific methods for their usefulness(17). As he
worked his way through the different social-scientific

theory-perspectives in his book, On the Logic of the Social Sciences, Habermas noticed the insufficiency of these methods for an embracing analysis of bourgeois society particularly at two points(18). While Habermas, in the case of Marx, still noticed that his method was limited, since humans and their thinking were seen as objects - as what indeed they also were to a large extent in reality, namely, alienated men deprived of their subjectivity by social conditions - he could discover in the different bourgeois social-scientific methods that they were no longer conscious at all of the unnaturalness of these collective compulsions. They did no longer draw any possible subjectivity of humans into their calculations. They accepted the very lack of subjectivity as natural. That is very obvious in Skinnerianism or in the different forms of functionalism(19).

According to Habermas, the bourgeois social scientists accepted the social analytical method based on the missing subjectivity of humans as alone possible. They no longer reflected upon the genesis and use-connections of their theory. That men, in a most stupid manner adapted themselves to the capitalistic conditions, could simply not be changed. Nothing could be done about it. Finally in the different forms of positivism, as the metaphysics of what is at hand and factually given, so Habermas criticizes, following Horkheimer, Adorno and Marcuse, the stupidity becomes a method(20).

In spite of the fact that today positive theology very often gets along very well with the dominant positivism, the latter is nevertheless the archenemy of any messianic eschatological-apocalyptical religion and theology(21). It is therefore the very anti-positivism of the critical theory in general and of Habermas's theory of communicative praxis in particular which can gain new space for messianic religion and theology as, e.g., described by the critical theorist Benjamin, or the critical political theologian Metz(22).

In his discussion with the German structural-functionalist, Luhmann, in the beginning of the 1970s, Habermas, following Hegel, asserted against system theory, that it sees the whole of society as a soulless mechanical system(23). Here men are represented - in Kantian and Hegelian terms - as mechanically functioning parts of machines, under which the socialized humans can no longer be recognized. This is likewise true of T. Parsons's cybernetic human action system(24). The philosophy of language, with which Habermas has occupied himself preeminently by now for over a decade, was among all bourgeois methods positively decisive for giving his new theory its start, for his new paradigm of communicative praxis(25).

Philosophy of Language

It is certainly not surprising that the positive in the philosophy of language was recognizable only for somebody who -like Habermas- is obliged to the Kantian and the early Hegelian philosophy, which emphasizes language as well as work and tools, sexual love, struggle for recognition, and nation, and for which not all cows are black because of sheer totality(26). Thus it is noteworthy only for somebody for whom reason is not merely narrowed down to its purpose-rational aspect, but has also a moral-practical side to it. Kant was, after all, not only interested in the star-covered heaven above him, i.e., the knowledge of the object world, the world of nature, the world of things around men, but also and particularly so in the moral law in man, man's social world, the world of expectations, norms and values. Both realms of knowledge, the natural and the social world, and the ability of man to know them, were Kant's and Hegel's main interest. As Habermas reconstructed and reactivated this interest, he saw that neither the Marxist critical analyses, which criticized merely the capitalistically limited ability to know in the cognitive realm, the world of things, nor the bourgeois social sciences which lost the subject, altogether comprehended sufficiently the realm of moral-practical reason.

When men think and act merely and exclusively in a purpose-rational or strategic manner, then, so Habermas argues, alienation is of course complete and human liberation is hopeless. In spite of all other theoretical tendencies and movements, Habermas recognized, nevertheless, that the realm of moral-practical reason is still present, however distorted and unconscious, in the life conditions also of people living and working in the late capitalistic society, namely, in the communicative everyday praxis. That is obvious, e.g., in the present women's movement, ecological movement, and peace movement(27). Habermas was stimulated to recognize those fragments of practical rationality in people's life world by the philosophy of language in the Anglo-American world. Both realms of reason, instrumental and communicative rationality, are contained in every speech act which underlies the communicative understanding of socialized humans.

This part can be made plausible very easily. A speech act consists of two parts: In one part I give a message about something, which I have noticed in the world, and communicate it to somebody else. By communicating the message to somebody else I take up an interpersonal relationship. This is accomplished by the second part of the speech act. Here is an example: "I warn you, I have seen a bear over there in the forest." That I have seen a bear is a statement about the world of nature. With my expression about the world of nature I connect a truth claim. With the warning I take up a very definite interpersonal relationship to the other individual, which is based on socially recognized norms. In this part of the speech act we also recognize the interactive social rules, which can ultimately be connected to the whole social norm system, to the entire social world. With my expression about the social world I connect a claim of rightfulness. Both the moral-practical as well as the cognitive-instrumental rules are contained in each speech act at one and the same time. It is particularly via the philosophy of language, more specifically the moral-practical aspect of such speech acts, that Habermas's new paradigm of communicative praxis is open and sensitive for religious worldviews and systems of interpretation and orientation, and the practical-rational elements in man. That does not, of course, necessarily mean that Habermas is in agreement with any of the mythical, religious metaphysical or mystical worldviews.

Discourse

According to Habermas we can test the claims of truth and rightfulness which are contained in each speech act by means of a rational discourse(28). Such discourse is of course a very old arrangement. Since a long time discourse has been for humankind the medium of its social and cultural development. There have been religious, philosophical and scientific discourses. Jesus was a master of religious practical discourse and quasi-discourse, i.e., parables, stories, illustrations and examples(29). Socrates was a master of philosophical practical discourse on justice, love and immortality(30). Einstein did not discover the formulas of his new quantum physics in the laboratory, but rather in scientific theoretical discourse with his colleagues on walks through the Alps.

Against this historical background we can define

discourse in the spirit of the Frankfurt Institute of Social Research as future oriented remembrance of human suffering with the practical intent to diminish it. We remember August 1914 – beginning of World War I– and September 1939 – beginning of World War II – and we ask: when again? We try to intervene practically and technically in the economic causation of World Wars I and II in order to prevent the immense human suffering of World War III. We remember the first economic convulsion in modern capitalistic society in 1828 and all the following depressions and recessions up to the great depressions of 1929 and 1981. We try to break the iron logic of the business cycle practically and technically and to prevent without war the next larger economic crisis, with all its human suffering: for each new percent of unemployment four more percent of criminality, insanity, divorce, abortion, wife beating, child abuse, alcoholism, drug addiction and other social problems. Habermas continues emphatically the rational practical discourse in the tradition of the Frankfurt School(31).

According to Habermas in discourse the speakers can relate themselves to four worlds: The world of nature, the inner world of the subject, the social world and the cultural world(32). In speaking about these four worlds the discourse partners must redeem four validity claims: The truth claims in relation to the natural world; the claim of honesty in relation to the inner world; the claim of rightfulness in relation to the social world; the claim of tastefulness in relation to the cultural world. Habermas stresses in his conception of discourse the world of nature and the social world and the correlated validity claims: The truth claim and the claim of rightfulness. Sometimes Habermas speaks even of a fifth world: the world of language.

According to Habermas, discourse must rest on an ideal speech situation, since the real speech situation in late civil society is systematically distorted as communication under domination of the controlling bourgeois class(33). Discourse anticipates under conditions of systematically distorted communication the universal communication community. As such discourse is continual ideology critique, ideology understood with Adorno as false consciousness, necessary appearance, rationalization of irrational power structures(34). As such discourse is also mythology critique, mythology understood, in opposition to enlightenment, as the attempt to instill once more into the masses of people new fears and to make them once more into slaves of their fate: the absolute domination, not only of nature overimagined, but also more specifically of the exchange principle over the living laborer in late capitalistic society(35).

Discourse in the sense Habermas and the other critical theorists understand it can not be satisfied with formal logic. It is rather dialectical(36). As such discourse allows the extremes to mediate themselves through each other: universal and particular, collective and individual, religious and secular. Dialectical discourse is an argumentative process. It consists of arguments and counterarguments. It is driven by objections and counterobjections. It is decided by the better argument. Dialectical discourse can be innovative. It can produce new technical or moral norms in a new historical situation. Dialectical discourse becomes innovative in the face of irrational traditions and authorities. Dialectical discourse is critical in the sense of phenomenology - critique as clarification - and in the sense of historical materialism - critique as emancipation.

More specifically, according to Habermas, in discourse we think in the case of truth claims of natural scientific laws(37). We assert of these laws that they are true. In the case of discourse claims of rightfulness we think of social norms. We assume that these norms are right. Both types of claims must be tested and proven in rational discourse: the better reasons alone must prevail. Every member of society must be able to participate in this discourse. It must be at least potentially universal. In such a rationally led discussion everybody must have the same chances. The dialogical roles must be exchangeable. Everybody must be enabled to open up a discourse and to continue the dialogue in talk and countertalk. Everybody must have the same chances to set up assertions, to give explanations and to put them to discussion. Everybody must be able to express his feelings without fear of action compulsion or repression. There must be equality in that everybody has the chance to give orders, to resist, to give promises and to receive them, to give an account and to ask for such an account.

Obviously these conditions demand a new life form. Habermas connects this new life form with the great bourgeois ideas of truth, freedom and justice(38). We act in our present-day world as if this ideal life form had already been produced and established in the midst of systematically distorted communication. If we would not pretend this, no communication would take place at all. But that this is not the case, we can see in every court procedure or in discussions between workers and intellectuals. That we pretend there is such an ideal speech situation guarantees, in a peculiar way, that such juridical processes or discussions take place at all; that our society still functions at all.

Insofar as Habermas assumes that premodern religious worldviews have become obsolete in modernity, because they can allegedly no longer produce social and personal identity under the conditions of highly complex action systems, e.g., the USA or the Soviet Union, and their rising contingency experiences and future orientation, he burdens rational discourse with that task to constitute brotherly-sisterly communication community, which religion can no longer fulfill(39). This is the enormously high rank that Habermas attributes to rational discourse. Interaction and intersubjectivity mediated through rational discourse is the very core of Habermas's extremely complex social philosophy. Only such philosophical and social-scientific complexity can hope to master the enormous differentiation of the late modern system of human condition and human action system including culture, society, personality and biological organism(40).

Ideal Speech Situation

Habermas finds the ideal presuppositions for the presence of reason, instrumental and communicative reason, on the different levels of discourse in the ideal speech situation(41). It is, of course, only an ideal which Habermas assumes. It is not yet realized. Habermas assumes the realization of reason in its unity counterfactually. Here Habermas measures society, like Marx before, by its own ideals. He engages in inner criticism. He holds the mirror up to civil society. He shows bourgeois society that it has not yet realized its ideals: freedom, equality, brotherhood, rational public discourse. Habermas remains faithful to this, his methodological procedure - inner criticism - from his first to his last work: from Change of the Structure of the Public Sphere to The Theory of Communicative Praxis. Habermas applies the same method also to religious worldviews(42). They promise to establish social integration, brotherly-sisterly communicative praxis and communication community. But they do not do so under the complex conditions of modern action systems and their contingency experiences. Precisely that makes them obsolete. That is Habermas's main indictment against premodern religious systems of interpretation of reality and orientation of action. They find their mirror in Habermas's critical theory of religion: the bishop says to his diocese, we are a family. But there is no real family. There is merely much economically conditioned alienation.

Also Habermas's conception of the changeability of civil society has never changed throughout his work: the bourgeois ideals – brotherhood, freedom, equality, justice for all, and rational public discourse – have been betrayed by capitalistic society and can no longer be retrieved by bourgeois society. They can be realized only in humanistic socialism. Therefore Habermas is committed to socialism. Only a socialistic society can be a society of reason and freedom. Habermas shares with Hegel the idea that only a future post-bourgeois society can realize the ideals of the previous bourgeois society(43). Habermas was only after going through the Marxian theory able to make fruitful for us socially the Kant and the Hegel of the bourgeois enlightenment. Habermas wants to bring about, against the opposition from the far Left and the far Right, through enlightenment as the attempt to free people from their fears and to make them into masters of their fate, a society of reason and freedom. We may call it in opposition to Future I – the totally technocratic and administered society, and to Future II – conventional and ABC (atomic, biological, chemical) wars, the Future III – the reconciled society, the brotherly-sisterly communication community, the victimless society, the society characterized by communication without domination, free mutual recognition of equal men and women, undamaged intersubjectivity and non-possessive devotion(44).

Thus Habermas intends to fight in late capitalistic society for the positions of the enlightenment. Like Horkheimer and Adorno, Benjamin and Lowenthal, Marcuse, Fromm and Sohn-Rethel, also Habermas unites in his critical theory the bourgeois, Marxian and Freudian enlightenment(45). Such enlightenment positions may, but must not necessarily be in opposition to prophetic messianic religion and theology. The dialectic of enlightenment – bourgeois enlightenment turning into guillotine, positivism and fascism, Marxian enlightenment into Stalinism, Freudian enlightenment into Pavlovianism and Skinnerianism – seems to indicate a need for correction. Messianic religion, having come home to itself from its self-alienation in feudal and bourgeois religion, could very well take over such a corrective role. Certainly in Benjamin's

critical theory, Jewish messianism plays a corrective role
versus the historical materialism represented by his friend,
Brecht(46). Such a messianic corrective we find also in
Adorno's critical theory(47). Neither is it missing in
Habermas's critical theory(48). Without the perspective of
redemption, latent as it may very often be, Habermas could not
have continued the critical theory of Adorno and Horkheimer,
Benjamin and Marcuse, Lowenthal, Fromm and Sohn-Rethel, so
ingeniously as he does, not even through the new paradigm of
communicative praxis(49). This paradigm is as powerful as it
is because of the remembrance of the Jewish-Christian
messianic, eschatological-apocalyptic brotherly-sisterly
communication community which it not only negates, but also
dialectically preserves and elevates: the early Christian
koinonia(50).

Misery and Protest Potential

As the fast spreading of his international reception in the
West and the East shows, Habermas has in the past decade
become one of the most influential figures in philosophy and
social sciences(51). The progression and the direction of
development of Habermas's works are already seen as proper
indicators in order to determine the position of the critical
theory of subject, society, history, art and religion. The
reason for this broad international reception is not, as
neo-conservative critics assume, Habermas's appeal to the
familiar images of sin and salvation as presented by Luther or
to the subconscious impact of these archetypes as discovered
by Jung(52). It is rather due to Habermas's insistence on the
human protest potential in the face of the misery of late
capitalistic society(53).

It is the great historical accomplishment of the
bourgeois thinkers from Descartes and Hobbes over Voltaire and
Turgot, Locke and Adam Smith to Kant, Fichte and Hegel, that
in the face of the immense destruction which the enfolding of
positive science, technology and capitalism caused for the
social order - in the face of the immense suffering of
innocent victims which it brought about in Europe and America
and then in the rest of the world, in the face of the distress
and misery of the overwhelming majority of mankind - they did
nevertheless consider the way of the bourgeoisie dialectically
as a way out of this same misery which the bourgeoisie itself
produced(54). They developed this bourgeois way rationally in

thought against the reactionary powers on the Right as well as against the powerlessly despairing dreamers on the Left. They consciously stood already on the position which Marx took from an economically and socially more developed situation and therefore also from a theoretically higher point of view. Hegel taught in his philosophy of law and religion, that whoever takes the cross of the contradictory present upon himself can pluck the rose of reason(55). Thus Marx wrote less mystically in his The Misery of Philosophy in 1847, that it is the "bad side," which calls into life the movement which makes history(56). The negative side does this by producing the necessary protest potential and conflict through which the instrumentalization, functionalization, reification, alienation of people by people and thus their misery can be overcome. It was the bad side of feudalism which produced the conflict out of which the bourgeoisie developed. It is the negative side of capitalism which mobilizes the proletarian protest potential and ignites the conflict out of which socialistic societies arise.

Habermas continues this great tradition of critical bourgeois and Hegelian-Marxian thought in his philosophy of communicative praxis by identifying the bad side of bourgeois modernization, its pathology, caused by a onesidedly developed and as such alienated instrumental or functional rationality, and its barbarous injustices and the protest and conflict potential which this pathological and unjust situation produces in late capitalistic society(57). This protest and conflict potential may make a difference in late capitalistic society, in direction of a post-bourgeois society, in which man is no longer a functionalized and as such degraded being, but is, in Kantian and Hegelian terms, self-purposive and as such autonomous and free. Habermas acknowledges the religious aspects of this protest and conflict potential(58).

Foundation Problems

Habermas's newest book, Theory of Communicative Action, is an attempt at a philosophical foundation of critical social theory(59). In an epoch in the evolution of science which is characterized by progressing differentiation and departmentalization of embracing philosophical perspectives to realms of competence and research of particular disciplines, this is a gigantic enterprise. This is so, since in the sphere of theoretical categories of philosophy and the sciences, the

division of labor has produced immense masses of theories. The
intellectual penetration of these masses of theories demands a
corresponding measure of scientific work. It was always
Habermas's intent and effort to keep in mind the possibility
of a philosophical reflection, at least in principle, and of
its significance as corrective for the empiricistic
self-assurance and arrogance of the positive social sciences.
They are sure that e.g., religion is good as a means of social
control, but they deny its truth claim(60). Sometimes the
sciences tend to inflate their knowledge into a new
religion(61). Habermas's philosophical reflection makes it at
least possible again, that in rational discourse the religious
truth claim can once more be discussed scientifically in order
then to be affirmed or rejected with good reasons. That is
certainly an advantage! Even when Habermas comes up with the
thesis that religious worldviews have become obsolete, we can
ask him for good reasons why this is so. That is no longer the
case in many of the positivistic social sciences.

The theoretically decisive progress in his effort to
remember the possibility of corrective philosophical
reflection was Habermas's penetration into the discourse on
the foundation problems of the modern theory of science, and
particularly the language-analytical philosophy in the 1970s.
That is one of the important categorical dimensions in
Habermas's thought. At the same time Habermas was able to
preserve critically the beginnings of his philosophical
thinking - particularly Kant's Critique of Pure Reason,
Critique of Practical Reason and Critique of Judgment, Hegel's
"Modes of Treatment of the Natural Law" in the Critical
Journal of Philosophy, edited by Schelling and Hegel, and
Hegel's Jena System Designs I, II, III and his Science of
Logic(62). Habermas remained faithful also, at least in
principle, to the critical theory of society as developed by
Horkheimer, Benjamin, Adorno, Marcuse, Fromm, Lowenthal,
Sohn-Rethel and others(63). Habermas gives a future to Kantian
and Hegelian thought and critical theory particularly by
critically negating, but also preserving and elevating them in
terms of his new paradigm of communicative praxis(64). Kantian
and Hegelian thought and critical theory constitute another
categorical dimension in Habermas's thinking.

His philosophical roots protect Habermas from a characteristic narrowing down of the philosophical perspective. They
let, e.g., that perspective, which makes the two positions in
the so-called positivism struggle in German sociology of the

1960s, between Adorno and Popper, as they run against each other or pass by each other like two ships in the night, appearing as masked and therefore falsely antithetical(65). In Habermas's view, in the meantime both positions have become useless as specifically limited ones for fundamental philosophical discourse. Nevertheless, the different perspectives of these positions must, besides many others, be superseded, corrected, and newly reformulated in the concept of an embracing practical rationality: in terms of language-mediated struggle for recognition(66). Habermas does this for Adorno's perspective in his theory of communicative praxis(67).

The third categorical dimension of his thinking disclosed itself to Habermas about a decade ago in his famous controversy with Luhmann's structural-functional system theory(68). It left behind important traces in his philosophy and sociology. It helped Habermas to penetrate finally Parsons's structural-functional system theory, which no critical theorist had done before him(69). The encounter with both forms of system theory, the German and the American one, made it possible for Habermas to sharpen further his critical theory of subject, society, history and religion(70). It enabled him to differentiate further between religion as systemic structure serving the functional requirements of pattern maintenance and integration on the one hand, and of messianic religion in terms of Jewish or Christian mysticism on the other(71).

On this theoretical and in a certain sense biographical basis, Habermas designs his new conception of communicative action. First of all he determines function and scope of the categories of rationality and action. In both respects Habermas receives critically the results of the theory of science and of sociology. Habermas broadens the foundations of the theory of action with the help of language-analytical and social-psychological categories into a new theory of communicative praxis.

Precisely in this process happens what in the philosophy of science is called a change of paradigm. It is an - in principle - different mode of perspective on the realm of problems, which corresponds with the systematization of another fundamental conceptualization of description. Habermas no longer conceives of action according to the Cartesian or Kantian model of a lonely subject entering a relationship with other subjects and the world(72). Habermas reconstructs, rather, action-theoretically inside the science-logically preestablished framework a complex social activity. In this activity among the members of a society, a symbolically, i.e., primarily linguistically structured social intersubjectivity constitutes itself. Only through this, so to speak, objectivated cate- gory, Habermas can comprehend adequately the formation of an individual identity, of a singular subject able to act: to speak, to work, to love, to struggle for recognition.

For Habermas, as for Hegel before, the conception of a singular personal identity presupposes the particular social identity and the universal cultural, especially religious identity - or its substitute - a universal communicative ethics developed, sustained and stabilized in rational discourse(73). Hegel's notion, the peak and summary of his logic - the dialectical unity of universal, particular and singular - has been the guiding force for his dialectical philosophy as well as the guiding principle for Horkheimer's and Adorno's critical theory and remains this also for Habermas's theory of communicative praxis(74).

With the thus grounded basis of a theory of communicative action, Habermas gains the <u>agens</u> for the enfolding of the social-theoretical categories for the conception of a life world, in which speaking, working, loving and recognition-demanding and -giving individuals live with each other and experience each other. Out of the perspective of structural-functional theories, Habermas posits against the life world a model of human condition as system(75). In the human action system as subsystem of the system of human condition as conceived by Parsons and Luhmann the introspection of socially integrated individuals does not play any role(76). The social scientists describe it from outside as a functioning totality, in terms of the positivistic rules of phenomenalism, nominalism, value freedom and quasi-natural science methodology.

Habermas promotes the development of those two conceptual strategies - life world and system - for the description of society by means of wide-reaching conceptual-logical, historical and theory-historical analyses. He explores the great philosophical designs which in this century Durkheim, Mead, Weber and Parsons have presented for his complex of problems(77). Against the background of Hegel's potentials of language, work, family, recognition and nation, Habermas develops these designs often far beyond the boundaries of their original theoretical scope and relates them to each other. The way of Habermas's thought leads him through a gigantic realm of theory and history to the construction of a philosophy of society, which executes a precise analysis of the problematic relationships and dependencies between system and life world.

Thus Habermas develops a grandiose dialectical image of the human enterprise called modernity. It connects the presentation of the historical unbinding of an immense potential of rationality with a ghostly pathogenesis of the present. Habermas shows how the life world of concrete speaking, working, loving and recognition-aspiring and -granting individuals is presently colonized, so to speak, by the abstract functional requirements and imperatives of the cybernetic human action system: pattern maintenance and tension management, integration, goal attainment and adaptation. Human life is overcome by the dead world of technology, bureaucratic organization and monetarization.

Habermas's theory of communicative praxis is the result of a precise science-logical enfolding of social theory. It is not merely the substratum of a moral feeling, which searches for the consensus of sympathy and thereby ruins its philosophical concern. Habermas's theory of communicative praxis finally flows into the conception of a new stage of the critical theory of society, including a critical theory of religion. It makes manifest its humanistic motive: that impulse of the occidental enlightenment, particularly the Kantian, Hegelian, Marxian and Freudian philosophy, which searches for ways to mitigate at least Future I – the totally technocratic, bureaucratic, monetarized one-dimensional society, to avoid under all circumstances Future II – thermonuclear war, and to promote and realize Future III – the reconciled society, the brotherly-sisterly communication community.

Rationality

As Habermas's new book, Theory of Communicative Praxis, serves the clarification of the foundations of a critical theory of society, the fundamental notion of communicative action discloses the entrance to three systematic complexes(78). These three complexes are interconnected with each other. The three complexes are: (1) the notion of communicative rationality, (2) a two-level conception of society, which connects the paradigms of action in life world and system, and (3) a new theoretical start, which explains the paradoxes of modernity by showing the actual subordination of the communicatively structured life world under the functional requirements and imperatives of independent, boundary maintaining, formally organized human action systems, e.g., the USA or Canada or East or West Germany or the Soviet Union or Poland.

In the introduction to the Theory of Communicative Praxis, Habermas lays the foundation for his thesis, that the problematic of rationality does not come from outside into social philosophy or sociology. It rather breaks into the open out of the inner structure not only of social philosophy but also of sociology. For every sociology with the ambition to be a real embracing theory of society the problem of the use of a notion of rationality with normative content posits itself on three levels at the same time. Such a sociology can not possibly avoid the connection among (1) the meta-theoretical question of the rationality-implications of the fundamental notions of action, and (2) the methodological question of the rationality-implications of a meaning-understanding entrance to the social world and its objects, and (3) the empirical question in which sense the modernization of a society can be described as rationalization, the word used in the Weberian sense(79). These three questions offer Habermas guidance for a systematic appropriation of the history of social-philosophical and sociological theory, since Hegel's great dialectical philosophy of reason and freedom(80).

For Habermas theory-historical reconstructions have the great advantage that they help him to move freely among action-theoretical categories, theoretical assumptions and illustratively used empirical evidences. Furthermore, such reconstructions have the advantage that they enable Habermas at the same time to hold on to his fundamental problem as reference point: how the capitalistic modernization can be comprehended as a process of onesided instrumental rationalization. Habermas tries to overcome the pathological functionalistic onesidedness of bourgeois modernization by complementing it with his new paradigm of practical, communicative rationality, communicative action and brotherly= sisterly communication community in the framework of the global capitalistic dominion of unbrotherliness and unsisterliness. In Hegelian terms Habermas makes the courageous attempt to subordinate the in modernity hypertrophied realm of work and tool under the in modernity atrophied dimensions of language and struggle for recognition(81).

According to Habermas, Weber's theory of rationalization extends on one hand to the structural change of religious worldviews and the cognitive potential of the differentiated value spheres of morality, art and science. It extends on the other hand to the selective pattern of capitalistic moderniza- tion. The aporetic course of the neo—Marxian reception of the Weberian rationalization thesis from Lukacs to Horkheimer and Adorno show Habermas the limits of the consciousness- theoretical starting point and the reasons for the necessity of a paradigm change from work to recognition, from purpose activity to communicative action, from instrumental action to brotherly—sisterly communicative praxis, from functional to communicative rationality. It necessitates for Habermas his recourse to Hegel's "materialistic" Jena System Designs I and III: his move from neo—Marxism over Hegel to Marx. With this move Habermas is in full agreement with Western Marxism, which always was able to retrieve the philosophical substance of historical materialism only for the price of the recourse to Hegel's historical idealism(82).

In this light Mead's communication—theoretical foundation of the social sciences and Durkheim's sociology of religion come together in such a way that the notion of the ling- uistically—mediated, norm—guided interaction up to the point of mutual unconditional recognition among equal persons can be explained in the sense of a conceptual genesis. The idea of making the Sacred into a matter of language — the linguification of the Holy — presents itself to Habermas as the perspective in which Mead's and Durkheim's assumptions converge in the rationalization of the life world of speaking, working, loving and mutually recognizing persons.

On the basis of Parsons's development of theory, Habermas analyzes the problem of the connection of system and action— theoretical fundamental notions or life world categories. Habermas takes, as Parsons before, Weber's theory of action as theoretical starting point in order to present the formal— pragmatic beginning of his theory of intersubjective, communicative action. Thus Habermas develops the originally phenomenological conception of the everyday life world(83). He traces the evolutionary trend down the modernization process to the original uncoupling of system and life world to the extent that he can reformulate Weber's thesis of rational- ization and can now apply it to the present conditions in the advanced capitalistic action system.

In the final considerations of his new book, Theory of Communicative Praxis, Habermas brings together the theory-historical and the systematic explorations of his research. Here Habermas opens up to examination his proposed interpretation of modernity by discussing tendencies of legalization in late capitalistic society. Here also Habermas makes more precise the tasks, which a critical theory has to face today, ten years after the death of Horkheimer and fourteen years after the death of Adorno(84). Habermas's theory of communicative praxis is a continuation of the critical theory of the Frankfurt School via the fundamentally Hegelian paradigm of the struggle for recognition between master and servant to the point of communicative praxis and communication community mediated by language and anamnesis(85).

Hegelian Foundation

Long before Habermas concerned himself intensely with the philosophy of language and the social philosophy and sociology of Weber, Durkheim, Mead and Parsons, he developed the roots of his own social philosophy and sociology of communicative praxis out of Hegel's and Schelling's Critical Journal of Philosophy, and Hegel's Jena System Designs(86). In the Critical Journal of Philosophy, for Habermas's social philosophy and sociology of communicative praxis, of greatest importance was Hegel's article on "Modes of Treatment of the Natural Law"(87). In the Jena System Designs, for Habermas, of greatest significance were Hegel's thoughts on the potentialities of language, work and tools, possession and family, struggle for recognition(88).

In his social philosophy and sociology of communicative praxis, Habermas traces Hegel's concepts of language, work, sexual love, struggle for recognition and nation through the latter's own mature philosophy, Marx's historical materialism, the philosophy of language, the critical theory of the Frankfurt School and the bourgeois sociologies of Weber, Durkheim, Mead and Parsons. Habermas finds traces of Hegel's philosophy of language, work, love, recognition and nation in all these critical and bourgeois social philosophies and sociologies. Habermas collects and brings home into his theory of communicative praxis all these Hegelian elements. As Habermas transcends Hegel and these post-Hegelian theorists and theories, on the Left and the Right, he also assimilates from them whatever they have to say on their own, about language, work, love, recognition and nation so that it may help and strengthen the development of his own paradigm shift from work and tool to struggle for recognition, instrumental rationality and action to communicative rationality and praxis. In this whole assimilation process Habermas remains, nevertheless, faithful to his roots in Hegel's treatment of natural law and his Jena System Design I and II - his characterization of the potentials of language, work, love, recognition and nation. These potentials guide Habermas throughout his philosophical work as once they gave direction to Hegel as he developed the foundations of his philosophy and explicated them. In this sense Habermas does indeed remain a Hegelian, no matter how critical he is at the same time of Hegel's logical presuppositions and his final system: He is a Hegelian on the Left, in the tradition of the Young Hegelians(89).

Like Marx before Habermas pushes himself off critically particularly from the mystical-theological aspects of Hegel's philosophy of the natural law and his Jena system designs(90). But these superseded theological elements do nevertheless guide Habermas as he moves critically through the Hegelian and post-Hegelian philosophy and sociology of religion. While these mystical elements are often latent in Habermas's almost continual discussions of religious worldviews and lifestyles, they do nevertheless surface here and there and that the more so the more his theory of communicative praxis matures(91). We shall concentrate in this essay on the religious dimension of Habermas's social philosophy and sociology of communicative praxis and in this dimension again on these mystical elements. They seem to us of greatest importance for the further development of Habermas's critical theory of communicative praxis: particularly for the resolution of its intrinsic aporia(92).

Habermas had in the very beginning of his philosophical life a controversy with Horkheimer concerning precisely the theological dimension of the critical theory: he was charged with neglect of this dimension. Since this time Habermas has often been criticized for his insensitivity for religious and theological issues. This criticism became the less justified the more Habermas's social philosophy and sociology developed. It is possible that Habermas's encounter with critical political theologians, like Metz, Moltmann, Solle and Peukert may have contributed to his growing receptivity for theological elements in Hegel's philosophy as well as in the critical theory, particularly in the work of Benjamin and

Adorno(93). There are elements of negative theology and even mystical atheism not only in Horkheimer's, Adorno's, Benjamin's and Fromm's social philosophy and sociology, but also in that of Habermas: Tendencies to leave God for the sake of God, to let go of God for God's sake, toward an atheism in God(94). Once Adorno hoped that Benjamin would deliver in his Passage Work a restitution of theology or better still a radicalization of the materialistic dialectic into its "inner theological glowing fire"(95). It would mean, so Adorno asserted, at the same time an extreme sharpening of the social dialectical, even the economic motif. Neither Benjamin nor Adorno nor Horkheimer have accomplished this restitution of theology in the critical theory completely. Also Habermas has not achieved this restitution, nor may he have intended to do so. But why should this task remain unresolved? The God who – according to Nietzsche – has died under the knives of instrumental rationality and functionalistic action could be redeemed and rise again in communicative rationality, in brotherly-sisterly communicative praxis and communication community, and unalienated man with him(96). It is true, Habermas has no sociological indication of this. But the mystical thought of it is not entirely foreign to him or to his theory of communicative praxis(97). What seems to be required is a "political proof of God"(98)! At present the political theologians Metz, Moltmann, Gutierrez, Solle, Peukert try to discover the theological glowing fire in historical materialism(99).

Formation of Subjectivity

Hegel's Jena system designs, out of which Habermas developed the very foundation of his social philosophy and sociology of communicative action, consisted of lectures Hegel held on the philosophy of nature and spirit at the University of Jena, Germany, during the academic years of 1803–1804 and 1805–1806(100). Hegel's Jena philosophy of mind follows and remains linked to his sytem of morality, his theologically grounded natural law position contained already in the Critical Journal of Philosophy of 1802, and even earlier in his Frankfurt System Program of 1797(101).

Habermas points out that Hegel's Jena system designs stand still very much under the influence of his study of the political economics of Adam Smith, Ricardo, Says, etc., which Hegel was pursuing at the time(102). Marxist studies of Hegel, like those of Lukacs, have always emphasized this fact of his interest in political economics during his Jena period(103). As a matter of fact, Hegel remained an admirer of political economics throughout his life(104). In spite of this, so Habermas criticizes, among bourgeois Hegel-scholars, the distinctive position of the Jena system designs I, II, and III within the Hegelian system has not yet received adequate consideration. Habermas argues particularly against the conception of the protestant Hegel scholar, Lasson, that the Jena system designs were nothing else than a preparatory stage for Hegel's Phenomenology of the Spirit. Lasson emphasizes the parallels between the Jena system designs and Hegel's later philosophical system. In contrast to Lasson, Habermas presents the thesis that, in his Jena system designs, Hegel offered a distinctive, systematic foundation for the formative process of the human spirit, of human subjectivity. In Habermas's view Hegel allegedly abandoned this basis, later on as he developed his system further. Habermas makes this Hegelian foundation of the formative process of human subjectivity into the very basis of his own whole philosophy and sociology of communicative praxis. As a matter of fact, also for Hegel it had been the foundation not only of the subjective spirit but of the objective spirit as well; of abstract right, personal morality, family, civil society and nation state, and even of the absolute spirit, art, religion and philosophy(105).

Since Habermas looks at Hegel's work through the eyes of Marx and finally a reconstructed dialectical materialism, it is understandable that he emphasizes the political-economical and thus materialistic elements in Hegel's early philosophy. In reality Hegel continued his study of political economics also later in life, as his Philosophy of Right clearly shows(106). Materialistic elements were never missing in Hegel's idealistic philosophy. Already before the Jena critical writings and the system designs, Hegel is in sympathy with the materialistic critique of civil society: its general fraud, corruption of nature, infinite lie, which calls itself truth and right(107). Benjamin quotes in his "Thesis on the Philosophy of History," Hegel's materialistic statement of 1807, when he completed his phenomenology of spirit: "Seek for food and clothing first, then the Kingdom of God shall be added unto you"(108). Hegel interpreted Christianity idealistically as well as materialistically as late as 1817 and even up to shortly before his death in 1831(109). He admits this in his Encyclopedia: "...the pure religious idealist and the pure religious materialist are only the two shells of the mussle which contains the pearl of Christianity"(110).

At the time when Hegel studied political economics in Jena, he was also very deeply involved in Dante Alighieri's Divinia Comedia(111). His article on the natural law and the very structure of his phenomenology of spirit reflect Dante's influence(112). In Jena Hegel even considered becoming a Catholic. But while for Hegel a complete philosophy could only be an idealistic one, he nevertheless appreciates materialistic arguments and his idealistic philosophy contains always strong materialistic tendencies(113). How else could he have become the teacher of Marx and Marxists up to Lukacs, Horkheimer, Adorno, Marcuse, and finally also of Habermas? Habermas continues to admire Hegel in spite of the fact that he believes he must transcend his religious-metaphysical worldview in the face of a modernity which, allegedly unlike Hegel, emphasizes subjectivity, contingency and future(114).

Habermas competes with the Hegel whom he continues to appreciate as the most modern of modern philosophers. Habermas's competition with Hegel centers in his accepting the latter's Jena philosophy of spirit, but without its theological presupposition contained in the article on natural law: the God who objectivates himself and sacrifices himself in the world as nature and history and precisely thereby reconciles himself with himself and with nature(115). For Hegel this theological presupposition is the prototype of and the foundation for the unity of the media of human self-realization: Language, work, sexual love, struggle for recognition and nation and thus for the unity of the human ego in this process of self-actualization(116).

It is Habermas's great ambition to supersede - i.e., critically negate, preserve and elevate - Hegel's still religious-metaphysical worldview and in and with it all previous mythical and religious-metaphysical systems of interpretation and orientation once originated from and situated in primitive, archaic, and historic-intermediate action systems, by his own philosophy and sociology of brotherly-sisterly communicative praxis and communication community(117). Habermas wants to realize this, his philosophical-sociological program, by continuing the critical theory of society of Horkheimer and Adorno by other means: by the paradigm of language mediated intersubjectivity and interaction retrieved from Hegel's Jena System Design I. This hermeneutics of retrieval balances Habermas's hermeneutics of destruction directed against supposedly obsolete mythical and religous-metaphysical traditions and authorities, which are allegedly no longer able to accomplish social integration and identity under conditions of highly complex modern action systems, their future orientation and increasing contingency experiences.

Fundamental Categories

For Habermas the five fundamental categories in Hegel's Jena System Designs I and III designate five equally significant patterns of dialectical relations: symbolical representation, labor process, sexual love, interaction on the basis of reciprocity and national solidarity(118). Habermas allows himself to be guided by all five of these categories. But most of the time he concentrates only on four of these categories – language, work, love and recognition – and ignores the nation. But it seems that the nation plays a more important role in Habermas's more recent work in the late 1970s and early 1980s(119). Sometimes Habermas concentrates on merely four categories – language, work, love and recognition – or on merely three potentials – language, work and love – or on merely two principles – language and recognition – and reduces the left out categories to the others which at that time are emphasized(120). At other times Habermas does not differentiate sharply and clearly enough language and the struggle for recognition. Each of the potentials is thinkable and can be practiced in the everyday life world without the other. That is why Hegel separates all five principles sharply from each other. He can afford such sharp distinction since his theological foundation guarantees the unity of the five potentials of human selfrealization and of the ego. This is no longer the case with Habermas or any other Hegelian on the left. This is indeed a problem for Habermas's universal pragmatic.

Habermas states in his discussions of Hegel's Jena System Design I that the categories language, work and sexual love designate three equally important patterns of dialectical relation: Symbolic representation, the labor process, and interaction on the basis of reciprocity(121). Here Habermas fuses the categories of familial love and recognition which Hegel kept apart sharply. According to Habermas each of the three patterns mediates nevertheless subject and object in its own way. The dialectic of language, labor and familial or

moral relations are each developed by Hegel as a specific
configuration of mediation between subject and object or
subject and subject. In Habermas's view what is involved here
are not stages constructed according to the same dialectical
logical form as it happens in Hegel's mature system, in which
language is the basis for the family, the family for work in
civil society and capitalistic society as production and
exchange process for the struggle for recognition in the
political sphere, or the state, and between states in the
historical process(122). Habermas is concerned with the young
Hegel, for whom the language, work, love and recognition as
elements of the immediate, empirically concrete life world
have not yet been objectivated into a system more or less
separated from this everyday world. Habermas refers to the
presystematic Hegel. Habermas's later concern with the modern
phenomenological differentiation between the life world of
immediately speaking, working, loving and reciprocally interacting subjects is latently present already in his early
occupation with Hegel's Jena system designs(123).

In Habermas's view what is involved in the Jena System
Design I and its fundamental categories are diverse forms of
construction itself. According to Habermas's radically
materialistic thesis, it is not God's or man's spirit in the
absolute movement of reflecting on itself, which manifests
itself in, among other things, language, labor, and familial
or moral relations. It is rather the dialectical
interconnections between linguistic symbolization, labor and
familial interaction which determine the concept of human
spirit, subject, self, ego. Here in his Jena System Design I
the presystematic Hegel still seems to Habermas to stand on
his feet. Only later, when Hegel produces his complete system,
does he begin to stand on his head. Thereby Hegel only
reflects in his system the real situation of bourgeois
modernity. Marx intended not only to put the systematician
Hegel on his feet but also the bourgeois world, which his
system reflected, so that the immediately speaking, working,
loving and mutually recognizing human subject of the life
world may no longer be a being instrumentalized and
commodified and as such degraded by the capitalistic system.

Habermas admits, of course, that the locus within the
later Hegelian system of the categories of language, work,
family, as well as of mutual recognition and nation, does
definitely speak against this, his radical thesis. These
categories do not appear in Hegel's logic but in his

philosophy of reality: in his phenomenology and psychology, in his philosophy of right and history(124). But Habermas insists, nevertheless, that in Hegel's Jena period the dialectical relations of language, labor and familial or moral relations still adhere so sensuously to the basic patterns of heterogeneous experience in the immediate life world that the logical forms still diverge according to the material context from which they were drawn. In Hegel's Jena system designs, so Habermas argues, externalization and alienation, appropriation and reconciliation are not yet integrated as is supposedly the case in his later system. For Habermas at least the tendency of Hegel's Jena lectures on language, work, family, struggle for recognition and nation is that only the aggregate of the three dialectical patterns – symbolical representation, the labor process, and interaction on the basis of reciprocity – of existing consciousnesss can render the human spirit, subjectivity, self, "I" transparent in its structure.

Habermas continues this tendency of Hegel's Jena lectures throughout the development of his social philosophy and sociology of communicative praxis. This unites him with and at the same time separates him from the Hegelian philosophical enterprise. It also unites him with and separates him from the enterprise of bourgeois modernization, which Hegel's later philosophy reflects so adequately. While Hegel's philosophy became in its development more and more the organic unity of the five categories of language, family, work, recognition and nation, Habermas's social philosophy of communicative praxis, following the trend of Hegel's Jena System Design I and III remains up to the present an aggregate of the five dialectical patterns of existing consciousness, self or "I", more specifically of the two dialectical patterns of symbolical representation and interaction on the basis of reciprocity: linguistically mediated intersubjective praxis.

From Cruelty to Respect

Habermas's paradigm shift from the dimension of work and tool or instrumental rationality, which underlies most of modern positive science, to the sphere of language mediated recognition or practical rationality, meets a need which today begins to be articulated in the sciences themselves. An example may illustrate this point. Between 1964 and 1974 Professor R. Ulrich, Psychology Department, Western Michigan University, Kalamazoo, Michigan, USA would place a couple of rats in a closed chamber, juice them up with about 600 volts of electricity, then watch them fight(125). His "battle of the rats" was called a "pain-aggression study." It drew many hundreds of students a year whenever it was conducted. Behaviorism became something like a religion at Western Michigan University. It gave simple answers to the most complex questions not only of animal, but also of human behavior.

Although the pain-aggression experiment was a great success with Ulrich's academic peers it was not well received with the simple people at home. The scientific community, or the behavioristic and positivistic part of it, was amazed about Ulrich's research and published it widely. Ulrich traveled far and wide to psychology conventions reporting his "data." When Ulrich's mother asked him once what the results of his scientific work were, he told her that "pain causes aggression." She looked at her son and said: "What is so unique about that? Grandfather always used to say that." Obviously everyday life experience and wisdom was far ahead of positive science concerning the connection of pain and aggression, not to speak of the experience and intuition of a Sade and a Masoch. Often positive science lives not only from the hunger for certainty, but also from the loss of memory.

Ulrich's scientific ambition was somewhat shaken by his mother's reaction. He nevertheless continued to conduct experiment after experiment, shocking the same animals day after day most cruelly. Ulrich's work grew into a widely recognized research center, which brought in half a million dollars of government grants each year, while there were at the same time only meager funds available for the Philosophy Department, the Religion Department, the Art Department, General Studies, etc. Ulrich's research on pain and aggression seemed to be very helpful to the government by providing a method of transforming e.g. a peaceful accountant into a most aggressive marine in the shortest amount of time, to be employed in Vietnam or elsewhere.

In 1974 Ulrich had a conversion. He moved his family to a 115-acre commune outside Kalamazoo: the Lake Village Farm Cooperative. When the chairman of the Psychology Department asked Ulrich to list his significant academic contributions for 1974, he replied that he has finally stopped torturing animals. He had moved from cruelty against animals to respect for them as well as for humans.

Between 1964 and 1974 Ulrich's laboratory at Western

Michigan University housed an assortment of pigeons, a dozen or so monkeys, and a colony of about 100 rats. After his conversion Ulrich set all those animals free in his commune. He recognized the limitation of the postivist concept of experience. He replaced the cruel abuse of the animals with real life experiments. Now Ulrich teaches his psychology students to simply observe the behavior of wild life in a natural environment and relate to the animals as friends. In the language of the history and philosophy of science Ulrich's conversion is really a paradigm change. In Habermas's language it is more specifically a paradigm change from work to inter-action, from subject–object relationship to subject–subject relationship, from functional to communicative rationality. Ulrich entered this paradigm change without any knowledge of Kant, Hegel or Habermas. His conversion was simply the result of an honest and courageous admission of the aporetical character not only of Skinnerian behaviorism but of much of positive science and philosophy of science and modern functional rationality in general. Skinner's behaviorism is after all the smaller brother of Parsons's functionalism. Both aim at Future I – the totally administered society, and Future II – the war society. Through his conversion Ulrich shifted his praxis toward Future III – the reconciled society.

Today Ulrich thinks that the whole behavioristic research is utter nonsense. There is no experiment, so Ulrich argues, other than the real life situation. Behaviorists study rats. But they do not know anything about rats. They merely know about white rats in a laboratory. When one studies white rats in a laboratory, the only thing one learns is about white rats in a laboratory: a creature so inbred, that it can only live in a laboratory. And from that data behaviorists think they can study human behavior to the benefit of the government, army and police: administrative research.

At present Ulrich lives with his family and 40 other commune members in his Farm Cooperative. When people come into this farm commune they move closer to the earth and it starts teaching them things. Early on the commune members go into basic research. They become animal lovers. As such they better have a real good reason as to why they are taking a pigeon and keeping it in a space where it can merely flap its wings or why they are placing electrodes in a monkey's head. In the 1950s Ulrich went to the Psychology Department of Southern Illinois University in order to get his Ph.D. Here Ulrich got the idea that he had to find out new things. So he started to do things to animals. Finally Ulrich realized that things positive science was doing and finding out about animals were things his family already knew for generations. Before Ulrich went to the university he grew up in his family with great fondness for animals. Now through his conversion or paradigm change Ulrich became a humanist whose solidarity is universal in the sense that it does not only include humans but animals as well.

Today Ulrich is aware that the primary goal of research in advanced capitalistic society is money. Researchers do their studies to get the grants which allow them to travel and to get promotions. Western Michigan University allowed its Psychology Department to turn into an almost pure Behaviorist Department without any alternative school of psychological thought being represented (e.g., all Freudians were removed). The only reason for this was that to be successful and to bring in massive grants, the Department had to concentrate on one single type of psychology. Ulrich fit well this model of a successful behavioristic researcher for over ten years. But after a few months on the commune Ulrich became aware of his own aggressive behavior and set out to change it.

When Ulrich first came out to the Lake Village Farm Cooperative one of the mares there kicked him and he did not know why. Ulrich is supposed to be an expert on behavior and controlling aggression and he could not even control this one horse. Ulrich began reaching back to his roots and looking at the animals around as equals and beings that deserved recognition and respect. Ulrich discovered for himself the principle of interaction and intersubjectivity not only among humans, but between men and animals as well. From that time on Ulrich got along with animals as well as with humans.

Then Ulrich began to feel that behavioristic research did not mean anything. It was meaningless. It is not helping us to be kind to one another or even helping the well being of humankind. Ulrich began to speak in categories which do no longer belong to the sphere of work and tool but rather to the realm of interaction, intersubjectivity and mutual recognition: meaning, kindness, helpfulness, respect, love, etc.

Ulrich's colleagues in the Psychology Department find this to be a rather strange language. They continue to disagree with Ulrich and his conversion and paradigm change. They refer to Ulrich as "nice but a bit off." It is their way to say that they are not willing to shift their methodology from the paradigm of functional rationality to that of commun-

icative rationality. It would simply be bad for business! What
Ulrich is doing is in the eyes of his colleagues almost as bad
as "theology." Behaviorism retains together with functionalism
a powerful position in an overwhelmingly positivistic
university, which had no difficulty to invite the theologian
H. Kung as visiting professor but has rejected Habermas twice.

Ulrich admits that he has difficulty with some of his
friends now because his and their paths are different. To show
what he means, Ulrich strolls almost habitually over to a
naying horse and gives him a firm hug around the neck. A lot
of things behaviorists have done to prolong human life, so
Ulrich reflects, mean merely that the greatest destroyers,
polluters, people who have been more cruel to other life
forms, have lived longer. But when the "Great Spirit" takes
all that into account, so Ulrich predicts, it is not clear
that we will be looked at as the greatest form of life.

Thus in his own way a former Skinnerian behaviorist has
diagnosed the pathology of modern positive science and of
modernity as such. It is not clear how far this kind of
diagnosis has spread up to today among scientists in late
capitalistic society. But one thing is for sure, that such
diagnosis prepares the ground for the reception of the kind of
paradigm change Habermas is promoting in Western civilization.

Universal and Singular

According to Habermas, Hegel recalls to mind in his Great
Logic, developed almost a decade after the Jena system
designs, that concept of the spirit, the subject, the "I", in
which his fundamental experience of the dialectic of language,
labor, family, struggle for recognition and nation and of
dialectic as such is contained(126). According to Hegel's
Subjective Logic, "I" is that initially pure unity or
universality relating to itself. Self is this universality not
immediately, but in that it abstracts from all particular
determinateness and content. In the freedom of unlimited
self-equality, the subject passes back to its universality.
Thus it is universality. Thus it is unity which is unity with
itself only due to that negative comportment. It appears as
abstraction from all particularity. It therefore contains all
the determinateness of language, work, love, recognition,
nation as dissolved in itself.

But according to Hegel's Subjective Logic, self, subject,
"I" is not only universality and unity, but also singularity.

Self   is   singularity   just   as   immediately   as   it   is   the
negativity   which   relates   to   itself.   Subject   is   absolute
being-determinate,   which confronts the other in the dialectic
of language, love, work, recognition and nation   and   excludes
it   at the same time. "I" is individual personality as well as
universality. The nature of both the ego and the notion, which
is the very peak of   Hegel's   logic,   consists   both   of   this
absolute   universality,   which is just as immediately absolute
singular individuation, as well as a   being-in-and-for-itself,
which is simply being-posited, and which is this being-in-and-
for-itself only through its unity with being-posited. The self
as   well   as   the   notion   is   the   dialectical   unity of the
universal,   the   particular   and   the   singular.   Neither   the
subject   nor the notion can be comprehended, if the moments of
universality and singularity are not conceived   simultaneously
in   their   abstraction   and in their perfect unity. "I" is the
universal   which   becomes   through   its   particularization   in
language,   love, work, struggle for recognition and nation and
thus   in   encounter   with   others,   singularity,   individual
personality.
       From   the   very   outset   of his philosophical work, Hegel
comprehends the self, in opposition to Kant and Fichte, as the
identity of the universal and the singular(127).   The   subject
is   for Hegel the universal and the singular in one. Spirit is
the dialectical unfolding of this   unity   in   language,   love,
work,   recognition   and   nation,   namely,   moral totality(128).
Habermas points out   that   Hegel   does   not   select   the   term
"spirit" arbitrarily. We still speak of the spirit of a nation
or   of   an   epoch   or   of a family. We appreciate team spirit.
Hegel chose spirit for his central term since   it   always   extends   beyond   the   solitary   self-consciousness   of   the
individual. The self as the identity of the universal and   the
singular   can   only be comprehended in terms of the unity of a
spirit, which embraces the identity of   a   self   with   another
subject   not   identical   with   it: the   unity of identity and
non-identity.   That   precisely   is   Hegel's   "definition"   of
spirit.
       According   to   Habermas,   following   Hegel, spirit is the
communication of individuals in the medium of   the   universal.
It is related to the speaking individuals as is the grammar of
a   language.   It   is   related to persons who love and work and
struggle for recognition as is a system   of   recognized   technical   or   moral norms. Habermas stresses, like Horkheimer and
Adorno before,   that   spirit   does   not   place   the   moment   of

universality before or above that of singularity, but instead permits the distinctive links between these singularities. Hegel calls this universal a concrete universal. Throughout his work Habermas translates Hegel's core concept "spirit" into "communication structure" or "world." Thus for Habermas, Hegel's subjective spirit turns into inner world, his objective spirit into social world, his absolute spirit into cultural world(129).

According to Habermas within the medium of this universal the single beings can identify with each other and still at the same time maintain themselves as non-identical. In Habermas's view the original insight of Hegel consists in that the "I" as self-consciousness can only be conceived if it is spirit: if it goes over from subjectivity to the objectivity of a universal, in which the subjects who know themselves as non-identical are united on the basis of mutual, reciprocal recognition. This insight of Hegel constitutes the very core of Habermas's theory of communicative praxis, which he has enfolded step by step during the past two decades. It is Habermas's critical theory of society in a nutshell.

For Habermas, self is the identity of the universal and the singular in this sense precisely explicated in Hegel's article on natural law, his Jena system designs and in his logic. Therefore Habermas can say that the individuation of a neonate, which in the womb of the mother has been an example of the human species as a prelinguistic living organism, and thus could be explained biologically in terms of a combination of a finite number of mechanical, physical, chemical and biological elements quite adequately, once born into the social world can only be conceived as a process of socialization, of learning. Habermas wants to make sure that here socialization can not be conceived as the adaptation to society of an already given individuality, but as that which itself produces an individuated being through the media of language, love, work, struggle for recognition and nation. Habermas, as Hegel and Durkheim before, can conceive the process of individuation only as a process of socialization(130). From this viewpoint Habermas develops the basis of his philosophical and sociological theory of communciative action: individuation through communicative praxis.

Struggle for Recognition

In Habermas's view the moral relationship was clarified by the
young Hegel in terms of the relationship between lovers, in
the dimension of the family(131). For Hegel in marital and
familial love the separated individuals still exist, but no
longer as separated(132). They are united. In love the living
feels the living. Hegel explains love as the knowing which
recognizes itself in the other. From the union of distinct
individuals results a knowledge which is characterized by a
double meaning. Each lover is like the other in that wherein
he/she has opposed himself/herself to the other. By disting-
uishing himself/herself from the other he/she thereby becomes
identical with her/him. This is a cognitive process precisely
in that for him/her the opposition is transformed into
sameness, or that the one lover, as he/she looks at himself/
herself in the other, knows him/her self.

In Habermas's perspective, Hegel does not explicate the
relation of recognizing oneself in the other, on which in turn
the concept of the self as an identity of the universal and
the singular depends, directly from the relation of intersubjectivity, through which the complementary agreement of
subjects confronting each other is secured. Rather, Hegel
presents love as the result of a movement. Love is the
reconciliation of a preceding conflict. The distinctive sense
of an ego-identity based on reciprocal recognition, so
Habermas argues, can be understood only if it has been seen
that the dialogic relation of the complementary unification of
opposing subjects signifies at the same time a relation of
logic and of social praxis in the life world. Hegel shows this
in the dialectic of the moral relationship. Hegel develops
this dialectic not only under the title of family possession,
but much more specifically so under the title of the struggle
for recognition(133). In Hegel's Jena System Design I and III
this dimension of the struggle for recognition is sharply
separated from the potential of family as well as from the
principles of tool and language. This category of the struggle
for recognition is the foundation of Habermas's theory of
communicative praxis. Habermas enfolds this category in his
theory and doing so mediates it dialectically with language,
and also sometimes with love and work. This category of the
struggle for recognition is the key not only to Habermas's
theory of communcative praxis but also to his critical theory
of religion contained in it and to political theology.

According to Habermas, in Hegel's <u>System Design I</u> and <u>III</u> the struggle for recognition reconstructs the suppression and reconstitution of the dialogue situation as the moral relationship. In this dialectical movement the logical relation of a communication distorted by power itself exercises practical force. According to Habermas only the result of this dialectical movement eradicates the power and establishes the non-compulsory character of the dialogic recognition of one self in the other: love as reconciliation. What is dialectical in this movement is not unconstrained intersubjectivity itself, but the history of its suppression and reconstitution. The distortion of the dialogic relationship is subject to the causality of split-off symbols and reified logical relations. These are relations that have been taken out of the context of communication and thus are valid and operative only behind the backs of the subjects. The young Hegel speaks of a causality of destiny. Later Hegel speaks of divine reason or providence governing the world(134). Here lay the roots for Habermas's critique of religion in the framework of his theory of communicative action. Hegel continues his elaboration of the struggle for recognition in his <u>Phenomenology of Spirit</u>, when he discusses the conflict between master and servant(135). Habermas's theory of communicative praxis and communication community is nothing else than the resolution of this conflict between master and servant in terms of mutual recognition among equals. Marx's <u>Capital</u> had the same intent(136). Habermas remains a <u>Marxist</u> in terms of a historical materialism reconstructed via the <u>Jena System Designs I</u> and <u>III</u>(137).

Media of Subjectivity

According to Habermas, Hegel does not link the constitution of the self, like Kant, to the reflection of the solitary "I" on itself(138). Hegel understands it rather in terms of a formative process, namely the communicative agreement of opposing subjects. Therefore, it is not reflection as such which is decisive, but rather the <u>medium</u> in which the identity of the universal and the individual is formed. Hegel speaks of the middle or <u>medium</u> by passing through which consciousness attains existence. Habermas expects that Hegel will introduce communicative action as the <u>medium</u> for the formative process of the self-conscious spirit, the human subject. Indeed in his <u>Jena System Design I</u> Hegel uses the example of the shared

existence of the primary group, namely family interaction, to
construct the family possession as the existing middle of
reciprocal modes of contact(139). However, besides the
potential of the family Habermas finds the two further
categories, which Hegel develops in the same manner as media
of the self-formative process of the subject: Language and
labor(140). Human spirit or subjectivity is an organization of
equally original media. According to Hegel that first
dependent existence – consciousness as middle – is the
spirit's existence as language, as tool, and as family
possession or as simple unity: Memory, labor and family. In
Habermas's view these three fundamental dialectical patterns
are heterogeneous. As media of spirit or subject language and
labor can not be traced back to the experiences of interaction
and of mutual recognition. In reality none of the five
fundamental categories of the philosophy of spirit in Hegel's
Jena System Design I – language, labor, family, struggle for
recognition or nation – can be traced back to any other of
these categories. But precisely their clear separation poses
the question of their unity and not only their unity but more
fundamentally the unity of the subject, spirit, "I," which
constitutes itself in and through these media and can be known
through them by others as well as by itself. For Hegel this
question was a theological one(141). For Habermas this
question points to the aporia of his theory of communicative
praxis: the contradiction of mutual unconditional recognition
and destruction of the other. It can only find a theological
answer or none at all.

Unity of Subject

When Habermas looks back to Hegel's Jena philosophy of spirit
then, indeed, the question of the unity of the self-formative
process of the subject forces itself upon him(142). This self-
formative process is initially determined by three and in
reality even five heterogeneous patterns of formation:
language, work, family, recognition and nation. This question
follows Habermas throughout the development of his theory of
communicative praxis. It becomes the more urgent the more he
leaves behind the religious-metaphysical and mystical
worldviews, which once gave unity to the self-formative
process of the subject and its media(143). Hegel's great
philosophy had for a last time provided this unity. But the
absence of this unity and how to restore it again is not only

the fundamental problem of Habermas's social philosophy and sociology but of all modern theories of action and of modernity as such.

In Habermas's view the question of the coherence of that organization of media and therefore of the unity of self is posed with special urgency once he recalls the historical effects of Hegelian philosophy and calls to mind the divergent interpretations that single out and elevate each of the fundamental dialectical patterns – language, work, family, recognition and nation – to the chief interpretative principle of the whole self-formative process of the individual subject and even the human species. Cassirer takes the dialectic of language or representation and makes it the guiding principle of his Hegelianized Kant interpretation. It is at the same time the foundation of a philosophy of symbolical forms. Marx stressed the dimension of labor. Lukacs, following Marx, interprets the movement of the intellectual development from Kant to Hegel along the guideline presented by the dialectic of labor. At the same time this guideline guarantees the materialistic unity of subject and object in the world-historical formative process of the human species. Freud emphasized the dialectic of love. Theodor Litt, a neo-Hegelian, leads to a conception of the stepwise self-development of spirit which follows the pattern of the struggle for recognition. Hitler and his followers posited the nation as the main medium of the self-realization of individual and collective. For Habermas's theory of communicative praxis the dialectics of language and of recognition is of greatest importance.

These positions, including that of Habermas himself, have in common the method employed by the young Hegelians, of appropriating Hegel at the cost of surrendering the identity of spirit and nature claimed by absolute knowledge(144). All these positions sacrifice Hegel's theology, which alone guaranteed unity to the media of language, work, love, recognition and nation and to the self-formative process of the human subject and the human species(145). However, for the rest these positions have so little in common that they only give evidence of the divergence of their approaches and of the media they stress, be it language, love, work, recognition or nation. They give thereby also evidence of the divergence of the conception of the dialectic underlying them. How, therefore, so Habermas asks, is the unity of the formative process of the self to be conceived, which according to Hegel's Jena System Design I and III goes through the dialectic of

language, labor, love, recognition and nation. If one rejects
Hegel's theological answer to this problem of unity, the only
answer which remains seems to be reductionism. The unity of
the self-formative process, which is no longer guaranteed by
the Absolute must be achieved by reducing four media to one or
three media to two. Thus one thinker reduces all media to
language, another one to work, another one to love, another
one to recognition, another one to the nation. Or one thinker
reduces all media to language and recognition, another one to
language and love, another one to love and work, another one
to work and nation. Habermas himself has at least the tendency
to reduce all media to language and recognition. There is a
price to be paid for this sacrifice of theology and for this
reductionism: the one-sidedness of the self-formative process
of the subject and of the self itself. Therefore it is of
utmost importance to refer once more to Hegel's theological
answer to the problem of the unity of the self-formative
process of the "I" and its media, before it can be admitted
with absolute certainty that it is obsolete and therefore
reductionism; and a one-sided self-formative process of the
ego and therefore an always somewhat damaged subjectivity is
the only alternative left. Too much is at stake here.

Divine Spirit

First of all, Habermas seeks the unity of the formative
process of the human spirit, the human subject, in an
interconnection of the three fundamental dialectical patterns:
language, tool and moral relationship(146). He searches for
this unity in the relation between symbolic representation,
labor and interaction. This distinctive interconnection,
limited to one stage, Hegel takes up again in his Phenomenology of Spirit in the relationship between master and
servant(147). According to Habermas this interconnection does
not reappear again in Hegel's system later. We may ask here if
it does not maybe reappear again in Hegel's Philosophy of
Right and in his late essay "On the English Reform Bill": in
the capitalistic society as relationship between the bourgeoisie and the class of the poor(148). It certainly reappears
again as relationship between bourgeoisie and proletariate in
Marx's Capital(149).
  According to Habermas this distinctive interconnection
between language, work and recognition is tied to a systema-
tics, which Hegel appears to have tried out only once in his

Jena period and which he abandoned later on. Habermas does indeed discover a tendency incorporated in the Jena lectures, that makes it understandable to him why the specific interconnection of labor with interaction loses, allegedly, its significance in Hegel's later systematic work. For in his Jena lectures, so Habermas argues, Hegel proceeded from that absolute identity of the spirit with nature, which prejudices the unity of the human spirit's formative process in a particular manner.

Habermas must admit, nevertheless, that in these Jena lectures Hegel constructs the transition from the philosophy of nature to the philosophy of spirit no differently than he does in his Encyclopedia of 1817, 1827, and 1830, the year before his death(150). In nature, so Hegel argues in his Encyclopedia, Spirit, the Divine Spirit, God's Spirit has its complete external objectivity(151). Therefore God's spirit finds its identity in the sublation of this externalization. Divine Spirit thus is the absolute presupposition of nature. The manifestation of God's spirit is as abstract idea immediate transition, becoming of nature. It is as manifestation of God's spirit, which is free, the positing of nature as his world. This positing is as reflection at the same time prepositing of the world as independent nature. God's revelation in the notion – the dialectical unity of universal, particular, and singular – is creation of nature as his being(152). In this being the Absolute as spirit gives to himself the affirmation and truth of his freedom.

For Hegel the Absolute is spirit(153). This is the highest definition of the Absolute. In Hegel's view the absolute tendency of all education, philosophy and theology is to find this definition of the Absolute as spirit and to comprehend its meaning and content. All history of religion and science pushed forward toward this point, this insight. Out of this urge alone world history is to be comprehended. The word and the repesentation of spirit has been found early. It is the content of the Christian religion, to make known God as spirit(154). In Christianity this insight, that God is spirit, was given to people's representation, their imagination. It is the task of philosophy to comprehend what is the essence in itself, the Absolute as spirit in its own element, in the notion. This task is not solved truly and immanently as long as the notion and the freedom is not its object and its soul. According to Hegel his own philosophy has solved the task to comprehend the Absolute as spirit not only in

representation, but also in the notion. For Hegel this
Absolute Spirit or Spirit of the Absolute, is the foundation
for the unity of the human spirit as it rises out of nature
and forms itself in the media of language, work, love,
recognition and nation. God's spirit is the absolute
presupposition not only of nature, but of the unified
self-formative process of the human subject as well. Hegel
agrees with Meister Eckehart that Ego, the word "I" is
nobody's own than God's alone in his unity(155). The human ego
is merely the example (Beiher-spiel) of the Divine "I".

The Other

According to Habermas under the presupposition of this thesis
of the identity of God's spirit with himself in the sublation
of the externalization of nature, Hegel has always interpreted
the dialectic of language and labor idealistically(156).
According to Hegel, together with the name we enunciate the
being of objects(157). In the same manner, that which nature
is in truth is incorporated in the tool. For Hegel, the
idealist, the innermost part of nature is itself spirit. This
is so, since nature only becomes comprehensible in its essence
and comes to itself in man's confrontation with it. The
interior of nature is expressed only in the realm of language,
in nature's names and in the rules of work in man's working
upon it. Of course, Habermas does not make completely clear
that the spirit present in nature is God's Spirit externalized
in nature. God's spirit is different for Hegel from man's
finite spirit present in language and work. Habermas does not
always clearly differentiate between Hegel's idealistic
position and his own materialistic interpretation of it.
      If, however, so Habermas argues, hidden subjectivity can
always be found by Hegel in what has been objectivated by man
in language and work, if behind the masks of named and
worked-upon objects, nature can always be revealed as the
concealed partner, then the basic dialectical patterns of
language and work can also be reduced to one common
denominator with the dialectic of moral action. The
relationship of the name-giving and the working subject to
nature can also be brought within the dimension of reciprocal
recognition. The intersubjectivity, in which an "I" can
identify with another "I" without relinquishing the
non-identity between itself and the other, is also established
in language and labor, when the object confronting the

speaking and the working subject is from the outset conceived
idealistically as an opposite with which interaction in the
mode of that between subjects is possible: when it is a
personal opponent and not a mere object. For Hegel the
Absolute is as Spirit before and in nature and is as such not
an object but - non-pantheistically - a subject, a
person(158). That is indeed Hegel's non-pantheistic absolute
idealism. God's Idea, Genus, Word or Logos is prior to the
mechanism of nature and to the human spirit, the human self
constituting itself in the media of language and work as well
as in love and the struggle for recognition and the nation.
This absolute idealism is present already in Hegel's Frankfurt
System Program and the Jena essay on the modes of treatment of
the natural law and constitutes the background for the later
Jena system designs(159).

     According to Habermas, as long as we consider each of
Hegel's determinations of abstract spirit by itself, a
specific difference remains. The dialectic of language and
labor develops as a relation between a knowing or an acting
subject on the one hand and an object as the epitome of what
does not belong to the subject on the other hand - the
personal totally Other. The mediation between the subject and
the object, passing through the medium of symbols or of tools
Hegel conceives as a process of externalization of the
subject. It is a process of externalization, objectification
and appropriation.

     In contrast to this, so Habermas argues, the dialectic of
love and the struggle for recognition is a movement on the
level of intersubjectivity(160). Here the place of the model
of externalization is therefore taken by that of separation,
disunion or division on the one hand and alienation on the
other. The result of this movement is not the appropriation of
what has been objectified, but instead the reconciliation, the
restoration of the friendliness which had been destroyed.

     In Habermas's view, Hegel's idealistic sublation of the
distinction between objects as objects and as adversaries
makes possible for him the assimilation of these heterogeneous
models. If interaction is possible with nature as a hidden
subject in the role of the wholly Other, then the processes of
externalization and appropriation which belong to the spheres
of language and work formally match those of alienation and
reconciliation which belong to the dimensions of love and
recognition. The unity of the self-formative process of the
"I," that operates through the media of language, tool, love

and recognition then does not have to be tied first to the interconnections of labor and recognition or interaction, which according to Habermas is still central to Hegel's Jena philosophy of spirit. This is so, since the unity of this self-formative process already subsists in the dialectic of man recognizing himself in the totally Other. In this dialectic of man recognizing himself in the wholly Other the dialectic of language and of labor can now converge with the dialectic of love and recognition or morality. Under the presupposition of Hegel's philosophy, which is for Habermas, not for Hegel, a philosophy of identity, the two forms of dialectic are only apparently heterogeneous.

Already here the fundamental theological problem of Habermas's theory of communicative praxis becomes manifest. Habermas's philosophy of communicative action is a philosophy of non-identity. In this philosophy the dialectic of language and labor on the one hand and of love and recognition on the other, remain separate. This separation threatens the unity of the self-formative process of the human subject. This is so, since Habermas as materialist can not accept the fundamental theological dialectic of man recognizing himself in the entirely Other, in which for Hegel and for all premodern mythical, religious-metaphysical and mystical worldviews the unity of the self-formative process of the human subject subsists. Therefore Habermas is forced in his critical theory of communicative action to tie the unity of the self-formative process of the human subject, that operates through the media of language, labor, love, recognition and nation, to the interconnection of labor and interaction.

This dialectic of labor and recognition is indeed central to Habermas's whole philosophy(161). It unites him with Marx and at the same time separates him critically from the Marxian position. For Habermas this dialectic between labor and recognition is to take the place of the dialectic of recognition between man and God and is to guarantee the unity of man's self-formative process, which once was accomplished by the latter. Habermas's theory of communicative praxis stands and falls with the success or failure of this replacement. In case it would fail, Habermas would have no other choice than to return to Hegel's position: namely, to base, maybe in a new form, the self-formative process of the human subject operating through the media of language, work, love, recognition and nation in the dialectic of man recognizing himself in God's absolute spirit instead of grounding it in the dialectical interconection of labor and interaction or of language and recognition, or on the dialectic of labor and recognition mediated through language(162). Historical materialism would return to its roots in historical idealism. This could happen in a Jewish and Christian mysticism. But Habermas counsels as emphatically against such return to Hegel as Horkheimer, Adorno or Haag, who explicates the theological element in the critical theory(163). Instead of such return to theology, Habermas rather opts, for the time being, for some kind of a phenomenological reductionism to the human self realizing itself in language mediated mutual unconditional recognition between the one and the other, into which the medium of work is integrated(164).

Self-Reflection

Habermas is sure that the dialectic of recognizing oneself in the totally Other, as Hegel comprehends it, is bound to the relationship of interaction between antagonists who are in principle equal(165). As soon, however, so Habermas argues, as nature in its totality is elevated to an antagonist of the united subjects, this relation of parity no longer holds. There can not be a dialogue between God's absolute spirit and nature, the suppression of the dialogic situation between the two, and a struggle for recognition, which results in a constituted moral relationship. For Habermas, not for Hegel, absolute spirit is solitary. For Hegel as for Meister Eckehart, God's absolute spirit is by "definition" trinitarian and as such communicative: Out of his absolute purity God the eternal Father drives forth the plenitude and the abyss of his whole divinity(166). He gives birth to all of this here in his inborn son and effects that we are the same son. And his birth is at the same time his remaining immanent and his remaining immanent is his giving birth. He remains always the One who foments in himself. We would not be unfaithful to Hegel, if we would speak of the communicative structure of God's spirit.

Habermas argues against Hegel, that the unity of Absolute Spirit with itself and with nature, from which it differentiates itself as its other, in the end can not be conceived in terms of the pattern of the intersubjectivity of acting and speaking subjects. Initially Hegel attained by this pattern of intersubjectivity the "I" as the identity of the universal and the singular, through the mediation of the

particular in language, work, love, recognition and nation.
The dialectical unity of spirit and nature, in which spirit
does not recognize itself in nature as an antagonist but only
finds itself again as in a mirror image, can, according to
Habermas, more readily be constructed from the experience of
the self-reflection of consciousness. Therefore, so Habermas
argues, Hegel conceives of the movement of Absolute Spirit in
terms of the model of self-reflection. But Hegel does this in
such a way that the dialectic of the moral relationship, from
which supposedly the identity of the universal with the
singular mediated through the particular originates, can enter
into it. Absolute Spirit, so Habermas interprets, is absolute
morality.
    The dialectic of the moral relationship which
accomplishes itself, e.g., on the criminal with the causality
of destiny in the same way as on those who struggle for
recognition, now proves for Habermas to be the same movement
as that in which the Absolute Spirit reflects itself(167).
This means, of course, that Absolute Spirit and absolute
morality are not only identical but different as well, since
otherwise the former could hardly reflect itself in the
latter. For Hegel the tragedy which takes place in the moral
world is a reflection of the tragedy which takes place in
God's absolute spirit(168).

Dialectic of Sacrifice

Habermas sees rightly, that in the theological writings of his
youth Hegel conceived that process of destiny from the
viewpoint of the members of a socio-moral totality, a nation,
as a reaction evoked by the subjects themselves(169). The
subjects evoked this reaction through the suppression of the
dialogic relationship. Hegel can subsequently reinterpret the
process of destiny all the more readily in the framework of
self-reflection as a self-movement of the socio-moral
totality, because he can link it to the dialectic of
sacrifice. Hegel has mentioned implicitly this dialectic
already in the Frankfurt System Program of 1797 and the System
Fragment of 1800, and he has developed it explicitly in the
Jena essay on the scientific modes of treatment of the natural
law(170). Here Hegel states, that the power of the sacrifice
consists in the perceiving and objectivating of the
involvement with the inorganic. By this perception this
involvement is dissolved. The inorganic is separated out and

recognized as such. Thereby the inorganic is itself incorporated into the indifferent. The living, however, by placing what it knows to be part of itself within the inorganic and offering it up to death in sacrifice, at the same time has recognized the rights of the inorganic and separated itself from it(171). Concretely this means that the socio-moral totality of the nations sacrifices the mechanical civil society and precisely thereby returns to itself as the realm of freedom(172). Hegel anticipates here the Marxian thesis that the realm of freedom presupposes the sacrifice of bourgoise society(173).

Tragedy of the Absolute

Hegel states in his essay on the natural law that the dialectic of sacrifice is nothing else than the performance of the tragedy in the realm of total morality, which the Absolute plays with itself eternally(174). Hegel presents the tragedy of the Absolute first in the Phoenician dialectical image of the Phoenix bird, which burns itself to ashes out of which a young most vigorous Phoenix bird rises again(175). It is the highest accomplishment of Eastern metaphysics. The Absolute gives eternally birth to itself into objectivity. In this its character of objectivity, the Absolute thereby surrenders itself to suffering and death. Then from its ashes − its selfsurrendered death − the Absolute ascends again to glory.
    Secondly, Hegel presents the tragedy of the Absolute in the Christian dialectical image of the crucified God(176). For Hegel the essence of Christianity is the unity of the Divine and human nature. The Divine in its form and objectivity has immediately a double nature. The Life of the Divine is the absolute unity of these natures. But the movement of the absolute conflict of these two natures presents itself in the Divine Nature, which has comprehended itself in this movement, as fortitude. With this fortitude the Divine Nature frees itself from the death of the other, opposing, human nature. But through this liberation the Divine Nature gives its own life. This is so, since this Divine Life is only in connection with this other human life. But the Divine Nature rises likewise absolutely out of the death of the other, human nature. This is so, since in this death, as the sacrifice of the second nature, death is overcome: the death of death, the negation of the negation.
    The Divine Movement appears also in the human nature.

Here the Divine Movement represents itself in such a way that
the pure abstraction of this human nature, which as such would
be merely a subterranean, purely negative power, is superseded
through the living union with the Divine Nature. The Divine
Nature shines into the human nature. The Divine Nature makes
the human nature through this ideal union in the spirit into
its reconciled living spirit. This body remains as body at the
same time in the difference and in finitude. This body
perceives through the spirit the Divine as something alien to
itself(177).
    In spite of the fact that Habermas is fully aware that
this double Eastern and Western description of the tragedy of
the Absolute is the same in Hegel's early essay on Natural Law
and the much later Great Logic, he insists that these two
works are not linked in their theological concern by a
continuous development(178). According to Habermas's
materialistic interpretation in the Jena System Designs I, II,
and III, Hegel's study of contemporary political ecomomics is
reflected in such a manner, that the movement of the actual
human spirit does not mirror the sacrificial as well as
triumphal march of the Absolute. It rather develops the
structures of the human spirit anew, as interconnections of
symbolically mediated labor and interaction. Language mediates
between work and the struggle for recognition. Hegel's
historical idealism always includes materialistic elements.
Benjamin knew this(179). But Habermas's historical materialism
is not supposed to contain idealistic elements! In reality it
preserves such idealistic elements as it rejects them and
rightly so.
    In Habermas's materialistic view the dialectic of labor
does not readily fit into the movement of such a spirit as
conceived by Hegel as absolute morality. Therefore the
dialectic of labor forces upon Hegel a reconstruction of the
self-formative process of man. Habermas insists that Hegel
accomplishes such a materialistic reconstruction in his Jena
system designs, but relinquishes it again after Jena. But
Habermas must admit that Hegel's materialistic reconstruction
of man's self-formative process leaves its traces behind in
his later idealistic work. Thus the position which abstract
right occupies within his later system, more specifically in
his Philosophy of Law, does not flow directly from the
conception of moral spirit(180). But Habermas finds,
nevertheless, elements of Hegel's Jena system designs,
particularly the philosophy of spirit, retained in the

dimension of private right. Other elements of the materialistic Jena reconstruction of the self-formative process of man are not incorporated in the later construction of abstract right.

Habermas could make things so much easier for himself, if he was able to admit that Hegel's historical idealism does contain at least seedlike a historical materialism. One consequence of this would be the insight that the tragedy of the Absolute and of total morality can very well include and accommodate the materialism of the modern science of political economics(181). Such a position would not unnecessarily have widened the modern contradiction between the religious and the secular(182).

Habermas develops his theory of communicative praxis out of the Jena system designs and out of the materialistic elements in Hegel's philosophy of abstract right, which were there retained form the materialistic reconstruction of the self-formative process of man in the Jena system designs. Habermas continues in his philosophy of communicative praxis the materialistic reconstruction of man's self-formative process, which Hegel accomplished in his Jena system designs but allegedly later abandoned. Habermas does this first, following Hegel and Marx, on the basis of the dialectic of labor. But Habermas goes, more than Marx, beyond the dialectic of work. Like Hegel in Jena, Habermas is interested in the movement of the actual human spirit. Unlike for Hegel before Jena and after Jena – and I would dare to say also during Jena – for Habermas the movement of the actual human spirit does not mirror the sacrificial march of the Absolute(183). The tragedy of absolute morality is not the reflex of the tragedy of the Absolute. In Habermas's materialistic view the tragedy of the Absolute disappears altogether. Also Habermas's perspective of the realm of right and morality is far from being tragic. His optimism separates Habermas's form of critical theory sharply not only from the pessimistic philosophy of Schopenhauer, but also from that of Hegel, Horkheimer and Adorno(184). Death appears nowhere in Habermas's philosophy of communicative praxis. While Habermas continues, where Hegel allegedly left off in his Jena system designs, and develops in his theory of communicative action anew the structures of the human spirit as interconnections of labor and struggle for recognition mediated through language and, while he does this obviously without connection to Hegel's tragedy of the Absolute in its Eastern or Western

religious metaphysical form, traces of this fundamentally
mystical conception do nevertheless surface sometimes in his
theory of communicative praxis(185). Of course, these traces
do in no way reveal an affirmative theology. But they indicate
the presence of a negative theology(186). They point to the
possibility of a mystical atheism(187).

Divine and Human Totality

The analogy of the _tragedia_ and _comedia_ of the Absolute and
the socio-moral totality, is of greatest importance for
Hegel's dialectical philosophy as well as for Marx's historical materialism as well as for the Hegelian Left in general,
the contemporary neo-Marxists, the critical theorists of the
Frankfurt School and particularly for Habermas's universal
pragmatic and the theory of religion intrinsic to it(188). It
is therefore necessary to develop further this analogy between
Divine and human totality and to show more concretely in which
sense civil society is the tragic difference in the
socio-moral totality, the organic state of reason, as the
crucified God is the tragic difference in the totality of God
as spirit. For Hegel as for Adorno later on the totality of
bourgoise society is the untruth: it is antagonistic(189). It
is the negative totality. It is not the real whole(190). The
untruth of capitalistic society is not the ultimate
socio-moral totality, but rather its very opposite. Civil
society has no social morality in itself: it shines into it
only from outside(191). The socio-moral totality comes into
its own only by superseding the difference of bourgeois
society inside itself: by negating and sacrificing its own
inner negativity. Doing so the socio-moral totality becomes
the truth: the truth is the whole(192). The socio-moral
totality or the organic state of reason presupposes the
sacrifice of civil society. The sacrifice of bourgeois society
is at the same time self-sacrifice. The dialectic of
capitalistic society moves beyond itself into the socio-moral
totality, the organic state(193). Since this analogy of Divine
and human totality is of such utmost importance for the
further development of Habermas's theory of communicative
praxis, including his theory of religion, as well as for the
critical theory of subject, society, history and religion in
general I would like to concentrate on it a little bit longer.

Dialectic of Civil Society

In 1873 Marx stressed in his "Epilogue" to the Capital that his dialectical method is according to its very foundation not only different from Hegel's dialectic, but that it is even its direct opposite(194). According to Marx, Hegel transforms the human process of thinking theologically under the name of "Idea" into an independent subject – the God. Shortly, he commits idolatry. Thus for Hegel, as Marx understands him, the human thinking process is the "Demiurge" of the reality of nature as well as of society and history. This reality is merely the external appearance of this God. To the contrary, for Marx, the ideal is nothing else than the material, which is transformed and translated in the head of man. Marx tries to separate Hegel's reality dialectic from his notion dialectic and turn the former against the latter. But Hegel's logos-theology does in no way hinder him from thinking dialectically on the subjective level and from thus penetrating most deeply into the objective dialectical process of civil society. It even grounds and reinforces and strengthens his dialectical analysis and critique of bourgeois history(195).

But already in the 1840s, only a few years after Hegel's death, Marx criticized intensely the theological or "mystifying" aspects of Hegel's dialectic(196). At this time Hegel's dialectic was still the intellectual fashion of the day in Germany. But precisely when Marx worked out the first volume of the Capital, the sour "epigones," who at that time were the prevailing force in educated Germany, treated Hegel as Mendelsohn had handled Spinoza in Lessing's time, namely as a "dead dog." Therefore Marx confessed openly and publicly as late as the 1870s, to be a disciple of the great thinker, the "Old Man." Marx used even Hegel's specific dialectical mode of expression still in the Capital, particularly in the chapter on value theory and certainly not only there. Hegel helped Marx greatly by his dialectical method, no matter how much theologically grounded, to criticize bourgeois political economy as the new science of civil society as production and exchange process.

Marx is nevertheless certain that dialectic suffers in the hands of Hegel a theologization to the point of idolatry, or, as he calls it, "mystification." But this mystification, so Marx admits, does in no way prevent Hegel from presenting the first time in the history of philosophy the general forms of the dialectic in an all-embracing and conscious mode. In

Marx's view, with Hegel, to be sure, dialectic stands theologically on its head. Thus Marx intended to turn around Hegel's
theological dialectic materialistically in order to discover
the rational core in the mystical form: to transform Hegel's
idealistic into a materialistic dialectic.

In Marx's view dialectic in its theological or mystical
form became for some time the great intellectual fashion in
German civil society, because it seemed to ideologically
transfigure and thus legitimate and stabilize its status quo.
In its non-theological or non-mystical, rational form, so Marx
argues, the dialectic is to the bourgeois class and its doc-
trinary spokesmen, its political economists, its ideologists
in general, a scandal, a horror and an abomination. It is to
be repressed under all circumstances! This is so, since
rational dialectic includes in the comprehension of the status
quo of civil society at the same time also the knowledge of
its negation, of its necessary decline and ultimate fall.
Rational dialectic comprehends every form of life in the
stream of its movement from its beginning over its climax to
its end, i.e., in terms of its very transitoriness and
finitude. Rational dialectic does not let itself be impressed
by any authority except the dialectical process of the form
itself, e.g., the form of bourgeois society. Rational
dialectic is according to its very essence critical and
revolutionary.

In Marx's perspective the practical bourgeois can feel
the contradictory movement of capitalistic society most
vividly and thoroughly in the occurrences of the periodic
economic cycle, through which modern industry moves regularly.
It points with its particular convulsions to the universal
crisis, when capitalistic society will "blow itself up"(197).
In January 1873, only three years after the foundation of the
Second German Empire, Marx saw the general crisis of bourgeois
society once more on the march, if also only in one of its
prestages. This coming crisis will, so Marx predicts at the
time, through the universality of its scope and the intensity
of its effects teach dialectic even to the luckiest characters
in Bismark's new holy Prussian-German Empire.

Hegel's dialectic, from which Marx learned much, does,
indeed, originate from the mystical-theological writings of
Master Eckhart, maybe of Nicolaus of Cusa, certainly of Boehme
and through him possibly also from the works of the Kabbalists
and the Hassidim(198). But at a time when the negative
Hegelian on the Left, Adorno, has serious doubts, if the

Marxian critique of the bourgeois political economy can, indeed, still be asserted as the rational core of Hegel's dialectic, we may at least be allowed to ask if there may not be present also in Hegel's fundamentally affirmative as well as negative theological and even mystical dialectic a rational, critical and revolutionary element(199)? Why else is Hegel by traditional and modern positivists considered up to today either to be as obsolete or as dangerous as Marx? We may also ask, if there may not also be present in Marx's rational, critical and revolutionary dialectic a prophetic, messianic and even mystical, shortly a theological element(200)? How else can Marx's materialistic dialectic justify a material, totalizing anticipation of the negation of the negativity of civil society resulting in the affirmation of the free association of rationally self-determining producers and even the realm of freedom, as indeed it does in the third volume of the Capital(201). While Hegel's dialectic does certainly stand on its head in terms of an affirmative as well as a negative theology, it can and does indeed, nevertheless, also stand materialistically on its feet, as particularly his dialectical analysis of civil society and bourgeois history does show very clearly(202). Hegel's idealistic dialectic contains in itself a strong materialistic element, without which Marx's materialistic dialectic would hardly have been possible. While Hegel does indeed reject on principle materialistic philosophies, he is nevertheless very much in sympathy with the materialist's grief and sorrow over the general fraud in civil society, its enormous derangement, disorganization and disorder of nature, the infinite falsehoods and lies which call themselves truth and right(203). In any case even today the idealistic-materialistic controversy is far from being settled. Hegel's notion of dialectic is not without reality and Marx's reality dialectic is not entirely without the notion.

A century after Marx wrote the Capital the business cycle still continues in European and American civil societies(204). But the universal crisis, which Marx foresaw, has still not yet occurred. The majority of the German, European and American bourgeoisie has still not yet learned dialectic from the process of capitalistic society, not to speak of from Marx or from Hegel, in spite of all the economic convulsions which have taken place since the two great thinkers taught their new method and in spite of the immense human suffering entailed in these crises up to the most recent depression of 1981-1983.

(Now managed by Keynesianism with other means: huge   military
investments,   up   to 2 trillion dollars in the USA alone.) But
all this does, of course, not mean that modern   civil   society
is   infinite   and   that   in   spite   of   all   the   particular
depressions and recessions the   universal   and   final   crisis,
which   Marx   predicted, will not occur some day in the future.
Considering at least this possibility   in   the   light   of   the
present economic, political, ecological and military situation
in advanced capitalistic society, it is not entirely unwise to
learn   dialectical   thinking   not only from Marx but also from
his greater teacher Hegel, in order to comprehend   better   the
contradictory   development of civil society and to engage in a
more adequate praxis and thus determine more   effectively   the
socio-ethically   most   desirable future. Logophobie should not
prevent us from doing so, not even in the name   of   idology   −
the destruction of the idol − the Demiurge of human thinking.

Alternative Futures

According to Hegel, civil society is characterized by the dialectic of particular and universal, individual and collective,
producer   and   consumer,   owner   and   worker,   rich   and   poor
classes,   luxury   and   misery(205).   This   dialectic   drives
bourgeois   society   beyond its own boundary. First, this inner
dialectic pushes this particular capitalistic society,   then
finally   civil society as such, as universal social formation,
beyond itself into different possible futures.
    We follow Hegel as closely and genetically as   possible,
as   in   his   highly mimetical dialectical thought he traces and
reconstructs the contradictory development   of   civil   society
from   his   Frankfurt   system program, system fragment of 1800,
his Jena critical writings and system designs over his   system
of   philosophy   and   encyclopedia   to his Berlin philosophy of
right and history and religion and   his   aesthetics: he   does
this   with   the   seven-mile boots of the dialectical notion as
universal,   particular   and   singular(206).   He   follows   the
dialectic   of   civil   society   through   Orient   and   Occident,
Antiquity and Modernity toward alternative futures: Future I −
the mechanized and automated society; Future II − always   more
extended   wars   with   always more abstract weapons, strategies
and tactics; Future III − the reconciled society(207).
    To be sure, Hegel is not a prophet and he does   not   want
to   be   one(208).   He   makes   his   astonishingly   precise
predictions, e.g. concerning the American and Slavic World   or

the history of art and religion, as Adorno remarks correctly, on the basis of the combination of an immense historical recollection and his dialectical logic, the first new logic since Aristotle(209). But Hegel does, indeed, sublate prophetic and messianic and even mystical content into philosophical form(210). Contrary to Bloch we must insist that Hegel has not betrayed the future beyond modern civil society and that precisely therefore he is so important for at least the mitigation of Future I, the resistance against Future II, and the realization of Future III, which can hardly come into existence without him and his theological, as well as rational, critical and revolutionary dialectic(211). At a time in which, as Adorno states, the moment of qualitative change has been missed in European and American civil societies, Hegel's social philosophy gains new actuality for social theory as well as for social praxis(212). This is particularly so, since Hegel has contrary to Marx, not only interpreted the dialectical history of civil society, but has also tried to intervene into it politically in terms of a future more rational and freer society(213).

As we proceed in following as mimetically as possible Hegel's dialectical philosophy of society, we concentrate on his most creative and fruitful time in Frankfurt and Jena: the Frankfurt system program, the Jena critical writings and system designs and the phenomenology of mind. They contain the fundamental themes concerning the dialectic of civil society and its resolution, which Hegel will elaborate later on in Nurnberg, Heidelberg and Berlin: in his system of philosophy, encyclopedia, philosophies of right and history, aesthetic and philosophy of religion. The limited space allows us no more than merely to indicate Hegel's later development of the fundamental aspects of the dialectic of bourgeois society and the remedy he tries to provide for it.

Mechanical State

From his Frankfurt system program of 1797 on, Hegel, by now being no longer a student of theology but rather being on his way to becoming a doctor of world wisdom, is highly critical of civil society as merely mechanical state(214). Guided by the idea of a free humanity Hegel moves from the world of nature to the world of man's work: society, state and history. Here he tries to show that there is no concrete idea of traditional or modern civil society as state. This is so,

since bourgeois society as state is something entirely
mechanical. There can be as little an idea of capitalistic
society as mechanical state as there can be an idea of a
machine. Only what is an object of freedom, so Hegel argues,
can be named idea. Civil society, is not an object of freedom.
We therefore must go beyond civil society as machine-like
state. This is so since every bourgeois society as
machine-like state must necessarily treat free men and women
as mechanical wheelwork. But capitalistic society as
mechanical state should not do this to free people. Therefore,
so Hegel concludes in a rather critical and revolutionray
manner, civil society as machine-like state ought to be
superseded. From the very beginning of and throughout his
sytematic philosophy Hegel recognizes in bourgeois society a
trend toward Future I - the totally mechanized and automated
society and resists it in the name of the idea of a free
humanity. Today the cancerous growth of civil society is
adequately expressed e.g., in the immense sprawl of the
metropolitan cities.

According to Hegel's Frankfurt system program beyond the
sphere of civil society as mechanical state lies the dimension
of the organic state. All ideas connected with this kind of
state, e.g. the Kantian idea of perpetual or even eternal
peace, are subordinated to the higher idea of human freedom.
Here at the same time Hegel wants to lay down the principles
of a history of humankind. He wants to unmask the whole
miserable human work of state, constitution, government and
legislation. Finally there come the ideas of a free moral
world order, divinity and immortality. In this context Hegel
intends to overthrow all superstitions. He plans to overcome
the traditional priesthood, which since recent times pretends
hypocritically to be rational itself, by reason itself. Here
in the dimension of history Hegel wants to present the
absolute freedom of all the "spirits," i.e. the nations. They
carry in themselves the intellectual world and therefore must
not search either for God or for immortality outside
themselves. From the very beginning and throughout his
systematic philosophy Hegel aims at Future III - the
socio-moral totality, the organic state of reason, the
community of nations, the realm of freedom, the realization of
a rational and free humanity.

Property

In 1801 at Jena, Hegel continues to describe in his essay "Difference of the Fichtean and Schellingean System of Philosophy" modern civil society, in which he himself lives, not as an internal state of reason or a substantial or organic state, but rather as an external state of necessity and understanding, of emergency and contingency(215). According to Hegel, the central interest of bourgeois society as state of necessity is property. The main constitutive purpose of capitalistic society as state of understanding is to prevent the violation of the property of its citizens, the bourgeois, rather than to prevent such damage after it has already occurred. Therefore, civil society as state of emergency must not only forbid real violations of property under punishment, but it must also obviate such damages. In relation to this final purpose the state of contingency must even forbid actions which in and for themselves do no immediate harm to any human being and as such appear to be completely indifferent. But these actions can make the violations of other people easier and thus can make the protection of the members of civil society or the discovery of the guilty individuals more difficult.

In his Jena critical writings, Hegel is fully aware of the fact that the dialectic of individual and collective in bourgeois society increases the chance of the unintended consequences of the actions of each of its members. The dialectic of capitalistic society requires its transformation into a state, which manages and controls the contingencies resulting from latent dysfunctions of the otherwise well intended actions of its members, set free precisely by that very dialectic.

In Hegel's view, the bourgeois does not subordinate himself to civil society as state of understanding out of any other motivation than in order to use and enjoy as freely as possible his or her property. There is, nevertheless, no action of the individual from which the consequent, functional and instrumental analytical understanding of civil society as state of necessity could not calculate and compute a possible damage for other people. The preventive understanding of bourgeois society and its force, the police fulfilling its duty, has to deal with this infinite possibility of damage, which one individual can do to the other quite unconsciously and without bad intent. Therefore there is in this bourgeois

ideal of civil society as state of emergency no action, move
or stir, which must not necessarily be subjected to a law and
taken under immediate supervision and control and to be noted
and paid attention to by the police and the other governing
bodies. Thus in bourgeois society as state of contingency,
which is based on and directed by the principle of analytical
understanding, the police knows very well where every
individual person is during every hour of the day and night
and what he or she is doing.

The dialectic of capitalistic society, which sets free
the particularity of the individual does, paradoxically
enough, also contain the tendency toward more and more
policing and administration, toward Future I: the totally
administered society, the police state. Fichte wanted even to
support this tendency by recommending that every citizen in
the state of understanding must carry all the time a passport
with his or her picture drawn into it(216). Hegel found it to
be under the dignity of a philosophy not of understanding, but
of reason, to support in civil society this tendency toward
more and more policing, the entirely administered society.

While Hegel's social philosophy of dialectical reason can
very well comprehend civil society as state of analytical
understanding, such state of necessity can hardly grasp such
philosophy. For Hegel philosophy is according to its very
nature something esoteric(217). It is not made for the "mob"
in civil society and it cannot be prepared for it. It is
philosophy only by the very fact that it contradicts understanding and thus even more so common sense. In relationship
to understanding and common sense of bourgeois society and
state, the world of philosophy is in and for itself a world
which is turned upside down: it moves from the universal to
the particular and not, like understanding, from the individual to the universal. The members of bourgeois society must
lift themselves up to the philosophy of reason. Philosophy
must not lower itself to them. As little as genuine art or
religion, true philosophy must ever make itself conform to
civil society as state of understanding. There exists a
dialectical tension throughout, from Frankfurt to Berlin,
between Hegel's philosphy of reason and civil society as a
state built epistemologically on analytical understanding.
This dialectical tension continues today in European and
American late capitalistic societies.

Hegel lived in German civil society, but as a philosopher
he was also out of it. Precisely this "extraterritoriality"

gave Hegel the possibility to penetrate so deeply into the
dialectic of civil society as state of necessity as indeed he
did(218). This its extraterritoriality makes Hegel's dialectic
so attractive to intellectuals, who share in it by their own
marginal social and political status in capitalistic society,
e.g. Jewish intellectuals from Marx over Freud to Bloch,
Lukacs, Horkheimer, Adorno, Marcuse, Kracauer, Fromm,
Sohn-Rethel, etc(219). It is a philosophy for all who suffer
from being at least to some extent in "exile." Rightly, E.
Wiesel remarked recently during a public discussion on
American National Television concerning the movie, "The Day
After," and the possibility of Future II – the thermonuclear
holocaust – that "the whole world is becoming 'Jewish,'" i.e.,
moving into exile. Hegel's social philosophy may be a guide
for Jewish and non-Jewish "exiles" to find their way home,
where, according to Bloch, nobody has been yet and where
everybody would like to be from childhood on(220).

Law

In Hegel's view the bourgeois natural law becomes through the
absolute opposition of the "pure" and the "natural" drive
intrinsic to it a representation of the complete dominion of
analytical understanding and the enslavement of the living
under the dead in civil society(221). Dialectical reason has
no part in the structure of bourgeois society as need system
and administration of justice including laws and courts and
police and corporations, and as state of understanding in
general. Therefore, reason rejects the structure of capitalistic society. Reason must do so, since it can find itself
most expressively only in the most perfect social
organization, which it can give to itself in its
self-formation: in a socio-moral totality, in a nation, in a
substantial state not of understanding, but of reason, in an
organic state.

     For Hegel, civil society as state of necessity is not a
rational organization in the sense of practical, communicative
rationality. It is rather merely a "rationalized" organization
in the sense of instrumental and functional rationality. In
bourgeois society as a state of necessity the nation is not
the organic body of a rich communicative life, but rather an
atomistic "army of life." It is a multiplicity, the elements
of which are substances absolutely opposed to each other.
These elements or substances are partially a variety of

points, the rational human beings, partially materials
modifiable by analytical understanding - commodities. The
unity of these elements is merely an abstract concept: the
law. The connection of these substances is an infinite
domination and control. Bourgeois society is a more or less
controlled aggregate of atoms. The dialectic of capitalistic
society, which emancipates these atoms produces precisely
therefore and thereby also a mania of control and of power
conformity. As such it tends from its very outset toward
Future I - the totally atomized, mechanized and administered
society! The "lonely crowd."

The absolute substantiality of the rational human points
and substances, the individual bourgeois, ground civil society
as a system of atomics, not of physics, but of practical
philosophy. In this practical philosophical system of
bourgeois society, like in the atomics of nature, an
analytical understanding, which is entirely foreign to the
particular atoms, becomes the law. In practical philosophy
this law of analytical understanding calls itself "right."
This law of understanding or right is a notion of totality.
This totality of right of civil society as state of understanding is supposed to oppose itself to every determinate
action of every particular individual and thus ought to
determine it and should thus kill the spontaneous living
element in it, the true personal identity.

The law of understanding or right is in civil society, be
it in Antiquity or Modernity, the Fiat justitia, pereat
mundus. This is the law of bourgeois society not even in the
milder sense, as Kant interpreted it: right must happen even
if all rogues, knaves and gangsters go under. It is rather the
law of capitalistic society in the harsh and radical sense:
right must take place even if thereby would be, by any chance,
eradicated, extirpated and exterminated all trust, pleasure,
delight, desire, love, all potentialities of a genuinely
socioethical identity with root and branch.

The dialectic of individual and collective has in civil
society as system of atomics, what Fromm calls a
"necrophilous" tendency(222). It gives preference to death
over life. It produces the bourgeois coldness, which
penetrates even, as Hegel observed, the heat of the passion of
lovers and the warmth of marriage and family, not to speak of
the communicative rationality and freedom of modern state and
history. There is nothing in bourgeois society itself, which
could control this necrophilia of which the administration of

justice is only one aspect. The cold subsumption of living labor under dead capital in the production and exchange process of civil society is another aspect.

By its very <u>necrophilia</u> the dialectic of capitalistic society anticipates and prepares its own historical sacrifice as self-sacrifice, departure and end. The most outstanding necrophilous characters, like, e.g. A. Hitler, are the products of the dialectic of civil society as well as the symptoms of its illness as well as its grave diggers, who hasten its movement to Future I - the neo-cesaristic society and through it to Future II - always larger and more abstract wars, finally ABC wars. Today the newly invented neutron bomb is the most adequate expression of the necrophilous character present in bourgeois society: it annihilates merely the living organisms and leaves dead property undamaged. But according to Hegel the same dialectic of individual and collective can also push beyond civil society as system of atomics, not toward Future I and Future II, but rather toward Future III: the absolute morality of the organic state and of a world society, in which a true unity of individual and community can be achieved. This is a matter not only of historical necessity, but also of human freedom.

Organic State

In Hegel's perspective man's subjective will in its limited passions is dependent(223). This dependent will finds the satisfaction of its particular purpose only inside of the general dependency of civil society as production and exchange process. But according to Hegel man's subjective will has also a substantial life, a reality in which it moves in the essential element and in which it has this element itself for the purpose of its existence. This essential element is itself the unification of the subjective and the rational will: it is the socio-moral totality, the substantial, organic state of reason in opposition to civil society as accidental, inorganic mechanical state of understanding. It is the reality, in which the individual has his or her freedom as absence of alienation and as identity in solidarity with others and enjoys it. The rational <u>citoyen</u> is the truth of the irrational bourgeois, the organic state of reason is the truth of irrational capitalistic society. As the rational state presupposes the sacrifice or self-sacrifice of civil society, so the citoyen the sacrifice or self-sacrifice of the bourgeois.

But the individual enjoys his or her freedom in the state of reason only insofar as he or she is the knowledge, faith and willing of the universal. This of course must not be taken in such a way, as if man's subjective will would come to its realization and enjoyment through the universal will and as if the universal will was a mere means for the self-realization of the subjective will and as if the subject would continually limit his or her freedom in relation to the other subjects. That happens in bourgeois society as state of necessity. Here in capitalistic society the common limitation, the mutual embarrassment makes a little space for each bourgeois, in which he or she can let himself or herself go. It is different with the freedom of the citizens in the rational state. For Hegel, concrete right, social morality, and organic state, and they alone, are the positive reality and satisfaction of freedom. The freedom, which in civil society is limited, is merely arbitrariness, which relates to the particularity of needs.

Bourgeois society is characterized by the dialectic of subjective and objective will, particular and universal freedom. In bourgeois society this dialectic of subjective and objective will reaches at best only a very relative and abstract identity. The dialectic of capitalistic society as state of necessity pushes beyond its boundaries toward Future III - the organic state of reason characterized by the reunion of particular and universal freedom. Here the objective essential will is no longer instrumentalized by the subjective accidental will of individuals or groups, nor is the individual will functionalized by the universal will. The substantial state is no longer the instrument of domination of one individual or one class in civil society over the other. It is no longer a class state. It is rather a state of reason, freedom and reconciliation.

Utopia

Hegel rejects the ideal of a philosophical utopia, in which the Absolute is already for itself prepared into something true and known and gives itself for complete enjoyment to the possibility of thought, which must only open up wide its mouth(224). From such utopian thinking is banned the troublesome assertoric and categorical work and construction. By such utopian thoughts' problematic and hypothetical shaking, the fruits fall from the tree of knowledge, which is planted in the sand of argumentation, all by themselves as already being cooked and digested. For the whole business of the reduced or half philosophy, which wants to be merely a problematic, hypothetical, preliminary, provisional and temporary attempt at thinking, the Absolute must necessarily already have been posited as absolutely true. Otherwise truth and knowledge could not result from the problematic and the hypothetical. Hegel's philosophy can not be counted among the utopian philosophies of this kind. It arrives at the alternative Futures only through hard dialectical work.

Likewise Hegel's philosophy is not one of the philosophical systems, which in his time are called "anti-socialistic" and which posit the being of the individual as the first and the highest(225). Hegel's philosophy has a more or less manifest tendency toward a humanistic socialism: Its central concern is Future III – the rational society, in which individual and community are truly reconciled and precisely, thereby, free. Of course, Hegel is not yet A. Blanqui or Marx.

War

During 1802-1803 Hegel published in Jena an essay entitled "On the scientific modes of treatment of the natural law, its position in practical philosophy and its relationship to the positive sciences of law"(226). During this time Hegel does not only study Dante's <u>Divina Comedia</u>. He also immerses himself critically into the new science of political economy. Hegel's Jena essay on natural law or social morality stands very much under the influence of a critical reception of Dante's theology as well as of Smith's, Ricardo's and Says's political economy.

In his essay on the natural law Hegel presupposes that the absolute social morality is nothing else than the nation or the organic state of reason. In this socio-moral totality the infinity or the form is the absolutely negative. As such the form is the mastering or restraining moment as received into its absolute notion. Here the form's overcoming or subduing function does not relate itself to particular determinations, but to the whole reality and potentiality of these determinations. The form connects itself to the life of civil society itself as the difference in the socio-ethical totality, the organic state. Thus the matter of bourgeois society is equal to the infinite form of the rational state.

But this happens in such a way that the positive element of this form is the absolute social morality. That means concretely: the individual belongs to a nation as rational state. The individual is not only bourgeois, but also and first of all citoyen.

The individual proves that he belongs to the nation as organic state negatively through the danger of death alone in an unambiguous way. The socio-moral totalities, the nations, constitute themselves through the absolute identity of the infinite element or the side of the relationship with the positive element, the organic state. Thereby the nations become individuals and posit themselves as individuals against other individual organic states. This position and individuality is the side of reality. If the nations are thought of without this reality, they are merely things of thought. It would be the abstraction of the essence without the absolute form. Such essence would thereby be essence-less. This relationship of individuality to individuality is a matter of proportionality and therefore a double relationship. The one relationship is the positive one: the quiet, equal coexistence of two states in peace time. The other relationship is the negative one: the exclusion of one national individuality by the other. For Hegel, both relationships are absolutely necessary.

Hegel comprehends the second relationship as a conquering function, which is taken into its notion; or as absolutely formal virtue, which is fortitude. Through this second side of the proportionality, so Hegel argues, is posited for the form and individuality of the socio-moral totality of the organic state, the necessity of war. In war there is present for Hegel the free potentiality, that not only particular determinations of civil society but the completeness of these determinations as life is destroyed. Bourgeois society is sacrificed and annihilated for the nation itself, the organic state, the socio-ethical totality, the inner difference of which it is.

The war, so Hegel states, maintains the socio-ethical health of the nations in their indifference against the determinations of capitalistic society and against the getting accustomed to these determinations of bourgeois life and against their petrification. Thus the movement of the wind saves the lake from rot into which a continual stillness would put it. A perpetual or even eternal peace, so Hegel argues against Kant, would lead to the decay of civil society as well as the organic state of reason.

According to Hegel, the inner dialectic of civil society pushes beyond its boundary into international wars. Without war bourgeois society would harden in its structures. It would stagnate. It would become ill. The dialectic of capitalistic society leads either to its petrification and ossification and thus to its ruin or to Future II - war among states, the dialectic of history. Paradoxically enough civil society itself pays for such wars, which originate from its own dialectic with the entirety of its own determinations, the life and property of its members, which the organic state is supposed to protect. It seems that not only Future I and Future III, but also Future II can be the result of the necessary dialectical sacrifice and even self-sacrifice of bourgeois society. Of course, Hegel is not yet O. Spengler.

Legislation and Courts

According to Hegel, to the civil society as system of abstract right belong in Antiquity as well as in Modernity the questions concerning the rightful ground or the legitimation of possession, contract and punishment(227). But in Hegel's view these issues are of subordinate interest and remain in the realm of formality. Furthermore, to bourgeois society as system of abstract right in general belongs the whole endless expansion of legislation concerning contracts of individuals with individuals related to things or types of labor, injuries, customs, duties and tolls at roads, markets and ports, etc. Here Hegel agrees fully with Plato, that it is under the dignity of "beautiful and good men" to legislate concerning such issues. Good and beautiful men will find the multitude of determinations, which have to be settled concerning these items, all by themselves, if God blesses them with a truly socio-ethical constitution. But if this is not the case, then the members of civil society will spend their whole lives to determine and to improve many of these issues. They shall hope and think that this way they will finally acquire the best type of human society.

But in Hegel's view, the bourgeoisie lives in an illusion or even delusion concerning such hope. In reality the members of civil society behave like sick people who because of intemperance and incontinence do not want to step out of their bad diet. Therefore, they do not effect anything else through their remedies and medicaments than to generate more manifold and greater illnesses. At the same time the members of bourgeois society do always hope, when somebody advises and counsels them concerning a new remedy or medicine, to become healthy through it. Likewise droll, funny, comical and ludicrous are for Hegel those bourgeois legislators who make laws about all these particular issues and continually improve them, in the hope to reach an end in this process. They do not know that they do, indeed, in a certain sense, cut to pieces the mythical watersnake Hydra: new heads are growing where old ones are taken off. More new and greater social problems arise in bourgeois society where old ones have just been resolved.

Hegel agrees with Plato that with the increasing licentiousness and illness in civil society more and more courts are opening up. No greater sign can be found for the bad, ignominious and disgraceful education and discipline in bourgeois society than that not only the bad people, the gangsters, and people of the lower, second estate, the craftsmen, artisans, mechanics and workmen, owners of factories and salesmen need more excellent medical doctors and judges. Even those people who belong to the higher first estate of philosophers, politicians and military men, who boast of their liberal education, are compelled to have a justice which is imposed on them by others as masters and judges. Even these educated people are forced to spend much time in the courts with suits and advocacies. But, according to Hegel, such legislation and these courts and the whole bourgeois administration of justice can not really heal the cancer in civil society, when once it has started to spread. They can not really arrest the dialectic of civil society as it moves toward the end of this social formation. This was not possible in the Phoenician, Greek, or Roman civil society. It is not possible today in modern Euro-American capitalistic society.

Remedy

In Hegel's view civil society as system of abstract right develops itself as universal condition and thus destroys the free social morality, wherever the latter is mixed up with those bourgeois conditions and can not be separated from them and their consequences(228). Hegel considers it therefore necessary, that this system of bourgeois society is taken up consciously and that it is recognized in its own right and that it is excluded from the first, the noble and universal estate of philosophers, statesmen and soldiers, and that it is granted and conceded its own particular estate as its own realm: the bourgeois class of artisans, manufacturers and merchants. In this bourgeois class as "middle class" between the first estate of philosophers, politicans and soldiers, and the third estate of farmers, civil society and its system of property can settle down for the time being. Here in the bourgeois class the system of abstract right can develop its whole dialectical activity in relation to its own confusion and the supersession of one turmoil by the other. It can move from one crisis to the other. In this concession Hegel does obviously go much further than Plato or Aristotle were willing to go or any other of the great philosophers of the Orient or the Occident, of Antiquity or Middle Ages. In this, like in other issues, Hegel was in spite of all his critique of modernity, an extremely modern philosopher. Hegel does not regress into Platonism in spite of his appreciation of the great thinker's world historical importance.

In terms of this concession, so Hegel argues, the potential of the bourgeois class determines itself in such a way that it exists in the possession of things as such and in the relative justice, which is possible here in relation to property. While, in Fromm's words, "being" is left to the first, the noble and universal estate of philosophers, statesmen and soldiers, "having" is relegated and attributed to the second estate, the bourgeois class. Hegel's remedy for modern civil society is precisely this kind of differentiation. His medicament is to leave modern civil society to itself and to its dialectic and its confusion and crises, and to its alternative Futures.

At the same time, so Hegel states, the bourgeois class constitutes a coherent system. In this system of civil society the relationship of possession is taken up into its formal unity. Thereby every individual, since he is as such able to have property, relates himself immediately against all others as universal or as citizen in the sense of bourgeois. The bourgeois finds for the political nullity, according to which the members of the bourgeois class are nothing else than private individuals, his compensation in the fruits of relative peace and acquisitions, earnings and gains in the complete if also transitory security of his enjoyment. This security goes toward the detail of this enjoyment as well as toward the whole. The security goes toward the whole of the enjoyment for every individual bourgeois, insofar as he is exempt from fortitude and from the necessity to sacrifice his life, which belongs as duty to the first, the universal and noble estate. The bourgeois is withdrawn from the duty to expose himself to the danger of a violent death. Such danger is, of course, for the individual the absolute insecurity of all enjoyment and abstract right.

Through this superseded mixture of principles, so Hegel assures us, and the constituted and conscious separation of the potential of the first and the second estate, each of the two principles receives its own right. What thereby has alone been achieved is precisely that, what ought to be accomplished according to reason, according to the notion as the dialectical unity of the universal, particular and singular: the idea of right, the reality of social morality as absolute indifference. Everything else in the social world is irrationality. From such irrationality the Phoenician, Greek and Roman state has died and the modern state may very well die from it.

At the same time the reality of social morality has been achieved as the real relationship in the existing opposition. In consequence this opposition is mastered, overcome, conquered and subdued by the reality of social morality as absolute indifference. In this process, this overcoming and mastering itself is indifferentiated and reconciled. That precisely is Hegel's remedy for the modern world: Future III – the reconciled society, the realm of social morality, the realm of freedom. It is precisely this Future III which, according to Hegel, philosophy is to promote in theory as well as in praxis.

Sacrifice and Tragedy

For Hegel the reconciliation consists precisely in the knowledge of the necessity and in the right, which the socio-moral totality, the organic state gives to its inorganic nature and to the subterranean, the underground powers – civil society and its dialectic – by leaving to them a part of itself as sacrifice(229). This is so, since social morality's power of sacrifice commits itself in the perceiving and objectivating of its entanglement with the inorganic, the mechanical structure of civil society. Through this perception social morality dissolves its entanglement with the negative, the inorganic, bourgeois society. The mechanical, capitalistic society, is severed, separated, detached and it is known as such. The inorganic civil society, is thereby itself taken up,

received, drawn up, absorbed and assimilated into the
indifference of the realm of social morality. The living
socio-moral totality has put that, what it knows as part of
itself, into the mechanical, bourgeois society, and has
sacrificed it to death. Thereby the organic social morality
has at the same time recognized the right of the inorganic,
capitalistic society, and purified itself from it. Future III,
the realm of social morality, is fully constituted by the
sacrifice of civil society as an integral part of itself.

For Hegel this whole process is nothing else than the
execution and performance of the tragedy in the realm of
social morality, which the Absolute plays with itself. The
Absolute gives birth to itself eternally into objectivity. The
Absolute thereby surrenders itself in this its form to
suffering and death. But the Absolute elevates itself again
out of its ashes into its glory. According to the Phoenician
religious worldview the Phoenix Bird burns itself to ashes and
out of it rises again a young Phoenix in new strength, vigour,
power and energy(230). According to the Christian religious-
metaphysical system of interpretation of reality and
orientation of action, the God surrenders himself to
crucifixion and then rises again from death. The historical
Good Friday is the representation of the metaphysical Good
Friday, and the historical Easter Sunday represents the
metaphysical Easter Sunday(231). The tragedy of the
socio-moral totality and its resolution reflects the tragedy
of the Absolute and its resolution. The Divinia Comedia is
first and the humana comedia is second. This sequence
constitutes Hegel's dialectical-theistic philosophy: as the
arrival of God as spirit presupposes his crucifixion, so the
rise of the socio-moral totality the negation of its intrinsic
difference - bourgeois society. Since Marx wants to build a
non-tragic human society, he feels compelled atheistically to
correct Hegel and to uncouple the socio-ethical totality from
its tragic theological prototype by transposing it into the
mere ideological reflection of the former in its present
antagonistic and as such tragic condition. By not making this
sacrifice of theology Hegel gives a depth dimension to the
revolutionary critique of and action in capitalistic society
which Marx's historical materialism does no longer have.

Hegel can resolve the problem of civil society and its
dialectic only in the context of this double divine-human
tragedy and comedia. In Hegel's theological-philosophical
perspective the necessary price to be paid for the

establishment of the realm of social morality or freedom is
the   sacrifice of civil society. In spite of the sacrifice of
theology and all demythologization and turning Hegel from his
head on his feet, Marx, Engels, Lukacs, Bloch and other
Hegelians on the Left have, nevertheless,   not   removed
themselves too far from Hegel after all: also for them the
development of the realm of freedom beyond the realm of
necessity presupposes the sacrifice and even self-sacrifice of
capitalistic society(232). Not only the dialectical idealist
but also the dialectical materialists plead for the cunning
and the power of reason: the instrumentalization of the
negative in the interest of the history of liberation. But
while Hegel is still able to ground and thus legitimate the
dialectical sacrifice and self-sacrifice of civil society
theologically and humanistically, Marx and his followers can
do this merely humanistically or not at   all.   Hegel's
philosophy is the more critical and revolutionary one without
which Marxism may easily yield to the   temptation   of
positivism, after the most urgent economic problems are once
taken care of.

Work and Tool

The potentials of language, work, family and recognition as
they appear in Hegel's System Designs I and III are in general
abstract and ideal(233). Work and possession, like language
and recognition become something other in civil society and
state than they are in their own abstract notion. Outside of
bourgeois society work goes for itself toward the need of the
individual as such. Likewise the possession is that of an
individual person. But in civil society work, as well as
possession, does in its singularity become universal. Here we
concentrate on the dialectic of the potential of work and tool
as it finds its universalization and concretization in civil
society and as such drives this social formation beyond itself
mainly toward Future I - the totally mechanized and automated
society. An iron logic seems to be at work here from Hegel's
time into our present.
     According to Hegel in civil society man supersedes his
merely formal work-activity in the machine(234). He lets the
machine work for himself completely. But every fraud which man
commits this way against nature and with which he remains
inside of its singularity, takes revenge against man himself.
The more man gains from nature and the more he subjugates it

to himself via the machine, the lower man falls himself. As man lets nature be worked over by different types of machinery, he does not really supersede – at least not for some time – the necessity of his own working. He only pushes it off and postpones it and moves it away from nature. Man does not direct himself in a living way toward nature as a living reality. This negative vivacity rather escapes. The working, which remains for man, becomes itself machine-like, extremely mechanical. Man minimizes work only for the whole, but not for the individual. He rather increases his workload. This is so, since the more mechanical the work becomes, the less value it has and the more man must work in this machine-like mode. Hegel anticipates to some extent Marx's value theory.

In civil society the singularization of work in terms of an intense division of labor increases immensely the quantity of things worked upon. In Hegel's time in an English manufactory 18 people work on one needle. Each individual has only one particular side of the work and only this side alone. One worker would maybe not be able to make 20 needles a day, not even one needle. These 18 work activities distributed among 10 people produce 4000 needles a day. To the labor of these ten workers, if they would work below 18 work activities, 48,000 needles would come in one day. But in the same proportion in which the produced quantity increases, the value of work falls. The productivity of civil society is a curse for its workers.

Furthermore, in bourgeois society the work becomes absolutely deadly. It turns into dead machine work. The skill of the individual worker becomes infinitely limited. The consciousness of the factory worker is degraded to the ultimate dullness. The connection of the particular kind of work with the whole infinite mass of needs present in capitalistic society can no longer be overlooked. It turns into a blind dependency. As a consequence a distant operation often very suddenly hinders or makes superfluous and useless the labor of a whole class of people, who were used to satisfy their needs through this kind of work. As the assimilation of nature becomes more comfortable through the moving in of in-between members in the production process, these steps of metabolism are infinitely divisible and the mass of the comfortable makes them again absolutely uncomfortable. Civil society is characterized by this dialectic of the comfortable.

In capitalistic society these manifold work activities

and needs as things must likewise realize their notion, their abstraction. The universal notion must likewise be a thing as they are. But this thing must, as a universal thing, represent all things. Money is this materially existing notion. Money is in bourgeois society a form of unity. Money is in capitalistic society the form of the potentiality of all things, of the need. The dialectic of civil society aims at total monetarization. Hegel anticipates Marx's and Habermas's theory of monetarization: the inner colonization of people's life world by the economic subsystem(235). Such inner colonization points to alternative Future I – the totally monetarized and bureaucratized society.

Thus the need and the work elevated into this universality forms for itself in a great nation a gigantic system of commonality and mutual dependence: The system of civil society. It is the in itself moving life of the dead. In its movement it moves back and forth blindly and in an elementary way. As a wild beast civil society needs a continual strict domination and taming. That is the task of the organic state, the socio—moral totality. The negative must be treated negatively, if the affirmative is ever to arise. Deregulation is not always the peak of political wisdom, particularly not in the long run. Hegel supersedes the negative dialectic of bourgeois society in the positive dialectic of the organic state of reason and freedom. Thereby Hegel does not only anticipate, but also transcend Adorno's negative dialectic.

But finally here in civil society the drive of man withdraws completely from work. It lets nature consume itself. It looks quietly at this self-consumption of nature. It governs with little work input the whole production process. This is the cunning not of reason, but of analytical understanding. That is the honor of cunning against the power of nature. The blind natural power must be grasped on one side, that it may direct itself against itself. It must be understood. It must be understood as determination. Drive must be active against this determination. Drive must make this determination as movement go back into itself, to supersede itself. Man is then the fate of the singular element in nature.

Since the individual's work in capitalistic society is this abstract work, he behaves as abstract ego or according to the mode of a thing. He does not behave as an embracing, content-rich, circumspect spirit, who dominates a large range

of things and is master over it. The individual in bourgeois
society has no concrete work and is not a concrete being. His
energy consists rather in analyzing, in abstracting, in
differentiating of the concrete totality into many abstract
aspects. The self of the worker is reified.

As in civil society the work of the individual becomes
completely mechanical, it belongs more and more to a manifold
determination. But the more abstract and machine-like the work
of the individual becomes in bourgeois society, the more he is
only the abstract activity. Thereby the individual is finally
able to pull himself out of the work process. He can
substitute the external nature in place of his own activity.
He needs mere movement. He finds it in the external nature.
The pure movement is nothing else than the relationship of the
abstract forms of space and time. It is the abstract external
activity. It is the machine.

More and more in civil society the worker can step back
from the machine and let it take his place: the dialectic of
civil society as working process leads to Future I - the
totally mechanized, automated, roboticized and cyberneticized
society. It will itself be a huge mega-machine with similarity
to the planetary system and its lawful movements. It will be
extremely productive and extremely reified and alienated. It
will be the very opposite of a reconciled society
characterized by absolute social morality, unconditional
mutual recognition, universal solidarity and freedom. It will
be as much determined by the instrumental rationality as the
reconciled society will be characterized by practical and
communicative rationality. Hegel spends his energy rather in
describing the realm of absolute social morality or reconciled
society, than the totally mechanized and automated society.
But the possibility of Future I is intrinsic to Hegel's
analysis of the dialectic of civil society as dialectic of
work and tools. Of course Future I is as much the end of
capitalistic society as Future II or Future III. In any case
the world historical transition is at hand.

Transition

It is not difficult to see, so Hegel states in his
Phenomenology of Mind toward the end of his stay in Jena, that
our period in history is a birth time, a time of
transition(236). The spirit of man has broken with the old
order of things so far prevailing in European civil society

and state, and with their old ways of thinking. The spirit of
man intends to let them all sink into the depth of the past
and to set about its own transformation. There are
contemporary thinkers on the Right and the Left who are
convinced, that the transition period Hegel was concerned with
continues today and will proceed for some time into the
future(237).

As the dialectic of European civil society proceeds and
moves beyond itself, frivolity and boredom are spreading in
the established order of things(238). Frivolity and boredom
are the foreboding of something unknown. Frivolity and boredom
in European bourgeois society betoken that there is something
else - something other - approaching. This gradual falling to
pieces of European capitalistic society, which first does not
alter very much the general appearance of its totality, is
suddenly interrupted by the sunrise, which in a flash and at a
single stroke, brings to view the form and structure of a new
world: a new socio-moral totality.

Later Hegel speaks of the possibility of the rise of a
new post-European and post-bourgeois American and Slavic
world(239). Hegel thinks particularly of a post-European and
post-bourgeois American world, which has moved through the
stage of civil society and its dialectic of rich and poor
classes. It can no longer arrest this dialectic through
external sporadic and systematic or through internal
colonization. It has through revolution achieved an organic
state and a living rationality and absolute social morality.
In this new socio-moral totality individual and collective are
reconciled to an extent never accomplished in the previous
European, Near Eastern, Asian or African world. Hegel rejects
any abstract cosmopolitanism, world republic or world state,
which relates itself mainly in "protestant" and
"revolutionary" terms to the concrete existing nations, but
does not open up any new vision of a concrete, living
socio-moral totality.

For Hegel, Future III - the reconciled society, can best
be realized in a new American and Slavic world. Beyond the new
American or Slavic World, Hegel envisions the self-realization
of the socio-moral totality of the world spirit, the spirit of
the human species, the community of nations, whose right is
higher than that of any particular mechanical or organic state
in history(240). Contrary to some Marxist critics, this world
spirit or spirit of the world is not identical with God's
absolute spirit. The world spirit must be in accordance with

the Absolute Spirit. It must elevate itself to God's reason,
providence, plan and purpose. But the world spirit is not
synonymous with or equivalent to God's absolute spirit. Hegel
is not a pantheist. The human totality is finite and remains
subordinate to the Divine Totality. Divine and human totality
remain different in their identity.

Ultimately for Hegel the dialectic of civil society does
not only move toward a reconciled post-European and post-
bourgeois American or Slavic world and the self-realization of
the socio-moral totality of the human species, the world
spirit, but into God's absolute love and freedom. Hegel does,
indeed, as Lenin states, find God in everything, but
particularly in the world-historical process as sequence of
social and political revolutions(241). For Hegel nothing in
history happens without God and all is his work: even the
dialectic of civil society and bourgeois history and their
teleology(242).

Anamnesis and Telos

According to Hegel, spirit comes to its existence not only in
space, but also in time; not only in nature, but also in
history(243). History is the process of becoming in terms of
knowledge, a conscious self-mediating process, a learning
process. Spirit is externalized and empties itself into time.
But this form of self-abandonment is, similarly, the emptying
of itself by itself. The negative is negative of itself. This
way of becoming presents a slow procession and succession of
spiritual shapes, spirits, a gallery of pictures, a series of
nations and thus also of civil societies. Each of these
nations and societies is endowed with the entire wealth of the
spirit of the human species. Each of these nations and
societies which follow each other in history moves so slowly
in time just for the purpose that its members, the individual
persons, can permeate and assimilate all this wealth of the
substance of the national and the world spirit. Modern civil
society is one moment in this long history of the spirit of
the human species.

The telos of this world history, is absolute knowledge or
spirit-knowing-itself as spirit. It finds its pathway in the
anamnesis of spiritual forms, the nations and civil societies
as they are in themselves and as they accomplish the
organization of their spiritual kingdom. Their conservation
looked at from the side of their free existence, appearing in

the form of contingency, is history. Looked at from the side
of their intellectually comprehended organization, their
conservation is the science of the ways in which knowledge
appears, i.e., philosophy, more specifically phenomenology.
Both together, history and philosophy — or history
intellectually comprehended — form the anamnesis and the
Golgotha of God's absolute spirit, the divine tragedy, the
metaphysical Good Friday, the reality, the truth, the
certainty of his throne, without which he would be lifeless,
solitary and alone. Only, so Hegel adapts from Schiller's poem
"The Friendship" and his "Philosophical Letters," out of the
"chalice of this realm of spirits foams forth to God his own
Infinitude"(244).

As civil society is sacrificed to the socio-moral
totality of the nation and the nations are sacrificed to the
socio-ethical totality of the human species, so this
socio-ethical totality elevates itself sacrificially into
God's absolute spirit. The tragedy of social morality of the
human species is superseded into the tragedy of the Absolute.
The pain of this elevation of individuals as well as of civil
societies and nations and the human species as a whole is
painless, so Hegel states following Meister Eckehart and the
whole Judeo-Christian mystical tradition, since it ends in
absolute enjoyment of the reunion of Divine and human nature:
divine and human totality(245).

When Marx was asked once what would come after the realm
of freedom built on the dimension of necessity, he answered
that he did not know. His greater teacher was not satisfied
with such agnosticism. For Hegel, the dialectic of civil
society does ultimately not end in Future I — the totally
instrumentalized, mechanized, automated, cyberneticized,
roboticized, administered society, or in Future II — more and
more extended wars with more and more abstract weapons,
strategies and tactics, finally ABC wars, or even with Future
III — the rational, substantial, organic state, a reconciled
American or Slavic world or the socio-moral totality of
humanity bound together by anamnestic and proleptic
solidarity, but in God's absolute spirit, freedom and love.
But while the telos of history is, as Hegel sees it, mystical
indeed, it does in no way render harmless, uncritical or
unrevolutionary the immediate historical process: the
dialectic of contemporary civil society. This goal of history,
as Hegel envisions it, can rather provide the potential and
motivation for modern men and women to act out the dialectic

of late capitalistic society: to try to mitigate at least
Future I, to resist Future II and thus to prepare as
passionately as possible a non-catastrophic transition to
Future III(246). In any case, much of Hegel's social
philosophy has not yet happened: While the present social
totality is indeed the untruth, it does nevertheless contain
in itself the potentiality to become the truth. It can be
actualized through critical thought and revolutionary praxis.

Forces and Relations of Production

Karl Lowith, to whom Habermas owes the most penetrating
analysis of the intellectual break between Hegel and the first
generation of his pupils, particularly the young Hegelians,
has also pointed out the subterranean affinity between the
position of these Hegelians and themes in the thought of the
young Hegel, particularly in his Jena System Designs I, II,
III(247). Habermas's theory of communicative praxis stands in
the tradition of the Young Hegelians, particularly of
Feuerbach and Marx, but at the same time differentiates itself
critically from them. The reason for Habermas's critique of
Marx is the latter's insufficient treatment of the dialectic
between labor and recognition or communicative interaction,
between forces of production and relations of production,
realm of necessity and realm of freedom.

Long before Marx wrote his "Paris Manuscripts" and the
"German Ideology" he declared in his "Contribution to the
Critique of Hegel's Philosophy of Right," that at least for
Germany, the criticism of religion had been largely completed,
namely by Feuerbach(248). For Marx, the criticism of religion
is the premise of all criticism, particularly the criticism of
state, society and family. The profane existence of error is
compromised once its celestial oratio pro aris et foci has
been refuted. Man, who has found in the fantastic reality of
heaven, where he sought a supernatural being, only his own
reflection, will no longer be tempted to find only the
semblance of himself - a non-human being - where he seeks and
must seek his true reality. Thus Marx has the critique of
religion behind himself and can now devote himself completely
to the critique of state, society and family. So at least he
thought! Habermas's very concern with religion shows, of
course, that Marx's statement that the critique of religion
had been largely completed, was somewhat premature, not only
for Germany, but also for France and the USA and other

capitalistic countries as well - even for socialistic Russia and China(249).

Marx, after having settled the religious question for himself, rediscovered in his "Paris Manuscripts" and in his "German Ideology" that interconnection between labor and the struggle for recognition in the form of the dialectic of the forces of production and the relations of production which for several years had claimed Hegel's philosophical interest, stimulated by his studies of political economics(250). Marx did this without any direct knowledge of Hegel's Jena system designs. Marx had, of course, indirect knowledge of them since the potentials of language, work, love, recognition and nation contained in them resurface again and again in later works of Hegel, which were known to him, e.g., the phenomenology, philosophy of right and history, etc. Marx develops in his "Paris Manuscripts" a critique of the last chapter of Hegel's phenomenology of mind: "Absolute knowledge"(251). Here Marx maintains that Hegel had taken the viewpoint of modern political economy, for he had comprehended labor as the essence of man, in which man has confirmed himself. It is in this passage of the "Paris Manuscripts," published for the first time only in 1932, in which Habermas finds the materialistic key to uncode Hegel's Jena system designs in the perspective of political economy and thus, by moving from Marx to Hegel, to reinterpret it in a materialistic and atheistic manner.

Marx stated in his "Paris Manuscripts" that what is great in Hegel's phenomenology and its final result - the dialectic, the negativity as the moving and generating principle - is, that Hegel comprehends the self-generation of man as a process(252). Hegel sees the objectification as de-objectification, as externalization and as sublation of this externalization. Thus Hegel comprehends the essence of labor and conceives objective man, the true man since he is the actual man, as the result of his own labor. The real, active behavior of man toward himself as species being, as the activation of himself as a real genus-being, i.e., as human being, is possible only through the fact that he really works out and brings forth all his species-forces. This again is only possible through the total action of men, i.e., only as the result of history. Man must relate himself to the species-forces as objects. This again is only possible in the form of alienation.

According to Habermas from this point of view Marx

himself attempted to reconstruct the world-historical process by which the human species forms itself in terms of the laws of the reproduction of social life(253). Marx finds the mechanism of change of the system of social labor in the contradiction between the power over natural processes, accumulated by means of social labor, on the one hand, and the institutional framework of interactions that are regulated in a "natural," i.e. primitive and pre-rational way, on the other. This corresponds to Hegel's dialectic of work and recognition.

But a precise analysis of the first part of the "German Ideology" reveals to Habermas that Marx does not actually explicate the interrelationship between the struggle for recognition and labor(254). But instead Marx, under the unspecific title of social praxis, reduces interaction to work, communicative action to instrumental action. Just as in Hegel's Jena system designs, more specifically, his philosophy of spirit, the use of tools mediates between the working subject and the natural objects, so for Marx instrumental action, labor, the productive activity, which regulates the material metabolism of the human species with nature, becomes the paradigm for the generation of all other categories – language, love, struggle for recognition and nation(255). Marx resolves everything into the self-movement of production. Because of this, so Habermas argues, Marx's brilliant insight into the dialectical relationship between the forces of production and the relations of production could be and was very quickly misinterpreted in a mechanistic manner(256).

Thus in order to guarantee the unity of the self-formative process of the human species after uncoupling it from the theological foundation it had in Hegel's philosophy, Marx first reduced all media of man's self-realization to the dialectic of work and recognition and finally to work alone. Habermas does not want to make this mistake. While he, like Marx, uncouples the sphere of morality from the Absolute Spirit, the human tragedy from the divine tragedy, world wisdom from divine wisdom, he tries nevertheless to overcome the subsequent disintegration of man's self-formative process and his "I" by reducing its media to the dialectic of labor and interaction, mediated through language. Doing this, Habermas remains, of course, still caught up in modern reductionism and in the dilemma, that the other media of man's self-formative process – love and nation – are short changed and that the unity of man's self-actualization is jeopardized or even made impossible. It must be expected that the neo-conservatives shall try to take advantage of this theological deficiency and this deficiency concerning love and nation and shall stress religion, family and nationalism in terms of their courage to education and to tradition(257). Our concern with the theological glowing fire in historical materialism and the consequent unity of all media of human self-realization in their difference has the intent to strengthen it against neo-conservative objections.

Liberation

Habermas is fully aware of the fact, that in contemporary late capitalistic action systems the neo-conservatives make the attempt to reorganize entirely the communicative nexus of interactions in the media of language, work, love, recognition and nation, no matter how much these interactions have been hardened into quasi-natural, highly instrumentalized forms: into the subsystem of systematically distorted language, and the no less instrumentalistically deformed economic subsystem, familial subsystem, political subsystem, and total national action system(258). This attempt of reorganization is being made according to the model of technically progressive systems of rational, goal-directed, instrumental, functional action, of the medium of tool and labor. In this situation, so Habermas argues, we have reason enough to keep these two dimensions – labor and recognition, forces of production and relations of production, instrumental action and communicative praxis – rigorously separated.

According to Habermas, a mass of wishful historical conceptions adheres to the idea of a progressive rationalization of labor. Although hunger still holds sway over two-thirds of the earth's population, the abolition of hunger is not a utopia in the negative sense. It could be done! The technology for doing it is available. But for Habermas to set free the technical forces of production, including the construction of cybernetic and learning machines, which can stimulate the complete sphere of the functions of rational, goal-directed, instrumental, functional actions far beyond the capacity of natural consciousness, and thus can substitute for human effort, is not identical with the development of practical norms which can fulfill the dialectic of recognition or moral relationships in an interaction free of any form of enslavement and exploitation, on the basis of a reciprocity allowed to have its full and non-coercive scope. Habermas thinks of communication without domination, of a brotherly-sisterly communication community.

In Habermas's view, liberation from hunger and misery does not necessarily converge with liberation from servitude and degradation. This is so, since there is no automatic developmental relation between work and recognition. Still, so Habermas argues, there is a dialectical connection between the two dimensions of labor and interaction. For Habermas neither Hegel's Jena system designs, particulary the reality philosophy, nor Marx's "German Ideology" have clarified adequately this dialectic between work and recognition. But in any case, Hegel and Marx can persuade Habermas of the relevance of this dialectic. Habermas knows that the self-formative process of the spirit of the individual as well as of the human species essentially depends on that relationship between labor and interaction. But, so we may add, it also depends on the dialectic of language and work, work and love, love and recognition, recognition and nation. Most of all, the self-formative process of individual and species must be unified in order not to have pathological, i.e. schizophrenic, results. Since Habermas wants, as little as Marx, to return to the tragic Absolute of Hegel's philosophy and of the whole Eastern and Western mythological and religious-metaphysical tradition, this unity of the self-constitutive process of the human individual and species remains a problem. It seems to me, that also Habermas's theory of the language-mediated dialectic of work and communicative praxis is not able to resolve this problem. As long as this is so, the Hegelian theological option should be kept open(259). While Habermas, like Hegel before, notices the disintegration of the religious-metaphysical worldviews, he is nevertheless like him also aware that these systems of interpretation and orientation are still very much around and as such must be taken seriously in practical discourse and its argumentative process(260). This is particularly also true for Hegel's own worldview, in which he intended to preserve the truth of Christianity and the other world religions through the present world historical transition period(261).

Transcendence and Immanence

According to Habermas, during the historical-intermediate stage of social evolution the dualism between divine tran-

scendence   and   an   almost   completely   desacralized   world-
immanence could still be mediated to some extent(262). In
order to legitimate the sphere right, which had been differentiated out of religion, and the rules of prudence of profane
exercise of power, the sacred interpretation of the king or
his office was sufficient. It was not even necessary to
transform the coronation of the king into an eighth sacrament.
In the occidental high cultures the two-realm theory was the
foundation for an, however tension-filled, coalition between
church and worldly regime. Transcendence and immanence were
different and maybe mutually exclusive, but they were still
held together by those and other mechanisms(263).

　　With the entrance into modernity these and other mechanisms of mediation between the transcendent and immanent have
become ineffective. Hegel sees himself confronted by the inefficiency of these mechanisms(264). In response to it, Hegel
develops his whole philosophy as a gigantic theodicy, as a new
conjugation of the transcendent and immanent, divine nature
and human nature, revelation and reason, religion and reason,
divine reason and world, divine providence and history, faith
and enlightenment, divine wisdom and world wisdom, absolute
and relative, infinite and finite, God and world, redemption
and freedom: shortly, a new <u>coincidentia oppositorum</u>.

　　In Habermas's view, there are different factors, which
are responsible for the inefficiency of the historical-
intermediate mechanisms of reconciliation between the transcendent and the immanent, the sacred and the profane in
modernity. With Protestantism disappear many of the pre-
Christian elements, which Catholicism had preserved. Thereby
is sharpened the demand of strictly universalistic commandments and correspondingly individualized ego-structures. With
the disintegration of the Catholic Church into several
confessions and a large number of denominations, sects and
cults (900 groups in the USA alone), the membership in the
community of the faithful loses its exclusivity. But at the
same time it loses also its rigid institutional character.
Europeans and North Americans learn in bourgeois society to
recognize the principle of tolerance and voluntarism of the
religious associations as being universally valid. It must be
noted here that exclusivity and rigid institutional church are
of course characteristics of Christianity, Judaism and Islam,
but are quite foreign to religions in the Far East, e.g., in
Japan(265). These characteristics belong to a rather extremely
differentiated stage in the evolution of mythical and

religious-metaphysical   systems   of   interpretation   and
orientation, which resists all forms of syncretism, be it in
the late Roman Empire or in modern advanced capitalistic
societies(266).

Finally, in most recent times theological currents gain
significance and influence, which interpret the message of
salvation in radically this-world terms. They flatten out and
make shallower the traditional dualism between the transcendent and the immanent, the religious and the secular.
Habermas thinks of liberal theology and particularly critical
political and liberation theology(267). According to Habermas,
in these theologies, particularly in political theology, God
signifies, almost exclusively, merely a communication structure. This communciation structure makes it necessary for the
participants to elevate themselves on the basis of mutual
recognition of their identity beyond the accidentality of a
merely external particular existence. This analysis does of
course not agree with the self-understanding of political
theology. For the political theologian it is rather the
communication structure of discipleship which helps   to
overcome despair in the absence of God's providence be it in
the world of nature, the personal world, the social world, or
the cultural world(268). The political theologian determines
God as the Reality who keeps history open and rescues the
innocent victims, who have been slaughtered, in their
annihilation(269).

In Habermas's view all these trends signify a development
in modernity, in which remains of the universal religions -
Judaism, Islam and Christianity - not much more than the core
content of a universalistic communicative morality. This
happens the more so the more purely the structures of these
world religions come forth. At the same time the ethically not
superseded mystical elements of a fundamental contemplative
experience, characterized by non-action, seem to split
themselves off in these world religions as an autonomous
realm. Unlike Marx, Habermas is equally sympathetic to the
ethical and mystical elements in the disintegrating religious-
metaphysical worldviews.

According to Habermas, Hegel had the beginnings of these
recent religious developments before his eyes, when he
developed his philosophy as theodicy or as proof of the
presence of God's rationality in the world as nature and
history. Hegel was also aware of the consequences of this
religious development. Hegel knew that with this religious

development the split between a single ego-identity, which is formed in universal religious structures and a particular collective identity, which is connected with a nation or state, becomes unavoidable. The ethical totality, in which every single individual has the possibility to perceive in the infinite independence of the other singular individual the complete unity with him or her, is split up in modern society. So at least it appears to Habermas.

Precisely because the universal religious identity is no longer able to unite in itself the singular identity of the individual and the particular identity of the nation in the framework of highly complex human action systems, religion has for Habermas become obsolete in the process of modernity, at least after Hegel. The modern dichotomy between the transcendent and immanent, the sacred and the profane, has led to the antagonism between individual and collective in modern action systems. We may conclude from this, that only if the transcendent and the immanent, the religious and the secular could be conjugated anew, also a new reunion between the individual and the collective would be possible again. That precisely was Hegel's theological and political program(270). In a certain sense, Habermas demands intrinsically a political proof of God. Only if religion would be able once more to unite personal and collective identity, could the charge of the obsolescence of religion be dropped. For such political proof of God Habermas does not so far see any indication in late capitalistic or socialistic action systems. It would be up to the political and liberation theologians to deliver the political proof of God which could newly establish the actuality of religion beyond the boundaries of modern civil society(271). It is obvious that Habermas can not accept the more recent fundamentalist upheavals in Judaism, Christianity or Islam and their political consequences as a new genuine reconciliation between the transcendent and immanent, the religious and the secular. The great value of Habermas's theory of communicative praxis is a negative one. It rejects courageously false forms of conjugation of the sacred and the profane. Precisely thereby it reopens practical discourse on the modern dichotomy between the religious and the secular and thus, possibly the way toward a new understanding, consensus and resolution of the modern abyssus between the collective and the individual.

Identity Problem

Habermas considers this identity problem – the disunity of universal religious, particular collective and singular, personal identity – in modernity to be the real motive force in Hegelian philosophy(272). Hegel would like to restore on the modern level and under conditions of highly differentiated modern action systems the unity of religious, collective and individual identity as it once existed on the primitive, archaic and historical-intermediate level of social evolution. Precisely because of this impulse of thought, so Habermas argues, Hegel has remained up to the present a contemporary thinker. Of course, Hegel sees the disunion of the subject and the society in connection with the disunion of subject and nature and the wholly Other in nature. Hegel thinks of a disunion of the subject with external nature on the one hand and with internal nature on the other. Thus the modern "ego" is characterized by a threefold disunion with external nature and the universal God, the particular society and the singular inner nature. Modern man is determined by a threefold alienation from the external world of nature and from the universal God in and behind it, from the particular social world and from the singular inner world. In his dialectical philosophy Hegel tries to conquer all three forms of alienation. In this sense his philosophy is one of freedom understood as negation of alienation. Freedom means man's being at home with himself in the world of nature, the inner world and the social world – in solidarity with others(273): Freedom is spirit as the identity of the identity of the one and the non-identity of the other.

Natural Science

According to Habermas modern natural science has usurped the realm, which the retreat of a transcendent God from a decisively desocialized and desacralized nature set free(274). In the progression of modernity a thoroughly ethicized system of faith began to compete with natural science. As this happened, a dedogmatization set in, which finally also put into question the religious interpretation of nature in its totality, nature as "creation." Now the knowing subject stands opposite a completely objectivated nature, in which no divine subject can any longer be intuited. The intuitive entrance into life and the essence of nature is repressed into the irrational realm. This is so except in the dimension of art, which has become autonomous in relation to faith and knowledge: religion and philosophy. Therefore, critical theorists like Benjamin, Adorno and Marcuse, had a particular preference for art(275). Marxists in Yugoslavia, who have lost their religion, turn to art instead. The same is true, if also to a lesser degree of Habermas. But for him besides art also mysticism continues to have some attraction(276).

In Habermas's view, the disunion of the modern "ego" with an objectivated nature without any subjectivity has consequences for the self-understanding of a secularized modern capitalistic or socialistic society. With the genesis of modern capitalism, the bourgeois society has been more and more uncoupled from the cultural system. No longer being legitimated by religion, it must now legitimate itself out of itself. In the perspective, which the new quantum physics has made successful in relation to nature, also the civil society and its members, the bourgeois, can understand themselves as contingent nature-phenomena. The constructs of the completely revised natural law, of utilitarianism and the bourgeois theories of democracy show the new connection between empiricistic fundamental conceptions and the universalistic principles of a completely secularized ethics(277). They have in common the attempt to put together the totality of the social life connections out of the universalistically regulated relations between singularized and natural individuals. Hegel speaks of bourgeois society as the "state of necessity and analytical understanding," in opposition to the socio-moral totality, the organic state of reason(278). For Hegel as for Adorno later on, the phenomena of capitalistic society are not the whole(279). They are the untrue totality, which must be superseded or sacrificed itself or make room for the true whole, the socio-moral totality, the realm of freedom. According to Habermas, this disunion of the modern "ego" with society finds its correspondence in the disunion of the acting subject with his or her own needs. The empirically interpreted nature of man, drives and inclinations, stand in unreconciled opposition to the universally justifed norms of the bourgeois abstract right and formalistic ethics. This opposition has again and again been articulated by thinkers from Kant's critique of practical reason over Hegel's philosophy of law and Freud's psychoanalysis to Habermas's theory of communicative praxis(280).

Disunion and Reunion

In Habermas's perspective, the threefold disunion of the
modern "I" signalizes the context in which Hegel himself sees
the driving force of modern philosophizing(281). When the
power of union, so Hegel argues, disappears from the life of
people and the opposites lose their living relationship and
mutual effectiveness, the need of philosophy comes about(282).
The disunion and reunion of life with which Hegel is
concerned, is first of all the life of the social world, the
social life-connections, not only of civil society as
mechanical state, but also of the socio-moral totality as
organic state. In this social world the identity problem poses
itself, from which Hegel starts and which he wants to resolve,
of course, always in relation to the divine totality(283).
What precisely is the task for which Hegel tried to find the
answer?
       According to Habermas the monotheism of historical-
intermediate society, particularly Christianity, was the last
thought formation, which had given a unifying interpretation
of the worlds of nature, self, society and culture as well as
a corresponding orientation, and which had been recognized by
all members of society(284). But in competition with modern
science and profane morality monotheism, particularly
Christianity, can no longer fulfill this truth claim of
interpretation or give orientation to action without a doubt.
Here, according to Hegel, philosophy must come in, not in
order to replace religion but to support its content by
sublating it into a scientific, i.e., philosophical form.
       But even if philosophy could take over the unifying
achievements of the universal religion by means of the notion
as the dialectical unity of the universal, particular and singular, so Habermas argues, the real problem would not yet be
resolved. This is so, because it is precisely this monotheism
that produced the opposition between the universalistic religious ego-and-community-structures, on the one hand, and the
particular identity of the nation or the state, on the other.
First, this opposition exists because the bourgeois mechanical
state is the form of organization of the capitalistic class
society. The inequality of the late capitalistic society can
not be justified in terms of a universalistic religious identity. Second, this opposition exists, because this form of
organization has as its consequence a self-assertion of
sovereign states against each other. This self-assertion is

incompatible with universalistic religious principles. More recent even papal and episcopal statements on "work" and "war and peace" affirm this incompatibility of capitalistic ine- quality inside bourgeois action systems and of the aggressive self-assertion among capitalistic and socialistic action systems, with universalistic Christian principles(285). But so far the universalistic Christian principles have shown themselves to be rather powerless and ineffective concerning the overcoming of internal inequality or the prevention of external, international wars. The recent letter of the American episcopate on peace is already as good as forgotten as far as the American public and government is concerned.

According to Habermas, if philosophy should solve the task of reunion, which religion so far has been unable to resolve, it must even transcend the unifying claim of inter- pretation and orientation of religion. It must restore that unity, which so far only the mythos was able to express and that mainly on the primitive and archaic level of human evo- lution and to some extent still on the historical-intermediate level. That explains to Habermas, why Hegel discusses the notion of absolute morality always, again, on the basis of the life of the Greek polis. Here in the universal Greek polytheism a singular identity of the individual could be formed, which was in harmony with the particular identity of the city-state. Here religious, social and personal identity were in unity. According to Hegel, this union of the singular individual with its particular political community in the horizon of a universal cosmic order, philosophy should restore again under conditions, which in the meantime are posited with the modern idea of freedom and the complete individuality of the individual. To be sure the philosophy Hegel has in mind is fundamentally a theological one: theological philosophy or philosophical theology(286).

Absolute Identity

All this means, of course, as Habermas sees clearly, that the modern identity problem, namely the disunion between the ego and society can not be resolved, if it is not possible to make comprehensible the absolute identity of the "I" or of human spirit with nature in its totality: no reunion between the singular identity of the individual and the particular identity of nation and state without the universal religious identity(287). It must be made comprehensible, that the world of nature and history are held together by a unifying power, which continually reproduces the disunion, which it also overcomes. For such an Absolute Spirit, who knows himself identical with himself in absolute identity, who has an Other, something absolutely different, namely nature, outside himself and opposite himself and who nevertheless keeps up between his identity and that non-identity a relationship of identity, Hegel had a paradigm before his eyes. This paradigm was the human "ego," or, better still, ego's achievement to relate itself as it knows itself as a completely individuated being, as absolutely different from all other "egos" and at the same time as immediately identical with the others, as an "I" in general: the unity of the singular and the universal "I". According to Habermas, the intersubjective maintenance of the "ego" identity is the original experience of the dialectic and "ego" is the original dialectical notion. For Hegel, of course, the dialectic of God's absolute spirit was original and the dialectic of man's spirit was its example, while Habermas like Marx intends to put Hegel from his head on his feet and to transform his idealistic into a materialistic dialectic, his alleged notion dialectic into a reality dialectic(288).

Subjective, Objective and Absolute Spirit

As soon as the philosophy of unification succeeds, so Habermas argues, to identify in nature God's absolute spirit in its absolute externality, also the disunion of "ego" and society can be overcome in the notion of the objective spirit or the social world(289). This is so, according to Habermas, since in the social world the spirit reproduces in itself a second time nature, this time in the naturalness of social institutions and of the historical process. With the help of this notion of objective spirit, Hegel can think the subjective spirit, the "ego" universally as free intelligent will and can, nevertheless, identify this "I" with the particularity of a determinate spirit of a nation and a particular state. This is so, since there is intrinsic to the objective spirit, universality and rationality, in spite of its particularity and the singularity of each of its members. The objective spirit as second nature, is destined to find its ground in the absolute spirit, particularly in art, religion and philosophy. The unity of the singular subjective, particular objective and universal absolute spirit, so Habermas admits, does indeed

solve the modern identity problem. It resolves the tension
between the universalistically formed identity of the "ego"
and the solid particular identity of the nation and the
nation-state. This state, not as mechanical state, i.e., civil
society, but as organic state of reason, is even allowed to
make the self-sacrifice of the individual in war into a sacred
duty. The organic state can do this, since it is as the finite
other of the absolute truly universal spirit of God, rational,
in spite of its obvious particularity. The state of reason is
the reality of the socio-ethical idea and as such, like "ego",
a finite reflection of God's absolute spirit. It is the
socio-moral totality which mirrors the tragedy of the
Absolute(290). In the same way Hegel can also supersede the
disunion of the modern "I" with its own inner nature or inner
world in the unity of the subjective with the objective
spirit. In spite of this admission, Habermas does not want to
return to Hegel. Why not?

Necessity and Freedom

Habermas concentrates on the strategy of resolution, which
Hegel chooses for the modern identity problem, and on the
means of construction which he employs(291). His approach to
Hegel is formal rather than material. After all, Habermas is a
Kantian Marxist or a Marxian Kantian(292). According to
Habermas, Hegel makes the attempt to produce for the modern
consciousness an identity-guaranteeing type of knowledge in
the same mode as the "concrete science" of mythical thinking
achieved it once for the primitive and archaic and still for
the historical-intermediate stage of human evolution and
consciousness. Habermas does not say that Hegel is a modern
mythmaker. He rather speaks of Hegel's attempt as immense in
its claim and unsurmountable in the power of its execution and
therefore fascinating to the present day. In principle, so
Habermas admits, Hegel can integrate all natural, psychological, social and cultural phenomena in the process of the
self-mediation of God's absolute spirit in such a way that
they throw light on the location, in which the modern "I"
finds its place. The universal religious communicative
structure, God's absolute spirit, which makes comprehensible
nature and history in their essential manifoldness, is at the
same time the structure over which the "ego" can establish and
maintain its singular identity. For Hegel to make
understandable, or, better still, to make comprehensible means

to work away all contingencies, which are threatening the singular identity of the self. "I" identifies itself through the acts of comprehension with God's absolute spirit. Hegel says of the Absolute Spirit that he accomplishes in himself the annihilation of what is nothing and the making vain of what is vain. This is biblical language! This is also mystical language as used before by Meister Eckehart or Nicolaus of Cues.

Of course, such universal comprehensibility as Hegel speaks of demands universal necessity. But Hegel does not want to think this universal necessity, like the mythos, as a fateful iron chain. Thus this universal necessity must not stand opposite the contingency, which, after all, it is supposed to annihilate. Therefore, Hegel has made the greatest efforts to preserve the idea of subjective freedom and free infinite subjectivity and the complete individuality which is Christian heritage, and to reconcile the absolute necessity with the contingency of the free, intelligent will, of the human subject(293). Habermas considers it possible that Hegel was successful in reconciling the absolute necessity of God's spirit and the freedom of the human spirit. We may add, that Hegel was at least as successful in accomplishing this reconciliation between freedom and necessity as the monotheistic Judeo-Christian tradition, from which he came as a former theologian.

But in spite of the fact that Habermas greatly admires Hegel's program to reunite under conditions of highly complex modern action systems once more the universal religious, the particular social and the singular individual identity and considers it possible that his reconciliation between absolute necessity and human freedom was indeed successful, he can, nevertheless, not continue this program in an unbroken way. Why not?

The reason for the discontinuity between Hegel's philosophy of reconciliation and liberation and Habermas's theory of communicative praxis is that for the modern consciousness not only the idea of freedom is constitutive, but also the unlimitedly objectivating thinking of the natural and social sciences and a radical future orientation incorporated e.g. in historical materialism or futurology(294). Through this post-Hegelian objectivating and future-oriented thinking categorically other contingencies come into existence. Hegel has, according to Habermas, not thought through in his notion of absolute necessity these new contingencies with the same great care with which he considered the contingency of man's free intelligent will. The main reason for Habermas's rejection of Hegel's accomplishment of a modern unity of universal, particular and singular identity in the power of the dialectical notion is of course his participation in the Marxian attempt to replace his idealistic into a materialistic dialectic. Such replacement destroys the power of the dialectical notion, which was originally a theological one. After the rejection of Hegel's theological notion there remains for Habermas nothing else to do than to replace it by the potentials of language and the struggle for recognition: discourse mediated mutual, unconditional recognition(295). For Hegel these potentials had an ultimate foundation in the theological notion as divine totality(296). Habermas sacrifices this ultimate foundation(297).

So Habermas counsels us, like Horkheimer, Adorno and Haag before, not to return to Hegel(298). But it very often seems as if Habermas himself, in his search for a new unity of universal, particular and singular identity, was moving from Hegel over Marx and the critical theorists to Durkheim, Weber, Mead, Parsons and then back again to Hegel. No matter how deeply Habermas is engaged in the critique of Hegel's philosophy, he remains, nevertheless, as much a Hegelian as Adorno, whom he so greatly admires and rightly so. Certainly Hegel's dialectic of the universal, particular and singular identity remains the guiding principle also still for Habermas, as for all critical theorists before, as he enfolds his universal pragmatic, more specifically, his theory of communicative praxis, of intersubjectivity, of interaction, of struggle for recognition(299).

But to be sure, what separates Habermas's universal pragmatic from that of Hegel is that the former is merely human pragmatic and is no longer, as the latter, a theological pragmatic including a human pragmatic. There can be no doubt Habermas would like to replace the universal religious identity, which supports in Hegel's philosophy the particular social and the singular individual identity by a universal communicative ethics, which is supposed to achieve what obsolete religious worldviews are no longer able to produce in post-Hegelian, modern highly complex future oriented and contingency-ridden action systems: social and personal identity. But Habermas himself has doubts, if such universal communicative ethics is indeed the only truth to be rescued from the collapse of religious systems of interpretation and orienta-

tion(300). This doubt is intrinsic to Habermas's critical
theory of religion. It points back to Hegel's critical
philosophy and forward to critical political theology.

Sexual Love

For Hegel the potential of the struggle for recognition
follows the principle of sexual love(301). Unlike Hegel,
Habermas does not stress the dialectical relationship between
marriage and family on one hand and reciprocal recognition on
the other. But it is precisely in this context, that the core
of Habermas's theory of communicative praxis can be made most
manifest and concrete: the mutual unconditional recognition
between the one and the other. I would like to make visible
once more this core principle of Habermas's universal
pragmatic in the context of the Frankfurt School's engagement
in sexual enlightenment and revolution.

The Frankfurt School's theory of subject, society and
history carries on the spirit of modern enlightenment(302).
The critical theory as it was developed from Horkheimer,
Adorno and Benjamin over Lowenthal, Marcuse, Fromm and Sohn-
Rethel to Habermas, includes in itself the heritage of bourgeois, Marxian and Freudian enlightenment and emancipa-
tion(303). The critical theorists understand enlightenment as
the attempt to free people from their fears and to make them
into masters of their fate. Critical theorists see the sexual
enlightenment, emancipation and revolution as an integral part
of the European enlightenment movement. Here we concentrate on
the critical theory insofar as it explores the sexual
enlightenment and emancipation.

While the critical theorists have an affirmative attitude
toward modern enlightenment, they are, nevertheless - following Weber - also keenly aware of its inner dialectic(304).
Enlightenment can turn against itself and increase fears and
dependence. Bourgeois enlightenment turned into guillotine,
positivism and fascism; Marxian enlightenment into Stalinism;
and Freudian enlightenment into Pavlovianism and Skinnerianism. But instead of being discouraged by this dialectic of
enlightenment, critical theorists reflect it into their theory
and precisely thereby are able to overcome it and to
strengthen whatever is true and good in the modern
emancipation process. Also the sexual enlightenment and
emancipation has its inner dialectic, which is creatively to
be overcome. Here we follow the critical theory as it

criticizes the dialectic of sexual emancipation and tries to find remedies for it.

Subjective and Objective Reason

In modernity, as in antiquity before, enlightenment means subjectification: reduction of all objective social arrangements to subjective reason(305). Thus from Horkheimer, the founder of the critical theory, to Habermas, who continues it in the sign of the new paradigm of communicative praxis, critical philosophers have opposed Neo-Thomism and any other conservative ontological attempt to restore more or less naively objective reason, which fell victim to modern enlightenment(306). To critical theorists a new moral-theological concept like "ontic sin" in sexual matters appears as relic of traditional thought characterized by the premodern mythical confusion between nature and culture, if not as mere cover for the seldom complete suppression of the sexual instinct in Western civilization and the chronic dishonesty connected with this.

But the dialectical philosophers do therefore not yield to subjective reason, more precisely instrumental reason(307). Science can not tell us why it is better to love than to hate, except that it may be better for business. It can not give us a final interpretation or orientation in sexual matters or in any other issue of moral concern. Horkheimer and Adorno criticize most rigorously subjective reason out of the ironically alienated perspective of an objective reason, which disintegrated with the decentralization of the religious-metaphysical worldviews in the process of modernization, rationalization, enlightenment, and disenchantment(308). If objective reason can be rediscovered at all, then this can happen only through precisely such ironical-dialectical critique of subjective reason: via negativa.

For the time being, Horkheimer and Adorno can do no more than to emphasize subjective as practical, moral reason against instrumental reason in sexual as in all other matters of human concern. Habermas stresses subjective as practical communicative reason against functional reason. Practical and communicative reason is the subjective foundation of religion and morality. At present nothing threatens religious systems of interpretation and orientation more than the pathological subordination of practical under instrumental rationality, for which critical theorists try to find a remedy. Therefore,

Horkheimer, Adorno, Benjamin and Marcuse are very much opposed to any alliance between religion and positivism in sexual or any other matter of moral concern(309). The same is true of Habermas.

Theology

As the critical sociologists move between theology and philosophy on one hand and science on the other, they are open in principle for the possible truths contained in religious worldviews, particularly Judaism and Christianity: Creation as self-negation, original sin, second commandment, messiah, redemption, communicative ethics(310). They try to rescue such truths by introducing them into the realm of the secular. This explains why critical theorists do sometimes take sides with theological ethics and ecclesiastical teaching against the sexual revolution, e.g., Horkheimer's support of Paul VI's encyclical "Humanae Vitae"(311).

Critical theory as such contains a theological dimension(312). Horkheimer understands theology as hope for absolute justice. For Horkheimer as well as for Adorno and Benjamin no genuine morality is possible without theology. In the midst of the eclipse of reason, these critical theorists hold on to the emphatic notion of absolute truth, which is not possible without the prophetic and messianic God who guarantees it(313). What is communicated to youth concerning moral impulses without reference to a transcendent becomes a matter of mere subjective taste and mood, as well as its opposite(314). For the critical theorists also sexuality is a matter of justice, truth, moral impulses and transcendence. Habermas, of course, here following Kant more than Hegel, tries to establish a genuine discourse ethic without any theological basis(315).

Self-understanding

The dialectical sociologists have traced the sexual enlightenment throughout modernity, but particularly through the 19th and 20th centuries(316). The sexual emancipation did not start in the 1960s and it has not ended with the 1970s. Hegel noticed great turmoil in the potential of marriage and family(317). The sexual revolution has become a rather permanent one, maybe since the beginning of modernity, certainly since the work of Freud, World War I and the "wild"

1920s, which transformed deeply the sexual mores of liberal
capitalistic society. On the shoulders of Kant, Hegel, Marx
and Freud, the critical theorists have not only observed,
described and analyzed the sexual enlightenment, but also
actively directed and corrected it. In a certain sense in the
critical theory the sexual emancipation has come to its
self-understanding and self-critique.

Species Relationship

From its very beginning dialectical philosophy identified the
sexual as species relationship(318). As such the sexual relationship is situated on the organic, anthropological and
sociological level. Critical philosophy contains a dialectical
biology, anthropology and sociology of sexuality.

Dialectical biology determines the sexual relationship as
reproduction of the species(319). The species relationship is
nothing else than the procreation of the individual through
the death of another individual. After the one individual has
reproduced itself as another individual, it dies off. Sexuality is the most differentiated and highest function of the
organism. Sexuality and death are closely interconnected.

The species relationship is process. It begins with the
sexual need of the individual. The need arises from the fact
that the individual is, as singular being, not adequate to its
genus and that it is at the same time the identical
relationship of the genus to itself and that it is both of
these in unity. Thus the individual has the feeling of
insufficiency. Therefore the genus in the individual is the
dialectical tension against the inadequacy of its singular
reality. The genus in the individual is the drive to achieve
in the partner of the other sex its self-feeling; to integrate
itself through the union with the other; and through this
mediation to close together the genus with itself and thus to
bring it into immediate existence. That happens in the genus
act or in copulation.

In dialectical anthropological perspective the species
relationship of humans rests on the biological differentiation
of the sexes(320). On one hand the sexual relationship is the
individual's subjectivity, which remains one with itself in
the feeling of social morality, erotic love, faithfulness,
honor, etc. The sexual relationship does not proceed to the
extreme of purposive universality: to society, state, history,
art, religion, philosophy and science. It is limited to

marriage and family. On the other hand, the sexual
relationship is the activity, which in the individual moves
into the opposition of universal, objective interests and his
or her own particular existence and external world. The
species activity realizes those universal interests in this
particular existence and produces them as unity. The sexual
relationship achieves in marriage and family its spiritual and
socio-ethical significance and determination.

According to dialectical sociology the species
relationship is, as marriage, the immediate socio-moral
unit(321). First of all, marriage contains the element of
natural vivacity in its totality, namely the reality of the
human _genus_ and its process. But beyond this, in the
self-consciousness of the marriage partners and their
communicative praxis, the unity of the sexes, which is merely
in itself and therefore existentially only external, is
transformed into self-conscious sexual, erotic and ethical
love. It becomes a moral relationship. The first element in
this love is that the lover does not want to be an isolated
independent person for himself or herself. Insofar as the
lover is such an isolated and independent person, he or she
feels deficient and incomplete. The second moment in love is
that the lover gains himself or herself in another person and
is thereby enriched. The lover finds recognition and validity
in the beloved person and the beloved person in the lover.
Therefore love is the most enormous contradiction. Analytical
understanding can not understand the dialectic of love. Only
dialectical reason can comprehend it. There is nothing harder
than the pointlike structure of a person's self-consciousness.
In love this self-consciousness is, nevertheless, negated. At
the same time the lovers have their self-consciousness as
something affirmative. Love is at the same time the production
and resolution of its own inner contradiction. As resolution
love is the socio-ethical unity which constitutes marriage and
family.

Historicity

Dialectical sociology emphasizes the historicity of sexuality,
erotic love, marriage and family as well as of the
theological, philosophical or scientific reflection upon
them(322). The natural lawyers of Antiquity, Middle Ages, and
Modernity have often looked upon marriage only according to
its biological rather than its dialectical anthropological and

sociological side. They often saw marriage merely as sexual or species relationship. Often to the natural lawyers every way to the many other determinations of marriage remained closed. Sexual enlightenment turned precisely against this one-sidedly biological interpretation of marriage and stressed its other anthropological and sociological aspects.

But it was equally rude, when bourgeois enlighteners tried to comprehend marriage only as a contract. According to bourgeois enlighteners, e.g., Kant, the mutual arbitrariness of the marriage partners comes to an agreement concerning the two individuals and their sexual parts. The bourgeois degraded marriage into the form of a mutual contractual use of the partner's sexual organs, a kind of exchange process dominated by the equivalence principle. Not even the church has been able to free itself from the wrong bourgeois concept of marriage contract. After Vatican II the church began to understand marriage as a covenant, but it regressed again to the bourgeois contractual understanding of marriage in the recently published new Codex Juris Canonici.

In opposition to bourgeois enlightenment the romanticists posited marriage merely into love. Of course, love, insofar as it is feeling, allows for contingency and arbitrariness in every respect. Social morality can not have this form of accidentality. Therefore dialectical philosophy determined marriage against natural lawyers, bourgeois enlighteners and romanticists as socio-ethical love by which transitoriness, moodiness and merely subjective arbitrariness are to be superseded and unconditional mutual recognition is made possible, which may transcend even the annihilation of the one or the other partner in anamnestic solidarity. Here the dialectic of sexual love and mutual recognition becomes visible.

Arrangement and Inclination

Dialectical sociology remembers that in traditional societies marriage and family began with the arrangement by the parents(323). The sexual and erotic inclination toward each other comes about in the persons who are destined for the union of love by their parents, through their learning about this their destination. In the modern society, the mutual sexual and erotic inclination of the lovers as these infinitely particularized individuals constitutes the beginning of their marriage and family. The traditional world stressed universality. From this perspective, the way in which the decision to marry constitutes the beginning and has the inclination for its consequence, so that at the point of real marriage both are united, is seen to be of a higher social morality. The modern world emphasizes particularity. From this view the way in which the infinite peculiarity of the lovers makes its pretense in conformity with the modern principle of free subjectivity, seems to be the more moral one. The modern sexual enlightenment, emancipation and revolution may indeed be said to begin with the shift from parental arrangement of marriages to the sexual and erotic inclinations of the lovers. This can be observed today in traditional countries, which find themselves in the process of modernization, e.g., Saudi Arabia, Iran, Iraque, Kuwait, etc.

The dialectic of sexual enlightenment appears early in bourgeois drama and other artistic representations, long before Baudelaire, Strindberg and Ibsen(324). In bourgeois artistic works, in which the love of the sexes constitutes the fundamental interest and all universality is forgotten, the element of penetrating frigidity, which can be found in it, is carried into the heat of sexual passion through the complete contingency and arbitrariness connected with it. This happens particularly through the fact that the artistic work represents the whole interest as resting merely on the sexes. This can be of infinite importance for the sexes, but not in and for itself. There was a price to be paid for the progressive shift from universality to particularity, from arrangement to inclination, and the price is bourgeois coldness even in matters of sexual and erotic passion.

Social Classes

According to Horkheimer, the feudal times, when the hand which used the broom on Saturday did also best caress the lord on Sunday, are indeed far removed(325). They have disappeared to such an extent that according to the psychoanalytically enlightened bourgeois consciousness the motive of the feudal lord who marries the chambermaid lies less in his generosity than in his neurotic feeling of guilt. In the critical theorists' view such acts of the lord are pure only in bad movies. A bourgeois who thinks well of himself will not leave the marriage, not even the caressing to the maid. The bourgeois has become ambitious. He demands from the women with whom he sleeps that they have become totally, with skin and

hair and everything, a luxury commodity. The declassification
of the woman of the lower classes does, indeed, also concern
her erotic value. The potential of sexual love seems to be
subordinated to the principle of struggle for recognition,
class struggle(326).

Correspondingly in the case of the man, his economic and
class position belongs to his erotic potentiality. Today the
American coed knows very well, if she dates a twenty- or a
fifty-thousand dollar boy. She estimates him in terms of his
future earning capacity and thus is willing to exchange sexual
favors for it. A man who is nothing in late capitalistic
society and has nothing and does not represent any real
economic chances of upward mobility has also no erotic value.
The economic power can even replace the sexual power. The
beautiful girl with the old man makes a fool of herself and is
compromised and ridiculed only if he does not have anything.
It is possible that with the consolidation of a worker's
aristocracy the limit of economic power will move downward.
The potential of sexual love şeems to be subordinated not only
to the principle of struggle for recognition, but also the
potential of work and tool(327). The critical theorist
combines Marx and Freud in order to assess sexuality, love and
marriage in liberal and advanced capitalistic society.

Social Product

In Strindberg's bourgeois theater the woman appears as evil
and revengeful creature, greedy for power(328). According to
Horkheimer this negative image of the woman stems obviously
from the experience of a man who is impotent in normal sexual
intercourse. In such an unsatisfactory relationship the woman
tends to develop in such a way as Strindberg portrays it. In
the view of the critical theorist Strindberg's perspective is
an example of bourgeois superficiality. Instead of going to
the bottom of things, Strindberg ascribes everything to nature
or better still to an infinite character structure. He
ontologizes the earthly woman into an eternal one.

But Horkheimer knows only too well that to make
responsible the man and his impotence for the malice of the
woman means, of course, to fall into the same mistake as
Strindberg himself. This is so since the impotence as well as
the valuation of normal sexual intercourse as the "rightful"
form of sexual pleasure and desire is itself a social product,
which changes with time. The inability of the man to perform

the sexual act which the woman wishes for and which even he
recognizes as the measure for the masculine erotic value, is
caused by the fact that he has either exhausted himself before
marriage in brothel or cohabitation or that he depends in
general on other forms of satisfaction. The critical theorist
explains the impotence of the man together with the derogatory
valuation related to it out of the history of liberal and
advanced capitalistic society and his fate in its process of
production and exchange. Horkheimer admits that Strindberg has
mirrored well the evil woman, the impotent man and the hell
which they live through together in a definite historical
moment. But he has ontologized and thus eternalized the
bourgeois condition as a biological one. He has mythically
confused the world of nature and society. The shallower Ibsen
is superior to Strindberg, because he connects the modern
marital problems consciously with a transitory form   of
marriage and family, the bourgeois form, and thereby with
capitalistic society and history(329).

Marriage

Horkheimer lived a long and happy marriage with his wife
Maidon: she became for him the highest and she would have
sacrificed her life for him(330). But he was nevertheless
aware of the fact that there takes place in this century a
regress in the respect for the one and only marriage which a
man or woman should enter and maintain during his or her life
time and that this belongs to the dialectic of enlightenment
in late capitalistic society(331). It becomes customary to
marry several times in order to reach higher and higher peak
experiences. The more this happens the more declines the
importance, significance and value of the individual(332).
That most divorced people remarry again one or two years after
their divorce shows to Habermas how shallow their marital
relationship and individualities were in the first place(333).
     Horkheimer explains the individual's loss of value with
the decline of strict monogamy out of the fact that the life
of the one marital partner is held together by his or her
reflection in the other partner with whom he or she lives and
grows older. In advanced capitalistic society the marriage
partners are very often no longer two persons who together
constitute the self of each of them and who make this "I" rich
through language, i.e., anamnesis, communicative remembrance,
and enfold it in reciprocal recognition, i.e., mimesis, mutual

imitation and empathy. In late capitalistic society the ego becomes similar again to the chaotic succession of experiences. At the same time, of course, the individual is freed from the myth of marriage and family. There is progress involved here. But the liquidation of the mythical is paid for by the regression into chaos. In a certain sense the truth itself manifests itself in the process of rationalization and enlightenment as mythical product. It looks as if man as the radical other than the animal is himself an error. While the critical theorist acknowledges the progressive aspects of sexual enlightenment and emancipation, he considers it his duty to point to the human costs involved: not only in the potentials of language and sexual love, but also in the principle of mutual recognition(334).

Children

According to Horkheimer, it is not possible that the children whose parents have married in the age of boys and girls and soon will get divorced again, since they do not form a good household team, can learn the external and internal gestures of sensibility and reflection(335). These children educated by those parents will finally not force themselves to do anything else than what the power of organized capitalistic society compels them to do when once the rebel leaders of the smaller societies, the motorcycle gangs, alliances and leagues come to their end. These children have not been educated and they have not learned any other motives than the brutal ones of getting ahead for any price. As far as another longing stirs in these children, which was a danger since childhood, it must be stunned and stifled through positive and negative reinforcement and further increase of brutality. In extreme exigencies this kind of education leads to that bourgeois icy coldness which makes a lie out of all the friendly gestures of the new man and the brotherly-sisterly communication community promised by religion and enlightenment alike. Sometimes the repression of longing comes forth in hate and murder. Children educated this way do no longer understand that there are other goals than those of success in empirical reality. They consider the bourgeois Christianity, which they receive on Sunday, during the week quite honestly as something completely bizarre and crazy. Family merely radicalizes the struggle for recognition, but does not contribute to it reaching its goal: mutual unconditional respect.

Fashion

From its very start, the sexual enlightenment has expressed itself in fashion. In recent decades the fashion of sexual emancipation reaches from muscle shirts and miniskirts over tighter and tighter blue jeans and smaller and smaller bikinis to the body worship of the me-generation. It fits together so well with the general commodity fetishism of late capitalistic society.

Benjamin describes fashion in his usual allegorical manner as the measure of time in the dialectical central station, which is death(336). In Paris, the capital of the bourgeois world, fashion opened up the dialectical transfer point between woman and commodity. Death is the long rude sales clerk of fashion. Death measures the bourgeois centuries according to the yardstick. In order to save money death makes itself the mannequin and personally leads the clearing sales. Its French name is social revolution. Sexual revolution is part of it. Benjamin stresses the subordination of the potential of sexuality under the principle of work, more specifically exchange.

For Benjamin fashion was never anything else than the woman's provocation of death. Even the woman who has terminal cancer will still dress herself "provocatively." In the past the woman's provocation of death has always ended with the victory of death. Fashion is the parody of the corpse. Fashion is a dialogue with the body, even with its decomposition. Today once more the fashion of the newest wave of sexual enlightenment and emancipation is provocation of death: longing for the resurrection of the body and the abolishment of death.

Perversion

According to Marcuse, originally the sexual instinct has no extraneous temporal or spatial limitations on its subject and object(337). Sexuality is by nature polymorphous-perverse. The modern societal organization of the sex instinct taboos as perversions virtually all its manifestations which do not serve or prepare for the genus act. Without the most severe restrictions, the perversions would counteract the sublimation on which the growth of culture depends. Marcuse's concept of the polymorphous perversity was one of the most important categories of the recent stage in the modern sexual enlightenment and revolution.

Horkheimer and Marcuse observe that people are always ready to become angry in late capitalistic society when the word perversion comes up(338). They explain this by pointing to a tremendous amount of repressed wishes for other than regular genital drive satisfaction. Any victim of a despotic regime in a national security state in Central America, South Korea, Phillipines or elsewhere, is in bad shape when the persecutor falls upon the motive of perversion. In this case no torture is terrible enough and sufficient for the masses to extinguish the inner fire, since none is strong enough. Hitler was able in his anti-communistic national security state to wipe out the whole left wing of his party, which demanded a revolution against the high bourgeoisie, by charging Rohm and his SA followers with homosexuality(339). The principle of sexuality is completely subordinated to the potential of the nation: the national interest however misunderstood.

No torture is strong enough to compensate the anti-perverts for their renunciation of perversion, which they can not overcome. The enjoyment which the anti-perverts imagine in connection with the perversion appears to them as so superhuman that the torture and the pains with which it is requitted must no longer be human. But there is almost no offense which imposes so relatively little suffering as the perversion. The exception is, of course, when force is used. But this is valid for any other business as well. As the murder attended with robbery is the non-plus-ultra of over-reaching, so is rape and murder the non-plus-ultra of sexual passion. This has as little or even less to do with the problem of the unusual sexual action as "money or life" with the empirialism of the multinational corporations.

Benjamin has pointed out the relativity of perversions. The horizontal position of the body had for the oldest female individuals of the human species the greatest advantages(340). It made pregnancy easier for them. Benjamin can see this already from the girdles and bandages which pregnant women use today. Benjamin asks the question, if the upright walk did not evolve earlier with the males than the females. Then the female would at times have been the four-legged companion of the male, like dogs and cats today. From this idea it is only one step to the other thought, that the frontal encounter of the two partners in sexual intercourse was originally something like a perversion. Maybe it was not at least this aberration through which the female was taught to walk upright. What once in human history was a perversion can become normal and vice versa.

In the perverse pornography of Sade and Masoch, so Horkheimer argues, cruelty can live itself out consciously as phantasy and can thus be enjoyed(341). The really infamous action makes use of rationalization. In times of war, which delivers such rationalization, as well as in dictatorial national security states, the perversion which is master of them, grows silently. Cruelty against the enemy as well as against one's own person, can live itself out, but it can very often not be satisfied. Since the cruelty is not conscious of its sexual nature, it stretches itself, so to speak, into bad infinity. It becomes insatiable. People who are enthusiastic about wars and dictatorships are usually not able to experience the perverse enjoyment. The more they find their account in the cruelties the more greedy they become for them. Education for the ability to enjoy constitutes a decisive element in the struggle against the arriving of Future I – the totally administered society, and Future II – the thermonuclear holocaust, and for the coming of Future III – the reconciled society. Education in the sphere of sexual love influences determinately the region of work and tool from which arises Future I and the dimension of the struggle for recognition from which comes either Future II or Future III.

Happiness

According to Marcuse the term perversion covers sexual phenomena of essentially different origin(342). The same tabu is placed on instinctual manifestations incompatible with high cultures and on those incompatible with repressive civilizations, especially those with monogamic genital supremacy. However, so Marcuse argues, within the historical dynamic of the sexual instinct, e.g. coprophilia and homosexuality have a very different place and function. The same difference prevails within the same perversion. The function of sadism is not the same in a free libidinal situation and in the activity of the SS officer, who takes a Jewish woman out of the concentration camp, feeds her, sleeps with her and then gasses her and then plays Chopin for the rest of the night. The inhuman, compulsive, coercive and destructive form of these perversions seem to be linked with the general perversion of human existence in a repressive civilization, e.g., that of late capitalistic society.

But, according to Marcuse, the perversions have an instinctual substance distinct from these forms. This substance may very well express itself in other forms compatible with normality in high cultures. Not all component parts and stages of the instinct that have been suppressed have suffered this fate because they prevented the development of man and humankind. The purity, orderliness, cleanliness, punctuality and reproduction required by the capitalistic performance principle are not necessarily those of any mature culture. The reactivation of childhood and prehistoric wishes and attitudes is not necessarily regression and to repress them is not necessarily progress. It may very well be the opposite: proximity to a happiness that has always been the repressed promise of a better future. According to Benjamin, origin is the goal(343). The critical theorists agree with Freud, when he defines happiness as the subsequent fulfillment of a prehistoric or childhood wish(344). Eschatology is present already in archeology. But such wish fulfillment and happiness noted in the potential of language, especially memory, and in the principle of sexual love is possible only if those potentials are freed from the oppression of the sphere of work and tool and its functional rationality as developed in late capitalistic society. The desublimation of the sexual instinct does not lead to happiness when it takes place under the control of the capitalistic class and merely serves the more intense subsumption of living labor under capital(345).

Recognition

The critical philosophers and sociologists have a name for the solution of the human problems involved in sexual enlighten-ment, emancipation and revolution: mimesis, imitatio(346). It is of mystical Judeo-Christian origin: messianic mimesis(347). For Horkheimer, Adorno and Habermas mimesis signifies a relationship between persons, in which the one leans upon the shoulder of the other or nestles to him or to her. One identifies with the other. One empathizes with the other. Imitatio aims at a relationship, in which the externalization of the one toward the example of the other does not mean the loss of himself or herself, but self-gain and self-enrichment. Shortly, mimesis indicates gestures of mutual, unconditional recognition, generosity, tenderness, exuberance, creative love and freedom without revenge. According to Habermas, the rational core of the mimetic impulse, ability, process and achievement can be set free when we are willing to give up in Western Civilization the pathological philosophy of work and tools, subject-object relation, instrumental rationality in favor of a new paradigm of the philosophy of language, recognition, interaction, intersubjectivity, practical rationality and integrate the partial functional rationality into the more embracing communicative rationality(348). Mimesis is understandable and practicable only in the context of the paradigm shift from the potential of work to the potential of language-mediated recognition which Habermas has promoted in his life work.

Adorno comes very close to this paradigm change, wherever he explicates Hegel's complementary ideas of reconciliation and freedom(349). In a comment on Eichendorff's poem, "Beautiful Stranger," Adorno explains that the reconciliation of the lovers does not annex imperialistically what is strange and foreign(350). The reconciled condition has its happiness in the fact that it remains in the granted nearness the distant and the different, beyond the heterogeneous and the homogeneous. Adorno describes reconciliation in terms of the undamaged, victimless intersubjectivity of the lovers. In Habermas's view such undamaged intersubjectivity comes about and maintains itself only in the reciprocity of an understanding, which rests on the mutual, free and unconditional recognition of the lovers in their being not instruments, but self-purpose.

Only once Adorno broke the critical theorists' self-imposed, radicalized obedience to the Second Commandment and called the Absolute by name: non-possessive devotion(351). Such devotion renders invulnerable the mutual unconditional recognition of the lovers as self-purpose even beyond the unavoidable death and destruction of the one or the other. But this can happen only in reference to an experience which makes possible the assertion of a Reality, who rescues the other who has been annihilated and thus enables the survivor to live in anamnestic solidarity with the beloved other who has been destroyed and redeemed, toward his own death and resurrection(352). For this Reality the Judeo-Christian experience reserves the name God. To live in such anamnestic solidarity with the other who has been annihilated and rescued is not superstition or instinctual fixation. It is rather the beginning of a new, post-bourgeois form of concrete, living universality, in which the lovers are not only emancipated, but also fulfilled. Ultimately there is no unconditional, mutual recognition, mimesis, reconciliation, freedom, victimless intersubjectivity and non-possessive devotion without resurrection and the Reality who guarantees it. If sexual enlightenment will end with the mutual instrumentalization of the sex partners, it will have failed. If the sexual emancipation will conclude with the mutual unconditional recognition of the lovers, it will have succeeded. The battle of the sexes remains undecided.

In any case, the core of Habermas's theory of communicative praxis – reciprocal recognition between the one and the other – having been prepared in the Frankfurt School is the foundation and criterion for his theory of religion as well. We shall now turn more specifically to Habermas's critical theory of religion as he has developed it in the framework of his theory of communicative praxis on the shoulders of the previous critical thinkers in the Frankfurt Institute of Social Research, particularly Benjamin, Horkheimer, Adorno and Fromm.

Chapter II
Critical Theory of Religion

Art, Religion and Philosophy

Habermas's theory of communicative praxis is rooted in Hegel's Jena system designs, in the sphere of subjective spirit: in the potentialities of language, work and tools, possessions and family, struggle for recognition, nation(1). Habermas concentrates in his theory of communicative action on the potentiality struggle for recognition. While the Jena System Design I differs from Hegel's later, mature system, by leaving out the logic in the beginning, it anticipates, nevertheless, the later Hegelian philosophy of nature, philosophy of subjective spirit and philosophy of objective spirit, particularly the philosophy of art and religion(2). The Jena System Design II anticipates the logic and the philosophy of nature in Hegel's mature system, but does not contain parts which would point to the later philosophy of subjective, objective and absolute spirit(3). The Jena System Design III does not contain any parts of the logic; but the philosophy of nature is well developed(4). The System Design III develops much further the philosophy of subjective spirit including language, work, love, recognition than the System Design I. Likewise System Design III evolves much further the philosophy of objective spirit than in the System Design I. But unlike System Design I the System Design III does not treat art and religion separately from objective spirit, but rather deals with art, religion and philosophy, which in the mature philosophy constitute the dimension of the absolute spirit, in the sphere of the objective spirit, under "Constitution," the organic state of reason.

As Habermas reconstructs in his Theory of Communicative Praxis the whole human pragmatic in Hegel's Jena System Designs, he includes in this reconstruction also religion.

Habermas develops his critical theory of religion as an integral part of his theory of communicative praxis out of as well as against Hegel's philosophy of religion insofar as it is contained in the System Designs I and III. We briefly develop Hegel's philosophy of religion insofar as it is present in his Frankfurt System Program and Jena System Designs I and III, in order to introduce Habermas's critical theory of religion in the most mature form it has reached in the most recent stage of his theory of communicative praxis. Furthermore we introduce Habermas's theory of religion by a short reference to the preceding critical theories of religion by Benjamin, Horkheimer, Adorno and Fromm(5). The critique of the critical theory of religion in general and of Habermas's theory of religion in particular will follow in the last chapter on "Critical Political Theology."

Esthetical Rationality: New Religion

In his Frankfurt System Program of 1797 Hegel moves from the "I" to the Absolute and from the Absolute to nature and from nature to the social world(6). Finally, for Hegel come the ideas of a moral free world, divinity and immortality. Hegel intends like the bourgeois enlighteners to overthrow all superstition. He wants to overcome the traditional priesthood, which in recent times pretends to be rational, by reason itself. For this the traditional priesthood has not yet forgiven Hegel up to today and punishes him by calling him a "rationalist" or worse, a "pantheist." Hegel aims at the liberation of all spirits, i.e., nations. They carry the intellectual world in themselves and therefore they must not search for God, freedom or immortality outside of themselves.

At the end of Hegel's Frankfurt System Program comes the idea which unites all other ideas. It is the idea of beauty, the word understood in the higher platonic sense. Hegel is convinced that the highest act of reason, the act in which it embraces all ideas, is an esthetical act. Truth and goodness are essentially connected only in beauty.

According to Hegel the philosopher must have as much esthetical power as the poet. People without esthetical sense are the literal philosophers who hang on single letters and miss the spirit. The philosophy of spirit is an esthetical philosophy. Man can not be ingenious in anything without esthetical sense. Not even about history can we think in a spirited way without esthetical sense. Here Hegel wants to make manifest what those people are really missing, who do not understand ideas and who even admit naively enough that everything is rather dark for them that goes beyond tables, tabulations, registers and number crunching.

Thereby, so Hegel argues, poetry receives a higher dignity again. Poetry becomes at the end what it was in the beginning at the time of Homer: the teacher of history, the teacher of humankind. There will be no philosophy, no history any longer. Poetry will survive all other sciences and arts.

At the same time Hegel hears so often that the masses must have a sensuous religion. But according to Hegel not only the masses, but also the philosopher needs a sensuous religion. What we need in Hegel's view is the monotheism of reason and heart and the polytheism of imagination and art.

Here Hegel would like to speak of an idea, which as far as he knows has not yet come into anybody's mind up to the present: we must have a new mythology. But this mythology must stand in the service of the ideas. It must become a mythology of reason. Hegel thinks of the development of an esthetical rationality.

Before we make reason or the ideas esthetical, i.e., "mythological," so Hegel argues, they do not have any interest for the people. Vice versa before the mythology is rational, the philosopher must be ashamed of it. Finally, enlightened and unenlightened people must shake hands with each other. The mythology must become philosophical. The people must become rational. The philosophy must become mythological, in order to make the philosophers sensuous. Then, so Hegel predicts, eternal unity will reign among us. No more will there be the contemptuous look. No more will there be the blind trembling of the nation before its wise men and priests. There only awaits us equal education of all forces of our being, of the singular individual as well as of all individuals. No power of our being will any longer be suppressed. Then there will reign universal freedom and equality and brotherhood and sisterhood of spirits. A higher spirit sent from heaven, so Hegel knows, must institute this religion among us. It shall be the last great work of humankind.

Absolute Presence

For Hegel, on the level of his <u>Jena System Design I</u>, religion is the form, the appearance of Absolute Independence, Absolute Presence(7). Here all depends on what the material is to which

each religion gives this appearance: if this content is absolute in itself? According to Hegel, we know this absolute content of religion: it is the Universal as something internal.
This Universal must necessarily be something internal,
something workless. This Universal is love. And when this love
forms itself, it is love for something, e.g., a woman. The
activity itself, the living work of the gods in different
religions, these heavenly, beautiful and energetic characters,
male as well as female indvidualities, can only be a singular
act, confusion in detail, a romantic adventurism. But the
figures in which these living individuals perceive themselves
as Absolute Consciousness, the founders of religions, are
essentially real persons, who exist in history. They are not
absolutely free individuals. But the heroes of these religions
are such, which represent the absolute pain in suffering and
tortures in the most extreme way. They have instead of a
beautiful appearance, which is satisfied and content in
itself, a highly dissatisfied, ugly appearance. Finally, the
relationship of that first individual consciousness to the
Absolute Consciousness is as living relationship, that a
nation as consciousness, in the form of singularity, achieves
a universal work, in which the individuals perceive their
Absolute Consciousness as form. The individuals find themselves superseded in the form of this Absolute Consciousness.
At the same time, this form is their own work. The individuals
are alive in the form of this Absolute Consciousness as their
work. But this Absolute Consciousness has no presence in the
individual consciousness as such, since it exists only as
notion. The Absolute Consciousness does not become a present
work, which completes itself here in a living way. This
Absolute Consciousness is an Absolute Beyond, before which the
individual consciousness can only annihilate itself. The
consciousness of the individual can not move in the Absolute
Consciousness in a living way. The stirring of individuality
before this Absolute Consciousness or Absolute Self-enjoyment
is therefore not an epic, but a comedy. But it is a divine
comedy, in which the action of man annihilates itself
immediately. Only the nothingness of man's praxis has here
absolute certainty. The consciousness of the individual is
only the dream of a consciousness, the Absolute Consciousness. The character of the consciousness of the individual is
eternally merely a powerless past. Thereby man, who
accompanies this drama, can only dissipate in tears.
      On the level of the Jena System Design I, religion and

art   are   not yet clearly differentiated as two distinct forms
of the dimensions of the   Absolute   Spirit,   as   this   happens
later   on   in   the   mature   philosophical system. According to
Hegel, the art, which   gives   presence   to   that   love,   those
romantic   deeds,   to these historical figures and this annihilation of the consciousness and actions   of   individuals,   can
not   take   from this content of religion its essential element
through the artistic form: namely, that it   has   no   presence,
but   is   merely absolute longing, longing for the Absolute. In
the course of the history of religions, the religious content,
in which the Absolute Consciousness appears, must free   itself
from   its longing, from its singularity, which has a beyond of
past and future. The world spirit, the spirit   of   the   world,
the   spirit   of   humankind   must   struggle   in   the history of
religions, in world history for the form of Universality.   The
mere   notion   of   the   Absolute   Consciousness,   the   Absolute
Self-enjoyment, must be elevated out of the reality into which
it has immersed itself as notion. As the   notion   of   Absolute
Self-enjoyment   it   gives   itself   the   form of the notion, it
constructs the reality of its existence and   becomes   Absolute
Universality.

Already   on   the   level of the Jena System Design I Hegel
projects, in a seedlike form, the whole history   of   religious
worldviews   and   systems   of   interpretation and orientation,
which Habermas almost two centuries later tries to reconstruct
once more in his universal pragmatic, his theory of communicative   praxis,   his   critical   theory   of   religion.   Like   the
Hegelian Habermas   later   on, so Hegel himself shows already,
from the very beginning of   his   philosophy,   the   history   of
religions   as   a   successive answer to the aporia of individual
and communicative human consciousness and praxis: the death of
the innocent other.   Today   political   theologians   point   out
precisely   this   aporia   against   Habermas's   theory   of
communicative praxis and   religion   and   try   to   find   a   new
religious   answer   for   it,   as   will   be   shown   in the final
chapter.

On the level of the Jena System Design III religion   and
art   have   become   almost as clearly differentiated as will be
the case in the Phenomenology   of   Spirit   and   in   the   later
Philosophy   of   Absolute   Spirit(8). But for Hegel here in the
Jena System Design III, as in his later philosophy, art is   in
its   truth   religion: religion   is   the truth of art as theological philosophy is the truth of religion. On the   level   of
the   Jena   System   Design   III, religion is the art world ele-

vated into the unity of God's absolute spirit. Hegel developed
the notion of absolute spirit from his Early Theological
Writings, through his Jena Critical Writings, and the logic
and metaphysics in his Jena System Design II to his System
Design III and beyond throughout his later mature
philosophy(9). In art every individual element gains through
beauty its own free life. But the truth of the individual
elements, the particular spirits, the nations which appear in
religion, is for them to be moments in the movement of the
divine totality: knowledge of God's absolute spirit of itself
as absolute spirit. God's absolute spirit is the content of
art as well as of religion and philosophy. Art, like religion
and philosophy, is only the self-production of God's absolute
spirit as selfconscious life in general, as being reflected in
itself. Art, religion and philosophy share the same absolute
material content. They are different only in form.

Hegel's universal pragmatic differs from that of his
successors in the history of philosophy up to Habermas by
being first of all divine rather than human pragmatic, i.e.,
theology: the knowledge of God's actions in himself as well as
in the world of nature, man's inner world, the social and cultural world(10). Lenin was right when he stated that for Hegel
all knowledge is knowledge of God(11). In this sense Hegel's
universal pragmatic is much more radically universal than the
universal pragmatic of all his successors, including that of
Habermas. Only secondarily Hegel's universal pragmatic is what
all pragmatics have been in the past 200 years of history of
philosophy and the social sciences, from Kant to Habermas:
human pragmatic. Thus for Hegel art and religion as well as
philosophy of natural, personal and social world are first of
all the work of God's absolute spirit and only then also of
man's spirit(12). God works through man's actions. Man acts in
God. Divine pragmatic realizes itself in human pragmatic.
Human pragmatic realizes itself in divine pragmatic and is
real only in conformity with divine pragmatic(13). God works
through the actions of the artist as he produces his work of
art. The artist acts and produces his work of art in God's
spirit. God works through the religious person and he or she
does his or her work in God's spirit. God works through the
philosopher and he in Him.

Absolute Religion

For Hegel on the level of the <u>Jena System Design III</u>, in art
this singular self is only a particular one – the artist(14).
The enjoyment of others is the selfless, general perception of
beauty. The determination of art is singular content. This
explains its immediacy as existence as well as the immediacy
of the self as separated from beauty as the unity of
individuality and universality or the unity of the self and
its universal existence.

For Hegel, in religion things are different from the way
they are in art, in spite of their common content. In religion
the divine spirit becomes object for himself as something
absolutely universal or as essence of all nature, of being and
action. He also objectivates himself in the form of the
immediate self. According to Hegel, Christianity is not only a
relative, incomplete religion, but the absolute, perfect
religion. Christianity as the absolute religion is this
knowledge that God is the depth of the spirit, who is
conscious and certain of himself. Thereby God is the self of
all. God is essence and essence is pure thinking. But
externalized from this inner abstraction, God is real self.
God is an individual human being who has common spacial and
temporal existence. This individual person is Jesus. This
individual is at the same time all individuals. In this
individual and in all the individuals, in whom he is, divine
nature is not other from human nature. Divine and human nature
are one.

In Hegel's view, in comparison with Christianity as the
absolute religion, all other religions are incomplete. They
are either only essence, the terrible essence of nature power,
where the self is merely nothing, or they are beautiful religion, mythical religion. As such they are a play, which is not
worthy of the essence, without foundation and depth. Here the
depth is the unknown fate. Later Hegel calls the Greek religon
the religion of beauty and fate(15). But Christianity,
absolute religion, is the depth which has stepped out into the
bright daylight of history. This depth is the "I". This depth
is the notion as the dialectical unity of universal, particular and singular. This depth is the absolute, pure power.

Hegel's universal pragmatic is at the same time transcendental pragmatic. Hegel's transcendental pragmatic is much
more radically transcendental than any pragmatic in the
Kantian tradition from Kant to Apel and Habermas(16). Hegel

does   not   only ask back, as Kant or Apel do, behind all human
pragmatic to its roots in human subjectivity, but behind   this
subjectivity   to   the   ground of all human, natural and divine
pragmatic, to God as the depth of   all   being.   God   as   depth
makes   possible   and gives validity to all divine, natural and
human pragmatic. No action in the world of nature, man's inner
world, social and cultural world is possible or valid   without
God   as   its   depth.   Hegel's radically universal pragmatic is
radically   formed and transcendental pragmatic insofar   as   it
penetrates   to   the   enabling   and   validating   ground   of all
praxis, into God as depth of being. In Hegel's   most   radical
theological-pragmatic   as foundation instance for human praxis
are united the deepest concerns of the transcendental and   the
universal pragmatics from Kant to Apel and Habermas(17).

Replacement

In   the   20th   century,   the   political theologian Paul Tillich
takes up this Hegelian notion of God as the depth or ground of
being(18). Tillich was one   of   the   few   theologians   closely
related   to the Institute for Social Research, particularly to
Horkheimer, Adorno and Fromm. Tillich was one of the very   few
theologians, in whom the members of the Frankfurt School could
recognize   a "loving Christian." Horkheimer was concerned with
Tillich's theological thought up to   the   last   years   of   his
life,   when   he ordered by testament a verse of Psalm 91 to be
written on his gravestone: "In   you,   Eternal   One,   alone   I
trust."   Even   on   his   last   trip,   before   his death, to the
hospital in Nurnberg, Germany, Horkheimer contacted once   more
the headquarters of the Tillich Society in Frankfurt. Habermas
is   as   familiar   with Tillich's theological thought as any of
the other critical theorists. He discovers Tillich's   concept
of   God,   the   "Ultimate   Reality," in Parson's structural=
functionalism(19). The Ultimate Reality is   precisely   God   as
being   itself,   ground   or depth of being. But neither Tillich
nor any other Christian thinker, e.g., K. Rahner, was able   to
convince   any of the critical theorists of the truth claims of
Christianity as Absolute religion: they rather opted   for   the
replacement of all religion by the critical theory of subject,
society, history and culture.

Following the classical Christian tradition of Nicaea and
Chalcedon   and particularly the teachings of Meister Eckehart,
Hegel makes the unity, the identity of human and divine nature
into the very core of his whole philosophy(20). Here   all   the

critical theorists, all of them being Jews except Habermas, depart from Hegel. Following Marx, Benjamin replaces the unity of the divine and the human in Hegel's philosophy with the Messianic and makes it into the key of his own philosophy and theology of history(21). Horkheimer and Adorno replace Hegel's unity of the divine and the human by the second commandment and make it into the very theological core of the critical theory(22). The divine can not be named and can not be known. The negative dialectician, Adorno, stresses the non-identity between the divine and the human until no identity whatsoever seems to be left(23). The second commandment turns into negative theology, philosophical agnosticism and idology: the struggle against idols(24). Idolatry lurks at least as temptation in any affirmative theology. Consequently for critical theorists, particularly for Habermas, transcendental and universal pragmatic is radically uncoupled from any divine fundamental pragmatic, which, if it exists, can not be known. For Habermas there seems to be no indication of any divine pragmatic: God, being at work in the world of nature, inner world, social and cultural world(25). Therefore with him human nature takes the place of divine nature and human pragmatic moves into the location of divine pragmatic. But the very aporia of a purely human transcendental or universal pragmatic, the temporal and deadly finite character of the struggle for recognition as well as of language, work, marrige and family and nation, the dilemma of unconditionality and annihilation in interaction as well as the political theological answer to this aporia and dilemma in intersubjectivity in the form of the assertion of a saving reality for the innocent other in interaction, who has been destroyed, will demand a return to the radically transcendental and radically universal fundamental pragmatic, which Hegel has developed in detail as no other modern philosopher in his Early Theological Writings, his Frankfurt System Program, his Jena Critical Writings, his Jena System Designs, his logic and in his philosophy in general(26).

Reconciliation

According to Hegel, in Christianity, the absolute religion, man's spirit is reconciled with the world(27). Man's spirit, as existing, is present in its objectification, organization and becoming through estates or classes, determinate social character and determinate social obligation and duty. Every

human self has a limited purpose and likewise limited action.
Against Kant, Hegel argues, that man's knowledge of himself as
essence, in right and duty, is as pure essence and pure
knowledge, empty. Man's knowledge of himself insofar as it is
filled is a limited manifoldness of things and actions. Man's
immediate reality, his life world, his environment is likewise
singular. According to Hegel, social morality in the Christian
sense is the elevation of man beyond his estate or class.
Christian social morality intends to carry further in its
action itself and the praxis of its estates or classes and to
do something for the universal, the nation, the international
community, God. For Hegel, Christianty has from the very
beginning a social, political and historical dimension. Hegel
is from the very outset a political theologian. He is the real
father of contemporary critical political theology, which
tends to supersede, i.e., negate, preserve and elevate his
philosophy of right and history, his political theology(28).
    In Hegel's view, in Christian social morality the
government stands above all citizens. The government is the
spirit, who knows himself as universal essence and universal
reality. In the Christian religion every citizen elevates
himself toward the absolute self. Here everybody comes to this
perception of himself or herself as a universal self. Here for
everybody his or her nature, estate or class disappears like a
dream image, like a distant island which appears and
disappears at the horizon like a thin little cloud(29). Here
in religion, before God, every citzen is equal to the
government, to the prince or the president. Here everybody has
the knowledge of himself as spirit. Here everybody is as
valuable for God as every other person. Here in religion
everybody is unconditionally recognized. Here the individual
empties himself or herself of his or her whole natural,
social, political and historical sphere, of his or her whole
existing world. This is not merely that kenosis, which is only
form, education, and the content of which is once more the
sensuous existence. Here in religion the individual finds
universal liberation from the whole of reality. This
liberation reality gives back to itself as something perfect.
    But for the political theologian Hegel, both realms, that
of earthly reality and that of Heaven, are still very much
separated. Man's spirit is reconciled with itself only beyond
this earthly world, but not in its earthly presence. If man's
spirit is satisfied in its earthly presence, then it is not
the spirit, which elevates itself beyond its existence. Man's

spirit must be shaken in this its earthly existence. Man's spirit is shaken in its earthly existence through war and other contingencies(30). Thus as a consequence, man's spirit flees out of its earthly existence into heavenly thought. But there is a longing for Heaven and likewise a longing for earth. That is the pis aller! Here Hegel anticipates Horkheimer's definition of religion as longing for absolute justice, which can not be achieved in society and history(31).

According to Hegel, man being satisfied through religion has the trust that the happenings of world history and nature are ultimately reconciled with the spirit. No contingency, no unreconciled, selfless necessity any longer dominates nature or history. But for Hegel, religion is only the represented, imagined spirit. Religion is not yet philosophy, which is spirit in the form of the notion. Religion is the self which does not yet get together its pure consciousness and its real consciousness. Religion is the self, for which the content of pure consciousness appears in the real consciousness as an Other. Here Hegel anticipates once more Horkheimer's definition of religion, for which religion is not only longing for absolute justice, but also longing for the entirely Other than what appears on the level of real consciousness: the absolute truth(32).

Christian Community

According to Hegel the thought, the inner idea of Christianity, as absolute religion, is this speculative idea that the self, the real is thinking(33). In Christianity the essence and being are the same. In Christianity this is posited in such a way that God, the transcendent, absolute essence, has become this real man Jesus. But likewise this reality has superseded itself and has become a past reality. This God, who is reality and superseded reality, i.e. universal reality, is the spirit of the Christian community. This God is spirit. This precisely is the content of Christianity as perfect religion. This is the object of Christian consciousness. God as spirit is the object of man's pure consciousness. First, God is eternal essence, son and spirit. Here all three "persons" are the same essence. Here the difference, the indifference of the immediate being is not yet posited. Secondly, God the essence of pure consciousness becomes an Other for himself, which is world. But this worldly existence is notion. It is being in itself. It is evil.

Nature, the immediate, must be represented as bad. Every
member of the Christian community must come to the insight of
his or her evil nature. He or she must come to the insight
that nature turns over into the notion, the evil, the being
for itself. It turns against the essence, which is in itself.
But, vice versa, nature is likewise the essence, which is in
itself. All this means that God appears in nature as real.
Every beyond has escaped.

Now it is for Hegel precisely the sacrifice of the divine
man Jesus on the cross, which demonstrates that this
opposition between God and nature is itself null and void(34).
The evil, the reality which is for itself, is not in itself,
but is universal. First the sacrifice of the divinity, i.e.,
the abstract, otherworldly essence, has already happened in
its becoming real. Second, the reality is superseded. It has
become universality. It has become universal spirit. But in
religion, this is merely a representation for consciousness.
Third, the universality of self must come into itself. That
means that the Christian community must renounce its
being-for-itself and its immediate nature. The Christian
community must recognize its immediate nature as something
evil. But this view of evil supersedes itself through the
comprehension of this representation. All this is represented
in the cult of the Christian community. In the Christian
liturgy that self gives to itself the consciousness of its
unity with the divine essence. In devotion the self knows
itself in this divine essence.

According to Hegel this universal spirit, or the spirit
of the Christian community, is the "state of the church." It
is the existing real spirit which has become object for itself
as spirit. But the spirit has become objective spirit, merely
in representation and faith, not yet in the notion. It is
true, this existing, real objective spirit is indeed the
spirit of the Christian community. But in the community's
representation and imagination the spirit flees beyond the
community's self, far away from it. That immediate knowledge
of the spirit and this being entirely other of the spirit are
not united in the Christian community. Everything in the
Christian community has the form of representation, of image,
of the beyond. Everything is accidental happening. To be sure,
the Christian community uses words like God's eternal
decision, providence, wisdom, plan, purpose, will, fullness of
time, etc. But such words are only said. They are not a matter
of insight. They are merely a matter of language. They are

merely words. In the Christian community there is no notion, no self, no comprehension. There is only selfless imagination and understanding. Only on the level of philosophy, insight, comprehension, notion, man is able to know God's reason as the rose in the cross of the present(35). Only the philosophical insight, that what has happened in history and nature and what is happening everyday and what will happen in the future, is not only without God, but is essentially his work, can reconcile man's spirit with history, state, society, family and nature and the catastrophes and contingencies taking place in them(36). Only the man or woman who takes the cross of the tragedy of the social world, the moral totality, upon himself or herself can gain this insight and this consolation(37).

Church and State

According to Hegel's Jena System Design III the church has its opposite in the state(38). The state is, for Hegel, the existing socially organized and institutionalized spirit. The church is the state elevated into thought. Man lives in two worlds, that of the church and that of the state. In the one world, the social world, the state, man has his reality which disappears, his naturalness, his sacrificial life, his deadly transitoriness and finitude. In the other world, the world of the church, man finds his absolute preservation. Here in the church, man knows himself as absolute essence. In the church man dies to reality with knowledge and will, in order to acquire the eternal, the unreal, life in thought, universal self.

But this eternal, so Hegel argues, has its existence in the spirit of the nation. The eternal is the spirit which is only spirit. It is the spirit which, through this movement, is still opposite to the form. But it is the spirit, which is, according to the essence, the same. The government and the spirit of the nation know that this spirit is the real spirit, which contains itself and the thought of itself.

In Hegel's view it is the "fanaticism" of the church, that it wants to introduce the eternal, the kingdom of God as such, on earth, i.e., in opposition to the state. When Hegel speaks of fanaticism he means the concentration of all the forces of an individual or group into one issue. The church has indeed only one issue: the realization of God's Kingdom(39). Hegel is aware of the fact that the fanaticism of the church intends to maintain fire in water. Church and state

are, indeed, two very different elements. But nevertheless, so
Hegel maintains, the state is precisely the reality of God's
Kingdom. This is the reconciliation in thought of the essence
of both with each other through the church. But if church and
state are unreconciled, then both are incomplete.

For Hegel the state is the spirit of reality. What
appears in the state must be conformed to it, and measure up
to it. The state must not respect the private conscience of
the individual as such and indeed very often does not,
particularly not in questions of war and peace. Conscience
belongs to the inner moral world of the subject. It is the
inner world(40). The state belongs to the external social
world. The state is the social world. If conscience is valid
as action or as principle of action, that must be shown and
demonstrated out of the action itself. This is an important
normative principle in Hegel's fundamental pragmatic.

In Hegel's perspective, the church is the spirit, which
knows itself as universal. As universal spirit the church is
the inner absolute security of the state. That must not be
misunderstood functionalistically in terms of external
functionality. The universal religious identity is the
foundation of the particular social and political identity.
Here in the church as universal spirit the individual is valid
as individual. The religious universal identity is not only
the basis for the particular social and political identity,
but also for the individual subject's singular personal
identity. Everything external is as such and in itself
insecure and unstable. But in the universal spirit of the
church the individual has his or her complete guarantee. What
man does out of religion, he does out of his self-thinking,
insofar as it is not yet philosophical insight. The universal
thought, which does not leave the religious person in all the
different manifoldness of his or her life is: that this is
duty! The individual must resign himself or herself into this
or that duty. It simply is. It is valid. It is justified in
the absolute essence. Here it has its absolute legitimation.
It is morality in the absolute essence, insofar as it is known
to me. It is absolute essence as such.

According to Hegel, on the one hand religion as such is
in need of existence, of immediate reality. It is the
universal. It is therefore under the dominion of the state.
The church is used by the state. The church serves the state.
The church is used by the state, since it is the reality-less
entity. It is that which has itself in the real spirit. It is
that which is as superseded.

On the other hand, so Hegel argues, religion is, vice versa, against the thinking, which elevates itself beyond its reality. Religion is this inner stubbornness, which surrenders its existence and which is willing to die for its thought, the eternal, the kingdom of God. Religion is the unforceable, which dies for the thought of the kingdom. For religion the pure thought is everything, the inner thinking as such or the thinking which has the meaning of action, which otherwise appears as something accidental. Religion has elevated thinking as such so highly, that many religious people have gone happily into death for it: the martyrs for the kingdom of God, the realm of absolute justice.

But according to Hegel, the state, which subordinates itself under the church, is either delivered to fanaticism and thus lost, or a regime of priests is introduced into the state. This priestly regime does not demand the surrender only of action and existence and certain thoughts, but of will as such and that in existence as such. The will as such is not to be sacrificed for the universal, for what is generally recognized as valid, but for the singular will of an ecclesiastical superior as such.

From the religious point of view, so Hegel argues, heaven escapes from the real consciousness in the process of modernization. The real consciousness becomes secular. A widening split occurs between pure and real consciousness, the religious and the secular(41). Man falls down to earth. Man finds the religious only in phantasy and imagination. Or the selflessness of religion is in itself such that religion is only the spirit, which represents itself in images. That means that the moments of that spirit have for it only the form of immediacy and of accidental happening. They are not comprehended. They are not a matter of insight. For Hegel, the content of religion is certainly true. But this being true of the religious content is merely an assertion or an assurance without insight. Ultimately, therefore, religion is to be sublated into philosophy, theological philosophy, philosophical theology(42). Only on the level of theological philosophy or philosophical theology the content of religion can, in the form of the notion, enter into discourse with philosophy and social science, with a transcendental or universal pragmatic. Only philosophy can reconcile pure and real consciousness, religious and secular, faith and reason, redemption and emancipation, revelation and enlightenment and thereby man and his world(43).

Theocracy

Following Hegel, Bloch has the cardinal merit in the 20th century to have repudiated in his book <u>Spirit of Utopia</u> with the utmost vehmence the fusion of religion and state by denying the political significance of theocracy(44). Benjamin following Hegel, as well as Bloch, has transformed Hegel's philsophical and theological view of the relationship between church and state into the language of the critical theory of subject, society and history(45). From Benjamin the transformed Hegelian position on religious and secular was taken over by Horkheimer and Adorno, Marcuse and Fromm and by Habermas in the framework of his universal pragmatic and his theory of communicative praxis as a new paradigm in the critical theory, and finally also by political theologians(46). To be sure, Hegel's view of the relationship between religion and political order was further modified in each new stage in the development of critical theory. But Benjamin's transformation of Hegel's position remained formative throughout all further developmental stages of critical theory and even of critical political theology.

In his "Theological-Political Fragment," Benjamin states that only the Messiah himself consummates all history, in the sense that he alone redeems, completes, creates its relation to the Messianic(47). Therefore, the kingdom of God is not the immediate goal of the state or of the historical dynamic. The Messianic kingdom can not be set up as the immediate <u>telos</u> of state or history. From the standpoint of state or history the kingdom of God is not goal, but merely end. Therefore, the order of the profane, state and history can not be built upon the idea of the divine kingdom. Therefore, theocracy has no political, but only a religious meaning. Like Hegel, Benjamin sharply differentiates religion and politics, but at the same time also relates them to each other. That precisely is the very core of Benjamin's critical theory of religion.

According to Benjamin, the order of the profane should be erected on the idea of happiness rather than on the idea of the Messianic kingdom. The relation of this secular order to the kindom of God is one of the essential teachings of Hegel's philosophy of history. It is the necessary precondition of a mystical conception of history, like that of Hegel or Benjamin. It contains a problem, that can be presented figuratively: if one arrow, so Benjamin argues, points to the goal, toward which the profane dynamic acts, and another marks the direction of Messianic intensity, then certainly the quest of free humanity for happiness runs counter to the Messianic direction. But the religious and the profane are for Benjamin, as little as for Hegel, only in opposition against each other. Just as a force can through acting, increase another, that is acting in the opposite direction, so the order of the secular assists through being secular, the coming of the Messianic kingdom. This core of Benjamin's theory of religion is the very starting point for Habermas's theory of religion.

While for Hegel the nations supersede each other in the dialectic of history toward the human species, which has the highest right and the latter again supersedes itself into God's kingdom, for Benjamin happiness is a decisive category of its quietest approach(48). For in happiness, so Benjamin states, all that is earthly seeks its downfall, and only in good fortune is its downfall destined to find it. Benjamin admits that the immediate Messianic intensity of the heart, of the inner man in isolation, passes through misfortunes and suffering. To the religious restitutio in integrum, which introduces immortality, corresponds a secular restitution that leads to the bad infinity of downfall. The rhythm of this infinitely transient profane extistence, transitory in its totality, in its spatial, but also in its temporal entirety, this rhythm of Messianic nature, is happiness. According to Benjamin, nature is Messianic precisely by reason of its eternal and total passing away. In Benjamin's view, to strive after such passing away of nature, even for those stages of man that are nature, his organic and anthropological dimension is the task of world politics(49). Benjamin calls the method of such world politics nihilism. Such "nihilism" is present already in Hegel's political theology, in his theological philosophy of right, history and religion(50).

Philosophy

According to Hegel's Jena System Design III, philosophy is precisely that insight, which is missing in religion(51). For Hegel, philosophy is the absolute science, the science of the Absolute. It is theological philosophy or philosophical theology. It is absolute pragmatic or pragmatic of the Absolute. While philosophy has in Hegel's view the same content as art and religion, in philosophy this content has the form of the

notion: The   self-particularizing   and   self-singularizing
Universal(52). Religion is consciousness of the Absolute   and
of absolute justice which has its only guarantee in the
Absolute and can not be without it(53). Art presents absolute
justice   and   the   justice of   the absolute   in the form of
representations. Philosophy does   the   same   in   the   form   of
notion, judgment and conclusion(54). Hegel does precisely that
in his Jena Critical Writings, his Jena System Designs and in
his later philosophy of right, history and religion: his whole
philosophy is one gigantic theodicy - the   proof,   that God's
justice has been done, is done, and will be done(55).
      For Hegel philsophy is first of all speculative philos-
ophy(56). As such it transcends the limitations of analytical
understanding. It is concerned with the absolute being, which
becomes Other for itself: relationship, life, knowledge,
spirit,   spirit's knowledge of itself(57). Speculative philosophy is logic as logos-theology, absolute pragmatic.   Second,
philosophy is philosophy of nature(58). It is the speaking out
of the Idea in the form of immediate being. Nature is going
into itself versus the Absolute, from which it flows. As such
nature is evil. But nature is also becoming of spirit, notion
existing as notion, subjectivity existing as subjectivity. But
subjectivity, spirit, this pure intelligience is likewise
again the opposite, the universal. It is the universal which
sacrifices itself. Thereby the universal becomes the real
universal. It is universal reality. It is the notion. It is
subjectivity. It is restored nature. It is the reconciled
essence. In this reconciled essence everybody can take his or
her being-for-himself or -herself through his or her kenosis
and sacrifice.
      In philosophy, as Hegel comprehends it in the Frankfurt
System Program and Jena System Design III, it is the   "I,"
which is also a universal(59). Here ego is not another nature,
not the non-present unity, not a reconciliation, the enjoyment
and existence of which is beyond and a matter of the future
only. For Hegel, as for Meister Eckehart before, it is rather
so, that here and now "I" knows the Absolute(60). Self
comprehends the Absolute. Ego is no other than the Absolute:
the unity of human and divine nature is real. They are
identical in their being non-identical(61). All dualistic
theology is passe. "I" is the Absolute in its immediacy. Ego
is this self. For Hegel self is this inseparable connection of
the singular and the universal and of the singularity as the
universal of all nature and of the universal of all essence,

all thinking. The immediacy of the spirit is the spirit of the nation or the spirit of the nation as existing absolute spirit, spirit of the Absolute. In Hegel's view religion is the thinking spirit, but the thinking spirit which does not yet think itself. Since the spirit does not think itself in religion, it is therefore not equal with itself. It is not immediacy.

For Hegel opposite to religion, the knowledge of philosophy is the restored immediacy. Philosophical knowledge itself is as such and always as immediacy. Likewise, the self-knowing spirit is consciousness, immediate sensuous consciousness, which is an Other for itself under the form of being. It is disunited into nature and knowledge of itself. The spirit knowing itself is a resting work of art. It is the existing universe, i.e., nature, as well as world history.

According to Hegel, philosophy frees itself from itself. It arrives at its beginning, the immediate consciousness, which is the disunited consciousness. Thus philosophy is man as such. As the point of man is, so is the world(62). As the world is, so man is. One stroke creates them both.

In Hegel's view, before this time in which we live, was the Other of time. But there was not another time. There was only eternity, the mere thought of time. In this thought of time the question concerning what was before time is superseded. This is so, since the question means another time before time. But in this case eternity would be itself in time. Eternity would be a "before" time. Therefore, eternity would itself be the past. Eternity has been. It has absolutely been. It is no more. As such eternity is limited. Hegel rejects this position, this contradictory concept of eternity, and rightly so.

For Hegel time is the pure notion, pure subjectivity. It is the perceived empty self in its movement, as space is the empty self in its rest. Before there is filled time, there is no time at all. The filling of time is the real, which has returned out of empty time into itself. Its perception of itself is time, the unobjective, the subjective. But when we speak about time before the world was, of time without filling, then we mean merely the thought of time. We mean thinking. We mean that which is reflected into itself. It is necessary for Hegel to go beyond this time, beyond every period, but in the thoughts of time. That is the bad infinity, which does never reach that toward which it moves.

According to Hegel, this disunion is the eternal

creating, i.e., the creating of the notion of spirit, this
substance of the notion, which carries itself and its opposite. But the universe, nature, which is so immediately free
from spirit, must again return to it. For Hegel the origin is
the goal! As a matter of fact, the spirit's task is precisely
this action, this movement, this return of nature to spirit.
Spirit must restore this unity between itself and nature for
itself. It must do that likewise in the form of immediacy. The
spirit is world history. Man does not become master over
nature until he has become master over himself. Nature is
moving toward spirit in-itself. That this in-itself of spirit
may really exist, spirit must comprehend itself. In world
history that very condition supersedes itself, that nature and
spirit are one essence only in themselves and not yet for
themselves. Spirit becomes knowledge of nature.

Time

Following Hegel, also Kraus and Benjamin think that the origin
is the goal(63). According to Benjamin, history is the subject
of a structure whose site is no homogeneous, empty time, but
time filled by the presence of the "nowtime" (Jeztzeit).
Benjamin says "nowtime" and indicates by the quotation marks
that he does not simply mean an equivalent of the usual
presence (Gegenwart) of everyday life. He clearly thinks of
Meister Eckehart's mystical nunc stans(64). Meister Eckehart's
mysticism is the common basis of Hegel's, Bloch's, and
Benjamin's philosophy of history(65).
       In Benjamin's view, to Robespierre ancient Rome was a
past charged with the time of the now which he blasted out of
the continuum of history(66). In Benjamin's view, the French
Revolution, of which Hegel was a contemporary and witness,
viewed itself as Rome reincarnate. It evoked Ancient Rome the
way fashion evokes costumes of the past. Fashion has a flair
of the topical, no matter where it stirs in the thickets of
long ago. It is a tiger leap into the past. This tiger jump,
however, so Benjamin argues, still takes place in an arena
where the capitalistic ruling class gives the commands. The
same leap in the open air of history is the dialectical jump,
which is how Hegel, Bakunin, Blanqui and Marx understood
revolution.
       Habermas, following Hegel, Marx, Kraus, Bloch and
Benjamin as well as Horkheimer, Adorno, Lowenthal, Sohn-Rethel
and Marcuse, develops further Hegel's Jena System Designs I,

II and III by transforming nature, self and history, as they
appear in Hegel's absolute fundamental pragmatic into the
evolving world of nature, the inner world of the "I" and the
social world in his own relative universal pragmatic(67). As
for Hegel, Kraus, Marx and Benjamin before, so is also for
Habermas the origin, the goal. But what is missing in
Habermas's theory of communicative praxis and what had been
missing already in Marx's, Kraus's and Benjamin's view of
history and revolution, is what was for Hegel the absolute
precondition not only of nature, but of self and history as
well, namely the Logic as Logos-theology: his absolute
fundamental pragmatic. But fragments of Hegel's logic and his
absolute pragmatic or pragmatic of the Absolute are nevertheless not only negated, but also preserved in Habermas's
theory of communicative praxis and particularly in his
critical theory of religion. It is, in spite of all rejection
of absolute idealism and of all totality claims, nevertheless,
not entirely notionless, "unspeculative" or "positivistic." We
shall search for fragments of Hegelian pragmatic rationality
in the most mature form of Habermas's critical theory of
religion as it stands in his present theory of communicative
praxis.
     Habermas follows in his critical theory of religion not
only Hegel's and Benjamin's philosophy of religion but also
Horkheimer's, Adorno's and Fromm's critical theory of religion. A short presentation of these theories will lead to a
better understanding of Habermas's theory of religion, which
continues them on the basis of the linguistic shift in the
critical theory: the paradigm shift from work and tools to
language-mediated interaction characterized by mutual unconditional recognition of the one and the other as ends and not
only as means.

Meaning

Along with Amery, Canetti, Steiner and Bloch, Horkheimer is
one of those Jewish intellectuals who, in 20th century Europe,
sought to re-examine the meaning of human existence(68). For
these survivors of the holocaust neither the reassurances of
liberal democracy nor the exhortations of a Zionist tradition
could inspire confidence in the future. The barbarity of
National Socialism had almost fully obliterated the Enlightenment, Western Christianity, and German Idealism. Thus,
Horkheimer undertook to carefully re-examine all of these tra-

ditions, especially Idealism, in formulating a critical sociology of religion that did not require a commitment to religious belief. In Western culture, where commodification is
highly developed, the transcendent element of theory and
practice has been almost eliminated. The transcendent, which
cannot be quantified, resists commodification - the process
that robs a thing of its otherness and expresses it in terms
of its similarities to all other things. European Jews experienced this commodity paradigm in a most personal way: in the
near annihilation of their otherness. Horkheimer's insight
into this situation led to a more positive evaluation of
certain metaphysical and theological trends that uphold the
conception of transendence and subjectivity without which
enlightenment decays into ideology and oppression(69). Hence,
the socio-philosophical importance of religion lies in its
appeal to the transcendent, to the wholly Other.
      Throughout his life, Horkheimer defended the importance
of subjectivity. While individuals are real for him, existing
society was but a false community of alienated relations
characterized by the horror of wars, concentration camps and
economic depression(70). Thus, in 1966, he stated that he
could not support any philosophy lacking a theological moment,
i.e., awareness of the Infinite or the wholly Other(71).
Without reference to the transcendent, the moral impulses
transmitted to youth - even if the latter are conscious
atheists - become a matter of mere caprice or dogmatism. In
this sense, the dialectical relation between the finite and
the Infinite, the very core of Hegel's philosophy of religion,
constitutes the innermost structure of Horkheimer's critical
sociology of religion. In his view, Western Civilization and
the Christan worldview cannot be separated, despite the fact
that the Christian principle of free subjectivity is undercut
by the cold subjectivity of bourgeois society(72).
      Horkheimer sought to extend Feuerbach's and Marx's cri-
tiques of religion, the correct understanding of which necessitates an analysis of Hegel's account(73). This led him to
explore the Hegelian philosophy of religion as well as positive sociology of religion, while at the same time remaining
critical of both. Other contemporary influences also contributed to Horkheimer's theory. Shortly after the end of World
War II, he and Adorno encountered Christian intellectuals such
as Kogon and Dirks(74). Although in many ways different, all
four shared an opposition to fascism and a common analysis of
the German political and cultural situation. With numerous

others in the liberal Frankfurt of 1946, they dreamed of a social-democratic future for Germany and the rest of Europe. Kogon and Dirks hoped for an alliance of Christians and socialists. But by 1948, the rigid German class system was re-established, and the Catholic and Protestant bourgeoisie united in opposition to the socialists. Hopes for a socialist Germany remained unfulfilled and a deep-seated pessimism toward change resulted(75).

All four men were controversial in their own circles. They all saw that Marxism had been misunderstood as the mere turning upside down of Hegel's dialectic. Horkheimer and Adorno, students of the Enlightenment, avoided becoming slaves to Enlightenment ideology. During their American exile, they had uncovered its dialectic: Enlightenment, which promises to liberate people from their fears and to make them into masters of their fate, can turn into its very opposite: fasicism, terror and the forced dependence on the Few. Dirks and Kogon believed in an "unknown God." Although they remained in the Catholic Church, they rejected the petrified Catholic and Protestant orthodoxies. They discovered a dialectic within religion paralleling the Enlightenment dialectic: Christianty, which Hegel had called the religion of truth and freedom, can also turn into its very opposite: ideology, the justification of unjustifiable relations of domination(76).

All four theorists fought the return of many Germans to ideological religion from their earlier commitments to National Socialism by attacking the ideological alliance between religion and positivity. Deeply concerned with the history of religion and of the Enlightenment, they emphasized the dialectic between religious and secular consciousness which Hegel had masterfully analyzed in the introduction to his Philosophy of Religion(77). Following Hegel's example of effecting a reconciliation between religion and reason, Kogon and Dirks tried, in their Frankfurter Hefte, to unite their own non-dogmatic Christianity with a non-ideological Enlightenment, i.e., one which would not decay into fascism. Horkheimer and Adorno, too, tried to bridge the gulf between their own demystified Enlightenment position and theology. They sought to heal the spiritual schizophrenia prevalent in late bourgeois and early socialist society, the rift between religion and secular culture, faith and reason, redemption and emancipation, by introducing theological contents into secularity(78).

Kogon's and Dirks's continuing dialogue · with Horkheimer

and Adorno was a result of their belief that Christianity
should confront important questions which Judaism poses to
Christianity. The Jewish prohibition of images of God
expresses the historical meaning of Judaism as expectation and
as still unfulfilled longing as contraposed to Christian
"fate," in which salvation is already attained. Judaism, the
historical root of Christianity, calls for a return to
Christianity's own utopian longing. The institutional corruption of Christianity, however, contributes to the forms of
disintegration in late bourgeois society, both by supplying
supportive ideology and by reproducing social divisions within
the Church. Recognizing that this corruption is part and par-
cel of present social decay, Kogon, Dirks, Tillich and others
sought to unveil the real and concrete utopian depth dimension
of the present world-historical period of transition, a period
whose possibilities include Future I - Walden II; Future II -
nuclear holocaust; or Future III - a solidary world feder-
ation(79).

Religion as Longing

Cognizant of the importance of faith for the future of the
world, in a 1970 interview Horkheimer argued that the liquidation of religion parallels the disappearance of meaning and
that the "death of God" entails the loss of absolute
truth(80). The European New Left and right-wing positivists
alike became indignant. To them, this statement implied that,
because of the loss of the dimension of truth and meaning,
faith in the transcendent had to be rescued. It cemented the
popular belief that Horkheimer had moved back from
enlightenment to religious faith - a belief supported by his
apparent "retreat into theology." But in 1973, Mansilla
visited him in Montagnola and reported that his a-religious
conception of theology remained unchanged(81). Theology, for
Horkheimer, is the expression of humanity's unappeasable
longing for justice. Its task is to help liberate reason from
its present positivist limitations. Faith in the transcendent
is the surpassing of what is immediately given, the
consciousness that the world is appearance, that it is not
absolute truth. Theology's efforts are identical with those of
Idealism from Kant to Hegel, i.e., to bring Enlightenment into
practice(82).
     According to Hegel, the image of the Absolute can be
represented as something hoped for, distant, transcendent; but

for the believer it presents immediate security, certainty and
enjoyment. Faith recognizes the image of the Absolute as the
substance of existence. It introduces happiness into the
present world of pain and darkness, and makes itself felt in
individuals' behavior. But religion can be revolutionary (as
longing) or reactionary (as certainty); its revolutionary
character depends on its secularization, on the smashing of
its idols. While Hegel was preoccupied with religious
consciousnesss as certainty, Horkheimer was more concerned
with it as longing, as hope for something transcendent in the
future. For Horkheimer, this longing can provide humanity with
a consciousness of truth in the midst of the horrors of
history.

Horkheimer's theory of religion shares with Hegel's the
analysis of the nature of religious consciousness as hope and
longing. Both Hegel and Horkheimer acknowledge that religion,
as longing for the Absolute, is essential to human beings.
Everything depends on the relation of religion to the
individual's secular worldview. Thus, the first task of the
philosophy of religion is to work through the meaning of the
various forms of secular consciousness at a particular
historical moment. The evolution of the principles of modern
culture from the Enlightenment on began outside what Hegel
would call philosophy, i.e., bourgeois society never sought to
unite religion and reason. Eventually, the principles of our
times began to struggle against philosophy and then to absorb
it, incorporating or accommodating whatever opposed it. The
opposition of Enlightenment to the original longing for the
Absolute begins in the universal difference between secular
and religious consciousness. At present, this split is much
further from true philosophical insight than in Hegel's time.
So the resolution is more urgent. Horkheimer's theory of
religion is essentially a reflection on this opposition and an
attempt to dissolve it. He reconciled religion and
secularization more profoundly by transforming the hope for an
absolute positivum (which underlies all positive religions)
into an absolute longing without such a positivum(83). By
secularizing religious hope, Horkheimer sought to preserve it
in an increasingly secular world, even into a future, totally
adminstered society. As early as 1935 he wrote: "Mankind loses
religion as it moves through history, but the loss leaves its
mark behind. Part of the drives and desires which religious
belief preserved and kept alive are detached from the
inhibiting religious form and become productive forces in

social   practice.   In   the   process   even   the   immoderation
characteristic of shattered illusions acquires a positive form
and is truly transformed. In a really free mind the concept of
Infinity is preserved in an awareness of the finality of human
life and of the inalterable aloneness of man and it keeps
society from indulging in a thoughtless optimism, an inflation
of its own knowledge into a new religion"(84).

Here   Horkheimer   understands   social activity as production, and philosophy not as other-worldly speculation, but as
struggle   toward   a   sane   world.   Marx had expected the total
disappearance of positive religion (in its opiate character).
Now, some generations later, Horkheimer reiterated this expectation   and emphasized, perhaps more than Marx, the mark religion would leave behind. Realizing that   secular   emancipatory
society   desperately   needs a corrective against the dialectic
of the Enlightenment, Horkheimer summoned the "immoderation of
shattered religious illusions" to preserve the theoretical
position   of   the   Infinite   and other   contributions of the
religious tradition(85). According to   Mansilla,   Horkheimer's
interest   in   the   Infinite   has   theological   roots(86). "The
concept of God was for a long time the place   where   the   idea
was   kept   alive   that   there   are other norms besides those to
which nature and society give expression in   their   operation.
Dissatisfaction   with   earthly destiny is the strongest motive
for acceptance of a transcendental being. If   justice   resides
with   God,   then   it is not to be found in the same measure in
the world. Religion is the record of the wishes,   desires   and
accusations   of   countless   generations"(87). Horkheimer never
substantially altered this definition of religion as the first
intellectual expression of humanity's greatest aspiration.

According to Hegel, religion contains three   constitutive
elements: God, the religious relation and cult. He criticized
bourgeois philosophers for their   agnosticism: their   concern
with   the   religious   relation rather than with God. Bourgeois
Enlightenment theologians were   entirely   indifferent   to   the
question   of   people's   real   knowledge   of the essence of God
since they   considered   this   knowledge   entirely   subjective.
Since   one cannot know what God is, the pretense of such knowledge was called absolute arrogance. Thus,   bourgeois   philosophers   promoted   agnosticism   as   a   means   of   emancipation.
Through this epistemological operation God   was   relegated   to
contingent   subjectivity,   and Hegel was amazed that bourgeois
agnostics attributed any objectivity to God at all.

Accepting Hegel's insight, Horkheimer rejected   bourgeois

agnosticism as ideology, for it relegates belief to mere subjectivism apart from social praxis. Yet Horkheimer appropriates the limited truth of bourgeois philosophy; God cannot be considered apart from the human subjective spirit, especially since God is unknown. He says much less than Hegel about the Infinite, but he understands that the relation between finite and Infinite underlies all religion. As a materialist and an atheist, Horkheimer sees all God-images as subjective human projections and all religion as the historical product of human longing. Since God is rooted in human feeling, he is not independent. Thus, Horkheimer can show that there is a feeling of God in many people, but he cannot show, as the metaphysicians tried to do, that God is(88). While Hegel thinks he knows that God is, Horkheimer hopes that God is, but fears that God is not(89). Both stress the finitude of the human subject and our consciousness of the negation of our sense of finitude. Both oppose Schleier-macher's definition of religion as a feeling of dependence and agree that in the consciousness of our sense of finitude lies already the consciousness of the negation of this limitation(90). But Horkheimer does not find that this negation of the negation necessarily leads to any positivum, certainly not to an absolute Positivum, i.e., God.

For Horkheimer, any positive objectification of the Absolute means dependence and unfreedom. The negation of our sense of finitude is a comparison between our true humanity and our immediate personal and social life: our limited existence. The very basis of his social criticism (that we are not yet ourselves) gives Horkheimer's theory its revolutionary character. Religion is not based on dependence, but on independence and freedom; not on the lack of correspondence between human existence and essence, but on the possibility of the elimination of this inappropriate disparity(91). While for Hegel religion seems to have already reconciled existence and essence, for Horkheimer, religion is only the hope that the negation of the negation of true humanity may become a positivum and that human existence may be appropriate to human nature in a future reconciled society(92).

Horkheimer's critical theory is doubtless influenced by the Jewish tradition, as were the theories of Marx and Freud. He shares with this tradition a sensitivity to human pain (especially as connected with evil or sin) and a longing for justice. His theory perpetuates the Jewish unhappy conscious-ness which preceded the Catholic unhappy consciousness analyzed by Marcuse(93). His theory is pessimistic, but it also contains the promise of reconciliation present in the myth of original sin. Horkheimer continually emphasized that reconciliation and ultimate satisfaction have not yet been achieved, so that the human feeling of pain of being split into the universal and the particular, and the longing to go beyond this dichotomy, remains. Horkheimer was not a stoic; negativity and pain exist and must be historically understood. In conformity with the Jewish spirit, Horkheimer remains in everyday reality and demands the reconciliation here, rather than after death. He broadens this fundamental idea of Judaism into an objective universal, the concrete essence of humanity. The loss of merely external reality, of the positive individuality of the Jewish people, drove Horkheimer to inward reflection, for in the face of negated reality nothing is left but subjectivity: the human will. Only through this subjectivity will reconciliation be possible, if at all. Dialectical reason must heal the old damage to human subjectivity caused by the separation of universal and particular.

Horkheimer's theory addresses not only the Jewish religion, but Christianity as well. He shares with Christianity the idea of the reconciliation of the world. But unlike Hegel, Horkheimer can no longer determine this reconciliation positively as the unity of God with the negatively posited reality, i.e., as Christ in history(94). He knows only of the radical non-identity of the human subject and the Absolute, and understands the Christian teaching on the Trinity in merely functional-historical terms(95). Although Horkheimer shares with Hegel the idea of the dialectical unity of the universal and the particular in individuality, he objects to Hegel's mystical speculation that the finite human spirit is a divine moment. He hopes for liberation from the restlessness of pain and, thus, with Hegel, he preserves a moment of Christianity: the announcement of freedom, the reflectivity and uniqueness of the human subject, the principle of free subjectivity(96).

Principle of Subjectivity

Today, this free subjectivity is rapidly melting away. The New Left's accusation that Horkheimer had escaped into religious faith reflects this demise. For Horkheimer, the young Marxists mistakenly measure human progress by the frozen objectivistic categories of the bourgeois order they criticize: production, consumption, exchange, expansion of power. The inability of dogmatic Marxists to recognize and appreciate positive moments in other contemporary systems of thought (e.g., Christianity's free subjectivity) compounds their error. In their malicious critique and in their right-wing counterparts, Horkheimer saw how far instrumental reason had already reached, and how close we have come to the end of serious philosophy and theology: Future I - the totally administered, subjectless society. In this desperate situation, Horkheimer's critical theory has, as always, a double task: to identify what should be changed in bourgeois or socialist society and to preserve the progressive elements in the great religious traditions, and to pass to future generations the goals of human emancipation as Western Enlightenment first comprehended them(97).

In 1973, Horkheimer expressed envy for the men and women who would inhabit the probable technological society of the future. In spite of the death of erotic love, they will be happy at least insofar as they will suffer no material want and will enjoy more material social justice than present or past generations(98). But their improved condition does not dispense critical theory from the obligation to direct public attention to the high costs involved in such technologically conditioned progress, e.g., the continuation of a negative moment of the present bourgeois order, namely human coldness(99). Without cold bourgeois subjectivity, Auschwitz, Hiroshima, Vietnam, El Salvador, Samosa-Nicaragua, the Shah's Iran, Grenada, Lebanon, Ethiopia, etc., would not have been possible. Horkheimer's early writings struggle to replace cold bourgeois subjectivity with a kind and loving post-bourgeois subjectivity, which necessarily had to be grounded in religion as hope and longing for the transcendent. His principle of concrete subjectivity is a secularized form of the Christian principle of subjective freedom as it appears in Hegel. Thus, Hegel is essential for full comprehension of Horkheimer.

Hegel set the Christian principle of free subjectivity against not only the abstract freedom of despots and oligarchs, but also against the false freedom of modern bourgeois society. He felt that the true idea of subjective freedom comes into the world through Christianity, because it teaches that the individual as such has infinite value and that every single person is the object of God's love. In Christianity the singular subject is the essential element: salvation is of the individual as individual. This Christian subjectivity or selfness, not bourgeois selfishness, is precisely the principle of Western Enlightenment, no matter how much the latter may continually oppose the former.

According to Hegel, the right of the particularity of the human subject to seek full satisfaction, or the right of subjective freedom (free subjectivity), constitutes the central difference between Antiquity and the Modern Age, for now a new relation between universality and particularity is made possible by the historical separation of the universal and the particular. This right to subjective freedom in its infinitude has been made into the universal real principle of a new form of the world as family, society and state. Hegel is fully aware of the fact that this principle of particularity is a moment of opposition(100). But it is at least as identical to the social universal as it is different from it. In Hegel's view, the independent development of the subject's particularity is the moment which has shown itself in history as the corruption which erodes the mores of the Old World and causes social disintegration. In general, the city-states of old were constructed on the basis of an original mythical-religious worldview which is lost in modern bourgeois society. Therefore, they could not endure the split between their social morality and the citizens' self-consciousness. The old states became the victim of abstract reflection as soon as it arose, first in the minds of a growing number of citizens and then in political reality. Their simple principle of universality lacked the infinite power of that social unity which first permits the opposition of reason (the opposition between the universal and the particular) but eventually overcomes it and maintains itself in it(101).

Particularity, as it appears abstractly in modern bourgeois society, is extravagance and boundlessness(102). The forms of extravagance are themselves boundless. Such abstract particularity is the very content of the principle of cold bourgeois subjectivity: the bourgeois' real, but false self-consciousness. Whereas an animal's instincts lead to a limited number of needs, people differentiate and multiply their desires continually, leading to a "bad infinity" of needs which demand satisfaction. For Hegel this disordered condition in bourgeois society can be harmonized only through control by the constitutional state. After both the right of subjectivity and the person's infinity have risen, the social totality must, at the same time, derive the strength to posit the particularity of the subject in harmony with its socio-

ethical unity. The socio—moral totality must supersede in
itself its as such necessary difference, civil society and the
principle of subjectivity it contains.

When in the Christian religion, one knows one's relation
to God's absolute spirit as one's essence, then the divine
spirit is present also in the sphere of one's secular
existence: in marriage, family, society, state, history and
culture. While human knowledge speculates that the essence,
purpose and object of humanity consists in subjective freedom,
this idea is the unfolding reality of men and women. According
to Hegel, Christianity has made it the very reality of
believers not to be slaves. If they were enslaved, if the
decision over their property and life resided in the
arbitrariness of despots or oligarchs, they would find the
very substance of their existence violated. For believers, the
willing of freedom is no longer merely a drive which demands
satisfaction, but is character, the spiritual consciousness
which is no longer instinctual. But this Christian freedom is
itself first just a notion, a principle of the individual's
subjectivity, spirit, the human heart. This freedom is first
merely destined to become objectified into rightful socio-
ethical, religious and scientific reality. Hegel believes that
the introduction of the Christian principle into the world
falls to the long, hard work of education(103). World History
is qualitative progress in the development of human freedom
and consciousnesss. The Christian principle is an important
and necessary moment in this progress. Hegel considers this
process of liberation internally necessary, in spite of all
the possibiltes of horrible regression and resistance in
history.

For Horkheimer, the right of free subjectivity or
subjective freedom has had tremendous consequences for the
development of the modern world. He knows that the idea of
Romantic love and of the right of the individual to eternal
happiness are of Christian origin, as are the modern concepts
of personal morality and conscience. Horkheimer preserves the
Christian principle in a secularized form as concrete sub-
jectivity(104). He radicalizes Hegel's position by accenting
the difference between the principle of subjectivity and the
social totality, although he does not fix the principle of
subjectivity in its difference and opposition against the
empirical whole. We are approaching the total demise of the
individual in modern society, and morality can be perennial
only as the individual's hostile struggle against the false

collective of civil society. Like Hegel, Horkheimer recognizes the dialectical character of the independent development of the particularity of the human suject. For Horkheimer, no path leads from the principle of Enlightenment subjectivity to the mythical, partriarchal religious principle of substantiality underlying traditional societies. Any attempt at such return under the conditions of advanced capitalism can lead only to fascism. Both theorists look toward a future society which would have the energy of a true social unity and which would allow the dialectical opposition of individuality and collectivity. The modern state has not been able to reconcile the individual subject with its own totality, but instead vacillates between anarchy and totalitarianism on the Right or Left. Neo-Caesarism in fascist or technocratic form constitutes a false synthesis of the individual and the collective because it does not allow the individual to develop fully his or her particularity, because it is abstract and has for its opposition an equally abstract subject. The real utopia of critical theory is the reconciled society, in which individual and universal would be in true harmony: it alone would be a rational and free society. Critical theory fights against false, ideological harmonies in order to make true reconciliation possible: Future III - the society of reason and freedom, into which civil society has been sacrificed or has sacrificed itself.

Like Hegel, Horkheimer believes in a substantial social morality, yet he defends more emphatically than Hegel the principle of independent subjectivity(105). Clearly the chaos of bourgeois society cannot and should not be helped by the elimination of the particularity of the individual subject. Unlike Hegel, however, Horkheimer cannot demand free subjectivity by recourse to the infinite right of the Idea. Horkheimer can do so only by recourse to human subjective reason, to the progressive elements in past religious and philosophical traditions and to the three Enlightenment movements, the bourgeois Enlightenment, Freudianism and Marxism. With Hegel, Horkheimer longs for a rational and free society in which the totality would no longer be false, but would assert people's concrete subjectivity into true harmony with its own socio-ethical unity: a real community of free individuals. For Horkheimer as for Hegel, free subjectivity is possible only in solidarity with others, even with the wholly Other. Horkheimer is emphatically committed to the Christian discovery that the person as person is free, that freedom constitutes human nature itself, that the individual is of highest value. For him, people must at some point in their lives establish an absolute relationship to the Absolute: an Absolute which is not, however, a loving God or spirit(106). Within us we cannot possibly carry God's absolute spirit, but only the hope for love and for spirit without which truly human action is impossible.

Horkheimer departs furthest from Hegel in rejecting the presence of God's spirit in the world as society and history. Hegel's claim of God's presence sounds to Horkheimer like utter blasphemy, for the substance of his world is a dark will to live(107). Social relations are not constituted in conformity to the Absolute. The social morality which the individual internalizes in family, society and state is neither better nor worse than the morality individuals have incorporated into such institutions in the first place. Horkheimer is much less sure than Hegel that the individual can internalize social morality through his or her existence in family, society and state, much less sure that this is the way the individual becomes really free. Both Horkheimer and Hegel agree that the essence of humanity is freedom and that the idea of freedom has become partially realized, although it is still a mere longing that demands satisfaction. The full application of the principle of concrete subjectivity to family, society and state remains a task and demands the long, hard work of Enlightenment.

Christian and Critical Views of History

In 1936, Horkheimer criticized Haecker's work and outlined his critical theory of religion(108). According to Haecker, finite things have only one real goal: death. No matter how long human accomplishments last, the storm which eventually extinguishes all finite goals will come. Finite goals are seen in the service of God and in the return of all things to God, who is the infinite goal. God uses the will of people and nations for his own unchangeable goals. In spite of his rejection of idealism, Haecker's philosophy of history resembles Hegel's. Horkheimer points out that Haecker does not propose a new theory of history, but only the Catholic conception, according to which the meaning of history consists in rescuing human beings from original sin. Although societies rather than individuals are the primary historical agencies, each individual must ultimately do this on his own. People, however, can abuse their freedom, so it becomes the Church's function to show them the way to salvation. This Church is not a natural community, race or nation but all Christian believers.

For Haecker, every attack against this religious view is vain, since opponents substitute temporal goods such as power, fame, money or enjoyment for God. But Horkheimer holds that this is correct only for the bourgeois who is indifferent to religion. It does not apply to self-conscious materialists and critical theorists, who recognize that the emancipation sought in oppposition to the Church must not be idolized. Critical theorists are safeguarded from idolatry by their solidarity with the real interests of a fettered and chained humanity, and by their dialectical thinking. In the same vein, Horkheimer finds idolatry in contemporary theology when it degrades the idea of the highest wisdom, love and justice, to the lord of history. For Horkheimer, it is possible to comprehend history without turning it into a process of salvation. Justice and wisdom are unreal as long as they remain mere images in people's minds. Critical theorists must not turn these images into a God in order to realize them, for the good, once realized, becomes historical and will pass away. The Enlightenment's finite goals are not at all like death, simply because they are not eternal. Critical theory neither looks to God for meaning in history nor diminishes the importance of progress and direction in history, but remains materialist and historical.

Horkheimer admires the wisdom of Catholicism, which unlike Protestantism, has not completely diluted the thought of eternity or separated it from material wishes. While bourgeois praxis represents in a certain sense the truth of Catholic theology, critical theory, which examines and understands that praxis, does not simply reject the theological motifs, but transcends them, thus rescinding the theological hypostatization of abstract human beings by developing the concept of God from determinate historical conditions(109). It teaches that free bourgeois subjects carry out their activities as equals, as individuals without time and place and without a definite fate. This representation is completed in the modern concept of God. But the real subjects beneath the abstraction and the real content of the bourgeois concept of God are historically determinate persons connected with each other through social life - its need-production-exchange system. The abstraction falsely reflects social being in bourgeois society. Since the concept of God during the last three or four centuries has been bound to a transient form of social being, Christian ideology represents a decisive cultural step beyond pagan religions. For Horkheimer and Hegel, Christianity is the fulfillment of the whole history of religion. Critical theory succeeds Christianity in assuming its progressive role; it rejects the resurrection of the dead, the last judgment, and eternal life as dogmatic positions, and it focuses on human needs for infinite happiness. Horkheimer thus opens Christianity to the truth and freedom it promised.

Materialists do not replace God with transitory goods. They know that the wish for eternal happiness cannot be fulfilled. Here Horkheimer explicitly points out the relation between religion and materialism: "All these wishes for eternity, and particularly for the entrance of universal justice and goodness, are shared by materialist and religious thinkers, as opposed to the dullness of the positivistic attitude"(110). But while religious thinkers acquiesce in the recognition that the Christian revolution has already taken place, materialists decry the limitless abandonment of humanity. Such sorrow is the price of longing for truth. Although materialist thought is concerned with pleasure and desire, Horkheimer realizes that they are transitory(111). Haecker examined the bourgeois personality and concluded that the perseverance of materialism is impossible, for the sense of transitoriness was drowned in the 1930s by false eternalisms. But according to Horkheimer, Haecker's religious consolation will lose its attraction with the creation of social conditions which no longer require myths: Faith in the re-creation of the world after its destruction goes too far in the fight against melancholy.

Roman Civil Society

In the preface to the Phenomenology of Mind, Hegel claimed that the contemporary era was one of birth and transition(112). He predicted three possible futures arising out of the decline of Western civilization: Future II – increasingly larger blocks of nations engaged in perpetual war (the result of the inner negativity of the individuality of modern nation states); Future I – entirely mechanized and automated society (the result of differentiation of needs and division of labor); and Future III – a new society characterized by a living universal rationality (the result of the extension of the principle of objective social freedom and of the Christian principle of free subjectivity). Hegel's whole philosophy points to the third alternative, to be realized either in a future American or Slavic world. In the last decade of his life (from 1821 to 1831), he witnessed the continual and irreversible decline of Western civiliztion. The Christian community was hopelessly split into three antagonistic sub-groups: those who held a naive and immediate faith; those who participated in modern Enlightenment while remaining members of the Christian community; and those like Hegel who were both dialectical philosophers as well as theologians.

Although with many thinkers before and after him, Hegel compared modern bourgeois society with the Roman Empire, more specifically with Roman civil society. In the last stages of the Roman Empire, the unity of religion disappeared: the divine became secularized while political life lacked wisdom and confidence. Reason took refuge in private property and contracts. The social totality became false and was given up under the Roman emperors; the particular well-being of individuals became the only worthwhile goal. According to Hegel, the same could be said of modern bourgeois society. The only valid feature of this society was the private moral view of the bourgeois. This is why justification through the notion (the dialectical unity of universal and particular in the individual) becomes an urgent need in modern bourgeois society. Such a philosophical need always appears at the end of a civilization(113). But Hegel knew that his reconciliation of religion and dialectial reason lacked historical specificity. Thus, he set up the philosophy of religion as an isolated discipline guarding the "truth" (the Christian principle of free subjectivity) pending bourgeois society's overcoming of its present contradictions into a free, rational organic state.

New World

A century after Hegel not only are we still in a "period of transition," but now there is even doubt that this is the birth of a new spiritual culture. During his lifetime, Horkheimer waited in vain for a qualitative break. Contemporary socio-political horrors muted his theological optimism. He saw the disintegration of the basic structures of Western civilization. What was for Hegel a certainty became for Horkheimer a mere hope. Horkheimer does not see a sunrise either in the near or distant future interrupting the decay of Western civilization with the rise of a new and just world. Unlike Hegel's world, the real post-European world is more like an unborn rather than a newborn child. If there is any beginning of a new world at all, then it is still very much hidden in the womb of the old Western world and may very well be suffocated in it. Yet, Horkheimer tried at least to outline a future true social whole. He also foresaw Hegel's three possible futures: Future II - perpetual international war, Future I - the fully mechanized society, or Future III - solidary, reconciled society. Social solidarity could rise out of the subjects' insight into their own finitude, suffering, and death. In such a society, individual and collective would be truly reconciled.

Both Horkheimer and Hegel foresaw the end of Christianity in the general decline of Western civilization, and both saw the Christian community fragment into the three aforementioned antagonistic sub-groups. Both valued highly naive believers, those who retained a genuine religious faith and both criticized the second group, the bourgeois Christian. Horkheimer predicted that the liberalization of religion in terms of Enlightenment theology would necessarily lead to the end of religion, for this liberalization plays into the hands of the daily politics of late capitalist society. "Enlightened" theologians compromise with the positivistically-oriented natural and social sciences. Of course, in order to avoid bourgeois corruption, religion cannot return to naively preaching the old divine commandments and prohibitions. Still religion can make modern men and women conscious of their finitude, conscious that they must suffer and die. Horkheimer finds himself in solidarity with the third group of believers, represented today by critical political theologians, liberal theologians, priests and expriests engaged in intense adaptation to bourgeois positive science and in the massive reproduction of bourgeois mass culture for great gains(114). Big business!. These dialectical theologians agree with Horkheimer that religion has lost its true function. In Catholicism, God was the creator of earthly orders of domination, and Protestantism traced the horrible course of history directly back to the almighty will of the Creator. Thus, any specific political regime bore the stamp of divine justice, while defamed by the rotten conditions of social reality. According to Horkheimer, Christianty forfeited its true cultural function to the extent that it allied with the state.

In agreement with Horkheimer, dialectical political theologians today decry the current ideological function of Christianty: the church should stop consoling believers by promising transcendent relief from evil earthly conditions. Rather, churches should be revolutionary agencies(115).

Horkheimer warns that religion cannot be secularized and still remain religion. It is vain to hope that the Church will preserve religion (and its spirit of freedom and justice) as at its beginnings, because contemporary solidarity with the oppressed has discarded its religious garment. None of the theological content can continue to exist as it is. But while truth cannot reappear in the form of traditional religion, something of religion will remain: the longing for the Infinite and for complete justice(116). Thus, Horkheimer urges that critical theologians transform the churches from ideological into critical institutions which would correct the false totality by presenting in secular form the ideals of justice, love and freedom. Horkheimer wants the hope for the Infinite to appear in the daily finitude of human lives and this finitude must appear as part of the horizon of absolute justice(117). The finite and the Infinite should no longer constitute two entirely separate dimensions, as in bourgeois Enlightenment theology, nor should the notion of the Infinite be swallowed up by the finite business of bourgeois science and politics. But the realization of religion is equal to its destruction, for the realization of its rational content (subjectivity, justice, etc.) entails the abolition of its religious form.

Enlightenment has overcome myth and has undermined once and for all the foundations of religion. The demythologizing which Horkheimer sees as necessary for the future, just society has made it difficult for simple people to express their longing for the absolute. As bourgeois society destroys the myth, it also destroys the Absolute without which morality is impossible. Thus, demythologization now means demoralization: the smashing of myths signals the end of morality. Horkheimer sought to resolve the dissonance stemming from the awareness of the end of Christianity, the tension between dialectical reason and religion, but his resolution is as partial as Hegel's. As an isolated intellectual elite, critical sociologists guard the truth (free subjectivity) against the present false totality, but they fail to provide modern society with a practical way out of the dichotomy between religiosity and secularity. Horkheimer falls short of Hegel's

philosophy of religion, insofar as he rejects the possibility
of rational, dialectical insight into the objectivity of the
Infinite or the Transcendent. But Horkheimer goes beyond Hegel
by specifying for modern society the shape of its future.
Unless interrupted by Future II - nuclear holocaust - he sees
the immanent logic of history unavoidably leading to Future I
- the totally administered, technocratic society. He does not
want to resign himself to such a prospect. On the positive
side, Future I - the administered society will not only be
able to satisfy people's material needs, but it might also
unfold productive forces which bring forth a not-exclu- sively
technical progress. No matter how inhuman this totally
administered world would be, it is still preferable to annihilation, since it contains the tiny potential for transition to
Future III - the solidary society(118).
      There is still a small chance that theology as the long-
ing for the Other, as the hope for justice, could survive in
Future I - the totally adminstered world - since even when all
material needs are satisfied, death remains inevitable. Horkheimer thought that post-modern people would perhaps become
more acutely aware of death precisely because they need not
worry about the satisfaction of material needs. His analysis
of religion will become most relevant if and when Future I -
the totally adminstered society - becomes a reality. He will
provide people with a way to resist it.

Humanistic Religiosity

More intensely even than Horkheimer, Fromm has devoted himself
to the explanation of the critical and rational elements in
religion. Fromm has nevertheless been criticized by his former
colleagues at the Frankfurt Institute for having
philosophically idealist theories, advising conformity to
present capitalist society, and paying only lip service to
social criticism. But an analysis of this theory of religion
shows that it is not only faithful to the essential elements
of critical theory but that it culminates in the very
foundation of critical theory: negative theology(119). As with
the theories of Horkheimer, Adorno and Marcuse, Fromm's theory
of religion is intended for those people in the twentieth
century who no longer ascribe to theistic religions and for
whom the crucial question is whether conversion to a
humanistic "religiosity" without the dogmas and institutions
of positive religions is possible. According to Fromm, these

people are not merely confronted with the choice between
selfish bourgeois materialism and the Christian concepts of
God, Trinity and Incarnation.

Born into a religious Jewish family in Frankfurt in 1900
Fromm recalls in his autobiography that the writings of the
Old Testament touched and exhilarated him as a boy more than
anything else he was exposed to(120). Fromm was particularly
moved by the prophetic writings of Isaiah, Amos and Hosea,
with their vision of the last days in which universal peace
and harmony would reign. This prophetic promise appealed to
the adolescent Fromm especially as he experienced minor
episodes of anti-semitism and the exclusionary clannishness of
the Christians as well as the Jews. But the autobiographer
believes that these experiences would not have impressed him
so deeply had it not been for World War I(121). As most
14-year-olds, Fromm was caught up in the initial excitement of
war, the celebrations of early victories and the reports of
the tragic deaths of individual soldiers. But by the war's
end, young Fromm was seriously troubled by the question of
what made war possible.

Having become deeply suspicious of all official religious
or secular ideologies, Fromm gave up the outward form of his
Jewish orthodoxy in 1926. In his search for an understanding
of the irrationality of human mass behavior, he followed a
path that led him to Hegel, Marx and Freud(122). Blending
empirical observation and Hegel's logic, Fromm revised both
Marx's theory of society and Freud's theory of the individual
and finally integrated them in The Dogma of Christ, published
in 1930. Here he set forth his theory of religion as well as
the essence of his critical theory of society. In this first
attempt to transcend the customary psychologistic approach to
historical and social phenomena, Fromm employed traditional
psychoanalytic methodology to show that ideas and ideologies
can be understood only by comprehending the real life
conditions of the people who create them and believe in them.

The roots of Fromm's theory of religion are to be found
not only in Marx and Freud but in the bourgeois enlightenment
as well. As described by Hegel in the introduction to his
philosophy of religion, enlightened bourgeois thought held
that the knowledge of God could not be posited by the
comprehending reason. Consciousness of God could arise only
from feeling. More consistent, he believed, were the
materialist or positivist theorists who reduced human thought
and spirit to sensation, and identified God as a product of

feeling and therefore without objectivity. But against both views, Hegel argued that the bourgeoisie had reified and privatized God into individual property. What was rooted merely in feeling existed only for the individual as his property, but not on its own. Hegel believed that any philosophy of religion was first of all under the obligation to prove that God exists(123).

Fromm, as most materialists in Hegel's time, considers God a product of human feeling without any independent existence. While for Hegel neither God nor people could be understood in isolation from each other, Fromm is confident that he can speak about people without reference to God. Whereas for Hegel, the foundation of religion was the dialectical relation between God's absolute spirit and human subjective spirit, for Fromm it is the individual's relation toward a wholly indeterminate X-reality(124). Hegel felt that the philosopher of religion at least had to establish the independent necessity of religion, if not of God. Only after he left the Frankfurt Institute in 1939 did Fromm go beyond religion's external, instrumental and functional necessity as an integrative social factor(125). In the past three and a half decades, he has increasingly emphasized an internal personal necessity of a humanistic religiousness.

Historical Materialism and Psychoanalysis

Fromm derives his critique of religion from the claim in Marx's historical materialism that man makes religion, and not religion man(126). Acording to Marx, religion represents an unreal world consciousness because it is a reflection of the false relations of state, society and family. Since the human essence lacks real objectifications, it seeks realization through fantasy in religion. Only by unmasking this fantastical self-realization for the sham that it is does Marx believe the philosopher can begin the critique of politics and social relations. For Fromm, Marx's work is the secular manifestation of the radical humanism expressed in the vision of the Old Testament prophets and the key to history. As in Marx's theory of religion, it is Fromm's intent to disillusion people so that they may come to their senses and think, act and change their reality.

Yet, critical theory developed partly because the German and European proletariat resisted such disillusionment and was reluctant to fulfill its historical revolutionary role. In Freud's psychoanalysis, Fromm found an explanation for the peculiar tenacity of religious ideas. According to Freud, primitive religion arises out of the need to personify the forces of nature in order for humans to react to them and overcome the feeling of complete helplessness. Even with the advent of a scientific understanding of nature, humanity's sense of helplessness remains, along with the longing for protection and Gods. Man's situation vis-a-vis nature, in Freud's view, is only the continuation of an infantile prototype. As small children, men find themselves in a state of helplessness in relation to their parents, whom they have reason to fear - especially their fathers - yet they are certain the fathers will protect them against the dangers of the outside world. With science, natural forces lose their human traits, but people still need to cling to the existence of a father, one more powerful than the biological one. Freud argued that the strength of religious ideas was due entirely to the power of humanity's oldest and strongest wishes and fears.

Fromm's concept of social character, introduced in The Dogma of Christ and later empirically verified in the Frankfurt Labor Study of 1931, mediates between Marx's notion of social reality and Freud's understanding of individual psychology(127). Character structure, shaped by socio-economic reality, determines not only what ideas one will choose, but also their strength(128). Further, Fromm argues that once created, the ideas influence social character and thereby the socio-economic structure(129). As in Hegel's dialectic, Fromm's middle term, social character, becomes more important than ideas or the socio-economic structure. This dialectical configuration gives his theory immediacy, empirical concreteness and humanistic warmth, but it leaves him open to his critics' charge that he psychologizes the family, state and history, and thereby promotes the adjustment of the individual to an antagonistic social reality(130). Fromm could have strengthened his analysis by showing how ideas mediate between social character and socio-economic reality and how, in turn, socio-economic structures mediate between ideas and social character.

In the peculiar stratification of class society, Fromm sees the infantile situation repeated for the individual. The individual at once fears the ruling minority while longing for the protection it affords. And everyone knows that resistance to that minority is always severely punished. Just as the child uncritically believes everything the father says, so does the individual accept whatever the ruling class or its political representatives decree. This infantile bondage of the masses, one of the main guarantees of social stability, cohesion and equilibrium, is maintained and strengthened by the power elite(131). According to Fromm, one of the best ways of doing this is through authoritarian religion. The ruling class always claims God as its ally while religion itself intellectually intimidates the masses, making them distrust their own senses. Paradoxically, says Fromm, religion also offers people a certain measure of satisfaction, giving life a tolerable appearance to discourage them from attempting to change from obedient to rebellious children or from wage laborer to revolutionary(132).

Fromm argues that the satisfaction religion offers are not those of ego drives such as self-preservation, better food or other material pleasures, but are libidinous satisfactions that occur in fantasy, especially collective fantasies(133). By virtue of their universality, the masses' social fantasies are perceived as if they were real by the individual. According to Fromm, religious fantasies function to console men and women for life's privations, encourage them to accept their class status by appealing to their emotions, and to assuage the guilt feelings of the ruling class by justifying their oppression of the masses(134).

Christian Proletariat

The Dogma of Christ describes the psychic situation of the Christian proletariat in the first three centuries of the faith. Fromm seeks to understand the social effect of the primitive Christian message and the changes in the early Christians' idea of Jesus(135). The first Christians were a brotherhood of the economically and socially oppressed held together by an enthusiastic hope and hatred. That hope sprang from the earliest Christian message: not a social or economic reform, but a promise of a not-distant future in which the poor would be rich, the hungry satisfied and the oppressed would gain authority. Not only is this hope expressed, but a hatred of the rich and powerful can also be seen in the Sermon on the Mount and the story of Lazarus(136). In fact, Fromm sees this understandable hatred for the oppressors in society run throughout the Gospels and the Christian tradition up to the Constantinian turn when the Church makes peace with the Roman establishment in whose name Jesus had been crucified three centuries earlier.

Fromm finds the oldest teaching on Jesus's nature to be adoptionist, i.e., that Jesus was not the Son of God from the beginning but became so only by a definite act of God's will. This is "Left-Wing Christology" or Christology from below since it starts out from Jesus's humanity. In many respects, Left-Wing Christology resembles the concept, familiar to the Jewish masses for many centuries, of a Messiah chosen by God to introduce a kingdom of righteousness and love. But Fromm finds two new elements in the early Christian faith: that the Messiah is exalted as the Son of God and that, no longer the powerful military hero of Jewish tradition, the Messiah gains his significance and dignity from his suffering and death on the cross. Fromm argues that the adoptionist belief is a new form of the old myth of the rebellion of the son against the father. Not only did the Christian proletariat hate their earthly fathers, the ruling class, but they also detested the divine Father who was always portrayed as the ally of their mundane oppressors. The early Christians did not dare consciously slander the powerful Father-God, but instead expressed their unconscious hostility by putting a man at his side, thereby depriving him of his privileged and unreachable patriarchal position(137). To Fromm, the adoptionist belief represents an unconscious wish for the removal not only of the divine Father but of earthly fathers as well.

The guilt these unconscious feelings generated was displaced by the figure of the suffering Messiah. In the first place, says Fromm, Christians identified with Jesus because he was a suffering human being like themselves. This identification then forms the basis for the fascinating power of the idea of the suffering man Jesus and its effect on the proletariat in the Roman Empire. Secondly, Christians shifted some of their death wishes against the Father to the Son. Fromm sees the father killed in the son's crucifixion in the early Christian myth(138). And thirdly, in their identification with the Son, Christians suffered death themselves, thereby atoning for their death wishes against their earthly and heavenly fathers(139). The focus on the early Christian fantasy of the crucified son, according to Fromm, lies not in the Christians' masochistic expiation through self-annihilation, but in the displacement of the Father by the suffering Jesus. Fromm sees in Christianity the end of religion and the beginning of humanism because for the first time a man has moved into the X-dimension, previously reserved for God(140). In the third and fourth centuries, "Right-Wing Christology," or Christology from above - the doctrine that Jesus was always God - became popular in the Church, a trend which Fromm claims represented an elimination of hostility toward God and a legitimation of the power both of the Father and of the ruling class(141).

Part of the psychic background of the belief in Christ was the cult of the Roman Emperor, which Fromm claims to have been closely related to monotheism in its belief in a powerful and righteous Father(142). The hostility toward the Emperor and Roman authority were not unique to the Christian proletariat nor were those goals the ones they hoped for. But while the non-Christian masses tried to realize their wishes through political praxis, the hopelessness of that path led the Christians to seek fulfillment of their wishes in fantasy. Hegel, to the contrary, argued that in the principle of subjective freedom - that the individual is of infinite value and destined to the highest freedom - can be found a revolutionary element, one that was a contributing factor to the final downfall of the Roman Empire.

Hegel emphasized that the validity of the society and of the state, as well as alienated human beings, will die with Jesus's death. What in the Romans' mind was the worst disgrace - crufixion as a criminal - was transformed into the highest honor, shaking all the bonds of human life in the process. The Christian proletariat connects the cross of the present with the rose of God's kingdom(143). Having no substantial claim on the Christian, the status quo could resort only to the application of the completely external force of the death penalty to gain allegiance. But since they believed in eternal life, Christians no longer shied away from death, and so the Empire lost its last weapon against the faith. Furthermore, that God dies, that the negation of everything is found even in God, is a most terrifying thought for Hegel. But, he argues, in the resurrection and ascension of Christ, God retains identity in the non-identity of death. For the early Christians that liquidation of the negative and the elevation of a man into heaven represented the highest verification of human value. For Hegel, this verification is the foundation of all Christian humanism.

Fromm agrees that there is a revolutionary element in the death of Jesus, but doubts that it actually gave the world a different form, Christianity being more fantasy than efective factor for social change(144). Nor does he find in Christianity the highest verification of human nature. For Fromm, God dies and there is no resurrection, and in that is to be found humanity's ultimate liberation. Accepting the principle of subjective freedom, Fromm believes that human powers alone give value to life, not the fact that people are the objects of divine love. While steadfastly believing in the possibility of humanism without God, Fromm has since The Dogma of Christ developed his critical theory of religion by recourse to the anthropological basis of Hegel's philosophy of religion: the disunity between immediate human existence and its mediate essence(145).

Essence and Existence

Fromm defines human essence as a contradiction inhering in human existence(146). On the one hand, we are animals, and on the other, since we are conscious, we cannot be one with nature, as animals can. This is the classical view, shared by Hegel, that humans are body and soul, angel and animal. Neither for Fromm nor for Hegel is the awareness of human limitations the subjective basis for religious consciousness. Rather, the awareness is the key to human transcendence of limitations through the development of freedom. In Hegel's view, a person's feeling of limitation is a comparison of one's nature with one's existence at this particular time in history. Immediate existence seems inappropriate, in conflict with human essence. Fromm points out that not only is human essence a contradiction, but it is also one that demands a resolution. Both Fromm and Hegel see in the search for such a resolution the dynamic source of the world's positive religions: how can people find relief from this inner tension and be at home in the world(147)?

Fromm claims that there is a progressive as well as a regressive resolution. The latter is exemplified by the attempt of primitive religion or severe psychopathology to do away with what makes us human - reason, freedom and self-awareness - and merge back into nature(148). In civil society, regressive self-reconciliation takes place in the form of fascism(149). The alternative is to find harmony through full development of all human productive and creative capabilities(150). According to Fromm, the progressive solution surfaced in the monotheistic teachings of Moses around 1350 B.C. The same idea was expressed in other times and cultures: by Lao-tse in China, Buddha in India, Zarathustra in Persia, and in Israel by Jeremiah and Isaiah. Whatever the form of this message, the idea was the same: to answer the question of life by becoming fully human. But in Fromm's view, this message of reconciliation is perverted and falsified as soon as people hear it for they immediately idolize and ideologize God(151). Fromm's theory of religion is an attempt to motivate people to return to the authentic search for inner harmony. He does this in the context of negative theology(152).

Negative Theology

The core of negative theology is that God is unknown - an idea that, according to Horkheimer, had its origins in Judaism(153). In his work You Shall Be as Gods (1966), Fromm traces the development of the concept of God in the Old Testament and later Jewish tradition. Formulated over a period of 1200 years, what is common to the idea of God in the Old Testament is that ultimate reality, or the highest value, can be found neither in nature nor in human history. Rather, only the One represents supreme value and the final goal of humanity(154). Fromm sees three stages in the evolution of this concept: first, God is visualized an absolute ruler who can arbitrarily destroy what he has created; second, in the Noah story, God makes a covenant with humanity, a step which prepares the way to complete human freedom, even from God; and third, to Moses God is revealed as the God of history rather than the God of nature(155). In that event, Fromm sees the most important distinction between God and idols: only idols have names, while Moses's God of history is nameless. According to Fromm, this uniquely Jewish prohibition against representations of God, expressed in the Second Commandment, finds its most advanced and radical formulation in the negative theology of Moses Maimonides, Nicolaus of Cusa and Meister Eckehart(156).

Fromm concludes by saying that in the Jewish view the only thing that matters is that God is(157). Since Jewish scholars attach little importance to speculation about God's nature, Judaism has not had a theological development comparable to that of Christianity. Rather, Jewish theology has always been a negative one in that the acknowledgement of God is fundamentally the negation of idols. Fromm's critical

theory of religion, then, insofar as it is a negation of
idols, is essentially negative theology. For Fromm, the
history of humankind is the history of idol worship: from
primitive idols of clay and wood against which the Jewish
prophets fought, to the modern idols — nation, race, the
leader, production and consumption, sex, car and career, the
fetishism of foot, legs and breasts, etc.

Fromm argues that negative theology can show that an
alienated individual is necessarily an idol worshipper since
by transferring living powers onto an external thing the self
must worship the thing in order to retain a measure of self-
awareness(158). In worshipping the idol, a person worships a
limited, partial aspect of the self, limiting the self to that
aspect and ceasing to grow. While the idol represents only an
isolated part of the person, God stands for the totality.
Therefore, one who tries to be like God approaches his or her
own totality — the full development of one's creative powers.

City of Being

According to Fromm, late medieval culture flourished because
people followed the vision of the City of God(159). Modern
civil society bloomed because people were energized by the
vision of the growth of the Earthly City of Progress. In
twentieth century advanced or organized capitalist society,
however, this vision deteriorated to that of the Tower of
Babel, which is now beginning to collapse and which will
ultimately bury everyone in its ruins. If the City of God and
the Earthly City were thesis and antithesis, then a new
synthesis is the only alternative to chaos, barbarism and
death: the synthesis between the spiritual core of the late
medieval world and the development of rational thought and
science since the Renaissance. In Fromm's vision, this truly
Hegelian synthesis is the City of Being. Fromm's critical
theory of religion is from its very beginning in the Dogma of
Christ, 46 years ago in Frankfurt, to its conclusion in his
latest book, To Have or to Be, entirely devoted to the coming
of this life-friendly City of Being. Throughout his life,
Fromm has worked against the actualization of alternative
Future I — the totally administered, technocratic, automated,
and bureaucratic society and against alternative Future II —
escalating wars and nuclear holocaust, and toward alternative
Future III — the reconciled, rational and free society, the
City of Being.

Behind non-believing Jews such as Fromm, Horkheimer, Adorno, Marcuse - searching today for a new meaning of human existence - rises a 3000-year history of faith of an intensity without comparison in world history, be it in relation to the faith itself or to the many attempts to liquidate it(160). In Fromm's critical theory of religion, it is obvious that the thorn of being chosen has bored itself deeply into the Jewish flesh, whether Jews try to rebel against this determination, repress it or transform it into the program of a non-theistic dialectical anthropology and eschatology, anticipating the City of Being, the humanistic society. Fromm's theory of religion is mainly a critique of ideology - the justification of unjust relations, false consciousness, necessary appearance, untruth. But something remains of religion after it is ideologized: the X-experience and with it, the anticipation of the City of Being, the truly rational and free society. In reality, Fromm does not transcend the negative theology of Judaism, but rediscovers in it the polemical revolutionary content it always had - perfect social justice.

Negative Dialectic

Neither Horkheimer's nor Fromm's critical theory of religion has influenced Habermas's critical theory of religion so deeply as that of Adorno. Adorno discussed everything, including religion, within the framework of Western Marxism, which had reactivated the philosophical aspects of Marx's work only at the high price of recourse to Hegelian idealism(161). It is thus not surprising that he returned to Hegel's philosophy of religion. Yet, while Hegel avoided discussing dissonances in religious reality in the context of declining Western Civilization, Adorno emphasized them(162). He continued Hegel's analysis of the dichotomy between religious and secular consciousness, but whereas the purpose of Hegel's philosophy of religion was to reconcile religion and reason, revelation and enlightenment, salvation and emancipation, Adorno sought to differentiate them. Where Hegel sought a balance between religious and secular consciousness, Adorno put all emphasis on secular consciousness.

According to Hegel's Phenomenology of the Spirit, religion is consciousness of the Absolute(163). While for medieval theologians this relation was not really essential, modern Protestant theology is concerned with it even more than with God as such. Hegel acknowledged the modern position, i.e.,

that   God   cannot   be   considered   separate   from   humanity's
subjective spirit(164). The reason for acknowledging this,
however, was not, as modern theologians assert, that God is
unknown, but because God is essentially spirit – a knowing
subject. Thus, the relation between God's infinite, and
humanity's finite, spirit underlies all religion.
      In Hegel's view, no one is so estranged from humanity as
to have no religion at all(165). Even hating religion presupposes preoccupation with it. What matters, however, is the
relation of infinite to finite consciousness. In modern times,
scientific, esthetic, social, and political consciousness, as
well as the experience of the Absolute, take form within this
relation. Before modern philosophy can reconcile faith and
enlightenment, it must work through these interconnections.
      Unlike Hegel, Adorno overlooked these relations and
focused instead on their social consequences. He was interested in cult only insofar as it survived in secularized form
in modern art – particularly in modern music and drama(166).
Although for Adorno religion was also consciousness of the
Absolute, the Marxist approach remained central in his
theory(167). His appeal to an Other, different from this world
as nature and history, had primarily a social-philosophical
impetus and led him to a more positve evaluation of certain
theological trends. Yet Adorno avoided the temptation of
transforming his critique of religion into a new religion,
thus repeating the dialectic of enlightenment – the turning of
enlightenment into myth(168). He opposed the tendency of
modern consciousness to elevate the fate of theological ideas
into a theologicum, because he felt it led to a lack of
theological meaning. For Adorno, the means for such an
experience was negative dialectic – determinate negation – the
very essence of negative knowledge(169).

Micrology

Pre-Hegelian materialists explained religion in terms of
humanity's break with itself. Adorno located the ground of
religion in humanity's consciousness of the negation of the
negation of self-consciousness, in the awarenesss of the
ability to transcend limitations, to overcome the gap between
existence and true nature, to become independent and
free(170). The negation of the negation of humanity's self-
consciousness did not lead, for Adorno, to a positive Abso-
lutum. This is why he was in solidarity with theology at the

time of its ruin(171). Enlightenment leaves behind almost no
residuals of the metaphysical and theological truth content,
thereby causing metaphysics and theology to immigrate into
what Adorno called micrology as a refuge from the totality.
     According to Adorno, totality becomes a radical evil in
Future I - the totally administered society(172). Totality is
the principle of domination of humanity over nature and
itself, inflated into the Absolute(173). A micrological view
of the world as nature and society demolishes the shell of the
particular and exposes the fraud that the particular is merely
an example of the universal. Since the whole is untruth,
metaphysics and theology can only survive in the most minute
and inconsequential particulars (i.e., in what Hegel called
foul existence: one indifferent to or opposed to the universal). According to Adorno, metaphysics and theology become
correctives to the objective reason which informs Future I -
the administered world. For Adorno Future I has already become
reality to some extent.

Faith and Reason

Adorno was a man of the Enlightenment, but not a prisoner of
its ideology. Along with Amery, Canetti, George Steiner,
Bloch, Wiesel, Benjamin, Horkheimer, Fromm, etc., he was one
of those unbelieving Jews who sought, in a century without
God, for a new meaning of existence(174). The brickle of being
chosen by God remains even when Jews try to repress it or
transform it into a program of atheistic anthropocentricity
and eschatology. Adorno's theory of religion was the climax of
his search for meaning in the context of Horkheimer's critical
theory.
     In Horkheimer's view, part of the high price the modern
world may have to pay for technological progress in the
totally administered society is human coldness(175). Adorno
saw this coldness as the principle of bourgeois subjectivity
which made possible Auschwitz and Hiroshima. To Horkheimer,
this bourgeois principle is the very opposite of the Christian
principle of free and loving subjectivity. In the struggle
with the bourgeois principle, the Christian principle lost
out. All of this and more was spelled out by Adorno during a
debate with Kogon and Dirks in Munster (1956) on "Revelation
or Autonomous Reason." In that debate, Adorno also summed up
what he had been thinking about religion since his early work
on Kierkegaard (1929-30): about faith and reason(176).

Like Hegel and Marx, Adorno felt he lived in a
world-historical transition period between the old Western
Civilization and a new world. He sought to help bring about
this new world with his theory of religion as a premise of all
criticism of personality, family, society, state, art,
philosophy, science, and technology. Thus, with Horkheimer, he
wrote in the Dialectic of Enlightenment: "Politics, which, be
it even in a highly unreflected way, does not preserve
theology in itself, remains, no matter how skillful it may be,
in the last analysis, mere business"(177). Whether God exists
and if someone has faith is important, because theology stands
behind all human action, not as the traditional science of the
divine or even of God, but as consciousness that the world is
mere appearance. For Adorno, theology was the hope that the
injustice characterizing the present world can be eliminated:
non-possessive devotion and the liquidation of death.

Adorno felt that none of the theological contents of
Christianity (e.g., the trinity, incarnation, redemption,
resurrection, miracles, eternal happiness or damnation) which
Hegel saw withering away and tried to preserve by translating
them from their mythological into a dialectical form, could
remain unchanged. All faith contents must emigrate out of
religious consciousness and into the continually expanding
secular consciousness. He pointed out that, during the Middle
Ages and Antiquity, religous representations were rich and
concretely elaborated. Contemporary opinion, however, sees the
life of modern people and the immanence of this world as
resembling a glass house, through whose walls they can look at
an eternally unchangeable philosophia perennis. In such a
situation, faith in revelation is even less widespread than
during Hegel's time and can be kept alive only by desperate
abstraction.

In Adorno's perspective, to defend faith in revelation in
the 18th century had a meaning completely different than it
has today. Then, theologians were concerned with defending
traditionally-given teaching content - the dogmas of the
trinity, incarnation, etc., against the attack of autonomous
reason. This reason would not accept anything other than what
could withstand its own test. Faith had to be defended against
reason by rational means. This task was hopeless from the very
beginning, and the rational argumentation Christian apologists
used appropriated the very same hostile principle of autonomous reason against which they sought to defend Christian
revelation.

Adorno charged that theologians in late bourgeois society preach stabilization of bourgeois society by the religion of revelation. People listen to them because they feel it would be good to have revelation, given the utter confusion surrounding them. Like Hegel, Adorno believed that it was the need for orientation rather than for truth which motivated people to return to the religion of their fathers. He found the same motivation in his contemporaries who returned to positive religion. He admitted also that such a return may be sparked by the hope that the disenchanted modern world may be given new meaning which can free humankind for full participation in their lives. Unlike Hegel, who wanted to save revelation through rational reflection upon it, contemporary apologists want to rescue revelation by rejecting autonomous reason itself. Adorno noticed in contemporary theologians an inclination to obscurantism much more inexorable and evil than all the limited orthodoxies Hegel felt were hostile to enlightenment and idealistic philosophy. According to Adorno, this occurred because contemporary theologians believe in their fundamental dogmas even less than theologians in Hegel's day.

The sacrifice of intellect to the faithful acceptance of revelation has been socialized in late bourgeois society, for too much thinking makes adaptation difficult in the administered world and produces suffering. According to Adorno, this lack of rationality resulted in the proliferation of apparatuses and means of domination. The consciousness of contemporary humanity no longer even contemplates the possibility of a rational society. With Horkheimer, Adorno knew that to escape domination, self-reflection is mandatory. Such self-reflection of human reason cannot happen by a leap of faith, as Kierkegaard suggested. Rather, reason must attempt to determine rationality itself; it must recognize its own natural structure. Although this motive is not foreign to the great world religions, Adorno felt it must go through the secularization process, or it will contribute to the same darkening of the world it seeks to avert: the eclipse of practical communicative rationality.

Truth

The renaissance of the religion of revelation appeals strongly to the notion of commitment. For Adorno, however, only weakness seeks commitment. The urge for commitment is, in reality, not directed toward the dignity of humankind. When human kind is unable to realize its own humanity, desperate fetishization of the extant social conditions in bourgeois and socialist society occurs.

Adorno believed that the turn to transcendence in the religion of revelation in late capitalist society functioned together with astrology, occultism, and the like to cover up the social hopelessness prevalent in bourgeois society(178). This turn to transcendence and the reactionary mode of behavior connected with it is based upon the world's division into two blocks of states rigidly opposed to each other. Every individual in them feels threatened with ruin. For Adorno, the innerworldly fear produced by this constant threat of destruction is hypostatized as existential or possibly transcendent anxiety, since there seems to be nothing available in the present to avert it.

Adorno was aware that whenever religion is accepted for any other reason except its own truth content, it undermines itself. God's absolute spirit did not prevent World War I or II or Auschwitz, nor will it prevent World War III. The very fact that positive religions today so willingly use internationally or nationally conditioned fears for their own external advantage attests to their intrinsic desperation.

In Adorno's perspective, the irrationalism of the positive religion of revelation was not always present. At its medieval height, the Christian religion of revelation rejected William of Ockham's nominalistic teaching of the double truth as self-destructive. The great scholastics achieved dignity precisely because they neither absolutized nor outlawed the notion of reason. It was in the age of nominalism that theologians moved to outlaw and degrade reason. As religious faith loses harmony with knowledge, or at least loses fruitful tension with it, it further loses its cogency, duress, and pressing invitation.

Modernity

In the contemporary modern period, the abyss between the traditional religion of revelation and knowledge grows ever wider and deeper. Adorno felt the abyss had become so deep that people no longer even recognized it, particularly in the US. Religion and knowledge exist as two separate entities in late bourgeois society.

Adorno saw the break between the social model of the

great world religions and today's bourgeois and socialist society as most decisive. Traditional religions were built on visible agricultural conditions or a low level commodity economy. Stemming from a much lower level of prediction and exchange fundamental categories of traditional religions are not contemporaneous with the base structure of modern civil society. In this sense, Adorno's theory of religion was materialist and therefore critical and scientific in the Marxian sense: stressing, like Hegel before and like Habermas later on, the enormous clash between traditional religion and modernity.

For example, the notion of the "daily bread" in the "Our Father" prayer was colored by the experience of scarcity through uncertain and insufficent material production. The notion cannot be simply transmitted to contemporary bourgeois society with its bread factories, its overproduction, and its depressive convulsions. In bourgeois or socialist society, famines like that recently in Ethiopia are social and not natural catastrophes. The Christian notion of "the neighbor" who is to be loved is also non-contemporaneous by the modern experience. This notion applied to groups in which members knew each other face to face. Help for the neighbor, urgent as it remains in the bourgeois world, is inconsiderable in relation to praxis' going beyond the mere immediacy of human relations to qualitatively change the world.

Yet, words like "daily bread" or "neighbor" cannot be simply eliminated from the Evangelium so as to express the revealed teachings in contemporary terms. If revealed teachings are adapted to the changed course of history, the authority of divine revelation is challenged. To do so would plunge the religion of revelation into complete indefiniteness; the religion of revelation would be totally liquidated. Therefore, Adorno saw no other possibility in the present historical transition period than extreme asceticism against any kind of faith in revelation. He strongly recomended prohibition against making any images of the Absolute. The unbelieving Jew Adorno remained as faithful to this Mosaic prohibition as any pious Jew of the past, and even more so.

Mystical Atheism

Neither Adorno nor Horkheimer could say anything positive about God. They believed the critical theorist could not represent the Absolute. Speaking about the Absolute, all that can be said is that the present world is a relative one; by saying what the world is, the critical theorist expresses what God is not. In this Adorno and Horkheimer stand in the great tradition of Western negative theology.

Adorno hesitated to admit his solidarity with Christian theologians, fearing that he would further divorce critical theory as negative theology from Christian positive theology, rather than to demonstrate their convergence. Nevertheless, he acknowledged, along with Christian theologians, the hope, longing and impulse that no person ever be hungry, that wars be abolished, and that concentration camps be eliminated. In these simple hopes consists the positive moment of Adorno's otherwise negative theology, the desire for and impetus toward universal justice, peace, freedom, solidarity, love, and reconciliation.

Adorno defined philosophy as the attempt to look at all things from the standpoint of redemption(179). Human cognition has no other light, for everything else eventually exhausts itself in mimetic construction and thus remains merely a piece of positivist technique. The world must be seen clearly as it will appear in the messianic light: displaced, alienated and contradictory. Such a perspective must be gained without arbitrariness and violence and by being completely in touch with the objective reality – an utterly impossible task. Any awareness stems from what exists already, thus it is inevitably affected by the same defacement, distortion, and indigence which it intends to escape in the first place. The more passionately thought tries to seal itself off from its being conditioned by capitalist society and history for the sake of the Unconditional, the more it falls into the evil world.

The truth of Adorno's life and work was the death of the innocent victims of Auschwitz and capitalist history in general. With Hegel, Marx, Kierkegaard, and contemporary critical political theologians, Adorno fought against bourgeois religion (non—redemptive Christendom)(180). He tried to overcome not only the dialectic of enlightenment and emancipation, but also that of religion. He struggled against evil religion, which gilds the ongoing catastrophe of capitalist history, but he welcomed good religion which he linked with the impulse toward justice and redemption.

Adorno called things by their name, so that they would disappear. But, he could not call God by his name. Thus, the

quest for the Absolute remained, without which there can be no
truth and no redemption and no truly human consciousness. In
the   tradition   of   mystical negative theology, Adorno negated
God for God's sake. He withdrew love from   creation,   Creator,
Trinity, God, so that it could be free for the Absolute beyond
the Absolute. He engaged in idology - the destruction of the
idolatry of race, nation, charismatic   leader,   and   commodity
fetishism. All   this   may be called a mystical atheism in the
Absolute. Adorno's negative   faith   and   negative   theology
express   the apocalyptic-eschatological hope that the murderer
may ultimately not triumph over the innocent victim   and   that
the destroyer may be destroyed.

Rationality of Action

Habermas, following Adorno and Benjamin as well as Horkheimer,
Fromm   and   other   critical   theorists,   begins   his new book,
Theory of Communicative Praxis, in which his   universal   pragmatic reaches its highest level so far, with the determination
of the rationality of human action(181). According to Habermas
the   rationality   of   opinions   and   actions is a theme, which
traditionally has been treated in philosophy. Habermas asserts
even that philosophical thinking originates precisely   in   the
becoming   reflexive   of   the   reason,   which   is   embodied   in
speaking, work, love, struggle for recognition.   For   Habermas
as   for his teacher, the Heideggerian Gadamer, the fundamental
philosophical theme is reason.   From   its   very   beginning   in
Ancient   Greece, philosophy is the effort to explain the world
in its totality: to explain the unity in the   manifoldness   of
particular phenomena through principles, which are to be found
in reason(182).
    Habermas   emphasizes   that these principles through which
philosophers tried to explain the world in its   totality,   are
not   to   be received in communication with the divinity beyond
the world. These   principles   are   strictly   not   even   to   be
discovered in reference to the ground or the depth of a cosmos
which   embraces   nature as well as society. In Habermas' view,
Greek thinking neither aims at a theology nor   at   an   ethical
cosmology   in   the   sense of the great world religions, but at
ontology. If the philosophical   teachings   have   something   in
common,   then   it   is, according to Habermas, the intention to
think the being or the unity of the world in   the   way   of   an
explication   of   the   experiences of human reason in encounter
with itself.

Unlike Hegel and like Horkheimer, Benjamin, Adorno, Fromm and the other critical theorists, Habermas is no longer concerned with objective reason or absolute reason or the reason of the Absolute, but mainly with subjective human reason(183). Habermas uncouples completely subjective from objective reason and considers only the former to be real and the later to be, in the Feuerbachian tradition, nothing else than the projection of the former(184). Habermas can no longer, like Hegel, agree with the discovery of Anaxagoras, that reason governs the world or with the prophets of the Old and New Testament, that Providence governs the world(185). Habermas differentiates as sharply and rigorously between philosophy and religion, knowledge and faith, as does Pascal(186). But unlike Pascal, Habermas stands entirely on the side of reason. He appreciates religion and faith and their consolation, but he can not share them. Unlike for Hegel, for Habermas philosophy and religion differ not only in form, but in content as well. Unlike Hegel, and like Horkheimer and Adorno, Habermas stresses only the non-identity and not at all the identity of faith and reason. Habermas gives up, what Hegel still tried to do throughout his philosophy: to justify faith by reason and reconcile reason with religion and to reunite them both(187). While Hegel stressed the theological element in Greek philosophy, Greek metaphysics, particularly in Aristotle, Habermas denies it(188). From the very beginning of his philosophical work, Habermas had a controversy with Horkheimer concerning the theological element in the critical theory. For Habermas, Adorno, not Horkheimer, was the "real atheist," in spite of the fact that Horkheimer and Adorno shared similar theological concerns with each other and with Benjamin: second commandment, negative theology(189).

Even if Habermas admits a theological element in philosophy, he stresses, nevertheless, that this is very different from the theological concerns of the great world religions. In discussions with theologians and religionists Habermas is willing to search for fragments of rationality also in the world religions(190). He likes most to discuss with critical political theologians(191). If Habermas would be interested in theology at all, it would be in the type of theology the political theologians are doing. But then, Habermas does not understand why these theologians call themselves still "theologians" at all, since most of the time they are concerned with communicative praxis anyhow and not with God. He finds the political theologians to be so similar to himself, the critical theorist engaged in theory of communicative praxis, the atheist. It will become clear in chapter III why political theologians, engaged in the transcendental or universal pragmatic, can, nevertheless, still call themselves theologians, and rightly so.

Paradigm

As Habermas starts his Theory of Communicative Praxis with the determination of the rationality of human action, he is very much aware of the fact, that this rationality has been very controversial since quite some time not only in practical philosophy but particularly in the social sciences and in the analysis of language(192). But the discourse on this matter of rationality has not yet come to an end. The determination of rationality hangs closely together with the specific notion of action, which has been accepted by this or that scholar. It remains separated from historical experiences as either a discipline-specific teaching of categories of social science knowledge, a logical order of our speaking about action or the fundamental conceptuality of practical philosophy is in view. Therefore Habermas turns with good reason in his discourse on rationality to Weber and his analysis of the origin of occidental rationalism and of the disenchantment of the religious worldviews(193). In spite of all reservations in relation to Weber's limitation to the phenomena of purpose rationality, which are particularly open to the researcher, here nevertheless lies the prototype of a theory of that rationality, which is rooted in the life forms of modernity.

In late capitalistic society there exists the deep despair, that emancipated reason, subjective reason uncoupled from the objective reason present in great philosophy and great religion, becomes enslaved to the will to life and thus destroys itself(194). Reason turning into functional reason, in order to make human survival possible, creates instruments and conditions, which make survival more and more impossible(195). Adorno, whom Habermas so greatly admires, reacted to this despair with a flight forward. He intended to grant the right to exist to the once, in the great world religions, revealed shine of reason, at least in an esthetical theory(196). Weber, whom Habermas follows rather closely in his theory of communicative praxis and particularly in his theory of religion, developed a sceptical worldview, which can be balanced only by the Credo of a responsibility-ethics on

the part of the sociological researchers(197). Whoever is   not
willing to follow Weber or Adorno, must search for a new level
for   his   social theory, where this disturbing experience with
subjective   reason,   which   has   become   historically   very
effective,   can   be   caught up with and worked over. Habermas,
who intends to go beyond Weber and Adorno, does precisely that
by a decisive paradigm   change,   which   leads   away   from   the
concentration   of the rationality problematic in the theory of
isolated subjectivity(198). Habermas puts into   the   place   of
the   supposedly   exhausted   paradigm   of   modern   subjectivity
thinking, to which after Kant,   Hegel,   Marx   and   Freud   even
still   neo-Marxism   from   Lukacs   to   all   the   members of the
Frankfurt School   remained   obligated,   his   new   paradigm   of
understanding-oriented   action or of communicative praxis, for
which,   nevertheless,   Hegel,   Durkheim   and   Mead   point   the
way(199).   After   Hegel   particularly   Mead   had   given   the
idealistic conception of subjective   identity   a   social-beha-
vioristic   turn   by   paying close attention to forms of interaction,   primarily   such   mediated   symbolically(200).   After
Hegel,   particularly Durkheim had analyzed the depth-layers of
the collective consciousness of society, which is   in   process
of   changing   from   religious   commitment   to morally grounded
social obligation(201). On the basis of   these   two   realistic
models,   both being very similar in their specific position to
aspects in Hegel's social philosophy, Habermas takes   off   the
steep   utopian peak from his earlier teachings about the ideal
communication community and diminishes somewhat the   blue-eyed
optimism   sometimes   contained   in them(202). He interprets the
ideal communication community into the mere   key   to   open   up
social   developmental   tendencies in modernity. It comes close
to the Weberian   concept   of   rationalization.   In   any   case,
Habermas's   new   paradigm determines   his   whole   universal
pragmatic, his theory of communicative praxis as well   as   his
critical theory of religion.

Mythical Worldview

In the framework of his new paradigm, rooted deeply in Hegel's
Frankfurt   System Program, Jena System Designs, Phenomenology,
Logic,   Philosophy of Right, and Philosophy of History, as well
as in post-Hegelian European and Anglo-American philosophy   of
language   and   social   science,   Habermas tries to explain the
notion of rationality by using the expression "rational"(203).
As Habermas does this, he must depend on   a   pre-understanding

of rational and rationality, which is anchored in modern
attitudes of consciousness. Habermas starts his theory of
communicative praxis from the naive presupposition that, in
the modern understanding of the world, structures of consciousness express themselves which belong to a rationalized
life world and make possible, at least in principle, a
rational life style. Habermas is very much aware of the fact
that with this occidental understanding of the world he connects implicitly a claim of universality. In order to see if
this universality-claim is valid or not, Habermas compares it
with the pre-modern traditional, mythical, as well as religious-metaphysical and mystical understanding of the world.

According to Habermas, myths fulfilled in primitive and
archaic societies the unity creating or integrative function
of worldviews in an exemplary way(204). At the same time,
myths form, in the cultural tradition which is open to us, the
sharpest contrast to the world understanding which is dominant
in modern action systems. Mythical systems of orientation are
far removed from making possible orientations of action, which
would be rational in the modern sense. These traditional
mythical worldviews constitute, insofar as the conditions of
rational conduct of life is concerned, an opposition to the
modern understanding of the world. In the mirror of mythical
thinking Habermas can discover the preconditions of modern
thinking. Modern self-knowledge leads through the knowledge of
traditional mythical systems of interpretation of reality and
orientation of action. As Hegel, Adorno and Horkheimer before,
Habermas develops his theory of modernity against the
background of traditional mythical, religious-metaphysical and
mystical worldviews(205).

Habermas has learned from Levy-Bruhl that the difference
between mythical and modern thinking does not lie on the level
of logic operations(206). The degree of rationality of mythical systems of interpretation and orientation does obviously
not vary with the stage of the cognitive development of the
individuals, who participate in them and understand the world
and themselves in their terms and orient their action and
interaction according to them. Habermas starts from the
assumption that adult members of primitive and archaic action
systems can acquire, in principle, the same formal operations
as members of modern action systems. It is, of course,
possible that the higher level competencies appear less
frequently in primitive and archaic action systems and are
applied more selectively, i.e., in narrower realms of
life(207).

Habermas insists, nevertheless, that the rationality of mythical worldviews can not be measured in terms of logical and semantic properties, but only in terms of the fundamental categories or thought forms, which they make available to individuals for the interpretation of their world and the orientation of their action. Habermas would like to speak of the "ontologies," which are built into mythical worldview structures(208). What prevents him from doing so is the fact that the notion "ontologies" stems from the tradition of Greek metaphysics and as such is limited to one special world relation, to the cognitive relation to the world of beings, to the objective world, the world of nature.

According to Habermas, a corresponding notion which includes the relationship to the subjective, social and cultural world as well as the relation to the objective natural world, has not been developed so far in the history of philosophy from China and India over Greece and Rome to Medieval and Modern Europe. Habermas has the highly ambitious purpose and plan to overcome this deficiency of the world history of philosophy by his own universal pragmatic and theory of communicative praxis. As a matter of fact, only if Habermas's theory of communicative praxis does succeed in this, will it be able to do something no less ambitious, namely to replace the mythical worldview of the primitive and archaic action systems as well as the religious-metaphysical systems of interpretation and orientation of the historical-intermediate action systems, which all have supposedly become obsolete in highly complex modern action systems, with his universal pragmatic.

While Habermas's universal pragmatic is indeed very different from Hegel's absolute fundamental pragmatic, since it usually pretends to know of no Absolute, he competes, nevertheless, with Hegel in that he wants, like him, to provide for modern man with the help of the post-Hegelian philosophy of language and social sciences, that interpretation of self and world and orientation of action, which once myths gave to primitive and archaic men and religious-metaphysical worldviews to historical-intermediate and still early modern men and to some extent even still late modern men, our contemporaries. The thesis of the end of religion is particularly not very plausible in recent years, when religious confessions seem to gain influence once more as identity forming factors not only in the Near East and in

Poland, but also in Central America and even in Habermas's own country, in Germany(209). Habermas carries out his very ambitious philosophical project with great genius, if also not the genius of a Hegel. It will remain to be seen if Habermas's competition with Hegel will be successful and if his universal pragmatic, including his discourse ethic can indeed be stabilized in advanced capitalistic and socialistic society(210).

Totality

The deeper Habermas penetrates the network of mythical inter-pretation of the world, the more he is impressed by the total-izing force of primitive and archaic thinking(211). On one hand, in myths rich and precise information about nature, inner world, social and cultural world are worked over: Geographical, astronomical, meterological knowledge, knowledge about fauna and flora, the animal world, the practice of healing, psychological impulses, complex familial relation-ships, economic and technical complexes, conduct of war, reli-gious rites, etc. On the other hand, these experiences are organized in the myths in such a way that every singular phenomenon is in its typical aspects similar to and stands at the same time in contrast to all the other appearances. Through these relationships of similarity and contrast, the manifoldness of observations comes together in a totality. The myths bring into relationship with each other and classify the different areas of phenomena under the perspectives of homology and dissimilarity, of equivalence and non-equi-valence, of identity and opposition. This analogy thinking weaves the phenomena into a singular network of corres-pondence. But its interpretations do not penetrate through the surface of what can immediately be perceived. Mythical thinking is not notional thinking and thus does not penetrate the depth of being. It contains a latent positivism.

According to Habermas, the concretism of a type of thinking, which is bound to perception, and the creation of relationships of similarity and contrast in terms of an embracing totality are two formal aspects, under which the primitive and archaic mythical thinking can be compared with ontogenetic stages of the cognitive development of the indi-vidual person. But the categories or fundamental concepts of mythical worldviews stem from areas of experience, which must be analyzed not psychologically, but sociologically. On the

one hand the reciprocity structures of the primitive and
archaic kinship system, the relationship of giving and taking
in and among families, between the sexes and generations,
offer themselves as schemes of interpretation to primitive and
archaic people. They can be used in many ways. On the other
hand, the categories of action gain a constitutive significance for mythical worldviews. Actor and ability to act,
intention and purposiveness, success and failure, active and
passive, attack and defense are the categories in which a
fundamental experience of primitive and archaic society is
worked over: the experience of being delivered without protection to the contingencies of an environment, which is not
under control. Primitive and archaic people can not bring
these risks under control because of the undeveloped conditions of their productive forces. Thus comes about the need in
primitive and archaic action systems to dam the flood of
contingencies, if not de facto, then at least in imagination. Primitive and archaic people in their totalizing myths
interpret away the contingencies and catastrophes inside and
outside their action systems and thus are able to orient themselves in their world. This is still true for likewise totalizing religious-metaphysical worldviews on the evolutionary
stages of historical-intermediate and even modern societies.
This is so since even here, in spite of the much higher levels
of the development of productive forces, the contingency
experiences are not yet completely under control. In some
respects they have even increased, e.g. in terms of weapon
technology(212).

Theodicy

Habermas sees the connection between mythical and religious-
metaphysical worldviews and the contingency experiences very
early in the development of his critical theory of reli-
gion(213). In world religions and world philosophies the
contingency problem is posed as the theodicy problem(214).
According to Kant all philosophical attempts in theodicy so
far, including the attempts of Voltaire and Leibniz, have
failed(215). Therefore Kant turns for a solution of the
theodicy problem to religion, to Judaism, to the faith of Job.
In the midst of the catastrophe of his life and of his most
vivid doubts, Job can say: "Until my end comes I shall not
deviate from my piety"(216). By this his pious attitude, Job
proved to Kant that he did not ground his morality on faith,

but his faith on morality. In this case, faith in the face of contingency and catastrophe is, as weak as it may be, nevertheless of a pure and genuine kind. It is a faith of that kind which does not ground a religion which looks out for favors, but a religion of a good conduct of life, in spite of all the injustices in the world.

Hegel finds, like Kant, the solution of the contingency or theodicy problem first of all in religion, more precisely in the Judeo-Christian faith in divine providence(217). From his Early Theological Writings on, Hegel is convinced that central and essential for the wise man is faith in a loving and benevolent providence(218). With this faith in providence is connected, if it is alive and of the right kind and not superstitious, a complete surrender to God. For Hegel this faith in providence is the main teaching in the Christian community. All that is presented in this teaching on providence reduces itself to the insurmountable love of God. Everything centers in this love. The doctrine of providence presents God as being near and present to us year in and year out, effecting everything that happens around us and in us. Hegel stands for a purified, realistic faith in providence, in which pain does remain pain and unhappiness remains unhappiness. According to Hegel, the only true consolation in suffering is trust in God's providence; everything else is empty talk, which glides away from the heart. For pain, there is no consolation at all. To pain only strength of the soul can be opposed.

In Hegel's view of religion to faith in providence, which embraces the whole life of man from his youth on, thinking is added later on(219). When man becomes older, he begins to think about the nature and properties of the essence whom religion calls God and providence. Particularly the more mature person reflects about the relationship of the world to this essence, toward whom all his feelings are directed. For Hegel faith and reason are not opposed. Reason explicates what faith has taught: Credo ut intelligam. Religious theodicy turns into philosphical-theological theodicy. Faith in loving providence is in no way unreasonable. Also for Hegel faith in providence which may be available to the masses of the people more or less, has always a social and political dimension(220).

According to Hegel, what lies between the subjective reason as self-conscious human spirit and the objective divine reason or divine providence as present reality, what separates the subjective reason from the objective reason, is that subjective reason is held captive by some abstractum, which is not liberated into the notion(221). For Hegel, to recognize the objective divine reason or providence as the "rose in the cross of the present" and thereby to enjoy it, this rational insight is reconciliation with reality. This reconciliation philosophy grants to those, to whom once has come the inner demand, to comprehend and to receive in that, which is substantial, God's providence, likewise subjective freedom. Thus these people stand with their subjective freedom not in something particular and accidental, but in that which is in and for itself, in God's absolute reason, providence, wisdom.

What Luther has begun as faith in feeling and in the witness of the spirit, is for Hegel the same as what the further matured human spirit intends to comprehend in the notion and to liberate for itself in the present and thereby to find itself in it(222). Hegel remembers that it has become a famous word in his time that half a philosophy leads away from God. Hegel argues, against Kant, that it is precisely this philosophy cut into half which puts knowledge into a mere "approximation to the truth." Hegel remembers the other part of this famous word: that the true philosophy leads to God. This has relevance also for the social world, for the political world, for the state. According to Hegel, as little as the mature, genuine human reason can be satisfied with the mere approximation to the truth, which, in terms of the New Testament, is neither cold nor warm and is, therefore, spit out, so little is it content with the cold despair which admits that in this temporal world things are bad or at best mediocre, but that there is nothing better to be had in it and that, therefore, one had to keep one's peace with reality. According to Hegel, faith in God's providence sublated philosophically, via the notion, into God's objective and absolute rationality present in reality, provides the true knowledge, which can bring about a warmer peace with reality than Kant's or aybody else's half philosophy, which misses the essence of God and the essence of the world: the world of nature, the inner world, the social world and the cultural world.

Hegel's philosophy of history is, in its totality, a theodicy, a justification of God in the face of the negativity of nature and more still of society and history(223). Hegel rejects the metaphysical theodicy attempt of Leibniz, because of the indefiniteness and abstractness of its categories.

Hegel's philosophy of history is a theodicy in that sense, that it intends to comprehend the evil in the world and thus to reconcile man's spirit with this world. According to Hegel, there is indeed no greater challenge to such reconciling knowledge than in society and world history. In Hegel's view, such reconciliation can happen only through the knowledge of the affirmative, in which that negativity disappears into something subordinate and overcome. Reconciliation with reality can come about only through the consciousness, partially of what in truth is the ultimate purpose of the world, partially of the fact that this ultimate telos has been realized in it, is realized in it and will be realized in it and that evil does not have validity besides this ultimate goal.

For this, so Hegel admits, the mere faith in Anaxagoras's nous or the prophets' providence is not at all sufficient. The reason, of which philosophers say that it governs the world, is as such as empty a word as the providence of which the prophets say that it rules the world. Hegel criticizes that people always speak about reason, without saying what precisely is its determination and its content, according to which we can judge if something is rational or irrational. Reason comprehended in its determination, that only is the thing as such. Otherwise, if people remain standing merely with reason as such, such words like reason or providence are merely words. For Hegel the question, what is the determination of God's reason in itself, falls together with the other question concerning the ultimate purpose of the world, insofar as God's reason is taken in relation to the world. For Hegel in this expression lies more concretely that this ultimate purpose should be realized. Here two things are to be considered: the content of the ultimate purpose, its determination as such, and the realization of it. For Hegel the telos of history is God's absolute freedom and the liberation of man into this freedom. The liberation of man's freedom into God's absolute freedom is realized through agents of change in the material of nations as they succeed each other in the different stages of world history from the freedom of the one, despotism, over the freedom of the few, oligarchy, to the freedom of all, democracy. For Hegel, this is the true theodicy, the justification of God in society and history, that world history is this developmental course and the real becoming of man's spirit and his freedom under the changing dramas of its particular national histories.

According to Hegel, only this insight, this historical theodicy can reconcile man's spirit with world history and reality: that everything happens from hour to hour with God and is his work.

For Hegel not only the political history, but also the history of religion is a theodicy(224). While the revealed religion was still latent throughout the history of nature religions - magic, Taoism, Hinduism, Buddhism - and of the religions of subjectivity - Zoroastrianism, Syrian religion, Egyptian religion, Jewish religion, Greek and Roman religion - and was thus not in its truth, it has, nevertheless, come in the fullness of time in the form of Christianity as the absolute religion. This time is not an accidental time, an arbitrary time, a mere whim, but a time, which is determined in the essential, eternal counsel and decision of God, i.e., in the eternal reason, providence and wisdom of God. It is the notion of the thing itself, the notion of religion, the divine notion, the notion of God itself, which has determined itself to this development of the history of religions and has posited its goal, the absolute religion, as revealed religious history, Christianity.

According to Hegel, precisely this course of the history of religion - from nature religions over the religions of individuality to the religion of freedom, Christianity - is the true theodicy. This course demonstrates all creations of the spirit, every form of its self-knowledge, as necessary, because spirit is alive and effective. Spirit is the drive to penetrate through the series of its appearances to the consciousness of itself as all truth. Likewise also the history of art and philosophy is a theodicy(225).

Death of God

For Hegel, since his Early Theological Writings, his Frankfurt System Program and his Jena Critical Writings, the theodicy problem reaches its climax in the Christian teaching of the death of God(226). That precisely is the absolute contingency: God has died. God is dead. This is for Hegel the most terrible thought. It is the most extreme atheism. Everything Eternal, everything True is null and void. It is not. The negation is in God himself. This is the highest, most awful pain. It is the feeling of completely being lost. With this feeling is connected the giving up of everything higher, of all morality, of all art, of all religion and philosophy. But his is only

half of the Christian theodicy. American God is dead
theologians have stopped precisely here.
    But, according to Hegel, the course of the dying and
death of God does not stop here. A reversal occurs. God
maintains himself in this process of his dying and death and
this his death is the death of death. God rises again to life.
The process of God's death turns into its opposite. This is
the Christian resolution of the theodicy problem. The
political theologians refer to this resolution, when they
discover the aporia of Habermas's universal pragmatic, as of
all other post-Hegelian types of pragmatic in Europe and
America, as we shall see in the last chapter(227).
    Hegel finds the resolution of the theodicy problem in the
story of the resurrection and ascension of Christ. Unlike
Kant, Hegel does not refer to the Old Testament and Job, but
to the New Testament and Jesus in order to find the solution
to the theodicy problem. As all the other events in Jesus's
life appeared to the immediate consciousness of his friends in
the mode of reality, so does also the event of this his
elevation in resurrection and ascension. For the perception of
Jesus's friends the death of death, the liquidation of the
grave, the triumph over the negative and the ascension into
heaven is as present and real as the execution of Jesus. The
murderer did not triumph over the innocent victim. The
innocent victim triumphed over the murderer.
    But for Hegel this overcoming of the negative is not a
taking off of human nature, but its highest proof even in
death and in the greatest love. For Hegel, Spirit is spirit
only as this negative of the negative, which therefore
contains the negative in itself. Thus if the Son of man sits
at the right hand of the Father, then in this elevation of
human nature its honor and its identity with the divine nature
have come most clearly and highly before the spiritual eye.
Thus this identity of human and divine nature is the resolution of the theodicy problem. This resolution must become
invalid as soon as human and divine nature are once more
separated, as it happens in the bourgeois enlightenment and in
the post-Hegelian history of philosophy and social science,
particularly in the Marxian and Freudian enlightenment.

Sacrificing Love

The anti-Hegelian, Kierkegaard, turns Hegel's theology and
philosophy of providence even more into a matter of

communicative praxis than his master had done already. In his
Edifying Talks in a Different Spirit, Kierkegaard says of the
doubter, sceptic or "backslider," that he may after all have a
living feeling for the good(228). If somebody wants to talk
about the good, particularly in the way of poets, then the
doubter is soon moved in his heart. Insofar as the world
brings a little bit of unhappiness to the sceptic and somebody
else would then tell him that God is love, that his love goes
beyond every understanding, that this love in its providence
embraces even the sparrow, which according to Jesus does not
fall to earth without God's will, then the backslider is
deeply moved. He grasps for faith like for a wish. Together
with the faith the doubter grasps for the wished-for help.
Then the sceptic has in his wish-faith a feeling for the good.
    But maybe the backslider is bypassed by the divine help.
Instead of the help a suffering person comes to the sceptic,
whom he could help. But this suffering man finds the
backslider impatient, rejecting. The suffering man must be
content with the excuse that the doubter is now not in a good
mood to care about the suffering of others, since he himself
is in trouble. But the sceptic nevertheless thinks that he has
the faith, that there is a loving Providence who helps the
suffering person, a Providence who also uses people as his
instruments. Kierkegaard connects Providence with human
intersubjectivity and interaction. Habermas speaks about
interaction without Providence. The political theologians
combine Kierkegaard with Marx. They find Providence, if at
all, through messianic mimesis, discipleship, friendship in
the social world - even on the Golgotha of history, on its
slaughterbench.
    According to Kierkegaard, it is possible that the doubter
receives his wished-for help from Providence. The sceptic
catches fire again in gratefulness to providence. He is
longing for loving Providence in a soft representation of its
goodness. Now, the backslider thinks he has rightly grasped
the faith in Providence. Now faith has won victory over doubt
and every objection. But now the doubter has completely
forgotten the suffering person. What is this condition,
Kierkegaard asks, other than scepticism and backsliding?
According to Kierkegaard, insofar as there can be any talk at
all about objections against faith, of bad happenings and
events which appear to object against it and against the
loving care of Providence, then this other suffering person,
who has not been helped and who has even been rejected in an

ugly way by the one who could have helped, with the excuse
that he was not in the right mood, is the stronger objection.
But the sceptic overlooks completely that, precisely in the
moment when he thought faith had gained victory over him, he
refuted this conviction in action. It is clearly doubt and
backsliding to think that one has a conviction if, at the same
moment, one oneself, refutes it in praxis. For Kierkegaard, in
truth the only proof for the possession of a conviction is the
one that one's own so-called conviction does not change every
moment in relationship to the different things which happen to
oneself, and change everything for oneself, so that one has
the faith today and has lost it tomorrow, and receives it back
again the day after tomorrow, until then something completely
unusual happens, so that one loses it almost completely, in
the opinion that one had it. That has happened to all the
critical theorists, more or less. From here the political
theologians argue with and against Habermas for a "political
proof" of God(229).

Kierkegaard assumes that there are two different people:
there is a doubter, who thinks that he has acquired the faith
in loving Providence since he himself has experienced that he
himself was helped, in spite of the fact that he has rejected
unmoved a suffering person whom he could have helped. There is
another man, whose life is, through self-sacrificing love, an
instrument in the hand of Providence, so that he helps many
suffering people while the help he himself wished for was not
given to him year after year. In Kierkegaard's view only the
second man is really convinced in truth, that there is a
loving providence. Kierkegaard comes to the following
beautiful and convincing conclusion: the One who has planted
the ear, he can hear. But for Kierkegaard the opposite
conclusion is equally beautiful and convincing: the one whose
life is sacrificing love, he really believes that God is love.
But, so Kierkegaard criticizes, in the daily hasty business
there is neither time nor rest for the quiet perspicuity which
teaches equality; which teaches to pull with other people at
the same yoke; which teaches the noble simplicity which
internally comes as an understanding to every man. There is
neither time nor rest in modern capitalistic society to gain a
conviction. Therefore, even faith, hope, love and the willing
of the good remain in the general hasty business merely loose
words and doubt. For Kierkegaard it is certainly doubt and
scepticism to live without conviction or, more precisely, to
live in the always changing deception to have a conviction

while one does not have it. This is Kierkegaard's solution to
the theodicy problem: faith in Providence through solidarity
with the suffering other, through sacrificing love. It is also
the solution of political theology(230).

Truth and Abandonment

Under the influence of Kant, Hegel, Schopenhauer, Marx and
Freud, Horkheimer's philosophy, his critical theory, came to
contain a theological idea, a theodicy(231). But Horkheimer's
theodicy is one not only in the sense of Weber. Weber
understood under theodicy every theoretical effort to explain
suffering in this world(232). In the original sense, which
still prevails in Hegel's philosophy, theodicy means the
justification of God in the face of the injustice, the evil
which is dominant in the world. In the Weberian sense all
religious, philosophical and scientific worldviews are
fundamentally theodicies. In the Weberian sense also the
teachings of Bakunin, Blanqui, Marx, Freud and Habermas can be
seen as theodicies in spite of the fact that, while they may
stress with Kierkegaard interaction, intersubjectivity,
equality and solidarity, they nevertheless deny divine
providence as mere illusion, infantility or ideology(233).
Political theology stays close to Hegel and Kierkegaard.
      Horkheimer's critical theory insists as theodicy that,
without the thought of truth and thereby of that which
guarantees it, the Absolute, God's reason, wisdom and loving
providence, there is no knowledge of its opposite, the
abandonment of humans(234). Because of this abandonment of men
and women the true philosophy must be critical and
pessimistic. Without the thoughts of truth, absolute,
providence, there is not even the sadness without which there
is no happiness.
      Horkheimer, as little as does Adorno, abstractly negates
the Other, the absolute truth, the truth of the Absolute,
loving Providence(235). For Horkheimer, the entirely Other –
absolute truth, absolute justice – is itself "determinate
negation" in the Hegelian sense of that, which on earth is
called injustice, human abandonment, alienation. Without the
thought of an unthinkable eternal Happiness there is not even
the consciousness of the earthly transient happiness, which in
respect of its unsupersedable transitoriness can never be
without sadness and grief: always one dies earlier than the
other in any intersubjectivity and communicative praxis.

Horkheimer tries consequentially to continue the tradition of the occidental philosophy, which is characterized for him by the fact that it had the task to support the Christian teaching, at least its postulates, through rational methods close to those of science. According to Horkheimer, truth in the emphatic sense, which outlives human error, can not be separated from theism(236). Otherwise positivism has validity. For Horkheimer and Adorno the newest, liberal theology is connected with such positivism, in spite of all contradiction between them(237). According to positivism, truth means functioning of calculations. Thoughts are organs. Consciousness becomes superfluous, insofar as the purpose-rational modes of behavior, which were mediated through it, have become firmly rooted in the collective. In Horkheimer's view, to rescue an unconditional meaning without God is utter vanity. Without reference to a Divine the good action, the rescue of an unjustly persecuted person, loses its glory, except if it corresponds to the interest of a collective on this side or on the other side of the border. Occidental historiography is in general one of the victors, not one of the victims: one of the oppressors, not one of the oppressed, one of the murderers, not one of the innocently slaughtered.

According to Horkheimer, morality can not be derived purely scientifically. This is so, since in positivistic perspective there is no difference between hate and love. In Horkheimer's view, whatever is taught to youth concerning moral impulses, without reference to the transcendent, becomes a mere matter of arbitrary taste(238). There is no doubt that Horkheimer understands the Transcendent as real Transcendent: as the eternal One in whom alone he trusts, as his gravestone reads(239). While the political theologians are here in full agreement with Horkheimer, Habermas does differ substantially.

Contingencies

At the present stage of Habermas's theory of religion in the framework of his universal pragmatic and theory of communicative praxis, we have the impression that for him the mythical and religious-metaphysical systems are necessary to deal with contingencies, since primitive, archaic and historical intermediate action systems are on the basis of their development of work and tools not yet able to control their environments more realistically(240). Habermas does not

seem to be fully aware of the fact that human interaction can
be threatened by contingencies and catastrophes, for which
there is to this day no science or technology available in the
realm of work or recognition, nor may there ever be: e.g.,
earthquakes, tornados, ice storms, cancer epidemic, heart
attacks, outbreaks of sadism, etc. It is here, where
Habermas's theory of communicative praxis, including his
theory of religion, moves into its aporia. All depends for
Habermas's universal pragmatic, if and how it will be able to
overcome this its aporetical situation. Ultimately the
universal pragmatic stands or falls, like previous
philosophies, with its solution to the theodicy problem(241).
This is, of course, also true for theologies, particularly
critical political theology.

Nature and Culture

When Habermas considers how the fundamental categories of the
myths, which are taken from the kinship system and interpret
experiences of interaction with an all-powerful nature, often
contingency experiences, are connected with operations of a
perceptively analogizing thinking, he can understand better
the known magic-animistic characteristics of mythical
worldviews(242). According to Habermas, most astonishing for
modern people is the peculiar fusion of the different
dimensions of reality in mythical thinking: nature and spirit,
nature and culture.

In Habermas's view the mythmakers project nature and
culture on the same level. Out of the mutual assimilation of
nature to culture and, vice versa, of culture to nature, there
arises on the one hand a nature which is equipped with
anthropomorphic traits; which is integrated into the
communication network of the social subjects; and which in
this sense is humanized. On the other hand, there is a culture
which, in a certain sense, is sucked up into the objective
effect connection of anonymous powers in a reified form; which
is naturalized.

According to such a mythical interpretation of the world
which fuses nature and culture, every phenomenon corresponds
with all the other phenomena through the workings of mythical
powers. Such a mythical worldview does not only make possible
a theory which explains the world narratively and makes it
plausible, but it makes possible at the same time also a
praxis by which the world can be controlled in an imaginary

way. The technique of the magic intervention into the world as
nature and society is a logical conclusion from the mythical
mutual relationship of perspectives between man and world,
spirit and nature, culture and nature. Mythical theory and
magical praxis work together in overcoming contingencies at
least imaginatively and thus in resolving the theodicy problem
in the form in which it poses itself on the level of primitive
and archaic action systems and their development of the
productive forces. From its magical beginnings on the history
of religion is the history of man's attempt to resolve the
theodicy problem(243).

     According to Habermas, the structures of the mythical
worldview as described so far do not permit an orientation of
action, which can be called rational by modern criteria(244).
Why not? In Habermas's view, modern people are irritated by
the fact that in the framework of a mythically interpreted
world they can not make certain differentiations between
nature and spirit - subjective spirit, objective spirit,
absolute spirit - as the extremely modern Hegel does, or
between nature and culture as post-Hegelian thinkers do(245).
These differentiations are fundamental for the modern
non-mythical understanding of the world. Habermas understands
the mythical fusion and confusion between nature and culture
as a mixture of two dimensions of reality, between physical
nature and the sociocultural environment. Traditional men's
myths do not allow for a clear categorical differentiation
between things and persons; between objects, which can be
manipulated, and agents, subjects able to speak and to work,
to love and to struggle for recognition and to be members of a
nation with a rational constitution, to whom we can attribute
interactions and linguistic expressions(246). So it is quite
consequential for Habermas when the magicians in the primitive
or archaic action systems of aboriginal Australians, ancient
Egyptians or Mesopotamians do not know as already Hegel
observed the differentiation between work and recognition,
instrumental action and interaction, teleological action and
communicative action, aim directed interferences via tools
into objectively given natural situations and the establishment of interpersonal relationships(247). In consequence of
the fusion of nature and culture, the lack of skill in primitive or archaic action systems, to which is related the technical or therapeutic failure of an aim-directed instrumental
action, i.e., work, falls for the mythmaker or the magician
under the same category as guilt for the moral-normative

failure of an interaction, which violates the existing social order. Again in primitive archaic action systems the moral failure is interwoven conceptually with the physical mistake, the evil with the detrimental, as the good with the healthy and the advantageous. The physical illness, e.g., cancer, is mixed up with sinful acts: She died from cancer because she committed this mortal sin.

Demythologization

In modern action systems, demythologization, which sets in already in historical-intermediate action systems in the framework of religious-metaphysical worldviews, reaches its peak(248). According to Habermas, the demythologization of the worldview means at the same time a desocialization of nature and a denaturalization of society(249). Habermas connects this process of demythologization with the differentiation between instrumental and communicative action. It occurs most definitely in the modern world, when it is at its best. In the modern world instrumental action is decommunified and communicative action deinstrumentalized. This happens when all goes well. But the pathology of modernity consists precisely in the fact that instrumental action was decommunified, while communicative action was not only deinstrumentalized: it rather fell victim to even more intense functionalization. In this consists the barbarism in modernity. Habermas's universal pragmatic and theory of communicative praxis is directed precisely against such barbarous instrumentalization of the struggle for recognition, interaction and intersubjectivity. The differentiation between instrumental and communicative action, which Habermas derived from Hegel's differentiation between work and tools, on the one hand, and struggle for recognition, on the other, and from Marx's distinction between the forces of production and productive relations is constitutive not only for his universal pragmatic and theory of communicative praxis, but also for his critical theory of religion(250). Also in his theory of religion, Habermas is, like Horkheimer and Adorno, a Hegelian Marxist or a Marxist Hegelian(251).

Worlds and Attitudes

In Habermas's view, the process of the demythologization of the worldview in modern action systems can be easily intuited and described(252). But it is much harder to analyze it thoroughly. Habermas intends such thorough analysis of the process of demythologization. Such analysis leads Habermas to a categorical differentiation between the object realms of nature and culture. According to Habermas, this categorical differentiation between object realms depends again on a process of differentiation which he can best analyze in terms of fundamental attitudes toward four different worlds: the world of nature, the inner world, the social world and the cultural world(253). Habermas sometimes fuses the social and cultural world. Depending on this, he operates either with a four or three world model.

In Habermas's perspective the mythical concept of "powers" and the magical concept of "conjuring" prevent systematically the separation between the media of work and recognition, between the objectivating attitude toward a natural world of existing things and the conform or nonconform attitude in relation to a world of legitimately regulated interpersonal relationships(254). This separation is characteristic for modernity. When Habermas considers nature and culture as object dimensions, then they belong to the world of facts, about which true statements are possible. But as soon as Habermas tries to identify explicitly in what precisely things are different from persons, causes from motives, events from actions, he must ask back behind the differentiation of object realms. Habermas must go back to the differentiation between fundamental attitudes toward the objective natural world of what is the case, and a fundamental attitude toward the social world of what can be legitimately expected, what is commanded or what ought to be. Habermas thinks that he makes the correct conceptual cuts between causal connections of nature and normative orders of society to the extent to which he is fully aware of the change of perspectives and attitudes, which he makes when he moves from observations and manipulations to following or violating legitimate norms of action.

Language

The fusion of nature and culture does for Habermas's modern, Hegel-inspired feeling not only mean the conceptual confusion of the objective world of nature on the one hand and the intersubjective inner world, social world and cultural world on the other, but also an insufficient differentiation between

language and world(255). Habermas criticizes in the mythical
worldview of primitive and archaic action systems an insufficient differentiation between the communication medium language, name, memory and content, about which an understanding
or consensus is to be achieved in linguistic communication:
the four worlds. Habermas insists, in Hegelian terms, not only
on the modern differentiation between work and recognition,
but also between language, on the one hand, and work, family,
recognition and nation, on the other(256). Modern man knows
that to talk about work is not yet work, to speak about love
is not yet love, to say something about recognition is not yet
recognition, to talk about a nation is not yet a nation. It is
traditional and mythical, to take the word for the work, which
is not there; or for the love, which is not given; or for the
recognition, which is not granted; or for the national spirit,
which is absent.

For Habermas, it is precisely the totalizing mode of
consideration of mythical systems of interpretation of reality
and orientation of action which makes it very difficult for
them to identify in a sufficiently precise manner the modern
semiotic differentiations between the sign-substratum of a
linguistic expression or a speech act - its semantic content -
and the reference point - the listener - to whom the speaker
can always relate himself with his expression(257). Modern
speakers are aware of this double structure of every speech
act. This dialectic of language and interaction escapes the
traditional speaker. That at least is Habermas's argument.

The mythmaker and the magician, as Habermas sees them,
are involved in a systematic confusion between internal
meaning and external connection among things(258). Habermas
finds this confusion proven in the magic relationship between
language or name and the signified objects, the concretistic
relationship between the meaning of expressions and the
represented connections among things. Internal relationships
exist among symbolical expressions in the medium of language.
External relationships exist among entities, which are the
case in the real world, in the dimension of work, the family
and familial property, the struggle for recognition and the
nation. For modern people the logical relationship between
ground and consequence is internal. The causal relationship
between cause and effect is external. There is a difference
between symbolical and physical causation. For traditional
people magical control over the world and mythical
interpretation of the world can flow easily into each other at

a certain point in the history of religions, precisely since
internal and external relations are still conceptually
integrated(259). They have not yet been differentiated. Such
differentiation will happen slowly in the religious-
metaphysical systems of interpretation and orientation on the
level of historical intermediate action systems and most
radically in the scientific worldview on the level of modern
capitalistic or socialistic action systems(260).

Validity Claims

Habermas does not find among primitive and archaic people a
precise concept for the non-empirical validity, which modern
people attribute to symbolical expressions(261). There are, of
course, also still among modern people, particularly among the
younger generation, those who have the greatest difficulty
grasping non-empirical validity. But in this case we must
speak of dedifferentiation, regression or rebarbarization.
This is not the case among primitive and archaic people. They
find themselves before the differentiation between validity
and empirical effectiveness. Modern people who mix up right
and might or what is right with social control, have gone
through their differentiation and have lapsed back again into
their original unity, without being able really to restore
this unity again. It is a false unity and the corresponding
condition is not original barbarity, but a new re-barbar-
ization. There is a world of difference between them.
     According to Habermas, primitive and archaic people
confound validity with empirical effectiveness in an original,
naive, entirely unreflected way. Here Habermas does not think
about special claims of validity. For modern people there are
different validity claims: propositional truth in relation to
the natural world, expressive honesty in relation to the inner
world, normative rightness in relation to the social world,
good or bad taste in relation to the cultural world. Among
primitive and archaic people these validity claims in relation
to the four worlds are as little differentiated out as these
worlds themselves. To be sure, such differentiation of
validity claims as well as of the worlds they are related to
can collapse again. Such collapse did indeed occur in the old
European fascist movement and is happening again in the
present worldwide neo-conservative and neo-fascist
movement(262).
     But modernity at its best - in its enlightenment movement

- has achieved and continues to achieve this validity
differentiation. Habermas is one of the best examples for the
modern enlightenment movement. In this movement the
differentiation of validity claims was carried furthest: from
Voltaire and Kant over Hegel, Marx, Schopenhauer and Nietzsche
to Freud, Bloch and the Frankfurt School. But among primitive
and archaic people, so Habermas argues, even the diffuse
concept of validity in general is not yet liberated from
empirical entanglements(263). Traditional people amalgamate
validity concepts, like morality and truth, with empirical
concepts of order, like causality and health. Therefore,
traditional people can identify the linguistically constituted
mythical system of interpretation and orientation to such a
large extent with the world order itself that they are not
able to look through it and to see it as one among many
possible forms of interpretation of the world. They are not
aware of the fact that this interpretation could be erroneous
and that it is, in any case, open to critique. In this respect
the fusion and confusion of nature and culture gains the
meaning of what Habermas, following the Hegelian-Marxist
tradition, calls a reification or "thingification" of
worldview(264). Habermas could take seriously such a
traditional worldview and its truth claims only if in
discourse it would be presented as criticizable in terms of
the better reasons and thus in an unreified form. Habermas
would not deny, a priori, that there are truths or fragments
of rationality contained in traditional worldviews. But the
validity claims of traditional systems of interpretation and
orientation are to be decided upon the basis of the better
reasons and nothing else, neither sacred authority, tradition
or texts.

Formalization

Habermas differentiates between linguistic communication and
the cultural world(265). The cultural tradition flows into the
linguistic communication. In the process of modernization
linguistic communication and cultural world differentiate
themselves from the world of nature, inner world and social
world only to that extent to which formal concepts of the
world and non-empirical validity claims are differentiated
out. Habermas argues that modern people arrive in theoretical
and practical discourse as processes of understanding at
formal presuppositions of commonality. These background

pre-understandings are necessary, so that the participants in discourse can relate themselves to something in the one objective world, which is identical for all observers, or to something in their intersubjectively shared social world. These formal presuppositions of commonality or this background knowledge actualize the claims of propositional truth or normative rightness always for one determinate linguistic expression. Thus, according to Habermas, the truth of a proposition means, that the asserted fact does indeed exist as something in the objective world of nature. The rightness which is made valid for an act in relation to an existing normative content, means that the established interpersonal relationship deserves recognition as a legitimate part of the social world. Honesty means that a statement which is made valid in relation to the inner world of a person, to which only he or she has privileged entrance, does indeed correspond to the conditions of this inner world. Tastefulness means that a statement made valid in relation to an object in the cultural world, e.g., R. Wagner's _Tannhauser_, does indeed correspond to its esthetical value. According to Habermas, since all these validity claims are based on formal world concepts, they can in principle all be criticized in theoretical or practical discourse. These validity claims presuppose a natural world, which is identical for all possible observers, or an intersubjectively shared inner, social or cultural world in an abstract form, i.e., in a form which is abstracted from all definite contents. Furthermore, the validity claims demand the rational position of another person.

Through these formal pragmatic statements the Hegelian Marxist, Habermas, shows himself to be deeply rooted in the Kantian tradition as well(266). This formalism must not necessarily degenerate into an escape from substantial issues. It does also not necessarily have conservative implications. It is compatible with revolutionary tendencies. So at least Habermas assumes.

Optimism

But Habermas's assumption of equal and rational and equally rational partners in theoretical and practical discourse is highly optimistic. As such it does indeed point to a weak spot in Habermas's universal pragmatic, theory of communicative praxis and theory of mythical and religious-metaphysical worldviews. It opens them up and renders them vulnerable not only for empiricists and structural functionalists, but also for critical political theologians. Habermas shares this enormous optimism concerning human rationality with other great enlighteners, certainly not with Schopenhauer, Nietzsche or Freud, but very much so with Kant, Hegel and Marx. Recent modern history does certainly not verify and justify such an optimism. There is such a thing as what Schopenhauer and Horkheimer call, on the basis of the Buddhist and Judeo-Christian tradition, the "original sin"(267). At least in actuality men are not equal in rationality. There are the young who have not yet reached rationality and the old who have lost it again and all the adults in between, who have a hard time to assert their rationality against the irrationality of their own instincts and the merely functional requirements of the collectives in which they live. Many revolutionaries, e.g., Blanqui and Marx, have run their heads bloody against the rockbottom reality of stupidity in large parts of the population of modern action systems(268). Often in this century fascist dictatorships were the result of highly irrational mass movements and majority decisions in liberal and advanced capitalistic action systems(269). No theoretical or practical discourse helped in these action situations(270). Will practical discourse help in the present or future to stop or prevent irrational fascist mass movements or dictatorial military governments? We can only hope so! But human rationality must not be absolutized. At the same time it must also not be stepped on in terms of a desperate misology(271). Human rationality must be recognized and appreciated in spite of its relativity and brokenness. Habermas himself speaks often of the "fragments of rationality," which we have to search for in the irrationality of society and history. It is very unlikely that even the most rational discourse will be able to replace the highest rationality the great world religions were once inspired by and once aspired to and from which modern subjective instrumental as well as communicative and esthetical reason has uncoupled itself(272). In modernity individual and society have become in Hegelian terms non-substantial(273). They are no longer grounded in the ground of God's reason, providence, wisdom, plan, telos, but rather in what is finite and accidental. It is very improbable that practical discourse as such can discursively and argumentatively restore substantiality to the modern individual or collective as they are engaged in "trivial pursuit."

Content

According to Habermas, actors, who raise validity claims in theoretical or practical discourse, must give up any attempt to prejudice content-wise the relationship between language and the reality of the four worlds, between media of communication and the content about which people discourse in them(274). The contents of the linguistically established worldviews must be abstracted from the posited world order itself under the presupposition of formal world concepts and universal claims of validity. Only under this condition can, according to Habermas, the concept of a cultural tradition, a temporalized cultural world, be formed. In this process people become conscious of the fact that interpretations in relation to the natural, inner, social and cultural world vary. Likewise the opinions and values of people vary in relation to the objective natural world and the intersubjective inner, social and cultural world. In Habermas's view, modern people are aware of all this.

But Habermas criticizes in this context mythical systems of interpretation and orientation in primitive and archaic action systems, since they prevent by their material orientation a categorical uncoupling of nature and culture. They do this not only in the sense of a confusion of objective natural world and intersubjective inner, social and cultural world. But they do this also in the sense of a reification of the linguistically constituted worldview. The consequence of this is that the mythical concept of the world is filled dogmatically with certain contents, which are then liturgically festgeschrieben, or fixed. These mythical contents or truths are withdrawn from a rational position and thereby from critique. There are no discourses about these truths or the discourses which do take place are internally limited in such a way that the mythical contents cannot really be put into question on the basis of good reasons. That happens, e.g., in the Catholic religion after a belief or moral norm has been declared by council or pope ex cathedra to be a dogma: Roma locuta causa finita. Pope John II does not want to discourse with his theologian Kung, since he suspects him of opening up once more questions concerning issues which are supposed to have been settled in the dogmatization process once and for all; e.g., creation, fall, incarnation, virgin

birth, redemption, church, infallibility, last judgment, etc.
Habermas himself does indeed once more open up and hold
open the discourse for non-dogmatic mythical or religious-
metaphysical or mystical truths, insofar as they are receptive
to a rational attitude and critique. Here lies the chance of
real discourse between critical theorists on one hand and
critical fundamental theologians with practical intent, theologians of communicative praxis, political theologians, not
only from Christianity, Judaism and Islam, but also from other
world religions, on the other. Here also new bridges can be
built via practical discourse as future-oriented remembrance
of human suffering with practical intent to diminish it,
between the religious and the secular. In such practical
discourse a new conjugation between revelation and
enlightenment, redemption and happiness, salvation and
liberation, grace and freedom should not be absolutely
impossible(275). Such practical discourse can also help the
different Christian churches to come to an understanding with
each other and with other world religions and to a
coordination of other plans and actions and to accomplish a
new manifold <u>coincidentia oppositorum</u> among each other(276).

Inner Nature

So far in his critical theory of religion Habermas meant with
his formula of the confusion of nature and culture mainly the
external nature and the objective social and cultural
world(277). But Habermas can demonstrate a similar fusion of
dimensions of reality in mythical thinking also for the
relationship between culture and inner nature or subjective
world. Only to that extent, to which the formal concept of an
external world, i.e., an objective natural world of existing
facts as well as a social world of valid norms, has been
formed, the complementary concept of an inner world or
subjectivity can result.
To this inner world belongs everything, which can not be
incorporated into the external world and to which the
individual has a privileged entrance. According to Habermas,
only against the background of an independent objective world
of nature, measured by criticizable claims of truth and
success, subjective opinions can appear as systematically
false; personal intentions of actions as systematically
hopeless; individual thoughts as sheer fantasies. Only against
the background of a normative reality, which has become

objective and is measured by the criticizable claim of
normative rightness, individual intentions, wishes, attitudes
and feelings can appear as illegitimate or also as
idiosyncratic, as not universalizable and as merely
"subjective."

In Habermas's view, to the extent to which mythical
worldviews dominate interpretations or cognitions of reality
and orientations of actions, the clear differentiation of a
realm of subjectivity is not possible. The development of
subjectivity presupposes demythologization. The mythmaker or
believer does not separate intentions and motives from actions
and their consequences. He does also not separate feelings
from their normatively established and stereotyped expressions. Habermas observes that the members of primitive and
archaic societies bind their own identity to a high degree to
the details of the mythically-liturgically fixed collective
knowledge and to the formal details of ritual prescriptions.
This observation seems to be characteristic for the situation
of the mythmaker and believer in general. The members of
primitive and archaic societies do not have a formal concept
of the world, which can guarantee the identity of the natural
and social world in relation to changing interpretations of a
temporalized cultural tradition. Likewise the individual in
primitive and archaic society can not depend on a formal
concept of the "I," which can secure his or her own identity
in relation to an independent and flowing subjectivity. The
individual who has not yet gone through the process of demythologization has also not yet learned to say "I." To learn
to say "I" means to break with myth and become enlightened.

According to Hegel, through Christianity the principle of
free subjectivity or subjective freedom came into the
world(278). With it the modern world started in seedlike form,
in the midst of the seedbed society of Israel and of the
historic-intermediate Roman action system. With the weakening
and loss of the Christian principle of subjectivity also
declines and shrinks the inner world of people in organized
capitalistic and socialistic societies(279). The Christian
principle presupposed a certain amount of demythologization.
Its loss results in the remythologization of modern action
systems - e.g., the fascist "myth of the 20th century"(280).
Can practical discourse give birth to a new subjectivity - a
post-Christian, post-bourgeois subjectivity? That is the
fundamental test question for Habermas's new discourse
ethic(281).

Closedness

Habermas emphasizes the closedness of mythical world-
views(282). He discusses this closedness of mythical systems
of interpretation and orientation under the perspective of the
lacking differentiation among the four fundamental attitudes
toward the objective natural world and the subjective, social
and cultural world. Furthermore, Habermas discusses the
closedness of mythical worldviews under the perspective of the
lacking reflexivity of the mythical systems of interpretation
and orientation. The participants do not understand their
mythical worldviews as systems of interpretation, which are
connected with a cultural world; which are constituted through
internal connections of meanings; which are related
symbolically to reality; which are connected with validity
claims; and which are therefore exposed to critique and able
to be revised. This way Habermas is able to read from the
dialectical structures of mythical thinking indeed important
presuppositions for the modern understanding of the world. All
this does, of course, not yet show that the alleged
rationality of the modern worldview does indeed reflect more
than the particular traits of the occidental cultural world
which is shaped by positive science and technology informed by
such a science, and can therefore rightfully raise a claim of
universality. As a matter of fact, Habermas does not assert
dogmatically such universal claim of occidental rationality.
He rather emphasizes the instrumental one-sidedness of
occidental rationality and thus its pathological aspect. Its
very particularism is, indeed, in need of balancing and of
complementation by practical rationality. We may add that
ultimately the likewise rather closed modern system of
interpretation and orientation is in need of correction by an
objective rationality, however this is to be comprehended, in
order to be redeemed from its obvious particularity,
relativity and pathology. Unlike traditional worldviews the
modern system of interpretation and orientation is closed
particularly in relation to objective reason as its
agnosticism and atheism on a mass scale makes only too
clear(283). Even the pseudo-religious neo-conservative
movements in late capitalistic society rather prove than
disprove this point(284).

Existential Themes

While Habermas stands much more radically on the side of modernity, secularity, scientific modern worldview and corresponding theoretical and practical discourse than Hegel or even Horkheimer, Benjamin or Adorno, he, nevertheless, admits that the traditional religious worldviews have articulated important existential problems(286). There is no doubt for Habermas that the linguistically articulated religious worldviews are closely interwoven with peoples' immediate life form and life world, i.e., with the everyday praxis of socialized individuals. That is the case in such a way that the religious worldviews must not be reduced to the function of knowing the external nature and to making it disposable. According to Habermas, following here Kant and Hegel, religious worldviews must not be understood only in terms of the dimension of work and tools and instrumental rationality, but also, and very much so, in terms of recognition, interaction, intersubjectivity and practical rationality(286). Particularly through this connection with the dimension of interaction and communicative rationality, religious worldviews are able to articulate fundamental existential problems, exigencies or contingencies.

According to Habermas in the framework of their religious worldview, the participants of a linguistic tribal or national community come to an understanding about central existential themes of their personal and social life. When modern people, so Habermas argues, want to compare the rationality standards which are built into different cultural systems of interpretation and orientation with each other, then they must not limit themselves to the dimensions of science and technology, which are offered by their own modern culture. Modern people must not make their possibility of statements and effective techniques into the measure for the rationality of traditional people. According to Habermas, worldviews are comparable only in respect to their ability to make sense of reality, particularly contingency situations. In Habermas's view worldviews throw light on important existential themes, which return again and again in all cultures: birth and death, illness, want, guilt, love, solidarity and loneliness. The worldviews open up equally original possibilities of making sense of human life. Thereby the worldviews structure the life forms and life worlds of people. These life forms are incomparable in their value. The rationality of life forms

can, according to Habermas, not be reduced to the cognitive
adequacy of the worldviews which underlie them.

Contradictions

While Habermas is fully aware of the fact that the religious
worldviews do indeed articulate these important existential
problems and themes, he does nevertheless not want to escape
into material aspects of the religious system. He is
interested first of all in their formal aspects. According to
Habermas the rationality of religious worldviews and life
forms must be read from their formal qualities. In Habermas's
view the cognitive adequacy of religious worldviews, namely
the coherence and truth of the statements possible in them as
well as the effectiveness of the action plans depending on
such coherence and truth, mirrors itself also in the praxis of
daily life conduct. Habermas points to contradictions in the
magic and myth of primitive and archaic action systems. He
recognizes that participants in religious worldviews often
interpret away their contradictions or refuse to face them.
They have a high toleration for absurdities. But for Habermas
such interpreting away, ignoring, refusal to face, and
tolerating of such contradictions in religious worldviews is
an indication for an irrational conduct of life. Habermas
calls irrational the orientations of action, which can be
stabilized only for the price of the repression of contradictions, dissonances, absurdities. Habermas insists, in
relation to the religious worldviews, on consistency. The
inconsistencies, contradictions, absurdities, shortly irra-
tionalities of religious worldviews, come to their culmination
in the sphere of the theodicy as apology of the world: the
justice of God or the gods in the face of the injustices of
the world; the assertion that the world is not as bad as it
looks(287).

Temporality and Finitude

At this point in the development of his theory of religion,
Habermas does not seem to be aware of the fact that this
aporetical aspect of traditional religious worldviews, which
appears most clearly in the unresolved theodicy problem,
reappears in exaggerated form in the secular modern world-
view(288). Here at least Habermas does not seem to be sufficiently conscious of the _aporia_ of his own extremely secular

universal pragmatic, theory of communicative praxis and
critical theory of religion concerning the important
existential problems once dealt with by religious worldviews.
The aporia of Habermas's universal pragmatic lies in his
neglect of the temporality and finitude of all human life and
action: the certitude of suffering and death as a phenomenon
of the everyday life world. There is a certain lack of
reflexivity in Habermas's theory of communicative praxis and
religion concerning this aporia. Not only the cultural world
is temporal and finite, as Habermas admits, but also the
natural world, the inner world and the social world. Likewise
temporal and finite are the speaker's four attitudes toward
these four worlds. Thus all language, work, love, recognition
and national life is, as being temporal and finite,
continually moving toward the end, toward death. There is a
certain repression of time, finitude, and death taking place
in Habermas's universal pragmatic, theory of communicative
praxis and even theory of religion. Annihilation threatens the
meaning of all human speech acts, work and tools, marriage and
family, mutual recognition and nation. Insofar as Habermas
does not sufficiently reflect upon the aporetical aspects of
his universal pragmatic, positivism and nihilism threaten to
penetrate all its aspects(289). Such nihilism can not simply
be banned by attempts to escape into formalism or to teach
people not only to live without consolation, but not even to
have any longer any need for it(290). The threat of such
nihilism, if it can not be overcome, will certainly always be
a "temptation" for people to return under the pressure of
contingencies, which will come sooner than later, to the
traditional religious worldviews, no matter how intense their
inconsistencies may be. Religious worldviews can always deal
with their absurdities at least to some extent by reference to
a highest rationality, providence and wisdom(291). Thus even
Horkheimer, who denied being a believer, nevertheless put, by
testament, on his gravestone a verse from the Hebrew Psalm 91,
which expresses trust in the Eternal One(292). Such trust
alone resists positivism and nihilism in the long run. It is
precisely the aporia in Habermas's theory of communicative
praxis and religion which drives the political theologians,
who build their fundamental theology with practical intent on
that theory, to refer back to experiences in Buddhism, Judaism
and Christianity, which are able to break through this dead
end street(293). All this does not mean that neo—conservative
thinkers could make use of this aporetical aspect of

Habermas's critical theory for their own apologetics of obsolete mythical or religious-metaphysical worldviews. They are anyhow, or should at least be sufficiently occupied with their own aporetical aspect: the theodicy problem. The specific Christian form of the theodicy problem is the parousia delay: that precisely is the catastrophe that things go on as they do in civil society and bourgeois history. Also the aporetical aspect of Habermas's universal pragmatic, theory of communicative praxis and religion in no way diminishes the great value of many of his substantial contributions to pragmatics as well as to political theology. Habermas can strengthen his position against objections from the side of religion concerning its central existential themes by retrieving insights into the problem of temporality, finitude and death in Hegel's Phenomenology of Spirit, Kierkegaard's Sickness unto Death, Benjamin's Passage Work and Adorno's Negative Dialectics(294). Here particularly Hegel's statement is in place:

> But the life of spirit is not one that shuns death, and keeps clear of destruction: it endures death and in death maintains its being. It only wins to its truth, when it finds itself utterly torn asunder. It is this mighty power, not being a positive, which turns away from the negative, as when we say of anything it is nothing or it is false, and, being then done with it, pass off to something else: on the contrary, mind is this power only by looking the negative in the face, and dwelling with it. This dwelling beside it is the magic power that converts the negative into being(295).

It seems that Habermas's theory of communicative praxis and of religion will come into its own the more it faces up to the fundamental existential "truths" of religious worldviews, and the less it shuns death and the less it keeps clear of destruction and the less it turns away from the negative and the more it looks the negative in the face and dwells with it. Whether it can really convert the negative into being, is another question. But one thing is certain: that there is no way to the affirmative except through the negation of the negative(296). The "rose of reason" can be reached only through the cross of the contradictory present(297). One must take upon oneself the cross of the negative present, in order

to be able to pluck the affirmative rose of reason contained
in it(298).

Closed and Open Worldviews

Habermas points to the rationality debate in England concerning the critical rationalist K. Popper's differentiation
between closed and open worldviews(299). According to the
critical rationalist position, the closed traditional
religious worldviews are characterized by a lack of awareness
of alternatives, sacredness of beliefs and anxiety about
threats to them(300). To the contrary, the modern worldview is
characterized by awareness of alternatives, diminished
sacredness of beliefs and diminished anxiety about threats to
them. According to Habermas, with the Popperian dimensions of
closedness and openness a context-independent criterion seems
to offer itself for the judgment about the rationality of
worldviews. But Habermas is fully aware of the fact that the
reference point of such a rationality criterion is once more
nothing else than modern science. The critical rationalist
reduces the sacred identity-securing character of closed
worldviews to their immunization against alternatives of
interpretation. The Popperians contrast these closed religious
worldviews with the free scientific spirit, which has for its
most important traits readiness to learn and the ability to
criticize. Mythical-magical worldviews are incompatible with
that reflexive fundamental attitude, without which scientific
theories cannot come into existence.

But Habermas knows only too well that the readiness to
learn and the ability to criticize are not at all merely
idiosyncratic traits of modern Western culture. Furthermore,
he considers it highly onesided to judge worldviews according
to the criterion of whether they hinder or promote a positive
scientific mentality. Habermas is not a "critical
rationalist." He is not a positivist(301). He is so far not
even in danger of becoming a positivist as some critical
theologians suspect. He holds very well his distance from
exclusively functional rationality.

The British rationalists define the closedness and
openness of systems of interpretation and orientation in the
dimension of the sense for theoretical alternatives. They call
a worldview closed insofar as it regulates without
alternatives the encounter with the external natural reality,
i.e., with that which can be seen and acted upon in the

objective world of nature(302). Habermas objects to the
rationalists that already this opposition of worldviews and a
reality with which they can be more or less in agreement,
suggests the impression that the formation of theory was the
main purpose of worldviews. In reality, so Habermas argues
against the Popperians, the structures of worldviews determine
a praxis of life which is not at all exhausted in the
cognitive-instrumental encounter with the external reality of
nature. The more Habermas stresses in his universal pragmatic
mutual, reciprocal recognition rather than work and tools, the
more he is willing to protect religious worldviews, at least
against the pathological inclination of critical rationalism
to reduce as much as possible all human activities to the
dimension of functional rationality and to neglect practical
rationality. In this sense religion and theology can indeed
find an ally in Habermas. There are, of course, Popperians who
explore religious systems of interpretation and orientation
with some sympathy. But they can never restrain themselves
from putting religion in the straight jacket of the
subject-object relationship and instrumental rationality. It
seems that the embattled religious positions find better
friends in Habermas and his followers than in Popper and his
disciples. The recent Telos issue on Religion and Politics has
demonstrated this(303).

Understanding and Socialization

Mythical worldviews, so Habermas explains, in relation to the
critical rationalist position, are very broadly constitutive
for processes of understanding and socialization, in which the
participants relate themselves as much to the orders of their
common social world and to experiences of their subjective
world as to processes in their one objective world of
nature(304). Habermas admits to the Popperians that mythical
thinking does not yet allow for the categorical separation
between cognitive-instrumental, moral-practical and expres-
sive-practical relations to the world. But this is for
Habermas merely a clear sign that the closedness of primitive
or archaic mythical worldviews must not be described exclusively on the basis of attitudes toward the objective world of
nature and that the openness of the modern understanding of
the world must not be characterized exclusively on the basis
of formal qualities of the scientific mentality. Habermas
intends emphatically in the context of his fundamental,

formal, universal pragmatic, to keep open the dimension of mutual recognition versus the dimension of work and tools. He intends to strengthen practical versus technical rationality. He thereby lays the foundation on which not only his own worldview, historical materialism, can be reconstructed against the context of the positivistic spirit of the times, the metaphysics of what is the case, but religion as well(305).

As Habermas discusses the differentiation between closed mythical worldviews and the open modern world-understanding in the framework of his own fundamental, formal, universal pragmatic, he connects this differentiation with the increasing categorical separation among the objective, subjective, social and cultural worlds and the specialization of cognitive-instrumental, moral-practical, and expressive problem positions(306). He emphasizes the differentiation of validity aspects, under which those problem positions can be worked through. Habermas sees the differentiation between closed and open worldviews in connection with the differentiation between linguistically articulated worldviews and reality and in terms of the separation of internal connections of meanings and external connections of things. The more differentiation there is among the world of nature, inner world, social and cultural world and the corresponding attitudes, the more open the worldviews become.

But according to Habermas, worldviews are not only constitutive for processes of understanding, but also for the socialization of individuals, for their learning processes. Worldviews have the function to form personal and social identities and to secure them. Worldviews fulfill this function by providing the individuals with a core of fundamental categories and presuppositions. They cannot be revised and changed without this change affecting the identity of the individual as well as of the social group. Individuals and groups may hang on to their worldview simply for the purpose of not having to change their identity. The thought of such identity-change alone may fill them with terror.

According to Habermas, the knowledge which guarantees personal and social identity, becomes more and more formal on the way from closed to open worldview. Christianity has gone through an intense process of formalization(307). This knowledge, which guarantees identity, is connected with cultural structures. These structures separate themselves more and more from the contents, which are given free for revision.

To these formal structures belong, e.g., protective attitudes. The formal arrangement of the tabu can be seen as an institution, which protects the original foundations of the worldview, where regularly dissonant experiences occur and threaten to confuse fundamental differences. Revisions do, nevertheless, occur in all worldviews. Protestantism is a massive revision of Catholic Christianity(308). But not only religious worldviews, but also modern secular worldviews, e.g. bourgeois or dialectical materialism, go through revisions(309). Habermas's own reconstruction of dialectical materialism is once more a new and very necessary revision of the historical materialism initiated by Marx(310). He is certainly revising Horkheimer's and Adorno's critical theory on the basis of his new paradigm of communicative praxis.

Hypostatization

When Habermas analyzes the Popperian dichotomy of closed and open worldviews in terms of his own fundamental formal and universal pragmatic, he comes to a perspective out of which he can make objections against the positivistic hypostatization of scientific rationality understandable and can uncouple them from all too fast conclusions(311). According to Habermas, scientific rationality belongs to a complex of cognitive-instrumental rationality in the wider dimension of functional action: work and tools. This complex can certainly claim validity beyond the context of particular cultures in particular action systems. But Habermas does not deny that there may be the possibility that modern people can learn something from the understanding of alternative, particularly premodern forms of life. In terms of their "wisdom" modern people can beyond all romantization of earlier stages of human development, which have been overcome, and beyond the exotic stimulation of foreign cultural contents remember the great losses and sacrifices and costs which their own way into modernity demanded. This is not only an insight of some critical rationalists. Since Horkheimer, critical theorists have pointed to the price which is to be paid for progress in the dimension of work and tools, i.e., instrumental rationality: e.g., the progress in the field of negative artificial birth control may have to be paid for, via detabuization, with the death of erotic love(312).

According to Habermas, the modern worldview has arisen from the differentiation between world concept and validity aspects, scientific statements and value considerations(313). Even some critical rationalists give their universalistic position in relation to cognitive-instrumental rationality a self-critical emphasis. Not the scientific rationality as such, but its hypostatization of functional rationality points to a pattern of social and cultural rationalization, which gives dominance to the cognitive-instrumental rationality not only in the encounter with the external world of nature, but also in the communicative everyday praxis in general(314). Habermas finds weak the argumentation of the critical rationalist, that there is intrinsic to every linguistically articulated worldview an incomparable notion of rationality or "wisdom." But Habermas is willing to differentiate clearly between the universality claim of functional rationality, which expresses itself in the modern understanding of the world and which is justified in principle, on one hand, and uncritical self-explication of modernity, which is fixed to the instrumental knowledge, the making disposable the external nature, on the other. In his Passage Work Benjamin has pointed to the hellish character of a modernity which is onesidedly bound to work, tools, production, exchange, functional rationality and intends to produce a theology of the capitalistic hell of the 19th and 20th centuries(315). Habermas's fundamental formal and universal pragmatic does not at all exclude the possibility that there are contained in traditional religious worldviews truths which could constitute a corrective for the onesided emphasis on work and tools and functional rationality and the neglect of mutual recognition and practical-communicative rationality: e.g., Messianic mimesis, Messianic impulse, Messianic realm, redemption(316).

Universal Rationality Structures

The rationality debate among Popperians in England suggests to Habermas the conclusion that universal rationality structures do indeed underlie the modern worldview(317). But the modern action systems of the West promote a distorted understanding of rationality, which is connected with cognitive-instrumental aspects and, insofar as this is the case, is merely particularistic in the sociological sense. Habermas points to some implications of such a conception.

When the rationality of worldviews, so Habermas argues, can be judged in the formal pragmatically determined dimension closedness-openness, then we must take into account the possibility of systematic changes in the structures of systemic interpretation and orientation. These changes cannot only be explained in terms of external psychological, economical, sociological or politological factors. But they can also be reduced to an increase of knowledge in the form of learning processes, which can be internally reconstructed. Habermas is aware of the fact that, of course, such learning processes must once more be explained with the help of empirical mechanisms. But Habermas conceives of these learning processes at the same time as problem-solving processes in such a way that they are open for a systematic evaluation on the basis of internal conditions of validity.

Learning Processes

According to Habermas, the universalistic position of the critical rationalists concerning the cognitive-instrumental rationality as such, makes cogent the evolution-theoretical assumption at least in principle, that the rationalization of worldviews does indeed happen via learning processes(318). That does not mean that Habermas wants to return to Hegel's philosophy of history and religion. It does not mean that the development must move continuously or in linear form or even with inner necessity in the sense of Hegel's idealistic causality, the causality of the Idea - the freedom-will of God(319). Habermas does not want to prejudice in any way with this, his assumption of the dynamic of the development of worldviews.

But whoever, so Habermas states, wants to comprehend historical transitions between differently structured worldviews as learning processes, must satisfy the demand for a formal analysis of connections of meaning(320). This formal analysis must allow the reconstruction of the empirical succession of worldviews as a sequence of learning steps, which can be followed by the participants with insight and which can be tested intersubjectively. At the same time, Habermas does not want to go so far as to assume that the scientist, who belongs to a modern action system, can not seriously understand the crucifixion of Jesus, before he has not reconstructed the learning processes which have made possible the transition from myth to a world religion or the transition from a religious-metaphysical worldview to a mystical system of interpretation and orientation or from such a system to the modern understanding of the world.

On the basis of Weber's sociology of religion, Habermas makes the attempt to comprehend the development of religious worldviews under the theoretical perspective of the formation of formal concepts of the world(321). He wants to understand the development of religious systems of interpretation and orientation as learning processes. In doing so, Habermas uses Piaget's concept of learning, which he has developed for the ontogenesis of structures of individual consciousness(322). With Piaget, Habermas differentiates among stages of cognitive development. They are characterized not only by new contents, but also by structurally described levels of the ability to learn. Habermas assumes that something similar does also happen in case of the emergence of new religious worldview structures. He transfers Piaget's insights into learning processes from the ontogenetic to the phylogenetic level. According to Habermas, the differentiation among the mythical, the religious-metaphysical, the mystical and the modern mode of thinking is characterized by changes in the system of fundamental categories: in Hegelian terms in the system of logic(323).

The interpretations of reality and orientations of action of a worldview stage, which has been superseded in human evolution, are devalued in the transition to the next stage, no matter what they look like contentwise. From one stage of worldview formation to the other not only this or that reason for this or that truth does no longer convince people. It is rather the whole type of reasons which no longer convinces anybody. According to Habermas, the devaluation of the potential of explanation and justification of whole religious traditions happened, indeed, when the mythical-narrative thought configurations were superseded in high cultures and when religious cosmological and metaphysical configurations of thinking were overcome in modernity(324). In Habermas's view, these pushes of devaluation of worldviews are connected with the transition to new levels of learning. In these transitions the conditions of learning change in the dimension of objectivating thinking in relation to the world of nature, in the dimension of personal reflections in relation to the individual's inner world, in the dimension of moral-practical insight in relation to the social world and in the dimension of the esthetical-practical ability of expression in relation to the cultural world. Since the conditions of learning have changed since Hegel's death, Habermas can no longer accept the Hegelian system of categories, the Hegelian logic as system.

Centralized and Decentralized Worldviews

Habermas differentiates sharply between the life world on one hand and the social and cultural subsystems of the human action system on the other(325). He introduces the concept of life world as correlate to processes of understanding. Communicatively acting persons come to an understanding always in the horizon of a life world. The subject's life world builds itself up out of more or less diffuse, always unproblematic cultural background knowledge. This life world background serves as source for the definitions of action situations, which the participants presuppose as unproblematic. The participants in a national or cultural community differentiate in their interpretations the one objective world of nature and their intersubjectively shared social world from the subjective worlds of individuals and of other collectives. The worldviews and the corresponding validity claims constitute the formal structures, through which the communicatively acting persons integrate the situational contexts, which are problematic and in need of consensus, into their life world, which is presupposed as being unproblematic.

According to Habermas, the life world accumulates the interpretational work done by past generations. The life world is the conservative counterpart and counterweight against the risks of dissensus, which comes about with every new actual process of understanding. This is so, since the communicatively acting subjects can achieve an understanding only over yes/no positions in relation to validity claims, which are criticizable. The relation between these weights of life world and dissensus-risks changes with the transition from traditional, centralized mythical, religious-metaphysical and mystical worldviews to the modern secular decentralized system of interpretation and orientation.

Nature of Religion

Hegel, following Meister Eckehart, describes centralized and decentralized worldviews(326). According to Hegel, in traditional religious worldviews the participants remove themselves from temporality. For the consciousness of traditional people, religion is the dimension in which all riddles of the world are resolved. All contradictions of deep contemplative thought are revealed. All pains of feeling are overcome. Religion is the sphere of eternal truth, eternal quietude, eternal peace. For Hegel man is man through thought in general, concrete thought. Man differs from the animal by being spirit: consciousness, self-consciousness, reason(327). From man as spirit radiate the manifold formations of sciences, arts, interests of political life, moral conditions which relate to his freedom, to his will. Here lay the roots for the modern decentralized worldview.

But for traditional man all these manifold social and cultural formations, so Hegel states, and the further interconnections of human conditions, actions, enjoyments, everything that has value and respect for him in his life world, everything in which he seeks his happiness, his recognition, his glory, finds its ultimate center in religion, in the thought, consciousness, feeling of God(328). Therefore God is for traditional people the beginning and the end of everything. As everything flows out of God, so does everything return again into God. Likewise, God is the center, which makes everything alive and maintains all those social and cultural configurations of traditional man's life world in their existence and animates them. In religion traditional man puts himself into absolute relationship to the Absolute as the center, in which all his other conditions come together and are centralized. Thus traditional man elevates himself to the highest level of consciousness and into the region which is free from any relationship to something other and which is the completely self-sufficient, the unconditional, the free and ultimate purpose for itself. Religion is the occupation with God as the ultimate Telos. Religion is completely free and purpose for itself. This is so, since into God as the ultimate purpose all other finite purposes return and in Him these purposes are centered and in Him these purposes, which so far were valid for themselves, disappear. Against God as the ultimate Telos no other finite purpose can stand up, and alone in Him all other purposes find their fulfillment. While in centralized traditional worldviews truth, quietude, peace, goodness, right, life, beauty are centered in the Absolute, in the decentralized modern worldview all these elements fall apart and constitute separate cultural and social departments. Here comes about a new modern polytheism(329).

According to Hegel, this dialectical image of the Absolute as beginning, end and center of everything can offer itself to traditional man's religious devotion as more or less present vivacity, certainty, enjoyment(330). This dialectical

image can also be presented as something longed for, hoped
for, as something distant and beyond(331). But always this
image remains certainty for traditional man. It radiates as
something divine into the temporal presence. It gives the
consciousness of the effectiveness of the truth inspite of all
the frightful, which still vexes the soul in this region of
temporality. Faith recognizes this image of the Absolute as
the truth, as the substance of all the existences at hand.
This absolute content of religious devotion is the animating
element in the present life world. It makes itself effective
in the life form and life world of the individual. It governs
the individual, in what he or she does or does not do. That
precisely is for Hegel the general concept, the feeling, the
consciousness of religion. It is the purpose of the science of
religion as Hegel sees it to consider, explore, and know this
nature of religion.

Religious and Secular

For Hegel there is, indeed, no human being who is so rotten,
lost, bad and miserable that he would not have anything at all
of religion in himself or herself. Everybody has at least fear
of religion or longing for religion or hate against religion.
Even if somebody hates religion he or she is still internally
preoccupied with religion and entangled in it. Religion is
essential to man as man and is not a foreign feeling to him.
But most important for Hegel is the relationship of religion
to the secular rest of a man's total world perspective. In
Hegel's view, philosophy relates itself to and essentially
works upon this relationship between the centralized religious
and the decentralized secular worldview. According to Hegel in
this relationship lies the source of the disunion against the
original absolute urge of man's spirit toward religion. In
this relationship the manifold secular forms of consciousness
and the very different relationships of these forms to the
interest of religion have constituted themselves. In this
relationship also lies the source for the possibility of the
modern decentralized worldview. It is precisely the disunion
between the traditional centralized religious worldviews and
the modern decentralized secular worldview, which has awakened
the need, which Hegel wants to satisfy in his philosophy of
religion. In his philosophy Hegel traces the, throughout modernity, continually deepening antagonism between centralized
and decentralized worldview and offers a reconciliation
between them.

and orientation.

Consensus

This Hegelian reconciliation is no longer acceptable to Habermas(332). While Habermas traces, like Hegel, the modern division between centralized and decentralized worldview, his whole sympathy is on the side of the latter. Habermas's theory of communicative praxis is much more radically modern and secularized than Hegel's dialectical philosophy. Habermas, as enlightener standing almost completely on the side of the modern decentralized worldview, is, nevertheless, open for centralized worldviews insofar as they can defend themselves in discourse with the better reasons.

According to Habermas, the further the worldview, which presents the accumulated cultural knowledge, is decentralized, the less the need for understanding among people is covered from the start by a life world, which is interpreted in such a way that it is no longer vulnerable by critique(333). The more this need for understanding must be satisfied by the interpretative achievements of the participants, i.e., over a consensus, which is risky, since it is rationally motivated, the more frequently we can expect rational orientations of actions. Therefore, Habermas can characterize the rationalization of the life world in terms of normatively ascribed understanding, on the one hand, and of communicatively achieved consensus, on the other. The more mythical, religious-metaphysical or mystical traditions present a prejudgment about which validity claims can be accepted when, where, for what, by whom and in relation to whom, the less the participants themselves have the possibility to make explicit and to test the potential grounds on which they base their yes/no positions. For Habermas, in the transition from pre-modern to modern action systems, communicative action, discourse-mediated interaction, step-by-step takes the place of the premodern worldviews. Habermas's theory of communicative praxis intends to supersede Hegel's dialectical philosophy of religion, in which the mythical, religious-metaphysical and mystical worldviews had been brought home as the cultural harvest from thousands of years of Eastern and Western history(334). The decentralized theory of communicative praxis tends to replace slowly the allegedly more and more obsolete premodern centralized mythical, religious-metaphysical and mystical systems of interpretation

World Order

In this perspective of the theory of communicative action, Habermas considers and judges the premodern and modern cultural worldviews(335). In this perspective the mythical worldviews become for Habermas an instructive border case. To the extent to which the life form of a social group is interpreted through a mythical system, to that extent the burden of interpretation and orientation is taken away from the individual participants. But at the same time the participants lose the chance themselves to bring about a criticizable understanding. In Habermas's view, insofar as the worldview remains centralized, it does not allow for a differentiation among the worlds of existing things, subjective experiences, valid social norms, and esthetical expressions. The language-mediated worldview is reified as world order. It can not be looked through as criticizable system of interpretation and orientation. Inside such a system − e.g., Taoism, Hinduism, Buddhism, Zoroastrianism, Syrian-Phoenician and Egyptian religion, Greek and Roman religion, Judaism, Christianity and Islam − the critical zone can not be reached in which a communicatively achieved understanding depends on autonomous yes/no positions in relation to criticizable validity claims(336).

   Here, as elsewhere, Habermas presupposes, of course, an enormous and at the same time equal rationality potential in all participants in discourse-mediated interaction. The rationality of the discourse partners from the present three generations must be greater than the rationality of all the mythical, religious-metaphysical and mystical worldviews, which are the result of the interpretations of reality and orientations of actions and corresponding experiences of hundreds of past generations. Habermas does not deny that there are at least fragments of rationality present in these traditional worldviews. But he puts, nevertheless, a tremendous burden of discursive thought and responsibility on the shoulders of presently living generations. It must also be taken into consideration that some of the human problems decided upon in the traditional worldviews may as such not be open at all to discursive procedures. Not only Hegel, but even Adorno was aware of such non-discursive subject matter(337).

Formal Properties and Concepts

Against this background of the description of the dichotomy of
centralized and decentralized worldviews, it becomes clear for
Habermas which formal properties cultural traditions must have
if, in a correspondingly interpreted life world, rational
orientations of action should be possible and if they should
be able even to densify themselves into a rational conduct of
life(338). These formal properties are also the criteria in
terms of which truths of traditional mythical, religious-
metaphysical and mystical worldviews can possibly be carried
over into the modern secular system of interpretation and
orientation. Such truths can range from God over original sin
and second commandment to the messianic mimesis, universal
solidarity and redemption(339). These criteria are of utmost
importance not only for a critical theory of subject, society,
history and religion but also, and particularly so, for any
critical fundamental theology with practical intent, theology
of the world, theology of communicative praxis, or critical
political theology(340).
    What precisely are these criteria, these formal
properties of cultural traditions, without which a rational
conduct of life is not possible? According to Habermas, a
cultural tradition which would enable its participants to live
and act rationally, must present formal concepts for the
objective natural world, subjective world, social world and
cultural world(341). It must allow through these formal
concepts for differentiated validity claims in terms of
propositional truth, subjective veracity, normative rightness
and esthetic taste. It must stimulate, through the formal
concepts, a corresponding differentiation of fundamental
objectivating, honest, norm—conform and expressive attitudes.
If a cultural tradition can provide such formal concepts, then
symbolical expressions can be produced on a formal level. On
this level these symbolical expressions are systematically
interconnected with reasons and are open to objective
judgment.

Reflexivity

Furthermore, in Habermas's view the cultural tradition, which
should make possible a rational life for its participants,
must allow for a reflexive relationship to itself. It must
have a high level of reflexivity. It must have freed itself
from its dogmatic aspects at least to such an extent that the
interpretations and orientations, which are saturated by

tradition, can in principle be put into question and can be
submitted to a critical revision. We may think of an
adogmatically reconstructed Judaism, Christianity or Islam. In
such case of de-dogmatization, internal connections of meaning
in the cultural tradition can newly be worked out. Alternative
interpretations and orientations can be methodically explored.
Cognitive activities of second order come into existence:
learning processes, which are steered by hypotheses and are
filtered through arguments. Such learning processes can take
place in the dimensions of objectivating thought, personal
reflection, moral-practical insight, and esthetic perception.
It is obvious that this principle of reflexivity is also to be
applied to Habermas's own work: his own philosophy and
sociology is as much part of that cultural world he discusses
as any other philosophical thought or any other piece of art
or any other positive religion. Therefore whatever criteria
Habermas applies in general in his discourses on culture are
valid for his own philosophical and sociological work as well.

Cultural and Social Institutionalization

Beyond this, in Habermas's perspective, in order to guide
people in rational praxis the cultural tradition must be able
to be coupled back in its cognitive and evaluative aspects
with specialized argumentations to such an extent that the
corresponding learning processes can be culturally institutionalized. Through such institutionalization cultural subsystems can come about for morality and right, for art, music
and literature, and science. In these cultural subsystems new
traditions can form themselves, which are argumentatively
based. They are, furthermore, made fluid by continual
critique. At the same time, they are professionally secured.
        Finally, according to Habermas, in order to make rational
conduct possible, the cultural tradition must interpret the
life world in such a way that success-oriented instrumental
action can be freed from the imperatives of an understanding
which must again and again be communicatively renewed, and
that instrumental action can at least partially be uncoupled
from communicative action, oriented through understanding.
Thereby a social institutionalization of purpose-rational
action for generalized goals becomes possible. In modern human
action systems, subsystems can form themselves over the media
of money and power. A rational economic subsystem, characterized by monetarization, and a rational political subsystem,
characterized by bureaucratization and administration, becomes
possible. While Habermas opposes the colonization of the life

world in terms of modernization and bureaucratization, he has, nevertheless, a positive attitude not only to the cultural subsystems of modern action systems - e.g., art, religion, philosophy or science, but also toward social subsystems, e.g., economy and polity(342). In doing so Habermas is much closer to Hegel than to Marx: he is as flexible toward civil society and its dialectic as Hegel was one and a half centuries earlier(343).

Spheres of Values

With Weber, Habermas understands the cultural and social subsystems in modern human action systems as a differentiation of spheres of values: goodness, beauty, truth, etc(344). For Habermas, as for Weber before, this differentiation of value spheres constitutes the very core of the cultural and social rationalization in modernity. According to Weber and Habermas, this differentiation is the consequence of the decentralization of the traditional mythical, religious-metaphysical and mystical worldviews(345). The value spheres of goodness, beauty, truth, etc., are no longer centered in the Absolute. The Absolute becomes entirely empty. Agnosticism and finally atheism prevails(346). At the same time, the decentralization of the traditional worldviews sets free the different dimensions of values. Thus it leads beyond agnosticism and atheism to a new, modern polytheism, its positive result is the possibility of the formation of rational autonomous value spheres or cultural and social subsystems in modern action systems. Like the old gods of Antiquity the newly instituted value spheres in modern action systems are continuously struggling with each other.

There is, of course, a price to be paid for such decentralization of the modern worldview and the consequential agnosticism, atheism and polytheism. It is now possible to present the untruth in the most beautiful form. Goodness may appear in the most ugly form. The artist dictator may present his immoral plans in an esthetic form most attractive for masses of people. Also this is a modern possibility! In his relatively optimistic attitude toward modernity, Habermas prefers to concentrate on the positive cultural and social possibilities arising from the decentralization of the traditional mythical, religious-metaphysical and mystical worldviews. But Habermas's awareness of the damage the life world can suffer from colonization by the autonomous economic and political subsystems, by monetarization and bureaucratization, shows the limits of his optimism(347). He sees, like

Horkheimer, Adorno, Marcuse and Fromm, the possibility of a totally administered, one-dimensional, technocratic society: Future I.

Habermas uses Piaget's concept of cultural decentralization in order to enlighten himself and us about the internal connections among the structures of a worldview, the life world as the context of processes of understanding and the possibilities of a rational life conduct(348). As he does this, Habermas encounters once more the concept of communicative rationality as opposed to instrumental rationality. Communicative rationality belongs to the dimension of recognition, instrumental rationality to the sphere of work and tools. For Habermas, the concept of communicative rationality relates the decentralized modern understanding of the world to the possibility of the discursive redemption of criticizable validity claims. Together with other critical theorists, Habermas considers the concept of communicative or discursive rationality to be complex enough, to include his scepsis concerning the onesided cognitive-instrumental self-explication of modern rationality as well as his motivation to learn from other cultures, in order to become aware of and to overcome this functionalistic onesideness of the modern self- and world-understanding. On the basis of this concept of communicative, discursive rationality, Habermas is able to overcome the incoherences, contradictions, and dissensions of traditional worldviews and to appropriate, through the formal properties of cultural traditions explicated above, more truths from traditional systems of interpretation and orientation than merely an universal communicative ethics as a result of their rationalization(349). That is the case at least in principle. So far Habermas has not yet sufficiently identified such other truths which could be rescued from allegedly obsolete traditional, mythical, religious-metaphysical and mystical worldviews. In the future, maybe such truths could best be identified in discourse between critical theorists and critical political theologians from different faith communities, be they Hindu or Buddhist, Jewish, Christian or Islamic.

Errors of Modernity

Like Hegel before, Habermas finds parallel processes and structures in the history of the individual and in the history of the human species(350). Thus Habermas applies the ontogenetic concept of egocentricity to the phylogenetic level(351). When Habermas conceives the concept of egocentricity as broadly as the concept of decentralization, which he also transferred from the ontogenetic to the phylogenetic level, and assumes that egocentricism renews itself in each stage of the development of the individual as well as of the species, then the processes of learning are again always followed by the shadow of systematic distortions and errors. According to Habermas, if this is true, then it could be possible, that also with the modern decentralized understanding of the world a special illusion could come into existence. This specifically modern illusion consists in the false assumption that the differentiation of an objective world of nature necessarily means the exclusion altogether of the subjective, social and cultural world from the realm of rationally motivated understanding. Habermas is very much concerned with this possible illusion of modern reifying functional thought. Habermas's core concept of communicative or discursive rationality is supposed to dispel this possible illusion. Should it be successful, it can once more open up rational discourse adequate to the specific structures of the inner, social and cultural worlds.

Habermas sees like Hegel before another possible error of modernity, complementary to this illusion of instrumental thinking, in modern utopianism(352). According to such modern utopianism, we are able to gain from the concept of decentralized understanding of the world and the procedural, discursive, communicative rationality at the same time the ideal of a form of life, which has become completely rational. Habermas warns that life forms do not only consist of worldviews which we can categorize under structural perspectives as more or less decentralized. Forms of life do also not only consist of institutions, which fall under the aspect of justice. For Habermas, life forms are concrete language games, historical configurations arising from habitual practices, group associations, cultural patterns of interpretation, forms of socialization and internalization, competences and attitudes. Habermas finds it senseless to judge such a syndrome of language, work, love, recognition, this totality of a life world, under particular aspects of rationality. For Habermas the model of illness and health is the standard by which he can – if at all – evaluate a form of life as failure, distorted, unhappy or alienated. A form of life is more or less healthy or sick. According to Habermas, we judge life forms and life histories at least secretly according to measures of normality, which do not allow for an approximation to ideal boundary values. The Kantian Habermas

is rather inclined to such approximation to ideals(353). But
the Hegelian Habermas suggests that we speak of a balance
among moments, which are in need of complementation, an
equilibrated playing together of the cognitive-instrumental
with the personal-intimate, the moral and the esthetic-
expressive(354). Habermas would like to strike a balance among
the highly differentiated media of human self-actuali- zation:
language, work, love, recognition, and national and
international community. Against the background of Habermas's
theory of communicative praxis a new equilibrium between some
religious truths to be retrieved from otherwise allegedly
obsolete traditional worldviews and secular truths intrinsic
to the modern systems of interpretation and orientation should
not be entirely impossible. This had been the purpose already
of Hegel's philosophy of religion and beyond that, of his
whole philosophy(355).

Good Life

Habermas is very much in agreement with the modern attempt to
identify a modern equivalent for what was once in the
traditional worldviews meant by the idea of the good
life(356). Today this idea is replaced by the sheer survival
of late capitalistic action systems, no matter how unjust they
are or how much their economic and political subsystems
colonize the immediate life world. But, according to Habermas,
this attempt to find an equivalent for the traditional idea of
the good life must not lead to the deduction of such an idea
from the procedural concept of discursive, communicative
rationality, with which the decentralized worldview of
modernity has left us behind. Also Habermas sees no
possibility of any reaching back to the fundamental categories
of traditional - in Hegelian terms - substantially rational
worldviews. Also Habermas can not return to Hegel's
substantial philosophy or to any of the substantial religious
worldviews sublated in it(357). Since Habermas does not think
any return to the substantial traditional or early modern
worldviews is possible, there remains for him merely the
critique of the distortions which are done to life forms in
capitalistically modernized action systems. These distortions
of life forms have come about through the devaluation of their
traditional substance and through their subordination under
imperatives of a onesided rationality, which is limited to the
cognitive-instrumental, the cognitive-functional. We should
conclude from this, that the distortions of life forms in
capitalistically modernized action systems can be corrected

only through a radical, critical reevaluation of some of the traditional substance of the life forms and the establishment of a new balance between work and tools on one hand, and of language, love, recognition, national and international community on the other. Habermas's theory of communicative praxis is the attempt to bring about a new equilibrium between instrumental and communicative rationality(358). Beyond that, political theologians try to find modern equivalents for the traditional religious message and thus to renew often in mystical terms the traditional substance of the life world of modern people(359). Thus critical theorists and political theologians cooperate more or less consciously and intentionally in correcting the distortions of life forms in late capitalistic action systems. All of this is, of course, immensely complicated and difficult. There are not only critical, but also conservative political theologians. How, e.g., is the central religious concept of "providence" to be restored critically – via a modern equivalent – after it has been distorted beyond recognition by Hitler or Reagan in their struggle against world communism: after the God who takes the powerful from their throne and sends the rich away with empty hands has been, for centuries, co-opted by and put into the service of the powerful and rich feudal and capitalistic oligarchies and thus has become the God of the owners rather than the God of the workers(360)? Critical political theologians will have to answer questions of this kind plausibly, particularly in a period in which neo-conservativism is as victorious politically as it is the case right now.

Habermas tries to base his critique of the distortions of life forms in capitalistically modernized action systems on the procedural concepts of communicative rationality(361). But, according to Habermas, this is possible only if it can be proven that the decentralization of the understanding of the world and the rationalization of the life world are necessary preconditions for an emancipated man and society. For Habermas, utopistic is only the confusion of a highly developed communicative infrastructure of possible life forms with the historical articulation of a successful life form. In his theory of communicative praxis, Habermas differentiates sharply between possible and actual life forms. he is in this respect as emphatically antiutopistic as Hegel in his philosophy of society and history(362). But what makes Habermas's theory of communicative praxis suspect of utopianism, nevertheless, is the fact that he neglects here, as in other places, the diachronical aspect of all actual as well as possible life forms, their universal finitude, their

negativity, their unavoidable destruction. The curse of all
human life forms is their finitude: therefore all true utopia
is sad(363). Unlike Hegel or Teilhard de Chardin, Habermas
does not take upon himself – at least not in theory – the
cross of the negativity of nature and of the even greater
negativity of bourgeois society and history in order this way
and only this way to discover in it the rose of reason(364).
He aims at emancipation and redemption without the cross. But
the history of freedom is also the history of suffering and
death.

Religion and Morality

Habermas takes the important concept of the rationalization of
worldviews and life worlds from Weber(365). According to
Habermas, Weber calls rationalization the cognitive separation
between right and morality, and religious worldviews: the
abstraction of moral practical insights, doctrines of right
and ethics, principles, maxims and rules of decision from
religious systems of interpretation and orientation, into
which they were originally embedded. In Habermas's view, in
any case, mythical–cosmological, religious–metaphysical and
mystical worldviews are constructed in such a way that the
internal differences between theoretical and practical reason
can   not yet have any validity. According to Habermas,
following Weber, the line of the rationalization or
autonomization of right and morality leads to the formal right
and the profane ethics of intentionality and responsibility.
Both formal right and secular ethics are systematized
contemporaneously with the modern experimental sciences. This
happens in the framework of the practical philosophy of
modernity. Rational natural law and formal ethics come into
existence(366). While Hegel sees and accepts the modern
separation between religion and morality, he still stresses,
nevertheless, the analogy between them as well as a structural
connection: between the divine Totality containing the
negative element of the crucified God and the socio–moral
totality containing the negative element of bourgeois
society(367).
    Habermas is fully aware of the fact that this process of
rationalization and autonomization of right and morality
starts still inside the traditional religious systems of
interpretation and orientation(368). The radicalization of
Jewish, Christian and other prophecies of redemption lead in
modernity to the sharp dichotomization between a search for
salvation, which is oriented in terms of internal, highly

sublimated means and goods of redemption, on the one hand, and
the knowledge of an external, objectivated world of nature, on
the other. Weber shows Habermas how the principles of an
ethics of intentionality develop out of this highly
spiritualized religiosity. This development follows from the
meaning of redemption and the nature of the prophetic teaching
of salvation as soon as it transforms itself into a rational
ethics, which is oriented according to internal religious
goods of salvation as means of redemption.

Brotherhood and Sisterhood Ethics

For Habermas, under formal perspectives this rational ethics
is characterized by the fact that it is no longer preconventional or conventional, but that it is post-conventional: it
is guided by principles and it is universalistic(369).
According to Habermas, the soteriological religiosity of the
religious community is the very ground for an abstract ethics
of brotherhood and sisterhood(370). It liquidates, in
reference to the next human being, the separation between
ingroup and outgroup morality, which is typical for the ethics
of kinship, neighborhood and state. Habermas agrees with Weber
that the challenge and the demands of the soteriological
community religiosity has always moved in the direction of an
universalistic brotherhood and sisterhood community beyond all
boundaries of the traditional social associations, often even
beyond one's own faith community. Universal brotherhood-
sisterhood is practiced today in Basic Christian Communities
in many countries(371). Brotherly-sisterly discipleship is one
of the core ideas of the most recent critical political
theology. It is precisely this truth of a universal brotherhood and sisterhood ethics which Habermas has been willing to
rescue from the allegedly obsolete traditional worldviews and
to carry over and integrate in secular form into his universal
pragmatic and theory of communicative praxis(372). What
Habermas calls the communication community characterized by
non-coercive communication is very much a secular translation
of the whole movement of Christian brotherly and sisterly
communities, beginning with the communistic early Christian
community(373). In this sense, Habermas's universal pragmatic
is a gigantic protest against the global dominion of
unbrotherliness and unsisterliness, carried and promoted by
late capitalistic action systems, in the name of an unlimited
universal brotherly-sisterly communication community. That the
neo-conservatives do not understand that is quite plausibe.

What is not so plausible is that the New Left seems not to be able to understand that neither(374).

Evolution

Habermas learns from contemporary Weber scholars that Weber stands with his sociology of religion in the camp of the evolutionists(375). Weber is indeed committed to evolutionism as far as his thesis of an equally directed rationalization of all world religions is concerned. This is the case in spite of the fact that Weber is in general rather sceptical in relation to laws of progress. Weber ascribes to the internal validity claims of religious worldviews and their autonomous logical evolution empirical effectiveness. The development of religious systems of interpretation follows a rational cogency. The genesis of religion contains a progress in terms of rationality. There is a specific learning process, which stretches through the whole evolution of the great world religions.

Habermas agrees with Weber and the most recent Weber scholarship, that the rational cogency which the religious worldviews follow in their evolution results from the need to receive a rational answer to the theodicy problem(376). The stages in the development of the world religions consist of the always more explicit comprehension of the theodicy problem and its solution. The process in which the mythical thinking of the primitive and archaic tribal religions is step by step rationalized through and is finally, via the religious-metaphysical and mystical worldviews of historical intermediate action systems, transformed into a universalistic brother-hood-sisterhood ethics of intentionality – i.e., ethicized, in modern action systems – produces continually new ideas concerning the solution of the theodicy problem. Long before Weber and Habermas, Hegel saw the whole development of religious worldviews as a theodicy(377). In this context Habermas's own thesis that mythical, religious-metaphysical and mystical systems have become obsolete appears in a new light. It could simply mean that once more the extant religious worldviews are not any longer able to give an adequate answer to the theodicy problem. Thereby another epoch in the evolution of religion has come to its end. But this could also mean that a new epoch with a better answer to the theodicy problem could begin. The obsolescence of religion would not be absolute, but merely relative. Habermas does not take this possibility seriously enough.

Structural and Material Aspects

Habermas, following Dobert and other Weber scholars, criticizes Weber for not sufficiently differentiating between the
material problematic of the theodicy, according to which the
rationalization of religious worldviews takes place, and the
structures of consciousness, which arise from the ethicization
of the religious systems of interpretation and
orientation(378). While the contents of the religious
worldviews mirror the different solutions of the theodicy
problem, so Habermas argues, the structural aspects become
manifest at the positions people are taking toward the world.
These positions are determined through formal world concepts.
As Habermas separates in this way structural from material
aspects of the religious worldviews, he is able to analyze the
playing-together of ideas and interests on the basis of the
material carried together in Weber's sociology of religion.
    Habermas is able to prove on the basis of Weber's
sociology of religion, that the paths of religious rationalization which branched off on the level of high cultures, do
indeed from their beginnings in myth to the threshhold of the
modern understanding of the world proceed from the same
problem: the theodicy problem(379). Furthermore, Habermas can
prove, on the basis of Weber's sociology of religion, that the
religious rationalization points towards the same direction of
a disenchanted understanding of the world, which is purified
from mythical and magical conceptions. Habermas points out
that only the occidental path of the evolution of religions
leads to a completely decentralized and secularized worldview.
Beyond this, Habermas assumes that the direction of the
development of the religious worldviews can be explained by
the autonomy of the core problem, the theodicy problem, and
the structures of the worldviews. The material
characterization of the structurally circumscribed
possibilities must be reduced to external psychological,
social, economical, and political factors. Out of his
assumption, Habermas gains a clear methodological
delimitation. According to Habermas, the work of the rational
reconstruction of the evolution of religious worldviews
extends to the internal connections of meaning and validity.
This work has the aim to order the structures of the religious
worldviews in terms of a developmental logic and the contents
in terms of a typology. For Habermas, the empirical, i.e., in
the narrower sense sociological, analysis of the development
of religious worldviews is directed towards the external
determinants of their contents and towards questions of the

dynamic of their evolution.

More precisely, according to Habermas, the sociological analysis of the development of religious worldviews is directed towards the following very specific questions concerning its dynamic(380). The sociologist would like to know what conflicts, which overdemand the structurally-limited interpretative capacity of an existing religious worldview, look like, and how they can be identified. He would like to explore in which socioculturally caused conflict situations a theodicy problematic comes typically into existence. The sociologist would like to find out who are the social carriers of the charismatic breakthrough or the rationalization of a new worldview. He would like to see in which social strata a new worldview is received and in which sector of society the new worldview orientates most effectively and to what extent people put it in their everyday praxis. The sociologist would like to discover to what extent new worldviews must be institutionalized in order to make possible a legitimate social order: if this must happen only inside elites or if it can happen also inside a total population. Finally, the sociologist would like to find out how the interests of the carrier strata guide the selection of the contents of the worldview.

Riddles

It is obvious that the sociologist is not a theologian or a philosopher and that he is therefore as such not interested or able to solve the riddles of God's providence as such, which are presented by nature and more still by society and history(381). Also it is characteristic for the critical theorists in general and for Habermas in particular, that they, contrary to Hegel, do remain standing rather melancholically in the more or less empty and sterile sublimity of the merely negative result, that history is nothing else than a huge Golgotha and slaughterhouse in which virtuous individuals, as well as happy nations and wise states, are senselessly sacrificed. For Horkheimer, in the face of the suffering of this world and its injustice, it is impossible to believe in the dogma of the existence of an almighty and all benevolent God(382). According to Habermas, in the face of the repetitive most outrageous and barbarous injustices, we must learn to live without consolation and we may even have to unlearn our need for consolation(383). Thus it is possible that the unresolved theodicy problem appears in Habermas's formal and universal pragmatic in the form of a new aporia:

the contradiction between unconditional recognition and annihilation in interaction and intersubjectivity(384). This aporia threatens the very core of Habermas's concept of universal communicative ethics and universal solidarity. This solidarity can be universal only if it includes also the innocent victims, who have been annihilated, often precisely because they were committed to such solidarity. But these innocent victims can be brought into universal solidarity only if they are not merely annihilated, but also rescued. It is here, where the political theologians refer against the aporetical aspect of Habermas's theory of communicative praxis to experiences of the Buddhist, Jewish, Christian or other religious traditions, which offer a resolution to the theodicy problem, which secular sociology and philosophy can not provide: e.g., the hassidic or kabbalistic theodicy and its struggle against melancholy and its consolation(385). Habermas is aware of this aporetical aspect of his theory of communicative praxis. He is willing to discourse on this problem with critical political theologians. He is willing to listen to Jewish mysticism as mediated to him by Benjamin and Scholem and to other religious answers to the theodicy problem.

Suffering

Habermas concentrates not only on the form but also on the content of Weber's sociology of religion(386). Weber has explored four of the great world religions: Chinese religion, Hinduism, Buddhism and Judaism(387). Weber was not able to complete his studies on Christianity and Islam which he had planned. Weber was engaged in a comparative study of the world religions. But according to Habermas, it is only at a few points that Weber condenses the comparative representation of the world religions to systematic comparisons. That happens particularly in the introduction of his sociology of religion, the excursion and the final chapter 8, on the Chinese religion(388). When Habermas takes into consideration only the most general perspectives in Weber's sociology of religion, he notices that he differentiates the religious worldviews, which all start from the common theodicy problem, particularly in the dimension of the representation of God, personal creator-God versus impersonal cosmic order, and in the dimension of orientation of action and salvation, affirmative versus negative attitude toward the world.

According to Habermas, in terms of Weber's sociology of religion the rationalization process of the world religions starts contentwise with a theme which is common to all of

them: the question concerning the justification of the unequal
distribution of earthly goods and happiness among people(389).
For Habermas this is the most fundamental ethical problematic.
It explodes the boundary of all myths(390). It results from
the need for a religious explanation for the suffering of the
people which is perceived to be unjust. That a person can
perceive his or her own personal misfortune as unjust needs,
first of all, a transvaluation of suffering. This is
necessary, since in the myths of the primitive and archaic
tribal societies, suffering was seen as a symptom of secret
guilt. The suffering person was possessed by a demon or was
burdened with the anger of a god, whom he or she had offended.

In general, so Habermas argues, following Weber, the
cults of tribal societies were directed toward the management
of collective contingencies(391). They did not aim at the
mastering of an individual's particular fate. What is new on
the evolutionary level of historic-intermediate and modern
societies is the idea that individual misfortune can hit a
person without his or her own fault, sin or guilt. New is the
idea that the individual person can have the religious hope to
be redeemed from all evils, from illness, want, poverty, even
from death. New is also the formation of religious communities
independent from ethnic associations. This religious community
arrangement aims at the salvation fate of the individuals. The
messages and promises of the religious communities turn toward
the masses of individuals who are in need of redemption. The
care of the souls is instituted. Now it becomes the typical
function of magicians and priests to identify the causes for
people's suffering. Sins are to be confessed. Sins are first
of all violations of ritual commandments. Counselling takes
place. Magicians and priests must show by what kind of
behavior suffering can be removed. The material and ideal
interests of magicians and priests can enter more and more the
service of plebian motives. Religion moves to the side of the
suffering people. This happens today emphatically in Latin
America, but also in the USA, where e.g. Lutheran churches in
the area of Pittsburgh have sided with the unemployed workers
against the "corporate evil," particularly the banks(392).

Here Habermas discovers a sociological explanation, which
Weber does not pursue any further(393). Habermas goes beyond
Weber, when he states that the new evaluation of individual
suffering and the appearance of individual needs for
salvation, do not fall from heaven. They make the question
concerning the ethical meaning of meaningless suffering into
the starting point of a religious thinking, which goes beyond
local myths. That does not just happen accidentally. According

to Habermas, this re-evaluation of personal suffering and the
appearance of individual needs for redemption are the result
of learning processes, which come into motion as soon as the
ideas of justice, which are established in primitive and
archaic tribal societies, clash with the new reality of high-
cultural class societies(394). Habermas goes beyond Weber's
positivistic sociology of religion in terms of a reconstructed
dialectical-materialistic theory of religion. In terms of
Habermas's historical materialism, we may anticipate that the
theodicy problem will largely disappear with the disappearance
of class societies and their injustices. But there are, of
course, also contingencies, which will occur even in the
classless communication community. Here theodicy turns into
anthropodicy: at stake is now no longer the justice of God but
rather the justice of man(395).

Prophets

According to Habermas's reconstructed historical materialistic
theory of religion, world religions develop without exception
in high cultures(396). That means that the world religions
develop in class societies, which are organized on the basis
of a state. In such politically organized class societies new
modes of production and corresponding forms of economic
exploitation come into existence, which are independent from
the system of family and kinship groups. Habermas admits in
relation to Weber that the conflict-potential arising from the
high-cultural politically organized class societies had, of
course, first of all to be set free by prophets(397). This was
necessary, in order to pull the masses of the people, who were
still held captive by magic and fetishism and myths into
religious movements of an ethical character. Habermas is able
to integrate the positive insights of Weber concerning the
function of the Judeo-Christian prophets into his own historical-materialistic theory of religion.
    Weber's sociology of religion does not, like Hegel's dia-
lectical philosophy or even still Horkheimer's critical
theory, contain a theology or, more specifically, a
theological theodicy(398). All theologies are at least
latently theodicies. In its original theological sense,
theodicy (theos dikae) means the affirmation of God's justice
in the face of the injustice, the evil which dominates the
world(399). Contrary to this, Weber understands under theodicy
any theoretical effort to explain suffering on this
earth(400). In the Weberian sense also the teaching of Marx
can be seen as a theodicy(401). In the Weberian sense also

Habermas's   reconstructed   historical   materialism   is   a
theodicy(402).   But   Habermas   is   a   philosopher   and   a
sociologist: he is not a theologian and he does not want to be
one, though he is open for   discourse   with   theologians.   His
theory   of   communicative   praxis   is   a   philosophical   and
sociological, rather than a theological theodicy.   While   all
theologies   are   theodicies,   not   all   theodicies   are
theologies(403).

In Habermas's dialectical-materialistic perspective,   the
world   religions   try   to   satisfy   the   rational   interest in
material and ideal equality   in   the   face   of   the   evidently
unequal   distribution of earthly goods and happiness among men
and women,   particularly   those   living   in   class   societies,
through   explanations,   which   are sufficient for increasingly
systematic rational demands(404). Habermas agrees   with   Weber
that there was alive always in the world religions an attitude
toward   something   in   the   real   world,   which was felt to be
specifically meaningless. Also there was always present in the
world religions the demand that the structure of the world   is
or ought   to   be in its totality a somehow meaningful cosmos.
This is still true for Hegel's great theological philosophy in
the midst of modernity. According to Hegel civil   society   is
the   difference   in   the socio-moral totality, its negativity,
the absence of social morality,   which   is   to,   and   will   be
superseded(405).   Nothing   else   is   the   intent of historical
materialism: the   sacrifice   or   self-sacrifice   of   bourgeois
society into the realm of freedom(406).

Habermas must admit that the world religions do not treat
the   question   concerning   the   justification   of   manifest
injustices as a purely ethical problem(407). They handle   this
question rather   as   an   integral   part   of   the theological,
cosmological and metaphysical question concerning the   justice
of   the   total   constitution of the world. The world religions
think this total world order in such   a   way   that   ontic   and
normative   aspects   are   blended   into each other. At present,
prophetic churches in the Americas and elsewhere   stress   once
more   global justice, the justice of the total constitution of
the world.

Solutions

Habermas discovers that in the framework   of   this   religious-
metaphysical order-thinking   the   world   religions found very
different solutions for the same theodicy   problem(408).   With
Weber,   Habermas   contrasts   particularly   two   categorical
strategies to solve the theodicy problem religiously.   There

is, first of all, the oriental strategy. It starts from the
representation of an impersonal, uncreated cosmos. There is,
secondly, the occidental strategy. It uses the conception of a
transcendent, personal creator-God. There is an oriental
immanent and an occidental transcendent conception of God.
There is Brahman, the God of order in Hinduism and Jahweh, the
God of action in Judaism. The believer must develop another
relationship toward the resting ground of the cosmic order
than toward the transcendent God of creation and liberation.
In the oriental strategy the believer understands himself as
vessel of the divinity, in the occidental strategy as God's
instrument. In the occidental strategy the believer tries to
participate in the Divine, in the occidental strategy the
believer wants to struggle for God's benevolence. It is
obvious that the differences between oriental and occidental
strategy are not always that clear-cut. Thus the occidental
mystic has, e.g., no difficulties in understanding man as
God's vessel as well(409).

Foundation

For Habermas, as for Weber, also the religious foundation of
ethics is different in the oriental and occidental
strategy(410). Habermas finds in the Asiatic religiosity the
idea of self-redemption through knowledge and in the
occidental religious tradition the idea of hope concerning
divine grace. Therefore, in the oriental tradition the cosmos
or being and in the occidental tradition the history of
salvation become the core of speculative world interpretation
and orientation of action. Habermas finds the opposition
between virtuosity and mass religiosity in all world
religions. But, according to Habermas, the oriental religions
have a greater affinity to the world-concept and life
experience of the intellectual strata. Habermas can not say
the same of occidental religions, in spite of Augustine,
Thomas Aquinas, Dante Alighieri, Eckehart, Nicolaus of Cusa,
Jacob Boehme, Kant, Schelling or Hegel.
      While Weber, in Habermas's interpretation, conceives the
world religions as very different solutions to the same
fundamental theodicy problems, they all move, nevertheless,
inside the same categorical play-space of religious-
metaphysical conceptions of order(411). They all blend into
each other different aspects not only of the ontic and the
normative, but also of the expressive: not only of nature and
the social world, but also of the inner and cultural world.

External Factors

Following Weber, Habermas explains the different contents of the religious worldviews with the help of external factors. Habermas thinks particularly of the psychically and socially conditioned situation of interest of those social strata, who are the carriers of the respective religious method of life in the decisive time of its formation. Here it does not matter if this carrier stratum was a literarily educated group of state officials as in Confucianism, migrating beggar-monks as in Buddhism, nature-bound farmers held captive by mythical thinking and magical praxis as in the case of medieval Catholicism, a nomadizing warrior group as in the case of Islam, or bourgeois city dwellers, e.g., artisans, merchants and home-industrial entrepreneurs, as in Protestantism. According to Habermas, these in the narrower sense socio-religious perspectives decide over the dynamic as well as the extension of the rationalization process. They also decide over the question of which selection is made from the structurally possible contents. It is obvious that the historical materialist Habermas can learn from Weber's sociology of religion concerning the connection between religion and types of work, since Weber had learned from Marx concerning the correlation between the economical and religious factor of social change and came even the closer to the Marxian base-superstructure theory on religion the older he became and the more he progressed in his own sociological work(412).

Affirmative and Negative World Attitudes

With Weber, Habermas differentiates the world religions in terms of their affirmative or negative attitude toward the world(413). Some religions motivate the believers to say "yes" to the world in its totality, others to say "no." Here Habermas does not think of active or passive attitudes toward life in the different world religions. Habermas is rather concerned with the question, if the believers evaluate the world, i.e., the surrounding world of nature, their own inner world, and the social and cultural world fundamentally positively or negatively; if these four worlds have for the believers an intrinsic positive value or not.

Habermas is aware of the fact that a negative attitude toward the world is, of course, only possible through that dualism which characterizes the radical religions of redemption. For Hegel, Zoroastrianism was the first of these

radically   dualistic   religions(414).   Hegel   showed   the
connection   between   dualistic   Zoroastrianism   and   later
religions   of   redemption   and   even   with   the   fundamentally
dualistic Kantian philosophy. The negative attitude toward the
world   demands   a   worldview   structure   which de-valuates the
world, like in the oriental strategy, as the   mere   phenomenal
foreground in relation to the essential background or, like in
the   occidental   strategy,   as   historically   transitory this-
worldliness   in   relation   to   the   external   other-worldly
creator-God. In case of the oriental as well as the occidental
traditions,   Habermas   finds   as   reference   point   in   the
individual search for salvation a reality   behind   the   world,
which   has   sunk down to or descended and immersed itself into
the world of appearance.

Habermas does not agree with Weber's assumption   that   a
world-affirmative   attitude   can   be   maintained only in those
religious worldviews in which   the   mythical-magical   thinking
and acting has not yet been radically superseded and the stage
of   a, in the strict sense, dualistic system of interpretation
and orientation has not yet been reached(415). But,   according
to   the   Kantian Habermas, only in comparison of Confucianism
and Taoism with Greek   philosophy,   could   Weber   have   tested
whether   this   assumption   of his is true or, if not, whether,
then,   radical   disenchantment,   a   dualistic   structure   of
worldview   and   affirmation   of   the   world can   very well go
together. Those three elements do indeed   converge   in   Kant's
philosophy and enlightenment(416).

In Habermas's   view, in case of the convergence of these
elements in religious worldviews, the   refusal   of   the   world
does   depend   on   the radicalization of the thought of redemp-
tion(417). This radicalization of the idea of salvation   leads
to   an   intentional   religious   emphasis   and   a   contrast
reinforcement of the dualism, which is present   in   all   world
religions,   and   certainly   also   in   many world philosophies,
e.g., Platonism and Kantianism(418). For   this   radicalization
of the thought of redemption, Weber offers to Habermas again a
sociological explanation. Weber points to the social conflicts
which   bring   about   the   appearance   of   prophets(419).
Particularly   mission-prophecies   favor,   as   e.g.,   in   the
Judeo-Christian tradition, an especially radical this-worldly/
other-worldly   split and, correspondingly, consequent forms of
world-refusal. Habermas finds this explanation acceptable.   It
conforms   to   his historical-materialistically oriented formal
and universal pragmatic and theory of communicative praxis.

Legitimation

Habermas engages in his formal universal pragmatic in a paradigm change(420). He shifts in his theory of communicative praxis from the medium of work and tools to the medium of recognition, from forms of objectivity to forms of understanding, from subject-philosophy to philosophy of intersubjectivity. The old philosophy of subjectivity starts from the fundamental relationship between a knowing and acting subject, and the realm of perceivable objects which can be manipulated and instrumentalized. In the philosophy of intersubjectivity, the formal properties of the intersubjectivity of possible understanding take the place of the conditions of objectivity of possible experience. For Habermas, forms of understanding always constitute a compromise between recognition and work, between the universal structures of understanding-oriented action and the compulsions of economic reproduction, which are not available thematically in a certain given life world, in the framework of a certain given action system. For Habermas the historically varying forms of understanding constitute, so to speak, the cutting edge, which comes into existence where systemic compulsions of the material reproduction intervene unnoticeably into the forms of social integration itself and thereby possibly colonize the life world.

Habermas illustrates the concept of the forms of understanding through those high cultural class societies in which religious-metaphysical worldviews take over ideological functions. Here ideology is understood in the critical sense of false consciousness, necessary appearance, rationalization of irrational power conditions(421). Habermas wants to gain from these illustrations the analytical perspectives for a systematic sequence of forms of recognition, interaction, intersubjectivity, and understanding. Here our main concern is the ideological or legitimating function of religious-metaphysical worldviews.

According to Habermas's dialectical-materialistic perspective, in politically organized class societies there comes into existence a deep need for legitimation(422). Such a need for legitimation could not yet exist in primitive and archaic tribal societies for structural reasons: mainly, lack of class antagonism. In Habermas's view, the systems of institutions of primitive and archaic societies which are organized on the basis of kinship-groups are anchored in rituals. They have their foundation in a praxis which explicates itself in mythical narratives. Such praxis stabilizes its normative validity out of itself. Contrary to these conditions in primitive or archaic action systems, the validity of laws in which a political total order, a state, including society and family, articulates itself, must first of all be guaranteed by the sanction-power of a king. But the political domain in archaic, historic-intermediate or modern action systems has social-integrative power only to that extent to which the disposition over the means of sanction does not rest on naked repression, but rather on the authority of an office, which for its part is anchored in the sphere of recognition or order of right. Therefore, argues Habermas, laws need the intersubjective recognition of the citizens of the state. These laws must be legitimated. Thereby the world of culture receives the task to give good reasons why the extant political order deserves recognition. The mythical narratives explicate a ritual praxis and make it understandable. But these mythical stories are themselves an integral part of this liturgical praxis. Contrary to this, the religious and metaphysical worldviews of prophetic origin have the form of teachings, which can be intellectually worked out. These teachings explain and justify an extant order of dominion in the framework of the world order, which they make explicit.

According to Habermas, the legitimation need, which originates from the structure of human action systems, particularly the societal structure, is especially precarious in high cultural class societies(423). When Habermas compares the old historic-intermediate civilizations with strongly hierarchical primitive or archaic tribal societies, he very clearly notices an increase in social inequality. In the framework of historic-intermediate or modern states dissimilarly structured units can be specified functionally. As soon as the realm of work and tools, the organization of social reproduction is uncoupled from kinship group relations, economic resources can more easily be mobilized and can be more effectively combined. But there is a price to be paid for this economic progress. The uncoupling of the economic subsystem from the familial subsystem in historic-intermediate and modern action systems and societies and the consequent extension of the material reproduction, must be bought with the transformation of the familial stratification system into stratified class society. This is, indeed, a high price to be paid for economic progress.

According to Habermas, under system integrative aspects this economic progress represents itself as integration of society on the level of a broadened material reproduction. But

under social integrative aspects this same economic progress
means an escalation of social inequality. It means the massive
economic exploitation and juridically covered-up repression of
the dependent classes. Habermas finds in the history of the
penal code and penal procedure of historic intermediate action
systems clear indicators for the high degree of repression
which the old civilizations without exception needed in order
to stabilize themselves. The crosses on which the 10,000
followers of Spartacus, who had fallen in battle for
liberation, and Jesus and some of his disciples and followers
were crucified, is one such indicator in the historic-
intermediate Roman action system(424).

Class Struggle

Habermas knows of social movements in historic-intermediate
action systems which, under social-structural perspectives,
can very well be analyzed as class struggles(425). This
remains true even if the participants did not engage in these
social wars as class struggles per se. These revolutionary
movements threaten the social integration. Therefore, so
Habermas argues in historical materialistic perspective, the
functions of exploitation and repression, which the office
authority of the King and the ruling class fulfill in the
systematic connection of the material reproduction, must be
kept latent as much as possible. The religious worldviews must
become ideologically effective. They must legitimate the king
and the ruling class and their repressive and exploitative
function. Feudal Christianity had this ideological
legitimating role to play in the historic-intermediate Western
medieval action system(426). Bourgeois Christianity fulfills
this same ideological, legitimating function to this day in
liberal and advanced capitalistic action systems(427).

On Wednesday, August 23, 1984, Pope John Paul II banned
Marxist "class struggle" in church support for the poor and
oppressed, stepping up the Vatican's efforts to reign in
leftist priests in the Third World and elsewhere(428). It was
the pope's most explicit statement in years against liberation
theology challenge to Vatican orthodoxy and ortho-praxis. The
pope warned that he would not tolerate the fundamental Marxist
principle of class struggle, evident in many Christian
movements aiding the poor. The forms in which the Christian
solidarity with the poor is realized, so the pope states, can
not be dictated by an analysis of "class distinctions" and
"class struggle."

Such statements are an attempt by the pope to interpret

away the fact of class distinctions and class struggle in spite of the fact that the hierarchy at least since Constantine has continuously participated in such conflict and usually not on the side of the poor, but rather on the side of slaveholders, feudal lords and owners of capital in theory as well as in praxis(429). Bishops like Archbishop Romero, martyr for the poor of Salvador, have been the exception through the centuries(430). By his statements John Paul II serves well, consciously or unconsciously, intentionally or unintentionally, the desperate legitimation needs of action systems characterized by democratic or authoritarian state capitalism in Latin America, South Korea, the Philippines, Africa, etc. In any case, the pope is far removed not only from Spartacus, but from Jesus as well. The cross on which Jesus was executed by the Roman class state and which the pope continuously carries with him, was the most cruel weapon in the hands of the slaveholders to control their insurgent slaves: an instrument of class struggle. The God of Jesus is a God of the workers, not of the owners.

Through the centuries, to be sure, the type of master has changed: the feudal lords have replaced the slave holders; the owners of capital have taken the place of the feudal lords. But the master-servant relationship as such remained(431). Critical Christians and critical theorists agree on this point(432). Also both agree that religion as such is more than mere ideology, legitimating unjust power structures. There is good and bad religion(433). There can be good religion: it can contain rational, liberating, utopian demands, e.g., by Jewish prophets and Jewish and Christian mystics(434). Class distinctions and class struggle are in process of becoming the criterion by which to differentiate between good and bad religion.

Long before Habermas, Hegel, Marx and Horkheimer pointed out the ideological, legitimating function of religion for repressive and exploitative human action systems(435). But in his critique of this ideological function of religion, following Hegel and Marx, Horkheimer starts from the insight that in the notion of God there was for a long time preserved the representation that there are still criteria other than those which nature and society express in their effectiveness(436). According to Horkheimer, the recognition of a transcendent being receives its strongest power from people's discontent with their earthly fate. In religion are deposited the wishes, longings and indictments of innumerable generations. For Habermas as little as for Hegel, Marx and Horkheimer before, religion is not entirely ideology and completely legitimation of the repressive and exploitative functions of kings and ruling classes: it is also the outcry of the oppressed for justice and the heart of a heartless world.

But also Horkheimer must admit even late in his life that in Western historic-intermediate and modern action systems the more Christianity brought into consonance God's world government with the bloody this-worldly happenings, the more the meaning of religion was perverted(437). Already Catholicism saw in God in certain respects the creator of the extant earthly order. Up to John XXIII the popes considered in their social encyclicals the medieval and modern class societies as a providential arrangement. Protestantism reduces the course of the world straightaway to God's almighty will. Thereby the churches do not only transfigure the unjust earthly regimes with the appearance of divine justice, but they also pull divine justice down into the foul and irrational conditions of reality. To the extent to which Christianity became, from Constantine on, the ally of the mechanical state, to that extent it has lost the cultural function to give expression to high ideals: freedom, justice, equality, solidarity, the good life. Up to the present, much of Christendom has still not yet learned from Hegel the great historical-philosophical principle, that God's eternal reason has determined also the great revolutions of world history as steps in man's liberation(438).

But contemporary critical political theologians reject particularly this role of Christianity to legitimate ideologically the exploitation and repression in politically organized historic-intermediate and modern class societies, with which Habermas is concerned(439). According to political theologians, churches are to play, rather, the dangerous role of a critical instance in modern action systems. Churches should no longer console the faithful over their bad earthly conditions with reference to a transcendent paradise. Churches should become carriers of revolution. This is not only wishful thinking on the part of critical theologians. While there is still everywhere a bourgeois service-church, which is overadapted to the functional requirements of late capitalistic action systems and tries hard to overcome their legitimation deficiency, there are also Basic Christian Communities, which are engaged in social revolutions for justice, equality, and universal solidarity or are in preparation to do so and this not only in Latin America, but also in the USA, Holland, West Germany, Philippines, in African states, and elsewhere(440). The concern with the

ideological and legitimating function of religion must not
lead to a situation in which its truth claims can no longer
adequately be discussed. Sociologism must be avoided in the
realm of religion as well as in the dimensions of art and
philosophy(441). Not every theodicy must necessarily be
ideology. There may be a theodicy which is true. To be sure,
it would have to prove itself precisely in the context of
national and international class struggle.

Privatization

Weber has shown, nevertheless, to Habermas, that the great
world religions are dominated by one all-embracing theme: the
question of the legitimacy of the unequal distribution of
earthly possessions and happiness among people(442). In
Habermas's view, the occidental theocentric worldviews develop
theodicies in order to reinterpret people's need for a
religious explanation of human suffering, which is perceived
as being unjust, into an individual need for salvation and
thereby to satisfy it. The further rationalization of
theocentric worldviews turns into their privatization. This
privatization reaches its peak in bourgeois Christendom in the
late capitalistic action systems(443). It is fought
passionately by critical political theology(444).

Dichotomic Structure

According to Habermas, the oriental cosmocentric worldviews
offer equivalent solutions for the same legitimation problem:
the inequality of human happiness chances(445). In Habermas's
perspective all oriental and occidental religious and
metaphysical worldviews have in common their more or less
sharply characterized dichotomic structure. This dualistic
structure of all worldviews allows the believers to relate the
sociocultural life world to a background world. The world
behind the visible world of the here and now and of
appearances represents a fundamental order. The dualistic
religious and metaphysical worldviews can take over
ideological, legitimating functions, if and when they are able
to represent the orders of historic-intermediate and modern
class societies as homologies of this world-order in the
background, beyond the immediate facts and appearances: the
foreground world as a mere doubling up of the background
world. According to Habermas, the world religions permeate
people's low cultures and high cultures at the same time. They
owe their overwhelming effectiveness to the circumstance that

they can satisfy with the same set of assertions and promises
a need for justification on very different levels of moral
consciousness at the same time. They can do this better, the
more positivistic they are(446). Their positivism may be
latent or manifest.

Here Habermas once more overlooks what Hegel and
Horkheimer still knew: theology, if not religion in its
totality, can also mean the consciousness of the fact that the
world as such is appearance in the sense that it is not the
absolute truth and the ultimate(447). Theology can be the hope
that the injustice by which the world is characterized will
not be the last word of the human species history. Then
theology or religion can be the expression of the longing that
the murderer may at least ultimately not triumph over the
innocent victim. This is originally Christian! The Christian
hopes for justice, for the punishment of evil people and for
the infinite happiness of good people. Christians hope for
this in historic intermediate and in modern action systems.
There are Christians living in primitive and archaic action
systems today, who hope for this. This hope is not only
originally Christian, but also originally Jewish. This longing
can be found in Buddhism and Hinduism. This hope is more or
less present in one form or another in all oriental
cosmocentric and occidental theistic worldviews. This must not
be forgotten when the ideological, legitimating role of
religious systems of interpretation and orientation is
analyzed. They are not only manifestly or latently
positivistic. They do not only contain an affirmative, but
also a complementary negative critical and revolutionary
theology and metaphysics.

Limitation of Communication

For Habermas on first sight, it is indeed a great riddle how
the world religions' ideological interpretation of the world
of nature, inner world, social and cultural world could assert
itself so well over centuries in the face of the most
barbarous injustice, suffering and death(448). According to
Habermas, the compulsion of material reproduction in the
economic subsystems of historic-intermediate and modern action
systems could not have so brutally permeated the strata-
specific life worlds of high cultural societies, if the
cultural tradition, the religious worldviews, could not have
been immunized and closed up hermetically against dissonant
experiences(449). Habermas explains this invulnerability of
the world religions through structural limitations of

communication.

Habermas admits that the religious-metaphysical worldviews have had a great attraction for certain stratas of intellectuals. The religious-metaphysical worldviews have indeed challenged the hermeneutical efforts of many generations
of mandarins, bureaucrats, preachers, theologians, teachers,
and all kinds of educated lay-people. The religious-metaphysical worldviews have indeed been argumentatively worked
out to the utmost extreme. They have been put into detailed
dogmatic form. They have been systematized. They have been
rationalized out of their own motives.

But in spite of all this head and brain work, so Habermas
argues, the religious and metaphysical categories of the traditional worldviews moved on the level of rather undifferentiated validity claims. In the religious-metaphysical
worldviews the rationality potential of speech remains bound
in a stronger way than in the trivial everyday praxis, which
has not been worked out so well intellectually. Thus the
experience is explainable, that today the problem consciousness of everyday life is often far ahead of the churches and
the theologians. While the theologies are either hermetically
closed up against the historical catastrophes or simply
explain away the suffering and destruction of the innocent
victims with great intellectual effort and sophistication as
punishment, test, sacrifice for God, country or family, etc.,
the common man on the street knows, only too well, that such
explanations do have little validity and wither away in the
face of Auschwitz, Hiroshima, Vietnam, Guatemala, El Salvador,
Samosa-Nicaragua, the Shah's Iran, Lebanon, Grenada, Ethiopia,
etc., and the immense human suffering these names stand for.

Language Regulation

According to Habermas, the fundamental categories of the world
religions carry, so to speak, the burden of legitimation for
their ideological effectiveness(450). These categories are
immunized and hermetically closed up against critical objections due to a fusion of ontic, normative and expressive
aspects of validity and due to the secured fixation in cults
of a corresponding faith attitude. The critical objections
against which the religious-metaphysical worldviews are
immunized do indeed already lie in cognitive reach of everyday
communication. But the immunization of worldviews is,
nevertheless, successful after the separation between the
religious and the secular has once been completely
institutionalized in historic-intermediate and modern action

systems. This institutionalized separation between the sacred and the profane takes care and makes sure that the foundations of the religious-metaphysical worldviews are not thematized in the wrong place and in the wrong time. Religious or metaphysical problems must not be discussed in the secular realm. At the same time inside the religious realm communication remains systematically limited because of an insufficient differentiation of validity spheres, i.e., on the basis of formal conditions.

This limitation of communication on the religious side has a variety of characteristics(451). In the religious sphere speech acts are formalized. They have a fixed loudness pattern. They have an extremely limited choice of intonation. They exclude some syntactic forms. They have only a very partial vocabulary. The sequencing of the speech acts is fixed. Religious speech draws illustrations only from certain limited sources, e.g., scriptures, proverbs, psalms, etc. In the religious realm stylistic rules are consciously applied on all levels. There exists a strong language regulation.

To the contrary, on the secular side everyday speech acts are characterized by a choice of loudness as well as a choice of intonation. To the everyday secular speaker all syntactic forms are available. He or she has a complete vocabulary. On the secular side there is flexibility of sequencing of speech acts. Here only a few illustrations are taken from a fixed body of accepted parallels. No stylistic rules are consciously held to operate.

Most recently, during the 1983 visit of John Paul II to Managua, Nicaragua, 16 mothers whose children had been murdered several days earlier by Samosa-counterrevolutionaries invading from Honduras, protested against him during his mass. The mothers did so because the pope did not pay attention to the pictures of their murdered children which they carried during the pontifical mass. The pope did not seem open to the barbarous injustice which had happened to the children and their mothers. The pope seemed to hide from the suffering of the mothers and the innocent death of their children behind fixed liturgical forms. In his sermon the pope remembered the natural catastrophe in Managua, the earthquake, but not the social catastrophes of long years of political oppression and economic exploitation in Samosa-Nicaragua. The pope's sermon and cultic interaction seemed to have a counterrevolutionary ring to it, in a Nicaragua in which a socialistic revolution had gained victory with Christian support. The protest of the mothers spread all over the plaza of Managua, where the pope celebrated his mass and where there stood still all the signs which welcomed him with most beautiful childlike and joyful images. The general protest on the plaza of Managua during the pontifical mass did not need any instigation by the Sandinista government or the Basic Christian Communites. It was a rather spontaneous explosion of the usual doctrinal and liturgical incapsulation of the theodicy problem. The protest of the mothers and the masses was directed against a pope who seemed in his religious speech acts not to be on the level of the secular Nicaraguan everyday problem–consciousness and seemed to justify the inequality and injustice of Nicaraguan class society, which the Sandinista revolution intends to overcome.

Reason and Religion

Hegel made a most powerful attempt to break through the institutionalized barrier between the religious and the secular, which makes successful the immunization of the fundamental categories of religious worldviews against critical objections and to reconcile reason with religion(452). But it was obvious to Hegel himself that his reconciliation between the sacred and the profane did not reach into the realm of everyday communication. This reconciliaton was sociologically partial. It had no sociological universality. For Hegel, philosophy and theology were a separate sanctuary. Its servants form an isolated priesthood, which must not go together with the bourgeois world. It must protect the possession of the truth. Hegel leaves it to the temporal, empirical present, the everyday life world and communication, how it can find its way out of the contradiction between the religious and the secular and how it can constitute itself. It is not the task of theology or philosophy to find for the common man a way out of this dilemma.

Following Hegel on the Hegelian Left, critical theorists like Horkheimer, Adorno, Benjamin, Lowenthal, Marcuse, Fromm and Kracover have broken through the institutionalized boundary between the religious and the secular(453). They have thematized religious issues like God, original sin, second commandment, prophets, Jesus, messiah, love, justice, redemption and salvation on the secular side. They have recognized progressive humanistic theologians and have been recognized by them(454). Following Hegel on the Hegelian Left, political theologians like Tillich, De Chardin, Kogon, Dirks, Metz, Peukert and Arens have broken through the institutionalized boundary between sacred and profane from the religious side(455). They have penetrated the theory of science and the theory of action and use their categories in defense of reli-

gious truths. They can not free themselves from the view of
the innocent victims of the past, the present or the future:
they take these victims extremely seriously(456). They look
for new non-ideological solutions of the old theodicy problem
in theological and sociological terms. These theologians are
engaged in open discourse inside and outside the church. There
are also today Basic Christian Communities in Central America,
Germany, Poland, Holland and elsewhere, whose every- day
problem-consciousness is quite high(457). Their partici- pants
discourse theological-political themes on the level of
everyday communication quite freely and openly. They carry the
bible in one hand and the newspaper in the other. They
conjugate anew the religious and the secular, revelation and
reason, redemption and emancipation. Instead of legitimating
the barbarous injustices of modern class societies ideologically, the members of Basic Church Communities work and
fight hard to overcome them, often sacrificing their lives for
the universal solidarity they propose(458).

Form of Understanding

According to Habermas, in general, nevertheless, the mode of
legitimation in high cultural, historic-intermediate and modern class societies is based on a form of understanding which
limits systematically the communication possibilities through
insufficient differentiation among validity claims(459).
Habermas hierarchizes the mythical, religious-metaphysical,
mystical and modern worldviews according to the degree of
decentralization of world understanding, which makes them
possible. Likewise, Habermas categorizes the orientations and
realms of action determined by the reality-interpretations of
those worldviews, according to the degree of differentiation
of the validity claims. This way Habermas reaches the relative a priori of the forms of understanding which are dominant
in human action systems at a certain point of social
evolution. Habermas admits that the structures of the dominant
worldviews do, of course, not reflect themselves symmetrically
in these forms of understanding as well as of recognition,
interaction and intersubjectivity. The established systems of
interpretation and orientation do not permeate with equal
intensity all realms of action and interaction. According to
Habermas, in high cultural historical-intermediate and modern
class societies the form of understanding receives its
immunizing power from a proper, structurally describable
falling level between two realms of action: the religious and
the secular. The sacred orientations of action have a greater

authority in relation to the profane orientations of action.
This is so, Habermas insists, in spite of the fact that in the
religous realm of action the sphere of validity is less
differentiated and also the rationality potential is
actualized to a lesser degree than is the case in the profane
realm of action.

Early Modernity

In Habermas's view, the cultural traditions of early modern
action systems show, that even in them the validity claims are
not yet completely differentiated(460). Habermas admits that
in early modern action systems independent cultural spheres of
values are formed. But first of all, only natural science is
institutionalized unambiguously under the aspect of precisely
one validity claim: truth. Art becomes autonomous: under the
validity aspect of beauty. But it retains its aura, as
Benjamin has shown, for centuries(461). The enjoyment of art
remains contemplative in character. This is so, Habermas
explains following Adorno, because of the religious, i.e.
cultic origin of art(462). The ethics of intentionality
remains connected with the context of faith traditions, no
matter how subjectivated they become. The post-conventional
ideas of right are still coupled up in the rational natural
law with religious truth claims. They constitute the core of
what, today, the neo-conservatives Bellah and Lubbe call state
or civil religion(463). It is particularly strong in the USA
and in West Germany.

There is no doubt that in the culture of early modern
action systems right, morality, art, and science already
constitute differentiated realms of value. But they do not
abstract themselves completely from the sacred realm as long
as their internal development does not yet take place
unequivocally under precisely one specific aspect of validity.
Habermas goes so far as to say that in modern action systems
the forms of religiosity on their part have by now given up
their fundamental dogmatic claim(464). They themselves destroy
their own religious-metaphysical background world. They themselves no longer pose the profane this-worldliness in terms of
a dichotomy against religious transcendence, the world of
appearances against the reality of an underlying being. This
is particularly true of liberal theology(465).

According to Habermas with the disintegration of the
Catholic church into a plurality of confessions and a large
number of denominations, sects and cults at the beginning of
modernity, membership in the community of believers loses its

exclusivity(466). It also loses its rigid institutional character. In early modern action systems the principle of tolerance and the principle of the voluntarity of religious associations becomes universally recognized.

Late Modernity

In Habermas's view in most recent times theological tendencies have gained influence, which explicate the Christian message of salvation in a radically this-worldly way(467). They level off the radical dualism of the traditional religious-metaphysical worldviews. God signifies almost only a communication structure. This communication structure makes it necessary for the participants to elevate themselves beyond the accidentality of their merely external existence on the basis of their mutual recognition of their personal identity. Habermas thinks here particularly of the new critical political theologies(468). He often does not see how they really do differ from his own theory of communicative praxis. These theologies seem to be nothing else than another version of a theory of communicative action. But that Habermas is not entirely correct in this becomes obvious as soon as the political theologians point to the aporia of the theory of communicative praxis in terms of mutual unconditional recognition between the one and the other and annihilation of the one or the other in interaction and intersubjectivity and try to overcome it in terms of corresponding experiences in the Judeo-Christian tradition(469). Metz, Peukert and Arens reject any attempt to make out of political theology merely another theory of communicative praxis.

For Habermas such trends of this-worldliness in the religious worldviews of late modern human action systems signify a development, in which nothing will be left of the universal world religions than merely a core construct of a universalistic brotherhood-sisterhood morality(470). In this process the mystical elements which arise from an inactive, fundamentally contemplative experience and which are not yet superseded in an universalistic ethics seem to split themselves off. The consequence of this development is that the split between an ego-identity, which is formed in universalistic structures, and a collective identity connected with nation and state is unavoidable. In late modern action systems the disunion of the socio-moral totality, in which every individual has the possibility to see in the infinite independence of the other individual the complete union with him or her, becomes definite(471). But thereby it becomes also

possible that in the secular realm action structures can   form
themselves which are determined by an unlimited differentiation of validity claims on the level of language and
recognition, argumentation and interaction(472).
    Here, according to Habermas, the syndrome of validity
claims differentiates itself on the level of language, of
discourses. The particpants of everyday communication can hold
apart not only the pragmatic fundamental attitudes, but in
principle also the levels of language and recognition,
discourse and interaction. There are secular realms of action
which are normed by positive laws. They are connected with
post-traditional institutions of right. They presuppose that
the participants are in the position to go over from naively
executed actions to reflectively directed argumentation. Now,
in late modern action systems the critical potential of the
ideal speech situation can be mobilized against the extant
institutions to the extent to which the hypothetical
discussion of normative validity claims is institutionalized.
The communicatively acting subjects, so Habermas claims, do,
of course, still encounter, like in the past, legitimate
orders as something normative. But in modern action systems
this normativity changes its quality to the extent in which
institutions are no longer legitimated per se through
religious and metaphysical worldviews.
    For Habermas, following Horkheimer, the religious realm
of action dissolves itself to a large extent with the
enfolding of late modern action systems(473). Religion loses
at least its function, its structure-forming significance. On
the level of a completely differentiated sphere of validity,
art strips itself from its cultic origin. Right and morality
abstract themselves from their religious and metaphysical
background. The cultural value-spheres separate themselves
sharply from each other in the process of the secularization
of the bourgeois culture in late capitalistic action systems.
The value spheres develop in terms of a validity-specific
autonomy. Thereby culture, particularly religious worldviews,
loses the formal properties which made it possible for it to
take over ideological functions and to legitimate the late
capitalistic action system and class society. To the extent to
which these tendencies assert themselves, the structural force
of the functional requirements of capitalistic action systems,
which intervenes into the forms of social integration itself,
can no longer remain latent. It can no longer hide behind the
falling level between the religious and the secular realm of
action.
    According to Habermas the modern secular form of

understanding is too perspicuous to grant a niche for the structural power of the functional requirements of late capitalistic action systems through unconscious limitations of communication(474). Under these conditions, Habermas expects that the competition between forms of system-integration and social integration in the life world comes forth more visibly than was the case in traditional or even early modern action systems. Finally, systemic mechanisms will repress forms of social integration also in those realms where the consensus-dependent coordination of action can not be substituted. That is precisely there, where the symbolical reproduction of the life world is at stake. In this case the mediation of the life world takes the form of colonization.

Total Administration

In Habermas's view, Future I - the totally administered society - may or may not become reality(475). In it the life world will be merely one subsystem in the human action system. According to Horkheimer, theology as the longing for the Absolute, as the hope for perfect justice, may continue to exist even in the totally administered society(476). This is so, since even then, when the entirely administered society should be able to provide for more material justice than the present late capitalistic society and can even satisfy all material needs, there still remains the fact that humans must suffer and die. Maybe people will then become more conscious of this fact, precisely because their material needs will be better fulfilled in the totally administered than in the late capitalistic action system. Maybe then genuine universal brotherly-sisterly solidarity will come about. Maybe such universal solidarity can contribute to the mitigation of the disadvantages of total administration, i.e., alienation, or even to a possible transition to Future III - the reconciled society.

It is, of course, also possible that theology as the longing that the murderer will ultimately not triumph over the innocent victim will be liquidated in the entirely administered action system. Thereby disappears from the world what was once called in traditional and modern action systems "meaning." People will, of course, be very busy in the totally administered, cyberneticized action system. But their activities will be meaningless and therefore boring. They will to a large extent be pseudo-activities. People will need

drugs: pharmaceutically produced dreams as a way out of boredom. Drugs will take on the ideological, legitimating role of
the obsolete religious worldviews. Then some day, together
with theology, also philosophy will be considered as a
childhood affair of the human species. Horkheimer predicted
for the near future that people will say that any discourse
about such religious and metaphysical issues as the relationship between the relative and the Absolute, immanence and
Transcendence, are foolish. Serious theology and philosophy
will come to an end(477). The colonization of the life world
by the action system will be complete. For Horkheimer the
coming of the administered world had not yet really happened.
For Adorno the administered society had already arrived(478).
For Habermas the total colonization of the life world by
monetarization and bureaucratization is not yet a reality and
may never become one. But whoever participates today in
collective bargaining conflicts in corporations or even
universities must get the impression that Future I has moved
much closer to us than it was at the time of the death of
Adorno in 1969 or of the death of Horkheimer in 1973.

Conflict

According to Habermas, Weber considers the Christian ethics of
brotherhood as an exemplary form of a rationally worked out
ethics of intentionality(479). In Habermas's view, following
Weber, the religious brotherhood ethics is characterized by
the strictly universalistic conception of the moral principles, the form of ego—autonomous self—control on the basis
of internalized, highly abstract orientations of actions and
the model of a complete reciprocity of relationships among the
members of an ulimited communication community. Such religious brotherhood and sisterhood ethics originated out of the
new community of a soteriologically oriented communicative—
religiosity created by prophecies. This happened precisely in
such areas where the rationalization and ethicization of the
redemption religion was pushed forward with greatest consequence. Habermas has inherited and secularized the Judeo—
Christian brotherhood—sisterhood ethics and has transformed it
into his universal communicative ethics(480). This discourse
ethics is opposed to Future I — the totally administered
society — as well as to Future II — ABC wars(481). This
universal communicative ethics, in which the Judeo—Christian
brotherhood and sisterhood ethics is superseded, points to

Future III - the reconciled society(482).

For Habermas, following Weber, in the development of late capitalistic action systems the Christian communicative ethics comes into the sharpest contradiction with the inner-worldly economic and political orders of life, which are essentially hostile to brotherhood and sisterhood(483). This conflict becomes the sharper, the more thoroughly these inner-worldly capitalistic orders of life are rationalized in terms of an instrumental or functional rationality. In late capitalistic action systems the dimension of work and tools and the dimension of recognition become incompatible. The instrumental-rational capitalistic economic and political subsystems become the more impenetrable by any religious brotherhood-sisterhood ethics, the more they follow their own immanent developmental laws. The brotherhood-sisterhood ethics must necessarily produce hindrances to the formal functional rationality of the economic and political subsystems of advanced capitalistic action systems characterized by the medium of money and by the medium of power. The universalistic brotherhood-sisterhood ethics based on practical rationality clashes with the forms of economic-adminstrative instrumental rationality. Economy and mechanical state reify themselves on the basis of this functional rationality into a brotherhood-sisterhood hostile social world.

All this is no less true for Habermas's own universal communicative ethics as integral part of his universal pragmatic(484). It is no less the result of the rationalization of religious worldviews than the Christian brotherhood-sisterhood ethics. It is based on the same practical rationality as the Christian brotherhood-sisterhood ethics. Thus it clashes as much with the functional rationality of the economic and political subsystems of late capitalistic action systems. In spite of all his optimism, Habermas plays as much the role of Don Quixote in late capitalistic action systems as the other critical theorists and the critical Christians(485). He fights against what Horkheimer called the "immanent logic" of history, which points toward a totally administered society based almost completely on functional rationality(486). He does so because he believes, like Horkheimer, Adorno, and other critical theorists and critical Christians before, that brotherly-sisterly love is better than hate.(487). He thereby respects ethical postulates in the Kantian and Hegelian sense(488). But unlike Kant, Hegel, and the critical Christians of today, Habermas and the other critical theorists do not appeal to God when they follow the ethical postulates(489). They are committed to a negative theology, a negative metaphysics, a negative ethics(490).

Mysticism and Work Ethic

According to Habermas, there are only two ways in which this conflict, which is grounded structurally in the opposition of brotherliness-sisterliness and unbrotherliness-unsisterliness in late capitalistic action systems, can be mitigated(491). One way is the retreat into "acosmistic" brotherliness and sisterliness of Christian mysticism. The other way leads into inner-worldly asceticism and thereby into the paradox of the protestant work ethic(492). Habermas sees in the Protestant work ethic a form of virtuosi-religiosity. As such the protestant work ethic renounces the universalism of brotherly and sisterly love. The work ethic obligates rationally all action in the world as service to God's will. God's affirmative will is in its ultimate meaning completely un-understandable. Paradoxically enough, at the same time, God's positive will is after all alone knowable. The work ethic obligates rationally all praxis as a test of man's state of grace. Thereby the protestant work ethic accepted the reification of the capitalistic economic cosmos, which is devalued together with the whole world as creaturely and corrupt, as willed by God and as material of the fulfillment of duty(493). For Habermas, the protestant work ethic means in principle and ultimately the renunciation of redemption as a goal, which can be achieved through men and for every man. The protestant work ethic renounces universal redemption in favor of the groundless, but always particularistic grace. The work ethic took the position of unbrotherliness and unsisterliness. As such unbrotherliness and unsisterliness, the protestant work ethic was no longer in truth religion of redemption.

Habermas, following Weber, cannot formulate the grace-particularistic regression of the egocentrically short-changed ascetic protestant work ethic more sharply than by saying that its position of unbrotherliness and unsisterliness is no longer religion of redemption. The ascetic protestant work ethic adapts itself only too well to the brotherhood-sisterhood hostility of the capitalistic economy. The protestant work ethic regresses in its grace-particularism far below the level which had been reached already in the communicatively enfolded ethics of brotherhood and sisterhood as a result of

the rationalization of the Christian worldview during the
Middle Ages. Habermas criticizes Weber for not having made
this insight fruitful in theoretical terms. This is even less
understandable for Habermas, when he looks at Weber's analysis
of the further fate of the protestant work ethic in the course
of the development of the liberal and advanced capitalistic
action systems. Habermas makes this insight fruitful in his
theory of communicative praxis.

Economic and Political Subsystems

According to Habermas, the practical, moral rationalityy of
the ethics of brotherhood and sisterhood as integral part of a
religion of redemption is incompatible with the two types of
men which are characteristic for the liberal and advanced
capitalistic development: the thoughtless specialist and the
heartless hedonist(494). The modern bourgeois world is dominated by orders of life, in which the two complexes of instrumental rationality, the economic and political subsystems,
come into dominance. The specialist and hedonist are best
adapted to the icy cold atmosphere of the economic and
political subsystems of late capitalistic society based on
functional rationality and thus can best survive in them.
      These two complexes of functional rationality cooperate
in the establishment of a world dominion of unbrotherliness
and unsisterliness. The capitalistic world is at the same time
cognitive-instrumentally reified and turned into complete
subjectivism. In this bourgeois world, moral ideas, which aim
at an autonomy of the individual rooted in communicative
reconciliation, have no real chance to assert themselves. In
the capitalistc world, the ethics of brotherhood and
sisterhood does not find any hold in institutions over which
it could reproduce itself culturally in the long run. The
result is the continual reproduction of the specialist and the
hedonist as dominant, all pervasive personality types of late
civil society.
      But for Habermas, it is not only the religious ethics of
brotherhood which is destroyed in the long run between the
millstones of the two complexes of functional rationality, the
economic and political subsystems, in late capitalistic
societies and action systems(495). Also that form of ethics
which adapts itself to the icy cold lovelessness of the
reified economic and political subsystems in advanced
capitalistic society, the protestant work ethic, will be and

is already to a large extent annihilated between the two complexes of instrumental rationality. Habermas admits that the work ethic first gains institutional validity in the protestant work culture. This happens to the extent that the starting conditions for the modernization process are fulfilled. But the modernization process itself undermines retroactively the value-rational foundations of the purpose rational action. According to Weber's and Habermas's diagnosis the intentional-ethical foundations of the work orientation are swept away in favor of a utilitaristically interpreted functionalistic work attitude. It is obvious that the two complexes of instrumental rationality which destroy the Christian ethics of brotherhood and sisterhood, and even the protestant work ethic, do also constitute a deadly threat for Habermas's own project of an entirely secular universal discourse ethic(496). The functional rationality, which destroys its own basis in practical rationality, thereby also liquidates the foundation of communicative action.

Dialectic of Rationalization

According to Habermas, after the destruction of the Christian ethics of brotherhood and sisterhood and the protestant work ethic, there remains completely unfulfilled in advanced capitalistic action systems the religiously articulated need which was the driving force behind all forms of rationalization of all human action systems: the claim that - in Hegel's terms - Reason or Providence governs the world or that the course of the world should be a meaningful process at least insofar as it touches upon the interest of humans(497). For Weber and Habermas the paradox of social rationalization is the experience of the meaninglessness of the purely inner-worldly self-realization of man toward a man of culture. In modernity the cultivated man was the ultimate value, toward which culture seemed to be reducible. Auschwitz and Buchenwald, Hiroshima and Nagasaki, Leningrad, Stalingrad and Kursk, Hamburg and Dresden, London and Coventry signal the end of occidental culture and cultivated man. So do Vietnam, Chile, El Salvador, Lebanon, Grenada and Ethiopia. Barbarism is at hand!

It is obvious to Habermas that Weber's intuitions point in the direction of a selective pattern of rationalization(498). Habermas speaks of an indented profile of rationalization. But Habermas is aware of the fact that Weber did not speak of the partial character of social rationalization but, rather, of its paradoxical character. Habermas explains this by the fact that Weber finds the cause for the dialectic of rationalization in the decentralization of the religious worldviews and in the differentiation of autonomous social and cultural value spheres. For Weber this differentiation process already contains in itself the seed for the destruction of the rationalization of the world, which it makes possible in the first place.

According to Weber, the seed for destruction of the rationalization of the world is not to be found in the one-sided institutional incorporation of the cognitive-instrumental potentials, which have been set free by this rationalization process. To the contrary, Habermas would be inclined to attribute the causation of the destruction of the rationalization of the world to the onesided overdevelopment of the functional rationality potential versus the practical rationality potential, of work and tools versus recognition, interaction and intersubjectivity. Habermas is optimistic enough to believe that we can overcome the dialectic of rationalization, enlightenment and emancipation, which is the result of the decentralization of the religious worldviews and the consequent differentiation of value spheres, by bringing into a new balance the spheres of work and tools and of recognition, instrumental and practical rationality, without a new centralization of the religious worldviews or reunification of the autonomous value spheres. He is optimstic enough to believe this balancing can be achieved via a discourse ethics.

For Habermas, Weber's explanation of the dialectic of rationalization has a certain plausibility only as long as he does not take into consideration for the practical, moral complex of rationality a form of religious brotherhood-sisterhood ethics, which is secularized on the level of modern science and autonomous art(499). Habermas thinks of a communicative ethics, which is uncoupled from any religion of redemption. According to Habermas, Weber does not take into consideration such an entirely secular universal communicative ethics, because he remains fixed on the dialectical tension between the religious and the secular, the sacred and the profane. Habermas is optimistic enough to believe that he can bypass the century-old modern dichotomy between the sacred and the profane on the secular side, or even overcome it(500).

Theological Foundation

Unlike Horkheimer, Habermas believes in the possibility of developing a communicative ethics without any theological foundation(501). According to Horkheimer, all attempts to ground morality in earthly prudence rather than in reference to a Beyond, the entirely Other, rests on harmonistic illusions(502). But not even Kant has always resisted the inclination to develop morality without theological grounding(503). The Kantian Habermas's inclination to do so is even greater than that of Kant(504). According to Horkheimer, all that hangs together with morality goes ultimately back to theology(505). It is grounded in theology in the oriental as well as in the occidental tradition and strategy. Horkheimer understands theology in terms of the Jewish and Christian religion of redemption as hope for absolute justice: that the present injustice may not be the last word of history. Perfect justice is not possible without the Absolute. In spite of Habermas's Kantian temptation to develop a communicative ethics without theological grounding, a deeper understanding of his theory of communicative praxis does not only show that he is willing to inherit from the Judeo-Christian worldview the ethics of brotherhood and sisterhood in secularized form, but that he preserves even a certain interest for Judeo-Christian mysticism, particularly through Benjamin and Scholem(506).

Nothing brings Habermas closer to the contemporary critical political theology and the Basic Christian Communities, in which it has its seat in life, than his universal communicative brotherhood-sisterhood ethics and his mystical interest(507). But Habermas forgets once more in all of this that all brotherly-sisterly recognition, interaction and intersubjectivity always moves unavoidably towards its end. All brotherly-sisterly communicative praxis is finally broken by death. All forms of subjective rationality, instrumental as well as practical are continually threatened and finally destroyed by death. This aporia calls for a resolution which non-dialectical or dialectical materialism may not be able to resolve(508).

Christian Communism

The Christian communistic brotherhood-sisterhood communities broke the bread and doing so, remembered the death and the resurrection of Jesus(509). In prayer, the members of the Christian communistic communities referred to the Reality who had rescued Jesus out of his execution and annihilation as well as other innocent victims, who had been destroyed, and who would rescue them, the survivors, from their death as well. Since the innocent victims had been rescued from their destruction, the participants in the Christian communistic communities could stay in remembering solidarity with them. This is no longer possible in entirely secular communication communities, since they can not refer to the Reality who rescues innocent victims and can therefore also not rationally engage in a solidarity which is truly universal. Annihilation is the last word(510). While the Christian communistic communities combined the ethical and the mystical elements, for secular communication communities these elements fall apart. There is a price to be paid for dropping the mystical elements by the secular communicative ethics: the price of its universality.

Abolishment of Death

While Habermas does not refer to death in the context of the possibility of secular universal communicative ethics, he does so when he deals with the bourgeois materialist and enlightener Condorcet's expectation that in the further progress of the world science can not only overcome all human suffering, but that science can even liquidate death(511). Habermas does not think that Condorcet's expectation concerning death is simply a curiosum. According to Habermas, behind Condorcet's expectation hides the conception that contingency experiences and problems of meaning, which so far have been interpreted religiously and have been worked over and away cultically, can be radically mitigated in a future, more progressive world. Habermas sees very clearly that if the contingency experiences and meaning problems can not be radically mitigated by science, a rationally unresolvable rest of problems remains, which must mean a very sensitive relativization of the value of the ability to solve problems, which is based on science. This precisely is one reason for Weber's attempt to pursue the processes of social rationalization not along the line of the development of science, but rather along the line of the evolution of religious worldviews. Habermas has to face this same problem once more, as he tries to develop an entirely secular universal ethics of brotherly-sisterly communication

communities: how   will they deal with contingency experiences
and problems of meaning? How will   they   approach   the
annihilation of their own members? When Habermas himself
speaks about the death of a person concretely, he does so,
strangely enough, or not so strangely after all, in the
context of mysticism(512). It seems that the aporetic   aspects
of a purely secular universal communicative ethics lead
Habermas to refer to experiences which are present in Judeo-
Christian mysticism. Will contingency and meaning problems
force the critical theorists some day to   recouple once more
communicative ethics with mysticism and to ground it once more
in it? This is an open question. It should be held open! In
any case, ethics without salvation seems to be as irrational
in the long run as salvation without ethics. Rationality seems
to point to a new coincidence of communicative ethics and
redemption: ultimately the abolishment of death(513).

Critical and System Theory

Habermas develops his critical theory of religion in the
framework of his formal and universal pragmatic and his theory
of communicative praxis not only in critical encounter with
Weber's sociology of religion, but also with the two most
important directions in Western social philosophy: Horkheimer's critical theory of subject, society and history, and
Parsons' structural functionalism and their respective theories of religion(514). Horkheimer's critical theory carries
on the tradition of the Hegelian Left, to which also Habermas's reconstructed historical materialism belongs(515). Parsons' structural functionalism stands in the tradition of the
Hegelian Right and its positivistic successors(516).
Horkheimer stresses, like his close friend Adorno, the
dialectical notion of universal, particular and singular,
which is of theological-mystical origin(517). Following Marx,
Horkheimer, Adorno and Habermas have in their critical
theories secularized the dialectical notion and put it into
the framework of a materialistic theory of society and
history(518). Parsons rejects the dialectical notion in
Hegel's philosophy altogether and concentrates on its
analytical elements and on its conservative systemic
content(519). Until Habermas, critical theorists were so
hostile toward the Parsonian system theory that they only very
seldom even mentioned it in their critical theories. Likewise,
Parsons very rarely referred to critical theory in his

analytical work. Habermas has started a critical reception of some aspects of the Parsonian system theory(520). A deep antagonism remains, nevertheless, between critical theory and system theory. We follow Habermas as he critically works over first Horkheimer's critical theory and then Parsons' analytical theory of religion and as he, thereby, further develops his own critical theory of religion(521).

Subjective and Objective Reason

According to Habermas, Horkheimer introduces the instrumental or functional reason as subjective reason into critical theory(522). Horkheimer opposes subjective reason to objective reason. Thereby, Horkheimer gains a philosophical and socio-logical perspective, which reaches behind Hegel's theological-philosophical notion of a unity of reason, which is differentiated in itself, and even back into mythical, religious-metaphysical and mystical worldviews(523). In Horkheimer's perspective, it is not Kant's critical philosophy, but religion and metaphysics, which constitutes the real contrast to a modern consciousness, which considers alone the ability of formal, instrumental rationality to be truly rational(524). The ability of formal, functional rationality seems to be competent in calculating probailties and in the coordination of correct means with a given purpose. Formal rationality is in Hegel's terms subjective rationality, in Weberian terms purpose-rationality, in Horkheimer's terms instrumental rationality, in Habermas's terms functional rationality. Formal rationality is opposed to what Hegel calls objective or absolute rationality, Weber value-rationality, Horkheimer practical rationality, Habermas communicative rationality. Formal rationality in Habermas's sense belongs to the sphere of work and tools, practical rationality to the sphere of recognition, interaction, intersubjectivity(525).

According to Horkheimer, in the center of the traditional theory of objective reason did not stand the coordination of behavior and goals, but rather the notions which were concerned with the idea of the highest good, with the problem of human destiny; and with the modes in which the highest aim could be reached. They were notions like divine reason, providence, wisdom, plan, goal(526). In the religious-metaphysical and mystical worldviews objective reason was originally God's reason and providence(527). For Horkheimer and the other critical theorists, as for Marx and Freud before, these theological notions sound very much mystical and even mythological, if not illusionary or even delusionary, nowadays(528).

Ontological Thinking

In Habermas's view, Horkheimer's expression "objective reason" stands for the ontological thinking which for centuries has driven forward the rationalization of the mythical and religious-metaphysical systems of interpretation and orientation(529). This ontological thinking comprehended the world of men as part of a cosmological order. In Horkheimer's perspective, the philosophical systems of objective reason, of which the Hegelian philosophy was the last great one, included the conviction that men were able to discover an all-embracing or fundamental structure of being(530). Men could deduce a conception of human destiny from this structure. To be sure, not all people could do so. From Parmenides to Hegel the many were excluded from the participation in being(531). It was an esoteric issue. This prejudice did not entirely cease even with Hegel(532). Paradoxically enough, even today many people have a hard time understanding the philosophy of Horkheimer, Adorno or Habermas, in spite of their continual reference to the everyday speech situation of the common man in his everyday life world. Likewise, many people have great difficulties today understanding the newest liberal and political theologies, in spite of the fact that they try to connect themselves to Basic Christian Communities and people's everyday life world. Philosophical and theological elitism have still not yet come entirely to an end.

Disenchantment

Habermas compares Horkheimer with Weber(533). According to Weber, the religious-metaphysical worldviews constitute the background for the modern history of consciousness, for the formation of subjective instrumental reason as the dominant form of rationality. Weber read from these religious-metaphysical systems of interpretation and orientation the process of disenchantment. He saw this process of disenchantment more under the perspective of ethical than of theoretical, scientific rationalization. Horkheimer sees, like Weber, the result of this rationalization of religious-metaphysical worldviews in the fact that cultural value spheres form themselves in the

culture of liberal and advanced capitalistic action systems.
They develop autonomously. For Horkheimer, the differentiation
of the cultural spheres, their decentralization, results from
the fact that extremely formalized, internally relativistic
subjective reason replaces universal, objective, absolute
reason and absolute truth, which was the very center of the
religious-metaphysical systems of interpretation and
orientation: God's reason, providence, wisdom, plan,
telos(534). In Horkheimer's view, to this subjectivism of
reason corresponds the fact that in modern culture and action
systems morality and art as well as religion and philosophy
become irrational. At least, they appear to be irrational to
people for whom instrumental subjective reason has become the
only criterion for their actions.

Dissociation

Horkheimer and Adorno saw, according to Habermas, that the
"dark" writers of the bourgeoisie, e.g., de Sade or Masoch,
were even in the paradigmatic century of enlightenment completely aware, down to the last consequences, of the
dissociation between objective reason and morality(535). These
dark bourgeois writers did in no way pretend that the
formalistic subjective reason stands in a closer connection
with morality than with immorality, or vice versa. This is
true today of all forms of positivism, in which formalized
instrumental subjective reason finds its most adequate
expression(536). For the positivist war is as good or bad as
peace, freedom as good or as bad as slavery and
oppression(537). He can not give good reasons why he should
not hate a decent person as long as this is fun for him,
except maybe that it may be bad for business. Positivism is,
in all its forms, by definition dissociated from objective
reason(538).

   According to Horkheimer in modern action systems not only
science and morality, but also art is dissociated from objective reason(539). This dissociation makes cultural commodities out of works of art. It transforms the consumption of art
into a series of accidental feelings, which are separated from
the consumer's real intentions. It leads to the regression of
hearing, seeing and touching(540).

   The same cultural commodification happens to religion and
philosophy as they are dissociated from objective reason in
the process of modernization(541). Modernity seems to return

into the primitive age, in which subjective instrumental
reason was not yet opposed by and coupled up to any objective
and absolute reason: the age of magic and fetishism(542). The
newest has great similarity with the oldest; the most modern
with the most primitive(543).

Truth

Habermas sees a difference between Horkheimer and Weber(544).
Horkheimer differs from the positivistically oriented Weber in
his evaluation of the separation of the cognitive, normative
and expressive value spheres in modern action systems. Unlike
the sociologist Weber, the philosopher Horkheimer remembers
the emphatic notion of truth in the religious-metaphysical and
mystical worldviews. At least Weber was never systematically
concerned with this notion of absolute truth which, according
to Horkheimer, is not possible without an Absolute which
guarantees it(545). In remembrance of this absolute truth or
truth of the Absolute, Horkheimer dramatizes the inner disunion of reason into objective and subjective reason, which
for Hegel were still in differentiated unity, in two direc-
tions(546). On the one hand, Horkheimer sees the normative and
expressive culture-spheres deprived of any immanent validity
claim. In the post-Hegelian era, we can no longer speak of
moral or esthetic rationality, as Hegel still could and
did(547). On the other hand, Horkheimer, like Adorno, still
entrusts speculative, i.e, dialectical thinking, which has
been transformed materialistically into critique, in spite of
all hesitation with a restitutive power(548). According to
Habermas, Weber, like all positivists, would have considered
such restitutive power of dialectical thought to be utopian in
the bad sense. For Weber such restitutive power of the
dialectical notion would have been suspect of a false charisma
of reason.

Meaning

But in Habermas's view, Horkheimer and Weber agree, nevertheless, in the thesis that the meaning-creating unity of the
religious-metaphysical and mystical worldviews disintegrates
in the cultural development of modern action systems(549).
This loss of meaning puts into question the unity of modernized life worlds. Thereby, this loss of meaning seriously
endangers the singular personal and particular social identity

of the subjects, who are socialized in modern action systems.
Hegel had seen the beginning of this development and reacted
to it creatively by showing with the help of occidental
mysticism from Eckehart and Nicolaus of Cusa over Boehme to
Baader, a new way to reestablish the unity of singular personal, particular social, and universal religious-metaphysical
identity under conditions of complex liberal capitalistic
action systems(550). Critical theorists and positivists still
owe conclusive proof as to why this Hegelian attempt to rescue
the differentiated unity of objective and subjective reason
should be entirely without validity and should thus be
completely discarded.
      Habermas agrees with Weber's and Horkheimer's analysis of
the loss of meaning in modernity(551). The purpose of
Habermas's formal and universal pragmatic, his theory of
communicative praxis and his theory of religion, is precisely
to restore meaning and to make it possible again for subjects
living in highly differentiated modern action systems to
constitute anew their singular personal and their particular
social solidarity via, not like in Hegel's case a mystically
reconstructed Christianity, but a universal communicative
ethics, which replaces the religious-metaphysical worldviews.
In Habermas's attempt to reunite once more under conditions of
highly complex modern action systems the unity of universal,
particular and singular identity, is indeed also at work the
restitutive power of critical dialectical thinking of the
notion, which once was a theological one(552). He is not a
positivist and so far not in danger of becoming one, in spite
of his commitment to an almost entirely autonmous subjective
reason and of his high appreciation for analytical thinking as
well. If his critical dialectical thinking makes Habermas a
"utopian" thinker, then this word is to be understood in its
most original and best humanistic sense: in the Blochian
sense(553).

Traditionalism

According to Habermas, Horkheimer and Weber agree concerning
another characteristic of modernity(554). For Horkheimer and
Weber the same rationalization and disenchantment, with which
religion and metaphysics once overcame the stage of
magical-mythical thinking, has now shaken the rationalized
religious-metaphysical worldviews themselves in their very
core, namely in the credibility of their theological and

ontological-cosmological principles. Habermas agrees with this analysis. It is precisely this same rationalization and disenchantment which makes his own formal and universal pragmatic, his theory of communicative praxis, his theory of religion, his paradigm change from philosophy of subject to philosophy of intersubjectivity, from work to recognition, from functional to communicative rationality, necessary and possible. Through this paradigm change Habermas intends, finally, to transcend not only the obsolete religious-metaphysical systems of interpretation and orientation, but also Weber, Horkheimer, and Parsons, the old critical theory and functionalism.

According to Horkheimer and Weber, as Habermas sees them, the process of rationalization and disenchantment leads to a cultural situation in modern action systems, in which the religious-metaphysical knowledge, which is mediated through teaching and learning, becomes petrified and rigid in the form of dogmas: revelation and culturally transmitted wisdom transform themselves into mere "traditions"(555). Today people speak rather innocently about the Jewish, Christian or Islamic "tradition," without noticing the death warrant contained in such scientific categorization. Religious or metaphysical convictions turn into a merely subjective "holding for true." The thought-form of the religious-metaphysical worldview itself becomes obsolete. Knowledge of salvation and world wisdom dissolve into merely subjectivated forces of faith. Only now, phenomena like religious fanaticism and educational traditionalism can appear. They are at work very powerfully in the present American protestant fundmentalist debate on creationism and evolutionism. Religious fanaticism and educational traditionalism are concomitant phenomena of protestantism on the one hand, and of humanism, on the other. Traditionalism is also at work in Catholicism, e.g., in Pope John Paul II's demand of sharp separation between church and Marxism(556).

As soon as the traditional knowledge of God, so Habermas interprets Horkheimer and Weber, in which the validity aspects of the good, beautiful, true and perfect are still centralized in the Absolute and undifferentiated, opposes modern systems of knowledge, which are decentralized and specialized in terms of propositional truth in relation to the world of nature, normative rightness in relation to the social world, authenticity in relation to the inner world and taste in religion to the cultural world, the mode of holding on to religious world-

views loses its ease and informality. A religious conviction
has such ease and informality only through good reasons. As
there are allegedly no good reasons any longer for traditional
religion, it turns into traditionalism, dogmatism, and
fanaticism.

Faith and Knowledge

According to Horkheimer and Adorno, as Habermas understands
them, in the further process of modernization, rationalization
and disenchantment of religious-metaphysical worldviews,
religious faith is characterized by the moments of blindness,
mere opinion and overpowering attitude(557). Faith and
knowledge separate themselves from each other. As religion
becomes privatized in bourgeois and socialistic action
systems, faith turns into an entirely private notion(558).
Faith and reason enter a dialectical relationship(559). If
faith does not continually assert its opposition to or its
agreement with knowledge, so Horkheimer and Adorno argue, it
is annihilated. Faith becomes limited itself as it becomes
dependent on the limitation of knowledge. That is the Kantian
dilemma! Protestantism has paid its attempt of faith to find
the transcendent principle of truth, without which it can not
exist, in the "word" itself, as once did the early Christian
community, and thus to give back to it its symbolical power,
with the obedience to the "word" in German fascism(560). The
same happens today again on the Christian Right in North
America(561). As faith remains unavoidably captive of
knowledge either as enemy or friend, it precisely thereby
perpetuates the separation in the struggle to overcome it. For
Horkheimer and Adorno, the fanaticism of faith is the mark of
its untruth. It is the objective admission that the man who
merely believes does thereby no longer believe. Faith becomes
ideology.

All these insights constitute the background for
Habermas's own theory of communicative praxis and religion.
They contain, without doubt, the remembrance of Hegel's most
gigantic attempt to reconcile anew faith and knowledge under
the conditions of highly differentiated modern action systems
and, at the same time, the assertion that the Hegelian
reconciliation attempt has supposedly failed(562). The
consequence of all this is for Horkheimer and Adorno,
faithfulness to an enlightenment which is aware of its inner
dialectic and precisely as such very much concerned with

religious issues like creation as self-negation, original sin, Messiah, messianic mimesis messianic realm, negative theology, universal solidarity(563). The consequence of all this for Habermas is an even more radical commitment to enlightenment, communicative rationality, universal brotherhood-sisterhood ethics, and unlimited communication community, which are, nevertheless, not entirely without some mystical remembrance(564).

Educational Knowledge

According to Habermas, following Horkheimer, on the secular side modern philosophy identifies itself as being at the same time opponent and heir of religion, ambiguously with science(565). Philosophy tries to rescue itself transitorily in the system of sciences. From this secular philosophy an educational knowledge splits itself off. It justifies itself primarily by continuing old traditions. This happens, e.g., in American Medieval Societies and Institutes. The difficulty of this educational traditionalism consists in the fact that it must cancel its own foundation. Only those traditions need conjuring which lack credibility on the basis of good reasons. Every traditionalism is neo-traditionalism: Neo-Thomism, Neo-Kantianism, Neo-Hegelianism, etc.

Spiritual Roots

For Horkheimer as well as for Habermas, the consequence of the formalization of subjective reason is that notions, like justice, equality, happiness, tolerance, freedom, which in past centuries had been intrinsic to objective and subjective reason or were supposed to be sanctioned by them, have lost their spiritual roots(566). They may still be goals and purposes for some people in advanced capitalistic societies. But there is no longer any rational instance which would have the right to attribute to them a value and which could bring them together with an objective reality, a positive Absolute(567). Those notions may still be affirmed by honorable documents, like the American Declaration of Independence and the Constitution of the USA. They may still enjoy some prestige for some time, particularly during national celebrations. But they lack, nevertheless, the affirmation through reason in its modern meaning: formalized instrumental subjective reason. Nobody can assert any longer

that any of these high ideals is more closely related to
absolute truth or the truth of the absolute than their very
opposites(568).

Polytheism

According to Habermas, this second push in the rationalization
and disenchantment process, carried through consciously and
consequentially by historicism, means the ironical return of
the repressed demonic forces(569). Habermas admits that they
had been overcome for some time by the unity-creating,
meaning-producing power of centralized religious-metaphysical
and mystical worldviews. In Habermas's view, Horkheimer's and
Adorno's thesis that enlightenment falls back into myth,
touches upon Weber's thesis that the rationalization process
carries the seed of its own destruction in itself(570). The
more the specific quality of each value sphere, which
establishes itself in modern action systems, comes forth
always sharper and less resolvable, so Habermas argues,
following Horkheimer and Weber, the more powerless becomes
people's search for wisdom and redemption in the face of a
renewed polytheism.

Hegel had pointed out the tremendous similarity between
the late Roman Empire and modern bourgeois society in terms of
private right, administration of justice, state and
religion(571). According to Habermas, following Weber and
Horkheimer, in the Roman Empire polytheism meant the struggle
among the gods(572). In modernity a subjective reason fights
this same struggle, of course, in the sign of impersonal
economic, political and cultural forces. This new modern
polytheism is stripped of its mythical form. Therefore, this
modern polytheism has lost its binding social-integrative
power. After the subtraction of its social-integrative
function this modern polytheism leaves to fate merely its
well-known blindness. In modernity this blindness of fate
consists in the accidental character of the dialectical
movement of the forces of faith, which have become irrational
with the loss of objective reason.

Science

According to Habermas, even science stands on shaky
grounds(573). It is, according to Weber, no more secure than
the subjective engagement of the scientists who have decided

to nail their life on this cross of science(574). For Hegel
the willingness of the philosopher to take upon himself the
cross of contradictory reality was the presupposition for any
penetration into the objective reason at work in private
right, personal morality, family, society, state, history and
religion(575). Such objective reason is no longer available to
the positive scientist. He must let himself be crucified for
much less: for the success of subjective, instrumental reason
and survival.

Weber gives witness with his own life to this heroic
self-understanding of the modern scientist(576). There is some
of this heroism in Habermas. His opponent, Popper, confesses
also to this heroic subjectivism(577). But unlike Habermas,
Popper reduces scientific critique not to a reasonable choice
between science and faith, but to an irrational faith or
trust, a decisionism: the arbitrary decision between two forms
of faith(578). While Horkheimer chooses knowledge, he does not
entirely lose his trust in the Eternal One, as his gravestone
with Psalm 91 indicates(579). While Habermas decides most
radically and heroically for scientific knowledge, he retains
nevertheless a mystical remembrance(580).

Self Preservation

In Habermas's view, following Horkheimer, Adorno and Marcuse,
in modernity subjective reason turns almost entirely into
instrumental reason(581). It has become a mere tool for individual and collective self-preservation. Subjective reason,
which has uncoupled itself from objective and absolute reason,
has become enslaved to the individual and collective will to
life and death(582). According to Horkheimer and Adorno, the
idea of self-preservation is the principle which drives the
formal, instrumental reason into utter insanity(583). In Marcuse's terms reason is no longer or not yet the victory of
eros over thanatos(584). Driven by the will to survive,
instrumental reason produces continually more and more productive and destructive tools, which push it with iron logic
toward Future I - the totally administered, cyberneticized,
militarized action system, and beyond this to Future II - ABC
wars(585).

Administered Society

Unlike Horkheimer, Adorno and Freud, Habermas is not influenced by Schopenhauer. Habermas has inherited Hegel's optimism, but without its theological basis in objective reason, except mystical fragments. His optimism seems to forbid Habermas to think about Future II - the thermonuclear holocaust. At least he does only very seldom, if at all, touch upon this possibility, which could put an end to all language and struggle for recognition as they appear in his writings. One must admit Future II is rather unthinkable.

For Habermas it is an open question if the bureaucratization process, described by Weber, or the administration process, described by Horkheimer and Adorno, will ever reach Future I - the totally bureaucratized and administered society, anticipated poetically by Huxley, Orwell and Skinner(586). But Habermas has, nevertheless, quite a clear concept of Future I. In the totally administered society, so Habermas argues, all achievements of social integration will be transfered from the continuing fundamental socialization mechanism of linguistic understanding to systematic mechanisms. Habermas is not certain and therefore leaves it open, whether such a totally administered human condition is at all possible without the transformation of social and cultural structures, which are deeply anthropo- logically grounded(587).

For Habermas, Future I - the totally bureaucratized society - means the absolutization of the system-functionalism developed by Parsons and Luhmann(588). Habermas sees the methodological weakness of such an absolutized structural-functionalism precisely in the fact that it chooses the theoretical fundamental concepts in such a way as if that process, the beginnings of which Weber, Horkheimer and Adorno have perceived in advanced capitalistic action systems, was already completed. Habermas denies that total bureaucratization or adminstration has already dehumanized the modern action system in its totality. According to Habermas, bureaucratization and administration have not yet closed together the modern action system into a kind of system, which has pulled itself completely loose from its anchorage in a communicatively structured life world, while this life world on its part has been degraded to the status of a subsystem besides other subsystems. For Horkheimer and Adorno, this totally administered world was the vision of the most extreme terror(589). Parsons

foresees no horrible administered world: the more differentiation in modern action systems the more freedom and mean-
ing(590). For his German counterpart, Luhmann, the administered world has become a trivial presupposition(591). Even
Habermas does not seem to be horrified by the totally administered world to the extent as Horkheimer and Adorno, but he
is also far away from the seeming indifference of Parsons and
Luhmann.

The Entirely Other

In Horkheimer's view, the principle of survival, nevertheless,
drives subjective reason into the insanity of Future I and II,
since the thought of an entirely Other, who transcends the
individual and collective subjectivity of self-interest, is
deprived of all rationality(592). While traditional theologians announced on the basis of the New Testament that God and
world had been reconciled by Christ, Horkheimer, Adorno,
Marcuse, Habermas and the other radical philosophers and sociologists of the Frankfurt School find the world until today
entirely unreconciled(593). No thought of the totally Other
can relax the will to survive and thereby bring back subjective reason to sanity. As Weber speaks of the global dominion
of unbrotherliness, so Horkheimer of the fraudulence of
traditional forms of solidarity(594). In Horkheimer's view,
the old religious and metaphysical systems of interpretation
and orientation have disintegrated or are in the process of
doing so, since the forms of solidarity, which they demanded
had become a fraud and the ideologies, which were bound up
with them, had begun to sound empty and apologetical. Habermas
agrees with Weber's and Horkheimer's analysis of the world
dominion of unbrotherliness and the end of traditional
solidarity in late capitalistic action systems.

In the meantime, critical political theology articulates
new forms of universal solidarity and Basic Christian Communities practice them(595). Of course, one swallow does not yet
make it summer. The new forms of religious solidarity may only
be transitory. On the other hand, Weber's, Horkheimer's and
Habermas's prediction of the end of religious brotherhood and
solidarity may be premature, as Marx's prediction that the
criticism of religion had been largely completed by 1841 had
been premature(596).

Freedom

According to Habermas, Horkheimer and Weber do not only agree
largely in their thesis concerning the loss of meaning in
advanced capitalistic action systems, but also in their thesis
concerning the loss of freedom(597). As they deduced the
thesis of the loss of meaning from the process of cultural
rationalization, so they deduce the loss of freedom from the
processes of social rationalization. Weber develops his thesis
of the loss of freedom in reference to the European
development of the 16th and 17th century(598). Horkheimer,
following Benjamin and Adorno, refers in the development of
his thesis concerning the loss of freedom to the 19th
century(599). Weber is concerned with the period in which
Protestantism, humanism and positive science began to put into
question the unity of religious and metaphysical worldviews.
Horkheimer is interested in the period of high liberalism on
the threshhold of the transition from liberal to organized
capitalistic action systems. Habermas agrees not only with
Weber's and Horkheimer's analysis of the loss of meaning in
modernity, but also with their analysis of the loss of
freedom. Habermas's formal and universal pragmatic, his theory
of communicative praxis, his discourse ethics and his theory
of religion are an answer to both analyses and an attempt to
resolve the modern problems of meaninglessness and
unfreedom(600).

Christian Principle

According to Weber and Horkheimer, as Habermas understands
them, the takeoff of the capitalistic development lives from
the quality of a conduct of life which owes its methodical
rationality to the unifying power of the medieval Catholic
ascetic ethics, which is universalized in Protestantism(601).
But Catholicism is relatively innocent of this development,
which finally ends in the Protestant work ethic(602). Except
for some psychoanalytically informed reservation, Horkheimer
shares Weber's conception that the principle-guided ethics of
Protestantism is the foundation for the cultural reproduction
of personal independence and individuality(603). According to
Horkheimer, precisely through the negation of the natural will
to self-preservation on earth in favor of the rescue of the
eternal soul, Christianity insisted on the infinite value of
each singular person(604). Hegel spoke of the Christian

principle of free subjectivity or subjective freedom(605). Horkheimer admits that this idea of the infinite value of each singular person fascinated even non-Christian or anti-Christian systems of thought in the occidental world. The Christian principle of subjective freedom or free subjectivity is certainly still present, if also in secular form, in the critical theory of subject, society and history and in its new form, the theory of communicative praxis.

Horkheimer is fully aware of the fact that the price which had to be paid for the Christian principle of subjective freedom was the repression of vital instincts(606). Horkheimer, informed by Marx and Freud, criticizes that such repression of vital instincts never succeeds completely: not only society, but also the individual psyche and organism have their realm of necessity, on which the realm of freedom is to be built, with more or less success(607). According to Horkheimer, one consequence of an only partial repression of vital instincts is the dishonesty which permeates Western Civilization. But Horkheimer must admit that precisely the renunciation of vital instincts which Christianity recommends and the consequent emphasis on inwardness increases human individuality. As man negates himself and takes upon himself his daily cross and thus imitates the sacrifice of Christ, he achieves at the same time a new dimension and a new ideal, which gives direction to his life on earth(608). All this is, of course, not a Protestant invention, but old Catholic heritage and is better represented in the Catholic mystical brotherhood ethics than in the Protestant work ethic(609).

Bourgeois Individualism

According to Habermas, Horkheimer simply repeats Weber's thesis of the religious-ascetical foundation of the economically-rational action of the capitalistic entrepreneur(610). But doing so, Horkheimer relates himself to the era of the liberal-capitalistic action system of the 19th and early 20th century, and not, like Weber, to the breakthrough of the new capitalistic mode of production at the end of the historic-intermediate action system of the Middle Ages. According to Horkheimer, individualism is the innermost core of the theory and praxis of bourgeois liberalism. It sees the progression of society in the automatic interchange of divergent interests in a free market. In the liberal-capitalistic action system the individual can preserve his or her social being only when he or she pursues his or her long-term interests for the price of the ephemerous, immediate enjoyments. In Habermas's view, the qualities of individuality, which had been produced through the ascetic discipline of Christianity, were strengthened by the renunciations of pleasures demanded by the early capitalistic economy.

Decline of the Individual

Against this background Horkheimer describes the modern tendency toward the decline of the free individual(611). Following Weber, Horkheimer finds the cause for the decline of the free subject in advanced capitalistic action systems in the progressing bureaucratization. Horkheimer understands under bureaucratization the growing complexity of the forms of organization, which comes into dominance in the economic and political subsystems of liberal and advanced capitalistic society and action system. Weber had spoken of the "steel-hard structure" of the advanced capitalistic action system. Adorno uses the equivalent of the "administered society." According to Habermas, the economic and political subsystems, determined by purpose-rationality, abstract themselves in the steel hard structure of the totally administered world from the motivational foundations in the individual. Weber researched these psychological foundations in terms of the Protestant work ethic(612). Horkheimer described this motivation basis in terms of the individualistic social character(613). In this process, Horkheimer conjures, like Weber, a loss of freedom in advanced capitalistic society and action system. The free individual disappears(614).

According to Horkheimer, as Habermas understands him, the free individual gained his or her singular identity originally from his or her orientation according to spiritual categories or principles, e.g., God's reason, providence, wisdom(615). In Horkheimer's view, the bureaucratization of advanced capitalistic action systems destroys this identity of the free individual(616). But for Horkheimer, the destruction of the individual's identity is also connected with the abstraction of systems of purpose-rational action, the economic and political subsystems, from the cultural subsystem. Culture means here for Horkheimer the horizon of the life world, which is experienced as rational. In Habermas's view, following Horkheimer, in advanced capitalistic action systems the individuation process of the free individual finds little

support in the realm of cultural reproduction. It is repressed
into the irrational. It is cut down completely to what is
pragmatic. This is the more the case, the more economy and
state transform themselves into an incorporation of
cognitive-instrumental rationality and subjugate also other
subsystems under their functional requirements and
instrumental imperatives. This is the more the case, the more
the instrumental rationality pushes all cultural actions and
institutions mercilessly to the fringes of the advanced
capitalistic action system and thus marginalizes them into
areas in which moral-practical and esthetical-practical
rationality can incarnate themselves, e.g., the family,
school, or religious groups.

According to Horkheimer, in pre-modern action systems
there still existed a dichotomy between culture and economic
production(617). This dichotomy left more space for the free
personality. The superorganization of modern capitalistic
action systems cripples the free individual fundamentally into
a mere mechanism of functional reactions. For Horkheimer, as
for Hegel before, the modern organizational units as, e.g.,
the totality of work, are mechanical parts of the socio-
economic system in advanced capitalistic action systems(618).

Reification

According to Habermas, for Horkheimer's analysis of those
processes which close the pre-modern dichotomy between culture
and production in advanced capitalistic action systems and
thus cut the individual off from ways of emancipation and
self-realization, the Hegelian and Marxist theory holds ready
the category of reification(619). Habermas's reconstructed
historical materialism aims at a new form of the negation of
reification in terms of a theory of communicative praxis and
of a universal communicative ethics, possibly one without
redemption(620). Its purpose is to overcome the loss of
meaning and the loss of freedom in advanced capitalistic
society and action system.

According to the Hegelian and Marxist Habermas, in
capitalistic societies and action systems the pattern of
rationalization is determined by the fact that the complex of
cognitive-instrumental rationality asserts itself for the
price of practical rationality(621). It reifies communicative
life-relationships. Therefore, Habermas finds it meaningful to
ask if the critique of the incomplete character of ration-

alization in capitalistic action systems, which appears as
reification, does not bring to consciousness a complementary
relationship of cognitive-instrumental rationality, on the one
hand, and moral-practical and esthetical-practical rationality, on the other, as the criterion intrinsic to the non-
shortchanged Marxian concept of praxis, i.e., in Habermas's
terms, to communicative action.

Projection

According to Habermas, following Feuerbach and Marx, it is
precisely this practical, communicative rationality which has
been projected and feigned in the religious-metaphysical
worldviews as a substantially unified rationality, as God's
reason(622). God is projected communication structure,
particularly the trinitarian God(623). But, so Habermas
argues, the notion of an objective and absolute reason has
fallen victim in the end to the rationalization of the
religious-metaphysical worldview itself(624). According to
Habermas, it is precisely the point of Marx's critique of
Hegel that here, in theory, the reconciliation which is
intended by Hegel, under the title objective and absolute
reason, must remain a fiction in spite of all dialectics(625).
    After the decentralization of the religious and
metaphysical systems of interpretation and orientation, so
Habermas argues, there exists among the differentiated moments
of objective reason only a merely formal connection produced
by subjective reason, namely the procedural unity of
argumentative reasoning(626). For the historical materialist
Habermas, discourse replaces objective and absolute reason
after the decentralization of the religious-metaphysical
worldviews. Thus in Habermas's view the reconciliation which
in theory represents itself on the level of cultural systems
of interpretation and orientation only as merely formal
connection can be realized at best in praxis in the life
world. Marx receives and appropriates under the catchword of
"philosophy becoming practical" the perspective of the young
Hegelian philosophy of action. Habermas's theory of
discourse-mediated communicative praxis is the dialectial
supersession-negation, but also preservation and elevation of
the young Hegelian philosophy of action(627).
    At present this philosophy of action is transformed by
political theologians, paradoxically enough, into a theology
of communicative praxis(628). It reintegrates at the

aporetical outskirts of Habermas's formal and universal
pragmatic anew the Reality which makes sure that absolute
justice can and will happen and that the murderer will not
ultimately triumph over the innocent victim and that finally
reconciliation will take place. That is the end of the
Feuerbachian and Marxian projection theory of religion.

Repressed Nature

According to Habermas, Horkheimer is maybe more than any other
member of the Hegelian Left aware of the enormous and tragic
price to be paid for a subjective rationality, which is
uncoupled from objective and absolute rationality and has
turned into functional rationality(629). According to
Habermas, here following Horkheimer, the social-psychological
costs of a rationalization which is limited to cognitive-
instrumental rationality are externalized by society and are
pushed upon the individuals and internalized by them. These
costs of functional rationality appear in many different
forms. They reach from clinificated mental illnesses over
neuroses, drug-addicton, psychosomatic disturbances, problems
of motivation and education, cancer and vascular diseases to
protest attitudes of estheically inspired counter-cultures,
religious youth sects, suicidal cults and criminal fringe
groups(630). Today these fringe groups also include anarch-
istic terrorism.

Horkheimer interprets fascism as the successful trans-
functionalization and as use and manipulation of the revolt of
the iner nature of man, in favor of the social rationalization
of late capitalistic action systems, against which this revolt
directs itself in the first place(631). In Horkheimer's view,
in fascism instrumental rationality has reached a stage in
which it is no longer conte simply to reprss nature. Now
functional rationality exploits nature by integrating the
rebellious potentialities into its own economic and political
subsystems. The National Socialists manipulated the repressed
wishes of the German people, particularly those of the petite
bourgeoisie.

According to Horkheimer, when the National Socialists and
their high bourgeois industrial employers, e.g., the Master's
Club of Dusseldorf, Germany, and the military backers started
the Nazi movement, they had to win over the masses, the
material interests of which were not their own(632). The Nazis
appealed to the regressive petite bourgeois stratum in German

capitalistic society, which had been condemned by the industrial development. They were pressed out and exploited by the, at that time, most advanced techniques of mass production. Here the Nazis could find among farmers, artisans, merchants, housewives and small entrepreneurs the champions of the repressed nature. These people were the victims of progressing instrumental rationality and its industrial incorporations. Hitler and his gang could never have come into power without masses of people situated in the lower middle classes. The money of the upper strata, particularly the high bourgeoisie, would not alone have been effective enough to catapult National Socialism into the window of power in the Weimar Republic.

Auschwitz signals the absolute triumph of instrumental rationality(633). It is no longer satisfied with the instrumentalization and commodification of living workers. It progresses to the functionalization and commodification of dead workers as well. The skin of the dead prisoners is made into lampshades and their hair is used in cushions and their bones are made into soap. Capital reproduces itself not only through the living, but also through the dead. Fascism accompanies and promotes this last consequence of capitalistic rationalization. It turns over dialectically, ironically and tragically into utter irrationality. Instrumental rationality becomes practical irrationality. Human suffering reaches through the instrumentalistic repression of nature a peak never known before in the history of the species.

Conservative Philosophy and Scientism

But in spite of the fact that Horkheimer has the deepest insights into the human costs of subjective reason, he does not recommend as remedy an easy, maybe mystical recoupling of subjective reason with objective or absolute reason(634). Habermas has even less than Horkheimer available as remedy such a recommendation for the reconnection of subjective and objective reason. Objective or absolute reason is simply no longer available to the majority of modern people, not in mythical or religious-metaphysical form and also not in mystical form.

According to Habermas, Horkheimer starts his critique of subjective instrumental reason with research into two contrary rememdies(635). There are two positions which react to the modern decentralization of objective and absolute reason and

its replacement by subjective functional reason and thus to
the disintegration of the religious-metaphysical worldviews by
turning into opposite directions: conservative philosophy and
scientism or positivism. In his Critique of Instrumental
Reason, Horkheimer develops at the same time a double-front
position against the tradition-oriented principles of contemporary conservative philosophy, on the one hand, and against
scientism on the other. This two-front position influences the
inner philosophical conflicts of critical theory up to the
present. It reflects itself still in Habermas' theory of communicative praxis, particularly in relation to Popper's and
his disciples critical rationalism(636). Horkheimer explicates his two-front position in relation to a controversy between representatives of neo-Thomism and neo-positivism(637).

Traditionalism

For Horkheimer, neo-Thomism has always stood representatively
for all attempts in the 19th and 20th centuries to renew, with
the help of Plato and Aristotle, the ontological claim of
philosophy, to comprehend the world in its totality, be it
pre-critically or in the sign of objective and absolute
idealism: the new ontologies(638). Neo-Thomism stands for all
traditional ontological attempts to overcome the decentralization of religious-metaphysical worldviews and to put
together again metaphysically the moments of reason which went
apart in the modern development of the human spirit: the
validity aspects of goodness, beauty, truth, being. In the
1960s and 1970s, Horkheimer and Adorno observed a general
trend in late capitalistic action systems to revive past
ontological theories of objective and absolute reason, in
order to give a new philosophical foundation to the fast-
disintegrating hierarchy of values accepted in advanced
bourgeois action systems and thus to restablize them(639).
Horkheimer sees medieval ontologies offered for use together
with pseudo-religions or half-scientific cures for the soul,
spiritism, astrology, cheap versions of past philosophies,
like Yoga, Buddhism or mysticism, and popular reconstructions
of classical objective philosphies. According to Habermas,
this neo-conservative trend continues today with Zen Buddhism,
transcendental meditation, Jesus and Maharaschi people, theosophies, "new revelations," Yoga, etc(640). Neo-conservatives
recruit themselves in large numbers from the schools of
J. Ritter and E. Voegelin(641). Most outstanding neo-con-

servatives are in Germany, R. Spaemann, G. Rohrmoser, H. Lubbe, and, in the USA, D. Bell, P. Berger, N. Glazer, S. M. Lipset, R. Nisbet, and E. Shils(642).

But Horkheimer can not emphasize enough that the transition from objective and absolute reason to subjective reason was not an historical accident(643). The process of ideas can not be undone arbitrarily in a certain moment of history. If subjective reason, so Horkheimer argues, was able to dissolve in the form of bourgeois and later Marxian and Freudian enlightenment the philosophical foundation of faith convictions, which have been an essential part of occidental culture, then this was so since this basis proved to be all too weak(644). Horkheimer finds the present neo-conservative revival of this basis to be through and through artificial and not, in the Hegelian sense, substantial. In these neo-conservative attempts to retrieve objective and absolute reason, the absolute itself becomes, according to Horkheimer, a means; objective reason a design for subjective purposes. Absolute and objective reason turns into ideology, the legitimation for the continuation of onesidedly instrumental and therefore pathological modernization process in late capitalistic societies and action systems.

At this point, Habermas agrees completely with Horkheimer(645). Habermas knows that neither philosophy, new ontologies, nor individual sciences or the system of sciences, nor both together can take over the integrative role, which the religious-metaphysical and mystical worldviews once fulfilled, when objective and absolute reason was not yet decentralized. The institutionalized philosophies and sciences produce changing and specialized opinions of teaching with merely hypothetical validity. Like Horkheimer, Habermas sees no other candidates to take the cultural and social role of the religious-metaphysical or mystical worldviews. Habermas believes as little as Horkheimer that the regressive forms of religious consciousness, in the sign of Zen Buddhism, theosophies, and pseudo-scientific therapies, which work with Yoga, self-hypnosis and group dynamics, can really be spread far. They remain small subcultures. According to Habermas none of these subcultures can bring back to life again what was once, in the great religious-metaphysical and mystical systems of interpretation and orientation, called God's objective and absolute reason, his wisdom, purpose, plan and man's related objective destiny. Their rationalization leads beyond them toward universalistic communicative ethics with or without telic, final structures or ultimate redemption(646).

Neo-Positivism

In spite of the fact that Horkheimer and Habermas reject neo-Thomism and any other new ontology or neo-conservative attempt to restore the objective and absolute rationality of religious-metaphysical and mystical worldviews, they do thereby not opt for neo-positivism: they are rather the "waiting" people(647). According to Habermas, what Horkheimer has against religion or metaphysics is not based on the false equation of reason and science, which is the essence of logical empiricism, or positivism(648). Horkheimer and Adorno object to the false complementarity between the positivistic understanding of science and a religion and metaphysics which only superelevates the scientific theories without contributing in any way to their understanding(649).

According to Adorno, the present religious mood goes very well together with the dominant positivism(650). To Adorno this is peculiar, but nevertheless not completely non-understandable. Here Adorno remembers Benjamin's smiling characterization that theology is today, as everybody very well knows, small and ugly and is in any case not allowed to let itself be seen in public(651). Sometimes it tries to rescue its content through the alliance with positivism. Liberal theology does precisely that, in spite of all objections to the contrary. But, according to Adorno, Horkheimer and Habermas, no element of theological content can continue unchanged(652). All must stand the test to immigrate into the secular and profane. Critical political theology is fully aware of this.

Horkheimer considers neo-Thomism and neo-positivism to be limited half-truths(653). Both try to assume a despotic role in the realm of thought. Logical empiricism and traditionalism refer back to self-evident highest principles. But the neo-positivism hypostatizes and absolutizes the scientific method, which is not clarified in its foundations. It takes the place of God, nature or being. At least, neo-Thomism and other forms of traditionalism do not replace objective or absolute reason by their own method. According to Horkheimer, positivism refuses to give good reasons for its identification of science and truth. Scientism limits itself to the analysis of the modes of procedures present in the praxis of science. In this positivists express their devotion for the institutionalized sciences. But the question, why certain procedures can be recognized as scientific, needs a justification. According to Horkheimer, positivism does not have such normative justification.

In Habermas's view, Horkheimer, in his struggle against scientism, appeals to critical reflection as a first step in the self-reflection of the sciences(654). Horkheimer and Adorno did not see their task in a material critique of the sciences. They did not want to connect themselves with the situation of the disintegration of objective reason, in order then to develop along the line of a subjective reason, which is externalized into its objects and which explicates itself in the most progressed sciences, a phenomenological notion of knowledge. It would then have to be broadened by self-reflection, in order thereby to open up the entrance to a differentiated and all-embracing concept of rationality. Instead of this, Horkheimer and Adorno saw the task of critical theory in the merciless critique of subjective reason out of the ironically estranged perspective of the unretrievably disintegrated and lost objective reason. In this ironical or negative way objective reason does remain present, nevertheless, in critical theory. Critical theory is to some extent negative metaphysics and theology(655). Thus critical theory is strangely situated between neo-positvism and neo-conservatism. It is hostile to both. But precisely because of its precarious middle position, it can easily be misunderstood from both sides, conservatively and positivistically.

Universal Reconciliation

According to Habermas, Horkheimer's and Adorno's paradoxical step to criticize subjective reason out of the ironical perspective of disintegrated objective and absolute reason of former, now obsolete religious-metaphysical and mystical worldviews, is motivated by the conviction that great religion and great philosophy can no longer systematically enfold and ground the idea of objective and absolute reason, the universal reconciliation of spirit and nature, out of their own power(656). Hegel's philosophy and theology was the point of culmination and end point of the history of the great religions and philosophies(657). Insofar as all this is indeed the case, great philosophy and great religious-metaphysical worldviews have gone under. Even mysticism can not rescue them.

At the same time, Horkheimer's and Adorno's paradoxical step is also motivated by the conviction that philosophy, in spite of the fact that the time of its realization, which was once possible and was proclaimed by Hegel and Marx, has been missed, is, nevertheless, the only place of remembrance of the promise of a truly human society, which is available to us here and now(658). Neither Horkheimer, Adorno nor Benjamin do exclude from such philosophy the theological element(659). Thus for Horkheimer, Benjamin and Adorno, under the ruins of philosophy as well as of religion lies buried also the truth, out of which thinking alone can draw its negating, reification-transcending power(660). Therefore, even Habermas does not only refer to Hegel and Marx, but also even to mystical messianism as it appears in the Hasidim and Kabala(661).

Mimesis

But in Habermas's view, Horkheimer's and Adorno's critique of subjective reason, more precisely formal instrumental reason, in the name of disintegrated objective reason, entangles itself in a paradox(662). This paradox resists most stubbornly even the smoothest and sharpest negative dialectic. This paradox consists in the fact that the critical theorists must establish a theory of mimesis or imitatio, in which instrumentalized nature can express its wordless complaint, but that at the same time they are not able to do so according to their own admission.

Horkheimer and Adorno call this mimesis an impulse(663). Mimesis or imitation does not mean, so Habermas explains, the form of man's immediate participation in and immediate repetition of nature. But Horkheimer and Adorno do still remember, so Habermas argues, in the category of mimesis, the model of a non-violent exchange between subject and nature. They do this even in the midst of the horror of the wordless adaptation to the suffered overpowering domination of a nature which strikes back chaotically against interventions of instrumental reason. For Horkheimer and Adorno, the constellation under which equality constitutes itself, the immediate equality of mimesis as well as the mediated equality of the synthesis, the adaptation to the thing in the blind process of life as well as the comparison of the reified realities in the scientific conceptualization, remains one of terror. According to Horkheimer, Adorno and Habermas, <u>mimetic</u> behavior is the organic nestling and clinging of the one to the other. Indeed, in modern action systems this <u>mimetic</u> praxis stands in the sign of horror. But that circumstances does not take away from the <u>imitatio</u> the role of the representative for an original subjective reason, the place of which instrumental reason has usurped. Hegel still knows of a subjective reason, the main task of which was to be open for and receive objective reason: to imitate, to nestle to, to cling to objective and absolute reason as it is present in the world of nature, inner world, social and cultural world(664). The main source of Hegel's notion of a subjective reason, which is essentially open for objective and absolute reason, and imitates it, is Judeo-Christian mysticism(665).

But in advanced capitalistic action systems, under the ban of functional reason, Horkheimer and Adorno can speak about this <u>mimesis</u> only as a piece of nature which can not be looked through and comprehended(666). Since, therefore, critical theorists can not develop a complete theory of <u>imitatio</u>, it is only consequential, according to Habermas, that Horkheimer and Adorno do not try to explicate the Absolute and the universal reconciliation, like Hegel still attempted to do, as unity of the identity and non-identity of spirit and nature, but leave it standing there as a <u>chiffre</u>(667). They also do this in strict obedience to the second commandment and as negative metaphysicians and theologians(668).

Astonishingly enough, Habermas thinks that Hegel's mystical idea of God as the identity of the identity and non-identity of spirit and nature, could still be circumscribed in the dialectical images of Judeo-Christian mysticism: e.g., messianic <u>mimesis</u>(669). For Habermas already Marx's formula of the dialectical connection of a humanized nature with the naturalization of man and his anticipation of the unity of reason and reality points in the direction of this Judeo-Christian mysticism(670). There is a mystical atheism, which reaches from Meister Eckehart over Hegel and Marx to Horkheimer, Adorno and Habermas(671). Already to Meister Eckehart, such mystical atheism alone makes a rational conduct of life possible(672).

Intersubjectivity

According to Habermas, Horkheimer's and Adorno's Dialectic of Enlightenment is a very ironical affair(673). It shows the self-criticism of subjective reason its way to the truth. But at the same time the critical theorists deny the possibility that on the present level of complete alienation in advanced capitalistic action systems the idea of absolute truth is still available. Habermas would like to dissolve this paradox in his theory of communicative praxis through his paradigm change(674).

Habermas admits that Horkheimer's and Adorno's mimesis does, in spite of the fact that they have no complete theory for it, nevertheless, as name, call forth several associations, which they indeed intend(675). Mimesis or imitatio point away from the realm of work and tools and to the realms of language and recognition, interaction, intersubjectivity. It signifies a relationship between persons, in which one person nestles to the other person and identifies and empathizes with the other person. Mimesis alludes to a relationship in which the exuberant self-giving of the one person to the example of the other person does not mean the loss of self for the first person, but the gain of self and enrichment. Imitatio points to the possibility of victimless intersubjectivity and non-possessive love(676).

But Horkheimer and Adorno see the mimetic ability, so Habermas criticizes, since it is not available to the conceptualization of cognitive-instrumentally determined subject-object relationships in the realm of work and tools, as the sheer opposite of reason, as mere non-rational impulse. Habermas must admit, nevertheless, that Adorno does not deny altogether any cognitive function to the impulse of mimesis(677). Adorno has tried to show in his Esthetics what the work of art owes to the disclosing cognitive power of mimesis(678). But, according to Habermas, moving here beyond Horkheimer and Adorno, the rational core in the mimetic achievement can be set free only when one gives up the paradigm of the philosophy of consciousness. It remains bound to the realm of work and tools. It knows only of a subject, which represents to itself objects externally and works them over and over. According to Habermas, the paradigm of the philosophy of consciousness must be given up in favor of the paradigm of the philosophy of language, the intersubjective understanding or comunication. It is related to the realms of language and recognition. It integrates the partial cognitive-instrumental rationality into an all-embracing communicative rationality. To be sure, Habermas accomplishes such paradigm change from philosophy of consciousness to philosophy of language and interaction on the shoulders of Horkheimer and Adorno, Weber, Mead and Durkheim in his universal pragmatic(679). The political theologians participate in Habermas's paradigm shift from work and tools to the dialectic of discourse and interaction(680). As Habermas finds in the dialectic of language and intersubjectivity a new foundation for the critical theory, so the political theologians discover in it a new basis for a fundamental theology with practical intent, a theology of communicative praxis, a political theology.

God and Religion

At this point, it must not be forgotten that Hegel traced long before Weber, Horkheimer, Adorno and Habermas the modern way from objective to subjective reason, and noticed their split and tried to find a rememdy for it(681). According to Hegel's philosophy of religion, in theology we have God as object as such and only by himself before us. Then, of course, also the relationship of God to man enters the consideration. According to the traditional religious-metaphysical worldviews, this relationship of God to man was not so essential. But newer modern theology speaks more of religion than of God. Modern theology demands that people should have religion. That is the main thing! The modern theologians pose as indifferent the question, if one knows something of God or not. The modern theologians think that the knowledge of God is something entirely subjective. In reality, modern theologians do not really know what God is. Contrary to this, so Hegel remembers, the medieval theologians were more concerned with the nature of God and its determinations than with the structure of religion.

Hegel does, nevertheless, recognize the modern truth, which lies in that God is not considered separate from man's subjective reason. But this, according to Hegel, should happen not because we do not know God, but because God is essentially spirit, a knowing God. There is a relationship of God's spirit to man's spirit. God knows himself in man, and man knows himself in God. For Hegel this relationship of spirit to spirit is the foundation of religion. Hegel finds this relationship most deeply expressed by Meister Eckehart:

> The eye with which God sees me is the eye with which
> I see him, my eye and his eye is one. In justice I
> am weighed in God and he in me. If God was not, I
> would not be, if I was not, he would not be. But
> this is not necessary to know, since these are
> things, which can easily be misunderstood and which
> can only be comprehended in the notion(682).

In Hegel's philosophy objective and subjective reason are
united(683). Subjective reason is a moment in objective
reason. Subjective reason is not yet entirely instrumental
reason(684). Functional and communicative reason are still in
balance in Hegel's philosophy, if also no longer in the social
world in which he philosophizes(685).

Rose of Reason

According to Hegel, what stands between man's subjective
reason as man's self-conscious spirit and the objective reason
as God's spirit present in reality and what separates
subjective reason from objective reason and does not allow
subjective reason to find satisfaction in objective reason is
the chain of some abstractum, which is not liberated into the
dialectical notion in theory as well as in praxis(686). In
Hegel's view the modern abstractions of statistical averages
or of social and cultural validity dimensions, which are the
result of the decentralization of the monotheistic religious
and metaphysical worldviews, block the relationship between
subjective and objective reason. This blockage has to be
removed! If it is removed, objective reason is comprehensible.
In the power of the dialectical notion the modern
differentiation and abstractions of statistical averages and
of social and cultural validity realms can not only be
negated, but also preserved and elevated in theory as well as
in praxis. The advantages of modern abstractions of
statistical averages or social and cultural decentralization
are not lost, but its harmful consequences are overcome in a
universal pragmatic which can combine a communicative ethics
with mystical elements. It seems to us that only if Habermas
can move in the direction of a new conjugation of
communicative ethics and mysticism, as understood by Hegel,
Benjamin or Scholem, can he ultimately avoid some kind of

positivism or post-positivism, or post-post-positivism. Bloch recommended the reading of Meister Eckehart to the political theologian Metz(687). It is recommendable also for the critical theorist Habermas.

For Hegel, in any case, to know objective reason as the rose in the cross of present irrational civil society and thereby not to despair, but to enjoy the fragments of rationality in bourgeois society, this rational insight is the universal reconciliation with reality: the socio-moral totality(688). Philosophy gives this universal reconciliation to those people to whom has once come the inner challenge, not only to understand civil society, but to comprehend objective reason in the social world on the level of dialectial subjective reason and the notion. These people will receive in what is substantial, in objective and absolute reason and freedom, also their own subjective freedom(689). They will stand with their subjective reason not only in something particular and accidental, be it in the world of nature or in the social world, in the inner world or in the cultural world. They will rather be rooted in what is real and rational in and for itself: God's universal and necessary, objective and absolute reason and freedom, and the socio-moral whole.

Habermas has gone as much through Hegel's dialectical philosophy as Horkheimer, Adorno or Marcuse(690). Most of the critical theorists had a lifelong preoccupation with Hegel's thought. But neither Habermas, Horkheimer, Adorno or Marcuse can see any longer in Hegel's philosophy, in the identity of the identity and the non-identity of spirit and nature or in the dialectical unity of objective and subjective reason, a remedy for the human suffering produced by the modern loss of objective reason and by a subjective reason, which has turned formal and instrumental to the utmost degree in late capitalistic societies and action systems. Therefore, they warn against taking refuge in Hegel's philosophy from the evils of present civil society. But the critical theorists have not offered any better remedy than Hegel, so far(691). Also Habermas's theory of communicative praxis is the function of and is entirely rooted in subjective reason, not instrumental reason of course, but practical communicative reason. No matter how practical or communicative subjective reason is, it becomes aporetical in the face of destruction and death, if it can not refer to Being and to objective and absolute reason: to God's spirit being present in men's objective and subjective spirit, in the social, cultural and inner world(692).

Death of God

Hegel subsumed the loss of objective and absolute reason in
modernity under the dialectical image of the death of God
taken from the oriental as well as from the occidental
religious-metaphysical and mystical worldviews(693). In
oriental and occidental religious systems of interpretation
and orientation, the Absolute plays eternally a tragedy with
itself, which reflects itself in the social world. The
absolute gives birth to itself into the objectivity of the
world. Thus, the Absolute surrenders itself to suffering and
death. Objective and absolute reason go under in the natural
and social world. But then, according to the oriental
religious-metaphysical and mystical worldviews, the Absolute
elevates itself again, like the Phoenix, out of its ashes into
its glory. With it rises again objective and absolute
rationality in the social world.

    According to Hegel, also in the Western religious-meta-
physical and mystical systems of interpretation and orientation, thinkers like Luther and Pascal state that God himself
is dead(694). But for Hegel, as for Luther and Pascal, the
death of God is only a moment and not more than a moment of
God as the highest idea: the crucified God rises again in the
resurrection. Hegel wants to give a philosophical existence to
what was once in the Christian worldview a moral prescription
of the sacrifice of one's empirical being or the notion of
formal abstraction. Hegel wants to restore to philosophy the
idea of God's absolute freedom. He thereby intends to bring
back to philosophy also the absolute suffering or the
speculative Good Friday, which so far in the Christian system
of interpretation and orientation was merely empirical and
historical, except, of course, with the mystics(695). Hegel
wants to bring back this Good Friday in the total truth and
harshness of its godlessness, its atheism. In the face of this
atheism the cheerfulness, but also particularity and relative
shallowness of the dogmatic philosophies as well as of the
nature religions and the religions of individuality - from the
religion of magic, Taoism, Hindusim and Buddhism over
Zoroastrianism, Syrian and Egyptian religion, to the Greek and
Roman religion and Judaism - must disappear(696). But
according to Hegel, out of the severity of this atheism alone
can and must arise God's highest totality in its complete

seriousness and out of its deepest ground, and at the same time being all-embracing and being in the most serene freedom of its form.

Double Nature

For Hegel, God has in his form and objectivity a double nature(697). God's life is the absolute oneness of these two natures. But the movement of the conflict of these two natures in the Absolute shows itself in the divine nature as the fortitude with which it frees itself from the death of the other, the human nature. Nevertheless, the divine nature gives through this liberation its own life. This is so, since the life of divine nature is only in connection with the other, the human nature. But the divine nature also rises absolutely out of the death of the human nature. This is so, since in this death, as the sacrifice of the second, the human nature, death has been overcome.

Dialectical Theism

Habermas is not exactly sure if Hegel is an atheist or not, and as for Haag, he is at the same time a pantheist and an arch-positivist(698). In reality, Hegel is as little atheistic, pantheistic, or posivitistic as is the Christian worldview, the Christian mystics, Luther or Pascal, when they assert the death of God(699). Hegel is neither an atheist, pantheist, or positivist when he asserts, with the whole Christian system of interpretation and orientation, the resurrection, the death of death, the negation of negation, and thus the ultimate affirmation of God's reality, wisdom and freedom(700). Hegel is not an atheist, pantheist or positivist, but a Christian dialectical theist. Contrary to this, critical theorists tend to stay with the death of God and thus with the loss of absolute and objective reason(701). But the theological or mystical element in Horkheimer's, Benjamin's, Adorno's and Habermas's critical theory puts this judgment once more into question(702). We can certainly say that while critical theorists do not assert, like Hegel and the political theologians, the resurrection, the negation of the negation, the death of death, the negation of the loss of objective and absolute reason, they do, nevertheless, long for the entirely Other than all what happens in the modern world with all its horror and terror and hellishness, from Auschwitz and Dachau, Leningrad and Stalingrad, Hamburg and Dresden to Korea, Vietnam, Nicaragua, El Salvador, Guatemala, Lebanon, The Philippines, Ethiopia and Grenada(703). That may even be true for the critical theorists' great resource person, Freud, who confessed to be "one of those unworthy people in whose presence spirits suspend their activity and the supernatural vanishes away(704). Even Freud was far from meaning to pass a sweeping condemnation of phenomena like presentiments, prophetic dreams, manifestations of supernatural forces, "of which so many observations have been made even by men of outstanding intellect and which it would be best to make the subject of future investigations"(705).

Breakthrough

Habermas's theory of communicative praxis is, like all of critical theory, once more a congenial and ingenious commentary on Hegel's philosophy of subject, society, history and religion. While Habermas's theory of communicative praxis derives from Hegel's early philosophy, its paradigm change from the medium of work and tools to the media of language and recognition, it does not really improve upon the remedy Hegel recommends for the pathology of modern subjective reason: The theoretical and practical breakthrough from subjective reason to objective and absolute reason and to the dialectical union of both(706). This breakthrough is for Hegel the solution of the theodicy problem. Habermas falls behind Hegel in the sense that he can not adequately balance the modern loss of objective and absolute reason and come to the dialectical union of both(707). Habermas falls behind Hegel in the sense that he can not adequately balance the modern loss of objective and absolute reason, meaning and freedom by a negation of this negation, as powerful as the one Hegel arrives at by referring to fundamental experiences in oriental and occidental religious-metaphysical and mystical world-views(708). While Habermas does not improve upon Hegel's remedy, he puts it, nevertheless, into a new and sharper light(709). That is, indeed, a great accomplishment under present conditions in modern action systems. Nothing is taken from the greatness of this accomplishment by the fact that Habermas may not have intended it that way.

Scepticism

The political theologians share in Habermas's and the other critical theorists' scepticism in regard to Hegel's philosophy and his mystical reconciliation between subjective reason and objective and absolute reason and freedom(710). They have difficulties with Hegel's mystical move from the historical to the speculative Good Friday and Easter Sunday and with his philosophical-theological sublation of historical Christianity. Sometimes they find Hegel too European, too bourgeois, too conservative or even reactionary, or in some parts, outright unhealthy. Sometimes they simply ignore Hegel, since they find, like the young Marx, his mountain melodies too hard to follow or his philosophical thought too hard to penetrate. Here and there they doubt if Hegel really understood fully the misery of the individual in capitalistic society.

The price the political theologians pay for this, their sceptical attitude toward Hegel, is that they do not really, like him, penetrate the details of the social world and that they can only assert where Hegel proves in terms of the dialectical notion on the basis of experiences contained in the Judeo-Christian worldview: in relation to the reality who makes it possible that the murderer will ultimately not triumph over the innocent victim(711). But the political theologians do, nevertheless, like Hegel and unlike Habermas and the other critical theorists, appeal once more, in the face of destruction and death, to God's absolute love, reason and freedom(712). The God who rescues the innocent victim from the murderer shows himself precisely thereby to be absolutely rational and free.

According to the political theologian, it would be absolutely irrational if the murderer would ultimately be allowed to triumph over the innocent victim: if the poor would not ultimately possess the Kingdom of God; if the gentle would not have the earth as well as heaven as their heritage; if those who mourn today would not be comforted in the future; if those who hunger and thirst for what is right and just would not be satisfied; if not mercy would be shown to those who are merciful; if those who are pure in heart would not see God; if the peacemakers would not be called sons of God; if the persecuted in the cause of right and justice would not own the Kingdom of God; if perfect justice would not be realized(713). The political theologian is fully aware of the fact that subjective reason alone, be it instrumental or practical and

communicative, can not help the dead man or dead woman who has
been destroyed unjustly and who has not had his or her day in
a just court(714). Even the most heroic man can not engage for
long in a rational form of life and daily conduct against the
background of the irrational triumph of the murderer over the
innocent victim, in late capitalistic society, after it has
once been declared to be absolute. In order to make a rational
form of life and conduct possible in the long run, reference
to objective and absolute reason is necessary. That at least
is the remembrance Hegel's philosophy contains for political
theologians as well as for critical theorists(715). Such
memory may not yet be a remedy. But at least such anamnesis
points in the direction in which the remedy is to be searched
for and may be found. In the meantime, the political
theologians assert the reality, whom the Judeo-Christian
tradition calls God and whom Hegel still thought to be able to
prove philosophically and theologically and who makes telic,
final, ultimate victory of the innocent victim over the
murderer possible, and who thereby enables the survivor to
conduct his life rationally toward his own destruction and
death as well as his own redemption in the midst of the highly
complex modern action systems and their subsystems(716).

System of Human Condition

Habermas develops his theory of religion not only out of his
critique of Weber's sociology of religion and Horkheimer's and
Adorno's critical theory of religion, but finally also out of
his critique of Parsons's analytical theory of religion, which
is embedded in and the coronation of his theory of the system
of human condition and particularly of the human action
system(717). According to Habermas, for Parsons the system of
human condition has four subsystems: telic system, physical-
chemical and biological nature, human organism, human action
system. Also the human action system has four subsystems:
Culture, society, personality and behavioral organism. Parsons
sees the human action system as a cybernetic system determined
by a control hierarchy(718). This control hierarchy has two
poles. At the lower pole of the control hierarchy, the action
system is limited by a natural or empirical environment: the
chemical, physical, biological dimensions of the earth and the
human organism. At the opposite pole, the action system is
limited by an environment of a non-empirical supernatural
kind: the ultimate reality(719). It stands for what Hegel

calls the Absolute, or God(720). It is the essential content of the telic system as aspect of the human condition.

According to Parsons, neither man's personality nor the social system, including its subsystems of family, economy, polity and religious organization, nor the cultural system have any direct relations to the cosmic environment(721). Their relations with the nature surrounding the action system in its totality are mediated entirely through the human behavioral organism. It is the action system's primary link with the natural environment.

In Parsons's view, in essentially the same sense, neither behavioral organism nor personality nor social system have direct contact with the Ultimate Reality, the final object of reference, toward which the action system is open upward(722). It can be reached only through the subsystem of culture, its ideas, values and symbols. When Parsons speaks of the Ultimate Reality above the human action system, then this is not only an equivalent to Hegel's Absolute but also to what Tillich calls Being(723). It is the center of the final structure, which constitutes the telic system in the system of human condition.

Ultimate Reality

According to Parsons, the Ultimate Reality poses problems of meaning in the sense of Weber's sociology of religion: theodicy problems(724). The objects that behavioral organisms, personalities and social systems know and otherwise directly experience are, in Parsons's terminology, cultural objects. They are human artifacts in much the same sense as are the objects of empirical cognition in nature. Hence, according to Parsons, the relations of behavioral organisms, personalities and social systems with non-empirical Ultimate Reality are in a basic sense mediated through the cultural subsystem of the human action system.

To be sure, the Ultimate Reality is not pantheistically identical with nature surrounding the action system, nor, in the sense of the early Durkheim, positivistically identical with the action system or society(725). Parsons is no longer a positivist in the sense Durkheim was one. Parsons's Ultimate Reality is rather a modern equivalent of the God of the prophets of the Old and New Testaments, who was above nature, society and history. But while for Parsons people living in action systems relate themselves via their culture to the

Ultimate Reality and while this, their relationship, makes a difference for their behavior, he can not, like the Jewish prophets or Hegel, see God or the Ultimate Reality being at work in nature and in human action systems and in their evolution(726). Here Parsons deviates from the Judeo-Christian worldview, according to which God was not only above but also at work in nature, society and history. But Parsons does remind sociologists, by his concept of Ultimate Reality, that nature and human action systems are not infinite or ultimate. Here Parsons agrees with Horkheimer(727). The thought of Ultimate Reality reminds the natural and social sciences of the finitude of nature and the whole system of human condition, and thus prevents them from engaging in an idiotic optimism concerning either of them and from hypostatizing themselves into a new religion.

Systematic Deviation

Parsons, according to Habermas, connects the cybernetic concept of the control hierarchy of the action system with the idea of the realization of values by the people living in them(728). Parsons thereby, so Habermas criticizes, transposes the transcendence of values and validity claims into the empiristic, fundamental conceptualization of the system theory. According to Habermas, in this Parsons does not succeed without break. While Parsons in his middle period took into account the intuition of value realization through a special position of culture, he asserts in his latest period that the culture, which is now integrated into the action system, receives its steering power from its connection with the non-empirical environment of the Ultimate Reality. Parsons emphasized this environment of the Ultimate Reality the more so, the older he became and the more the legitimation deficiency of the American action system of which he and his work were a part, and of the late capitalistic action systems in general became obvious to him(729).

But according to Habermas, the notion of the non-empirical environment of the Ultimate Reality is a very strange element, indeed, inside Parsons's system theory(730). This is so, since the system theory does in general conceive of the self-steered maintenance of system patterns in such a way that the system boundary is in principle threatened at all front sections in the same mode. Everywhere the system boundary must be defended against invasions from overcomplex environments.

The processes of pattern maintenance are controlled exclusively by values which are immanent to the human action system itself, more precisely, its cultural subsystem. Outside the system boundary, Parsons finds usually only limiting conditioning, not steering variables. The environment of the Ultimate Reality constitutes an exception to all of this.

In Habermas's view, Parsons is fully aware of the fact that his concept of action system deviates in this important respect of the environment of the Ultimate Reality from the general idea of a system theory(731). Parsons admits that directionality may usually be conceived as internal to the human action system. However, so Parsons argues, on the action level what is more important are attempts to legitimate decisions concerning alternative actions by referring to an authority outside the human action system itself: the Ultimate Reality. Parsons does not undertake, so Habermas criticizes, any attempt to show how the model of cybernetically self-steered action systems and subsystems can be adapted to the needs of a theory of culture, which is of completely different, namely not sociological, but theological origin, and how this can be done in such a way that the structural-functional paradigm is thereby not changed fundamentally.

Of course, this is possible since Parsons's theory of culture is not so theological as it looks. The Ultimate Reality is, after all, not entirely the "living God" of the prophets of the Old and New Testaments, or of Hegel, who actively intervenes in history(732). Parsons's Ultimate Reality legitimates the status quo of action systems and, beyond that, only such changes which restore its equilibrium after it has been disturbed. But it does not intervene actively into cybernetically self-steered action systems and their own evolutionary differentiation(733). Parsons's Ultimate Reality is not a revolutionary God like the God of Isaiah and Jeremiah, of John the Baptist and of Jesus, of Hegel and of the critical political theologians(734). It is the static God of Parmenides, rather than the dynamic God of Heracleitos; the God of being rather than the God of becoming(735).

Cultural Determinism

According to Habermas, as soon as Parsons introduces the cybernetic control hierarchy into his theory of human action systems, the four fundamental functions of the four subsystems of the action system - pattern maintenance as the function of

culture, integration as the function of society, goal
attainment as the function of personality, and adaptation as
the function of the behavioral organism - lose their equal
status(736). The sense of direction with which Parsons puts
the four functions behind and above each other receives,
beyond the temporal significance, a hierarchical meaning(737).
According to Habermas, Parsons's idea of value realization
sublimates itself into an abstract order of ranking in which
culture and its function of pattern maintenance takes the
highest position. Parsons secures this ranking order a priori.
He makes sure that the functionally specified subsystems of
the action system - culture, society, personality, behavioral
organism - can work upon each other not arbitrarily, but only
in the one-way sequence of the functions of pattern
maintenance, integration, goal attainment and adaptation.
This, of course, constitutes a cultural determinism. And this
cultural determinism is a form of idealism, at least for
Habermas.

Idealism

There is an idealistic bias built into Parsons's functional
theory. Habermas points out that this idealistic prejudice of
Parsons in favor of cultural determinism is unconsciously
introduced into his technique of the cross-tabularization of
the system of human condition: telic system, physical, chemical, biological nature, human organism, action system(738).
In Habermas's view, the latent sense of this formalism of
cross-tabularization consists in that, on the one hand, the
aspect of validity of symbolical expressions is reinterpreted
empiricistically and that, at the same time, on the other
hand, the change of values is made immune against
materialistic assumptions and objections. According to the
historical materialist Habermas, Parsons secures with the
technique of cross-tabularization the more or less latent
idealism of his system-functionalism. Habermas gains this
insight from the external as well as internal differentiation
of the cultural subsystem in the human action system.

Constitutive Symbolism

In earlier periods of his work, so Habermas observes, Parsons
followed in the inner differentiation of the cultural subsystem Weber's threefold division of cognitive interpretation

patterns, moral-practical value patterns and esthetical-practical expressive patterns(739). But by the 1970s, Parsons's formalism of cross-tabularization makes necessary a fourfold division. In his new cross-tabularization Parsons keeps open the fourth field of the culture system for constitutive symbolism. For Habermas, this means nothing else than religion. Parsons does this, so Habermas states, in spite of the fact that science and technology, right and morality, as well as autonomous art have in modernity differentiated themselves out of the connection with religious-metaphysical worldviews. According to Habermas, these cultural components are therefore neither structurally nor historically on the same level with the religious symbolism. Parsons is obviously willing to put on equal footing religious-metaphysical worldviews, science, technology, morality and art in order once more to gain contact with what Hegel and Horkheimer call objective reason and of which late capitalistic action systems are in desperate need for ideological and legitimation purposes. Contrary to this, Habermas tends to subordinate religious-metaphysical systems of interpretation and orientation under art, morality and science in his critical theory of culture(740).

Telic System

According to Habermas, Parsons' formalism of the cross-tabularization of the system of human condition makes manifest completely the more or less secret idealism in his late social philosophy and sociology(741). Here Parsons subordinates the general action system to a transcendence, which is reified into a telic system. Here comes fully to light for Habermas the religious idealism Parsons has smuggled into his theory of the human action system with the introduction of the conception of the control hierarchy. What precisely is the telic system?

Parsons, as Habermas understands him, takes the general action system, which embraces culture, society, personality and behavioral organism, on its part merely as one of the four subsystems of the system of human condition: besides the telic system or final structures, physical-chemical-biological nature and human organism. Parsons relates the action system in its totality to the integrative function. From this results the compulsion for Parsons to construct a system of fundamental human condition. In this system of human

condition, Parsons attributes to the function of pattern
maintenance the telic system. Its final structures connect
themselves to the action system at its upper pole. Thus the
telic system replaces, or better still, includes, what Parsons
called earlier the super-empirical environment, the Ultimate
Reality. The final structures take the place of what Hegel,
Horkheimer, Adorno and Habermas call objective and absolute
reason, in a depotentialized form(742). Parsons attributes to
the goal attainment function of the system of human condition
the subsystem of the human organism and to the adaptive
function the subsystem of physical-chemical-biological nature.

According to Habermas, here in the system of human
condition Parsons conceives of the cultural subsystem in the
action system in such narrow terms that everything which so
far had the connotations of a highest instance of steering or
an Ultimate Reality moves likewise into the position of an
environment for the action system in its totality(743). This
action system borders with its cultural subsystem at the
Transcendence which has been reified into the telic system.
According to Parsons, the telic system stands in a relation of
cybernetic superordination to the action system in its
totality. Its final structures have to do specifically with
religion. In the view of Parsons, the son of a Protestant
minister, it is primarily in the religious context that
throughout so much of cultural history belief in some kind of
Ultimate Reality of the non-empirical world has figured
prominently. According to Habermas, with this speculative step
into the telic system with its final structures, Parsons
enters into his late social philosophy. According to this
philosophy the system of human condition consists at its upper
pole of the telic system with its final structures, and at its
lower pole of the physical-chemical-biological nature, and in
between of the action system with its subsystems of culture,
society, personality, and behavioral organism and the
subsystem of the.non-behavioral organism.

In Habermas's view, Parsons's system of the human
condition has, in methodological perspective, another status
than all other systems with which social theory or particular
social sciences are usually concerned(744). According to
Habermas, since the telic system is traditionally the realm of
religious faith, it can not be introduced like other
subsystems, e.g., the economic and political subsystems of
society, as a scientific realm of objects. Habermas admits
that the telic system could be introduced as social scientific

realm of objects if religion could find its place in the framework of the cultural subsystem of the action system. Parsons does indeed emphasize that all the talk about a telic subsystem presupposes the faith in a sphere of Ultimate Reality. Parsons's conceptual strategy reminds Habermas of the one with which the late F. W. J. Schelling, who started from the experience of the existence of God as basis, introduced his positive philosophy(745). It led via Muller to the contemporary positive science of religion(746). Tillich, from whom Parsons received immediately his concept of Ultimate Reality, admits that the influence of his Schelling studies on his theological and philosophical development was very strong(747). With full recognition of the philosophical difficulties of defining the nature of the Ultimate Reality and the telic system, so Habermas states, Parsons wishes, nevertheless, to affirm his once more, sharing the age-old belief in their existence(748). Parsons said this only a few years before the celebration of the fiftieth anniversary of his doctoral dissertation at the University of Heidelberg and his fatal heart attack in Munich, Germany, shortly after. Habermas met Parsons a last time during his last visit in Germany for the purpose of his dissertation anniversary. While Habermas appreciates the tremendous social-scientific effort of Parsons, certainly his theory of religion does not sound more plausible to him than that of Schelling, Hegel or Tillich. It appears to be as obsolete as the religious-metaphysical worldviews it reflects upon.

Epistemological Interpretation

According to Habermas, Parsons's system of human condition enjoys a unique position in social theory and the social sciences, since it needs an epistemological interpreta-tion(749). It presents the world in its totality from the perspective of the human action system. Parsons does not only conceive of the religious subsystem, but also of the subsystem of the human organism and the physical-chemical-biological nature in such a way as they can be perceived from the perspective of the action system as environment. According to Parsons, the structural-functional paradigm categorizes the world in its totality as being accessible to human experience in terms of the meanings its various subsystems and aspects have in relation to humans.

Habermas and Parsons do not only share Hegelian, but also

Kantian background knowledge(750). According to Habermas, in the Kantian transcendental interpretation Parsons's telic system constitutes the general and necessary conditions under which the action system relates itself to the external nature, man's inner nature and to itself. Thus the telic system determines the transcendental orders, under which the objective world of nature, the subjective nature of man and the action system stand for the action system itself. According to Parsons, the general proposition of his structural-functional sociology is that for each of the modes of human interpretation and orientation there is a meta-level which is concerned with conditions or assumptions which are necessary in order for an interpretation or orientation to be meaningful and to make sense. Habermas observes that Parsons attributes to the final structures of the telic system a similar function as the Kantian Weber ascribes to the religious-metaphysical worldviews. Parsons does this to the extent to which he derives, like Weber, from the religious-metaphysical system of interpretation and orientation abstract attitudes toward the world. Only determinate attitudes toward the world were supposed to make possible the decentralized worldview which forms itself in modernity. In Habermas's view, also Parsons connects himself with his system of human condition to the modern decentralized, secularized system of interpretation and orientation.

According to Habermas, Parsons relates himself to the Kantian critique of theoretical reason, practical reason and judgment(751). Parsons conceives of the three Kantian critiques as so many attempts to reconstruct the transcendental condition for the objectivation of the external nature under cognitive-instrumental perspective, for the constitution of the action-connections under practical-moral perspective, and for the non-objectivating encounter with man's own inner nature under esthetical perspective. In Habermas's view, out of this Kantian perspective there results for Parsons' sociology, religion as the hybrid product of an objectification of transcendental order-achievements(752). Parsons reifies these order achievements into Transcendence in the sense of the existence of a Divine Being. In Habermas's view, also the Kantian view of religion in the boundaries of mere reason, i.e., to be sure, subjective reason, can be interpreted in this way(753).

But Habermas knows only too well that such a Kantian religion of reason, which is already too much for him, is not at all sufficient for Parsons(754). According to Parsons, there is in his structural-functional paradigm a fourth sphere of transcendental ordering, to which Kant did not devote a special critique. Parsons thinks it has to do particularly with religion. It seems possible to Parsons that Kant, as a good child of the bourgeois enlightenment, was sufficiently sceptical in this sphere of religion not to venture to say anything positive about it. He rather rested content with stating his famous denial of the probability of the existence of God(755). Parsons finds here a logical gap in Kantian thought which he intends to fill.

Habermas admits that Parsons does not want to fill this fourth sphere of transcendental ordering in his system of human condition, the dimension of religion, which Kant left to a large extent empty in terms of philosophical agnosticism or negative theology, merely because of his own personal religious needs and experiences(756). According to Habermas and to Parsons himself, it is most of all the compulsion of the construction of the system of human condition itself which demands the filling of its empty fourth sphere. But in Habermas's view this filling does not only happen simply because there is a fourth cell to be taken care of in the system of human condition, like in any other system. It is rather so, according to Habermas, that the system-theoretical principle itself resists Parsons's intended transcendental interpretation of the human condition and precisely this forces an objectivistic understanding. In Habermas's view, Parsons is compelled by his own construct to reinterpret the system of the achievement of order into a system of the highest cybernetic control values or final structures of the telic system in such a way that it can interact as a world of supra-empirical entities with the other worlds: the physical-chemical-biological world, the world of the human organism and the world of the human action system.

According to Habermas, this perspective leads Parsons to wild speculations which he does not want to pursue any further(757). In Habermas's view, as in the case of the St. Simonists and of Comte, the father of positivism, so does also in the case of Parsons the development of structural-functional theory lead into the powerless attempt to create a social-theoretical substitute for the social-integrative function of a religious-metaphysical worldview, which is affected and eroded in its very substance. Habermas himself is, of course, not entirely free from this temptation, neither. Certainly Habermas's formal, universal pragmatic and theory of communicative praxis and universal communicative ethics is to fulfill the social-integrative function which allegedly obsolete religious-metaphysical systems of interpretation and orientation can no longer perform and thus to provide the possibility for the formation of new social and personal identities. Also Habermas overlooks that Parsons's concept of the telic system and the final structures contains in itself the insight that neither the anorganic and organic nature, nor the human organism, nor the human action system is its own telos and that they are not final structures in themselves, but that they are appearances. Parsons knows at least that anorganic and organic nature, the human organism and the action system do either have their telos beyond themselves or that they have no telos and thus no meaning at all(758).

Understanding

Habermas understands Parsons's system of the human condition as the analytical level on which the actions must be located which are coordinated through understanding(759). Doing so, Habermas finds that the field which Parsons calls the "telic system" contains the general structures of the understanding of the world. It corresponds to the Logic in the Hegelian system(760). The final structures of the telic system determine how the participants in the system of human condition can relate themselves with their communicative expressions to something in the world. The field physical-chemical-biological nature in the system of human condition represents the objective world, the field of human organism the subjective world, and the field of action system, i.e., culture, society, personality and behavioral organism, the social world of possible relationships. Parsons himself speaks, like Hegel and Habermas, of different worlds. He mentions the physical world, the world of the human organism and the world of interpersonal relationships. In this perspective, so Habermas argues, Parsons's telic system represents the relational system on which the communicatively acting subjects base their processes of understanding. The three other subsystems of the system of human condition - physical-chemical-biological nature, human organism and human action system - represent the totality of that over which the subjects can reach understanding. Such an understanding can

take place insofar as the communicative actors relate themselves in discourse exclusively to something in the objective
world of nature, the subjective inner world, the social world
or the cultural world.

Life World

So far Habermas can understand the four-field scheme which
Parsons introduces under the title "System of Human Condition"
as a variation of his own Hegelian scheme of four world
relations, which the communicative actors establish with their
communicative expressions and actions(761). But Habermas is
irritated by the circumstance that Parsons introduces the
system of human condition by the way of the complementation of
the action system through three further subsystems: the final
structures of the telic system, the physical-chemical-
biological nature, and the human organism. If Habermas would
allow this objectivating consideration of Parsons to stand as
being correct, the action system in Parsons's system of human
condition would fall together with what he himself, following
Schutz, has called the life world(762).
    According to Habermas, this action system as life world
offers with its components culture, society, personality and
behavioral organism, the background and the resources for
communicative action mediated and oriented through understanding achieved in discourse. Then Habermas can understand
the three other subsystems of Parsons's system of human
condition - telic system, physical-chemical-biological nature,
and human organism - as well as also the action system or the
life world itself, as regions which cooperate in the production of communicative action. But, so Habermas insists, the
subsystems - telic system, physical-chemical-biological nature
and human organism - do not, like the components of the action
system or the life world - culture, society, personality and
behavioral organism - cooperate in the generation of communicative action in a direct, but only in an indirect way.
Nevertheless, here Habermas admits that the telic system can
participate in the production of communicative praxis, if also
only in an indirect way. This is important for the further
development of Habermas's theory of communicative praxis and
religion.

Communicative Praxis

For Habermas, the action system or the life world and communicative praxis are interdependent(763). Precisely therefore,
the components of the action system or the life world –
culture, society, personality and behavioral organism – can
participate in the generation and communicative interconnection of interactions. In Habermas's view, communicative
praxis depends on cultural knowledge, legitimate orders and
competences, which are developed in the process of socialization. Furthermore, communicative action feeds upon the
resources of the life world, more precisely of culture,
society, including family, economy, polity and religious
organizations, personality, including id, ego and superego,
and the behavioral organism. Finally, communicative praxis
constitutes on its part the medium through which the
symbolical structures of the action system reproduce
themselves. Not only does communicative action depend on the
life world, but the life world also depends on communicative
praxis. Communicative action and life world stand in a
dialectical relationship with each other. They are separate,
but also inseperable. They reproduce each other.
     But according to Habermas, all this is not valid for the
material substratum of the action system of the life world:
the physical-chemical-biological nature, with which society is
connected through the metabolism process of the human
organism; the genetic disposition of the human organism, with
which society is connected through the processes of sexual
reproduction. Of course, social processes do intervene into
the physical-chemical-biological nature as well as into the
human organism and the processes of the distribution of human
gene material. But the physical-chemical-biological nature and
the human organism do not need, like the life world or the
action system, for their own reproduction the medium of
communicative action mediated and oriented through understanding reached in discourse. Human action only works back on
the physical-chemical-biological nature and on the human
organism, more or less constructively or destructively.
Contrary to physical-chemical-biological nature and the human
organism, the telic system, so we may add here, anticipating
possible future developments of the theory of communicative
praxis, does indeed also need, like the action system or the
life world, the medium of communicative action mediated
through understanding for its reproduction. This can be best

made   clear further in reference to Judeo-Christian mysticism:
the redemption of God as presupposition for the   salvation   of
man(764).

According to Habermas, in this understanding of Parsons's
system   of   human   condition   the fields of physical-chemical-
biological nature and   human   organism   represent   regions   on
which communicative praxis depends indirectly, namely mediated
through   the   material   substratum of the action system or the
life world,   particularly   the   behavioral   organism   and   the
id-sphere   of   the   personality(765).   Here physical-chemical-
biological nature and human organism   appear   in   their   functional   interconnection   with the material reproduction of the
action system or the life world. They do not come up as object
realms of possible knowledge and also not as reference   realms
of communicative action.

Transcendence

In Habermas's view, according to Parsons, the telic system is
supposed to take an analogous position to   the   physical-chemical-biological nature and the human organism in the system of
human   condition.   This   is   so, since Parsons understands the
telic system as a region which influences communicative action
indirectly   over   the   symbolical   reproduction   of   the   action
system or the life world in which the communicating actors are
situated.   It   is   obvious to Habermas that Parsons postulates
with the telic   system   a   supra-natural   counterpart   to   the
physical-chemical-biological nature and the human organism and
its   genetic   structure.   The   final   structures   of the telic
system   are   supposed to enjoy   the   same   autarchy   and
independence   from   the structures of the action system or the
life world and the communicative   praxis,   with   which   it   is
connected,   as   the physical-chemical-biological nature and the
human organism. At this point   Parsons   regresses   far   behind
Hegel,   who   has   overcome   in   his   dialectical philosophy as
theology, on   the   basis   of   Judeo-Christian   mysticism,   such
premodern,   reifying dualistic theology and has emphasized the
mystical differentiated unity   of   divine   and   human   nature,
divine and human subjectivity and intersubjectivity(766).

In   Habermas's   perspective   there   are   no   indicators
whatsoever available to social theory and the social   sciences
in general for a transcendence which is completely independent
from the action system or the life world and the communicative
praxis   of   faithful people - their prayers, devotions, sacri-

fices, conjurations, and even indictments and curses(767).
According to Habermas, there is no indication for a God who,
in terms of Judeo-Christian mysticism, would not have to be
redeemed through the efforts of men before he can redeem them.
Therefore, in Habermas's view, the autarchic and independent
position, which the telic system is supposed to take in
Parsons's system of human condition owes itself to an
unjustified doubling up of the cultural components of the
human action system or life world as part of the system of
human condition. While Habermas stresses the identity of
culture and ultimate reality, final structures or telic
system, he overlooks their differences. The mystics and Hegel
have emphasized the identity as well as the non-identity of
the Divine and the human, their dialectical relationship: for
them God is precisely the identity of identity and non-
identity of the Divine and the human(768). In Habermas's
interpretation of Parsons's theory of the telic system, this
dialectic of the human and the Divine is in danger of being
arrested and of collapsing.

From Functionality to Intersubjectivity

According to Habermas, only if Parsons transfers the
transcendental perspective from the subject-object model of
human knowledge to the intersubjective understanding among
individuals, who can speak and act not only instrumentally but
also communicatively, can he give the final structures of the
telic system and its order achievements a theoretically
acceptable and empirically redeeming meaning(769). In this way
Habermas invites Parsons to join him in his own paradigm
change from work and tools to recognition, from functional
rationality to practical rationality, from instrumental action
to communicative action. This would, of course, mean a radical
transformation of the structural-functional system theory.
    In case Parsons could participate in such paradigm
change, it would be possible to establish a direct connection
between the telic system and its final structures or the
Ultimate Reality on one hand, and the action system or the
life world and communicative praxis on the other. The
dialectic between telic structure and communicative praxis
could become manifest. It could become visible, how Ultimate
Reality, telic system, final structures on one hand and action
system or life world and brotherly-sisterly communicative
action, mediated through understanding, and communication

community on the other can reproduce each other. In this case, Habermas could possibly be open and receptive for the meaning of what Parsons calls the telic system, final structures or Ultimate Reality. In reference to Judeo-Christian mysticism, Habermas could think of a God, who must first be redeemed by men and women engaged, in the framework of their life world, in brotherly-sisterly communicative praxis and communication community, in order then to be able to redeem them. In this way experiences from Judeo-Christian mysticism can provide the theological foundation for Habermas's universal communicative ethics and this ethics, as integral part of Habermas's formal and universal pragmatic and theory of communicative praxis, could provide a new foundation for a mystically oriented political theology(770).

Habermas himself has not yet established such new conjugation between communicative ethics and mystically oriented political theology. But Habermas's formal universal pragmatic, theory of communicative praxis and theory of religion, developed out of as well as against Kant's, Hegel's, Marx's and Freud's philosophy of religion, Weber's sociology of religion, Horkheimer's critical theory of religion and Parsons's analytical theory of religion, contain in themselves the potential for such a conjugation of Judeo-Christian mysticism and a politics of Messianic mimesis or imitatio(771). Such conjugation could make immune Habermas's universal pragmatic and theory of communicative praxis against all objections, which may validly be raised against them on the basis of experiences preserved in religious-metaphysical and mystical worldviews and on the basis of truths validly to be rescued from such systems of interpretation and orientation(772). Political theologians have begun to actualize the potential in Habermas's universal pragmatic and theory of communicative action concerning a new conjugation of meaning and rationalization, objective and subjective reason, telic and action system, Ultimate Reality and life world, final structures and communicative praxis, the messianic and history, redemption and happiness, grace and freedom, revelation and enlightenment(773).

Mysticism

Habermas sums up his theory of religion contained in his universal pragmatic and theory of communicative praxis in the most concrete and deepest form in relation to Scholem's work on Jewish mysticism(774). He does this in reference to two public occasions: Scholem's eightieth birthday in 1978 and Scholem's funeral four years later, in 1982. In his Laudatio for Scholem on his eightieth birthday, Habermas confesses to the mystical elements he has learned from the great Jewish scholar of the Kabbala. During Scholem's funeral in Jerusalem, Habermas tests the mystical elements he has learned from him against the background of death and destruction. Habermas, who had deeply involved himself in the writings of Benjamin, the friend of Scholem, became himself a friend of Scholem and the mystical Judaism he stands for(775). Habermas, the non-Jew, gave his daughter a religious Jewish name: Rebekka.

In his Laudatio, Habermas declares that he has learned particularly from Scholem's "Ten unhistorical sentences about Kabbala." Habermas is interested particularly in two motifs in Scholem's "Ten unhistorical sentences on the Kabbala": an epistemological and a history-philosophical motive(776). For Habermas, the first motif is circumscribed by the concepts of revelation, tradition, teaching(777). The starting point of this epistemological motif is the rabbinical parable, that the sacred writings of the Jewish people are similar to a big house with many rooms(778). Before each room there lies a key. But it is not the right key. The keys have all been exchanged. It seems to Habermas that tradition has here been immersed into a Kafkaesque light(779).

Epistemological Motif

For Habermas tradition means first of all teaching(780). The teaching of the prophetic word is the medium for the communication of knowledge. This medium has come into existence, so Habermas admits, only with the great religious-metaphysical worldviews. Rabbinical Judaism has developed the praxis of teaching, the exegesis of sacred texts, into a very high form.

According to Habermas, the mystic is a man or woman who appeals to illuminations(781). He or she refers to an immediate, intuitive entrance into God's inner life-process or inner history. As such, the mystic is the born competitor to the ordained administrators of the authentic divine word, to the priests. Habermas admits that the Jewish mystic appeared as orthodox up to the 17th century. Up to then mysticism was effective mainly as conservative force. The kabbalists have, nevertheless, so Habermas argues, a natural interest to revalorize the oral Torah in relation to the written Bible.

They give a high rank to the commentaries, with which each new generation appropriates to itself anew the revelation. The mystics do no longer identify the revelation with the written Torah. For the mystics the truth is not, like for the priests, fixed once and for all. It is not positively expressed in a well-circumscribed amount of statements, so that the tradition could exhaust itself as revelation. The revelation depends on the creative commentary. It hopefully produces and invents timely equivalents.

Habermas feels a certain affinity to the mystics. He applies the critical instrumentarium of his formal and universal pragmatic, his theory of communicative praxis and theory of religion, to the teachings of the Kabbalists(782). According to the mystics, as Habermas understands them, the written Torah becomes complete only through the oral, the spoken Torah. The voice of God speaks through the interpretative arguments of the scribes of all generations down to the Last Judgment(783). If this argumentative discourse among the scribes of all generations should stop, the divine source of revelation itself would cease to flow. Later on, this kabbalistic concept is radicalized once more. Now already the written Torah is seen as a translation of the Divine Word into the language of men. Already the written Torah is a mere interpretation. It is as such criticizable. Everything is oral Torah! The written Torah is a mystical notion. It points to the messianic condition of a future complete knowledge. The mystics know of the revelation. But all the keys to the revelation are exchanged and mixed up.

For Habermas, informed by Scholem and the Kabbala, the Torah turns, in the exuberant fullness of its meaning, a different face to every generation and even to every individual(784). But the Torah remains, nevertheless, always the same. The Torah from the tree of knowledge is a covered and veiled Torah. It changes its clothes. These changing clothes are the tradition. Only in the status of messianic redemption-theory and praxis the tree of knowledge and the tree of life are united. Only then the Torah enters into the messianic light as uncovered and unveiled. Only in this messianic light of redemption the manifoldness of the contradictory interpretations of revelation in the argumentative discourse of the individuals and generations will manifest its unity. It was there from the very beginning, if also in disguise.

The mystical notion of tradition, so Habermas explains,

covers   a messianic notion of truth, which is strong enough to
resist historicism(785). The discourse of individuals and
generations continues through the dimension of time, through
the centuries. The centuries are directed toward the point of
a universal consensus, which will ultimately be achieved.
According to Habermas, the secularized form of this process
toward universal understanding is what Pierce calls "in the
long run"(786). According to Habermas, this dimension of time,
these centuries of discourse directed toward ultimate
understanding, make it possible for the mystics that they must
not pretend any infallibility. The permanent discourse makes
it possible for the kabbalists to reconcile the fallibility of
the process of knowledge with the perspective of unconditionality of knowledge, the stages of knowledge with absolute
knowledge, the steps of knowledge with the absolute truth or
the truth of the absolute(787).

For   Habermas, in this perspective also the objectivating
modern human sciences can lose the horror of historicism, of
the relativization of all validity claims(788). As human
knowledge in general, so do also the human sciences share with
the traditions which they appropriated the ambiguous status of
a covered and veiled Torah. This Torah hides the spark of
messianic light. It does not grant the light of certitude
before the Last Judgment arrives. Of course, this messianic
theory of truth, which Habermas explicates here on the basis
of Scholem's work on the Kabbala, does take into account a
notion of tradition which is not only turned backward.
Tradition is for the mystics not any longer valid merely as a
writing on and renovation of the once given, old truth. As in
the mystical illumination the truth forces its way into the
mind of the mystic, so the truth can also break into and
explode the old tradition. It can interrupt the continuity of
tradition. In this sense, Jesus's communicative actions mediated through his innovative speech about the Kingdom of God in
the form of parables, illustrations, examples and stories,
broke the continuity of the Jewish tradition of his time(789).

According to Habermas, tradition does not ground in an
unambiguous, manifest knowledge, but in an idea of knowledge,
the messianic redemption of which is still to come(790).
Therefore, the tradition lives from the dialectical tension of
its conservative and its utopian content components. This
Kabbalistic notion of tradition receives in itself revolutions
no less than restorations. It frees what e.g., Catholics and
Protestants call "tradition" from its dogmatic character.

Habermas's theory of religion is certainly open for such non-dogmatic religious tradition.

Historical-Philosophical Motif

For Habermas, at this point the epistemological motif in Scholem's "Ten unhistorical sentences about the Kabbala" leads over to the historical-philosophical motif(791). In Habermas's view, as the complex revelation, tradition, knowledge, teaching, so is also the thought of God's creative power of negation, God's self-negation, a further systematic fruit of Scholem's unhistorical reading of the Kabbala. Scholem concentrates particularly on the Kabbala of Isaak Lurian(792). Habermas penetrates with the help of Scholem into Lurian's mystical philosophy of history. From there a way leads to Schelling's, Hegel's and Baader's philosophy of history(793). In the mystical theology of the divine self-negation lie the roots of Hegel's dialectical notion(794).

According to Habermas, following Scholem, Lurian speaks a materialistic language particularly in his deduction of the Tzimtzum, the self-enclosure of God(795). Lurian's materialistic language brings close to Habermas the thought that the mystical symbolism, which uses such dialectical images and speech as the Tzimtzum — God's self-limitation and self-concentration — could very well be the thing itself. Here lie some of the roots not only for the idealistic messianic mimesis in Hegel's historical idealism, but also for the materialistic messianic mimesis in Marx's historical materialism(796). Also in Habermas's reconstructed dialectical materialism this materialistic messianism is not entirely extinguished(797). It is certainly no less strong in Habermas's than in Benjamin's critical theory of subject, society, history and religion(798).

Creatio ex Nihilo

Habermas observes that the processes of creation in mythical as well as in pre-Judeo-Christian religious-metaphysical worldviews, have always been thought of as creation out of something, out of chaos or out of matter, which lies ahead of the creative principle(799). But a completely new thought, so Habermas argues with Hegel and Scholem, comes up in the history of religion and philosophy with the Judeo-Christian formula of the creatio ex nihilo(800). God's absolute will creates the world out of nothing. In the Judeo-Christian worldview this nothing must not any longer be represented as a potentiality outside of God's creative power(801). According to Habermas, particularly mystical thinking, which immerses itself into the God's life process and history, concentrates continuously on this formula of the creatio ex nihilo(802).

According to Habermas, Lurian starts, like the Christian mystic Boehme before, from this concept of God's creatio ex nihilo: That God descends into his own ground, in order to create himself out of it(803). On the basis of this concept, Lurian can think, like Boehme, the creation out of nothing according to the dialectical image of a God, who pulls himself together or contracts himself(804). Thereby, the God generates an abyssus in himself, into which he descends and into which he withdraws himself, in order in this way to give free the space, which the creatures will occupy. According to the kabbalist Lurian, the first act of creation is God's self-negation. It is the first negation in the notion of God. Thereby, God calls forth, so to speak, nothingness. According to Habermas, this kind of mystical thinking and teaching stands in the strictest opposition to the emanation theories, which stem from neo-Platonism. The first negation in the notion of God calls forth and makes necessary a second negation: the negation of negation - redemption.

Alienation

At this point, Habermas remembers the theodicy problem(805). It was the very core of all mythical, religious-metaphysical and mystical worldviews. It also was the very center of Hegel's philosophy of religion, Weber's sociology of religion, Horkheimer's theory of religion, and Parsons's sociology of religion. Here Habermas understands the theodicy problem not only in the Weberian sense as any theoretical attempt to explain suffering in this world. But he rather understands it in the Hegelian sense as justification of God's objective and absolute reason, his providence and wisdom and justice in the face of the horror and terror in the world of nature, and more still in the world of society and history. According to Habermas, Lurian's mystical model of God's inner life process offers the only consequential solution of the theodicy problem in the context of mythical and religious-metaphysical systems of interpretation and orientation. In Habermas's view, informed by Scholem and Lurian, God can not create a perfect

world. This is so, since a perfect world would be God himself.
But   God can not double himself up. He can only limit Himself.
The kabbalist is not so naive to expect from God that he would
repeat himself. The repeated God would be a created God and
thus would be finite, and thus would be no God at all.
Precisely because God can not repeat himself, creation must
exist in this, its present alienation, the word understood in
the Hegelian sense(806). In this alienation creation must, in
order to be itself, put evil outside itself.

Exile

In Habermas's view, the self-enclosure of God as the mystic
describes it, is the archetypical form of the exile which the
Jewish people experienced and suffered again and again(807).
God himself goes into exile. God bans himself. This God's
exiling himself and banning himself explains why all being
from God's original act of self-enclosure, self-negation,
self-banishment on, is being in exile and thus needs to be led
back and to be redeemed. In his "egoism" God withdraws into
the abyss, or matter or anger or whatever form his self-
negation may take. From this notion of God's self-negation
lead different lines over to Schelling, Hegel and Marx.

The Unconditional

Before Habermas, Horkheimer saw the close connection between
Hegel and the Jewish tradition(808). According to Hegel, as
Horkheimer understands him, the answer to the question concerning the Unconditional lies in the enfolding of the dialectical notions. In this dialectical development of the notions,
the thinking person is not allowed to stay with one of them as
the absolute truth(809). Horkheimer tells the old anecdote
about the disappointments of the students concerning Hegel's
lectures in Berlin. The students came to Hegel with the high
expectation to receive the key to the mystery of the Absolute,
the Unconditional. They hoped to hear what the Absolute means.
Hegel began his lecture series with the logic and went over to
the philosophy of nature. In the following semesters the
professor lectured on anthropology, phenomenology and
psychology as well as on private right, personal morality and
social morality. He showed in his philosophy of history how
the historical development moves from despotism over oligarchy
to democracy. Hegel enfolds the dialectic in the development

of art, religion, philosophy and science. He tries to make the
truth of each particular philosophy in the history of
philosophies to speak for itself. Hegel does this until the
deficiency of each particular truth, its finitude, generates
the impulse to go beyond it. When Hegel came in his lecture
series to the point where his own philosophy had to follow, it
seemed to the students that now, finally, the decisive word
about the Unconditional had to come, because of which they had
participated in the whole process of knowledge in the first
place. But instead, Hegel began again with the logic.
      To Horkheimer this anecdote about Hegel sounds like a
story from the Talmud. To Horkheimer the similarity between
Hegel's philosophy and the Talmud is not accidental. Both are
concerned with the absolute truth. But the thinker can not
point to this truth positively. He can not say this truth af-
firmatively. But this truth is, nevertheless. The contradiction lies in the Jewish tradition as well as in Hegel's
dialectical philosophy. The dialectical philosophy explicates
the contradiction as moment of the thinking which aims at the
truth. The Jews have preserved their revelation, tradition,
teaching through many centuries of persecution and exile. In
this Jewish teaching neither the reward of individual eternal
happiness nor the eternal damnation of the individual was
decisive. The Jews remained loyal to a law, even after their
state had disappeared, which could have enforced it. The Jews
obeyed the law merely on the basis of the hope which was valid
for the just people of all nations in the future. All this
together constitutes the contradictoriness which connects the
Jewish people and the Talmud with Hegel's philosophy as well
as with the philosophy of Hegel's friend, the earlier Schelling and with the philosophy of the young Marx, Hegel's great
student, and finally with the philosophy of Freud and the critical theory of subject, society, history and religion(810).

Nature, Revolution, Nihilism

According to Habermas, one of the lines which lead from
Lurian's mystical model of God's self-negation to Schelling,
Hegel, Marx and Freud ends in the materialistic dialectic of
nature(811). Already for the mystic God's permanent creation
meant that his contradiction renews itself in each particular
process of nature. The encounter with nothingness repeats
itself in each process of life. For Hegel death is present in
the genus process of each organism(812). In Habermas's view,

another line leads from Lurian's mystical theology to the
revolutionary theory of history. A third line leads to the
nihilism of a post-revolutionary enlightenment. Scholem was
very intensely preoccupied with the revolutionary theory of
history and with nihilism(813).

Apocalyptic Meaning

Here it is far from Habermas to follow Haag and to argue that
a God who thinks nothing is nothing. But it is, nevertheless,
obvious to Habermas that a God who negates, exiles and bans
himself loads the Jewish people's historical experience of
exile and diaspora with heavy meaning(814). The God who
negates himself fills the Jewish historical experience of
exile with apocalyptic meaning. This is particularly the case
where the power of the negative, the suffering from the
catastrophe of being driven out, oppression and isolation, are
already interpreted as signs for the creative power of the
negative, for a turn toward the good. According to Habermas,
here in the Kabbala, Hegel's friend, Holderlin's, word has
been anticipated: "Salvation grows in the greatest danger"(815). When even the whole creation begins with a self-
negation and self-exile of God, so Habermas argues with
Scholem and Lurian, then the moment of the greatest danger
means an indication of the chance of redemption. "When you
have sunk to the lowest level," so God announces in the
Kabbala, "in that hour I shall redeem you"(816). The first
negation in the notion of God leads to the second negation: to
the negation of negation - to salvation(817). Today critical
political theologians like Metz speak about a political-
theological "hermeneutics of danger."
    But, according to Habermas, the mystical world of Lurian
did not really support the apocalyptic representations of
spontaneity and incalculability of redemption(818). It rather
gave support to the messianism of those mystics who wanted to
force the redemption. The act of God's self-banning does also
mean, so Habermas explains, that God withdraws and opens up
for humans a realm of freedom and responsibility. Habermas is
very much in favor of this thought. As a matter of fact, it
gives a theological foundation to his theory of communicative
praxis. To be sure, Habermas may not at all intend such a
theological grounding of his version of the critical theory.

Catastrophes

God's retreat is, according to Habermas, the condition for the catastrophes which begin with the "breaking of the vessels" already in God's own inner life process itself(819). Since Adam's fall these catastrophes repeat themselves in the history of nations. Habermas emphasizes particularly the mystical thought that God has withdrawn so far that the return of things to their original location is given into the responsibility of humans. As every sin repeats the original process of God's self-banning, so every good deed contributes to the return home of the banned people. The withdrawn God makes room for the enfolding of universal communicative ethics(820). Here if anywhere, Habermas can find the negative theological basis for his communicative ethics and praxis.

Messianic Activism

In Habermas's view, following Scholem, the coming of the Messiah means for Lurian no more than the signature under a document, which the humans write themselves(821). Finally, for Adorno and Habermas it does not matter any longer if the Messiah and his redemption do really come or not(822). What counts is that the humans themselves bring home themselves, the exiled. For Habermas they do this in language and under-standing-mediated communicative praxis. In communication community the exiles redeem the God who redeems them(823).

According to Habermas, mystics always knew well of the magic power of contemplation which can force movements in the heart of God and can overcome his anger and his negativity and which can in the innermost core of the world prepare the pro-cess of the resurrection of the fallen nature(824). The later Kabbala, so Habermas explains, turns this inner contemplative movement toward the outside, into messianic activism. Finally, this activism receives the profane meaning of economic and political liberation from the exile of oppressive action systems. The program of "no resurrection of nature without revolutionization of society" reaches on the Hegelian Left from the young Marx to Bloch and the later Benjamin as well as to Adorno and Habermas(825).

Antinomism

In Habermas's opinion, following Scholem, the messiah of the
seventeenth century, Sabbatai Sevi and his prophet Gaza, did
make of these mystical ideas, reported by Lurian, not only a
messianic, but also an antinomistic use(826). Jesus, the
Messiah of the first century, resisted all temptations and was
without sin and criticized the antinomistic trend in John the
Baptist's Kingdom-of-God movement(827). But when the Sultan
put Sabbatai Sevi before the choice, to suffer martyrdom or to
convert from Judaism to Islam, he decided for apostasy(828).
The Kabbalists understood this apostasy of the messiah,
Sabbatai Sevi, according to the archetype of the Tzimtzum, the
self-enclosure and self-negation of God, as creative act of
descendence into darkness. Thus his apostasy was justified.
The apostasy, so Habermas explains, is the tragic component of
the mission, which is to overcome the power of the anti-Divine
out of its own innermost realm. Thus the messiah is to conquer
the anti-Christ(829).

Nihilism

According to Habermas, Scholem has studied the nihilistic
consequences of this Lurian teaching about the messiah Sabbatai Sevi in the case of the Frankistic sects(830). Scholem
has traced the phenomenon of religious nihilism through the
history of Christian heretics from the Taborites and Adamites
over the Begines and Begardes, the Brothers and Sisters of the
Free Spirit, down to the early gnostic sects(831). All these
sects wanted to fulfill the true messianic meaning of the law
through a lawbreaking praxis. In Habermas's perspective, the
model of the Tzimtzum, of God's self-limitation, self-negation, descendence into the abyss, covered well the heretical
messianism of the Sabbatai's enormous visions of the redeeming
power of the subversive. The model has also justified the
related rituals, which were supposed to make manifest the
power of negation in the execution of actions which were at
the same time destructive and liberating. The same political
nihilism can still be found in Hegel, Nietzsche and
Benjamin(832). Rasputin personified the sectarian antinomistic
nihilism in the Orthodox Church of modern Russia shortly
before the socialistic revolution of 1917.

Enlightenment

When Habermas reads Scholem's description and analysis of the
religious nihilism of the eighteenth century, toward the end
of the twentieth century, parallels impose themselves on him,
which he dares to draw only very carefully(833). Scholem
emphasizes and proves, through biographical examples, the tendency toward a dialectical turn of mysticism into enlightenment. According to Habermas, the religious nihilism of Frank
seems to drive the Jewish mysticism to a point where the
religious form is exploded from inside. Thus its deeper
impulses can converge with the new ideas of the bourgeois
revolution: egalite, fraternite, et liberte(834). The
sublation of religious contents into political contents has
happened, of course, so often in modernity without specific
mediation that Habermas must ask himself if the mystical
antinomism does not already, on its part, react against the
disintegration of the religious-metaphysical worldviews. In a
similar way surrealism reacted against the disintegration of
auratic art in modernity. Habermas knows of Benjamin's and
Adorno's interest in surrealism(835). Habermas sees here
parallels for Scholem's interest in mystical antinomism.
    According to Habermas, the cases of religious and artis-
tic nihilism are similar in the demand that the real content
of religion and the real content of art, the substance of what
Weber calls the religious and esthetical value sphere, ought
to be rescued in the moment of their disintegration through
radical liquidation or destruction(836). That explains to
Habermas the show-character of the self-consuming religious
and artistic actions and the shock which they aim at. Habermas
finds similar traits in a certain form of contemporary
terrorism, e.g., West German terrorism in the 1970s, or
Lebanese terrorism in the 1980s(837). According to Habermas,
this terrorism can, from the perspective of the participants,
be directed toward the goal to save the true content of the
revolution, which has been missed or has been repressed,
through shocking exhibitions and shows(838). This happens
precisely in the moment when not only revolution is almost
impossible in advanced capitalistic action systems, but when
also the modern state and that revolutionary praxis which
corresponds to it, disintegrate or go at least through a
transformation which is hard to assess.

Atheistic Mysticism

Habermas remembers that Scholem was asked, during an interview in Germany in 1970, concerning the actuality and significance of the Kabbalistic thinking for the Jewish people in the present historical process(839). At this time Scholem had serious doubts if the Kabbala could still find a vital answer for the present situation of the Jewish people. But in his answer, so Habermas observed, Scholem used, nevertheless, a kabbalistic configuration of thought. Scholem prophesied that God will appear as non-God. Scholem admitted that all the divine and symbolical things can also appear in the garb of atheistic mysticism. Scholem knows that the voice which says "I am the Lord, your God" is no longer unquestionably valid. In this situation there remains alone a tradition which is transformed according to its notion. This transformed tradition only knows one crime. This crime is committed by those people who cut the living bond between the generations. Among the modern societies, so Scholem predicts, only that nation will be able to save the substance of the humanum, which is able to carry the essential contents of its religious tradition which points beyond the humanum into the realm of the profane. The critical theorists wanted to do precisely that.

Habermas is not, as some theologians argue, a bourgeois atheist. Habermas is rather, like Horkheimer, Adorno, Benjamin, Fromm, Marcuse and Lowenthal, committed to that atheistic mysticism or mystical atheism which has arisen from Judeo-Christian mysticism(840). Under the garb of this mystical atheism at least some of the truths of the obsolete religious-metaphysical worldviews can reappear in secular form(841). Habermas's mystical-atheistic universal pragmatic strengthens the living bond between the generations. Habermas's atheistic-mystical theory of communicative praxis helps to rescue the humanum under conditions of highly complex modern action systems precisely by transcending it, but at the same time without reifying this transcending once more in terms of final structures, telic systems or ultimate reality. The self-expansion of the people in communicative praxis and communication without domination and in communication community may overcome God's self-contraction. The redemption of God by the people may lead to the redemption of the people by God.

Death of a Friend

During the funeral of his friend Scholem on February 22, 1982, in Jerusalem, Habermas confronts the materialistic messianism and atheistic mysticism which he has learned from him, with the harshness of immediate death and destruction(842). One hour after noon, so Habermas reports in his reflections on the funeral, the small stretcher with the body of Scholem, who had died the day before, stood in the middle of the square before the Academy of Sciences in Jerusalem. Scholem had been the president of this Academy for a decade. First the stretcher with Scholem's body stood there on the square somewhat forsaken and lost. There was no coffin to protect the body. Scholem's body was merely enveloped in a blue cloth covered by the white letters of the University of Jerusalem.

For Habermas's eyes and those of his friends, this unprotected arrangement of the stretcher, with Scholem's body, standing on the square under the free sky, meant two things: the fragility of man, his being delivered up to the contingencies of a blind and merciless nature, on the one hand and the need for protection, the dependence on the community of the family, the friends and neighbors, on the other(843). As for Hegel before, so for Habermas only family, friends, neighbors, shortly brotherly-sisterly communicative praxis and communication community can protect the sick and suffering and dead from the senseless destructive power of nature(844). Such is the human condition.

In the course of the following hours, so Habermas continues his story about Scholem's funeral, a large community gathered on the square where the stretcher with Scholem's body was(845). Then, first of all, the older people gather, and, of course, those Jewish people who emigrated with Scholem, or before or after him, from Germany. They are called the "Jeckes." Habermas recognizes among the Jeckes the old E. Simon and many other persons, whose names he knew from Scholem's letters and books. The restlessness of the news reporters and camera people directs attention to the arrival of Navon, the President of the state of Israel. But a really solemn mood does not come up in the huge crowd, which by now forms a half-circle around the stretcher. Distant from all Protestant inwardness, so Habermas explains, the cantor's ritual of announcement and prayer connects itself with the formlessness of a rather everyday process in the everyday life world of Jerusalem.

Divine Sparks

First E. Urbach, the president of the Academy of Sciences, speaks. The speech is given in Hebrew. Habermas can recognize only a few singular words from Urbach's eulogy: Tzimtzum, the self-enclosure of God, and Tiqqun, the redeeming return to the beginning(846). Habermas is not sure if Urbach also speaks of the "breaking of the vessels": the catastrophic even in the process of creation. According to the Kabbalists, this catastropic event produces inside God himself an original disorder. Thereby the catastrophic event also brings forth that problem which drives forward the process of the history of salvation. The problem is, how the dispersed and scattered divine sparks can be freed from their incapsulation into the world of matter, into nature, and how they can be re-collected. That is, indeed, the fundamental mystical problem. It is the problem of Meister Eckehart(847). It is still the problem of Hegel's philosophy of nature, subject, society, history and religion and its dialectical logic(848).

According to the Kabbalists, so Habermas remembers, by now God has withdrawn himself so far from the world that the task to collect the scattered divine sparks and to write the document for which the Messiah means no more than the missing signature and to lead things back to their original location is entirely surrendered to the effort of humans(849). Habermas understands Scholem's own life story out of this same mystical drive to collect the dispersed sparks of the divine light, to save and salvage and retrieve the fragments of a messianic future. Out of this mystical motivation Habermas understands the scientific life work of the great Judaist Scholem as well as his life long effort to woo his friend Benjamin over from historical materialism to Judaism and mysticism, which Benjamin never really left behind(850). Very similarly, Habermas's own life work consists in the collection of fragments of rationality in late bourgeois culture and society, including its religious worldviews.

Dialectical Notion of God

It never becomes entirely clear if Habermas, the historical materialist, is entirely conscious of the dialectical notion of God hidden behind the dialectical images of the mystical story about God's self-enclosure, the redemptive return of all things to the beginnings, the catastrophe and chaos in God, the dispersion of the sparks of divine light, the salvific recollection of the sparks imprisoned in nature, time, body, multitude, the negation of negation, man's participation in the redemptive process, the role of the Messiah at the end of the whole process and the recollection of the Messianic future(851). This dialectical notion of God is the foundation of Hegel's philosophy and it is still at work in secularized form in Marx's and Freud's work and in the work of critical theorists, including Habermas himself(852). It is fundamentally precisely that notion which interconnects Judeo-Christian mysticism, historical materialism, psychoanalysis, critical theory and critical political theology. Sometimes all this seems to be manifest to Habermas. Then again, all this seems to be latent in him and his work.

Positivism

Habermas remembers that Scholem has used with great and sovereign skill and competence the positivistic instrumentarium of the tradition of the human sciences for completely non-positivistic, basically mystical purposes(853). Scholem has secured, so Habermas explains, the lost traces of the School of Safed, which is connected with the name of Lurian. He has brought to light once more the mystical movement inspired by Sabbatai Sevi. Scholem has devoted his main work to this mystical messiah, who around the middle of the seventeenth century put into a state of great excitement and expectation a large part of the Jewish people living in the diasporas of Europe and the Near East(854).

Power of the Negative

According to Habermas, Lurian interprets the Kabbalistic tradition in such a way that the Jewish people's experience of suffering in exile is dramatized in an extreme way(855). According to Lurian's interpretation, the exile of the Jews only repeats a fate to which God subjected himself, when he had to withdraw into himself and to begin an exile inside of himself in order to make room for creation. In Habermas's view, Lurian lays in dialectical images the foundation for a tradition which breaks with the representations of emanation, which are too lazy to think dialectically. The new tradition throws light on the affirmative, creative role of the negative. The power of negation, so Habermas explains, becomes

the pushing force in the salvation process. This idea takes a
practical form in the law-breaking praxis of the mystical
messiah, the Sabbatai Sevi. In Habermas's view, even still the
Sabbatai Sevi's forced conversion to Islam can be understood
as an extreme act of the overcoming and surpassing of evil by
the means of sin. According to Habermas, Scholem follows the
traces of this mystical messianism, which turns over
dialectically into enlightenment and nihilism, to the Jewish
poet Kafka and his impact on modern literature and even life
world. "Kafkaesque" has become part of everyday language in
late capitalistic society.

Renewal of Judaism

Scholem knows, so Habermas argues, that the passionately
longed for renewal of Judaism stands under the conditions of
modernity(856). Therefore, this renewal cannot be accomplished
out of the sources of orthodoxy. Thus, Scholem turns to the
sources of the heterodoxy of mystical messianism. Obviously,
the Christian political theologians are in a similar
position(857). In order to be able to renew Christianity under
the conditions of highly complex modern action systems, the
political theologians, following the example of Hegel and the
advice of Marxist thinkers like Bloch, Benjamin, Adorno,
Habermas, connect themselves to the often at least allegedly,
heterodox sources of Judeo-Christian mysticism(858).

Friendship

Scholem's intention to renew Judaism under the conditions of
modernity can not be separated, so Habermas believes, from
that stubborn impulse which has carried his friendship with
Benjamin(859). This friendship did not only last during Benjamin's lifetime, but even four decades beyond his sacrificial
suicide in true, what he called anamnestic solidarity(860).
This communicative relationship between Scholem and Benjamin
maintained itself almost exclusively over the medium of the
written word. It continued first through the intensive
exchange of extremely scrupulous letters and then, on the part
of the survivor, through an almost detective-like work of
reconstruction. Scholem's detective work becomes visible in
his biographical notes about the mysterious Mr. Noeggerath. He
must have been for Benjamin a fascinating significant other
during his studies in Munich, Germany. It becomes also obvious

in   Scholem's   well-documented   conjectures   concerning   the
puzzling content of the handbag which Benjamin is supposed to
have carried with him immediately before his death and which
he gave to a woman to carry to the USA and which in the
meantime got lost. Habermas suggests that in his detective
work Scholem searched in the mentality of his friend Benjamin
for the ability of that saving glance, which is present in
Judeo-Christian mysticism.

Transforming Glance

According to Scholem, there can be found in the Kabbala
something like a transforming look(861). It is doubtful to
Scholem if he should characterize this glance as magical or
utopian. For Scholem this look reveals, nevertheless, all
worlds. It discloses even the most insignificant location,
where one just stands. According to Scholem, one must not
argue about what is above or below. One must only(!) look
through the point where one stands. Habermas repeats the word
"only" with an exclamation sign, in order to express the
tremendous difficulty to precisely that: to look through
the point where one just stands. Also Bloch had pointed to
this enormous difficulty.

Religious Experiences

Scholem has not only, so Habermas closes his reflections on
his funeral in Jerusalem, opened his own and his friends' eyes
for the Jewish fate and suffering and for centuries of Jewish
exile(862). But most important, Scholem has instructed
Habermas about religious experiences, which mirror themselves
in the messianic movements. Habermas can refer to such
experiences as reflected in Judeo-Christian mysticism, when
the aporetic aspects of his own formal, universal pragmatic
and his theory of communicative praxis become overwhelming.
    Political theologians have begun to refer precisely to
such experiences when they are faced with the aporia of
unconditional recognition and merciless annihilation   in
communicative praxis and communication community. They are as
open for the paradoxical character of human experience as
Scholem and Benjamin. They stand somewhere in between Scholem,
the Kabbala scholar, and Benjamin, the historical materialist,
who remains, nevertheless, in contact with Judeo-Christian
mysticism.

Neo-Conservatism

Habermas finds the most passionate opponents of his philosophy
of communicative praxis among German and American neo-con-
servatives(863). According to Habermas, the neo-conservative
thinkers in Germany and the USA and in other late capitalistic
action systems demand at present that the programmatic departure from cultural modernity, which they see in all Left-wing
movements, should make room for a healthy consciousness of
tradition, particularly also religious tradition. As soon as
the cultural modernity closes all locks which are open to
everyday praxis, so the neo-conservatives argue, and as soon
as the expert cultures are adequately cut off from people's
everyday interaction, the pattern-maintaining forces of common
sense, of historical consciousness and of religion will enter
almost automatically into their own right. It is obvious to
Habermas that the neo-conservative post-enlightenment movement
suffers severe birth pangs and that it is, indeed, very much
in need of neo-conservative midwives. And they are available
plentifully in the USA as well as in West Germany and
elsewhere.

Courage to Education and Past

The neo-conservatives concentrate their work first of all on
the "courage to education"(864). This means a neo-conservative
politics of education, which cuts down elementary eduation to
the most primitive intellectual skills and secondary petite
bourgeois virtues, like industriousness, discipline, cleanliness. At the same time, the neo-conservative politics of
education concentrates itself secondly on the "courage to the
past" in family, school and state. The neo-conservatives see
their task, on the one hand, in the moral neutralization of
those past times, which could only elicit criticism and
refusal, e.g., Auschwitz and Dachau, Stalingrad and Leningrad,
Hiroshima and Nagasaki, Vietnam, the Shah's Iran, Samosa's
Nicaragua, El Salvador, Guatemala, Lebanon, Grenada, Ethiopia,
etc.

Innocent Victims

Habermas remembers that Benjamin had once called in his
"Thesis on Philosophy of History," the empathy with the victor
a characteristic of historicism(865). After World War II,

G. Heinemann, former president of the German Federal Republic, admonished the Germans and others, in the spirit of Benjamin, to take also the perspective of the vanquished, of the conquered insurrectionists and revolutionaries when they look at society and history. Heinemann had to let himself be told by the neo-conservative Lubbe, that this, his orientation toward the innocent victims and his identification with them, is in accordance with the wishful image of his own past and that as such it is a fixation at immaturity(866). For Habermas in the same connection stand the attempts to interpret national socialistic domination in Germany and elsewhere so skillfully that every reference to any form of fascism can be done away with as a sign of - as the neo-conservative Rohrmoser put it - the dominion of sophistry, which has become universal.

Religious Truths

In Habermas's view, the neo-conservatives know, of course, that the simple truths of common sense and the historical continuities can not alone carry the burden of the moral-spiritual renewal in late capitalistic action systems, which they hope for(867). Therefore, for the neo-conservatives most important is the appeal to the binding forces of religion. Habermas must admit that the bourgeois, Marxian and Freudian enlighteners have indeed not been successful in satisfying the people's need for consolation. They were also not able to make this need for consolation disappear. For Habermas, religion is mainly consolation. Habermas himself confesses like Freud not to be able to console or to be consoled(868). Habermas has decided to live without consolation. Thus the neo-conservatives can try to instrumentalize a religion, which the enlighteners have rejected or not adequately understood and dealt with(869).

Furthermore, Habermas must admit that the bourgeois, Marxian and Freudian enlighteners have not answered so far the central question in relation to religious-metaphysical and mystical worldviews: namely, if there is not something more to be rescued from the truths of the religious-metaphysical-mystical systems of interpretation and orientation after their decentralization and disintegration, than merely the profane principles of a universalistic and communicative ethics of responsibility. Should it not be possible to take over, with good reasons and out of real insights, from obsolete

religious-metaphysical-mystical worldviews into secularity and
modernity fundamental categories like redemption, salvation,
resurrection, Messiah, messianic age, messianic light,
messianic impulse, second commandment, negative theology. The
older members of the Frankfurt School, like Horkheimer,
Benjamin, Adorno, Marcuse, Fromm, Lowenthal, have, indeed,
been able to retrieve some theological categories of this kind
from Judaism and Christianity into their otherwise extremely
secular critical theory. Even Habermas himself is able to
rescue some truths from allegedly at least partially heterodox
Judeo-Christian mysticism beyond the universal communicative
ethics and the brotherly-sisterly communication community into
his even more extremely secular formal, universal pragmatic
and theory of communicative praxis: self-enclosure of God,
creation as self-negation, breaking the vessels, collection of
divine sparks, messianic perspective, messianic redemption,
etc. His description of Scholem's lifework and his concern
with him and his friend Benjamin do at least point in this
direction, in spite of all his reservations concerning any
renewal of religious-metaphysical-mystical worldviews under
the conditions of extremely differentiated and complex modern
systems of human conditions and action systems.
      Habermas is fully aware of the fact that he moves with
this, his question concerning the retrieval of religious
truths, still very much in the circle of modernity. But in any
case, this question, as Habermas rightly argues, does, indeed,
lead away from the traditionalistic renewal of the religious
consciousness, which the neo-conservatives have in mind and
intend to accomplish. According to Habermas, this question
puts us all under the obligation to understand and better
comprehend the whole spectrum of movements and impulses which
today fill the programs of church events, e.g., the "Days of
Catholicism" in Germany: the struggle between the church from
above and the Christian Base Communities and the conflict
between liberal and critical theology in the church from
below(870).

Protest Potential

Habermas knows very well that even religious fundamentalism
feeds upon many different sources. Its questions are often
important, if also its answers are insufficient and
obsolete(871). Beyond that, it is obvious to Habermas that the
non-fundamentalistic forces in religion, e.g. liberal and

critical political theology, do unbind precisely that pro-
test-potential and those forces of problematization which the
conservatives would like to dam in(872). This is shown very
clearly by the religiously inspired and motivated parts of the
peace movement in Germany, Great Britain, and the USA(873). In
this context, the American Jesuit Berrigan is a most outstanding figure. Precisely here, Habermas finds those interesting people whom the neo-conservative sociologist Schelsky
calls the exploitative mediators of meaning, and which the
neo-conservative Lubbe names ironically the ideological sign-
posts, openers of horizons, experts of goal reflections and
pathfinders.

Force of Integration

But Habermas does, nevertheless, praise the American neo-conservative D. Bell for analyzing without any prejudice the
different orientations which carry a new community-religiosity
inside and outside the official churches in the USA. Contrary
to this, the German neo-conservatives, so Habermas criticizes,
have only one thing in mind: the social binding-forces of
faith-traditions. Religion is to be a force of integration and
legitimation in late capitalistic action systems. They quite
obviously suffer from a legitimation deficiency in the face of
the inequalities and injustices of their class societies(874).
Religion has to fill this deficiency.

    According to Habermas, the neo-conservatives can imagine
such a faith-tradition merely as a substantial tradition in
the Hegelian sense of the word. Such substantial tradition is
completely set free from and made immune against any demand
for good reasons. For Habermas, as for Hegel before, also
substantial traditions are criticizable in their validity
claims(875). According to Habermas, Lubbe considers precisely
this functionalistic interpretation of religious faith-
traditions as a praxis to conquer contingencies to be a great
advantage, because it brackets out the question concerning the
truth claim of religious faith. Religion is good for integration, social control, the management of contingency experiences. If it is true is of no concern whatsoever. Hegel
foresaw this development on the Hegelian right(876). In the
USA the entente between religion and structural-functional
social sciences has rested now for sixty years on the understanding that religion is good, but not true(877). This deal
was to the advantage of the late capitalistic American action

system. It was to the disadvantage of the validity claim of the religious worldviews. This deal has now obviously spread to other advanced capitalistic action systems, e.g., West Germany. Thereby it becomes not less, but more problematic. Habermas rightly points out that we can not revive religious traditions by showing instrumentally and functionalistically the good things they can bring about in organized capitalistic action systems(878). In Habermas's view, such retreat into functionalism does not at all remove the embarrassment in which every traditionalism is caught up after the historical enlightenment. Habermas agrees here with Horkheimer, who pointed out already in 1946, shortly after his return from American exile from Nazi Germany, that precisely the very fact that religious tradition must be conjured so forcefully by conservatives in late capitalistic action systems indicates that it has lost its substantial power over people(879). That precisely is the embarrassment of the contemporary neo-conservatives.

Protection

But Habermas does not want to be misunderstood in religious matters: the non-renewable resources of our natural environment and the symbolical structures of our life world, the historically grown religious-metaphysical worldviews as well as the modern life forms, need protection(880). In spite of all his criticism concerning the obsolescence of religious-metaphysical-mystical systems of interpretation and orientation, Habermas wants them, nevertheless, to be protected. This is so possibly because of some unexplored truths still contained in religious-metaphysical-mystical worldviews; or possibly because of the need for support for the life world threatened by colonization through the extremely instrumentalized economic and political subsystems of late capitalistic societies and action systems.

But Habermas is convinced that the religious and secular life forms can be protected against colonization by money and administrative power only when we know very precisely and specifically, through which factors the life world is indeed threatened. The neo-conservatives exchange, like the Fascists before, cause and effect. The neo-conservatives put into the place of the real source of the crisis of late capitalistic action systems, the economic and administrative imperatives, the so-called reality compulsions, which monetarize and

bureaucratize always wider realms of the life world and
transform always wider communicative human relationships into
commodities and objects of administration, the specter of a
deviant, subversive transcendent left-wing culture. This false
analysis explains to Habermas why the neo-conservatives, when
they have to choose, do not find the life world, particularly
its familial and religious aspects, so sacred as they usually
pretend them to be. If neo-conservatives in the USA have to
make a choice under financial pressure, e.g., during an
economic depression, whether they should close in a university
the Religion Department or the Business Department or the
Engineering Department, they do not hesitate very long to find
out that it is the Religion Department which has to be phased
out(881). Political theologians intending the renewal of
messianic religion under conditions of highly differentiated
modern, late capitalistic or socialistic action systems, find
better allies among critical theorists like Habermas, than
among neo-conservatives. Precisely, therefore, the critical
encounter between Habermas and the political theologians is of
greatest importance.

Ideology or Utopia

Throughout the 19th century and into the early decades of the
20th century, the Hegelian Left freed itself from belief in
the existence of a divine power independent from society and
history but nevertheless governing both. Without this kind of
"atheism"--which one finds from Feuerbach and Marx all the way
to Bloch, Lukacs, Korsch, and Horkheimer--there can not even
be the beginning of human emancipation. This atheism is also
present in Habermas's universal pragmatic.

But between the two world wars it became clear to this
Hegelian Left how difficult it is to avoid turning precisely
this atheism into a new religion, thereby jeopardizing human
enlightenment and liberation once more. As long as the horror
and terror of nature, of society and history, of life and
death has not been overcome at least partially through the
work of a just society, people will be inclined to take refuge
in an attitude which has about it something of the other-
worldly silence of the old temples. In a world historical
situation in which human society has not advanced further than
we are now, a society in which evil increases qualitatively,
even the most "progressive" human beings still experience
moments in which they are drawn toward religion. It also

happens, when people are thrown into dark times, that the concept of God becomes the place where discredited, non-instru-
mental values and norms are kept alive. Western Marxists
retrieved the insight that men's and women's dissatisfaction
with their earthly destiny is the strongest subjective motive
for the acceptance of a transcendent being--not, of course,
for its objective existence. If absolute truth and justice
reside with God, then it is not to be found in the same
measure in the world of nature, the personal world, or the
social and cultural world. Religion as system of
interpretation and orientation is the record of the wishes,
hopes, longings, desires and accusations of countless
generations. It is the expression of a people's real distress
and their protest against that distress; it is not a hindrance
to human emancipation, but a reservoir of ideals for
liberation. Habermas is willing to admit this.

Particularly after World War II, it seemed to many that
humankind was losing its sense of religion as it moved through
history. But this loss left its mark behind. Part of the
drives and desires, longings and hopes for absolute justice,
which religious belief once preserved and kept alive, have now
been detached from an inhibiting religious form and have
become active forces for human enlightenment and emancipation.
In this process, the immoderation characteristic of scattered
religious illusions acquires a positive form and is truly
transformed. Thus, in a really emancipated person, the concept
of the Absolute, the Infinite, the Ultimate Reality is
preserved in the awareness of the finality of human life and
of the unalterable aloneness of men and women on this earth.
For Habermas the concept of the Absolute is superseded in a
discursive universalistic ethics in which people try to deal
rationally and realistically with their finality and their
aloneness(882).

The Hegelian Left, in the process of de-mystifying
religion, never confused the sharp boundary line between
emancipation and redemption. Only the Messiah or Christ
Himself consummates all history. Nothing social, political, or
historical can relate itself on its own account to anything
messianic. The Kingdom of God is not the goal of the social,
political, or historical process. In historical perspective,
the messianic realm is not the goal but the end. The order of
the profane cannot be built on the idea of God's kingdom.
Theocracy has only a religious meaning. It has no political
significance. It is the goal of redemption, not of

emancipation.   Habermas   agrees   completely   with   Bloch   and
Benjamin on this point(883).
The order of the secular must therefore be erected on the
idea of emancipation and happiness. But this does not elimin-
ate   the   important   ties   that   link   the   profane   order   to   the
messianic realm. This point can be   represented   figuratively.
If   one   arrow points to the goal of emancipation toward which
profane history moves, and another arrow marks   the   direction
of   messianic   intensity toward redemption, then certainly the
quest of free humanity for   emancipation   and   happiness   runs
counter to the messianic direction toward redemption. But just
as   a   force   can,   through   acting,   increase another that is
acting in the opposite direction, so the order of the   secular
world   assists   through   being profane, the coming of the messianic kingdom. The profane, therefore, although not itself   a
category of God's kingdom, is nevertheless a decisive category
for   its   silent approach to the process of world history. The
main concern of the Hegelian   Left   is   emancipation.   But   it
gives   rise   to   the idea of redemption and vice versa. Emancipation and redemption are separate, but also inseparable. They
reproduce each other in their utter   difference.   Emancipation
withers   away   into   the   totally adminstered society if it is
uncoupled   from   the   idea   of   redemption. The   emancipatory
impulse   needs   the redemptory corrective, if it is not to end
up in   individual   or   collective   terrorism.   The   redemptive
impulse needs the emancipatory corrective if it is to have any
impact on the political and historical process. While Habermas
cultivates   in his   universal pragmatic mainly the emancipatory
impulse, he is also aware   of   its   need   for   the   redemptive
corrective.
Today,   for   the   Hegelians of the Left there is good and
bad religion. Good religion is the   impulse,   carried   through
counterfactually and not yet suffocated by overadministration,
which   demands   that   the   ban of injustice be broken and that
things turn toward what is right. Where life   stands   in   this
sign   of   emancipation   down   to   every   single   gesture, there
indeed is good religion. But not everywhere,   where   there   is
religion,   is   there   also   emancipation. Bad religion is this
very   same   impulse,   but   perverted   into   affirmation,   into
<u>kerygma</u>.   It   is   the   impulse   to   gild   the reality of evil.
According to this perverted religion, the   suffering   of   life
and   the   terror of history have a "meaning," be it a relative
earthly meaning or an absolute heavenly one. This lie does not
even need the cross.   It   lives   already   in   the   ontological

notion of "transcendence" or "being." By contrast, when the religious impulse is for justice, or for the hope that the murderer will not triumph over the innocent victim, it is honest and does not need any apology. In his universal pragmatic, Habermas sides unequivocally with good religion against bad religion: with the innocent victim against the murderer.

It has become only too obvious that religion contains ideological as well as utopian, integrative as well as emancipatory elements. It has been the mistake of the Hegelian Left for some time to share in the error of the Hegelian Right and its positivistic heirs, that religion is nothing else than a mechanism for social control, integration, equilibration and stability. But many people on the Hegelian Left, now, have begun to correct this mistake. They have started to discover in feudal and bourgeois religion the hidden seeds of messianic religion. For a long time the dialectical materialists were not dialectical enough in their relation to religious worldviews. They took religious systems of interpretation and orientation as homogeneous instead of contradictory. All this means that the Hegelians on the Left must from now on treat religion as they have treated art and philosophy before, namely, dialectically. The irrational aspects of religious authorities and traditions, which suffocate human emancipation, must be attacked. The prophetic, messianic elements in religious traditions and authorities, which enhance the emancipatory process, must be retrieved. Habermas is prepared to do this.

Theological Glowing Fire

Habermas does indeed find good, emancipatory, utopian elements in religious worldviews: sparks of light, fragments of rationality. But Habermas has so far done as little or even less than Horkheimer, Benjamin, Adorno, Marcuse, Fromm or Sohn-Rethel what Adorno expected in the 1930s not only Benjamin, but the critical theory as such, to accomplish: to discover the theological glowing fire in the depth of historical materialism and thereby to strengthen its revolutionary impulse and make it immune against metaphysical objections(884).

For Hegel the tragedy of the Absolute was the foundation for the tragedy of the socio-moral totality(885). In Hegel's view that precisely was the theological glowing fire in the realm of social morality, that it reflected in its tragedy the tragedy of the God. Hegel comprehended in the power of the dialectical notion as universal, particular and singular the divine totality as a trinitarian one: the divine whole surrenders part of itself in the Christ and thus sacrifices itself to the other of itself, the world, and thereby reconciles it with itself and with nature in the spirit and returns into its own original unity(886). The spirit can not arrive before the Christ has not died(887). Likewise in the power of the dialectical notion Hegel comprehends the socio-moral totality as trinitarian: the socio-moral whole surrenders part of itself in civil society and sacrifices it and thus is able to return to itself in the organic state of free citizens(888). The organic state of living rationality can not come about as long as bougeois society as mechanical state has not been sacrificed or has not sacrificed itself(889). Hegel determined capitalistic society as the tragic difference in the realm of social morality. It is entirely mechanical, instrumental, functional. It is without any social morality(890). Legality takes the place of morality(891). Civil society is the negative totality which has to be superseded into the positive totality. The socio-moral whole comes to itself only through the sacrifice, more precisely the self-sacrifice of bourgeois society. Capitalistic society as mechanical state must be negated, but also preserved and elevated into the organic state of citizens recognizing each other not as instruments, but as ends in themselves. Bourgeois society moves beyond itself into the organic state by the power of the dialectic of its own inner contradictions between religious and secular, individual and collective, man and nature, producer and consumer, owner and worker, luxury and misery, rich and poor classes(892). That precisely is the revolutionary element in Hegel's philosophy of society and history. This revolutionary element is reinforced in Hegel's social philosophy by its theological element: the crucified God.

Marx put Hegel allegedly on his feet(893). He uncoupled the tragedy of the socio-moral totality from the tragedy of the Absolute with the practical intent to resolve it. He believed to unmask the tragedy of the Absolute as mere ideological reflection of the tragedy of the socio-moral totality, which was to be overcome by dialectical theory and revolutionary praxis. As Marx transformed Hegel's historical idealism into his historical materialism he neglected or repressed its theological glowing fire. Marx replaced Hegel's idealistic dialectic by his materialistic dialectic(894). Marx looks at the socio-moral totality in purely humanistic and scientific

terms. But Marx continues to agree with Hegel's revolutionary
position that the development of the realm of freedom
presupposes the supersession of capitalistic society: it is
driven beyond itself by its own immanent dialectic of capital
and labor, bourgeoisie and proletariat(895). As for Hegel, the
organic state does still preserve in itself elements of
bourgeois society as mechanical state or the citoyen elements
of the bourgeois, so for Marx the realm of freedom is still
based on the realm of necessity, the necessary work and tools,
the necessary metabolism between society and nature(896).
Unlike in Hegel's historical idealism the revolutionary
element in Marx's dialectical materialism is no longer
reinforced by the theological presupposition of the God who
sacrifices himself in history and rises again to himself.
Historical materialism is thus rendered extremely vulnerable
in theory and more still in praxis by metaphysical objections.
        Horkheimer and Adorno continue like Marx to turn Hegel
upside down. But at the same time they try to rediscover again
the theological dimension in historical materialism, which it
has by the very fact of its origin from historical ideal-
ism(897). With Hegel they stress against Marx and the Hegelian
Left the tragic character of the socio-moral totality. They
see in late capitalistic society the negative totality, which
has to be overcome. With Schopenhauer, Baudelaire, Benjamin,
Brecht, Pasternak and many other thinkers and poets of the
19th and 20th centuries, Horkheimer and Adorno describe
bourgeois society as "hell"(898). They are much less
optimistic than Hegel or Marx concerning the sacrifice or even
self-sacrifice of bourgeois society or dialectial transition
from the hell of capitalistic society to the realm of freedom.
Informed by the fascist experience Horkheimer and Adorno doubt
very much that the negation of the negative totality must
necssarily lead to a positive socio-moral totality. The iron
logic of bourgeois history seems rather to lead to the social
megamachine of the totally administered society or into the
holocaust of thermonuclear war(899). Small, if at all present,
is the probability and possibility that capitalistic society
will move by its own inner dialectic toward the reconciled
society. Precisely this pessimism may have motivated
Horkheimer and Adorno to look for the theological glowing fire
in historical materialism so that as theory it may not fall
victim to positivism and as praxis may not turn into mere
business or pseudo-activism.
        Habermas, like Marx before, uncouples the socio-moral

world with which he is mainly concerned in his formal and universal pragmatic and theory of communicative praxis from the theological foundation which it still has in Hegel's dialectical philosophy and which it tries to regain again in Horkheimer's, Adorno's and Fromm's theory of subject, society and history. While Habermas is indeed concerned with the tragedy of the Absolute in the framework of Jewish mysticism, he does not find or identify its reflection in the tragedy of the social world. As the social world does not mirror the crucified God, so it does also not reflect his resurrection. It seems that in Habermas's formal and universal pragmatic linguistic and social action takes the place theology once occupied in Hegel's philosophy(900). In a dialectical move originating from Hegel's Jena System Fragments and worthy of his further philosophical accomplishments Habermas in his formal and universal pragmatic, theory of communicative praxis and theory of religion takes recourse to language, more specifically practical discourse and communicative action in order thereby to supersede late capitalistic society as negative totality of work and tools toward the struggle for recognition with the final telos of a communication community characterized by mutual unconditional respect between the one and the other not as instruments, but as ends in themselves. It must remain doubtful, however, if discourse mediated social praxis can really motivate and effect, legitimate and stabilize the paradigm change from the negative totality of work and tools to the positive totality of a community characterized by communication without domination, from the bourgeois to the citoyen, without theological grounding, without theological glowing fire. This is the main deficiency in Habermas's reconstruction of historical materialism. The revolutionary transition from late capitalistic society to a society characterized by mutual recognition needs beyond discourse mediated communicative action a kind of sacrifice which may not be forthcoming in the long run without motivation rooted in the Unconditional.

Habermas agrees with Hegel and Marx that the civil society must not only be negated, but also preserved and elevated. Habermas does not want to do away with instrumental or functional rationality, but rather integrate it into the broader practical, communicative rationality. The communication community without domination will contain in itself instrumental rationality as being superseded. But in his preoccupation with language and intersubjectivity Habermas neglects, unlike Hegel and Marx, the contradictoriness of late capitalistic society as the motor for its transformation. By this very fact Habermas's version of historical materialism seems to be much less revolutionary than Hegel's historical idealism or Marx's dialectical materialism, or even Hork- heimer's early critical theory. There remains, nevertheless, in Habermas's formal and universal pragmatic and theory of communicative praxis the concern with the protest potential in late capitalistic society(901). The question is if the protest forces and protest initiatives are strong enough to push advanced capitalistic society beyond itself into a victimless society characterized by mutual recognition. It certainly does not help the revolutionary deficiency of Habermas's reconstruction of historical materialism that whatever revolutionary element it still contains has no theological foundation as it is the case with Hegel's dialectical idealism. This is particularly important at this point in history when it seems that the moment of a revolutionary transition from civil society to an organic state of living rationality or the realm of freedom, as Hegel and Marx had envisioned it, has been missed at least for the time being. At this point in history the theological dimension is of utmost relevance as source of hope for what is not yet, as it is strangled and suffocated by what is the case.

Unlike Hegel, Adorno, Benjamin and Horkheimer, and like Marx, Habermas still believes in spite of his by now much more positive attitude toward religious systems of interpretation and orientation, that he must make the sacrifice of theology in order to come to a reconstructed historical materialism. Unlike Hegel and like Marx and Freud Habermas does not see the tragedy of the socio-moral totality grounded in the tragedy of the Absolute. He can not, like Hegel, reach behind language and nature in order to find the theological basis for the revolutionary supersession of capitalistic society into the realm of freedom. To be sure, Habermas does not, like Popper, make the sacrifice of theology for positivism, the metaphysics of what is the case in late capitalistic society(902). He makes this sacrifice for dialectical materialism. He can not penetrate to the theological roots of the tragedy of the social world: the tragedy of the Absolute. He can not discover the theological glowing fire in the depth of his reconstructed historical materialism. This is so in spite of the fact that his interest in Jewish mysticism has brought him very close to such discovery. In case Habermas will some day discover the

theological   glowing   fire   in   the   depth   of   dialectical
materialism in the power of the dialectical notion, which
according to Adorno was originally a theological one, he may
be able to rekindle again its original revolutionary impulse:
that bourgeois society must be sacrificed or must sacrifice
itself so that a socio-moral world can be established on the
level of the nation and the species(903). According to Hegel
half a philosophy leads to atheism and anarchy(904). Only a
whole philosophy can reach the dialectical notion of God and
the dialectical notion of the organic state. Only a whole
philosophy can rescue from despair and can console those who
have to live in the tragic difference in the state as positive
moral totality: the negative totality of bourgeois society.
     Critical theorists as well as critical Christians are
under the obligation while living in the negative totality of
organized capitalistic society, i.e., in hell, to accomplish a
kind of existence which anticipates the positive socio-moral
totality, be it called with Hegel organic state of living
rationality, or with Marx realm of freedom, or with Horkheimer
and Adorno reconciled society, or with Habermas communicative
community characterized by communication without domination
and by mutual respect. It is of course possible that the
negative totality of bourgeois society will harden itself
further in its negativity. Then there will be no organic state
or realm of freedom. There will be Future I - the escalation
of the necrophilous mechanical state, the totally monetarized
and bureaucratized society. It is possible that the negative
totality of late capitalistic society will push under the
pressure of its inner contradictions and crises into Future II
- ABC wars. It is possible that a transition from the negative
totality of civil society to the positive totality of a
materially democratic state will take place but that it will
be a catastrophic one. It is the obligation of critical
theorists and critical Christians to prepare a non-catastrophic, victimless transition from the negative to the
positive totality characterized by practical, communicative
rationality.
     Such non-catastrophic transition from the negative to a
positive social world can, of course, be tried on purely
humanistic grounds. That precisely Habermas attempts to do
when he uncouples the obvious tragedy of the socio-moral
totality from its theological prototype, the tragedy of the
Absolute, in his sacrifice of theology. Contrary to this we
suggest that a recoupling of the social world to the Absolute

would not do any harm to Habermas's critical humanistic
position, but would rather reinforce its revolutionary intent
to supersede the instrumental world of capitalism into a world
of discourse-mediated communicative praxis. The divine tragedy
is resolved in the resurrection(905). The human tragedy is to
be resolved in the revolutionary supersession of the negative
totality of capitalistic society as mechanical state, which
transforms speaking, working, loving and recognition-aspiring
people into machines, into the positive totality of the
organic state of living practical, communicative rationality,
in which free citizens come to mutual understanding with each
other and recognize each other as ends in themselves and
coordinate their life plans with each other(906).

According to Hegel's philosophy of right and religion in
order to pluck the rose of objective reason of the organic
state of free citizens, we must first take upon ourselves
daily the cross of civil society as mechanical state of
necessity and abstract analytical understanding(907). In his
critique of Hegel's philosophy of right Marx does not only
rephrase the relationship of rose and cross in terms of
flowers and chain, but also tries to turn it upside down(908).
In Marx's view we must first pluck the ideological flowers of
religion which legitimate the chain of bourgeois society and
only then can we break the capitalistic chain. But in his
reinterpretation of Hegel's dialectical image of rose and
cross, Marx remains much closer to his great teacher Hegel
than he may have been aware of. For Hegel as for the mystics,
particularly Eckehart and Nicolaus of Cusa before, man
overcomes death not by running away from it but rather by
facing it(909). Likewise the cross is overcome precisely by
being carried(910). For Hegel the rose of objective reason
does not legitimate the cross of bourgeois society, but rather
its revolutionary supersession or self-liquidation into the
rose of the reason of the socio-moral totality, of the organic
state of the free humanity, of the kingdom of God(911). In
this sense the truth is the whole(912). Mysticism and
revolution do not necessarily exclude each other, but rather
reproduce and reinforce each other(913). In any case, Hegel
and Marx agree that the cross or the chain of capitalistic
society must be overcome before the organic state or the realm
of freedom can come into being. The self-estrangement of the
positive socio-moral totality in its immanent difference, the
immoral civil society as mechanical state has to be cancelled
or must do away with itself via its own inner contradictions

and the corresponding convulsions toward Future III – the reconciled society(914). Otherwise the socio-moral totality itself will be pulled deeper and deeper into its own difference and self-alienation and thus will either be hardened further and further in itself toward Future I – the totally monetarized and bureaucratized society – or it will destroy itself in Future II – ABC wars.

Critical theorists and critical fundamental theologians agree in the longing and in the hope that the socio-moral totality can overcome in itself its own negativity, bourgeois society, and can thus reconcile itself with itself on the national and international level. Particularly in discourse with Habermas, theologians of communicative praxis are preparing the theological-humanistic foundations on which cooperation between critical Christians and critical theorists will be possible in the future(915). On this theological-humanistic basis critical theorists and critical Christians can cooperate in at least mitgating Future I – the social megamachine, in resisting Future II – the thermonuclear holocaust, and in promoting Future III – the communicative community characterized by communication without domination in the national and historical dimension(916). Critical theorists and critical Christians can cooperate in such a way, if they are able to combine two statements by Benjamin, related to each other in an ironical-dialectical manner: First, there is a sphere of human agreement, which is free from power to such an extent that force can not even penetrate it: the real sphere of understanding, language(917). Secondly, there must be pessimism all the way, yes, and throughout: particularly, there must be distrust in all understanding among classes, among nations, among individuals, and there must be unlimited trust alone in I. G. Farber and the peaceful perfection of the air force(918). Since Benjamin we have, of course, made much progress: today we must rather speak of infinite trust in General Electric, Westinghouse, Martin Marietta, General Dynamics and the peaceful perfection of space weapons; trust in and perfection of the military and industrial complex, and the politics of the total market(919). Without such ironical-dialectical pessimism there can be no real mutual understanding and no real mutual unconditional recognition of the one and the other as self-purpose, and no Future III – the reconciled society.

Chapter III
Critical Political Theology

From Critical Theory to Fundamental Theology

After consideration of the newest and most mature form of
Habermas's critical theory of religion, as it is contained in
his universal pragmatic and theory of communicative praxis,
the question arises, of course, again and again with
increasing urgency, why and how after his critical conclusion
that religious worldviews are obsolete because they can no
longer resolve adequately on the present level of human
evolution and learning the theodicy problem and thus can no
longer provide any basis for social and personal identity in
highly differentiated modern action systems, religion and
theology can at all be possible? Why and how can they at all
be protected as integral elements of the life world threatened
by colonization through the economic and political subsystems
of contemporary and future capitalistic or socialistic action
systems?
Habermas challenges with his critical theory of religion
particularly the most progressive theologians, those closest
to his universal pragmatic, the critical fundamental
theologians, the theologians of communicative praxis, the
political theologians, to say why and how they can still call
themselves theologians and why they do not also simply call
themselves critical theorists or theorists of communicative
action? What precisely is the difference between universal
pragmatic and critical fundamental theology or theology of
communicative praxis or political theology? Certainly the
challenge of the theory of communicative action aims at the
very heart of the new critical political theology as well as
all other types of theology.
The fundamental theologian responds to this challenge by
penetrating the universal pragmatic to the point where it

reveals its own aporia in the face of contingency, catastrophe
and paradoxy, and by trying to resolve this aporia through
recourse to the Jewish and Christian and other world
religions. Thereby the theologian of communicative praxis
tends to strengthen the universal pragmatic against all
theological and metaphysical objections, which could be made
against it, and to fortify at the same time religion and
theology against all the objections which could be made
against them by the critical theory, especially by Habermas's
universal pragmatic. Critical theory and political theology
meet their common interest in particularly Jewish and
Christian mysticism: from the Kabbala and Hasidism over Moses
Maimonides, Master Eckehart, Nicolaus of Cusa, and J. Boehm to
Hegel, Marx and Freud(1). We shall concentrate particularly on
Peukert's and Arens's fundamental theology, theology of
communicative praxis and political theology(2). In our
critical discourse on the new fundamental theology we shall
combine personal and reflexive, existential-practical and
cognitive-theoretical elements. We shall engage in narrative
as well as reflexive argumentation about the theology of
communicative praxis with special emphasis on the theodicy
problem.

Discovery

We encountered Peukert's new fundamental theology in a very
tragic moment of our life together here in the USA and in
Canada(3). My late wife Margie and I "discovered" Peukert's
theology of communicative praxis in September 1977, when we
found out that she had cancer of the colon which then spread
fast to liver and lung. The science which had produced the
carcinogenic compounds in the commodities which we had bought
as consumers from the producers had made Margie ill, but was
not able to stop the destruction it had initiated.
    The theodicy -the justification of the all-loving and
all-powerful God in the face of the horror and terror of
nature and particularly of society and history- had always
been a central problem for Margie and me. Margie's father had
died from a heart illness three months before her birth in
Washington, DC, and my father had died from cancer of the
colon early in my childhood in Frankfurt a.M., Germany. Margie
and I experienced and participated in World War II on
different sides of the front, she on the American and I on the
German side. Later in our married and family life as our seven

children were growing up, we often visited the bloody
battlefields in Europe on which I had fought and the graves of
the slaughtered and vanquished which mark them until today.
Doing so, we had often faced the dilemma of the theodicy
problem as Scheler had posed it after his participation in the
butchery of the battle of Verdun: if God was indeed, as
Christianity teaches, all-loving and all-powerful, he would
intervene in and stop the catastrophe of history. Since he
obviously does not, he is either power without love or love
without power. In the goodness of his heart, Scheler decided
for the latter possibility and developed a dynamic pantheism,
in which God is love only slowly acquiring power as well.
Scheler's solution to the theodicy problem always appeared
impressive to us, if also being somewhat theoretical.

During the last apocalyptic year of our life together,
the theodicy became for Margie and me indeed a most practical,
most personal and intimate, and most cruel problem. At this
moment, Peukert's fundamental theology became our theodicy
and, as such, gave us and our children a possibility of
interpretation and orientation in the midst of utter
absurdity.

While Modernity started with the quest for the
justification of man, it ends with the quest for the
justification of God. Peukert has faced this problem. In his
theology of communicative praxis Peukert struggles for a new
and more concrete and plausible theoretical and practical
answer to a problem which is much older than modernity, the
problem of Job and of Jesus: the theodicy—God's justice and
the unequal distribution of happiness chances, shortly, the
barbarous injustices in society and history.

Death of the Other

During the "good times" in the agony of 1977 and 1978, in the
USA and Canada, between operation, chemo-therapy and radiation
treatment, Margie and I discussed different aspects of
Peukert's political theology, which seemed to us to be most
relevant to our situation. As a result of our discussions,
together we composed an article, "Peukert's New Critical
Theology," for the Ecumenist as we slowly moved toward
Margie's death(4). This article became something like our
spiritual testament. Together we concentrated and meditated on
each subchapter of the article: "Science and Action,"
"Communicative Competence," "Obsolescence of Religion,"

"Theological Basis Theory," "The Death of the Innocent Other,"
"Political Proof of God," "A Christology from Below." When we
came to the subchapter, "The Death of the Innocent Other,"
Margie felt that this was another indication of her
approaching end. She was never afraid of death. Yet she wanted
to live so much and see and enjoy her grandchildren. I tried
to console Margie that the "other" in this case was Jesus, and
that she was not him and therefore she did not have to go up
to Jerusalem and to Golgotha and die. However, as we would
know only too soon, these were human thoughts, not God's
thoughts. The last miracle we hoped for to the end was not
performed. We had to let ourselves be corrected in our hopes
and our thoughts.

Margie received her death sentence--malignant tumor in
the colon--over the phone from her internist at Bronson
Hospital in Kalamazoo, Michigan on Friday, September 30, 1977,
at 3:00 p.m. The operation was to take place a week later.
After having heard the bad news Margie called me and invited
me to drive out with her into the countryside, to celebrate my
50th birthday at an inn. While Margie was driving our family
car to the country inn she told me her last wishes. She would
never repeat them again, so she promised, in order not to
cause us further pain. Her wishes were: I was to be strict and
good in educating our seven children; during her funeral the
coffin was to be closed in order not to arouse feelings of
guilt among our children and friends; her small life insurance
of $1,000 was to be used for her funeral and should suffice;
after some time when a friendly woman would come along I was
to marry again. Soon after Margie had expressed her last
wishes we arrived at the country inn and began our birthday
celebration.

On the following Monday the surgeon, who was to operate
on Margie, showed us her fist-sized tumor on an x-ray screen.
He was a Catholic. He told us how beautifully and wisely God
had created the anatomic structure of man and of woman. It
gave him the chance to operate effectively. He asked us for
our informed consent. We gave it to him. The surgeon's
theology did not include the cancer which was in the process
of destroying Margie's life. After the operation had failed to
remove together with the malignant tumor all of the
Lymphosarcomas, the surgeon told Margie to distribute her
jewelry and silver, of which she had little, among her
children and to put her things in order and to prepare for the
end. She was to take all the trips, she always wished to make

throughout her life and could not, in the months still left to her. The doctor did not tell us how to pay for the operation he had performed, and the following radiation, chemotherapy, blood transfusions, pain medications, and the hospital visits in general, not to speak of the costs for the trips still to be taken. He ended up once more on a theological note: Margie was to forgive before her death all that people and society had done to her.

On a beautiful sunny day in May 1978, we went to Borgess Hospital here in Kalamazoo, only to find out that in spite of operation, chemotheraphy and radiation, the cancer had spread from colon to liver and into the already damaged right lung. On our way home from the hospital, Margie fell into utter despair. She felt that God had forsaken her completely. I tried to console her by saying that God is with us. But she asked: "Where is he?" And he was, of course, nowhere to be found. He seemed to be as dead as Margie would be only too soon. In the coming summer weeks Margie prayed out of D. Berrigan's Uncommon Prayers(5). There she discovered the "dialectic" between Psalm 73--"And where in the World are you?" and Psalm 46--"The Lord is Lord, Our Refuge, Our Strength!" She wrote a little note under Psalm 73: "I know God is in this world--but really--where is he at times?" One day, I told Margie that a terrible injustice had happened to her. She remained silent. She did not want to speak to us about this injustice so as not to make us even sadder. Yet shortly before her death, she told a friend: "I have lived a good life. I have no regrets." The injustice was not on her side. It was on the side of society and, ultimately, on God's side, if indeed there was a God.

One day in June 1978 Margie and I went to a movie together. We did not know exactly what the story would be. It happened that in the end of the movie the lover left his beloved girlfriend, who was terminally ill, and did not wait for the hour of her death. As so often during Margie's history of suffering this event was rather ominous to us. Margie saw in the movie another sign of her own fast approaching death. She asked me to stay with her to the very end and not to leave her and to allow her to die in my arms. I promised.

For many years Margie, an American citizen, had prayed that God's providence may guide us someday to Canada where she hoped we could find more recognition for the emancipatory form of education we were engaged in. By 1978 we had received an invitation to teach in Canada. When I departed on July 1,

1978, by car with some of our children from Kalamazoo to
Canada where I was to teach as visiting professor during
Summer and Fall 1978 and Winter 1979 and Margie was to follow
next day by plane with one of our daughters, she said in our
bedroom: "When it is already so hard to say Goodby for only
one night, how terrible must it be to say Goodby for Eternity.
It is so long." A heavy thunderstorm raged above our house. A
few months later Margie died without saying Goodby.

During the long summer of 1978 when Margie's health went
downhill continuously and with great spead, she agreed with
friends and myself in Kitchener, Ontario, where I taught at
this time as a visiting professor at Waterloo University, that
we should call a priest to give her the Sacrament of the Sick.
A Jesuit priest came with one of his parishioners and
performed the ritual. Margie received the sacrament with great
seriousness, dignity and hope. On his way out the young Jesuit
and I spoke about the many priests and sisters who had left
their vocation in recent years in Canada, the USA, and
elsewhere. The priest admitted quite honestly and
realistically that there were indeed many good reasons for
doing so. When the Jesuit left, he told me as a matter of
consolation that many people call him up in the morning after
the performance of the Sacrament of the Sick and tell him
joyfully that the condition of the patient had improved. But
next morning Margie felt as bad as before and her excrutiating
pain and deterioration continued with most cruel regularity.

Throughout her long suffering Margie never lost her
faith. But often she did not know what to make of the New
Testament. It seemed to be ambiguous. What did the New
Testament really say to her concrete situation? Was she to
pray and hope for a miracle? Or was she to prepare for death?
In reality she did both.

Toward the end of the summer Margie had one of her
happier dreams. We always discussed them with each other.
Margie had taken one of the pills which her doctor prescribed
and which supposedly were to mitigate her pain, but never did.
The morphine pills were to be saved for the bloody end. In
Margie's dream her grandmother and her mother, who had raised
her, and her father whom she had never seen since he died
three months before her birth, appeared to her from Heaven in
most beautiful forms and waved to her and asked her to follow
them. But Margie told them that she would like to wait a
little while at the door of heaven, until we all, her family,
could follow her and be together again. The dream expressed

Margie's wish to be redeemed from the months of horror, to wake up every morning to the continuing terrible reality, like on deathrow, as well as her longing to stay and live with us happily. After Margie had told her dream she stood up from her bed, but then suddenly fell without us being able to interfere and cut her lips at the corner of the night table. It was the third time that she had fallen in such a sudden way.

During the last months of Margie's life, as we discussed together our article on Peukert's fundamental theology, we spoke about the destruction of the innocent other, about the anamnestic solidarity, and about God's reality which saves before death, as in the case of Job, or in death, as in the case of Jesus; a Reality which can be experienced in solidary interaction between the one and the other and can be named in the dialectic of love. We knew that it happens again and again: that good men and women have tried to live in solidarity with others, particularly with the oppressed, exploited, poor, suffering, dying, (i.e. men and women to whom others owe their own possibility of living, speaking and acting) and have, nevertheless, been annihilated due to no fault of their own. We also spoke about the survivor who is threatened with inner destruction by the death of the other in his or her own inner center of self and ego—identity. Once Margie told me, as her illness came to a new climax, that she was moving further and further away from me. Then she asked: "Can you give me up?" And I answered: "No!" We did not want to yield to, surrender and capitulate before the forces of darkness, which were in process of separating us.

Daily Margie and I read the stories by and about Jesus from the New Testament. We thought of Jesus in terms of his discourse—mediated solidary interaction with his friends and his opponents as he moved toward his execution. We knew that through the continual assertion of the gracious reality of God for the oppressed, ill, suffering and dying others posited practically in his communicative existence, Jesus has provoked and opened up the possibility of asserting God to be the saving actor even in the case of his own death. God has rescued the just other, Jesus, in his destruction on the cross in the form of the resurrection. He has affirmed and justified him before the establishment that murdered him in the framework of power conformity and, thus, of systematically distorted communication. Thereby, God has justified himself. That is Christian theodicy! Ultimately, the murderer did not triumph over the innocent victim. That was our central hope,

through which we understood all of Christanity and Judaism.
On Monday, September 19, 1978, one of our younger sons,
to whom in baptism we had given the name of Thomas More, the
saintly statesman, humanist and socialist, ran away from our
home in London, Ontario, where I taught at this time as
visiting professor at Western Ontario University. It happened
when I visited Margie in the cancer clinic of Victoria
Hospital in London, where she stayed for a week to receive
entirely ineffective, but nevertheless painful chemotherapy
and also blood transfusions. Thomas could no longer stand the
smell of death in our house. He moved in with a much older
woman in our hometown of Kalamazoo. When we brought Margie
home from the cancer clinic at the end of the week and she did
not find her son, she searched for him and fought for him with
all the energies still left to her. We found no effective
support in our attempts to bring our minor son home from his
cohabitation with the older woman, who was also his employer
and teacher: neither from lawyers nor from priests or
ministers or university administrators. Bourgeois decadence
had undermined the law and the noblest institutions. To the
very end of her life Margie hoped that her "prodigal son"
would return. But when Thomas was called to his mother's
deathbed in the last hours of her life, he refused to join his
brothers and sisters and to see her a last time. Margie had
found her Judas.

As Margie's death approached at our London home, she was
more concerned with the crucifixion than with the
resurrection. Twenty days before her death she asked me, since
she could no longer walk, to buy a cross for my birthday in
her name. It was to be a cross with the crucified Jesus on it
and not the resurrected Christ. Margie intended us to look at
the crucified Messiah in the hour of her death and then to be
consoled in the midst of death and then, after her funeral, to
go on with our lives and our work.

We knew during all of this, that the assertion of the
resurrection of Jesus is real only as practical anamnestic
solidarity with all innocent victims of history. We also knew
that our Christology from below needed the Christology from
above in order to be fully true: not only a prophet, but God
himself had died on the cross and had killed death and, thus,
had made possible through the negation of negation, through
the death of death, resurrection and ascension.

Our completed article had appeared in August 1978, two
months before Margie's death. I could still read the article

to Margie and she with her emaciated hands would applaud particularly those parts which were concerned with the theodicy problem: the discrepancy between God's love and justice and the absurdity of our contingency situation. She was happy with the article.

On the evening of October 19, 1978, after conventional medical technology and traditional religion had become almost equally aporetical, Margie thanked us for all the good things we had done for her, particularly during the terrible year of her suffering. We also thanked her for all the love she had given to us through 22 years of marriage and family life. Then Margie told me very quietly, that the end would come during the night. She asked me to stay with her. I promised to stay with her always. Margie's end did, indeed, come early in the morning of Friday, October 20, 1978, in the protective circle of her family. The theodicy problem reached its climax. Not only a good and to the end non-possessively loving woman, God himself seemed to have died.

In my sermon at Margie's funeral, which she had prepared in detail down to location, readings, prayers, and songs, I followed the core issues of our article on Peukert's fundamental theology, which we had meditated upon throughout the past year so full of pain, suffering, tears and disappointments. I spoke about Margie's good life as wife and mother, as social worker, as pianist and organist, as teacher, and most of all about her non-possessive devotion to family, friends and students here in the USA, in Canada, Germany and Yugoslavia.

Then, I talked about the possibilities of action for the survivors. They can, of course, make the attempt to eliminate completely the memory of the innocent other who has been destroyed and thus refuse to acknowledge reality by simply repressing it. The survivors can cynically draw the conclusion from the experience of the annihilation of a good person that everyone should optimally utilize all possibilities of action only for himself or herself as long as there is still time: Carpe diem! In this case the survivors would abandon universal solidarity, including the anamnestic solidarity with the destroyed other, who, nevertheless, has been rescued by God's saving reality, as the fundamental principle for finding their own singular identity. Finally, the survivors could let themselves fall back into a cruel process of mutual annihilation a la Social Darwinism and thus drop behind the evolutionary threshhold of the achievement of the fundamental norm of communication: mutual, unconditional recognition and universal solidarity. In the spirit of our article, I rejected all these options and pleaded for the continuation of loving recognition of Margie beyond her death in anamnestic and proleptic solidarity, asserting her being rescued by God's gracious reality in the Christian community and beyond.

Later on, I erected upon our common grave our symbol: the Rose in the Cross. It took me two years until finally I received permission from the mayor of Kalamazoo to put up the cross with the rose, since it was a religious symbol and the cemetary is secular, and thus the religious symbol may irritate secular people. A huge cross of South Dakota granite contains a small rose cut out of the rock, under which is written the first verse of Psalm 4, which Margie and I prayed together every evening throughout the year of her suffering and death as we waited for the always postponed execution, up to the last night: "When I call, You hear me, o God of my justice, in distress you set me free!"(6) While the symbol of the rose of God's wisdom in the cross of the contradictory present stems from Hegel's philosophy of right, his political theology, it expresses at the same time the core issue of Peukert's new theology of communicative praxis: God's saving reality and the contingencies of nature, personal life, society and history. It is the problem of theodicy.

Fundamental theologians like Peukert, Metz, Arens, have come to stand in deep respect before Margie's life and dying, which as praxis of faith is indeed ahead of all theoretical reflection. But political theologians find it necessary nevertheless to translate this experience theologically and philosophically into principal and radical question to such an extent that formally and contentwise nobody can bypass any longer the problem which it contains: the theodicy problem. The fundamental theologian may be somewhat afraid of the expectations which direct themselves toward him concerning such philosophical and theological translation of such experience. But he consoles himself with the hope that a whole community of political theologians will work together in solidarity to pose and to answer those unresolveable radical questions arising from such experiences. Together the theologians of communicative action will find the courage they need in theory and praxis as they face these questions. I would like to turn to and engage in such philosophical and theological translation of experience.

Dialectical Construct

Peukert's fundamental theology can be understood as an answer to Habermas's thesis, that the traditional religious worldviews have become obsolete because of their inability to resolve the theodicy problem and the consequential identity problem in spite of all the psychological and sociological mechanisms for their protection against the onslaught of modernization, rationalization and disenchantment which in recent centuries and decades have become less and less effective: the inner limitations of religious discourse; liturgical fixation of insufficient theodicy answers; interpreting away of the most dreadful evils in personal, social, political and historical life; forgetfulness; repression of deviant theological thoughts; and most of all, an extreme tolerance of religious people for the most outrageous inconsistencies, contradictions, paradoxes and absurdities in reality as well as in the religious systems of interpretation of reality and orientation of action(7).

Peukert answers Habermas with an ingenious dialectical construct worthy of Hegel: the aporia of the philosophy of science leads to the philosophy of action and the aporia of the formal and universal pragmatic leads to fundamental theology, theology of communicative praxis, critical political theology(8). There arises, of course, the serious question, if fundamental theology does not have its own aporia, which again drives the philosophers and natural and social scientists back into their philosophies of action or of science, no matter how aporetical these philosophies may be or how much they may require them to live without any consolation or even in despair. There is, indeed, an aporetical point in fundamental theology itself, which must be faced squarely, if it is not to be reached and overtaken by Habermas' indictment of alleged obsolescence before it has even been fully developed: the theodicy problem. The specific Christian form of the theodicy question is the parousia delay: the present continuation of the horror and terror in nature, society and history, which no maranatha seems to be able to break. The greatness of Peukert's theology of communicative praxis consists precisely in his willingness to face courageously the theodicy issue(9). This is the more astonishing if one takes into consideration that there were many earlier Christian attempts in modernity to deal with this problem, which were far from being sufficient, plausible, and convincing(10).

The Problem

Voltaire experienced the devastating earthquake which on All Saints Day killed thousands of people in Lisbon under the ruins of their churches. Leibniz spoke of the best of all possible worlds(11). In his Candide Voltaire laughed Leibniz out of court. In response to Voltaire and Leibniz, Hegel constituted his whole dialectical philosophy as a theodicy in the theological sense: the justification of God's reason, wisdom, love and providence in the face of the enormous negativity in the world of nature, the personal world, the world of society and history and the world of culture(12). Hegel's philosophy is the last great systematic attempt to deal with the theodicy in Christian terms. It even illicits Habermas's greatest respect in spite of the fact that he can no longer accept it because of the intensification of the modern contingency experience and future orientation after Hegel's death(13).

Unlike Hegel, his disciple and opponent Kierkegaard avoided to answer the theodicy problem directly by simply pointing fideistically to the sinfulness of man and thereby regressing somewhat into mythology(14). This way, he tried to ward off all rebelliousness and revolutionary impulses, which may arise from the unresolved theodicy problem. Where God's providence was obviously missing in the face of horrible contingencies, man himself had to replace it with his own providence in discipleship and brotherly love. Human pragmatic replaces divine pragmatic or theology proper.

Hegel's most outstanding student and opponent, Marx's historical materialism can be understood as theodicy in the sociological sense a la Weber: as a theoretical explanation of the injustices in civil society and bourgeois history but with the practical intent of overcoming them through revolutionary action(15). Yet when Marx's beloved wife Jenny died and soon afterwards his daughter who was closest to him, the great man broke down and walked disconsolately and in despair the beaches of the French Riviera. He died himself a little bit more than a year after his wife. There was no answer in the Capital for these very personal contingencies, this very intimate theodicy. Marx wrote the Capital and everything else without considering concretely the tragic end of individuals, families, nations or species. Marx did this in spite of the fact that he often read Shakespeare's tragedies to his children. Marx even took his children to church in London in order to listen to the music. Being asked by his children what this religion was all about Marx answered: there was once a poor man and the rich people murdered him! But the materialistic interpretations of the death of the other and one's own death and the corresponding orientations of action are insufficient. The theodicy problem remains unresolved.

In this century, the great Marxist playwright, Brecht, read the Bible daily, but turned it all materialistically upside down as Hegel had done sometimes before and as Benjamin would do later: "Seek for food and clothing first, then the Kingdom of God shall be added on to you"(16). Brecht's plays contain not only an inverse theology, but also an inverse theodicy, which according to Adorno is as such to be rescued some day in the future by the critical theory of subject, society and history(17). But neither Benjamin, Adorno nor Habermas have really been able so far to retrieve concretely Brecht's inverse theodicy. Peukert's fundamental theology contains in itself the potential to do so.

For Horkheimer, the Christian dogma of an all-loving and all-powerful God is almost unbelievable in the face of the horror and terror of nature and history(18). Horkheimer, therefore, deemphasizes the messianism in his own work, which was still very strong in Marx's dialectical materialism(19). It is reawakened again in Benjamin's conjugation of dialectical materialism and Jewish mysticism in the framework of his political theological fragments, the article on the historical materialist Fuchs, the collector and historian, his passage-work and his theses on the philosophy of history(20). Horkheimer, however, with his friend Adorno retreats into the most extreme obedience to the Second Commandment; not to make any images of the Absolute, not to name it or in any way pull it down into the malum metaphysicum or the mala physica of nature and history, or to justify, gild and transfigure them by it in terms of a bad religion(21). Adorno recommends in the name of autonomous reason the strictest asceticism against all forms of religious revelation, including the Christian one(22). Horkheimer and Adorno were committed to a negative theology and theodicy a la Moses Maimonides, Meister Eckehart and Nicolaus of Cusa as idology: the destruction of idols, including the fetishisms of sex, car and career, which characterize the bourgeois personality; the fetishisms of shoes, legs, breasts and commodities in general; and the cults of nation, race and leader(23).

However toward the end of his life, Horkheimer discussed

the question of death and immortality with his beloved wife, Maidon, who had converted from Christianity to Judaism. Before his wife's sudden death from a heart-attack in 1969, Horkheimer had spoken with her about their meeting again in Eternity. The verse from Psalm 91 on Horkheimer's gravestone: "In You, Eternal One, alone I trust" is at least the beginning of an affirmative theodicy in the framework of negative theology and historical materialism.

Christian Response

On his deathbed the outstanding Catholic theologian R. Guardini confessed to a friend concerning the theodicy problem: "When I shall come before God, he shall certainly ask me many questions. But I shall have to ask God some questions as well: why all this terrible suffering in this world?" "And I hope," so Guardini continued, "that God's angel will give me a sufficient answer." Guardini had not found an adequate answer to the theodicy problem in any of the many theologies he had studied or even in his own rather extensive one.

For the convert and devout Christian on the Right, Schneider, the theodicy problem posed itself strangely enough only very late in his life(24). It happened in his fifties when he fell ill and was looking through the microscope at the cells in his blood feeding upon and destroying each other. In a long cold and desperate winter in Vienna, Schneider lost his faith in resurrection and ascension and was merely longing for the rest of the grave.

Peukert's saintly teacher, Rahner, in spite of his intellectual dependence on Hegel and his participation in the Marxist-Christian dialogue, never treated the theodicy problem explicitly in his huge theological opus. His whole theology remains hermetically closed up against the horror and terror of nature, civil society and bourgeois history. When Rahner, following Nicolaus of Cusa and Hegel, speaks of God as one who does not will or allow the death of the innocent victim as a bloody tyrant, but rather kills out of love, then this argument as such does not really resolve the riddles of the theodicy, but rather sharpens and intensifies them beyond measure(25). This is so, even if such divine killing out of love takes place in the process and context of reconciliation. Here obviously traditional theology comes to its utmost limitation. Even in one of his last prayers, which his friends put on his memorial card after his death, Rahner admits implicitly his inability to resolve the theodicy problem and leaves its solution to his own very personal eschatology: "I wait, o God, in patience and hope. I wait like a blind man, to whom is promised the rise of light. I expect the resurrection of the dead and of the flesh." The rest is most cruel abandonment and capitulation.

For a long time Rahner left the resolution of the theodicy problem to his colleague, the Frankfurt Jesuit F. Nink. He spent over half a century constructing a neo-scholastic theodicy. When Nink's student, Haag, demolished his theodicy during his habilitation presentation on the newer ontologies at the University of Frankfurt in 1956 in the presence of his old teacher as well as of his new mentors Horkheimer and Adorno, he said very humbly: "How do we say it better from now on?" This is, indeed, the question with which also Peukert is still faced and with which critical political theologians will have to struggle for some time to come, for better or for worse.

The outstanding and very popular liberal theologian, H. Kung, is fully aware of the whole problematic of the theodicy at this point in the history of the world religions in general and of the Christian church in particular. He knows how questionable the biblical concept of "Providence" has become for many people living through the dialectics of civil society and bourgeois history and their contingencies, e.g., economic depressions, ecological destruction, hot and cold wars, etc. Kung is an immensely kind, compassionate, loving, generous and tolerant man. He certainly has his own share of suffering. His own Catholic church, which he defends so well in the present religious crisis situation, has stabbed him in his back by withdrawing from him the venia legendi in theology. He is very much aware of the fact that the affirmation of his theological lifework and his reconciliation with Rome may occur only after his death. Kung shares intensely in the human suffering around him. He was deeply shocked when he heard of the senseless tragedy of our family. He suffered to the point of despair with the young priest who committed suicide since he could not resolve his personal conflict which arose from his obligatory promise of celebacy. Kung knows that no paradigm or theory really helps the victim in the hour of catastrophe, in the face of the factum brutum of the bitter end, not even the best theological paradigm, not even his own. Kung is aware that Horkheimer and Adorno criticized Hegel following Schopenhauer precisely because of

the allegedly all too positive and affirmative and ultimately
optimistic way in which he resolved the theodicy problem in
his philosophy of right and history(26). Kung is in agreement
with this critique.

     However, none of Kung's 26 books or so contains a whole
specific chapter on the theodicy problem, nor can his whole
theology be considered as a plausible and conclusive theodicy.
No matter how deeply Kung feels with and sides and identifies
with the innocent victims of senseless tragedies, he, nevertheless, always trusts in their speedy resolution. That is his
temperament. His trust and optimism is fascinating. It is
uplifting. But there are, nevertheless, tragedies which are
lifelong and for which there is no resolution in sight in time
and not even in Eternity. This remains true even if there is
no self-stigmatization at work in the victims, as we find it
e.g., in the so-called Sermon on the Mount. What society has
done to the innocent victims of Stalingrad, Kursk and
Petrograd, London and Coventry, Auschwitz, Treblinka and
Buchenwald, Hamburg and Dresden, Vietnam and Lebanon, Iran and
Nicaragua, El Salvador, Grenada and Ethiopia, etc., can never
be undone. To say the opposite and simply point to the Last
Judgment, Heaven or Hell, would be idealism in the worst sense
of the word, i.e., ideology, untruth. We may not know what
happens in the other world, if there is one, but we do know
very well what society has done to the innocent victims in
this world and that their bloody end in all its cruel details
can never be cancelled out by any power in heaven or on earth
as if it had never happened. While Kung does indeed call the
bad things inside and outside the church by their name, he
nevertheless often seems to glide over them all too easily in
his brilliant style rather than to dwell with the negative
until being arises from it, if indeed it does. Kung likes to
tell the story of the Pharoah, who ordered his slaves to build
a ship for him and put it into his pyramid so that after his
death he can cross in it the river which separates time and
Eternity. For Kung the Pharoah's order is not only an
expression of human longing for eternal life, but rather a
well-founded trust. The question if the Pharoah was willing to
bring his slaves along on his ship is not even asked.

     Kung's optimism is more of Catholic than Protestant
origin. Kung may have learned it in the Catholic youth
movement of the 1930s and 1940s, in which we both were
members. In this movement we sang the most trustful and
hopeful songs even when around us cities were falling into

ashes and people were gassed in masses in concentration camps
and we did not much else while the socialistic armies drove
the fascist invaders with all their many army chaplains from
Stalingrad and Kursk, where their crusade against atheistic
bolshevism ended catastrophically, to Berlin, where they had
come from in the first place. Kung is far removed from
Luther's radicalization of the Pauline anthropology and his
renewal of the tragic image of man of Sophocles and Aeschylos.
Kung's temptations come more from the religions of the Far
East than from Zoroastrianism and its religious and philosophical consequences up to Kant; more from Nestorius than from
the monophysitists; more from Pelagius than from Augustine;
more from Erasmus than from Luther or Barth; more from Hegel
than from Schopenhauer; more from the positivists than the
negativists, the critical theorists. What enormous idealism
and optimism does it take to state with Kung that there will
be no world peace without peace among the world religions
rather than the other way around – if peace at all(27)?

The declining Western bourgeoisie is desperate for such
idealism and optimism as Kung's work provides and is willing
to pay a high price for it. Unintentionally, Kung has become
the patron theologian of the American and European business
community. While Kung is indeed very much aware of the human
suffering which is produced by the capitalistic system at home
and abroad, he nevertheless affirms, like John Paul II and the
Canadian and US bishops, the very essence of capitalism, its
innermost law which underlies most of the suffering
criticized: the private appropriation of collective surplus
labor and value, or the subsumption of living collective labor
under dead private capital, or the law of exchange not only of
things but of people as well. He considers private profit
maximization to be absolutely necessary. Only late did Kung
discover the destructive tendencies in the over-optimistic
Reagan administration and its policies at home and abroad.
While Kung is humbler than people may give him credit for, he
does, nevertheless, admire greatly bourgeois scholars, particularly theologians, who have turned into "grand seigneures"
as, e.g., my teacher J. Lortz, the Christian on the Right, the
church historian. To be sure, the truth of the Catholic is not
necessarily the bourgeois, as Horkheimer asserts, but rather
the citoyen in the free state and the member of a free
humanity and ultimately the member in the kingdom of god. But
it must nevertheless be a warning to us, that the optimistic
prophets in the Old and New Testament were all false prophets,

while the true prophets were all pessimistic, at least in   the
short run: the true utopia is sad(28)!

   While   Kung   is very much in sympathy with the liberation
theologians and endorses   them   officially   and   defends   them
against   Rome   and   would   be   one of them in case he lived in
Latin America and not in Germany, he   is,   nevertheless,   like
John   Paul   II   and   Cardinal   Ratzinger, opposed to class all
emphasis on distinctions and class struggle. When   his   friend
Greinacher   collects   in German churches money for hospitals in
Nicaragua, Kung approves. But, when his friend collects   money
for   weapons   for   the defense of the revolution in Nicaragua,
Kung is opposed. Even Jesus' disciples carried weapons on   his
own   order(29).   How are the poor to defend themselves against
their   oppressors and exploiters after   all   other   means   have
been   exhausted without weapons? In all this Kung is closer to
Cardinal Ratzinger, than in general he would like to be.   Kung
is   very   much   afraid   -   and   that   with   good reason - that
political or liberation theology   will   endanger   further   the
lives   Christians   living   e.g.,   in   Latin   American national
security states. Once more,   Kung   is   more   in   the   camp   of
Erasmus than, e.g., in that of Thomas Muntzer(30).

   Kung   does   not   like   positivism   to   be   used   as   a
"Schimpfwort." He would like to take a middle position between
positivism, the metaphysics of   what   is   the   case,   and   the
Frankfurt   School,   which   denies   it.   Kung   sees   and fights
courageously against the mala physica in church,   society   and
history, but he seems not to be aware ofthe possibility of the
malum metaphysicum.   Kung   has   promised   toread   again and more
thoroughly Horkheimer's   and   Adorno's   critical   theory: the
negative   dialectic.   It would be even more important for Kung
to analyze more deeply the teacher of Horkheimer   and   Adorno:
Schopenhauer, the father of metaphysical pessimism. While Kung
has   devoted   whole parts and chapters to many modern thinkers
in his Incarnation of God and Does God Exist?,   he   has   given
only   small   segments   in these books to Schopenhauer and that
mainly in connection with Nietzsche(31). Schopenhauer deserves
more penetrating analysis! This is Schopenhauer's century,   if
we like it or not! Not only Horkheimer and Adorno learned from
and lived Schopenhauer's works, but also such different people
as   Freud,   Th. Mann,   Hitler and Goebbels. No matter how cold
his bourgeois style of thought may be,   Schopenhauer   must   be
faced for better or worse. Kung's theological work does indeed
try   to give witness to the great Christian statement: "See, I
make all things new!"(32) It will be an   even   better   witness

for this statement after it has fully received and hopefully conquered Schopenhauer's metaphysical pessimism. Hegel has tried to do this. His work is to be continued.

Rahner's student Metz combines Marx and Kierkegaard in his theodicy attempt. While Metz stresses the sinfulness of man, he does not want to let God get away with murder neither. He has certainly become aware of the theodicy deficiency in his teacher's transcendental theology. Precisely therefore, Metz develops his political theology with its face toward Auschwitz(33). Metz is still shocked by the fact that the parish in which he grew up was so completely unconcerned during World War II with a concentration camp which was only fifty kilometers away and in which many innocent victims were gassed and destroyed in bright daylight. Metz finds in discipleship the only help against the despair which arises from the experience of the absence of God's providence, be it in nature, in personal life, or most of all in the apocalyptic dialectic of late civil society and advanced bourgeois history. Metz answers historical materialists, like Adorno or M. Machovec, who ask how one can still write poetry or even pray after Auschwitz, by saying: Because the victims prayed in Auschwitz! In the future Metz intends to construct his political theology in its entirety as theodicy on the basis of Messianic mimesis. Hegel tried to do this in his dialectical philosophy of right, history and religion, his political theology(34). However that was before Auschwitz, Treblinka, Hiroshima and Nagasaki.

G. Baum, convert from a Jewish family to Catholicism and, at this time, one of the most popular proponents of the papal and episcopal natural law position on work and peace in Canada and the USA, does not go so far in his theodicy attempt as to say with Nicolaus of Cusa, Hegel or Rahner, that God kills out of love. He speaks, nevertheless, in the Augustinian spirit of God wounding some people more than others who then can do nothing else but to surrender and to follow him no matter how irrational and absurd the situation may be. Baum wants to be practical! The rage of the victim about the injustices he or she has experienced is to be transformed into sadness and then into complaints against God, and then finally into lamentations before God, so that the original anger does not strike out at innocent bystanders and thus produce new injustices. While Baum's attitude and relationship to nature is rather weak, he notices, nevertheless, sadness even in the faces and gestures of animals, e.g. owls, no matter where they are situated in the food chain. Existentially, Baum is more afraid of the death of the other than of his own. He knows that one can escape from the theodicy as little into the natural law as into historical materialism, psychoanalysis, philosophy of language, theory of action, activism or even overwork. He is aware, that the German adage, "Was ich nicht weiss, macht mich nicht heiss" is nowhere so ideological and untrue as in relation to the theodicy problem. With Hegel, Baum shares the insight that there is no real consolation for the one who has just been struck by the death of the other. Not even the remembrance of the happiness which the one and the other gave to each other in their life together may provide a sufficient counterbalance against the absolute negativity of the death of the other. Baum is sensitive to the fact that here all language and theory fails and that brotherly love and solidarity in interaction and intersubjectivity may be the most humane and Christian praxis. Here, all linguification of the Sacred comes to its end! Here, one can only silently lean against the storm! Gregory Baum and his wife Shirley proved all this when they assisted Margie and me in our great tragedy in Canada. Margie looked to Baum during her last months of life like the "Madonna." In this may lie the unspoken clue for a better answer to the theodicy.

Peukert's friend W. Dirks has thought about the theodicy problem throughout his long and spiritually very rich life, characterized by the sacrament of marriage, the Eucharist, and democratic socialism(35). Like his friend E. Kogon, Dirks has been somewhat in sympathy with Hegel's attempt to explain human suffering in capitalistic society and bourgeois history as sacrifice for the purpose of human liberation. However Dirks has difficulty in telling this solution of the theodicy problem to the suffering victims. Thus, even in his eighties, Dirks continues to search for a better answer to the horrifying riddles of history, e.g. the catastrophe of European Fascism(36). For Dirks, as for Margie and myself, Peukert's fundamental theology as theodicy attempt came at the right moment in life(37). Peukert's theology of communicative praxis has helped Dirks in the dilemma between his peace with God on one hand, and the lack of peace in society and history, on the other. Dirks is longing for the peace of the heart, which he so well deserves. Yet he can not forget the innocent victims of the past, the present, or the future. For Dirks, Peukert communicates a new solution to the old theodicy problem as he takes seriously the victims and thinks from

their   position about society and history in messianic mimesis
and develops out of this a   great   salvation-historical
perspective with the help of modern philosophy of science and
action.
        Peukert continues his teacher's, Metz's, tendency toward
a political theology as theodicy in his fundmental theology
with great personal commitment and sacrifice. He looks through
the theodicy problem to its utmost limits in the most humane
way and he does not shy away from the awesome negativity it
contains. It is certainly not right to call with the "Father"
in A.Gides, The Return of the Prodigal Son, "proud" those
thinkers like Peukert, who can not stay in the "house," i.e.
in a closed Christian system of interpretation of reality and
orientation of action, since they are not satisfied with the
insufficient traditional responses to the theodicy prob-
lem(38). It is also not right to put those thinkers with Dante
Alighieri into the Inferno or at least into the Purgatorio and
burden them with heavy rocks in order to punish them for or
purify them from their "pride"(39). That only multiplies and
intensifies the problematic of the theodicy! It seems that the
survival of Christianity and the other world religions in and
beyond modernity may very well depend on the resolution of
this theodicy problem. Here the main question is, whether
Peukert's own answer to the theodicy--God's gracious reality
saving the innocent victim if not before, then in his or her
annihilation--is sufficient to reverse at this moment in
history the alleged obsolescence of the religious worldviews,
as asserted by Habermas and his many followers, and to
retrieve their fundamental existential themes beyond the mere
reception of their communicative ethics in secular form(40).

Openness of History

Most important for Peukert's fundmental theology as theodicy
has been and must be in the future the controversy between
Benjamin and Horkheimer concerning the closedness or openness
of history(41). It is obvious that if history is closed and
the murderer has definitely triumphed over the innocent
victim, there can no longer be any resolution of the theodicy
problem(42). Then Brecht is right with his statement at the
end of his City of Mahagonny: Nobody can help the dead
man(43). This is the most untheological and desperate
statement thinkable. A resolution of the theodicy problem is
possible only when history is open in principle and the

Critical Political Theology

neural356   Critical Political Theology

murderer will at least ultimately not triumph over the
innocent victim(44). It seems that Peukert intends to stay
with this most fundamental issue of the openness of history
and not let himself be distracted by secondary concerns, no
matter how important they may appear to be in themselves, or
due to circumstances. It would be better still if Peukert
would stay with the dialectic of the openness and closedness
of history.

The controversy concerning the openness of history
surrounded Benjamin's article on the dialectical materialist
E. Fuchs in the 1937 issue of Horkheimer's Zeitschrift fur
Sozialforschung(45). According to Benjamin's article, the
abstraction in which bourgeois history of culture presents its
content is a matter of mere appearance for the dialectical
materialist. It is instituted by a false consciousness. The
historical materialist relates himself with great reservations
to this abstraction of culture from the dialectic of
traditional or modern civil society as production and exchange
process. In Benjamin's view, the dialectical materialist is
justified in such reservation by the mere inspection of what
has really happened in history: what he sees in terms of art,
religion, philosophy or science is all of an origin which he
can not consider without horror. These cultural dimensions do
not only owe their existence to the efforts of great, ingenius
men and women who have created them, but also to the drudgery
and pain of nameless masses of slaves, serfs and wage
laborers. For Benjamin, there is no document of culture which
is not at the same time also a record of utter barbarism.
Bourgeois cultural history has not done justice to the core of
this sad fact so far and it can hardly hope to do so in the
future.

However for the historical materialist and political
theologian Benjamin all this is not yet what is most decisive.
When the concept of culture as such is already problematic for
the dialectical materialist, then the disintegration of the
cultural goods, which can become for humankind commodities and
objects of possession (in the framework of what Weber and
Habermas have called the modern decentralization of God's
attributes of beauty, holiness, truth, justice, into autonomous cultural areas like art, religion, philosophy, social
morality in the form of a new polytheism), is for him an
entirely unthinkable idea. For the historical materialist and
political theologian Benjamin it is most decisive that the
work of the past is not closed. This is indeed the foundation

of his, as well as of any present or future critical political
theology as theodicy.

According to Benjamin the dialectical materialist does
not see the work of the past or any part of it fall into the
lap of any epoch like a thing nor is it simply at hand. For
the historical materialist, the notion of culture, as conception of artistic, religious, philosophical, scientific or
socio-moral forms, which are considered by bourgeois thinkers
as being independent, (if not from the process of production,
in which they came about, then at least from the labor process
in which they continue to exist) carries a fetishistic trait.
Culture appears as reified. For Benjamin, the bourgeois history of culture is nothing else than the residuals which the
memories of men and women have formed and which have not been
disturbed in their consciousness by any political experience.

Idealism and Materialism

Criticizing Benjamin's article on Fuchs, Horkheimer states
that he has thought for a long time about the question of
whether or not the work of the past is really closed(46). For
Horkheimer, Benjamin's assertion of the openness of history is
"idealistic" in the Hegelian sense, if the closedness of
history is not included in it. For the historical materialist
as Horkheimer understands him, the past injustices which have
happened to the innocent victims who have been slaughtered
without having had their day in court, has happened and is
definitely closed. What has happened to the innocent victims
who have gone under, no present or future can ever heal any
longer. They shall never be called upon to receive their
happiness in Eternity. Nature and society have done their
destructive work on them. According to Horkheimer, whoever
assumes the openness of history must believe in the Last
Judgment. However the idea of a Last Judgment, into which the
infinite longing of the oppressed, exploited, tortured and
dying has been superseded, is merely a naive residual of the
primitive and archaic "wild" thinking, which misunderstands
the utter unimportance of the role of man in the history of
nature and simply humanizes the, as such, inhuman universe
mythologically.

Finitude

Benjamin and Horkheimer were at the time of their controversy
about the closedness or openness of history aware of the work
of the convert to Catholicism and committed opponent of
Fascism, not in exile, but inside of National Socialistic
Germany, Th. Haecker(47). He anticipates in many ways
Peukert's concern with the theodicy: the deadly finitude of
man and God's saving Infinite Reality. Haecker stresses more
than Peukert the demonic and Satanic element in civil society
and bourgeois history. He was in immediate contact with
totalitarian state capitalism. Finally the Nazis did forbid
him to teach or write, which did not happen to Guardini,
Schneider, Rahner or Nink. He died in Germany toward the end
of World War II.

Horkheimer admits in his critique of Haecker's The
Christian and History, that the historical materialist has in
common with the religious thinker all these wishes, hopes and
longings for Eternity and particularly for the arrival of
absolute perfect and universal justice(48). Thereby, the religious idealist and the dialectical materialist differentiate
themselves from the utter dullness of the positivistic
attitude. At that time positivism was newly reimported from
Germany into the USA where Horkheimer lived in exile from Nazi
Germany and from where he criticized Benjamin as well as
Haecker. This happened right at the time when in Nazi Germany
the concentration camps began to accelerate their destructive
work.

Yet, so Horkheimer continues his argument against
Haecker, while the idealistic Christian thinker acquiesces
concerning the thought that the wish for Eternity is already
fulfilled, the consciousness of the historical materialist is
deeply permeated by the feeling of the limitless abandonment
of man. This is the only true answer to the impossible hope.
That, of course, is the end of all theodicy.

In his critique of Haecker's Christian idealism
Horkheimer reaches the utmost extreme of his own materialism
and atheism. According to Horkheimer, the thought is of course
monstrous, that the prayers of the persecuted victims in their
most extreme need do not reach any goal; that the prayers of
the innocent, who must die without clarification of their
cause, do not reach any goal; that the last hopes for a
super-human instance does not reach any goal; and that the
night which no human light enlightens is also not permeated by

any divine light. Horkheimer is fully aware of the fact that
without God eternal truth has as little any ground or hold as
infinite love. The infinite non-possessive devotion and love
becomes an unthinkable notion without God. Yet for Horkheimer
such monstrosity is not a compelling argument against the
assertion or denial of a matter of fact. Logic does not
contain the law that a judgment is wrong simply because its
consequence is despair. Here, for Horkheimer, the chorismos
between the Infinite and the finite seems to be absolute.

Nevertheless, Horkheimer does assert that in a truly free
consciousness the notion of the infinite remains as the
consciousness of the finality of all earthly happenings and of
the unchangeable abandonment of man(49). Thus, the notion of
the infinite preserves late civil society from an idiotic
optimism, from the inflation of its own knowledge, its own
positive sciences, into a new religion. Yet for Horkheimer,
the notion of the infinite remains merely a concept. The
ontological proof of God, which constitutes the very core of
Hegel's dialectical philosophy as theodicy, has broken
down(50). In contrast to the idealist Hegel, there is no
reality for the materialist Horkheimer to the idea of God.
Without this reality all theodicy must fail.

Benjamin agrees fundamentally with Horkheimer's harsh
critique of Haecker's idealism(51). He finds most significant
the Chinese story it contains, according to which the good man
and the bad man are likewise forgotten soon after their death:
Nihilism.

The Dead

Nevertheless, Benjamin does resolve his controversy with
Horkheimer in his own way. He does this not so much in his
immediate letter to him of March 28, 1937, but rather in his
theses "On the Notion of History" in the larger context of his
Passage Work, which remained a torso(52). A straight line
leads from Benjamin's article on the historical materialist
Fuchs to the "Historical-Philosophical Theses." Here, Benjamin
no longer merely talks about cultural goods or the work of the
past, but more personally, directly, and concretely about the
enslaved ancestors and the generations of vanquished people
and finally, simply about the dead. In the Theses, Benjamin
makes clear his opposition to Horkheimer's historical-
materialistic insight that history is closed. He is not
frightened by Horkheimer's charge of idealism. He agrees with

Horkheimer that the openness of history is ultimately a
theological issue. He does not shy away from the idealistic or
theolgical consequences of his assumption that history is
open. There is ultimately only a theological answer to the
theodicy problem.

Anamnesis

According to Benjamin's Passage Work, the corrective to
Horkheimer's thoughts about the closedness of history lies in
the consideration that history is not only a science, but also
a form of remembrance(53). What the science of history states,
anamnesis can modify. Memoria can make what is not closed in
history, the happiness, into something which is closed, and
what is closed, the suffering, into something which is open.
Benjamin admits that this recollection is, indeed, theology.
However, in remembrance, so Benjamin argues against Horkheimer, we make an experience that forbids us to comprehend
history in principle unhistorically, as little as we are
allowed to try to write it in immediately theological terms.

Theology and Historical Materialism

Adorno never believed in Horkheimer's atheism. In his famous
Hornberg Letter to Benjamin of August 2, 1955, Adorno stated
that it was most important that Benjamin preserve the
theological elements of his glorious first design of the
Passage Work in his second design(54). Adorno was afraid that
with Benjamin's conception of the dialectical image in the
second design of the Passage Work, not only the original power
of the Hegelian notion as dialectical unity of the universal,
particular, and singular, which was originally a theological,
mystical one, is threatened but that thereby particularly that
social movement in contradiction in civil society is missed,
which historical materialism is essentially concerned with and
for which he made the sacrifice of theology(55). Shortly,
Adorno admonishes Benjamin not to surrender to his friend
Brecht's vulgar atheism and to give up the conjugation of
dialectical materialism and theology by which the first design
was characterized(56). This conjugation has become essential
for Metz as well as for Peukert. A future political theology
must pursue further this coincidentia oppositorum, this
coincidence of redemption and happiness, grace and freedom.
    In his Hornberg Letter, Adorno demands nothing less from

Benjamin than that he should restore again theology in his second design. Adorno wants Benjamin to achieve, in other words, a radicalization of the materialistic dialectic or historical materialism into its innermost theological glowing fire. This means at the same time an extreme sharpening of the social-dialectical, even political-economic motive. According to Adorno, the notion of false consciousness, as well as the connection between theology and materialistic dialectic can be achieved only by critical recourse to the Hegelian origin.

Future political theology must not try to carry theological elements into dialectical materialism, but rather penetrate into its own theological foundation: to set free its own theological potential. According to Benjamin, theology can serve historical materialism against metaphysical objections(57). Vice versa, historical materialism can protect theology against psychological and sociological objections which arise against it from the dialectic of late capitalistic society and history.

Past and Future

Benjamin answers Horkheimer and Adorno in his Theses by stressing the at the same time theological and revolutionary tiger's leap into the past(58). This has become the core issue of Metz's political theology and of Peukert's theology of communicative praxis: anamnestic remembrance of the innocent victims of the past who have been slaughtered and have been rescued by God's gracious reality(59).

However Benjamin is at the same time fully aware of the fact that this tiger jump into the past does today still take place in the arena of civil society, where the capitalistic ruling class gives the commands. The same leap in the open air of post-bourgeois history is the dialectical one, which is how Marx, Bakunin and Blanqui understand the revolution(60). The contemporary critical political theologian must not forget that the jump into the past must necessarily lead to the leap into the future: from the remembrance of the innocent victims to the hope for the realm of freedom beyond the boundaries of late capitalistic society and beyond that for God's kingdom. A theology which merely stresses the jump into the past will necessarily become reactionary. A historical materialism, which merely emphasizes the dialectical leap into the future, will necessarily become rootless, shallow and sterile. Theology and historical materialism must reproduce each other

dialectically. Only a fundamental theology which is at the
same time concerned with anamnestic and proleptic solidarity
in the sense of dialectical materialism can also approach the
solution of the theodicy problem with greater hope for
success. Political theology as theodicy will come into its own
only as dialectical leap into past and future in the open air
of post-capitalistic history, beyond the control of the
dominant bourgeois class.

Recourse to Hegel

Western Marxists like G. Lukacs and K. Korsch, Horkheimer,
Benjamin and Adorno, H. Marcuse and Habermas were able to
develop a more humane form of dialectical materialism only by
critical recourse to Hegel(61). From Hegel, Horkheimer,
Benjamin and Adorno received their negative theology,
including its method, the determinate negation, as well as
their concern with the theodicy problem(62). The fundamental
theologian should not let himself be hindered by post-Hegelian
logophobie and anti-metaphysical prejudices from seeking help
concerning the theodicy problem in Hegel's dialectical
philosophy and theology. Horkheimer admonished us that we all
must suffer and die and that every end is bloody and
catastrophic and E. Bloch told us that we are continually
exposed to brutal metaphysical experiences in the form of such
contingencies(63). The last great Western metaphysician,
Hegel, may have some worthwhile insights for the future
development of a fundamental theology as theodicy not based on
what he called in his Jena System Designs I and III the
potential of "work and tool," or functional rationality of
subject-object relationship, but rather on the paradigm change
to what he named the potentials of "memory and language" and
"struggle for recognition" or practical rationality of
subject-subject relationship(64). Peukert has learned not only
from Benjamin and Habermas, but also from Hegel. Much more is
to be learned by political theology not only from the Hegelian
Left, but also for Hegel himself.

Telos

For Hegel there is indeed no greater need, demand and challenge for a reconciling theodicy than in society and his-
tory(65). According to Hegel such a theodicy can be achieved
only through the knowledge of the affirmative telos of

history, in which the social and historical negativity
disappears into something subordinated and superseded. This
happens through the consciousness, partly of what is indeed
the goal of history, namely human liberation, partly of the
fact that this purpose has been, is and shall be realized in
the God-produced and -determined revolutions of world his-
tory(66). Besides this _telos_ the evil of history--war, hunger,
oppression, exploitation, torture, death of the innocent
victims--do indeed exist, but have no reality in the emphatic
sense. Only what in society and history is conformed to the
revolutionary goal of liberation is rational and only what is
rational is emphatically real(67). But for this, so Hegel
argues, the mere abstract and thus empty faith in God's
providence or mere discipleship in his absence is not
sufficient. God's providence must be determined concretely in
terms of human freeedom, agents of change, social units,
course of events in order to be able to be the foundation of
rational revolutionary conduct.

Hegel sees the negativity, the irrationality, the immense
suffering in society and history as clearly and thoroughly as
his opponent Schopenhauer(68). Hegel anticipates P. Klee's and
Benjamin's angel of history(69). The angel's face being turned
toward the past sees one single catastrophe which keeps piling
wreckage upon wreckage and hurls it in front of his feet. The
angel would like to stay, awaken the dead, and make whole what
has been smashed. Doing so, he would indeed resolve the
theodicy problem.

However, according to Benjamin, a storm is blowing from
paradise. It has got caught in the angel's wings with such
violence, that he can no longer close them. This storm
irresistably propels the angel into the future to which his
back is turned, while the pile of debris before him grows
higher and higher. This storm is what we call progress in the
scientific and technological society.

When Hegel looks at the tragedy of human passions in
traditional and modern civil society and bourgeois history and
sees the consequence of their violence, of stupidity and evilness and the destruction of the most blooming civilizations
which the human spirit has produced, then he can only be
filled with utter sadness about this finitude and transitor-
iness(70). He falls into moral melancholy and indignation,
since the destruction of the great cultures is not only the
work of nature, but much more so of the free will of men.
Hegel can easily lift those destructive consequences without

any rhetorical exaggeration and merely through the correct
compilation of the misfortunes which the most virtuous individuals and the most beautiful nations and states have
suffered, into the most terrible painting. By this painting
grey in grey, Hegel can escalate the feeling to the deepest
and most confused sadness, for which no reconciling result can
hold the counterweight. We can fortify ourselves against this
melancholy arising from this negative incompleteness of
history, or escape it provisionally only by thinking
positivistically: what has happened, has happened! It is fate!
It can not be changed! Then we step back again out of the
boredom which that reflection of sadness can produce for us
into our own narrow life world and myopic feeling, into the
present of our particular purposes and self-interests, shortly
into our bourgeois selfishness. This egotism stands at the
quiet shore and enjoys securely the distant view of the
confused ruins. Precisely this historicistic perspective
Hegel, Marx, Benjamin and Peukert try to overcome in
anamnestic solidarity.

When Hegel sees history as this slaughterbench, this
Golgotha, in which the virtue of individuals, the happiness of
nations and the wisdom of states is continually sacrificed,
the question arises for him with necessity, for which ultimate
telos these outrageous sacrifices have been, are and will be
made. This leads Hegel to the question concerning that which
he has made into the universal beginning of his whole
political theology: the a priori principle that God's
providence governs history(71). From the very beginning Hegel
determines the happenings, which that dark and tragic picture
of history presents to the melancholical feeling and the
corresponding reflection as the field in which must be seen
merely the means for that what he predicts that it will be the
absolute, the true result of world history: not only a new
post-European, post-modern, post-bourgeois American and Slavic
World characterized by a better balance between individual and
collective never achieved before in Africa, Asia, Near East or
Europe; or the final community of nations as the result of the
dialectic of history; but its sublation into God's absolute
spirit, love and freedom(72). That precisely is Hegel's
solution to the theodicy problem: he transforms the negative
into a positive incompleteness of history. The historical
process is open in principle. Hegel's philosophy of history is
indeed a theology.

From the very beginning of his political theology Hegel

has despised the option to walk the way of the reflection of
analytical understanding and the fetishistic abstractions it
produces and to ascend from the horrible particular events in
society and history to the redeeming universal goal(73). Hegel
anticipates critically some of the Schopenhaurian critical
theorists when he charges that it is anyhow not the interest
of the melancholical feeling and reflection to elevate itself
beyond the tragic painting of history in order to truly
resolve the riddles of God's providence, which are indeed
posed correctly in this historical picture of ruins. It is
rather the nature of these sad reflections to please
themselves in the empty and sterile sublimities of that
entirely negative result. Against such totally negative
dialectic Hegel returns in his political theology to the a
priori point of view, that God's wisdom governs the social and
historical world as well as nature, and the inner and cultural
world and that it is powerful enough to assert itself against
the negativity not only of nature, but even of society and
history. Hegel's political theology contains the promise that
the moments of God's providence, plan, and purpose—human
freedom, agents of change, social system, course of
action—will contain the essential determinations for the
answer to the question which arises from the dark picture of
history: the theodicy problem.

Divine and Human Reason

For Hegel what lies between reason as man's selfconscious
spirit and God's reason, wisdom and providence as being at
work in the systems and revolutions of history and what
separates human reason from divine reason and does not let the
former find satisfaction in the latter, is merely the claim of
some fetishistic abstraction of analytical understanding, so
dominant in civil society, which is not liberated into the
notion as the dialectical unity of concept, judgment and
conclusion(74). To know God's reason as the rose in the cross
of the present dialectic of society and history and precisely
thereby to enjoy it, this rational insight is for Hegel the
solution of the theodicy problem and the reconciliation with
reality, in spite of all its irrationality and contingency.
The theological notion is to be confronted with reality and to
be found in its transitoriness. Social philosophy as political
theology gives such reconcilition to those to whom has once
come the inner demand to comprehend and to receive in that

what is substantial, the socio-ethical totality as the result
of the sacrifice and self-sacrifice of civil society, and
God's providence, likewise their subjective freedom and to
stand with their free subjectivity at the same time not in
something merely particular and contingent, but in that what
is in and for itself, the socio-moral totality and ultimately
God's providence, will, plan, purpose and task.

As little as for Hegel man's reason does acquiesce with
the Kantian mere approximation to the truth, which is in
biblical terms neither hot nor cold, but lukewarm, and as such
must therefore be spit out, so little is it content with the
cold despair, which admits positivistically, that things are
indeed bad or at best mediocre in this temporal transitory
social and historical reality, but that just nothing better is
to be had: that, therefore, one must make peace with the
world, bad as it is, and hold it(75). In Hegel's view it is a
warmer peace with reality which the insight provides that
nothing in society and history happens without God and that
all is his work(76).

Of course, so Hegel states, in order to pluck the rose of
God's reason in the cross of the contradictory present, the
antagonistic social totality, one must take upon oneself the
cross itself(77). For Hegel the cross has a polemical,
revolutionary meaning: it means first of all the negation of
the natural will(78). It means, furthermore, the negation of
the system of traditional as well as modern civil society, in
which bourgeois needs, desires and passions find their
satisfaction. Finally it means the negation of the negation,
the death of death, resurrection and ascension. If it is true
that the citoyen can not become a citoyen without sacrificing
in himself the bourgeois with all his fetishization of sex,
car and career and all other commodities, then this is even
truer for the Christian who, in conforming to the so-called
Sermon on the Mount, wants to enter the Kingdom of God(79).

According to Hegel for the one who takes upon himself the
cross in messianic mimesis the unity in difference of divine
and human reason becomes reality(80). Hegel agrees with
Meister Eckehart: "The eye with which God sees me, is the eye,
with which I see Him. My eye and His eye are one. In justice I
am weighed in God and He in me. If God was not, I would not
be. If I was not, He would not be"(81). But for Eckehart as
well as for Hegel there is no real need for the masses of the
people in civil society to know this, since these are things
which can easily be misunderstood and which in any case can be

comprehended only in the theological notion as the self-
particularization and self-singularization of the Universal.
In spite of this esoteric attitude Eckehart continued to
preach and Hegel continued to teach these things and the
notion to the people.

Eschatology

In Hegel's view for the one who takes the cross upon himself
and who has replaced the traditional dualistic theology by a
mystical dialectical theology, history can be comprehended and
the comprehended history constitutes the recollection, the
memoria, the anamnesis and the Golgotha and the historical and
metaphysical Good Friday of God's absolute spirit, love and
freedom(82). Such comprehended history is the reality, the
truth and the certainty of God's throne, without which he
would not be the living communicative, trinitarian God.
According to Hegel out of the realm of finite spirits of
individuals as well as of nations foams back to God his own
living and spiritual Infinitude.
    In the perspective of Hegel's eschatology the pain which
finite beings, individuals as well as nations, feel in this
their supercession—their negation, preservation and elevation
—into God's infinite spirit, love and freedom, is not really
painful, since they turn into moments in God's eternal
history(83). Should this pain pain us, so Hegel asks with all
mystics, since it increases only our joy? In any case, in
Hegel's view God does not leave his just one in the grave. God
does not let rot his saint. God rescues the innocent victim in
his or her annihilation.
    Hegel, following Meister Eckehart and Boehme and through
him the Kabbalah and Hasidism, states that God as spirit in
the process of knowing himself excludes himself from himself
into finite sparks of light, the consciousnesses of individuals and nations(84) Then God recollects himself again out
of this finitude and comprehends himself as in the finite consciousnesses arises the knowledge of his own trinitarian
nature and thus his own selfconsciousnes. Out of the fomenting
of finitude as it transforms itself dialectically into foam,
God's spirit exhales and fragrances and arises and returns
into itself.

Reconciliation

Hegel sees the church divided into Catholics and Protestants, as well as into naive believers and educated believers, who participate in secular enlightenment, in spite of Jesus' demand that his followers should be one as the Father and the Son are one and his insight that a realm that is split in itself can not survive(85). Therefore, the church looks to Hegel after the bourgeois enlightenment and revolution as if it was going under once and for all. But Hegel has no doubts that the Kingdom of God has, nevertheless, been founded for Eternity. God's holy spirit lives eternally in his community. The pillars of hell can not overcome the church.

In Hegel's view political theology is a separate sanctuary. Its servants form a priesthood. It is set apart. It must never go together with and conform to civil society and bourgeois history. It must preserve the possession of the trinitarian truth through the dark transition period from the old European World toward a new post-modern, post-bourgeois American and Slavic world and beyond that toward a community of nations, a free humanity, and the Kingdom of God.

Political theology must represent in theory as well as in praxis the reconciliation of God with himself and with nature: that nature as God's being-other-in-itself, is nevertheless divine in its roots and that man's finite spirit is in itself precisely that, partly to elevate itself to the reconcilation with God in the present, partly to come to this reconciliation and liberation in the process of history. This reconciliation is ultimate liberation and redemption. This is Hegel's political theology as theodicy.

Non-possessive Devotion

To be sure, Hegel's political theology as theodicy is historical idealism no matter how strong the cryptic materialism maybe it indeed contains. But as long as the controversy between idealism and materialism has not come further than where it stands now, the contemporary political theologian must not be too prudish about it(86). There is no reason why he should not continue to argue with Hegel, that materialism and idealism are the two shells of the muscle in which is hidden the pearl of genuine Christianity(87). On this basis political theology can integrate into itself historical materialism.

Of course, Hegel's political theology as theodicy contains strong mystical elements. But that does not mean that, therefore it must necessarily be uncritical and unrevolutionary. Marx has argued this once, when at the same time he declared himself to be the disciple of the great thinker Hegel and expressed his respect, like Habermas today, for the overwhelming philosophical accomplishment of his teacher(88). On the contrary, Hegel's mystical dialectic provides the fundamental categories for and thus reinforces the critical and revolutionary potential of the materialistic dialectic, which is present in his social philosphy as political theology as well as in Marx's theory of civil society and history(89). Thus Hegel can possibly also strengthen the critical and revolutionary character of a contemporary fundamental theology, theology of communicative praxis and political theology, which neither in theory nor in praxis intends to shy away from the theodicy problem but plans to resolve it concretely by helping people living under formal democratic state capitalism to attack successfully the global problems of war, hunger, political oppression, ecological destruction and alienation(90).

Peukert knows, of course, only too well, that critical political theology is rather powerless today against the factual conditions in late capitalistic actions systems including bourgeois Christendom, and against their functional requirements(91). But Peukert agrees with the negative Hegelians Horkheimer and Adorno, that true revolutionary praxis depends on a theory, which does not make any compromise with the unconsciousness with which late bourgeois society allows thinking to be instrumentalized and reifed and to become hardened and petrified and ossified(92).

Furthermore, true revolutionary praxis depends on a theory which does not close itself up against the knowledge of the Absolute, against theology. Only once in his entire dialectical philosphy and sociology did Adorno break his self-imposed strictest obedience to the Second Commandment in the context of Hegel's thought on reconciliation and freedom and named the Absolute: Non-possessive devotion(93). This name indicates the theological glowing fire in historical materialism. This name constitutes the connection between theology and dialectical materialism. This name is the key to the solution of the theodicy problem. This name signifies the very core of a critical political theology which can inspire anamnestic as well as proleptic solidarity.

Such political theology centered in the Absolute as
non-possessive Love can indeed help people who live in
advanced capitalistic action systems to mitigate at least
Future I—the totally monetarized and bureaucratized society;
to resist Future II—ABC wars; and to promote passionately
Future III—the reconciled society, the realm of freedom, the
communication community without domination, the victimless
society, the society characterized by mutual unconditional
recognition. Peukert has done excellent work in direction to
develop such uncompromising political theology centered in the
Absolute as non-possessive devotion. Peukert continues bravely
to do so. He is not afraid of the uncomprehended difficulties
of the Job question, the Jesus question, the theodicy problem,
to which great art, the great world religions and their
theologies and the great philosophies, including historical
materialism, have been more or less sufficient, plausible and
convincing commentaries.

Liberation

Theology must speak of God and his action or it is not
theology at all. The political theologian can call himself a
theologian only if he can still or again speak of God and his
work in nature, personal life, social and historical world and
cultural world in a valid way and with volume in the framework
of modern highly complex action systems. The political
theologian Peukert does indeed speak of God and his praxis.
Having worked his way through the modern theory of science and
theory of action, particularly Habermas's universal pragmatic,
Peukert speaks of God, as Hegel before, as absolute love and
freedom(94). The fundamental theologian can speak of God as
liberating freedom only insofar as he can speak of man's
freedom, as it is liberated by God's freedom. The theologian
of communicative praxis talks with Hegel and Kierkegaard about
the carrying out of man's deadly-finite, temporal existence,
which precisely as temporal carrying out, as praxis, is the
movement towards God as absolute freedom, who initiates and
makes possible this very existence in the first place(95). For
Peukert, this freedom of man liberated by God as absoltue
freedom, has as praxis of love a non-limitable horizon of
universal solidarity. Following Hegel, Kierkegaard and
Benjamin, the political theologian includes into this horizon
of universal solidarity also the dead, the innocent victims,
whose freedom has been deadly frustrated in society and

history and who have never had their day in court. The
horrendous injustices against them have never been expiated in
the historical process up to the present: the murderer does
still triumph over the innocent victim(96)! Whoever forbids
himself to forget the dead, the unjustly destroyed, so Peukert
argues, must certainly forbid himself to forget those who are
hungry, oppressed, alienated and tortured now or will be in
the future. Universal solidarity embraces the innocent victims
of past, present, and future in the hope that ultimately
absolute justice will be done: that ultimately the murderer
will not triumph over the innocent victim(97). The prophets of
the Old and New Testaments share this solidarity and this
hope. Political theologians refer, beyond the critical
theorists, to these prophets(98).

Precisely insofar as political theologians are really
theologians and speak of God as absolute spirit, love and
freedom, do they throw light on the aporetical aspect of
Habermas's universal pragmatic, his theory of communicative
praxis(99). This aporetical aspect consists mainly in
Habermas's neglecting to a large extent the diachronical
character of the struggle for mutual recognition as well as of
language, work, family and nation. While Hegel and Marx were
fully aware of the temporal character of language, work, love,
the struggle for recognition and nationhood and therefore also
of the finitude and the element of death involved in these
media of human self-realization, Habermas's theory of
communicative praxis is almost as synchronical as Parsons's
structural functional theory of action(100). Therefore death,
which plays such an important role in Hegel's as well as in
Horkheimer's, Adorno's and Benjamin's philosophy, seems to be
as much repressed in the theory of communicative praxis as in
the system theory and in the everyday life of late
capitalistic action systems, which both try to reconstruct
systematically(101). While Hegel in his philosophy of right
and history is fully aware of the massive destruction of
individuals and whole nations and civilizations, the theorist
of communicative praxis and the structural functionalist seem
to ignore the gigantic annihilation of action systems and of
the people interacting in them, even in the evolutionary
aspects of their theories(102). For Habermas and Parsons there
is simply no dying going on in human action systems nor do
these systems seem to die themselves, and history is for the
two theorists no longer the huge slaughterhouse and Golgotha,
which it was for Hegel as well as for his great opponents,

Schopenhauer, Kierkegaard, Nietzsche, and even Blanqui and
Marx and certainly for Benjamin, Horkheimer, Adorno and Fromm,
and which it is again today for the political theologians Metz
and his disciples Peukert, Arens and Lamb: history has
happened once, but it does not happen any longer(103).
Habermas rejects Benjamin's thought, that precisely the
remembrance of the innocent victims helps to initiate and
sustain political revolutionary praxis(104). Habermas overlooks or represses the very fact that, since all human interaction as well as all language, work, love and nationhood move
in time towards their end, death, as the most everyday fact
and as what Bloch has called the great "anti-utopian," threatens all human intersubjectivity with absolute meaninglessness
and makes it as such invalid and impossible as soon as its
illusionary repression is once lifted(105). Political theology
addresses itself precisely to this dilemma of meaning
threatened by deadly temporality and finitude in the theory of
communicative praxis(106). It can help to resolve this dilemma
only by precisely not being once more merely another form of
theory of communicative action, but by referring to essential
truths in the Judeo-Christian and other religious worldviews,
other than merely universal communicative ethics as the result
of the rationalization of the great religious systems of
interpenetration and orientation.

Contingency

One reason why Habermas considered mythical as well as religious-metaphysical and even mystical worldviews to be obsolete
in modern systems of human condition was the increase of
contingencies in them as result of science and
technology(107). It is certainly true that the contingency
experience has sharpened in modern action systems in recent
decades(108). These contingency experiences do not only
concern the disappearance of external resources in time, like
trees, oil, coal, clean water, clean air, etc., but also the
limits of institutional and psychic abilities to resolve
crises: the dwindling resources of freedom and meaning(109).
This contingency experience strengthens the call for a type of
religion which would merely have the task to reabsorb such
experience of psychic and social systems and thereby to
stabilize the latter. The German functionalist, Luhmann, has
called such religion "contingency management praxis"(110).
Habermas has resisted rightly in his theory of communicative

praxis such a functionalization of religion for the purpose of
the management of contingency experiences and the stabilization of capitalistic action systems(111). Religion, which is
functionalized in such a way - bourgeois religion - has indeed
become obsolete as medium of identity formation, even if it
could fulfill such a contingency management function in highly
complex human action systems. Like Habermas, the political
theologian resists such system-functional integration of
religion(112). Here theorists of communicative praxis and
political theologians are in full agreement.

For the political theologian Peukert the experience of
contingency reaches its peak and its complete aporia
particularly where attempts to make possible greater self-
determination in intersubjective freedom turn over into and go
under in even greater barbarism(113). Horkheimer and Adorno
speak of the dialectic of enlightenment or emancipation(114).
Hegel had recognized that the history of human freedom leaves
behind the ruins of beautiful civilizations(115). Benjamin,
going even further than Hegel, can comprehend history only as
a field of ruins(116). Out of this comprehension of history,
Benjamin formulated the dialectical notion of anamnestic
solidarity(117). It has become one of the core concepts of
critical fundamental theology. Benjamin stands, together with
Horkheimer and Adorno, for experiences which have not been
more explicitly documented only for that reason, that those
who made these experiences have been destroyed. Critical
theory intends to be nothing else than the mouthpiece for the
innocent victims of history who have been destroyed and can no
longer speak for themselves. The same is true of theology of
communicative praxis.

The political theologian explicates this experience of
the innocent victims, who have been annihilated, in detail,
because it is, according to the action-theoretical
reconstruction of the notion of contingency, the most decisive
experience(118). According to the basic norm of communicative
action, the universal solidarity, which in principle excludes
nobody, is the condition for one's own identity(119). But in
such a horizon of universal solidarity, the political
theologian experiences and learns that men and women, who have
tried to exist and act in such a mode of universal solidarity,
have precisely therefore, paradoxically enough, gone under and
have been destroyed. Their attempt at a solidary existence
ended in annihilation. For the fundamental theologian this
paradoxical experience has important consequences for the "I"

of the survivor and its own identity. It could destroy the surviving "ego's" identity. Therefore, the theologian of communicative praxis looks for a possibility to work through once more such catastrophes in history or in "I's" own personal life on a higher level and thereby to rescue or regain "self's" identity. The political theologian looks for a possibility to integrate this kind of negative experience in some totality and thereby to preserve "I's" identity and integrity or even to regain them.

The critical fundamental theologian is, of course, aware of the possibility that the price for "ego's" being able to remain itself may very well be the repression of the catastrophic experience. In this case, "I" would, of course, have to impose on itself an amnesia of world historical proportion, extension and dimension. But such amnesia would cripple "self's" own consciousness and would annihilate any attempt to regain its own identity in all seriousness. A communicative rationality, which understands itself normatively, moves here against its ultimate limit. Habermas's universal pragmatic ends precisely in this dilemma. That is its aporia.

In order to resolve this dilemma, the political theologian goes back behind Habermas to Benjamin and his controversy with Horkheimer in the 1930s(120). This controversy was concerned with the question, if there can be in the experience of historical contingencies or catastrophes, an escape forward in terms of consolation through the happiness of future generations, in terms of a merely future-oriented solidarity? What are the consequences, if such future-oriented consolation is impossible? How is the relationship between a future generation and the past generations to be determined? Is it possible at all for "ego" to keep firmly in consciousness an ultimate, non-revisable annihilation of the victims of the historical process, out of which "I" itself has arisen, and at the same time to be happy and to come to itself and to find its identity? Hegel had denied such a possibility of happiness at least for the makers of history(121). But if "I" bans the memory of the contingencies and catastrophes of history out of its consciousness, then "self" betrays the solidarity, which alone makes it possible, that "ego" can find itself, be itself, have its identity, be at home with itself, be free. In this case, human existence becomes a self-contradiction. The remembering, anamnestic solidarity turns into an utter paradox.

The political theologian sees the whole philosophy and theology of Benjamin, following Kierkegaard, as the attempt to keep open this existential contradiction and to prevent its repression(122). The experience of this contradiction, this type of negativity, is for the political theologian methodologically of elementary significance and has as such a particular rank. This is so, since in this contradiction the attempt to develop out of general science-theoretical insights a normatively dimensioned theory of action and to move from a theory of power-oriented science and action to a theory of communicative, freedom- and solidarity-oriented praxis, comes into its crisis. In this contradiction, the normative foundation structure, out of which orientations for action and scientific rationality should likewise be able to be grounded, breaks into pieces. It does not point into a utopian future, but proves itself in the factual history as Kafkaesque and absurd. In addition, this experience becomes unavoidable, when "ego" achieves a certain niveau of action toward others and at the same time begins to live consciously in the historical dimension. Beyond this, the political theologian points to the fact that historically this experience determines the Judeo-Christian tradition at its very core(123). It is obviously also at the roots of another world religion, Buddhism, the religion of inwardness, and may also be at the roots of Zoroastrianism, the religion of light and darkness, and the Syrian religion, the religion of pain(124).

Intersubjective Action

In order for the political theologian Peukert to be able to resolve the aporia of the universal pragmatic, he must first of all demonstrate the fundamental principle of intersubjective action as it has been dealt with from Hegel's Frankfurt System Program, Jena Critical Writings, and Jena System Designs, and Marx's historical materialism over the sociologies of Durkheim, Weber, Mead and Parsons to the critical theories of Horkheimer and Adorno, and Habermas's theory of communicative praxis(125). This principle, as Hegel already formulated it, states that one can find his or her identity only in relationship to the other(126). The condition for the being oneself of the one is the free being oneself of the other.

For the critical fundamental theologian, as for Hegel before, this intersubjective existence of the one and the

other is strictly temporal(127). The ability of the one and
the other, to exist here and now and to turn toward each
other, originates from the ability of both to move toward
death as limit of their existence in an anticipatory mode and
from this anticipated death to come back to the momentariness
of communicative existence here and now. Peukert grasps
intersubjective existence in its temporal extension as well as
in its decision-structure, which transforms time into
ultimacy. But insofar as this temporal existence is strictly
intersubjective, the moving of the one toward his own death in
interaction with the other means also the movement toward the
death of the other. It means the recognition of the temporal
existence of the other as the possibility of exstasis into
ultimacy, Ultimate Reality, God's absolute love, spirit,
freedom, eternity. Thus the other can become a source of
meaning, freedom, energy, love and rest even after his or her
death, without danger of idolatry.

In the perspective of the political theologian this
communicative movement of the one and the other as mutual
recognition of the existence of the other and as the
possibility of transformation into ultimacy is in the
unconditionality of this recognition at the same time the
practical assertion of God as the reality for the other, who
does not allow him or her to be destroyed in death and who
therefore grants to the other the hope to be affirmed also
even in death. The communicative praxis toward death is the
hopeful movement toward death as movement toward God as the
reality, who proves himself in death as redemptive power. With
Hegel the political theologian speaks of the death of death,
the negation of the negation of the other and therefore also
of the one(128). With Luther and Hegel and the whole Christian
tradition the political theologian confesses: "You do not
leave your just one in the grave; you do not let rot your
saint." Here God's love and providence reveals itself fully.
This is the Christian solution of the universal theodicy
problem. This is the Christian consolation!

From all this it follows for the political theologian
that this type of temporary, intersubjective, communicative
action has a non-limited horizon, in the direction of the
future as well as of the past(129). Death is not a limit.
There can be solidarity here and now only as solidarity not
only forward into the future, with the not-yet born
generations, but also into the past with the innocent victims,
who have unjustly been destroyed. Peukert refers to what

Benjamin has called in his "Theses on the Philosophy of History": The revolutionary "tiger jump into the past"(130). It had been prefigured in Hegel's philosophy of history.

All this means for the fundamental theologian that the solidary affirmation of the other here and now always already starts from the assertion of the indestructibility, even the rescue of the past, of the innocent victims, who have been unjustly annihilated: the death of death. Like Meister Eckehart, Hegel and Kierkegaard, the theologian of communicative praxis sees and understands the resurrection of Jesus as an event, which can not be isolated(131). It rather makes possible our own existence in discipleship and in the attempt of communicative action in unconditional, universal and unlimited solidarity. Thus the political theologian agrees with Kierkegaard that God's reality, love, providence and the consequent rescue of the innocent victim in death is comprehended by the survivor only if such comprehension proves itself in the unconditional recognition of the suffering others here and now.(132). Political theology can not be done with one's back toward Auschwitz, Hiroshima, Vietnam, El Salvador, Lebanon, Ethiopia, Nicaragua, Granada.

The foundation of political theology and thereby the introduction of responsible talk of God in highly complex action systems is in consequence of all that has been said so far, bound to the analysis of such communicative praxis as described by philosophers, sociologists and psychologists from Hegel's Frankfurt System Program, Jena Critical Writings, Jena System Designs I and III and Phenomenology of Spirit to Habermas's theory of language-mediated interaction(133). The foundation of theology of communicative praxis and the new God-language is thinkable and possible only out of the realization of such communicative action. Only out of intersubjective praxis, which is structured that way, God becomes as reality identifiable and nameable: as the one who resurrected Jesus and who rescues all innocent victims, so that the murderers will not triumph over them ultimately. In this connection the political theologian can and must, as Hegel before, introduce the word "God:" God as absolute love, providence, freedom, justice, truth(134). Critical fundamental theology comes out of communicative praxis and points toward and leads into this interaction of the one and the other. In consequence, theology of communicative praxis is already in its theoretical beginning and in its fundamental conceptions and categories a practical science, constituted by a specific

form of action: not so much by work, sexual love, or nationhood, but by language-mediated struggle for unconditional,
mutual recognition of the one and the other as self-purpose in
family, society, state and history. The political theologian
agrees with Kant and Hegel, that the faith in God arises
formally from practical reason(135). Practical reason,
communicative praxis, human freedom are the subjective bases
for religion and the notion of God as absolute freedom. For
Kant this notion of God is merely a postulate of practical
reason, a mere "ought." For Hegel the notion of God is
provable reality, the most real reality. The eclipse of
practical reason means necessarily also the decline of
religion. Such eclipse does occur at present and explains most
sufficiently the contemporary religious crisis.

Political theology is the explicit theory of a type of
praxis, which makes possible a social and personal identity in
modern highly differentiated action systems, even in
aporetical experiences, which tear the person apart, e.g., the
loss of a father or mother, brother or sister, husband or wife
through heart attack or cancer(136). This identity owes itself
to God's unconditionally turning toward the partners in
communicative praxis and mutual recognition. This turning of
God toward the interacting partners must always be presupposed
and practically realized in action for the other. God makes it
possible for the interacting partners to overcome the
master-servant relationship in all its many forms between
themselves toward unconditional mutual recognition of each
other as self-purpose and free subjects(137).

According to the fundamental theologian such communicative praxis between the partners aims in its societal,
political and historical dimensions at the structuring of a
common social world and of institutions, in which the
overcoming of the master-servant relationship in the form of
class domination and the consequent unconditional mutual
recognition among people is the condition of "I's" identity
and the location for the experience of that absolute
liberating freedom, which in the Christian tradition is called
God: absolute love, truth, spirit, providence, justice.
However, unlike Hegel, Blanqui and Marx, but very much like
Habermas, the political theologian does not take seriously
enough the class struggle, which lies between the principle of
unconditional mutual recognition and its social, political and
historical realization(138). Hegel always warned: the
principle of freedom is not yet its application. This

practical realization of the principle of universal freedom is a long, painful process, the process of world history itself. It is the praxis of the history of class struggle, the history of liberation, as well as the endurement of most terrible human suffering.

Execution

According to the political theologian Peukert, the Christian tradition is no less than the theory of communicative praxis challenged by the question, how human interaction can be possible and valid in the face of determinate boundary experiences: personal, social, political, historical catastrophes, e.g., World War II or the threat of a thermonuclear World War III with an "absolute" Stalingrad(139). Therefore, Peukert, Arens, Lamb and others consider it to be legitimate and necessary to ask back as Hegel before to the origin of this communicative praxis – as far as Christianity is concerned – in the speech acts and communicative interaction of the historical Jesus(140).

In the perspective of political theology, Jesus's discourses and communicative praxis are obviously concerned with making the beginning of God's dominion experiential for the people as the event, which liberates men and women into freedom and which creates for them the possibility to recognize and accept each other, because everybody is already recognized and accepted by the redeeming Reality called God: the prophetic messianic God's loving providence(141). Peukert states that Jesus "asserts" in his speech acts and in his communicative praxis, God, the Father, as the unconditionally affirming and saving Reality not alone for himself, but also, and particularly so, for the others(142). The media of work and tools, of marriage and family, and even of the nation are strangely neglected not only in the New Testament, but also in the theory of communicative praxis and the political theology. Here much work is still to be done.

The theologian of communicative action is aware that the word "assertion" as it is used in relation to the historical Jesus's discourses and interaction is rather provocative(143). Peukert intends the provocative use of "assertion" to direct attention to the fact that Jesus insists here on being concerned with reality. But Jesus's pointing toward this reality does not happen in a purely verbal statement of fact. It rather happens that way, that a man moves toward God as

Reality for the others and in that, as Reality for himself in
the temporally structured, deadly-finite realization of his
existence. Precisely that way Jesus asserts God as Reality,
who on his part can only out of this intersubjective mode of
existence be called by his name. Thereby, all talking of
theology is bound back to a certain communicative praxis. That
excludes a reifying understanding of the reality of God, since
God is experienced as a liberating Reality, who as absolute
liberating freedom puts into motion transformations in the one
and the other. To be sure, Jesus's "assertion" of God's
reality for the other and himself, be it in discourse or in
communicative praxis, is not a proof of God. It is
particularly not an ontological proof of God, a la Anselm of
Canterbury or Hegel(144). It is entirely a matter of faith.
But this faith remains connected with communicative reason.

But in case Jesus's speaking of the reality of God is
understood this way and also introduced this way, so the
political theologian argues, then with his execution as with
the unjust destruction of all innocent victims, questions must
break into the open, which concern the interpretation of
reality in its totality, as well as the orientation of action
in it(145). These are the questions which constitute the
fundamental problems of Benjamin's thinking(146). They are
deeply rooted in Judeo-Christian tradition, particularly in
the Job and Jesus stories. These are also those questions
which stimulate attempts, like that of Habermas, to
reconstruct the history of religions in terms of a theory of
communicative praxis and to retrieve from it a normative core
of intersubjective action, an universal communicative ethics.
Habermas himself knows that there are more truths to be
retrieved from the world religions than just such an ethics or
social ethics(147).

For the immediate life world and environments of Jesus,
the question had to come up with his execution, if his
assertion that God is the saving Reality for the poor, the
exploited, the excommunicated, the tortured, the lost, the
innocent victims, who had been unjustly destroyed, was also
valid for himself in his own death(148). Jesus, who had
asserted this redeeming Reality, this Providence, with his
communicative existence for the others, had been annihilated.
It looked as if Jesus's assertion had not been valid for him
personally. His execution appeared as the factual refutation
of his assertion of the saving reality of God. It seemed that
thereby the attempt of a communicative existence, which

asserts in the being for others an unconditional, had been led
ad absurdum. This problem constitutes the background of the
narratives about Jesus's suffering, even of the Evangelia in
their totality. This problem remains also, if one rejects the
answer to it by the New Testament, as do all Jews and all
Muslims and all critical theorists, including Habermas. This
problem - the destruction of those who engage in universal
solidarity - must be resolved, at least in its general form,
if not only the New Testament, but also the whole modern
theory of pragmatic, including Habermas's theory of
communicative praxis and the critical political theology
depending on it, should not become obsolete from their very
start.

Resurrection

The answer of the Evangelia to this problem as well as of the
whole Christian Kerygma, is clear: God has resurrected Jesus
from the dead and has proven him as saved, as not ultimately
annihilated(149). The answer of modern theory of science and
of theory of action concerning the destruction of those who
have developed this likeness to universal solidarity, the
triumph of the murderer over the innocent victim, is much less
clear(150). This is true also for Habermas's universal
pragmatic.

The political theologian tries to explore the meaning of
this answer of the Evangelia and what it does mean, to
understand this answer fully(151). It has become quite
customary in Christian theology in the exegesis of this
answer, to ask back right away and exclusively to the reality
of the risen Christ. But if theology had really understood the
essential norm of communicative praxis - mutual unconditional
recognition as fundamental norm of human existence - then, so
the theologian of communicative praxis argues, it would have
to follow e.g., the theology of Rahner and would have to
start, vice versa, from the question, which transformation of
one's own reality, one's own self-understanding, one's own
identity, this event of resurrection can set in motion, if one
tries to comprehend it practically as the possibility of the
completion of one's own existence(152). According to the
fundamental theologian, theology stands only at the very
beginning of such comprehension. Theology must assimilate
theoretically modern theories of action, particularly the
transcendental and universal pragmatic, in order to explicate

what it means to exist as a Christian out of the
eschatological perspective of the resurrection(153). Such
theology would indeed be the answer to Adorno's secular
longing for the removal of death(154).

After having assimilated modern pragmatics, political
theology sees clearly in which way, according to the
understanding of the New Testament, the deed of the
resurrection of Jesus makes possible a kind of existence which
asserts in its own solidaristic action God as the redeeming
Reality for Jesus and, in anticipation of the eschatological
completion, for all innocent victims of the past, present and
future(155). But the faith in the resurrection is, then, in
itself a praxis, which as praxis, as communicative action,
asserts the prophetic and messianic God for the others and
which tries to express Him in intersubjectivity and
interaction and in granting unconditional recognition
particularly to the weaker other: the oppressed, exploited,
tortured, betrayed, murdered innocent victim.

This specific kind of communicative praxis makes it clear
to the political theologian that also the extreme contingency
experience of the annihilation of the other in cruel death
does not make meaningless for the survivor an existence in
universal solidarity(156). As anamnestic solidarity with the
crucified Jesus, this faith in his resurrection, is at the
same time practical solidarity with all other innocent victims
who have been unjustly destroyed in one way or another. This
faith is as anamnestic solidarity, genuine universal
solidarity in the horizon of the one human history of freedom
and suffering.

In such faithful communicative action the possibility is
given to the survivor to find a new identity in the face of
the death of the innocent other and of his or her own death to
come in the future: this is not an identity which originates
from the clinging to rigid structures in a religion of
anxiety. It is rather an identity which develops out of the
experience of liberation into an unlimited, universal
solidarity. It does prove itself practically in modern highly
differentiated action systems. In this case, religion is not
obsolete! While such faith-directed communicative action
disproves Habermas's thesis of the obsolescence of religion,
it at the same time strengthens his theory of communicative
praxis by breaking through its aporetical aspect.

Humane Survival

For the political theologian Peukert, the first essential question is whether critical fundamental theology posits the framework of its consideration in such a way that it has, indeed, in view the urging and threatening problems of human praxis in its totality, as newspaper, radio and television report them daily(157). Hegel suggested already that people should find what God wills and does in the morning paper(158). The political theologian thinks of that type of human praxis in which men and women try individually or in groups to secure out of an oppressive exigency a humane survival and to determine the meaning of their existence. The global capitalistic economical and political crises, which announced themselves already in Hegel's time in an always sharper form, are also crises of consciousness and culture. They demand elementary transformations of subjective interpretation of reality and orientations of action, i.e., anthropological revolutions, as well as qualitative changes of the social and cultural structures in modern action systems. Hegel's dialectical philosophy was, as philosophy of revolution, a first answer to the apocalyptic contradictions of late Western civilization, and to the transition from the old European to a new American and Slavic and finally world culture: from contradictory civil society to the free state and the free humanity and ultimately to the Kingdom of God(159).

In the perspective of the political theologian, the contemporary crisis in the economic, political and cultural subsystems of modern capitalistic and socialistic action systems as well as in the consciousness and life world of individuals, challenges to the utmost all resources of thinking and acting in the Judeo-Christian tradition(160). If theology does not keep in mind this challenge of human praxis in its totality and with all its threats and dangers, contradictions and pathologies, then it misses its object and objective at the very start. This is so, since political theology must not allow that from the very outset only a segment or region of human praxis is attributed to its concern by modern action systems or that theology ascribes such area to fundamental theology as to one of its own subdisciplines or that it itself chooses such a segment or region of human action as its own area of retreat. The universality of a political-theological problem-position must not fall back behind the everyday problem-consciousness and problem-discourse of an average newspaper reader or television viewer. Only against this background Christian and ecclesiastical praxis can be sufficiently determined. Following political theology, members of Christian Base Communities have begun to combine the daily reading of the newspaper, listening to the radio and looking at television with the daily reading of the Bible(161). Motivated by the "Sermon on the Mount," the base communities identify with the innocent victims and resist the murderers, of whom the newspapers, radio and television daily report so plentifully(162).

Power

For political theologian Peukert, the second essential question is whether a critical fundamental theology, which tries to orient itself in terms of the science of action, follows in its theoretical determination of Christian and ecclesiastical praxis technical-strategic models or paradigms of mutual recognition, interaction, intersubjective praxis(163). In the latter type of paradigms the partner in action is not seen as an instrument, but is recognized as an equal, autonomous, free other, who can judge on his own, particularly when he or she is in the position of the weaker. Here the partner is looked upon as the one who can contradict the other with good reasons and can ask him or her questions, which lead behind his or her position. Thus both partners can find out of their own discourse and interaction a common orientation of praxis and thus can gain their own social and personal identity. In consequence, the question for the theologian of communicative praxis is, whether political theology does in principle depart from the subtle manipulatory forms of a power-conform instrumental rationality and functional action and does indeed not diminish, but rather radicalize the fundamental ethical norm, to recognize the freedom of the other. This is so, since political theology has to be witness to and must preserve the liberating and life-giving power of God for the other in the structure of its action.

Instructed by Hegel and the Hegelian Left up to Habermas, the political theologian must be careful to see the struggle for recognition in its world historical totality(164). The unconditional mutual recognition of the one and the other as ends in themselves, in their self-purposiveness and freedom, is the idea as well as the notion, the result as well as the beginning of the struggle for recognition. The notion is not yet the idea. The result must not let the political theologian forget its genesis. We are still living very much in class societies in which the masters are onesidedly recognized by their workers, but see and treat them not as ends in themselves, but as instruments, as means of production. Communication without domination has not yet been achieved. While neither in capitalistic or socialistic action systems, we must act as if unconditional mutual recognition was already the case, the critical fundamental theologian is right, neverthless, when he stresses the telos, which is to be achieved in the struggle for recognition step by step: universal dignity and freedom in universal solidarity.

Ecclesiastical Action

According to the political theologian, Peukert, a test for all of this lies in the determination of the structure of ecclesiastical action(165). Political theology starts from the assumption that also the church, as institution, can submit – and that even in exaggerated form – to the pathologies arising from the onesided instrumental-rational orientation of modern capitalistic or socialistic systems of human condition and action systems. In terms of these pathologies, structural-functional requirements and mechanisms can not only disturb a Christian praxis, they can even prevent such Christian action. A church can turn from an ecclesia of brotherly-sisterly communio and communication, a communication community into a church of administratively ordered and by the ecclesiastical environment factually executed excommunications: the dialectic of religion. If the churches, and following them, the theologians dispense themselves from the question, if their own form of organization contradicts the very cause, which is to be witnessed to and which is to be communicated to the people, the cause of Jesus, the Messiah, the absolute recognition of God's reign and thus the end of all domination of man over man, then most certainly comes into existence for the church members only so much stronger the danger of that double-bind situation, of that pathogenic drop of relations, in which by building up of commitments identities are endangered and even destroyed. This happens not through fruitful transformation, but through enforced regression. Such paradoxes of relations are particularly aporetic and painful in religious institutions. In case these paradoxical relations become the fundamental ecclesiastic structures, then it is put into question, if the core of the Judeo-Christian tradition - God's reign and the communication community of men and the unconditional mutual recognition of their freedom can at all still be witnessed in the church. According to Peukert the rule which is valid for the case, that religious systems participate in the pathologies of modern action systems and thereby endanger men and women because of systemic reasons, i.e., structural-functional requirements, has never been formulated and expressed more clearly than in the statement of the New Testament: "The Sabbath is there for man, not man for the Sabbath"(166). Liberal theologians, like Kung, and political theologians, like Metz and Peukert, have suffered very personally and intensely from these ecclesiastical pathologies in the 1970s and 1980s alone(167). So have many other believers, priests and laymen alike. Because of the power-conform petrified bureaucratic structure of the church and its rigorous functional requirements and the consequent lack of Christian freedom and brotherly-sisterly solidarity, many theologians did not let themselves be ordained in the first place or left their ecclesiastical position after ordination, before and more still after Vatican II.

Praxis

The political theologian Peukert is fully aware of the fact that the modern notion of "praxis," which has been developed since Kant and Hegel, constitutes a challenge not only for the sciences, but also for practical theology as well(168). Not only the social sciences, but also the natural sciences stand before the challenge of the modern concept of communicative praxis, to examine their own theoretical and practical foundations. It is particularly important that also the natural sciences are bound into a humane conception of action. For the political theologian it is most important that the determination of Christian and ecclesiastical action through political theology corresponds to the demands of that notion of praxis; in it the central concern is communicative, liberating, innovative action, which enables people to accomplish common self-knowledge and self-determination and thus to overcome systemic resistances and contradictions. Beyond this, theology in its totality, as political theology, must be ready and able to participate in this horizon in interdisciplinary discourse and cooperation, not only with the social, but also with the natural sciences.

Identity Crisis

Like Hegel and the critical theorists before, the political
theologians are very much concerned with the modern identity
crisis(169). It signifies for the political theologian Peukert
the experience that one does not understand oneself any longer
nor is one able to make oneself understandable for others:
confusion of language as once it was connected with the tower
of Bable. This breakdown of the ability to engage in
intersubjectively reflected self-understanding, can happen to
individuals and groups as well as to whole societies, and
action systems and systems of human condition. The fundamental
theologian has the impression that the present identity crisis
has its root in the fact that our encounter with experiences
of contingency has a power-conform character(170). More
precisely, our action is determined by systemically petrified
mechanisms of accumulation of power, be it in the form of the
increase of economic power or be it in the form of the
escalation of administrative power of disposition. This leads
obviously to a colonization of all aspects of our life world
by money power or bureaucratic power. The increase in the
capacity to threaten and to annihilate, as intrinsic principle
of politics, is for such colonization only one, if also a most
outrageous indication. The theologian of communicative praxis
considers possible the overcoming of the identity crisis,
which has turned into a threat to our existence, only if the
systemically rigidified and ossified mechanisms of accumulation of power are broken through. This again can be achieved
only when praxis orients itself according to the principles of
practical, communicative rationality and intersubjectivity. In
conformity with these principles, the right to life, the
dignity and integrity of persons, i.e., intersubjectively
reflected self-determination, guides all actions. Thereby in
many respects a new level of orientation of action can be
reached. This is so, since the self-determination of every
individual binds itself to the reflection on the possibility
of the self-determination of all others. That way
self-determination reaches the niveau of an ethics of
universal solidarity, universal communicative praxis,
universal communication community, shortly the level of
universal communicative ethics. The political theologian does
not differentiate sufficiently between power as medium of the
dimension of interaction and political activity and money as
the medium of the sphere of work and economic activity. In the

most precise sense, power belongs in the realm of interaction
and only in a derivative way in the dimension of work. In
order not to glide into mythical thinking, it is necessary not
to fuse work and interaction, money and power, but to separate
them sharply. Only then their interrelationship can be seen
clearly.

According to the political theologian, this reflection on
self-determination includes the systemic preconditions of
intersubjectively reflected existence in the evolutionary data
of the world of nature, in the ability of the inner world of
the human psyche to endure stress, in the recoupling of the
mechanisms of material reproduction and of the administrative
steering in the social world. This happens in such a way that
these preconditions themselves are vice versa related and
bound back to the horizon of understanding of intersubjectively reflected existence. The fundamental normative
principle of such action does not only consist in the
recognition of the factual existence of the other, but much
more so in the will to secure and broaden the life possibility
of the other. Intersubjective creativity becomes a life form.
Thus the mechanisms of the accumulation of money in the
economic subsystem and of power in the political subsystem and
the colonization of the life world by money and bureaucratic
power is broken through. Now a peace, which makes life
possible, is the goal of action. So far, of course, wars are
still a fact of daily life and they are not only economic
wars, but also wars of recognition, wars for power over other
people. The superpowers do not only want the natural and human
resources of smaller nations but also wish to be recognized
fully by smaller powers without paying back to them the same
respect, e.g., the relationship of the U.S.S.R. to Afghanistan
and the relationship of the U.S.A. to the Central American
states, particularly Nicaragua, Grenada and Cuba.

The political theologian is aware that with all this
reflection there is connected an enormous learning problem. He
tries to define this learning problem as precisely as
possible. He does this by showing, that in the process of such
transformation of human action structures as demanded by the
present identity crisis, aporias arise, which concern in their
core the central starting points of all world religions,
particularly Hinduism and Buddhism, Zoroastrianism and Syrian
and Egyptian religion, Judaism and Christianity, i.e., the
religious dimension of human action and interaction(171).
Particularly an ethics of universal solidarity or communi-

cative praxis, which as a result of the rationalization of the world religions, does not exclude historical remembrance, sharpens the experience of the possibility of annihilation, even the factual destruction of the other, who has been recognized in his or her unconditionality. Thus a communicative rationality, which explicates itself normatively, threatens to become paradoxical for itself. How is this paradox of practical rationality to be resolved?

Sociological Directions

The reflection on the death of the innocent other and its consequences for communicative rationality and praxis enables the political theologian Peukert to ask the question concerning religion in modern highly differentiated action systems more precisely(172). The sociology of religion after World War II regressed very often into sociology of religious institutions. It was primarily concerned with the efficiency of the institutional administration of religion. By now it has become clear not only that particularly religious institutions can take part in the pathologies of modern action systems, but also that the question concerning religion must be posited more radically in terms of the question concerning the constitution of the identity of individuals and societies, in the face of existence-threatening crisis experiences. In principle, the older sociology of religion had included this heuristic horizon(173). Present attempts to connect the older evolutionistic with the structural-functional methodology developed by Durkheim and Malinowski aim at the preservation of the dimension of that problematic(174). In the face of the new challenges of the general crises and contingencies in Western civilization, which demand also theoretically a new level of dealing with them, two types of solutions seem to present themselves to the fundamental theologian. In the political-theological perspective, both of these sociological directions carry with themselves their own aporia.

Functionalism

On the one hand stand the neo-conservative attempts to determine religion functionalistically and system-theoretically as contingency experience management praxis(175). Religion, purified from all mythical, metaphysical, mystical, as well as ecstatic utopian and eschatological elements, becomes part of a post-enlightenment instrumental rationality(176). This functional rationality has become aware of the limits of its power, particularly of the limits of the controllability of the impact problems of its own scientific and technological will to change the face of the earth. Instrumental rationality finds its peak in the recognition of the unavoidability of that which is factually the case. It has its most adequate expression in the different forms of positivism as the metaphysics of what is the case(177). The American sociologist, Bellah, conceives of this functionalized religion as new "civil religion"(178). It is supposed to stabilize capitalistic action systems, which are threatened by crises of ungovernability and of socialization-refusal, by legitimation deficiency and withdrawal of loyalty. It can not be denied that some functionalistic elements found their way even into the New Testament: by their fruits the good people are to be known!

According to the fundamental theologian who is committed to practical rather than functional rationality, the aporia of this type of structural-functional sociology of religion lies in that the problems of learning, which are posed by the present individual and collective identity crises, are resolved merely resignatively and regressively(179). Functionalistic sociology breaks off reflection concerning the moment of the Unconditional, which gives itself validity in the struggle for recognition, in interaction, and thereby also ceases reflection on the experience of the annihilation of the innocent other, which occurs in such intersubjectivity. Instead, functionalist sociology bends back reflection to the problem of stabilization of contingent organized capitalistic action systems. But precisely thereby it becomes entirely unclear to the theologian of communicative praxis, how the systematically ossified life world and system-threatening functional mechanisms can be overcome in advanced capitalistic action systems, particularly the mechanisms of power-motivated monetarization and bureaucratization.

According to the political theologian, as to Horkheimer and Habermas before, any attempt to rescue free subjectivity and intersubjectivity in the framework of functional sociology must fail(180). In the framework of structural functionalism, of course, also the question concerning the reality of the Unconditional in the struggle for recognition, of which religious people speak, is extremely uninteresting, since it cannot be decided upon in instrumental categories. For the

functionalist, the modern placebo-suspicion against religion
has lost its disillusioning and disintegrating effect. Even if
religion were a healing panacea for all contingency
experiences, it would not effect more than a placebo at the
time of actually happening placebo-effects. In functionalistic
perspective, a true religion is equivalent with an illusionary
one. Religion is good, i.e., eufunctional, for the survival of
late capitalistic action systems, but it is not true(181). In
functionalistic perspective, modern critique of religion from
Hegel to Feuerbach, Marx, Nietzsche and Freud to Horkheimer,
Adorno, Benjamin, Bloch and Habermas has become as obsolete as
true religion(182). In functionalistic perspective, we find
ourselves today merely in a post-critical age of a socially,
functionally required religious activity, which must be
efficiently organized and administered. Hegel's statement that
in civil society what counts is no longer to know God, but
merely to have religion, to prove religion, but not God, has
in late bourgeois society become fully accepted(183). Today
even some theologians agree.

Critical Theory

Since the fundamental theologian is interested in overcoming
the petrified life world and system-threatening functional
mechanisms in modern action systems, he searches for an
alternative to structural-functionalism(184). He finds this
alternative in the critical theory of Horkheimer, Adorno and
Benjamin and particularly in Habermas's universal pragmatic,
his critical analysis of the present social, political and
world historical situation(185). But Habermas starts from the
assumption that religion has in principle been overtaken by
practical, communicative rationality(186). According to this
analysis, the evolutionary tendencies toward the further elevation of human autonomy, system differentiation and reflexivity, which have asserted themselves throughout modernity,
make the interpretations and orientations of traditional
religious worldviews appear as obsolete(187). But according to
the political theologian, particularly a practical or
communicative rationality, which does understand itself
normatively, is in danger of going under, because of its own
paradoxes, when it breaks off reflection concerning
experiences of unconditionality and annihilation in the
struggle for recognition, interaction, intersubjectivity and
represses in communicative praxis the Absolute and suffering

and death, as Habermas indeed does to a large extent in his
universal pragmatic and theory of communicative praxis(188).
Therefore the political theologian must go beyond critical
theory.

New Theory of Religion

The political theologian, Peukert, proposes a third theory of
religion as alternative to the aporetical structural-functional sociology of religion and to the likewise aporetical
critical theory of religion(189). At least, he delivers the
design of such an alternative. Such an alternative theory of
religion, which intends to do justice to the by-now reached
level of problematic in the theory of science and the theory
of action, and which wants to give guidance to the next
learning step, which is demanded from the individual as well
as from society at this point in history, must obviously
fulfill certain requirements. Such an alternative theory of
religion must start from the question, how subjects can find
in a certain social and historical situation their identity in
the struggle for recognition, in interaction and intersubjectivity. With Kierkegaard the fundamental theologian speaks
of the possibility of the subjects' being themselves(190). At
this point the new theory of religion must pay attention to
the systemic deformations of identities. At the same time, it
must ask for a praxis, which can overcome these deformations.
Thereby, a new notion of praxis is introduced. Then praxis
means, to act in a transforming way toward a non-alienated
form of life, under experienced and suffered-through systemic
contradictions, which deform one's own life world, and thereby
under conditions of alienation. In such a non-alienated form
of life, subjects can find their identities together. Thus
with their conditions, subjects can change themselves and with
the subjects their conditions can change. This kind of communicative praxis is in itself, in its innermost core, a learning
process. It is characteristic for this new alternative theory
of religion, that it keeps open the paradoxy of communicative
rationality between unconditionality and annihilation in
intersubjectivity, interaction, communicative praxis. It
allows to signify those kinds of actions which, in the face of
this paradoxy of unconditionality and annihilation, assert an
Unconditional, Eternal, God in intersubjective action itself
and which free this Unconditional from the economic and
political increase of power, which threatens our existence:

like Habermas, so also does Peukert agree to some extent at
least with Jewish mysticism, that God himself has to be
liberated through the efforts of men and women, before he can
redeem them(191).

According to the political theologian, such an alternative, new theory of religion can no longer fall into a positivistic or behavioristic self-misunderstanding(192). It can
connect itself science-theoretically with those human and
special social sciences, in which the observer, in his attempt
to understand, is himself an existential part of what is to be
observed and understood. The alternative theory of religion
receives into itself the self-reflective character of
Horkheimer's critical theory, which self-reflectivity has long
been prepared in Jewish and Christian mysticism and in
Kierkegaardian existential thought(193). At the same time this
new theory of religion is defined from its very start, i.e.,
in its very methodology and in its relation to the object
realm, by a niveau of reflection, which is achieved in the
face of evolutionistically and structurally determinable
crises and by the matter-of-fact relation to problems, which
then arise and which can be connected to specific phenomena.
Thereby, the new theory of religion also receives the possibility, to analyze certain social, political and historical
objectifications of religious consciousness in their structure
and on their specific level. That includes the possibility to
determine the elementary learning steps of religious consciousness. It makes possible also the critical reception of
the new beginnings of an evolutionistic theory of
religion(194).

Thus also for theology a new basis of discourse comes
into existence. Theology must try to reformulate its central
statements in the face of a thus radicalized theory of
communicative praxis and to realize the learning steps, which
are demanded from it in the present personal, social,
economic, political, historical and cultural situation. The
result is a very much radicalized political theology, which is
much more than a mere theory of communicative action.

Radical Political Theology

Such a political theology, radicalized on the basis of a
theory of communicative praxis being aware of its own _aporia_
in the face of crises, contingencies and catastrophes, and
thus turning into a radical theory of religion, defines the

Judeo-Christian prophetic and messianic religion as hope for absolute justice: as longing that the murderer may at least ultimately not triumph over the innocent victim(195). This reduction of Judaism and Christianity to the hope for absolute justice is far from being naive. As radical political theology starts with the execution of Jesus as the climax of a long history of annihilation of innocent victims, which continues today, it allows for a new interpretation of Judaism and Christianity in the contemporary phase of the world historical struggle for recognition on the level of subject, society, state and culture(196).

For the radical political theologian, Jesus's execution means first of all very realistically and brutally, that the murderers have indeed, for the time being, triumphed over the innocent victim, as they have done so often in the past and will do in the future. But the resurrection means the reversal of this triumph of the murderers. Resurrection means that the murderers have not triumphed over the innocent victim ultimately. The innocent victim has received the highest recognition. God has rescued the innocent victim and thereby justified him before his murderers and has thus also justified Himself. That is the Christian theodicy! God's justice consists in the ultimate triumph of the victim over the murderer. From the resurrection arises the hope for us living in the present phase of the world historical struggle for recognition, that also we can successfully resist and conquer the murderers, at least ultimately. We can act justly in the face of massive injustice.

In the perspective of radical political theology, "hell" as it is presented in the gospels, is more than a mere metaphor and must not at all be interpreted away as Origines did in the past and the Jehovahs Witnesses do today. Nor must hell be repressed by telling people that they should concentrate on the here and now. Even theologians engage in such repression. Hell means, demythologized, that the life of the murderer will ultimately not go well, in spite of the present impressions to the contrary. Heaven, demythologized, means that the life of the innocent victim will ultimately go well, in spite of all present appearances to the contrary. In opposition to Brecht's City of Mahogonny and in agreement with Benjamin's slightly modified "Theological-Political Fragment," the radical political theologian can say that the dead man can be helped - by God through the crucified and resurrected Messiah, who binds the innocent victim who has been slaughtered to God's Kingdom(197).

According to the radical political theologian, as we ourselves are deeply involved in the struggle for recognition at this point of world history, in the apocalyptic conflict between producers and consumers, owners and workers, rich and poor classes, nations and continents, misery and luxury, the prophets of the Old and New Testaments can help us to break through the sophistry of the murderers, which declares the victims to be guilty no matter if they stigmatize themselves or not(198). The New Testament leaves no doubt concerning the question, who are the murderers and who are the innocent victims: Herod, King of Judea, is the murderer and the children of Jerusalem are the innocent victims. Herod, governor of Galilee, his wife and stepdaughter and his soldiers are the murderers and John the Baptist is the innocent victim. Pilate, his soldiers, the Sadducees, the party of Herod, Judas and parts of the people are the murderers and Jesus is the innocent victim. Saul is the murderer and Stephanus is the innocent victim. The murderer can repent and become a victim himself: Saul turned into Paul and was executed by the Roman authorities: they were the murderers and he was the innocent victim.

For the radical political theologian the struggle for recognition between murderers and victims described in the New Testament throws light on present recognition conflicts on the personal, social, economic, political, historical and cultural level and vice versa. In the light of the gospels there can be no doubt that, in the twentieth century the SS man, who takes out of the labor camp a Jewish prisoner, feeds her and makes her his prostitute, and after he is tired of her takes her into the gas chamber and afterwards plays Chopin for the rest of the night, is the murderer and that the Jewish woman is the innocent victim. In the light of the New Testament, there can really be no doubt who are the murderers and who are the victims in contemporary history: in Vietnam, El Salvador, Nicaragua, Honduras, Guatemala, Argentina, Brazil, Lebanon, Grenada, Ethiopia, etc. In the light which contemporary history throws on the Old and New Testament, there can really be no doubt who, then, were the murderers and who were the innocent victims. Radical political theology contains a political hermeneutics of danger, which connects clearly the struggle for recognition in antiquity and modernity, the prophets then and the prophets today, the murderers then and the murderers today, the innocent victims then and the innocent victims today.

Radical political theology contains a universal communicative ethics. It arises from the struggle for recognition as
portrayed in the New Testament. Its fundamental norm is that
the Christian must never side with the murderer. The Christian must always identify with the innocent victim, in present
or in anamnestic or in anticipatory universal solidarity.
Through its communicative ethics radical political theology
advises Christians to engage always in those political parties
which by their actions fight against the murderers in high
places and for their innocent victims. Thus radical political
theology helps Christians today to interpret personal, social,
economic, political, historical and cultural reality and to
orient their praxis in this reality here and now, as well as
in the immediate and more distant future. Thus radical political theology can help to overcome the terrible indictment
against Christianity by critical theorists that it has sided
again and again with the murderers(199). Political theology
helps Christianity to gain back for itself its own dangerously
liberating memoria vitae, passionis, mortis et resurrectionis
Jesu Christi(200). Thus radical political theology also
reemphasizes anew the criterion by which the true and the
false church can be differentiated. The church is false
insofar as it identifies with the murderers. The church is
true insofar as it identifies with the innocent victims in
past, present and future(201).

Dialectical Learning

According to the political theologian Peukert, the new
alternative theory of religion, which serves radical political
theology as basis, is complete only then, when it also
contains a theory of the development of individual religious
consciousness(202). Such theoretical attempts will have a
future, which conceive the development of religious consciousness according to the paradigm of genetic competence - and
identity - theories. These theories differentiate in encounter
with things, with persons and with themselves, two types of
learning.
The one type of learning is essentially cumulative. In
the framework of a given fundamental structure of interpretations and orientations and modes of behavior always more
details are learned. These particulars only affirm these
fundamental interpretations and orientations. But there are

experiences which, if they are really allowed to enter the
students' minds, explode their so far acquired modes of
dealing with reality as well as their own self-understanding.
The adequate working through of those experiences forces the
students to self-finding and to the building up of action
competency on a very different level. This self-finding on a
new niveau happens out of the experience of the negative.
Catastrophes are not forgotten! The innocent victims, who have
been destroyed, are remembered. Contingency experiences are
not repressed. They are not interpreted away. They blow up
firmly structured and petrified and ossified systems of
interpretation and orientation. This is another type of
learning. Peukert calls it, in terms of the classical use of
language, a dialectical learning process.

In a broader sense, the fundamental theologian can speak
of the stage theory of development inspired by Piaget as dialectical learning(203). In the meantime, scholars do explain,
according to Piaget's theoretical paradigm, not only learning
in the cognitive instrumental, but also in the practical-
interactive, intersubjective and motivational realm. Most
important in this tradition is the work of Kohlberg, particularly his theses about the development of moral
consciousness(204).

The theologian of communicative praxis can explain out of
Kohlberg's methodology the problem position of dialectical
learning(205). According to Kohlberg, the development of moral
consciousness tends via the stages of preconventional,
conventional and post-conventional morality to always greater
autonomy, justice and intersubjective reflexivity. However
Kohlberg is fully aware of the fact that precisely on the
highest level of moral consciousness, on the niveau of post-
conventional and principle-guided ethical consciousness once
more elementary questions can break into the open and undo the
whole moral development achieved so far. Such questions are:
Why should we be moral in the face of overwhelming contingencies or catastrophes, which have happened, are happening,
and will happen? Why should we be just in a universe which is
obviously unjust to a large extent? According to Kohlberg, the
answer to those contingency questions and thus the resolution
of despair only a religious consciousness can achieve, which
tries to keep up the principles of justice even in the face of
suffering and death and of an unjust reality: which does not
allow the evil reality to crush the hope for absolute
justice(206). But for Kohlberg here at the same time a

theoretical problem of construction arises. Kohlberg speaks
tentatively of a seventh stage in the development of moral
consciousness after the sixth stage of the orientation
according to universal human and ethical principles. But at
the same time Kohlberg stresses that this radical fundamental
problematic of absolute justice in the face of contingencies
and catastrophes exists coextensively to all stages of moral
development and that therefore one must start in another
dimension of human pragmatic.

        This leads the political theologian to the development of
a theory of ontogenesis of religious consciousness(207). To be
sure, it can be successful only when it starts from the
dimension of dialectical learning processes. It must determine
the becoming of the subject out of the struggle for
recognition, interaction and communicative praxis in the
dimensions of subject, society and history in relationship to
an unconditional, absolute, eternal Good, which is not
coextensive with this action and which is not posited by this
praxis. In these dimensions it can then be determined on which
level identity can be found and preserved in the face of
extreme experiences of contingency. Here orientation happens
in terms of universal communication and solidarity(208). In
the center stands a communicative praxis with a universal
claim, directed toward universal solidarity: communicative
praxis with God mediated through intersubjectivity and
interaction(209). Man's own autonomous freedom is constituted
intersubjectively. Man trusts in his being accepted by God as
absolute love and freedom particularly in failure, pain and
death. God is experienced as the one who makes possible and
fulfills absolute meaning mediated through relative, finite
freedom in the fragmentary happening of powerlessness and
love.

        According to the fundamental theologian the task of an,
in this sense, highly differentiated new alternative theory of
religion is not only to reconstruct the history of religion
and stages of the development of individual religious
consciousness(210). It is rather like political theology,
itself, a practical science. Out of the consciousness of the
participation in the historical process and the entanglement
in social crisis, the new theory of religion stands under the
challenge to throw light on our present action situation in
its most extreme boundary dimensions and to help to work out
the transforming steps of learning to acquire that kind of
praxis which makes possible, under conditions of more and more

sharpening experiences of contingency, an existence in
universal solidarity.

Theological Legitimation

The political theologian Peukert remembers, like Hegel before,
that the problem of the theological legitimation of the moral
order appears in Plato's writings toward the end of the Greek
city-state(211). Plato experiences the breakdown of the
universal mythical background of the particular city-state,
Athens, under the impact of the new principle of singular
subjectivity represented by the sophists(212). He notices the
insufficiency of a purely poetical-exegetical-hermeneutical
making certain of meaning. This breakdown and this
insufficiency poses the question concerning the legitimation
of the normative order of the polis as well as also the
question concerning the virtue of the free citizen. Here the
controversy arises, if the virtue, which is determined through
freedom in the center of practical rationality, must be
thought of as one which unites all capacities of the soul and
if, then, it is in general teachable as are the abilities,
knowledge and skills which are demanded for the subordinated
particular virtues of the lower estates and classes in the
framework of instrumental rationality.

According to the fundamental theologian, in the Judeo--
Christian tradition the faith in man's being affirmed by God
unconditionally provides the ground for the possibility and
the obligation for "I" to affirm the other human being
likewise unconditionally(213). This is particularly so, when
the other has wasted and destroyed already his life
possibilities in terms of the criteria of a mere morality of
the law. The political theologian is fully aware of the fact
that such a supersession of a law-morality develops, of
course, historically according to its own dialectic in the
social-political realm. Against the claim which is raised by
Christendom that ethical norms have once more to be
subordinated under socially-politically mediated religious
claims for their legitimation, arises out of the same
tradition the protest of a radicalized consciousness of
freedom. For this modern consciousness of freedom only the
consensus of free subjects, equipped with unalienable human
rights, can provide the basis for the binding power of rules
of action. The political theologian thinks particularly of the
nominalistic discourse on the natural law, the notion of human

rights, the theory of contract(214).

In German idealism, the theologian of communicative praxis finds the positions of Kant and Hegel standing opposite each other in an irreconcilable fashion(215). Kant rejects any foundation of morality on the basis of existing mores and norms and determines morality as the quality of the autonomous subject, who tests the reasons or determinations of his or her actions in accordance with the maxim of the categorical imperative(216). Hegel, on the other hand, as the fundamental theologian sees him, knows only of an affirmative freedom which receives its morality from the consensus between the individual conscience and a given rational social order(217).

Thereby political theology and a consequent morality and moral education stand before an aporia(218). Political theology can not with Kant simply presuppose the autonomy of the will of the human subject, particularly of a young person. Political theology can also not simply assume with Hegel the existence of a just social order. It must rather ask its own questions which aim at the genesis of autonomy and morality and are in no way exhausted in ethics and social theory.

According to the political theologian, after Kant and Hegel and German idealism the explicated problematic sharpens(219). This is so, since the morality of self-determination, which in German idealism was thought to be possible, in principle at least, comes under ideology suspicion. It is under suspicion of being the product of something else. Marx and Engels see the idealistic morality of self-determination as ideology of the ruling class for the legitimation of its exploitation of the oppressed class(220). Nietzsche sees in the idealistic morality of self-determination the survival rule of a species, which has not yet struggled its way through the principle of the accumulation of the life possibilities through creativity, i.e., will to power(221). Instead, its individuals degrade themselves mutually. Freud sees in the idealistic morality of self-determination the forced internalization of an authority, which pretends to secure the life of a needy being and precisely thereby prevents the satisfaction of its essential needs in freedom(222).

Against the background of this post-Kantian and post-Hegelian critique of morality, the fundamental theologian stands before the alternative, either to drop the foundation of social morality and a consequent moral education, which is likewise directed toward autonomy and solidarity, altogether, or to sharpen it in terms of a critical theory of action.

Durkheim represents the first case, when he understands
morality and moral education positivistically as mere internalization of orientations, which are interpreted as survival
rules of a society(223). The individual goes under, when he or
she does not obey these rules. Skinner demonstrates that in
this first case the notion of human freedom does indeed get
lost(224). Luhmann represents the first case when he reduces
moral problems to technical problems of system-steering of
individual and social systems and their interdependence(225).
For Lubbe, in the first case there remains nothing else than
the flight into resignation as well as subordination under
natural and social contingencies(226). Futurologically the
first case points to Future I - the totally administered
society(227).

The political theologian chooses the second case(228). He
holds on to the moral principle of the unconditional, mutual
recognition and respect among humans as free subjects. He
intends to develop this fundamental moral principle further
toward a universal theory of action, which can gain validity
for the whole human praxis. Such a moral principle is not
possible without theology. Horkheimer and Adorno stated with
Hegel and against Kant clearly and rightly that without
theology all morality, politics and education turn into sheer
business(229). Here the fundamental theologian sides with
Hegel, Horkheimer and Adorno against Kant and Habermas, who
consider possible a morality without theological founda-
tion(230). The second case points to Future III - the reconciled society(231).

Negative Theology

According to the political theologian Peukert, the contingency
experiences of the forced emigration to the USA and the fascist annihilation strategy strengthened in critical theorists
the consciousness of the connection between critical theory
and theology(232). This came out most powerfully in Benjamin's writings(233). But it is present also in the writings of
Horkheimer and Adorno, Marcuse and Fromm and even Haber-
mas(234). At the same time, there grew in these thinkers,
particularly in the face of the bourgeois need to call something positive by its name in the all-darkening catastrophes
of contemporary history, the refusal to do this. Horkheimer
and Adorno articulated this refusal in their Dialectic of
Enlightenment(235). Here they explicated the Second

Commandment of the Decalogue more radically than this had ever been done in Jewish tradition: the prohibition against making positive images of the Absolute. Here they stated very clearly that the Jewish religion does not tolerate any image or word, which would give consolation to the desperation of anything mortal. For both thinkers hope is connected only with the prohibition to call upon the false as God, upon the finite as Infinite, upon the lie as Truth. The guarantee of redemption lies alone in the turning away from all faith, which substitutes itself for it. Knowledge lies alone in the denunciation of illusion and delusion.

In this emphasis on the Second Commandment, Horkheimer and Adorno also see the difference between Judaism and Christianity. For Horkheimer and Adorno it is precisely the will of the Christians to become certain of something positive, an absolute Positive, a positive Absolute, which is the real cause of their anti-Semitism(236). They charge that the Christians, who talked themselves into Christianity as secure possession, had to confirm their eternal salvation through the earthly misfortune of the Jews, who did not make the dark sacrifice of reason. This precisely is the origin of anti-Semitism. Horkheimer and Adorno can accept the crucifixion of Jesus, but not his resurrection. They can not follow Hegel, when he justifies the faith in Jesus's resurrection in terms of positive dialectical rationality, in which the negation of negation, the death of death is followed by a position and affirmation: resurrection and ascension(237). They remain committed to a negative dialectical rationality, which exercises the most extreme asceticism against the truth claim of any revelation(238). They do this in the name of the Second Commandment.

The political theologian must admit that this is without doubt one of the most sensitive spots in the discourse between theologians of communicative praxis and critical theorists(239). But the fundamental theologian points out, nevertheless, that the tradition of theologia negativa, most clearly formulated by Meister Eckehart, Nicolaus of Cusa, and Hegel and a corresponding anthropologia negativa is not only in the center of the Jewish tradition and of the critical theory, but also at the very core of the Christian religion(240). Second Commandment, negative metaphysics, ethics, theology, anthropology, and philosophical agnosticism are points, at which political theology and critical theory can agree to a large extent.

The political theologian must also admit that Horkheimer's and Adorno's judgment concerning the Christian origin
of anti-Semitism can quote sufficient historical evidences for
itself(241). This is so, since there is the issue of
anti-semitic background attitudes, which are sedimented also
from religious traditions. They play an important role
particularly in the reception of the critical theory in
theological as well as in other circles, e.g., social and
pedagogical groups. Such religious background attitudes do
certainly make most difficult the reception of the critical
theory as well as of the political theology in West Germany
and the USA up to the present. In psychoanalytical terms, the
resistance against the critical theory and the consequent
political theology is rooted in the repression of a long and
guilt-loaded history of anti-semitism.

In any case, the political theologian refuses to blame
the critical theory which subordinates itself completely and
radically under the Second Commandment, that it aims with its
unconditional critique of late capitalistic and socialistic
action systems at nothing else than a struggle, in which only
the decisiveness and the means decide, which those are ready
to use, who have firmly made up their mind to turn the
conflict in their favor(242). Political theologians reject
also the assertion that Adorno's statement that the first
demand on education is that Auschwitz will not happen again
and that to give reasons for such demand would be something
outrageous in the face of the outrageous which has happened,
starts simply from an experience of negativity which says
nothing about what is good for man(243). In case of such
assertion, the possibility is no longer far away to find
connections between the radically emancipatory cultural
revolution and terrorism(244). The challenge, in which the
most extreme contingency experiences of world history so far
mirror themselves, to realize humanity precisely under the
condition that one does not, like Hegel, claim to have any
general meaning of history, which would be comprehensible here
and now, and that one does also not ask others to have such a
claim, constitutes one of the central demands of Jewish
theology. It is also the central demand of the critical theory
for the occidental way to interpret reality and to orientate
one's action in it. It is thus also a central demand for
philosophical and theological thinking in general(245).
Political theology takes this challenge of Jewish theology and
critical theory extremely seriously. This of course does not

excuse fundamental theology from again and again testing this
challenge against the power of the original dialectical notion
in Hegel's logic, philosophy of right and history, which was
and is and will be a theological one(246).

Non-Possessive Devotion

According to the political theologian Peukert, Horkheimer and
Adorno,   following   Hegel, intend in their Dialectic of
Enlightenment to reveal a connection of blindness and
illusions and delusions dominant in late capitalistic action
systems(247). Horkheimer's and Adorno's thinking is negation
of negation, negative dialectic, which does not go over, like
Hegel's affirmative dialectic, into positing something
affirmative(248). Dialectic is for the two thinkers the
self-consciousness of the objective connections of blindness,
illusions and delusions in advanced capitalistic society. But
dialectic as such does not yet escape this connection of
blindness. The objective goal of dialectic, nevertheless, is
to break out of these blinding illusionary connections from
inside(249). Horkheimer's and Adorno's analysis of a condition
of late capitalistic action systems, in which dominion over
external and internal nature and over other humans has become
a destructive principle, brings out into the open what ought
to be freedom from domination precisely where it refuses to
draw   up positive counter-utopias. Under the contingency
experience of the industrial annihilation of humans in peace
or war, Horkheimer and Adorno even transcend the Marxian
protest against their reification and transformation into
commodities. The commodification of people under capitalism
has reached its all-time peak in Auschwitz. Here even dead
people were turned into profitable commodities: their skins
being turned into lampshades and their bones into soap. The
triumph of the capitalistic exchange principle in its
application to humans! Horkheimer and Adorno erect in
negativity the unconditionality, the inviolability, the
integrity of the other. The possibility of another form of
intersubjectivity appears in this negative dialectics.
Precisely here Habermas connects himself with the critical
theory of Horkheimer and Adorno. Instead of freedom from
domination, Habermas speaks of communication without
domination(250).
    Beyond this, Habermas states that, for Adorno, the
devotion to the other completely separated from the will to

ownership over him or her, is the only dialectical image or
word with which he violates the tabu over the hoped-for
condition of the future(251). According to Habermas the Second
Commandment, the prohibition of making images of the Absolute,
is for Horkheimer and Adorno as strictly valid for utopia as
for the messianic future of the Jews(252). As far as Habermas
can see, Adorno breaks through this prohibition of a
constantly negative philosophy and theolgy only at this one
point, when he speaks of the non-possessive devotion to the
other. The determinate negation in Hegel's logic ends with the
absolute idea or spirit(253). The determinate negation in the
critical theory ends with non-possessive love. The two
determinations of the Absolute are not too far away from each
other. They may very well be identical.

        Horkheimer finds this non-possessive devotion to the
other expressed in an exemplary way in Jesus. According to
Horkheimer, Jesus died for all humans(254). He could not keep
himself avariciously for himself. He belonged to everything
which suffers. Jesus's non-possessive love to the others was
the unheard-of deed, which broke through the icy-cold
atmosphere of the late Roman action system. Political
theologians hope that Jesus's non-possessive devotion to
others can once more bring warmth into the icy-coldness of
technical manipulation and the struggle for recognition in and
among modern capitalistic and socialistic action systems.

Integrity

According to the political theologian, Peukert, following
Hegel, the radicality of an ethics, which concentrates on the
invulnerability and integrity of the other, becomes clear only
when it is explicated toward the whole of world history(255).
From the very beginning of his critical philosophy Horkheimer
had felt with and against Hegel and Schopenhauer that the
annihilation of innocent victims in the historical process was
ground for an unconsolable sadness(256). Horkheimer's
controversy with Benjamin at the end of the 1930s concerning
the rescue of the past and the spiritual heritage of Benjamin
written down in his thesis "On the Notion of History" after
the Hitler-Stalin Pact and shortly before his own death,
radicalized the question concerning the solidarity of all
finite beings as question for a new relationship to
history(257). Now for Benjamin, the hope that future
historical progress could compensate the injustice against the

victims of Nazi or other state terror appears as utter blasphemy. For Benjamin the catastrophe is the progress and the progress is the catastrophe(258). Catastrophe is the continuum of history. The oppressed, not human kind, are the subject of history. The continuum of history is that of the oppressors. It is the task of the historian to explode the present out of the continuum of historical time. Later, for Benjamin's friend Adorno, that precisely is the catastrophe, that things go on in history as they do under the domination of the capitalistic masters(259). From Benjamin's perspective, the Marxian impulse to see history through the eyes of the weak and the victims of the social and historical process, gains a new quality(260). Historical consciousness as solidary anamnesis of the disappointed, unlived, broken off, destroyed life of the innocent victims breaks open the continuum of the world historical struggle for technical control over external and internal nature and for recognition of the master by the slave. Then also confrontation occurs between an epoch treated by an historian and prehistory(261). In the power of this confrontation the treated epoch becomes solidaristic with the actual situation of the historian. Also in historical consciousness arises a new form of interaction and intersubjectivity, which is characterized not by the recognition of the master by the slave, but by unconditional mutual recognition of and respect for the invulnerability of the one and the other human being.

The political theologian does not have the impression that this principle of unconditional mutual recognition of the integrity of the one and the other, which not only Benjamin, but also Horkheimer, Adorno, Sohn-Rethel, Marcuse, Fromm and Habermas have begun to formulate, has been pursued much further and has led to any important methodological consequences in the human and social sciences, particularly in historiography or in pedagogics. Historiography has not gone beyond social history. Pedagogics has not worked out a concept of education, the normative core of which is a historically differentiated consciousness of universal solidarity. In the dimension of theology, critical political theology alone has made the principle of the new intersubjectivity, characterized by unconditional mutual recognition of the other as end in himself or herself, its very core and has begun to apply it to family, society, state and history(262).

Innovative Praxis

The political theologian Peukert agrees with the fundamental
thesis of critical theory, which moves consistently through
all its developmental stages: that the mechanism of modern
action systems which aim at the accumulation of money and
administrative power and are ultimately self-destructive,
increasingly endanger the construction of a communicative life
world, in which human consciousness, spirit, can awaken and
can find itself and be at home with itself and be free in
solidarity with others(263). This thesis does not only
challenge the human and social sciences, e.g., historiography
or pedagogics, but also fundamental theology, to develop in
this area of the struggle for recognition, interaction,
intersubjectivity, communicative praxis its own essential
categories and principles. They must be gained out of
interdisciplinary discourse and cooperation. They can beyond
that achieve foundation-theoretical significance for the human
and social sciences in general. This is so, since what is of
concern in these principles and categories, is the connection
between the constitution of subjects out of their
intersubjectivity and interaction and communicative praxis in
their specific life worlds, on the one hand, and the material
and cultural reproduction of modern action systems on the
other. Metz, Peukert and Arens have begun to develop in a
fundamental theology the foundation principles and categories
for a critical political theology with the help of the
critical theory from Horkheimer to Benjamin, Adorno, Marcuse,
Sohn-Rethel, Lowenthal and Habermas.

According to the political theologian Peukert, decisive
for all stages of critical theory, from Horkheimer to
Habermas, is the quest for that kind of innovative praxis
which breaks open and can transform the systematically
distorted and petrified psychic and social mechanisms of
advanced capitalistic and socialistic action systems and can
open up a life world for intersubjectively reflected self-
knowledge and self-determination(264). Adorno, Marcuse and
Benjamin attribute this kind of innovative liberating praxis
almost exclusively to art or the metaphorical language move-
ment(265). Following Habermas, the political theologian tries
to demonstrate in a new start that this kind of innovative,
emancipatory praxis is a fundamental characteristic of human,
intersubjectively oriented action in all action systems in all
historical epochs.

In the perspective of the fundamental theologian, human
action can objectivate itself in structures, in given or historically developed, self-designed schemata(266). They constitute human action systems(267). Sociology lives from such
objectifications. But these objectifications are also the
existential ground of formal sciences, like logistics, system
theory and cybernetics. But – and that is most important for
the political theologian – human action can also transcend
these objectifications and posited structures in action
systems and can transform them and keep them open for further
transformations. For the theologian of communicative praxis,
intersubjective action in its complete form is then
characterized by the fact that it is able to realize such
innovations and transformations in action and counter-action
and thereby to find new common interpretations and
orientations. The fundamental theologian can show this in the
case of innovative linguistically mediated action(268). First
attempts to move beyond behavioristic, constructivistic and
structuralistic developmental and learning theories can show
the direction of the necessary enfolding of an action theory
as basis theory not only for the human and social sciences in
general, but also for political theology(269).
    In the view of the political theologian, such a new
conception of the notion of innovative praxis has consequences
for the normative foundation of intersubjective action(270).
Also post-conventionally conceived communicative ethics can
come under the suspicion that they do not posit the fully
developed subject, who is conscious of himself or herself and
in full disposition of himself or herself, in any anticipatory, but merely a factual way. The fundamental theologian
admits to Habermas that ethics can be grounded only in the
basic structure of interaction itself(271). If this is so,
then with the conception of intersubjective action also the
fundamental starting point and methodology of ethics changes.
    According to the political theologian, there would be no
greater misunderstanding of ethics than to assume that it had
to reproduce merely the mechanism of equalization among the
claims of subjects of right. The fundamental theologian is on
the level of a theory of innovative, transformative action
rather concerned with the obligation, first of all, to help
the other to come to the knowledge and articulation of himself
or herself and thereby of his or her claims. In the view of
the theologian of communicative praxis, the fundamental postulate of ethics is the mutually making possible of the acquisi-

tion of self-understanding and competence of communicative
action, i.e., creative intersubjectivity. In the view of
political theology, a pedagogical ethics, which imposes
responsibility for the making possible of the self-knowledge
and self-determination of the other, is no longer merely a
secondary and derived, but a primary orientation of
intersubjective action in general. Fundamental theology must
include such a pedagogical ethics, if it really wants to apply
itself and reproduce itself in highly differentiated modern
action systems.

Democracy

All this has, in the perspective of the political theologian,
Peukert, also consequences for the structure of democratic,
i.e., freedom-insuring institutions in modern action
systems(272). The work, e.g., in educational institutions, is
burdened with the fact that they are the location in which the
contradiction between the functional requirements of human
action systems and their subsystems and the postulates of
life-world-oriented ethics, particularly pedagogical ethics
and action, becomes obvious and is carried out. The
fundamental theologian agrees with Habermas that the normative
core of the most significant achievement in modern action
systems, the democratic constitutional state, consists in that
claims of system-conform-functioning do not only find their
limits at the border of codified essential human and civil
rights, but that they are completely subordinated under common
public discourse and formation of will(273). Thus the
political theologian can show that the critical ethics,
particularly the critical pedagogical ethics, agrees entirely
with the will to democracy(274).

According to the political theologian, such a critical
ethics and a pedagogical engagement conforming to it, demand
rightly social institutions in which the priority of communicative self-knowledge and self-determination is secured. They
also demand educational institutions, in which the ability to
such self-knowledge and self-determination can be acquired.
The fundamental theologian is aware that all these connections
between critical ethics, pedagogics and the constitutional
state are not yet very well worked out. In addition they were
rather darkened in the second developmental stage of critical
theory. But there is no doubt for the theologian of
communicative praxis that a pragmatic of dealing with human

action systems and their subsystems, particularly the economic
and political subsystems, must be enfolded in the framework of
a theory of democratic institutions.

Nature

As the political theologian Peukert posits a theory of action
in the described way, he encounters two fundamental
categories, which have been developed in classical critical
theory(275). They signify two interconnected boundary problems
of modern action systems. They are the notion of an unlimited,
all-embracing solidaristic community, which includes also the
victims of the historical process, and the notion of nature.
Hegel anticipated these categories in his philosophy of
nature, right and history(276).
     The political theologian finds in the works of Hork-
heimer, Adorno and Marcuse a notion of nature which points
toward an inner contradictoriness of the eccentric position of
man as a natural being(277). Man is also in his inner world,
in his inner conscious self-awareness, a part of the external
world of nature. Man is forced to manipulate this external
nature in terms of work and tools, in order to secure his
survival. Thereby, man's way to deal with external nature
hangs inseparably together with his way to deal with his inner
nature. In the perspective of the fundamental theologian, it
is an unavoidable, practically consequential task, to tie the
notion of instrumental action, which underlies the causal and
functional thinking of the natural sciences, the medium of
work and tools, consequentially into a human-specific,
temporal, situative-reflective, intersubjectively oriented
conception of communicative praxis, which does not aim at the
accumulation of monetary or administrative power: the medium
of unconditional mutual recognition. Like Habermas, the
theologian of communicative praxis sees no other way to
overcome the contemporary dichotomy between work and
interaction, or between nature and culture(278). He sees also
no other way to find the basis for an integrative notion of
education. Here, as elsewhere, the political theologian
overlooks the medium of marriage and family, as well as the
medium of nation. Both media have to be included in a future
political-theological reflection, which intends to cover the
totality of human action in terms of a universal pragmatic
embracing language, work, love, recognition and nationhood.

Universal Solidarity

In the view of the political theologian, Peukert, the demand for a solidarity of all finite beings was radicalized in the controversy between Horkheimer and Benjamin about the conclusiveness or inconclusiveness of history(279). For the fundamental theologian this solidarity is universal in the sense that it relates itself to the present and future generations as well as to the innocent victims, who have been destroyed and annihilated in the past. In the perspective of the theologian of communicative praxis, the memoria of the victims of history has not only the functional meaning to motivate the struggle for a better future. Progress only toward the future, without any tiger jump into the past, was for Benjamin merely the continuation of the catastrophe. For Benjamin, the anamnesis of the innocent victims who have been annihilated in history transcends the mere appropriation of cultural goods. It aims at a more embracing formation of human solidarity consciousness.

The political theologian agrees fully with Benjamin's conception of solidarity with the innocent victims who have been destroyed in one way or another, and of whom he himself or herself may become one himself or herself in the process of messianic mimesis only too soon(280). But the fundamental theologian must also admit that theoretical efforts of this kind seem to be outrageously powerless in the face of conditions, which daily annihilate more and more innocent victims in the Near East, Central America, Africa and elsewhere. The political theologian, nevertheless, remains in full consensus with the position not only of Benjamin, but also of Horkheimer and Adorno, that transforming true praxis depends entirely on the uncompromising attitude of theory against the unconsciousness, with which civil and socialistic society allows its thinking to harden itself and to become petrified(281).

The political theologians Metz, Peukert, Arens, etc., are helping many Christians in their dilemma, that they cannot forget the innocent victims, who have been annihilated in the past, are annihilated in the present, and will be annihilated in the future(282). They communicate new solutions for the old theodicy problem: God's justice in the face of the horror and terror of nature and history. The fundamental theologians take these innocent victims seriously. Following Jesus's example, the theologians of communicative praxis think from the

perspective of these victims. Out of this perspective of the
vanquished, the political theologians develop with the help of
the modern theory of science and theory of action,
particularly the theory of communicative praxis, a historical,
salvation-historical perspective of the world of nature, man's
inner world, the social and historical world, and the cultural
world.

Parables of Jesus

Political theologians do not only criticize Habermas's universal pragmatic, because of its aporia - the temporality of all
interaction and intersubjectivity and the annihilation of the
interacting partners in spite of their unconditional mutual
recognition - and try to overcome this aporia out of the
Judeo-Christian religion and other religious traditions, e.g.,
Buddhism(283). They also learn from Habermas and apply his
theory of communicative praxis to the Judeo-Christian
religion. As the political theologian Metz applies Benjamin's
mystical-materialistic notion of history to the Christianity
of the New Testament, so does the theologian of communicative
praxis, Arens, student of Metz and Peukert, apply the theory
of communicative action, especially the dialectic of language
and recognition, to the historical Jesus and his discourses
with his friends and opponents, particularly his parables,
illustrations, examples or stories about the Kingdom of
God(284). The fundamental theologian Arens sees the historical
Jesus as partner in discourse and storyteller as he is
passionately engaged in the struggle for recognition of God's
reign and of himself and thus in the liberation of the
people(285).

According to the political theologian Arens, from
Habermas's universal-pragmatic reflection on the double
structure of everyday communication results the insight, that
every text must be seen as communicative action between
subjects in respect to a certain thing or subject matter(286).
Following this insight, the fundamental theologian develops
his own pragmatic theory of the parables of Jesus(287). In the
explication of his pragmatic theory of parable, the theologian
of communicative praxis takes recourse to the double structure
of speech acts worked out by Habermas(288). He hopes to be
able to clarify the communicative functioning of the illustrations of Jesus with the help of Habermas's universal-
pragmatic reflections. Habermas has, indeed, influenced

strongly with his universal pragmatic not only philosophy and the human and social sciences, but also theology, even exegesis(289).

Double Structure

In Habermas's perspective the double structure of everyday communication or speech signifies the fundamental bipolarity of all textually mediated speaking(290). Habermas takes this bipolarity for the starting point of his analysis of speech achievements as well as of the question concerning the validity claims raised in speech. He elevates this double structure of speech to the level of the notion and clarifies it through the standard version of the speech act. In this standard form an illocutive part executed with the help of a performative sentence and a propositional part formed with the help of a sentence with a propositional content are put together. According to Habermas, in the face of the speech act invariance of propositional contents, understanding between listener and speaker, comes about only when they come to a consensus at the same time on the level of intersubjectivity by means of illocutive acts about the interpersonal relationship to be established between them, and on the level of experiences and things, by means of the propositional content, about this very content(291). In Habermas's view, the partners in communication must connect an illocutive understanding of something with a predicative understanding, which aims at understanding about something. They must connect dialectically the struggle for recognition with language. The double structure of everyday speech consists of the language-mediated struggle for recognition, interaction, or intersubjectivity.

The political theologian Arens discovers in Jesus's parabolic speech acts, his illustrations and examples about God's Kingdom, what Habermas calls the double structure of speech, the language-mediated struggle for recognition(292). He reconstructs this bipolarity, this dialectic in Jesus's stories. This double structure reflects itself in the New Testament texts. For the fundamental theologian each of Jesus's parables is as determinate, concrete expression first of all a speech act. The political theologian is concerned with the pragmatic theory of parables as the theory of the speech acts of Jesus, not with the pragmatic analysis of parables as analysis of a speech act.

In Jesus's parabolic speech acts, the original illocutive act, as far as it is preserved at all, is of course objectified. That means that the original illocutive act is portrayed on the level of the propositional content in the narrative framework. The political theologian asks in relation to Jesus's parables, about what and for what he wanted to come to an understanding with his listeners. The fundamental theologian thereby relates the content aspect and the relational aspect of the parables of Jesus to each other. For the theologian of communicative praxis, Jesus's interactive, behavior itself is the real framework of his kerygma. The political theologian comes to this insight by binding back the content of Jesus's parabolic speech to his intersubjective behavior understood as his verbal and non-verbal communicative praxis. The fundamental theologian understands both parabolic speech and interactive behavior as mutually throwing light upon each other: the parabolic content is a help for the interpretation of Jesus's intersubjective behavior and his behavior is the self-explication of the content of his speech. With Jesus, language and interaction or struggle for recognition stand in a dialectical relationship(293).

Facts and Fiction

According to the political theologian, Arens, Jesus speaks in parables about processes in the world of nature and about human actions in the personal, social and cultural world(294). Jesus speaks about facts which are open to the experience of his listeners and which are known to them and with which they are familiar. Sometimes Jesus speaks also about fictitious matters. But the listeners have, nevertheless, also insight into these invented matters on the basis of their own experience. The listeners are in the position to understand these fictitious matters as well as the real facts before. To be sure, the propositional content of Jesus's stories have theological references: "The Kingdom of God is like..."(295). These theological references are certainly of utmost importance. But first of all, the fundamental theologian brackets out these theological references. Then statements about objects of experience of the lifeworld of Palestinian proletarians, small farmers and petite bourgeois constitute the propositional content of Jesus's parables, his images and image stories. The meaning of the images and, thereby, of the semantic content of the parables of Jesus is, so the theologian of communicative praxis formulates in terms of Habermas's theory of communicative action, fully understandable only in the synthesis or coincidence of the propositional content with the illocutive act, which determines that content in its communicative function. In Jesus's stories, so the political theologian argues, a large amount of illocutive acts can be identified through a pragmatic analysis of parables and can be characterized with corresponding performative verbs.

Mutual Understanding

Following Habermas's theory of communicative praxis the political theologian Arens directs his pragmatic parable theory toward a paradigm of understanding of Jesus's stories as speech acts, which aim at a consensus(296). The pragmatic theory of parables tries to achieve this understanding through an analysis of the structure of parabolic communication. The existing theological parable theories support more or less the concern of the fundamental theologian's pragmatic parable theory, to emphasize in Jesus's illustrations the orientation toward mutual understanding(297). This is so, since according to the theological theories of parables, also the intention of the examples of Jesus, seen under the aspect of the speaker-listener relationship, is a consensus to be achieved through understanding.

Beyond the level of intention reflected in the theological theories of parables, the political theologian Arens, is in the position in his pragmatic theory of parables to answer the question concerning the "where to" of the stories of Jesus as a question concerning the form of intersubjectivity, which in them is made a matter of language and which in them is aimed at with their help(298). Arens can answer this question through the consideration of the illocutive act, which is performed in the parable and through the reconstruction of its illocutive power or role. As far as the illocutive and proleptically envisioned perlocutive intentions of the speaker Jeus is concerned, the fundamental theologian can say, on the basis of the analysis of his speech acts, that he tries to come to an understanding with his opponents, mostly the Pharisees, by wooing for them. Jesus tries to convince his oppositional listeners of his new understanding and interpretation of reality and of his new orientation of action. He does this by telling his opponents plausible stories, e.g., about the joy in the face of the found-again

prodigal   son,   about   the   solidaristic   goodness,   and   by
communicatively acting with them in away which corresponds to
the attitude which is mediated in these illustrations.

Evidence

The political theologian Arens speaks in a double sense of the
evidence of Jesus's deed, i.e., his communicative praxis(299).
According to the fundamental theologian, the evidence of the
content of Jesus's story corresponds to the evidence of his
interactive behavior in a mode which lets appear as evident
the understanding of the world, which is implicated in his
parables and in his communicative actions. The theologian of
communicative praxis signifies as communicative understanding
the interpersonal relationship, which Jesus offers to his
opponents in his telling his parables. Jesus has produced this
interpersonal relationship unilaterally and anticipatorily as
offer and invitation to his opponents. The opponents are
challenged to ratify this intersubjectivity on their part
through their own corresponding encounter aand communicative
praxis not only with Jesus, but also with other people as
well. Arens determines these illocutive acts, which are
performed in Jesus's so understood speech acts in relation to
his listeners, as "communicating," "offering," "inviting."
Jesus communicates to his opponents an understanding of
reality, which is expressed in the texts as well as in his
communicative praxis. Jesus offers his interpretation of
reality to his opponents. Jesus invites his oppositional
listeners to enter a new form of action. The political
theologian signifies the perlocutive act or effect, which does
not stand in the power of the speaker and which is envisioned
proleptically through the parable, as "convincing" or as
"converting."

Form of Mediation

For the political theologian Arens, the relationship of the
propositional content of Jesus's parables to the illocutive
act, which is performed in the telling of the story, means
that the "thing," which is mediated in the presentation of the
illustration - the Kingdom of God - does not represent any
content   which   can   be   abstracted   from   the   form   of
mediation(300). In a good Hegelian sense, form and content are
separate, but at the same time inseparable(301). Form and

content are dialectically one. They reproduce each other. The content of Jesus's parables, which is to be mediated, constitutes itself as semantic content of the stories only together with the form of its communication. The semantic content of Jesus's parables receives from this form its situational pragmatic meaning as, vice versa, the form is made non-ambiguous or universal through its content. The communication or interaction, structure, which is addressed by a series of Jesus's parables, is mediated as their content – in respect to the dominion of God and the freedom of men and women as the always co-thematized "thing" of his stories – by the fact that this communication happens in a form which realizes precisely this structure. Jesus does this, so that this intersubjective structure may be shared by the opponents.

In the perspective of the political theologian, in this precisely lies the specific double structure of the parables of Jesus: propositional content and illocutive acts are related toward each othr in such a way that that, about which something is said, is woven together most closely with that, for which this happens(302). Therefore, so the fundamental theologian argues, the reality of God and his dominion and the liberation of the people, which in Jesus's parables is linguified very often at least indirectly, must be understood from the perspective of how and where it is put into language, namely, in the practical-communicative action free of domination(303). For the theologian of communicative praxis, out of the discussion of the double structure of Jesus's parabolic speech results finally in relation to the talk of the Kingdom of God and human freedom, the consequence that nothing can be said about God's <u>basileia</u> without it being communicated at the same time and without people being invited into it in this very communication, that happens in the mediation of the Kingdom of God, which invites and challenges to participation(304).

Truth and Rightfulness

The political theologian Arens formulates in terms of Habermas's universal-pragmatic categories that Jesus's parabolic talks, illustrations, examples or stories about God's kingdom do obviously deal with the problematization of two validity claims of his communicative praxis: the truth of his verbal expressions and the rightfulness of his actions or of the norms underlying his praxis(305). Between Jesus and his pharisaic opponents, so the fundamental theologian argues, there exists no longer any background consensus, which would allow him and them to continue unproblematically communicative, understanding-oriented action. There exists rather a deep dissent in reference to the correctness of Jesus's communication with tax collectors, prostitutes and sinners of all kinds, his commensalism with them as well as his violation of ritual and cultic commandments, which constitute and stabilize the pharisaic interpretation or construction of reality. Jesus breaks through the "fence of the law." According to the theologians of communicative praxis, Peukert and Arens, the controversy concerning the legitimation of Jesus's action is at the same time a controversy about the truth of what he says about God: a controversy concerning the reality of God(306). Most fundamentally, it is a struggle for the unconditional recognition of Jesus's truth claims and of God's reign, and the liberation of the people.

In the political theologian Arens's view, the truth claim of Jesus's speech and the claim of the rightfulness of his interactions, which are to be discussed between himself and his opponents, do not constitute two validity claims, which are separate and independent from each other(307). According to Habermas's reflection on theoretical and practical discourse, these two validity claims of truth of speech and correctness of action converge only at the point of the radicalization of discursive engagement as final step in the practical discourse concerning the question of what should be valid as knowledge(308). But in Jesus's case, so the fundamental theologian argues, the two validity claims converge in that mode, that the truth of his verbal expressions can not at all be asserted without rightful actions, which correspond to these expressions. Here theory and praxis are indeed one. The Hegelian/Marxian theory-praxis dialectic is anticipated in the dialectic of Jesus's discourse and struggle for recognition(309). According to the New Testament, the truth makes free only when it is done(310).

All this is so, according to the political theologian, since in Jesus's case what is of concern is not the assertion of the truth of facts in the world of nature, which is logically neutral and understandable in an impersonal way and which can be tested through repeated observations and even in laboratory experiments(311). What is at stake in Jesus's case is, rather, a self-obligating assertion of truth. The truth claim of this assertion can be proven only in a communicative praxis which is related to this very claim of truth. The theologians Ladriere and Evans argue that in the context of the bible religious knowledge is a form of action(312). To know God, means to recognize or to acknowledge God: to let God be God! Thereby is implicated a certain mode of behavior and an obligation. The parable of Jesus is a message which tells the listener which is the proper attitude toward God. Jesus's stories do not contain directly a teaching about God. Jesus's illustrations tell the listeners that their behavior toward God shall be right, insofar as they consider God in that determinate mode, which the example indicates. Jesus's parabolic theology is an indirect theology.

But according to the political theologian, the performative character of the talk of God is not correctly represented with what Ladriere and Evans indicate with the term "religious knowledge" or "teaching"(313). For the fundamental theologian Evans's expression "my faith does involve a belief that..." means really that the faith asserts religious expressions as true. Therefore, the theologian of communicative praxis speaks instead of "religious knowledge" or "teaching" rather of the assertion of the truth of speech acts. The truth claim of these speech acts can be proven as one, which is self-obligating, personal and withdrawn from testing by observation, and effective only in actions which correspond to it. According to the political theologian all this does, of course, in no way exclude the discursive grounding of theoretical religious truth claims or practical claims of rightfulness. Such discursive grounding must, of course, take place in the framework of a practical discourse, which justifies the taken-over obligations of action.

Theoretical and Practical Discourse

According to Habermas, discourses serve essentially the finding of a consensus(314). In theoretical and practical discourses arguments are exchanged. In practical discourses these arguments take the form of suggestions for the justification of a norm which is recommended for acceptance and is looked upon as being able to be universalized. The norm finds a rationally motivated recognition, when in it on the basis of the logic of practical discourse a universal interest receives a validity which has been stated and affirmed without illusions.

There is no doubt that Jesus continually entered argumentative practical discourses with his friends and enemies. Beyond this the political theologian Arens acknowledges Jesus's parables, illustrations, examples and stories as discursive arguments in the framework of his practical discourses(315). The fundamental theologian finds the suggestion to understand illustrations as arguments in several parable theories(316). The theologian of communicative praxis affirms this suggestion, that parables are arguments, against the parable theorists, theologians and religionists, who see the stories of Jesus rather as analogies and therefore fight passionately against the idea that they are arguments in the framework of practical discourse.

Narrative Argumentation

The political theologian Arens understands Jesus's parables as narrative argumentation(317). He comprehends Jesus's stories as quasi-discursive. The fundamental theologian calls Jesus's illustrations quasi-discursive, instead of simply discursive, since in his stories as contributions to discussions no complete discourse takes place. Such discourse always consists of speech, counterspeech, and consensual unification. Jesus merely simulates a complete practical discourse in his illustrations. They are interconnected narratively with the arguments of the opponents. Arens follows in his interpretation of Jesus's parables as quasi-discursive, Habermas's advocatory model of simulated discourse(318).

Often in Jesus's quasi-discursive stories, his opponents and he himself appear in antagonistic advocatory positions in a covered-up form. Jesus's quasi-discursive parables reflect as integral parts of practical discourse between himself and his opponents his struggle for the recognition of God's kingdom with them. Jesus tells the stories with the intent to come to an understanding with his opponents about this unconditonal recognition of God's reign and the likewise unconditional recognition of the freedom of the people. Precisely such emphasis on the quasi-discursive character of Jesus's parables constitutes foundationally political theology as such. Its roots lie precisely in the struggle for recognition: first of all Jesus's struggle for the recognition of God's sovereignty and then, consequentially, his struggle for the recognition of the people, i.e., their emancipation, the realization of their humanity in the context of alienated and oppressive human action systems, their sovereignty, be it on the primitive, archaic, historical-intermediate, modern or postmodern or any other level of human evolution.

The political theologian calls Jesus's parables quasi-discursive since he justifies in them his own behavior and the reality of God, which grounds it, and the liberation of the people on three levels(319). On the level of his communicative behavior toward tax collectors, prostitutes, and other sinners, Jesus argues substantially for his turning toward such fringe existences or "foul existences," since they need most the solidaristic acceptance he offers them(320). Jesus shows from his own understanding of himself and of reality, the rightfulness of his orientation of action and of his behavior toward the "foul existences" in society and history as well as the falseness of the behavior of his addressed opponents toward them. He does this in the - to speak with Brecht - narratively alienated presentation of their excommunicating interaction with tax collectors, whores, and other sinners, which in reality is not legitimated by God(321). In this parabolic presentation, the opponents are supposed to recognize themselves and to see themselves confronted with the Abba of Jesus, who is friendly to men and good and solidaristic with them. From the perspective of God, the opponents' interaction with the stigmatized tax collectors and sinners appears senseless and inhuman. It illicits the self-stigmatization of Jesus and his friends and followers in protest against the domination of men by men and as effective means to overcome it(322).

Forgiveness and Repentance

To be sure, nowhere does Jesus argue in his stories for the abolishment of the law or for the legitimation of the false norms underlying the behavior of tax collectors, prostitutes or sinners(323). For Jesus as for all the prophets of Israel before him, forgiveness is bound to repentance. There is no forgiveness without repentance: <u>metanoia</u>, anthropological revolution! Without repentance forgiveness means the legitimation of the sinful acts, and the false norms guiding them. Jesus was far from such legitimation. The Messiah Jesus is not an antinomist as some of the friends of John the Baptist. On the other hand, also the Abba of Jesus appears in his parables not to be entirely unambiguous. He can lead people into temptation. When the perfection of the heavenly Father consists in his indifference with which he lets his sun shine and rain fall on the good and the evil, he lets, nevertheless, also a tower fall on sinful people, and he lets them be slaughtered by Pontius Pilate in the Temple of Jerusalem. He kills his enemies and lets his enemies kill his enemies and even his friends. He will finally abandon him, Jesus, himself on the cross and later on destroy Jerusalem and disperse the whole Jewish nation as Jesus had prophesied. Sometimes the political theologian Arens is hesitant to face the inconsistencies in Jesus's narrative theology. He is particularly hestitant to deal with the negativity of God, mythologically expressed in his "wrath." The negativity of God does nevertheless appear in Jesus's parabolic theology even to the extreme of the imposition of eternal hell and damnation on non-repentant sinners(323). Political theology must take this negativity of God seriously. This is the theodicy problem of Jesus, which is resolved for the Christian community only after his death through its faith in his resurrection: God justifies himself by justifying Jesus before his murderers through his resurrection. But this theodicy problem breaks into the open again with the parousia delay: that the Messiah does not return to break the continuum of that hell which is contemporary society and history.

Obsolescence

According to the political theologian Arens, on another level Jesus justifies his parabolic action toward his opponents by making understandable for them in discursive communication, which anticipates the goals of the discourse, the following: the opponents' norms of behavior, which they believe are legitimated and sanctioned by God as their guarantor, have become obsolete(324). These norms of behavior have become obsolete through communicative action, which breaks through these norms, the fence of the law. This communicative praxis is innovative, liberating, and joy-inspiring. Jesus engages in this communicative praxis toward his opponents out of the experience of the "Abba." It is interesting to observe that Jesus's declaration of obsolescence of at least large aspects of the Jewish worldview is today by Habermas applied not only to the Jewish, but also to the Christian and all other religious systems of interpretation and orientation. Habermas does indeed find himself in good company. He radicalizes and universalizes decisive aspects of the Jesus position.

Foundation of Action

Finally, according to the political theologian Arens, on a third level Jesus grounds the truth claim of his speech about God and the dominion of God by demonstrating this claim, which is bound to the praxis of the practical proof of this truth claim, in his inter- active behavior toward the discriminated people as well as toward the discriminators, as foundation of his action. In this, Jesus justifies his action at the same time out of this ground(325). Jesus opens up his praxis on this basis as self-evident - as a matter of unconditional insight and as, vice versa, making this foundation a matter of insight.

Justification

The political theologian Arens can understand Jesus's parables as quasi-discursive speech, since they serve the justification of the claim of the rightfulness of his action(326). Arens compares Jesus's illustrations in decisive traits to Habermas's model of practical discourse and explicates Jesus's examples in their communicative function out of Habermas's paradigm(327). According to the political theologian, Jesus pursues with his stories the aim not only of an apology of his praxis, but also of the consensual overcoming of the conflict which exists between himself and particularly his pharisaic opponents. Jesus tries to convince his opponents of the rightfulness of his actions or of the norms which underlie them, in such a way that he struggles in discursive and quasi-discursive speech, in a mode which anticipates understanding with his opponents, for recognition and thereby for consensus and vice versa. Jesus does this by showing to his opponents in metaphorically - ironically - alienated parables the nonsense of their intersubjective behavior, which is bound to particularistic interests and norms. Jesus does this in the face of what Habermas calls in his theory of communicative praxis the universality, egality and reciprocity of human communications as condition and normative foundation of being human. Jesus does this in the face of what he himself calls the Kingdom of God, which is close and into which all people are invited to enter. Jesus does this in the face of what systematically-theologically is called the universality of God's will to redeem.

God and Satan

Also here the political theologian can, of course, not over-
look that the stories of Jesus contain strong indication that
not all people shall make it into the Kingdom of God and that
many remain in the "outer darkness"(328). Jesus does not
indicate any solidarity with non-repentant whores, murderers,
or idolaters. Jesus differentiates clearly in his parables
between the kingdom of God and the kingdom of Satan(329).
Jesus takes seriously in his stories the power of Satan and
the possibility of eternal damnation even of the majority of
the people. The political theologian can not deduct from
Jesus's illustrations good reasons for what Schopenhauer calls
unjustly against Hegel an outrageous optimism(330). The
political theologians' fundamental mood of hope and joy will
always be mixed with the sadness about the continuing
possibility that the recognition of God's reign as well as the
liberation of the people may remain fragmentary for some time
to come. In the context of the present dark situation in
bourgeois history, the political theology needs, as Bloch
suggested, a new demonology and satanology.

Linguistic Difference

Of course, the political theologian, Arens, does not want by
his parallelization of the language of Habermas's theory of
communicative praxis, the language of the historical Jesus and
the language of systematic theology, to identify these lan-
guages(331). There exists here a clear linguistic differentiation. The fundamental theologian's pragmatic theory of
Jesus's parables, which explicates the theologically relevant
structure of action by action-theoretical means, does in no
way pursue the interest of a reduction of theology to theory
of action. The political theologian Metz warns emphatically
against such turning of theology into just another theory of
communicative praxis. The theologian of communicative praxis,
Arens, rather pursues with his pragmatic theory of Jesus's
stories the clarification of essential theological problem-
positions in the fundamental-pragmatically grounded action-
theoretical framework and with the help of the categories,
which have been worked out by modern pragmatics, particularly
Habermas's theory of action. Thereby the fundamental theologian tries to get into focus the public, i.e., political
intention and effect of Jesus's communicative action and his

parabolic political theology, which is implicit in this communicative praxis, in opposition to a merely historical, existential or linguistic-literary-scientific entrance to him as a storyteller. Likewise, it is possible for the theologian of communicative praxis in this framework to enfold the political implications of speaking about Jesus's intersubjective action and theology, the confession toward him and the praxis in his mimesis after his death and resurrection in the sense of a political hermeneutics: messianic imitatio as the very core of Christianity.

Ideology Critique

According to the political theologian Arens, Jesus's parables are as elements of discourse and as quasi-discursive, ideology critique(332). They are also argumentative and analogical. Jesus's illustrations take away all false pretenses from the Jewish religious worldview as system of interpretation and orientation. They uncover the principles of the pharisaic interpretation of reality as ideology, i.e., false consciousness, necessary appearance, rationalization of irrational conditions, for the purpose of the legitimation of their collective identity(333). This pharisaic identity is based on the exclusion of fringe groups of marginalized and alien people. Jesus brings into the open the Pharisees' system of interpretation and orientation as ideology for the legitimation of their own "being set apart" from the rest of the people, which is the very meaning of their name. The Pharisees identify themselves in opposition to the impure as the perushim, the pure. Jesus's stories tear down in fictionally-metaphorically mediated narrative argumentation the fence of the law, which sanctions the pharisaic interpretation of reality. In opposition to the pharisaic construction of reality, Jesus propagates in his examples an understanding of self and world, which is carried by the principle of universal communication. This principle is grounded in God as absolute love, freedom and spirit. This new comprehension of self and world tries to realize the principle of universal communication in practical engagement, i.e., in the communicative movement toward the other and in the other toward God. Thus the fundamental theologian applies Habermas's atheistic theory of communicative praxis to Jesus's discourses and his struggle for unconditional mutual recognition, between man and man and man and God.

In the political theologian's perspective, Jesus makes manifest in his mutually interpreting language-mediated as well as non-verbal communicative actions the Pharisee's construction of reality as a life world and a social order, which is built upon the excommunication of stigmatized impure people, like publicans, prostitutes and sinners in general(334). The Pharisees claim God's will ideologically for the legitimation of their life world and social system. Jesus demonstrates on the basis of his experience of the reality of God and his dominion, God as preceding absolute love, freedom and goodness, which can be experienced in his interaction and intersubjectivity. As Jesus does this, he puts into question together with the Pharisees' interpretation of reality, which is built upon the antagonism between in-group and out-group, at the same time also their ideological image of God, which corresponds to their particularistic ideological construction of social reality. At the same time, Jesus represents the reality of God as unlimited love, freedom and goodness, which excommunicates nobody, particularly not any repentant sinner. For the fundamental theologian precisely in this consists the ideology-critical character and achievement of Jesus's parables. Jesus withdraws through his stories from the Pharisees' interpretation of reality and from their orientation of action their legitimating theological basis. Jesus does this in his examples by not simply - in Habermas's terms - reclaiming their ultimate unity-producing principle, God, as the founding principle of another worldview, but by demonstrating the reality of God in communicative praxis as the Reality, which breaks through the all too narrowdomination-determined life world and social order constructs. The kingdom of God is not repressive(335). The kingdom of God means the end of all domination of man over man. The kingdom of God is the liberation of all men and women, who are willing to accept their being liberated.

Scenic Understanding

Jesus uses the parables, so the political theologian Arens, argues following Habermas, in order to put into process on the side of his opponents, mainly the Pharisees, a scenic understanding(336). In this scenic comprehension the opponents should be able to see in the light of the textually imagined situation the repressiveness of their own previous interpretation of reality and orientation of action and the latent structures of power, which they have produced. The Pharisees should be able to do this from the perspective of what the fundamental theologian calls with Adorno, Benjamin and Habermas, the undamaged life or the right or rational life(337). Jesus presents this undamaged or right life paradigmatically. This is indeed a messianic perspective(338). Jesus intends this imaginative anticipation of successful communicative praxis to be likewise a practically anticipated offer to his opponents, to change their previous structure of action, which has been systematically distorted by force. This should happen out of the messianic perspective of the liberating experience of communication without domination among All, which is grounded in God's reign and which is made possible through it.

According to the political theologian, Arens, Jesus's ideology critique is proven in its truthfulness through his own communication without domination, which is completely carried by his experience of God's providence, governance and guidance. For Jesus, God does indeed govern the world(339). Therefore, communication without domination among all men is possible in principle and ultimately. The murderer shall not triumph ultimately over the innocent victim.

Direction of Change

The consistency of Jesus's language-mediated or non-verbal communicative praxis without domination and force, so the political theologian Arens argues, makes at the same time transparent, in which direction the ideologically sanctioned power relations in his life world and social system are to be changed(340). Jesus presents in his stories his ideology-critical destruction of the pharisaic interpretation of reality in metaphoric language. The fundamental theologian applies Adorno's deconstructionism to the Jesus story. But beyond this the theologian of communicative praxis finds that Jesus's speech acts are oriented toward a real consensus between himself and his addressees, particularly the Pharisees, precisely because they undo the false appearance of the pharisaic worldview. All this makes it possible for Jesus's opponents, the Pharisees, to follow his speech acts at all and lets them become an offer and an invitation to them to enter the kingdom of God and man's realm of freedom. The political theologian's application of Habermas's universal pragmatic to Jesus's parables makes it very clear why socialists from Blanqui to Horkheimer and Bloch loved Jesus as great enlightener and emancipator, but hated the "pharisaic" clergy and church(341).

Synthesis

According to the political theologian, Arens, the illocutive and intentional perlocutive potential of Jesus's stories results out of their specific connection of ideology critique, argumentation and analogy(342). Therefore neither parable theories, which emphasize one-sidedly the argumentative aspects of Jesus's illustrations, nor parable theories which emphasize merely the analogical character of Jesus's examples really do full justice to them(343). The fundamental theologian makes the attempt to synthesize the advantages of both types of parable theories in his pragmatic parable theory based on Habermas's theory of communicative praxis: argumentation, analogy and ideology critique. Precisely this synthesis gives the pragmatic parable theory its exciting uniqueness.

From the political-theological perspective the parable theorists, who emphasize the argumentative character of Jesus's stories, miss their adequate understanding and particularly their communicative function. They do this, since they misunderstood the direction of Jesus's illustrations toward the opponents, mainly the Pharisees, on the basis of an argumentation which is understood through a model of antagonism, as defensive and apologetical in the sense of the argumentative defense and justification of Jesus's message of liberation against his critics. Most of these theorists also neglect the understanding-oriented intention and understanding-enabling function of Jesus's speech acts. They refer to quasi-psychological opinions rather than to the communication structure of Jesus's parables and the process of parabolic understanding.

In political-theological perspective, the parable theorists who emphasize the analogical or metaphorical character of Jesus's stories, rightly give weight to the movement of the narrator toward his listeners. The reality of the listeners is alienated in the text of the parables, so that they can see it in a new way(344). But these theorists of parables, who emphasize their analogical character, can not point out with whom which reality is alienated in which direction and imaginatively changed. These theorists emphasize in relation to the other parable theorists, who concentrate on the argumentative character of Jesus's parables, that moment in them, which liberates the listeners and invites them to participation and moves them to a new discovery of reality. But the analogical parable-theorists are not in the position to make clear how the ana-logon, the word in movement, functions and which movement it carries into Jesus's action situation in relation to his listeners. The fundamental theologian sees the reason for this deficit in the fact that the analogical parable-theorists are to a large extent caught up in a merely existentially determined understanding of language and text. Thus they do not get into their view the situationality of speaker and listeners, text and thing.

The political theologian overcomes the mutually demonstrable shortcomings, which appear on the side of the argumentative parable theorists, through the understanding of Jesus's illustrations as arguments in the antagonistic sense and on the side of the analogical parable theorists through the understanding of his stories as analogies or metaphors, in a pragmatic parable theory, which follows Habermas's theory of communicative praxis(345). On the basis of his pragmatic parable theory, the fundamental theologian recognizes in Jesus's parabolic speech acts narrative arguments, which are directed toward understanding with his opposition. Jesus uses in his narrative arguments the analogical or metaphorical speech form, in order to bring before the eyes of his addressees scenically, by means of interconnecting, estranging and discovering imagination, their interpretation of reality and their orientation of action in the face of a praxis which is grounded in, made possible, and demanded by God's dominion, his reign, his governance, his sovereignty. As understanding-oriented elements of communication between Jesus and his opponents in relation to the kingdom, his arguments struggle with them narratively for a consensus, which they anticipate at the same time in their quasi-discursive communication structure.

Subversion and Revolution

According to the political theologian, Arens, the interconnection of ideology critique, argumentation and analogy in discourse, makes the parables of Jesus into subversive and revolutionary stories(346). Jesus's illustrations invite his opponents and challenge them to revise their interpretation of

reality and their orientation of action. Jesus's narrative
presentation of his ideology critique contributes finally, as
it is put into inviting metaphorical language, to the fact
that the discourse can be continued with his opponents. This
happens in spite of the fact that the consensus, which Jesus
intended to find in discourse with his opponents, was
factually never realized. The result of Jesus's discourses was
his execution. Jesus's opponents, Pharisees, the Sadduceeic
hierarchy, Herod's party and the Roman occupation authorities
denied him recognition by killing him. Jesus lost the
language-mediated and non-verbal struggle for recognition with
his opponents. His subversion and revolution ended in his
death. Jesus's friends granted him unconditional recognition
after his death by accepting in faith and announcing publicly
in words and interaction his resurrection. Jesus's subversion
and revolution continued after his death. Political theology
renews once more the dangerous memory of Jesus's subversive
and revolutionary parable theology and interaction.

Christology from Below and Above

The political theologian Arens is, like other political theologians on the Hegelian Left, and unlike the political
theologians on the Right, engaged in a Christology from below,
for which his exegesis and his pragmatic parable theory give
him the foundation(347). Being concerned with the historical
Jesus and his subversive, polemical, revolutionary
language-mediated or non-verbal struggle for recognition for
his Father and himself, the critical fundamental theologian
somewhat neglects what traditional Christology from above
called the divine nature of Jesus(348). It does not seem to
surface even in the description of Jesus's death(349). What
Hegel was still able to do, namely to make the unity of the
human and divine nature in Christ the center of his philosophy
and theology, seems no longer to be possible in the pragmatic
theory of Jesus's parables and the corresponding political
theology(350). There is a danger of Nestorianism rather than
monophysitism. But this danger can certainly be banned by a
deeper penetration into Jesus's discourse-mediated struggle
for recognition, particularly his subversive, polemical,
revolutionary parables. There is no reason why political
theologians on the Hegelian Left should not be able to
conjugate once more what was still together in Hegel's
political theology and Christology: that not only the man

Jesus but God himself died on the cross and rose again(351). They should be able to reunite a Christology from below with a Christology from above. Without such a new coincidentia oppositorum, the Christology from below is itself in danger of becoming aporetical. There are forms of political theology and Christology, in which this danger of aporia is faced and attempts are made to resolve it by gaining new contact with elements in the Christology from above(352). Their goal is a new coincidentia oppositorum: the coincidence of grace and freedom.

Communicative Structure

The political theologian Arens sees in the framework of his pragmatic parable theory, based on the critical theory and mainly on Habermas's theory of communicative praxis, the actuality of Jesus's parables, stories or illustrations for the present personal, social, economic, political, historical and cultural situation, particularly in the com- munication structure which reveals itself in his examples(353). According to the fundamental theologian, the concept of the communication structure undermines the opposition of form and content(354). It binds form and content together by demonstrating their common relation to the struggle for recognition, interaction and intersubjectivity(355). Actors mediate in their interaction in determinate forms always certain contents. The theologian of communicative praxis knows, of course, that with changing historical situations the concrete formation of these contents does change as well(356). Therefore, the political theologian, who wants to say today: "The Kingdom of God is like..." must confront the old images and metaphors used by Jesus with new ones, precisely for the sake of the communication structure, which manifests itself in his parables. In no way, so the fundamental theologian insists, must the old images and metaphors simply be repeated or replaced. The old illustrations and stories must rather be reinterpreted through new ones, which today can take over their former critical function. The theologian of communicative praxis intends to realize the communicative, i.e., ideology-critical, argumentative and analogical potential of Jesus's parables in a new personal, economic, social, political, historical and cultural situation with new opponents, e.g., in the present worldwide class struggle between the multinational corporations and the fascist

military or civilian dictators who protect their interests and
the   neo-conservative   religious   ideologists   who   try   to
legitimate both, on one hand and the   exploited   masses,   who
produce   their   surplus   labour   and   value and accomplish the
maximization of their profit on the other.

Equivalents

The political theologian, Arens,   does   not   believe   that   he
should or could preserve the communication structure, which is
manifest   in Jesus's illustrations through the mere recitation
of the sacred texts or through the   mere   application   of   the
contents   or   through the mere allegedly time-neutral analysis
of the   parable   form(357).   The   fundamental   theologian   can
actualize   the   communication   structure   only   through   the
localization of such communication   models   in   our   concrete
action situation.   For the theologian of communicative action
the parables of Jesus are relevant only to the extent to which
he can find and invent here and now in the face of the kingdom
of God, which has broken into history in Jesus's communicative
praxis, equivalents of his parabolic communication.   According
to   Arens,   the   characteristics   of Jesus's speech acts, which
the pragmatic parable theory has worked   out,   guarantee   that
the   judgment about the equivalence of the equivalents is left
neither to the subjective nor to the collective intuition. The
criteria of Jesus's speech acts function at the same   time   as
criteria   for   the   judgment   over present-day speech acts, to
which equivalence is attributed.

According to the political theologian, speech   acts,   in
which   the   communication   structure,   manifest   in   Jesus's
parables, should   be   actualized today,   must   be   situation-
al(358).   They must be situated in concrete action situations.
In these situations they pursue an innovative intent. They aim
at   changing   the   oppressive   situation   as   well   as   the
participants   in the situation, in order to move them to a new
interpretation of self and reality and to a new orientation of
action. Such speech acts move, in terms of their intention, by
means   of   textual   communicative   actions,   which   use   as
communication elements between subjects fictional-metaphorical
texts.   At   the   same   time,   in   these texts God's kingdom is
indirectly and practically thematized. Present day equivalents
of   Jesus's   parabolic   communication   are,   as   the   latter,
oriented   toward   understanding,   comprehension and consensus.
Insofar   as   no   consensus   can   be   presupposed   among   the

participants, the equivalents will try to come to such a
consensus via discursive and quasi-discursive speech. In
present day equivalents ideology critique, argumentation and
analogy must interconnect themselves.
According to the political theologian, Jesus's communicative action asks for repentance and for application to our
own social and world historical situation(359). The
fundamental theologian gives two contemporary examples, in
which the connection of ideology critique, narrative
argumentation, and metaphorical analogy in communicative
intent is realized. In them Arens sees paradigms of Christian
communicative action in the tradition of Jesus's parabolic
speech acts and the corresponding struggle for recognition.
They are true equivalents of Jesus's communicative praxis.
They show the actuality of biblical texts in the present
economic, political and historical situation. They show in
which direction a new conjugation and coincidence of the
religious and the secular, revelation and enlightenment,
redemption and happiness, theology and revolution, grace and
freedom is possible(360).

Christian Encouragement

The political theologian finds an equivalent in Cardenal's
adaptation of the psalms(361). In his Psalms of Struggle and
Liberation Cardenal, the Nicaraguan priest and political
revolutionary, and now cultural minister, confronts the texts
of the bible with the brutal reality of the Latin American
bourgeois dictatorships and corporate power structures, e.g.,
the United Fruit Company and its subsidiaries(362). According
to the critical fundamental theologian, by doing this Cardenal
restores to the biblical texts their relation to the everyday
life world as well as to the social system and its sinful and
therefore extremely oppressive economic, political and even
ecclesiastical structures. Thereby, Cardenal renews the
communicative potential of cry, accusation, and at the same
time of encouragement. These are uttered illocutionary acts.
They are arguments in favor of qualitative change, critiques
of the governing ideology of national security, and analogies
concerning the presence of God in the Latin American liberation movement. In the view of the theologian of communicative
praxis they are revolutionary parable acts, appealing to God
in the contingencies of concentration camps and torture
chambers in Latin American national security states. This is

e.g. exemplified in Cardenal's translation of Psalm 129, "I Call Out in the Night from the Torture Chamber":

From the depth I call to you, Lord,
I call out in the night from prison
from the concentration camp.
From the torture chamber
in the hour of darkness
hear my voice,
                my S.O.S.

If you draw up the record of sins,
Lord, who would have a clean slate?
But you pardon sins,
You are not implacable like them in their investigations.

I trust in the Lord and not in the leaders,
Not in slogans,
I trust in the Lord and not in their radios!

My soul hopes in the Lord
more than guards watching for dawn
more than prisoners counting the night hours.

We are jailed,
              while they are partying.
But the Lord is liberation,
freedom for Israel(363).

In Arens's perspective the uttered illocutionary acts of cry, accusation, and encouragement are also revolutionary acts, which appeal to God, who invites to universal communication, in which the whole cosmos praises him. This is exemplified in Cardenal's translation of Psalm 148, "Praise the Lord you Nebulae":

Praise the Lord
nebulae like specks of dust on photographic plates.
Praise the Lord
    Sirius and your companions
    and Arcturus and Aldebaran and Antares.
Praise the Lord you meteorites
    and elliptical orbits of comets
    and artificial satellites.

Praise the Lord
   atmosphere and stratosphere,
   Hertz waves and X-rays.
Praise the Lord
   atoms and molecules,
   protons and electrons,
   protozoa and radiolarians.
Praise the Lord
   sea dwelling mammals and atomic submarines.
Praise the Lord
   birds and airplanes,
Praise the Lord hexagonal crystals of snowflakes
and emerald prisms of copper sulfate
   - under the electron microscope -
flowers flowering in the bottom of the sea,
diatoms like a diamond necklace
   and Diadema Antillarium,
   Anurida maritima and Ligia exotica.
Praise the Lord
Tropic of Cancer and Polar Arctic Circle
storms in the North Atlantic and Humboldt Current,
dark forests of the Amazon,
   islands of the South Seas,
volcanos and lagoons
   and the Caribbean moon behind the silhouette of palms.
Praise the Lord
   democratic republics
   and United Nations
Praise the Lord
   police and students and pretty girls.
His glory surpasses the earth and the heavens,
   telescopes and microscopes
and he has done great things for his people
   for Israel, his ally,
                 Alleluia(364).

According to the political theologian examples which have become stimulating for many peace movements in America and Europe and elsewhere, have been and still are, the antimilitaristic actions of Philip and Daniel Berrigan and the Plowshare Group(365). The Jesuit priest, Daniel Berrigan, confronts the texts of the bible with the American economic, political and military establishment. In his Uncommon Prayer he connects the ancient psalms with the American life world

and action system and its sinful economic, political and
military structures, and its oppressive functional require-
ments(366). Thereby Berrigan renews, like Cardenal, the communicative potential of cries of pain, despair and disappointment, and accusations of suffering poor people. Berrigan
exemplifies this in his translation of Psalm 10, "They Call
You Blind Man: Call Their Bluff":

> Lord why do you stand on the sidelines
> silent as the mouth of the dead, the maw of the grave -
> O living One, why?
>
> Evil walks roughshod, the envious set snares
> high and mighty the violent ride
> Applause for maleficence, rewards for crime
> Yourself set to naught.
>
> Eyes like a poiniard impale the innocent
> Death cheap, life cheaper
> The mad beast is loosened, his crooked heart mutters
> Fear only me!
>
> Lord, they call you blind man. Call their bluff
> extinguish their envy.
> See: the poor are cornered
> marked for destruction, grist
> for a mill of dust.
> At the bar of injustice
> they tremble, wind-driven birds
> under the beaks and stares
> of the shrouded Big Ones-....(367)

At the same time, Berrigan also renews in his Uncommon
Prayer the communicative potential of encouragement and trust
in the face of contingency and catastrophe. He exemplifies
this in his translation of Psalm 31, "The Trusting Heart Shall
Prevail":

> How great is your goodness Lord
> poured out on the one who loves you.
> Face to face with iniquity
> the trusting heart shall prevail.
>
> Far from intrigue, from malice

I run to your presence, take sanctuary
in your eyes. Hands aloft, you encompass
a holy tent, a refuge.

The war of tongues, a babble, a rout
        rages, goes nowhere.
        I would dwell
        tongue stilled, mind subdued
        in your holy temple.

Come make me your temple
deep founded, touching high heaven.

All you who fear the Lord
        exult, take courage
        come shelter in him(368).

Berrigan translates the dialectic of the experience of
the absence and the presence of God, of pain and trust
expressed in the ancient Hebrew psalms into the present action
situation of the American late capitalistic system of human
condition and action system. In this American action system
one half of a percent of the population of over 200 million
people own as much as twenty-five percent of the nation's
wealth and forty-nine percent own as little as two percent of
the national wealth. Since the great depression of 1981-83 the
so-called middle class, earning between twenty and forty
thousand dollars a year, and its American Dream are gliding
down into the working classes and the underclass of the
chronically unemployed. Over thirty-five million Americans
live in slums and utter poverty and over ten million are
starving to death in the "richest country of the world." Even
in the present stage of recovery in the business cycle
produced by huge military investments up to 300 billion
dollars a year, 7.4% of the American working force is still
unemployed.
    The communicative cries of pain, despair, disappointment
and accusation of the poor and the communicative expression of
encouragement and trust, which Berrigan articulates in the
present American life world and action system are arguments in
favor of metanoia, anthropological revolution, radical qualitative systemic change in the interest of the diminishment and
finally abolishment of the unnecessary suffering of the many.
They are a thorough critique of the official American ideology

that there is no real poverty or hunger in America; that such things belong to the "Evil Empire," Russia; that everything is alright the way it is in America, with few little exceptions easily dealt with; and that what is the case in America is positive and good and that everybody is happy in America, particularly the workers, except maybe a very small minority of chronic troublemakers or welfare loafers. The cries of pain and expressions of encouragement are analogies concerning the presence of God in the midst of the massive epidemic of cancer and heart attacks, unemployment, armament, racism, nationalism, sexism, exploitive capitalism. They are polemical, subversive, revolutionary narrative acts appealing to God in the midsts of what Benjamin called the "hell of the arcades," the commodity fetishism of idolatrous department stores(369). Thus God invites to universal communication beyond the particularism of capitalism, nationalism, racism, sexism, youth centeredness and militarism(370).

According to the political theologian, the Berrigan brothers are engaged in a variety of symbolical acts as Jesus once was, but now in another action system and action situation: digging a grave in the garden of the White House, shedding their blood on draft files, or in view of the Pentagon, symbolic damage to a cruise missile, etc(371). All these symbolic acts are a warning anticipation of Future I – the totally administered, militaristic society, and of Future II – the thermonuclear holocaust, a last crusade against atheistic communism, the universal atomic grave the American military-industrial complex is about to dig(372). In the fundamental theologian's opinion these symbolical acts are also a challenge to Christian theology to understand and even comprehend itself as a theology of communicative action with the intent of contributing to the arrival of Future III – the reconciled society(373). It would mean the survival of mankind and humane life for all in the presence of both, the bomb as the universal power of death and the kingdom of God having germinally arrived through Jesus's word and interaction and person(374). In Habermas's view the Berrigans are still too individualistic, to the point of elitism. He considers that to be morally dangerous. He wishes them to be more communicative in terms of a broader solidarity. Such criticism is certainly well taken.

Marxist Encouragement

The political theologian, Arens, stands on the Hegelian left: he learns from the Marxist Kantian or Kantian Marxist Habermas(375). Cardenal combines in his psalm translations Judaism, Christianity and Marxism. He cooperated in the Nicaraguan socialistic revolution. At present he is a member of the Sandinista government. But the difference between the critical political theology and historical materialism becomes very clear when the psalm translations of Cardenal and Berrigan are compared with the way one of the greatest Marxist playwrights of this century, Bertold Brecht, translates the bible, which he read daily, into the late capitalistic action system and world historical action situation(376). Also here, particularly in his plays St. Joan of the Stockyards and The City of Mahagonny, we find the biblical connection of ideology critique, narrative argumentation and metaphysical analogy in communicative intent and the renewal of the communicative potential of the biblical cry, accusation and encouragement, but unlike in the case of Arens, Cardenal and Berrigan, not in terms of an affirmative, but rather of a negative dialectics and theology(377). When Brecht's Saint Joan, herself dying from pneumonia in the stockyards of Chicago, demands radical, qualitative change of the American capitalistic action system, which produces so much suffering and pain and degradation, the salvation army girls, to whom she herself had belonged until recently, the Black Straw Hats, say to her:

Be a good girl! Hold your tongue!....
Keep conduct high and spirit young.
But do not forget to rue it!...
But always do it
with a twinge of conscience, for –
Being given to contemplation
and to self-vituperation –
your conscience will be sore!
Men of trade be informed:
You can not afford
To forget the splendid
Quite indispensable
Word of the Lord,
Which is never ended
and ever transformed!(378)

Brecht's Saint Joan unmasks this ideological translation of
biblical motives by the Black Straw Hats in the face of the
murderous capitalistic system in the form of her own newly
gained humanistic atheism:

> Therefore, anyone down here who says there is a God,
> When none can be seen,
> A God, who can be invisible and yet help them,
> Should have his head knocked on the pavement
> until he croaks....
> And the ones, that tell them, they may be raised in spirit
> and still be stuck in the mud, they should have their heads
> knocked on the pavement. No!
> Only force helps, where force rules,
> and only men help, where men are(379).

Brecht's Saint Joan is indeed engaged not only in ideology
critique, but also in narrative argumentation and metaphorical
analogy as well as in cry, accusation and encouragement. But
Saint Joan does not get through the "obduracy," to use the
biblical term, of the owners in the Chicago Stockyard. Thus
the Chicago businessmen sing together with their ideologists,
the Black Straw Hats:

> Fill the full man's plate! Hosanna!
> Greatness to the great! Hosanna!
> To him that has shall be given! Hosanna!
> Give him city and state! Hosanna!
> To the victor a sign from Heaven! Hosanna!
> Pity the well-to-do! Hosanna!
> Set them in Thy path! Hosanna!
> Vouchsafe Thy grace! Hosanna!
> And Thy help to him that has! Hosanna!
> Have mercy on the few! Hosanna!
> Aid Thy class, which in turn aids Thee, Hosanna!
> With generous hand! Hosanna!
> Stamp out hatred now! Hosanna!
> Laugh with the laughter, allow, Hosanna!
> His misdeeds a happy end! Hosanna!
> Humanity! Two souls abide
> Within thy breast!
> Do not set either one aside:
> To live with both is best!

Be torn apart with constant care!
Be two in one! Be here! Be there!
Hold the low one, hold the high one –
Hold the straight one, hold the sly one –
Hold the pair(380).

To the bourgeois church such translation of the bible
into the present action situation must appear as blasphemous
as once Jesus's discourses and quasi-discourses and struggle
for recognition appeared to the Pharisees and Sadducees and to
the priests(381). The emerging messianic church sees in such
translation ideology critique and narrative arguments and
metaphorical analogies as well as outcries, accusations and
encouragement directed against an alienated late capitalistic
action system, which is legitimated by a reactionary bourgeois
Christendom(382).

In his opera, The City of Mahagonny, Brecht lets the men
and women of Mahagonny, a metaphor for the late capitalistic
action system, sing their song of God(383). It translates, in
an alienated form biblical eschatology, into the present
capitalistic society and bourgeois history. The men and women
of Mahagonny sing at the end of the song, "God in Mahagonny":

...On a somber forenoon
In the midst of the whiskey
God came to Mahagonny.
In the midst of the whiskey
We noticed God in Mahagonny.

Off you go to hell!
Put your cigarettes away!
Foreward march, into my hell, boys,
Into hell and no delay!
They looked at each other, the men of Mahagonny.
Yes, answered the men of Mahagonny.

On a somber forenoon,
In the midst of the whiskey,
You come to Mahagonny.
In the midst of the whiskey
You begin in Mahagonny!
Let nobody move an inch.

We're on strike. Keep calm, steady!

You can't drag us off to hell,
When we live in hell already.
They looked at God, the men of Mahagonny.
No, answered the men of Mahagonny(384).

Inverse Theology

The ideology critique, narrative argumentation and metaphorical analogy as well as the outcry, accusation and encouragement contained in this as well as in other poems and plays by Brecht, are the result of the at least existentially and socially unresolved theodicy problem: God does obviously not help the helpless and defenseless(385)! Much of this Brechtian atheism, grounded in the terrible injustices of the late capitalistic action system, is, at least latently, present in Habermas's critical theory of communicative praxis(386). Not Adorno, as Habermas thinks, but Brecht is the real atheist(387). The Brechtian atheism represents much of the disappointment with the God of Judaism and Christianity in the Western action system, not only in elites, but also in the masses of the people: mass atheism. It is the greatest challenge for the political theologian Arens's pragmatic theory of parables, Peukert's pragmatic fundamental theology and Metz's political fundamental theology as they try to give actuality to the gospel in the present historical action situation. Political theology can succeed only when this Brechtian atheism, which is born out of massive unjust human suffering in modern capitalistic action systems, can be, not ideologically, but truthfully superseded. It will not be possible to find equivalents for Jesus's parables in the present historical situation, if such supersession of Brechtian suffering-motivated atheism is not possible and really achieved. Adorno has shown a negative theological way of how such supersession of Brechtian bible-rooted atheism may be accomplished(388). Bible-rooted political theology can learn from Adorno. Even Habermas may learn still more from Adorno's theological via negativa than he has already.

In his famous Hornberg letter, Adorno demands from Benjamin against his friend Brecht nothing less than a purification of theory in his Passage Work II and a restitution of theology; a renewal of the originally theological notion, i.e., the dialectical process of universal, particular and singular; or better still a radicalization of materialistic dialectic down into its theological foundation(389). Adorno

did not want to agree with the way of Benjamin's thinking
toward the kind of ontological materialism and atheism which
underlies Brecht's work. Benjamin's thinking had led from a
hasidic-mystical beginning over Hegel's Philosophy of Law and
History, Lukac's History and Class Consciousness to Marxist,
socialistic positions(390). Benjamin's thinking had found
clarification and sharpening in his controversy with Brecht.
Adorno insisted that Benjamin should turn away from objections
which Brecht's materialistic and atheistic metaphysics
provokes(391). Brecht is for Adorno, in biblical terms, the
"stone of contradiction," "the apostate," the "atheist"(392).
Adorno warns Benjamin and woos him at the same time. Adorno
would like to hold Benjamin back from the methodological
consequences of a philosophical position change by Brecht.
Adorno saw in Benjamin's Passage Work truly that given piece
of prima philosophia which to develop was the task of the
critical theory: a negative metaphysics and theology(393).
Adorno hoped that Benjamin would realize in the Passage Work
everything concerning theologial content and language in the
most extreme theses, which was present in it potentially from
the very beginning(394). This should happen without
consideration of the objections coming from Brechtian atheism.
Adorno resists any reception of the Brechtian atheism into
Benjamin's Passage Work or into critical theory in general.
Adorno considered it possible that it could be the task of
critical theorists some day in the future to rescue Brecht's
atheism as inverse theology(395). No critical theorist has
done such rescue work so far. Also Habermas has not done this.
Maybe it is more the task of political theologians than of
critical theorists to save Brecht's atheism as inverse
theology. Metz's political theology, Peukert's pragmatic
fundamental theology and Arens's pragmatic parable theory have
at least prepared the basis on which Brecht's atheism can be
rescued as inverse, i.e., negative theology. This could very
well happen via Hegel's Frankfurt System Programs, Jena
Critical Writings, and Jena System Designs I and II, and most
of all his Phenomenology of Spirit, which Brecht studied
intensely in Leipzig after World War II and which he allowed
to change his "epic theater" into a "dialectic theater."
Brecht's atheism points out as inverse or negative theology,
including ideology critique, narrative argumentation and
metaphorical analogy as well as cry, accusation and
encouragement, what God is not and thereby makes room for a
new search for an affirmative theology: who God is and what

his work is in nature a well as in the inner world, in the
social and historical world and in the cultural world, and
what man's action is in the context of this divine pragmatic:
man as speaker, worker, lover, fighter for unconditional
mutual recognition and member of national and international
communities, directed   toward   a universal communication
community and the messianic kingdom.

Prodigal Son

The political theologian Arens lets himself be inspired and
guided by Jesus's situation-related personal and theological
parables, illustrations, examples and stories in his search
for such positive modern equivalents for his discourses and
quasi-discourses and struggles for recognition as the psalm
translations of Cardenal and Berrigan, as well as for such
negative modern equivalents as the plays and poems of
Brecht(396).   In those equivalents the communicative structure
of Jesus's parables is actualized in a modern form for the
present world historical action situation. In those modern
equivalents the relevance of Jesus's parabolic communication
is practically demonstrated for the action situation in
contemporary late capitalistic action systems. The critical
fundamental theologian lets himself be directed by Jesus's
ideology-critical, argumentative and analogical invitation to
the praxis of God's kingdom.
     For the political theologian, such invitation is para-
digmatically present in the parable of "The Prodigal Son," one
of the most ingenious biblical stories: "Now the publicans and
sinners were drawing near to Jesus to listen to him. And the
Pharisees and the Scribes murmured, saying, 'This man welcomes
sinners and eats with them' ... And Jesus said, 'A certain man
had two sons. And the younger of them said to his father,
"Father give me the share of the property that falls to me."
And he divided his means between them.'"
     "And not many days later, the younger son gathered up all
his wealth, and took his journey into a far country; and there
came a grievous famine over that country, and he began himself
to suffer want. And he went and joined one of the citizens of
that country, who sent him to his farm to feed swine. And he
longed to fill himself with the pods, that the swine were
eating, but no one offered to give them to him."
     "But when he came to himself, he said, 'How many hired
men in my father's house have bread in abundance, while I am

perishing here with hunger! I will get up and go to my father, and will say to him, 'Father, I have sinned against Heaven and before you. I am no longer worthy to be called your son; make me as one of your hired men.' And he arose and went to his father."

"But while he was yet a long way off, his father saw him and was moved with compassion, and ran and fell upon his neck and kissed him. And the son said to him, 'Father, I have sinned against Heaven and before you. I am no longer worthy to be called your son. But the father said to his servants, 'Fetch quickly the best robe and put it on him, and give him a ring for his finger and sandals for his feet; and bring out the fattened calf and kill it, and let us eat and make merry, because this my son was dead, and has come to life again; he was lost, and is found! And they began to make merry."

"Now, his elder son was in the field; and as he came and drew near to the house, he heard music and dancing. And calling one of the servants, he inquired, what this meant, and he said to him, 'Your brother has come, and your father has killed the fattened calf, because he has got him back safe.' But he was angered and would not go in."

"His father, therefore, came out and began to entreat him. But he answered and said to his father, 'Behold, these many years I have been serving you, and have never transgressed one of your commands; and yet you have never given me a kid, that I might make merry with my friends. But when this your son comes, who has devoured his means with harlots, you have killed for him the fattened calf.'"

"But he said to him, 'Son, you are always with me, and all that is mine is yours; but we were bound to make merry and rejoice, for this your brother was dead, and has come to life; he was lost and is found"(397).

This parable lucidly shows to the political theologian the discursive character of Jesus's parabolic action towards his pharisaic opponents(398). In the story, the fundamental theologian sees the different perspectives of the dramatized persons - the good father, the two sons, the servants - cross one another and thus present a panorama of understandings of action. In this panorama the opponents of Jesus, the Pharisees and Scribes, can not help to recognize their own understanding of action, since it is put up against the horizon of other understandings and is thus, in the Brechtian sense, alienated. The Pharisees and Scribes must see themselves as clearly in the son who stayed at home with the father, the "good" and

"just" son, as the publicans, prostitutes and other sinners
must find themselves in the younger son who squandered and
wasted his wealth and life.

Intention

On the basis of the political theologian Arens's pragmatic
parable theory, the intention of Jesus's story "The Prodigal
Son" is quite clear in the context of his life. It is a
narrative argument for non-excommunication. It comprises non-
self-excluding table fellowship. It has been made possible by
the goodness of the Divine Father who forestalls all human
action, rights, sins and merits. For the fundamental theologian the parable is a discursive argument, which crosses
different perspectives. By doing so, it brings the hearer into
imaginary contact with different understandings of reality and
orientations of action, with the aim of proving the Heavenly
Father as the person, who does justice to all and who evokes
rejoicing. The story invites and challenges the opponents, the
Pharisees and Scribes, to accept its plea by following their
counter-argument up to a point where its ideological basis is
unmasked. There are for the theologian of communicative praxis
distinctive hints that the Pharisaic position is interwoven
into the text of the illustration. That is the result of the
analogical and metaphorical character of the story. The elder
son "is" not a Pharisee or a Scribe. the younger son "is" not
a publican. The father "is" not God. But the actors in the
parable show, nevertheless, by their action in a metaphorical
and alienated way, how Pharisees act or how publicans could at
least act and how God acts. At the same time, the speakers and
actors show all this in a way critical to the ideology of the
Pharisees and Scribes, which legitimates their power position
in the traditional Jewish life world and system. According to
the political theologian, the combination of ideology
critique, argument and analogy give Jesus's story its
elocutionary force.

The political theologian observes that the end of the
parable remains open. The total reaction of the older son is
not narrated. The parable does not end. It is open-ended. But
it challenges the opponents, the portrayed persons - Pharisees
and Scribes, publicans and sinners and God - to complete it.
Whether Jesus's parable act succeeds or not, is, according to
the fundamental theologian, dependent on the reaction of the
listeners. They may or may not accept the offered

understanding   of   the   action situation and   the   action
possibilities.
The story, as it remains open-ended, calls on the addressees to participate in it and to complete it. In the view of
the theologian of communicative praxis, the illustration is a
call and an invitation to accept the rightness of Jesus's
action in relation to publicans and sinners and the truth of
his narrative theology, the goodness of God, which are
involved in the story. In the parable, Jesus invites his
opponents, the Pharisees and Scribes, to recognize God's
loving governance and providence and his own love and to
include those publicans and sinners who are repentant into the
community and commensalism.

Social Models

The critical theorist Adorno has pointed to the break between
the social models of the great world religions and contemporary capitalistic and socialistic systems of human condi-
tion(399). The world religions were formed according to perspicuous agrarian conditions, at best according to a very
simple commodity economy. The critical theorist quotes affir-
matively a Jewish poet, who stated that in Judaism and Christanity village air is blowing. Adorno can not abstract from
the premodern origin of Christianity without doing violence to
the religious content through reinterpretation. Christianity
is not contemporaneous to all times. People are not timelessly
concerned with what they once heard as "good message." The
premodern concept of "daily bread" from Jesus's prayer "Our
Father," which originates from the experience of scarcity in a
premodern condition of uncertain and insufficient material
production can, according to the critical theorist, not simply
be transferred into the modern world of bread factories and
over-production,   in   which   massive starvation of whole
populations are "natural" catastrophes of society and not of
nature. In Adorno's view, the concept of the neighbor in
Jesus's command to love is related to groups in which the
members know each other face-to-face. The help for the
neighbor, as urgent as it remains again and again in a world
which is devastated by the "natural catastrophes" of the
capitalistic action system, is insignificant in relation to
the transcendence of praxis beyond any mere immediacy of human
relations: in connection with a transformation of the world,
which would stop once and for all the social nature of

catastrophes, e.g., the recent starvation catastrophe in Ethiopia.

The political theologian Kogon admits to Adorno that most of the parables of Jesus have a somewhat village character(400). But that does not mean that they cannot be understood in every later civilization without adaptation as they were understood once in the cities of Jerusalem, Alexandria and Rome during Jesus's lifetime and shortly afterwards. According to Kogon, Jesus's parables must not be adapted, since they fit always. Kogon can apply the parable of "The Prodigal Son" to the present world historical action situation without distortion of the value which stands behind the story and without diminishing it. Kogon, the Christian socialist, would feel the greatest joy when, e.g., a Bolshevik would come to the knowledge of the true way to salvation. Such a knowledge would have revolutionary effects.

The socialist poet and playwright Andre Gide wrote, following Hegel, a play on the parable "The Prodigal Son," directed mainly against P. Claudel, who tried to convert him to Catholicism(401). It is quite obvious that in this play the younger son represents the socialists and the older son stands for the Christians. It is also quite obvious that Gide takes the poetical freedom to continue the open story of Jesus and add new inventions, e.g., a third son. Furthermore, in his play "The Prodigal Son," Gide asks everybody to try it once: to be the younger son, to be a socialist! Critical Catholic underground youth groups in Nazi Germany played Gide's "The Prodigal Son" during World War II in Frankfurt and elsewhere. Underground Christianity and Socialism found each other under Nazi oppression. There is no doubt that equivalents can be found for Jesus's parables among Christians and non-Christians in modern capitalistic and socialistic action-systems and that they thus can gain new actuality once more in the present world historical action situation.

Future

Cardenal and the Berrigans announce in their psalm translations the absence as well as the presence of God, who looks for and accepts what is lost. Brecht proclaims mainly the absence of this God. Also Habermas sees no indication of such a God in late capitalistic action systems(402). The critical theorists do in general accept the ideology critique and the narrative argumentation, the cry and the accusation in

Jesus's stories and in political theology, but not their affirmative metaphorical analogies of the Absolute. They remain most strictly bound to the Second Commandment(403). But to be sure, the political theologians would never have come to search for modern equivalents for Jesus's parabolic communication without being motivated to do so by the critical theory of religion as developed on the Hegelian Left from Feuerbach and Marx to Bloch, Horkheimer, Adorno, Benjamin, Brecht and Habermas(404). Thus the political theologian Arens is inspired by Habermas's universal pragmatic, which declares religious worldviews to be obsolete and at the same time wants them, nevertheless, to be protected as elements of the life world against colonization by the capitalistic or socialistic economic and political subsystems, since there could be more truths in them than the Hegelian Left has discovered so far(405). Habermas does indeed criticize traditional religion in his theory of communicative praxis. But so does Jesus in his parables. Jesus gave in his stories at the same time a new interpretation of reality and a new orientation of action. So does Habermas in his theory of communicative praxis(406). So does the political theologian(407). The future will be the test of the better interpretation of reality and the better orientation of action, the future alone, the immediate and the more distant future. The better interpretation and orientation will be the one which helps to mitigate at least Future I – the totally monetarized and bureaucratized society, to avoid Future II – conventional and ABC wars, and to promote Future III – the true communication community based on mutual understanding and recognition.

Jesus's Theology

The political theologian Arens has presented in his pragmatic parable theory, following Habermas's theory of communicative praxis, Jesus's indirect and practical speech of God in fictional-metaphorical texts as the essential characteristic of his theology(408). Jesus's theology represents as narrative talk of God in practical action situations and connections a situational, practical and narrative theology. The fundamental theologian thinks that he is justified to speak of the theology of Jesus, since he linguifies his experience of the reality of God and his providence and governance in dialectical images and metaphors in the framework of discourses and quasi-discourses; and since he explicates in

his illustrations, examples and stories his interpretation of
self and world in relation to the Reality which determines him
and which he calls God, even more personally and intimately,
Abba, Father. This explication takes place in such a way that
it can intersubjectively be reconstructed and practically
followed. The theologian of communicative praxis starts his
talk about Jesus's theology from his teacher's, the political
theologian Metz's statement, following Kant, that there is a
narrative deep structure to critical reason(409). Following
Metz, the political theologian Arens can say that the logos
which thematizes theology, enfolds itself in a narrative way
in Jesus's stories about the reality called God or Abba(410).
According to the fundamental theologian Jesus's narrative
theology gains paradigmatic character for the Christian speech
of God in general, and for political theology in particular.

Theological Notion

Long before the present-day political theologians, Hegel found
in Jesus's narrative theology the paradigm for his political
theology and for his attempt to reconstruct theologically not
only nature and the inner world of the individual, but also
the social and cultural world as the product and work of God's
reason, providence, governance, wisdom, spirit, love and
freedom(411). Following Eckehart, Hegel transforms the dialectical images of Jesus's theology in the original power of
the theological and mystical notion – as dialectical process
of universal, particular and singular or, more concretely, as
dialectical process of notion, judgment and conclusion(412).
Hegel gives the theological content of Jesus's images and
metaphors the most adequate form in the dialectical mystical
notion. He does this not only in his Christology, but also in
his philosophy of law and history, i.e., his political
theology(413).
    Since Hegel found Jesus's dialectical discourses and
quasi-discourses as well as his struggle for recognition to be
most revolutionary, he had no difficulties whatsoever, to see
particularly in world historical revolutions the product of
God's reason and freedom(414). Thus Hegel's whole philosophy
and theology became a philosophy and theology of revolu-
tion(415). Hegel was in all that obviously much closer to the
theological and sociopolitical truth of Jesus's discourses,
quasi-discourses and social and political interactions than
the conservative churches of his day or our day and was

precisely,   therefore,   rejected   by   them(416).   Present-day
political   theologians   finally   bring   home   the   harvest   of
Hegel's   political   theology   and   they   do   this   interestingly
enough with the help of the Hegelian Left from Feuerbach, Marx
and Kierkegaard to Bloch and the   critical   theorists   of   the
Frankfurt   School,   particularly   Horkheimer,   Adorno,   Benjamin
and now Habermas(417). They do this in spite of the fact   that
they have not reached the level of the dialectical theological
notion.   In   the   process   of   the   further development of the
theology   of   praxis,   political   theology   must   not   remain
notion-less. But that will take time!

It   seems   to   be   most important that with the political
theologian's concentration on Jesus's theology in the form   of
parables,   illustrations,   examples   and stories, the original
theological power of the dialectical notion is not   endangered
and   that   political   theology   does   not   become   a victim of
simplification(418). This question not only touches   upon   the
form,   but   also upon the theological and sociopolitical truth
content of Jesus's discourses and   quasi-discourses.   Furthermore,   without the dialectical notion the political theologian
must also miss the contradictory movement of   modern   capitalistic   action   systems   and   history,   for   which most of the
members of the   Hegelian   left   have   made   the   sacrifice   of
theology(419).   Political   theology,   in   order to realize its
full ˙potential, must, better sooner than later,   move   to   the
level of the dialectical notion. It can do this with the help
of Meister Eckehart and Nicolaus of   Cues,   Kant   and   Hegel,
Bloch,   Horkheimer,   Adorno   and   Benjamin,   Marcuse   and
Habermas(420). No matter how interesting exegesis and the many
details it unearths may be, ultimately there always stands the
question of truth and it refers to the totality of   the   Jesus
phenomenon   and   it   can   be   comprehended   adequately   by the
dialectical notion(421). This is a matter not only of   theory,
but of practice as well.

Critical Theology

Only on the   level of the dialectical theological notion can
political theologians today, as   Hegel   before,   defend   themselves   more   effectively   against objections from artists and
philosophers concerning the evilness of the world and of God's
abandonment of the helpless or his absence(422). This is   particularly important in the face of the qualitative increase of
evilness   in   late capitalistic action sytems in the twentieth

century. Brecht sums up these objections in his play, <u>The Good Woman of Setzuan</u>(423). The good woman of Setzuan, Shen Te, must also be the mad man of Setzuan, Shui Ta, in order to be able to survive at all in Setzuan, another metaphor for the late capitalistic action system. So Shen Te confesses to the Three Gods who come to bad Setzuan in order to find at least one good person:

> Shen Te, yes. Shui Ta and Shen Te. Both.
> Your injunction
> To be good and yet to live,
> Was a thunderbolt:
> It has torn me in two.
> I can't tell how it was.
> But to be good to others
> And myself at the same time,
> I could not do it.
> Your world is not an easy one, illustrious ones!
> When we extend our hand to a beggar,
>   he tears it off from us.
> When we help the lost, we are lost ourselves.
> And so,
> Since not to eat is to die,
> Who can long refuse to be bad?
> As I lay prostrate beneath the weight of good intentions,
> Ruin stared me in the face.
> It was, when I was unjust, that I ate good meat
> And hobnobbed with the mighty.
> Why?
> Why are bad deeds rewarded?
> Good ones punished?
> I enjoyed giving.
> I truly wished to be the Angel of the Slums.
> But washed by a foster-mother in the water of the gutter,
> I developed a sharp eye.
> The time, when pity was a thorn in my side,
> And, later, when kind words turned to ashes in my mouth
> And anger took over,
> I became a wolf.
> Find me guilty, then, illustrious ones.
> But know:
> All that I have done, I did
> To help my neighbor,

To love my lover,
And to keep my little one from want.
For your great, godly deeds,
    I was too poor, too small(424).

Brecht's Three Gods depart from evil Setzuan and the only
good woman of Setzuan, Shen Te, who at the same time was a bad
man, Shui Ta, and both in one person, with a valedictory hymn:

What rapture, oh, it is to know
A good thing, when you see it.
And having seen a good thing, oh,
What rapture 'tis to flee it.

Be good, sweet maid of Setzuan,
Let Shui Ta be clever.
Departing we forget the man,
Remember your endeavor.

Because through all the length of days,
Her goodness faileth never.
Sing halleluja! Make Shen Te's
Good name live on forever(425).

Brecht's divine trinity leaves Shen Te behind in evil
Setzuan and she cries for help which is not granted by the
gods. That is, indeed, modern experience! Brecht's Three Gods
cheerfully answer Shen Te's, the good woman of Setzuan's
ideology critique, argumentation, analogies as well as her cry
for help, accusations and encouragement with their old
ideology, the old justification of their own problematic power
positions and of an evil world. Brecht's atheism is precisely
directed against such ideological theodicy and rightly so.
Brecht's atheism can not be converted into theology by a
blue-eyed, cheerful, all too optimistic liberal theology,
which simply corrects some words in his poems full of
seriousness and dignity in the face of the horror and terror
of nature and history(426). This liberal theology shares the
same unjustified optimism which we find sometimes in Habermas
and for which Hegel was unjustly criticized by Schopenhauer
and which in Brecht's atheism is rightly overcome. What
society has done in theory and practice to Jesus, the innocent
victim alone, then and through the centuries up to the present
- not only his enemies but even his friends - makes such

optimism impossible.

Political theology must answer the very justified objections of Brechtian or any other atheisms, born out of the suffering, pain and death of innocent victims, with a non-ideological and much less cheerful and triumphant, rather sad theodicy. True philosophy and theology must be sad in the face of a world, the mere continuation of which is a catastrophe(427). Political theology must in its totality be a critical theodicy. But it can be a critical theodicy and bring together the rose of God's reason and the cross of the contradictory present only when it can unite content and form: Jesus's theology and the theological notion, the theological content of Jesus's dialectical parables, images, metaphors, illustrations, examples and stories and the form of the mystical notion(428). Form and content must be equal, adequate and one, if half truths and despair are to be banned and real encouragement is to be given in the present capitalistic and socialistic system of human condition(429).

The Tragic End

According to the political theologian Arens, Jesus discloses in his communicative praxis for his friends and his opponents, the Pharisees and Scribes, his providential, loving and liberating God, his Abba(430). Jesus brings his God closer to his friends and opponents than they may find it comfortable. Jesus makes God's loving providence and governance a matter of immediate experience, as being present in his own discourses and quasi-discourses and in his own interaction and intersubjective relations. Jesus explicates his providential God in the interconnectedness of language and struggle for mutual, unconditional recognition rather than of work, family, or nation(431). Jesus linguifies God, in his interaction-embedded discourses and quasi-discourses. Therefore, Jesus's theology is an integral element of his communicative praxis. Jesus's speech and interaction, which interpret each other mutually, together let become transparent the reality of God and let it become a matter of experience. Jesus communicates in language and struggle for recognition the reality of God in communicating, communicative praxis.

The political theologian knows, of course, very well that Jesus did not reach his goal: that his communication of reality, providence and governance of God may be shared in the praxis of the kingdom of God in Jerusalem and elsewhere(432).

He could not break through people's hardness of the hearts,
their   unwillingness   to   learn   and to evolve. Jesus's
communication remained foreign to his pharisaic opponents and
to the largest part of his family and his nation and to this
day to the largest part of world society, if not even to the
largest part of feudal and bourgeois Christendom. According to
the fundamental theologian, Jesus's message of liberation
never reached the Zealots and the Essenes. The Sadducees may
have had premonitions of the potential danger of Jesus's
indeed dangerous messianic communication and communique. Jesus
did not achieve the always again and again in argument and
counter-argument searched-for consensus with the Pharisees and
Scribes. They never recognized Jesus's claims concerning the
truth of his speech about God or the rightfulness of his
action in relation to publicans, prostitutes and sinners in
general. The group of Jesus's friends and followers remained
small. The political theologian is not sure if Jesus was ever
able to win the masses of the people over to himself for a
longer time span. The socialist Blanqui may very well be right
when he argues that the pharisaic and priestly elite in
Jerusalem was finaly able to turn the masses of the people
against Jesus and that they crucified him, while the masses
screamed for joy(433).
    According to the political theologian, Jesus finally went
to Jerusalem in order there to await the last decisive phase
of God's kingdom to break into the people's life world and
into society, state and history(434). Jesus had a last meal of
departure with his friends. It became the peak and summary of
Jesus's symbolical action. In this action of the last supper,
Jesus collected speech and interaction and his whole life into
the signs of bread and wine. Jesus offered his speech,
struggle for recognition and his whole life in these signs to
his friends. Then Jesus was imprisoned by the Romans and the
Sadducees. Jesus was finally, through the cooperation of the
Roman occupation forces, particularly Pilate, and the Roman
temple cohort, the Sadducee-hierarchy and the party of Herod,
sentenced to death and executed.

Assertion Validity

The political theologian Arens is fully aware, as the
fundamental theologian Peukert before, that in the face of
this execution, this violent end of the man who had asserted
and communicated through his speech and interaction and

through his person God as the Reality, who does not exclude
anybody from his love and freedom, who is good and liberating,
who searches for what is lost and who is the saving Reality
for others, the elementary question had to impose itself upon
his friends: if this assertion had not also validity for him,
Jesus himself, in his own most cruel suffering and death(435).
Can they, the friends, assert God as redeeming Reality, not
only for the others, but also for Jesus himself in his
suffering, pain and death? The political theologian emphasizes
that this question certainly posed itself first in time to
Jesus's friends(436). But in logical perspective, this
question concerns every human being, who sees himself
confronted with Jesus's assertion of the reality of God and
his communicative action in the face of his death and the
annihilation of any other innocent victim in history(437).

The political theologian is very much aware also of the
other alternative: that Jesus's shameful death on the cross
has refuted his assertion and communication of God's saving
reality and has exposed his solidaristic communicative praxis
as being deadly(438). The murderers have triumphed over the
innocent victim. When the man Jesus, who has asserted in his
language and his struggle for unconditional recognition and
with his whole existence God as providence for others, is
himself annihilated, then there seems to be a very good
possibility that this assertion has, indeed, been refuted by
the historical fact, the factum brutum of his most terrible
death. It looks as if in this case there can be no longer any
speech of God as providence at all. Beyond this, it seems that
with the death of Jesus any attempt toward a good life, which
asserts in the existence for others an Unconditional, is led
ad absurdum(439). Brecht's atheism and much of modern atheism
born out of terrible suffering and death points very
effectively in the direction of this alternative, if it can
not be brought home in terms of a critical political theology:
the providential God of Jesus is dead. With Jesus has died his
providential God.

Parable of God

In the face of this most aporetical situation, this seemingly
absolute dead-end street, the political theologian Arens
engages in the Kierkegaardian leap of faith: he confesses with
the Christian church in messianic faith to Jesus's
resurrection by his providential God(440). Jesus's friends

asserted a short time after his death that he is alive: God
has resurrected Jesus! The storyteller Jesus proves himself to
be the living parable, illustration, example of God out of his
resurrection. It ultimately affirms and puts to right Jesus,
the innocent victim's language, his parbolic theology, his
struggle for recognition, his interaction with others, his
intersubjectivity, his person against his murderers. This
happens out of the providential, eschatological action of God
in relation to Jesus as the living parable of God. The man
Jesus who had told all these innumerable stories about God had
himself turned into a story of the providential God.

Theological Significance

For the political theologians the theological significance of
Jesus's death is as central as it has been for the whole
Christian tradition(441). For Hegel, with the death of Christ
begins the transformation of consciousness(442). The death of
Christ is the center around which Christianity turns. In the
notion of Jesus's death lies the difference between an
external, merely historical conception of Jesus on one hand
and a faith conception of Christ out of the Spirit of truth,
the Holy Spirit, on the other. For Hegel, Jesus's death is the
teststone, at which faith proves itself, since here its
understanding of the phenomenon of Christ represents itself
fully. Jesus's death has for Hegel first of all the meaning
that Christ has been the God-man, the God who had at the same
time human nature, even to death(443). It is the fate of human
finitude to die. Thus, death is the highest proof of humanity,
of its finitude. Beyond this, Christ has died the intensified
death of a criminal. Jesus did not only die a natural death.
He died even a death of social shame and degradation on the
cross. The cross is a class struggle instrument. The cross is
used by the Roman latifundia owners to control their slaves.
Jesus died a polemical and revolutionary death. Thus humanity
appeared in Christ to the most extreme point. That is Hegel's
Christology from below.
     But for Hegel, the death of Jesus has still a further
determination(444). In Jesus's death God has died. God is
dead. This is, according to Hegel, the most terrible thought:
that everything eternal, everything true is not. The negation
is in God himself. The greatest pain, the feeling of being
completely lost, the giving up of everything higher is
connected with the death of God. God himself has been

crucified. The rest is nihilism! Recently the political
theologian Moltmann, following Hegel, speaks again about the
"crucified God"(445). The American God-is-dead movement ends
with the death of God. There is no resurrection or acension.
   But according to Hegel, the story of Jesus's life does
not end here with his death and the death of the crucified
God(446). A turn occurs! God maintains his identity in the
non-identity of this process of Christ's death and his own
death and this process is only the death of death, the
negation of the negation. God arises again from death to life.
Things turn into their opposite: the negative into being. This
is the resurrection and ascension of Christ. In this death of
death, overcoming of the grave, triumph over the negative and
this elevation into Heaven, God does not strip himself of
human nature. It rather receives in this negation of the
negation its highest recognition, even in death and in the
deepest love. When the Son of Man sits on the right side of
the Father, then in this elevation of human nature its honor
and its identity with the Divine Nature has come most clearly
before the spiritual eye. Today the political theologian
Moltman follows very much this notion of Hegel not only for
the crucified but also for the arisen God and the consequent
psychic and political liberation of man(447). That is
Christology from above.

Divine Identification

Contrary to the political theologians Hegel and Moltmann, the
political theologian Arens, following the fundamental theologian Peukert, stresses the crucified and resurrected Jesus
rather than the crucified and risen God(448). They proceed
consequentially in a Christology from below rather than in a
Christology from above also in their interpretation of Jesus's
death and his resurrection by God. The political theologian
agrees with Becker that God identifies himself through his
resurrecting action with the providential image of God, for
which Jesus of Nazareth stood up during his life(449). The
fundamental theologian also agrees with Jungel that the resurrection of Jesus from the dead means that God has identified
himself with this dead man(450). That means right away also
that God has identified himself with Jesus's God-forsakenness.
It means, furthermore, that God has identified himself with
the lived life of this dead man. The theologian of communicative praxis agrees with Crossan, when he formulates with the

help of the word "parable," the personal continuity in the
discontinuity between the storyteller Jesus and the Christ, to
whom the Christian community confesses: the parable-teller,
Jesus, becomes the parable(451). Jesus announces the kingdom
of God in parables. But the primitive church proclaimed Jesus
as the Christ, the parable of God.

Messianic Mimesis

According to the political theologian Arens, whoever recognizes after Jesus's death and resurrection him as the living
parable of God and confesses him as such, is invited and challenged to act in the imitatio Christi(452). For the fundamental theologian the following of Christ means the attempt to
take over the structure of his communicative action out of the
experience of the reality of God. This Reality has been
brought close in Jesus's speech and interaction. It has been
made a matter of experience in Jesus's discourses and quasi-
discourses and struggle for recognition. The reality of God
has rescued Jesus in his death and annihilation. This reality
of God searches for what is lost and creates life out of
death. It is the very foundation for the messianic mimesis:
the tendential imitatio Christi.

Theology of Praxis

The political theologian Arens draws the lines which result
from the presentation of the person of Jesus, his discourses
and quasi-discourses, his parabolic theology and his communicative praxis to his death and resurrection(453). According to
the political theologian, this his theological design must now
be worked out in an embracing theological theory of action, a
theology of communicative praxis. The enfolding of such a
theology of praxis must not only bring about an action-
theoretical understanding of Jesus's execution, annihilation
and resurrection as well as an explication of the relationship
between the earthly storyteller Jesus and him as the proclaimed parable of God, but likewise a theory of Christian
speaking and struggle for mutual and unconditional recognition
as well as of work and of family and of membership in the
national and international community. In such a theology of
action must be explicated in detail what it means to apply
Jesus's structure of communication to late modern situations
of speaking, working, loving, struggle for recognition in the

framework of highly differentiated national and international action systems and to adapt it in this context, if that should be necessary(454). Furthermore, such theology of universal pragmatic must demonstrate, how this actualization of Jesus's communicative structure happens in the present world-historical situation. Like Nicholas of Cusa's, Meister Eckehart's, and Hegel's mystical theology and philosophy before, political theology must make explicit God's reality and rationality and the fragments of this his rationality in the language-mediated struggle for mutual unconditional recognition as well as in the whole social-historical world, the natural world, the inner world, the cultural world and the world of language(455). Finally, this political theology must give orientation to the corresponding ethical-political praxis. It must be political theology in the fullest sense of the word. Only such a fully developed political theology can successfully refute the thesis of Habermas's universal pragmatic, that religion has become obsolete, since it is no longer able to resolve the theodicy problem and to grant social and personal identity in highly differentiated modern capitalistic or socialistic action systems and in the face of growing contingency experiences and future concern(456).

Interdisciplinary Approach

The fundamental theologian's pragmatic theory of the parables of Jesus aims at a political theology, which is conceived in terms of Habermas's theory of communicative praxis: a theology of communicative action(457). The political theologian Peukert has developed a fundamental-theological methodology for such a theology of communicative, universal, solidaristic praxis(458). He has done so against the background of Metz's political theology, who is his as well as Arens's teacher(459). According to the political theologian Arens the theology of praxis prepared by Metz, Peukert and himself, will, as fully developed political theology, achieve a theological concentration of the fundamental questions concerning the Christian speech of God in relation to what happens in, with and through Jesus as well as in a tendential following of Jesus(460). Beyond this, the theology of praxis will contribute to an integration of the theological disciplines among themselves. It is committed to an interdisciplinary approach to theology as a whole.

    In the process of their specialization the theological

disciplines have moved further and further apart from each
other not only in their material aspects, but also in their
very foundations. A theological theory of communicative praxis, which will follow Arens's pragmatic theory of parables and
Peukert's pragmatic fundamental theology and Metz's political
theology will necessarily correlate historical, systematic and
practical problem positions. This is so since such a theology
of praxis must work out its fundamental concern of a practical
and political hermeneutic of Christianity(461). The theology
of praxis will start from the foundation of the practical,
political hermeneutic of Christianity, which is to be derived
historically—exegetically. This foundation is rooted in
Jesus's language mediated communicative action. The development of the theology of praxis will start in the face of the
systematic—theological questions concerning the christological, theological, ecclesiological and ethical consequences of
Jesus's communicative—practical explications of the reality of
God and the self—explication of this Reality in Jesus's life,
suffering, death and resurrection.

Paradigmaticality

The political theologian Arens's pragmatic theory of parables
wants to introduce paradigmaticality into the project of a
theological universal pragmatic(462). It intends to contribute
to the constitution of a theology of praxis in cooperation
with Peukert's fundamental theology and Metz's political
theology. It wants to take the first steps into such a theology of universal pragmatic. It itself remains a task for future interdisciplinary theological research. According to the
political theologian this task can be pursued only in inner-
theological, interdisciplinary cooperation among the historical—exegetical, the systematic and practical theological
disciplines. This must happen at the same time in continuous
interdisciplinary discourse between theology and those disciplines in the human sciences and philosophy which work on
action—theoretical problems.

Hermeneutics

In this sense the political theologian Metz demands rightly
that a hermeneutic of Christian praxis must also be made clear
in relation to the non—theological theories of action(463).
This precisely is the reason for the continuous discourses

between the political theologians and Habermas in Munich,
Frankfurt, Munster, Boston and elsewhere. According to the
political theologian Arens, the theological universal pragmatic must clarify its methodology, status and scope once more
in relation to the human-scientific and philosophical action-
theoretical methodologies, which co-constitute it. Such confrontation includes likewise a theological critique of and
theological separation from non-theological forms of pragmatics. Such confrontation also implies that every theological theory of action must once more put itself theologically
into question and relativize itself in the face of the practical intention and constitution of Jesus's speech-mediated
communicative praxis and the Christian talk of the reality of
God and of his work in nature, personal inner world, social-
historical, cultural world and world of language, from one
hour of history to the other.

Theological Universal Pragmatic

The political theologian Arens has established, with the help
of Pierce's reflection on the irreducible triplicity of the
sign relation, Habermas's universal pragmatic and Apel's
transcendental pragmatic as common functional-pragmatic basis,
a fundamental-theologically oriented theory of Jesus's para-
bles(464). Therefore, for the political theologian theological confrontations with Habermas's and Apel's pragmatic
methodologies are very relevant in view of the aimed-at theological universal pragmatic. After having gone through the
pragmatic theory formation and its reflective foundation and
through the design of a pragmatic theory of parables, which
builds on these non-theological pragmatic theory formations,
the fundamental theologian looks forward to the kind of work
which has still to be done if an embracing theology of praxis
should become reality, which will not simply be another pragmatic, but a specifically theological universal pragmatic. It
is obvious from all this that political theology intends,
paradoxically enough, to renew and defend Christianity with
categories out of Habermas's universal pragmatic and Apel's
communication community which contain elements of that same
bourgeois, Marxian and Freudian enlightenment, by which it has
been fought for over two centuries and has now been declared
to be obsolete and which it itself set into motion in the
first place. The goal of the political theologians is, nevertheless, a new, post-Hegelian critical reconciliation of

unideological   enlightenment   with   unideological,   messianic
religion: a new conjugation of freedom and grace(465).

Exchange Relation

The political theologian Metz criticizes Habermas's   universal
pragmatic as well as Apel's transcendental pragmatic, by saying that the universal solidarity, which they intend, has tendentially the character of a bourgeois exchange relation(466).
It is a reflection of the late capitalistic exchange   society.
It   does   not   go   dialectically   beyond the late capitalistic
society(467). Political theology tends to go beyond   the   late
capitalistic action system: formal and universal pragmatics do
not go that far. Shortly, they do not go far enough!
    The   fundamental theologian Peukert criticizes Habermas's
and Apel's pragamtics because   of   the   elementary   _aporia_   in
their very center(468). This _aporia_ becomes visible to Peukert
as   soon   as Habermas's and Apel's conception of the unlimited
communication community and its elementary   aspects   of   reciprocity   and universal solidarity are enfolded in direction of
their historical dimension: the history of liberation is   also
the history of suffering and death.

Total Emancipation

Metz   sees   in   Habermas's   attempt   to reconstruct historical
materialism on the basis of a developmental logic   a   form   of
evolutionistic   disintegration   of   the   dialectic   of   libera-
tion(469). It has allegedly already been at work   in   Hegel's,
Marx's   and   Benjamin's   philosophy of history(470). Metz dis-
cerns in the differentiations between   work   and   interaction,
technique   and   praxis,   the empirical and anticipation, which
Habermas enfolds on the basis of Hegel's Jena System Designs I
and III in his theory   of   communicative   praxis,   an   _instru-_
mentarium   for   the   dialectically   working   through of social
contradictions in the   interest   of   total   emancipation(471).
Metz   is   extremely   critical   of such total emancipation, and
rightly so.

Idealism

Metz charges Habermas and Apel that   they   propose   solidarity
merely   among   rational people, a highly particularistic soli-
darity(472). What happens to the irrational people? Metz sees,

in any case, in the background of Habermas's universal
pragmatic and Apel's transcendental programatic Hegelian
idealism at work. They connect this Hegelian idealism with a
subtle logic of evolution. Like Hegel, Habermas and Apel
presume transcendentally the rationality of the subjects.
Where Habermas and Apel become aware of the inequality of the
partners in discourse or in the struggle for recognition, they
compensate, allegedly like Hegel, this inequality reflexively
and valuate it upwards. Habermas and Apel engage, allegedly,
like Hegel before, in the transcendental simulation of the
equal rank of the partners in discourse and interaction. For
Metz, Habermas's universal pragmatic as well as Apel's communication community seem to imply this Hegelian idealism in the
way in which they both presuppose the reciprocal recognition
of the subjects which are envisioned in their universal rules.
According to Metz, all relations which are developed in Habermas's and Apel's pragmatics and in similar theories of communicative action, the postulated unlimited communication community as well as the intended universal solidarity, have tendentially the character of a bourgeois relation of exchange(473).
Shortly, Metz opposes the real speech situation to the ideal
speech situation and the real class struggle in civil society
to the ideal of mutual recognition.
   The practical, political-fundamental theologian Metz criticizes and unmasks Habermas's and Apel's discourses of the
rational and equal people, which is directed toward universal
freedom, as pseudo-solidaristic(474). All relevant contemporary theories of science and action circle around such
discourses. To Metz these theoretical and practical discourses seem to be pseudo-solidaristic in the face of the
objective history of the suffering and death of innumerable
victims, which have accompanied the history of liberation and
solidaristic action from the very beginning. In the framework
of his practical, political-fundamental theology, Metz opposes
Habermas's and Apel's reciprocal solidarity by a Christian
solidarity. It is accompanied by the categories of the dangerous memory and story: memoria vitae, passionis, mortis
Christi and of all other innocent victims who have been
destroyed.

Master and Servant

Hegel takes more seriously in the dimension of interaction the
terrible struggle between master and servant and then, on the

social economic, political and historical level, the conflict
between the classes - slaveholders and slaves, feudal lords
and serfs, bourgeois and proletarian and all the human
suffering involved in this class struggle than Metz is willing
to admit(475). For Hegel, reciprocal or Christian solidarity
do not stand at the beginning of history as class struggle,
but at its end(476). According to Hegel, the universal
freedom, which will be the result of the history of despots
and oligarchs, the freedom of All, is only potentially and
seedlike present at its beginning. It takes the whole long
history of human suffering in order to actualize the first of
all merely potential universal freedom. Benjamin, whom Metz
opposes to Habermas and Apel, is closer to Hegel than Metz is
aware of(477). Hegel never shied away from the awesome negativity of civil society and bourgeois history: he saw as
clearly the hell of capitalistic society and the need for its
supersession as later on Marx, Benjamin or Adorno(478).

Differentiation of Levels

According to the political theologian Arens, when Metz objects
to Habermas that his developmental-logical conception destroys
evolutionistically the dialectic of liberation, then this
objection rests on a confusion of two levels(479). Metz
confuses the level of real history, which also according to
Habermas does not move in stages reconstructable in terms of a
logic of development, with the level of the development of the
structures of instrumental-technical and moral-practical
action as well as of the development of social organization,
which makes social evolution possible, but does not determine
it. Habermas would say that Metz confuses the logic of
development and the dynamic of development(480). According to
Habermas, the dynamic of development does indeed proceed
discontinuously. It can be reversed. It is always threatened.
It underlies the dialectic of rationalization, enlightenment,
emancipation and progress(481). What in Hegel's philosophy of
history constituted a dialectical unity, the logic of historical development and the dynamic of historical development,
has fallen apart for Habermas. He insists on the
differentiation of these levels.

The political theologian, Arens, is right when he defends
Habermas against Metz, stating that he is not a vulgar Marxist
of the kind, as Benjamin denounces them in his "Theses of the
Philosophy of History"(482). According to the fundamental

theologian, Habermas is as conscious of the discontinuity of the history of freedom and the human suffering which develops it as Hegel and Benjamin, Horkheimer and Adorno(483). Therefore, Habermas can not be simply put practically into the history of the victors. Habermas also does not sanction such a history of the victors theoretically. On the other hand some must argue against Arens, suffering and death of innocent victims of history do not take the same central position in Habermas's Theory of Communicative Praxis, which they have in the philosophies of Hegel, Horkheimer, Benjamin and Adorno and which they have in Metz's and Peukert's political theology and which they deserve and must have precisely for the sake of the future - Future III - the reconciled society(484). Arens has so far left the whole theodicy problem to Metz and Peukert and also does not intend to deal with it in the near future.

Habermas's differentiation between work and interaction is as little carried by an interest of total emancipation as Metz alleges, as Hegel's differentiation between language and work or work and familial love, or love and the struggle for recognition or interaction and nation(485). For Habermas as for Hegel before, human freedom is finite and relative(486). Only God's freedom is absolute(487). Human liberation can not be total, because of the limitations imposed on it by external and internal nature. Habermas knows this as well as Kant, Hegel, Marx, Horkheimer or Adorno. But even if Habermas's differentiation between work and recognition was really based on an interest in total liberation, so the political theologian Arens judges rightly, this does not yet say anything about the correctness of this differentiation as such(488). The fundamental theologian points out that these differentiations are, of course, at least for Habermas, not of a theological nature(489). At the same time, in the perspective of the theologian of communicative praxis, nothing speaks against it that a fundamental theologian who is interested in discourse with other sciences and dependent on such discourse, could take up this Hegelian differentiation insofar as it is scientifically communicable. The political theologian may do so precisely in order to make clear with the help of the differentiation, e.g, of work and recognition, the specific theological interest in an interdisciplinarily responsible way. It would be to the advantage of the fundamental theologian Arens and his further work if he would reach behind Habermas to his roots in Hegel's critical Jena Writings and Jena System Designs I and III. So far Arens has not done so. Hegel's

mountain melodies are too steep or deep for him. But Hegel's
early presystemic system designs could give Arens's theology
of communicative praxis a depth dimension, in which also the
theodicy problem could be approached anew in a creative way.

Theological Interest

The political theologian Arens admits that Metz is, of course,
completely right when he states that this specific theological
interest in interdisciplinary discourse can not be one of
total emancipation(490). The political theologians Metz,
Peukert and Arens can not agree to the interest in total
emancipation out of the experience and the knowledge that
human history of liberation does fail again and again. It is
characterized by frequent regressions into barbarism. During
this century such a regression took place in Central Europe:
Fascism. The liberation history is aporetical insofar as it is
not able to take into itself and supersede in itself the
history of redemption and the history of meaninglessness,
suffering, death and guilt. Hegel's philosophy of history is
not aporetical precisely to the extent to which it does take
into itself the history of redemption and supersedes in itself
regression, meaninglessness, boredom, suffering, death, guilt:
It is an open history(491). The notion of history includes its
negativity, its horror. It is precisely therefore a theod-
icy(492). The same is true of Benjamin's design of history,
which has the messianic for its very center as well as the
immense human suffering and death(493). Both conceptions of
history are so similar since they are both rooted in
Judeo-Christian mysticism. Both designs of history are full of
contingencies, which are nevertheless ultimately superseded.

Reciprocity

According to the political theologian Arens, in every merely
human history of freedom the attempt to live in a universal
solidaristic way must lead into what Peukert calls, following
Benjamin, the paradox of anamnestic solidarity(494). This does
not mean for the fundamental theologian that Christian
solidarity can be played out against reciprocal solidarity, as
Metz does. The theologian of communicative praxis frees the
concept of reciprocity from the connotations it has for Metz
and also for Horkheimer and Adorno in the context of late
capitalistic society: its connection with the bourgeois

equivalence principle. For the political theologian, taught by
a view into the history of the thing, which is meant by this
notion of reciprocity, and into the history of this notion
itself, from Hegel's Jena Critical Writings, Jena System
Designs, and Phenomenology of Spirit, over Mead, Durkheim,
Weber, Parsons, to Habermas and Peukert, this notion of reciprocity has nothing to do with the capitalistic exchange or
equivalence principle(495). The fundamental theologian asserts
even that reciprocity means precisely the interpersonal
relation, which in the New Testament is called love of the
neighbor. Then reciprocity does not mean do ut des, "I give to
you that you may give to me" which characterized the human
relations in the Roman civil society as well as the relations
of the humans with their gods in the Roman political religion
of utility(496). Do ut des determines also what human
relations are in the modern civil society and in the
corresponding bourgeois religion(497). Genuine reciprocity, on
the other hand, means for the political theologian the
recognition of the other for his or her own sake and for my
own sake(498). It means recognition of the other as equal and
equally needy person, who depends on love and understanding as
I do. Horkheimer, following Hegel, translates the
Judeo-Christian commandment to love: love your neighbor, he is
as you(499).

According to the political theologian, this reciprocity
is executed as recognition out of the, at least, intrinsic
common knowledge about the fact that we are unconditionally
dependent on each other(500). Therefore, we must come to a
consensus with each other about what we do, what we want and
what we should do and should want to do in the interest of the
one humanity and before God's face. Therefore, love of the
neighbor as reciprocal solidarity seeks as such the discourse.
It moves from recognition to language. It struggles for
understanding and consensus. For the fundamental theologian,
this becomes particularly clear in the case of the love to the
enemy. It is not merely a special Christian virtue. It is
rather a deeply humane form of communicative action. It wants
that the enemies may change themselves in their enmity. The
Sandinistas practiced this love of the enemy most beautifully
during and after their revolution in Nicaraguan and continue
to do so today as their amnesty offers show which they extend
to Samosa counterrevolutionaries paid by the president of the
USA and private capitalistic circles in the USA and else-
where(501).

Anamnestic Solidarity

The political theologian Arens takes most seriously Peukert's
critique of Habermas's universal pragmatic and Apel's transcendental pragmatic and his demonstration of the aporetical
character of both conceptions in the paradox of the anamnestic
solidarity(502). Peukert sums up this demonstration in the
statement that the normative implications of a theory of communicative praxis for the identity of subjects as for the
structure of society becomes aporetical, where the theoretician tries to think the historical constitution of the one
solidary human species(503). Habermas does, indeed, recognize
Peukert's critique that in his theory of communicative praxis
the temporal dimension is neglected(504). But so far Habermas
has not yet stated how he will counter Peukert's and Arens's
critique without drawing his own theological consequences out
of the aporia of his own theory of communicative action. The
question is if this aporia can be resolved on the secular side
of enlightenment and in the framework of a dialectical notion,
which is no longer theological, or without such notion since
it has fallen victim not only to secularization but even to
deconstruction, or if reference is to be made once more to
religion and to the theological roots of the dialectical
notion, as Adorno recommended to Benjamin.

Absolute and Finite Freedom

According to the political theologian Arens, Peukert directs
attention to the fact that Habermas's theory of communicative
praxis, which determines the normative foundation of struggle
for recognition, interaction and intersubjectivity as unconditional equality, reciprocity and universal solidarity, moves
in a threefold mode against a boundary which it can not supersede on its own in its conception developed so far(505). In
the political theologian's perspective, first of all the limit
of Habermas's theory of communicative praxis becomes visible
in the face of the question, from where the indisposable
freedom of the intercommunicating and interacting partners is
itself once more provoked(506). This indisposable freedom must
be mutually imposed and given to the partners of communication
in such a mode that both subjects let themselves be engaged in
the event of intersubjective historical freedom. For the
political theologian, the first boundary of Habermas's and
Apel's pragmatics is their inability to at least thematize,

not to speak of answering, the question concerning the
absolute freedom as the presupposition of finite historical
freedom. Hegel had been able in his divine and human universal
pragmatic to formulate and to answer this question: man's
freedom was grounded in and directed toward God's absolute
freedom(507). Since Hegel, this question has never adequately
been articulated or answered again on the Hegelian Left. It
was continually loosely formulated and answered on the
Hegelian Right(508).

Temporal Structure

Second, for the political theologian Arens the temporal structure of communicative action has so far not been considered or
enfolded as systematically relevant either in Habermas's
universal pragmatic or in Apel's transcendental pragmatic or
in any other pragmatic methodology(509). Peukert states
against the background of Heidegger's analysis of the temporal
structure of human existence that a theory of temporal
communicative action, which includes the death of the one and
the other as the most extreme horizon of consciousness, has
not yet been developed(510). Even today, Heidegger's analysis
has not yet been superseded by any theory of communicative
action, which will take into consideration the temporality and
the death of the one and the other partner in speech, work,
love, recognition or nationhood.

Unlimited Solidarity

For the political theologian Arens, the third limit which constitutes the elementary aporia of action-theoretical reflection so far, is its failure to assert really as unlimited the
universality and solidarity which are demonstrated in it as
normative elements of interaction(511). Universal solidarity
can eo ipso not be limited merely to the present generation.
Essentially unlimited universal solidarity must by its very
notion embrace the past and present as well as the future
generations, the past and contemporary victims as well as the
future heirs of history(512). Radically and paradigmatically
the question poses itself to the political theologian, how
solidarity can be lived particularly with the dead who have
been annihilated precisely for the realization of this universal solidarity. The fundamental theologian denies that the
question for a reality toward which solidarity moves precisely

in the face of the question concerning the solidarity with the
innocent victims of history, who have been annihilated, can be
excluded from practical discourse. If anywhere, then here the
question poses itself out of a theory of communicative praxis
concerning the Reality which is meant in theology: the Reality
which is witnessed for the other in communicative action in
the face of his or her death(513). Thus the husband witnesses
for his despairing wife who, poisoned by carcenogenic material
fed to her by its producers, is dying from cancer, God's
reality, who will rescue her, the innocent victim, out of
annihilation. The husband witnesses this also for himself in
relation to his own death to come later.

Achievement Capacity

The political theologian Arens is fully aware of the fact that
also his own pragmatic theory of parables, which has been
developed out of Habermas's universal pragmatic and Apel's
transcendental pragmatic, must stand up to Peukert's demonstration of the aporia of these conceptions of communicative
praxis(514). Peukert's questions are valid also for the political theologian's own pragmatic theory of Jesus's parables.
The fundamental theologian can give only a tentative answer.
His answer is that Peukert's demonstration of the elementary
aporia of Arens's fundamental pragmatic and of Habermas's
integrative pragmatic theory which is built on it does not
negate entirely their limited achievement capactiy. The fundamental theologian Arens has explicated paradigmatically in
his pragmatic theory of parables this limited achievement
ability. The theologian of communicative praxis has shown that
an analysis of the speech and interaction of Jesus, his
language mediated communicative praxis on the fundamental-
pragmatic basis of Habermas's universal pragmatic makes possible a series of theologically relevant insights. It constitutes at the same time a paradigmatic introduction to a practical-fundamental theological theory of action. The fundamental theologian admits that his pragmatic theory of parables
can not give a perfect foundation to a theology of communicative praxis.

Foundation

According to the political theologian Arens, Peukert has
achieved such foundation of a theology of communicative praxis

by going through the problem positions of the theories of science and action(515). Peukert demonstrates the convergence of the theory of science and the theory of action in a theory of communicative praxis. Peukert has also shown the aporia of the present-day theories of language and interaction, of communicative praxis. Peukert develops the foundation of pragmatic-fundamental theology with the enfolding of two theses. First, Peukert asserts that the Judeo-Christian religion is concerned with the reality which is experienced in the foundation – and boundary experiences of communicative praxis(516). Judeo-Christian religion is also concerned with the mode of communicative praxis which is still possible for the survivor in the face of these foundation and boundary experiences. Similar assertions could, of course, be made for Buddhism and other world religions(517). Secondly, Peukert asserts that a pragmatic-fundamental theology can and must be developed as theory of this communicative, anamnestic-solidaristic action of the survior, who moves toward death, and of the Reality which is experienced and disclosed in this communicative praxis(518). The political theologian Arens accepts both of Peukert' assertions. But a future political theology can and must also overcome the deficiency of Peukert's fundamental theology as well as Arens's pragmatic parable theory. This deficiency consists in the merely "assertive" character of their aporia-solution: the Kierkegaardian leap of a faith, to which dialectical reason is not reconciled(519). Hegel had achieved such reconciliation between faith and dialectical reason in the context of modernity(520). Political theology as such must develop a post-Hegelian conjugation of faith and dialectical reason and thus build a bridge to non-ideological enlightenment. Only such a new coincidentia oppositorum of faith and reason would give political theology the desired foundation.

Narrative Character

According to the political theologian Arens, Peukert's science-theoretical foundation of fundamental theology has an elementary and narrative character(521). It is certainly not a theoretical, ontological proof of God of the kind Hegel developed up to his death(522). Whoever takes the theology of communicative praxis as an ontological proof of God overlooks its narrative and practical character(523). Peukert is not an Anselm of Canterbury, Descartes or Hegel of the twentieth cen-

tury(524). He is not engaged in the ontological argument as an
analogous movement of thought. He does not deduce the material
truth of the existence of God out of the formal science of
logic. He is like Habermas, much closer to Kant, who forbids
precisely such deduction(525). Neither Peukert nor Arens
present any proofs of God, not to speak of an ontological
proof. If, indeed, they try, like Hegel, to reconcile reason
with religion, then it is communicative reason which they want
to reconcile with the Christian religion, particularly the
faith in the resurrection and this in very practical and
narrative terms(526). If the political theologians intend,
like Hegel, to know religion in its manifold formations as
internally necessary, then they mean the necessity of that
Reality in Judaism and Christianity and other world religions,
which rescues men in their annihilation and thus makes
possible communicative praxis and mutual unconditional
recognition and reciprocity among the one and the other. When
the political theologians intend to rediscover, like Hegel, in
Christianity, the truth and the idea, then it is once more the
truth that God did not let his just one rot in the grave: that
God has resurrected Jesus out of his annihilation; death of
death; negation of negation; and that such resurrection is
promised to all innocent victims destroyed in history(527).

   According to the political theologian Arens, Peukert
refers, like Metz, anamnestically back to experiences of the
Judeo-Christian religion(528). In the face of these Judeo-
Christian experiences and the reality of God asserted and
communicated in them, Peukert gives an account about the
Christian faith. He does this by starting out in an interdisciplinarily responsible and theologically fundamental way
to demonstrate the possibility of a responsible speech of God
out of these fundamental Judeo-Christian experiences(529).

Theological Tasks

The political theologian Arens's design of a pragmatic theory
of parables has explicated the communicative praxis of Jesus
in the light of mainly Habermas's fundamental-pragmatically
grounded theory of action(530). Doing this, the fundamental
theologian has started with one of these essential experiences
of the Judeo-Christian religion: Jesus's discourses and
quasi-discourses, his parables, illustrations, examples and
stories. From there the theologian of communicative praxis was
able to enfold the question concerning the reality of God to a

point where it poses itself once more most radically and
paradigmatically in the face of the execution of Jesus, the
man committed to the reality of a loving God and universal
solidarity, as well as in the face of the annihilation of all
the innocent victims of history, past, present and future.
Peukert has shown this radicalization and universalization.
This radicalization and universalization has substantially
relativized the political theologian's, Arens's, design of a
theory of Jesus's parables as being enclosed in the aporia of
all modern theories of action up to Apel's transcendental
pragmatic and Habermas's universal pragmatic.

The embracing theology of praxis, which the political
theologian envisions for the future, has the task of working
out in terms of a practical-fundamental theology, the question
concerning the reality of God in the face of the death of Jesus and of the annihilation of all the other innocent victims
in history. This is to be done in the sense of an action-
theoretically conceived theology, an eo ipso political
theology.

Furthermore, the future theology of praxis has the task
of enfolding the theological, Christological, ecclesiological
as well as ethical-political consequences of such political
theology for contemporay Christian action, including theolo-
gizing as one form of such Christian praxis. In spite of all
its necessary output of energy and spirit, so the political
theologian Arens warns, the theology of universal pragmatic
must recognize out of its own analysis at the same time that
it is and ought to be something secondary and mediated.
Theology of praxis is as reflecting political theology of
subject, society and history primarily the reflex of the
communicative action of subjects. Political theology must
relativize itself once more in order to be really effective.
Political theology must find its subjects in the praxis of the
kingdom of God and must let them go into his praxis of the
Basileia: into the acting out of the truth, which makes free
only when and if it is done(531).

Dialectical Imagination

As Metz, the father of critical political theology, has been
inspired by Rahner so he on his part has inspired Peukert and
Arens and many other friends and disciples, including myself.
At the same time Metz has developed very close intellectual
ties to Habermas. The two scholars have several points of

intellectual contact: one is personal and social morality.
Beyond this, Metz's political theology is characterized by a
great wealth of thematic interrelationships, speculative penetration and a special sensibility for social and cultural
connections. Metz has always been interested in a productive
work of mediation in relation to different cultural traditions
and backgrounds. He deals again and again with themes of great
intercultural relevancy.

Metz's political theology has certain visionary traits.
It contains, e.g., a vision of a new epoch in the history of
the church - the decentralized church of the poor, a pro-
phetic-messianic church. Following Benjamin, Metz translates
back Hegel's dialectical notion into the dialectical image,
the dialectical imagination, where it came from in the first
place. Metz admits that he considers such dialectical
imagination to be important in a time and a situation which is
globally more or less characterized by precisely the absence
of great visions. The loss of dialectical imagination and
visionary energy appears to Metz to be ultimately more
dangerous than the danger that visions may dissipate into and
go under in vaguely moving abstract utopias.

According to Metz, exact dialectical imagination is a
necessary starting point for the new critical political theology in which he shares with Peukert, Arens, and many other
disciples and friends in different nations and on different
continents. Ultimately, Metz is concerned in his political
theology with a future-oriented work of reconciliation: the
productive reconciliation among different cultural traditions.
There is an affinity between Metz's socio-economic ideas and
the considerations based in the natural law tradition which
the Canadian and American bishops have presented recently in
their pastoral letters in answer to questions concerning the
American capitalistic economic order. This affinity exists in
spite of Metz's very justified scepticism toward the natural
law tradition, which historically is rooted in Greek and Roman
domination philosophy. But while Kung has left the natural law
far behind, Metz is willing to accept it, if it serves the
poor and oppressed classes.

While Metz is highly critical of Hegel, he is, nevertheless, willing to make his world of thought and effect history,
characterized as "dialectical tradition," fruitful for his
work of reconciliation and for the fundamental problems of the
future of our civilization. Metz shares in the old liberal
prejudice, that Hegel's famous statement in the "Preface" to

his Philosophy of Right, what is rational is real; and what is
real, is rational, is extremely conservative, if not even
reactionary. But at the same time Metz is not entirely
unwilling to admit that Hegel may indeed have seen in his
Frankfurt System Program, his Jena Critical Writings, his Jena
System Designs I and III, his Phenomenology, and even still in
his late Philosophy of Law and Philosophy of History the
immense suffering of the workers in modern civil society as
mechanical state of necessity and analytical understanding,
making mere cogs in a machine out of them. However that may
be, it is, nevertheless, particularly this dialectical
tradition which originates from Hegel and has been developed
further by the Hegelian Left up to Bloch and Lukacs and the
critical theorists in the Frankfurt School, which Metz invokes
in the framework of German philosophy and social science in
order not to have to respond to the present crisis symptoms
and crisis experiences with a more or less explicit
intellectual defeatism.

However, one may judge in detail the problems and perspectives contained in Metz's political theology: they are
without doubt of greatest importance for the present global
North-South and East-West conflict, on the outcome of which
depends the fate of the human species. In his political theology Metz limits himself to a large extent to philosophical-
theological-cultural question positions. He exercises a strong
semantic control in relation to the religious-political
language of German idealism, particularly Hegel's work. But
such limitations do in no way diminish Metz's political theology in its global significance, but even unbind and increase
its innovative force and creativity. Metz is guided in his
critical political theology by the pathos and ethos to achieve
a helpful work of reconciliation in the face of his own bitter
experiences under German Fascism and during World War II.   In
his political theology Metz tries to actualize anew and renew
creatively those traditions in the German history of culture,
which under National Socialism were miserably misunderstood
and treated with contempt - particularly the dialectical
tradition: the dialectical imagination!

European Dilemma

In the present world historical action situation, the political theologian Metz remembers very acutely that there is such
a thing as a European dilemma not only for the extremely Euro-

pean critical theory of subject, society and history, which
Habermas continues on the basis of a new paradigm in his
theory of communicative praxis, but also for European Chris-
tianity(532). Metz's, Peukert's and Arens's own political
theologies seem to break through Eurocentricity as little as
Habermas's theory of communicative praxis inspite of the best
intent. At least many Americans seem to have a hard time to
"understand" these "continental" theologies and philosophies.
This must be changed!

The charge of Eurocentricity is particularly true for the
Catholic church which followed and accompanied the European
history of modernity more or less passively and defen-
sively(533). It did not participate productively and innova-
tively in the so-called modern history of freedom. It not only
made no essential contribution to the bourgeois, Marxian and
Freudian enlightenment movements represented so competently in
this century by the critical theorists, particularly Habermas,
but even resisted it as much as possible. The church has
mostly opposed with all means available the modern European
history of emancipation. This opposition started with the
Catholic resistance against the first reformation(534). The
so-called "Catholic times" in modern European history were
almost always times of counter-movements: counter-reformation,
counter-enlightenment, counter-revolution, political restoration and romanticism. Catholics have been slow learners in
modern liberation history. All this makes, of course, understandable the furious critique of church and religion by Voltaire, Marx, Blanqui, Freud and many other enlighteners(535).
Therefore most astonishing is the contemporary encounter
between Catholic theologians and modernity: the dialogue of
Rahner and Kung with the philosophy of Kant and Hegel, the
discourse of Metz, Schillerbeeckx, Peukert and Arens with the
critical theorists, more recently with Habermas, shortly the
whole phenomenon of a modern Catholic humanism(536). After the
church has fought democracy so long inside and outside itself,
it is amazing suddenly to hear American bishops say that
political democracy is not enough, but that we need economic
democracy as well.

According to the political theologian Metz, Catholics
can, of course, also say something in defense of their conservative attitude toward modernization and enlightenment(537).
In the political theologian's view this conservative attitude
contains indeed much sensibility for what Horkheimer and
Adorno called the dialectic of enlightenment and which also

Habermas does not deny(538). Catholics felt somehow the inner
contradictions and the fateful and tragic aspects of the
modern history of emancipation.

But the political theologian does not want to and can not
deny the historical neglect, omission and failure, which has
been connected with this conservative Catholic attitude toward
and refusal of the whole project of modernity and enlightenment, which Habermas describes so well and stands for and
intends to and does indeed continue in his universal pragmatic. The negative Catholic attitude has made it at least very
difficult for Catholics to develop a new conjugation of grace
and freedom, adequate to the challenges of modern liberation
history. Precisely such conjugation or coincidentia oppositorum is the essential intent of the critical political
theology.

Messianic Church

For the political theologian Metz, the supersession of this
Catholic dilemma in the late European, late bourgeois, early
socialistic action situation points beyond the monocultural
space of the occidental Christendom toward a messianic world
church(539). This global messianic church learns to invoke and
to represent the grace of God as the holistic liberation of
man(540). It is no longer satisfied with a worldless God or a
Godless world, with unfree grace or graceless freedom. This
messianic church no longer holds captive the God of the
prophets of the Old and New Testament as the feudal and bourgeois church have done. It lets the prophetic and messianic
God loose in the midst of the modern and post-modern liberation history. This messianic church takes seriously the apocalyptic contradictions in late capitalistic action systems
which drive daily closer to the thermonuclear holocaust, and
tries to overcome them in God's grace(541). This messianic
church is ready to pay the price for this, its new historical
conjugation of grace and freedom. The many recent martyrs of
Central America and elsewhere give witness to this(542).

Poor Churches

In the perspective of the political theologian Metz, particularly the poor churches of the third world send messianic as
well as socialistic impulses throughout the global
church(543). Christians of the First World, in Europe or North

America, can not receive and accept these messianic as well as
socialistic impulses when they subordinate themselves all too
fast to all too familiar and not seldom obsolete patterns of
theological images and thoughts. What is at stake in these
messianic and socialistic impulses is a new unity of
experiences of redemption and liberation; a church community,
which enfolds in itself a new relationship of religion and
politics and which understands its fundamental Christian
experience of grace as political mystique of resistance againt
the idolatry of an unjust world, which holds its people in
utter contempt.

Here in the poor churches of the Third World, particularly in the Christian Base Communities, the political theologian
sees the <u>Evangelium</u> positively intervene in a new mode into
modern liberation history, which is also always a history of
suffering(544). Many conservative Christians are frightened by
this new intervention. Habermas and other critical theorists
are not sufficiently aware of it. Particularly the Basic
Christian Communities search for a reflection of the new City
of God among men and women, a mirroring of the messianic polis
in the human history of suffering and liberation. The Base
Communities announce this messianic and socialistic message
and fight for it heroically.

Conservative and Critical Christians

The time is obviously over once and for all in Christian history, when Christians were almost exclusively allied with the
forces on the Right, even fascism(545). We refer to sixteen
centuries of Constantinian Christianity and its own right-wing
political theology. To be sure, Constantinian Christianity has
not yet come to its end. It produces even new shoots in terms
of a new neo-conservative bourgeois Christendom in the USA,
West Germany, Lebanon, Guatemala, and elsewhere, which is
politically rather effective in elections as well as in the
defense of the interests of multinational corporations. But it
is likewise obvious that there is an increasing number of
critical Christians today who are deeply engaged, together
with socialists, in the process of solving conditions of utter
misery in late capitalistic and socialistic action systems and
beyond that in the process of its redemption as well(546).
These critical Christians try to overcome in their speech of
the prophetic and messianic God the conflict between word and
experience(547). These Christians make the attempt, to answer

the quest for meaning posed by non-believing Jews inside and
outside the Frankfurt School, from Marx over Freud to Bloch,
Horkheimer, Adorno, Benjamin, Marcuse and Fromm(548). After
the "death of God," these Christians reflect on the God of the
godless and announce a messianic God to the people, who are
condemned to misery and death in advanced capitalistic and
socialistic action systems(549). They look for the historical
Jesus as the Messiah and for his cross in and through the
Evangelium rather than for the dogmatic Jesus of the
churches(550). They are engaged in a meta-dogmatic interpretation of what is essentially Christian(551). In the midst of
the present world crisis, these Christians are committed to a
communicative, universal ethics of brotherhood and sisterhood,
very much like the one envisioned by Habermas. But they are at
the same time conscious of its roots in the New Testament.
They are living out of this messianic ethics.

At the same time these critical Christians are aware of
the aporetical aspects of this ethics in its secular form,
being no longer theologically grounded(552). In the midst of
the late capitalistic action system, characterized by an
intensive collective as well as individual death drive, which
is even sometimes theologically transfigured in terms of a
last crusade and the Battle of Armageddon, these Christians
stand, work and fight unideologically for world peace and
peace at home: of course, peace with justice(553). They follow
courageously their prophetic impulses in a new messianic
church from below.

Productive Assimilation

Habermas has objected against Benjamin that such messianic
impulses and the anamnestic solidarity connected with them, as
can be found today in Basic Christian Communities, can not
really be transfered from simpler traditional action systems
to highly complex modern action systems(554). They can not be
applied politically and made historically effective. They are
precisely therefore obsolete. The political theologian Metz
takes Habermas's critique very seriously. But then the
political theologian does not really speak of transfering the
messianic impulses and the anamnestic solidarity with the
innocent victims, who have been slaughtered, to present-day
organized capitalistic or socialistic action systems. He
rather speaks of a productive assimilation. It happens in the
learning space and process of the global church. The political

theologian, inspired by Habermas, has himself some doubts if this application or assimilation of the Evangelium, particularly Jesus's "Sermon on the Mount" and his other discourses and quasi-discourses, his parables, illustrations, examples and stories are not after all too immediate, too naive, too much pre-enlightenment, too pre-hermeneutical and finally too reductionistic in relation to our own situation in over-differentiated and overcomplex and as such very abstract and imperceptible late modern action systems. But the political theologian overcomes his doubts, elicited by Habermas's objection and refutes them step by step.

Hermeneutics of Danger

What the political theologian Metz sees at work in the present breakthrough of a new messianic church is not simply bad imme-diacy, the word understood in the Hegelian sense(555). It is rather another form of hermeneutics. It is, to be sure, a po-litical hermeneutics. We can call it in the horizon and framework of Benjamin's "Theses of Philosophy of History" a historical-materialistic hermeneutics of danger(556). Accord-ing to the political theologian, the lightening of danger shines through the whole biblical landscape, particularly the New Testament scenery. Danger and risks permeate axiolog-ically all New Testament statements. The imitatio Christi stories of the synoptics are, as is well known, not simply entertaining narratives. They are also not merely didactic stories. They are rather stories in the face of danger. Jesus enters his discourses and quasi-discourses with and tells his illustrations and examples to opponents, who have long planned to kill him and he is aware of this(557). Jesus's parables are dangerous stories. According to John, Jesus states: "When the world hates you, then you know, that they have hated me already before you. Think of the word, which I told you: the servant is not greater than his master. When they have persecuted me they shall also persecute you"(558). Paul states: "From all sides we are driven into the corner, but we find still room. We do not know where to turn, but we do not despair. We are hunted down, but we are not abandoned. We are cut down, but we are not annihilated"(559). We can not understand the New Testament, when in our hermeneutic the axiological presence of danger is systematically bracketed in. A political theology needs a political hermeneutics and it must be a hermeneutics of danger. Such political hermeneutics is not naive.

The hermeneutics of danger, which the political theologian observes in the breakthrough of a messianic church is indeed reductionistic(560). Praxis returns into pure theory. Mysticism turns into logic. Resistance and suffering returns into the experience of grace and spirit.

According to critical theorists and political theologians all hope of the prophets of the Old and New Testament is reduced to the hope for absolute justice(561). All longing of the prophets of the Old and New Testaments is reduced to the longing that the murderer shall ultimately not triumph over the innocent victim. The "Sermon on the Mount" sides with the innocent victims, who now weep and moan and are hungry for justice against the murderers(562). In the New Testament it is clear who are the murderers and who are the victims. The victim, who has been destroyed, will still have his or her day in court. It is not true, what Brecht says at the end of the City of Mahagonny: that nobody can help the dead man.

The political theologian learns from Benjamin's "Theologico-Political Fragment" that the Messiah will connect the innocent victim with the Messianic realm(563). Thus the dead man or woman can be helped and he or she can help the living. So, Dom Paulo Evaristo Arns, Cardinal of Sao Paolo, tells his Toronto audience, that in case he should be shot by the agents of the Brasilian national security state, he will rise with the Risen Lord and then will help his people in their liberation struggle even better than he can do now. The church can only console the innocent victim, never the non-repentent murderer, who continues his evil work in always new forms. When the church begins to console the non-repentent murderer, it can no longer console the innocent victim.

According to the political theologian the political hermeneutics of danger pulls and pushes Christianity together into this hope and into this longing for perfect justice(564). It throws Christianity back to its very essence, to what is specifically Christian. Certainly such a reduction can not be theologically underestimated. It is also obvious that the Judeo-Christian longing for absolute justice need no special adaptation to modern capitalistic or socialistic action systems. It is easily understood by modern people and precisely therefore all too often furiously resisted.

Faith and Reason

From his early theological writings over his essay on natural
law and the Jena system designs to his late philosophy of
right, history and religion, Hegel is engaged - long before
critical theorists and critical political theologians - in a
new conjugation of the religious and the secular, which in
modernity had moved from difference over antagonism and hate
to indifference and false forms of reconciliation(565). Hegel
reconciles in his philosophy as theodicy, faith and reason,
the divine and the moral, divine and worldly wisdom, divine
and human nature, divine tragedy and tragedy in total morality, divine providence and right, divine reason and wisdom and
history. Hegel's reconciliation remains valid today(566). It
is the basis from which critical theorists and political theologians begin their search for an even better solution(567).
    Hegel's new coincidence of the religious and secular
faith and reason begins in his early theological writ-
ings(568). It continues in the Frankfurt System Program, the
Phenomenology of Spirit, the Jena Critical Writings and the
Jena System Designs, and it is completed in the philosophy of
right, history and religion(569). It is present already in the
Jena System Designs at the same time when Hegel is deeply
engaged not only in the study of Dante, but also of the
political economists(570). In religion, so Hegel argues, in
the Jena System Designs III, spirit becomes object for itself,
as absolute universal or as essence of all nature, of being
and action and in the form of the immediate self(571). Self is
universal knowledge and thereby the return into itself. The
absolute religion, Christianity, is precisely this knowledge
that God is the depth of the spirit, who is conscious of
itself(572). Thereby God is the Self of all. Christianity is
the depth which has come out into the bright daylight(573).
This depth is the "I." It is the notion. It is the absolute
pure power. In Christianity the spirit is reconciled with its
world.
    Habermas breaks once more the Hegelian conjugation of the
religious and the secular, faith and reason, God and world,
redemption and happiness, grace and freedom(574). Thereby he
opens up anew the discourse on the antagonism and the reconciliation of the sacred and the profane, now in the context of
highly complex modern systems of human condition and action
systems.
    Like Horkheimer, Adorno and Benjamin before, Habermas

knows that religion can not be rescued fundamentalistically in opposition to enlightenment(575). Religion has lost all rear-guard struggles against enlightenment for four hundred years. Religion can only be rescued by being rediscovered in the depth of secularity itself. Adorno advised Benjamin to dis-cover the theological glowing fire, the theological and mys-tical notion, in the depth of extremely secular historical materialism and precisely thereby help both alike, theology and dialectical materialism(576). That precisely was the pro-gram of the old Frankfurt School and it remains at least the latent program of Habermas. Maybe Habermas does not even want to realize this program(577). But the fact is that Habermas's theory of communicative praxis does, indeed, have the poten-tial to realize this progam(578). It does this already at present negatively by resisting passionately false forms of conjugation between the religious and the secular, faith and reason in the critical theory as well as in the sociologies and philosophies of Durkheim, Weber, Mead, Parsons, in Amer-ican and German structural functionalism(579). Habermas does help to realize this program by inviting political theologians into practical discourse on the spiritual situation of our time and on politics and culture and by providing for them a paradigm by which to understand newly the texts of the Old and New Testaments as forms of communicative praxis: the dialectic of language and interaction(580).

Christian and Marxist Roots

But Habermas's theory of communicative praxis can help political theologians only, because his brotherly and sisterly communicative action and communication community has itself a religious, specifically messianic and Christian core: "And all who believed were together and held all things in common and would sell their possessions and goods and distribute them among all according as anyone had need. ...Now the multitude of the believers were of one heart and soul, and not one of them said that anything he possessed was his own, but they had all things in common"(581). Those are the Christian roots of Habermas's secular theory of communicative praxis. Habermas may or may not be fully aware of these roots.

But Habermas's theory of communicative action has still other, humanistic roots. It combines in itself the dialectical image of the early Christian brotherly-sisterly communication community with the other dialectical image, which Marx

projects into the future: according to Marx the realm of
freedom, the true communication community, begins indeed only
there, where the realm of necessity, the instrumental
dimension, the realm of work and tools, which is determined by
need, want and external purposiveness, ceases(582). The realm
of freedom lies by its very nature beyond the sphere of
material production: mutual recognition beyond work. As
primitive man must struggle with nature in order to satisfy
his needs and to maintain his life and to reproduce it, so
also civilized man must do. Man must do this in all forms of
society and under all possible modes of production. With man's
development this realm of natural necessity broadens itself,
since his needs become more differentiated. At the same time
the productive forces widen themselves which satisfy these
needs. Freedom in this realm of natural necessity can only
consist in that the socialized man, the associated producers,
regulate rationally this, their metabolism with nature, and
thus bring it under their common control instead of being
dominated by it as a blind fate and power: recognition within
the dimension of labor and tools.

In Marx's view the freely associated producers will
perform the metabolism between society and nature with the
least amount of energy possible and under conditions which are
most worthy of and adequate to their human nature. But this
realm of production will always remain a realm of necessity.
Only beyond this realm of necessity begins the development of
the specific human energies. It is end in itself, purpose for
itself, self-purpose. It is the true realm of freedom. The
limiting of the medium of work and tools is the precondition
for the increase of the medium of mutual recognition, of
interaction and intersubjectivity, of communication without
domination, of brotherly-sisterly communication community
characterized by freedom and equality. The dimension of work
and tools is included in the realm of mutual unconditional
recognition. Habermas is fully aware of the Marxian roots of
his theory of communicative praxis: the dialectic of work and
recognition as well as of interaction and language(583).
Habermas's universal pragmatic is essentially the result of
his reconstruction of historical materialism(584).

Precisely because Habermas has opened up once more in his
extremely secular reconstructed dialectical materialism, his
universal pragmatic, his theory of communicative praxis the
discourse on the disunion and reunion of the religious and the
secular, messianic faith and reason, universal religious

identity and particular secular social identity and singular
secular personal identity, is he able to help political
theologians as they search for a new coincidentia oppositorum,
the coincidence of religious and secular, grace and freedom,
redemption and happiness(585). Habermas opens up in his
discourse on communicative praxis anew the possibility of a
new consensus between enlighteners aware of the dialectic of
enlightenment and believers conscious of the dialectic of
religion, concerning not only religion, but universal solidarity as well(586). Habermas also points in the direction of
alternative forms of communities, in which universal solidarity can be practiced(587).

Basic Christian Communities

One such new form of community life is the Basic Christian
Community in different nations and on different contin-
ents(588). One inspirational force in the worldwide Basic
Christian Community movement is Metz's political theology as
fundamental theology with practical intent(589). The political theologian Arens is not only a theoretician of the Basic
Christian Community movement in Germany and Europe, but he is
also practically engaged in it(590). He is an active member of
the Basic Christian Community of Frankfurt a.M., Germany. The
Basic Christian Community movement is part of the praxis
fundamental theology intends as theology of communicative
praxis. Political theology has its seat in life in this movement. It is rooted in this movement. It is the reflection of
this movement. It finds its realization in and through this
movement. In spite of the fact that Habermas lives and works
mainly in the German Federal Republic, in Munich and now again
in Frankfurt, and that he is in continual communication with
political theologians in Frankfurt and Munster, Germany, and
Boston College, Boston, Mass., USA, he seems not to be sufficiently aware of the German, European or international Basic
Christian Community movement and its protest potential(591).
    According to the fundamental theologian Arens, the
Frankfurt Basic Christian Community is part of the "Coordination Circle of Basic Groups and Communities" in the German
Federal Republic(592). This Coordination Circle embraces more
than thirty German Basic Christian Communities. The first aim
of the German Coordination Circle and of the particular Basic
Communities which carry it, is to broaden and intensify the
network of the still relatively small German Basic Christian

Community movement and to invite more groups and communities
to extend and to intensify the network. The basic community
groups meet regularly on Sundays. The members read the bible
with each other and pray and break the bread and share a meal
and in discourse discuss their projects and coordinate their
life plans.

Provocation

In the German Federal Republic, as in Holland, Italy, Poland,
USA, Nicaragua and elsewhere, the Basic Christian Communities
constitute a problem for the larger, more conservative Christian Churches(593). Their very existence can mean a provocation for a hierarchical church too well adjusted to the
overall bourgeois action system of which it is a part. The
Basic Christian Community is very often a thorn in the flesh
of the hierarchical church, warning and acting in the name of
the prophets of the Old and New Testaments against the
Church's overadaptation to capitalistic society. But even in
the non-conformist German Catholicism, which insists against
pressure from above, the hierarchical church, on a self-
responsible and accountable appropriation and continuation of
the Second Vatican Council from below, by the critical laity
and clergy, scepticism has arisen concerning the Basic Christian Community movement. To some critics from the otherwise
rather progressive "Priest and Solidarity Groups" in the
German Federal Republic the Basic Communities appear as a
"fad." According to the critics, Basic Communities may have
their place in the underprivileged strata and poor majorities
of the populations in Latin America. Such Basic Communities
may be imitated in the Federal Republic. But such _mimesis_
appears to be a rather cocette enterprise. The Basic Christian
Communities take this criticism seriously and reflect it into
their theory and praxis.

Imitatio Christi

Political theology contains the biblical category of the "following of Christ," the Messianic _mimesis_, the _Imitatio
Christi_: Jesus's discourse mediated communicative praxis is to
be followed tendentially in the modern action situation(594).
The political theologian Arens takes this category of
"following Christ" very seriously(595). Therefore the
fundamental theologian can comprehend very well how it differs

from a mere "imitation." He knows that Basic Communities in
Europe and the German Federal Republic are not just a matter
of foreign import of the exotic lifestyle of the "little
people" in Latin America. In the view of the theologian of
communicative praxis, the following of Christ does indeed have
its place in the German ecclesiastical as well as social
reality. This is so, since considered in world perspective,
the German social reality is an exploiter-situation and the
German ecclesiastical reality a situation of hierarchical
power and administrative colonization with broad and basic
effects, which can be very much felt and experienced by the
people below. The Theology Department at the University of
Frankfurt, situated only a few steps away from Horkheimer's
Institute for Social Research, can, e.g, not train theologians
for the Catholic dioceses, because some of the members of its
staff are laicized priests. The rather liberal bishop of
Limburg, Germany, in whose territory Frankfurt lies, has
decreed precisely this policy. The intellectual quality of the
theologians is not in question. Arens is a lay theologian and
as such a member of the Theological Faculty at the University
of Frankfurt. He has never been a priest. But he shares the
difficulties imposed on his Department by the hierarchical
church.

Metanoia

To be sure, Basic Christian Communities in the German Federal
Republic are not yet a church of the poor as it is the case in
Latin American countries(596). As in other Western European
countries, the members of the Basic Communities originate
mainly from the lower and middle bourgeoisie. According to the
political theologian Arens, the German and other European
Basic Christian Communities are, nevertheless, the sign of a
church which turns away from the total identification with the
existing conditions in late capitalistic action systems. They
are signs of metanoia, of an anthropological revolution(597).
In the fundamental theologian's view, he who today wants to
engage in metanoia must understand the word of God in what is
given and demanded here and now in this present action
situation(598). Once the political theologian Hegel demanded
that people should find out what God is doing in the world
through the morning paper(599). The new Basic Christian
Communities take the bible in one hand and the newspaper in
the other(600). The Basic Communities engage in what Habermas

calls interaction and discourse, and they constitute what he
identifies as   protest   potential in late capitalistic action
systems(601).

Word of God

The political theologian Arens reports that in many places in
the German Federal Republic men and women begin in small
circles, house communities, initiative circles to take up the
bible and begin to comprehend the words of the God who "has
pulled down princes from their thrones and exalted the lowly;
the hungry he has filled with good things, the rich sent empty
away" in the context of their familial, professional, occupa-
tional, ecclesiastical, social, economic and political action
situations(602). They read the parables of Jesus, the stories
of the primitive Christian Community and the reports about the
conflicts in the Corinthian Church and thus, through scrip-
ture, come to a deeper Christian interpretation of their reality and orientation of their action. They read the psalms a-
gainst the background of the armament insanity in late capitalistic action systems and the creation story in the face of
the environmental destruction.
       Franzioni, the former abbot and present-day member of the
Basic Community of St. Paul Before The Walls, in Rome, calls
the reappropriation of the word of God the central element in
the Basic Christian Community movement. The Basic Christian
Communities rediscover once more, as Hegel before, the revolutionary God of the prophets of the Old and the New Testaments.
They are Christian-socialistic in content in late capitalistic
as well as in bureaucratic-socialistic action systems(603). As
they remember their own dangerous memoria vitae, passionis,
mortis et resurrectionis Christi, and practice it they are
able to call upon bureaucratic socialists to remember their
own dangerous revolutionary remembrance and to act out of
it(604).

Ecclesial Community

The political theologian Arens stresses that the Basic Communities are ecclesial communities(605). Like the primitive
Christian Community they pray with each other and break
bread(606). In the German Federal Republic as well as in other
European countries, the members of the Basic Communities can
break bread only in the consciousness that they belong to a

rich, satisfied nation and rich and satisfied church, who have
occupied the first place at the table(607). Therefore Basic
Communities give to the last at the table as much as possible.
They try to share with the poor, particularly in Latin
America, at least two percent of their income. Beyond that,
the Basic Communities in Germany and Europe let themselves be
questioned by the poor churches of Latin America. They are
even willing to accept a present from the Latin American
churches: the Basic Christian Community.

The political theologian is fully aware of the fact that
Latin American Christianity has been delivered for centuries
to the Christian occidental colonialism and empirialism and is
still held captive by it under the mask of the multinational
corporations, e.g., the United Fruit Company and its sub-
sidiaries. The European Basic Christian Communities give
highest recognition to the poor nations of Latin America and
to their suffering. Out of this highest respect, the European
Basic Communities accept the spiritual fruits of such suffering. The Basic Christian Community movement itself is such a
fruit.

Revolutionary Ferment

The fundamental theologian Arens remembers that the Bishops
conference of Medellin has called the Basic Christian Community the "Church of Christ itself"(608). Marins, former direc-
tor of the clergy section of the Brasilian Conference of
Bishops says of the Basic Christian Communities that they,
precisely because they are the church, are something extremely
dangerous(609). That is so, since the church itself is dangerous. The Basic Community is not only containing protest
potential. It is a revolutionary ferment in history, since it
tries to rebuild the world with the values and criteria of
Christ. The Basic Christian Community rediscovers as ecclesial
community Hegel's insight into the revolutionary character not
only of God, but also of Jesus and the church(610). The Basic
Christian Community overcomes the split, which Hegel had
discovered between God as absolute freedom and the unfree
church allied with reactionary political forces(611).

Biblical Message and Social Reality

According to the political theologian Arens, people in Germany
need Basic Christian Communities, precisely because the Church

from above, the hierarchical church in the German Federal
Republic, is not at all dangerous and revolutionary, but
rather well adapted to the late capitalistic action system and
well known for such adaptation(612). Often the language of the
parish priest in German bourgeois churches has great
similarity with that of a travel guide, who most cheerfully
accompanies his comfortable guests on their trip through the
Alps telling them about the beauty of the landscape and the
delicious lunch coming up in the next inn. Sometimes priests
who leave their vocation do in reality join the travel
industry.

Of course, the German Basic Christian Communities themselves are still far away from being revolutionary ferment.
They do not yet have the revolutionary spirit of the Basic
Christian Base Communities in Chile, Nicaragua, El Salvador
and other Latin American countries(613). But in the German and
European Basic Christian Community movement there do take
place, nevertheless, first beginnings, attempts, steps toward
a new connection between biblical message and social reality.
In practical discourse with each other and in common prayer,
the German and European Basic Communities learn to take the
word, to open the mouth, to stand up, to walk upright, to make
public use of faith and reason in matters of war and hunger,
political oppression, ecological destruction and general
alienation. The German and European Basic Christian
Communities are fully aware of their historical position
between World War I, fascism and World War II, on the one
hand, and the threat of World War III and of thermonuclear
annihilation, on the other(614). Therefore, the Basic
Christian Communities make the attempt at a new conjugation of
revelation and reason, redemption and happiness, faith and
enlightenment, grace and freedom, in advanced capitalistic and
socialistic systems of human condition and action systems.

Solidarity and Identity

According to the political theologian Arens, the German Basic
Christian Communities make continually the very important
experience of their powerlessness in relation to the powerful
forces in the economic, political and ecclesiastical subsystems of the highly differentiated late capitalistic German
action system: big business, party bosses, bishops and arch-
bishops(615). The Basic Communities experience the closeness
of Jesus particularly in their experience of such helplessness

in the face of their being colonized in their very life world
by the economic, political and ecclesiastical subsystems, by
monetarization and bureaucratization(616). They share this
experience of helplessness with the friends of Jesus during
the sea storm, when they cried: "Lord, we go under!" Paradoxically enough, thus precisely they find help in Jesus.
German Basic Community Christians belong to the powerless.
They identify with the powerless. They share in the solidarity of the powerless among each other. They participate in
this solidarity of the powerless in common protest and resistance against economic, political and ecclesiastical violation
of the right of the people to a dignified, good and free life
of All. Such solidarity binds German Basic Community Christians together among each other and connects them with the
Basic Christian Communities of other countries and continents:
Poland, Holland, Italy, USA, Chile, Brazil, Nicaragua, etc.
Through such solidarity the Basic Communities gain their
Christian identity.

Messianic Imput

In the perspective of the political theologian Arens, the
Basic Christian Communities in the German Federal Republic
have originated from the experience of deficiencies in the
German bourgeois church: the lack of Eucharistic community in
the traditional parish, the lack of liberating praxis in
communication with each other and of solidarity with the
exploited in the German Federal Republic, particularly foreign
workers from Turkey, Greece and elsewhere, and with the
oppressed and exploited in other parts of the world, the lack
of a Christian inspired connection and conjugation of faith
and politics(617). The German Christian Democratic Party can
provide Christian or democratic inspiration as little as the
same type of party can do this in Italy or in Chile or in El
Salvador or elsewhere. Where such deficiency experiences tend
to come together and to accumulate and to be shared in the
parish, the messianic impulses of individuals call out and
call together. A Basic Christian Community comes into
existence.

Ecumenism and Internationalism

According to the political theologian Arens's observations,
Basic Christian Communities look beyond the boundaries of

their church and the borders of the nation, to which they belong(618). They are ecumenical as well as international in their orientation. Basic Christian Communities, being ecumenical and international in inspiration, see that revolution fermentation takes place also in other European countries and on other continents at the basis of the church, which is not everywhere also the social basis, but basis, nevertheless. This revolutionary fermentation is much more pronounced in the Netherlands, most intensely before the doors of the Roman Curia, in Italy, in France, Spain and Portugal as well as in Poland and Hungary, than in Germany or the USA. The Bolletino Europeo, a contact letter of the European Basic Christian Communities, starts from Isolotto, Italy and appears in Italy, German Federal Republic, the Netherlands, Belgium, France and Portugal. It contributes to the direct exchange of different Basic Christian Community movements in Europe among each other.

Prophetic Power

Basic Christian Communities are not, so the political theologian Arens insists, a better or other church than the one which has existed so far through almost twenty centuries(619). The Basic Christian Community movement rather reclaims the prophetic power of the biblical message in an all too administered church for this very church. The Basic Christian Communities are a critical force in the powerful bureaucratic, ecclesiastical institutions of the Roman Catholic, Orthodox or Protestant church. They are not other ecclesiastical organizations or ecclesiastical counter-institutions outside the bureaucratic ecclesiastical institutions of the main traditional churches. They are the traditional church's internal, loyal but prophetic opposition(620).

In the political theologian's view to be revolutionary fermentation inside of all the traditional churches, from which the members of the ecumenically oriented Basic Christian Communities originate, means for the Basic Communities themselves to resist the inclination toward an elitist immunization against and self-isolation from the defective power churches(621). It means not to give up the friction with the traditional bureaucratic ecclesiastical institutions and at the same time to avoid the danger of sectarianism. Basic Christian Communities must endure in the old churches, even if that is very difficult in the face of the hardening of the traditional church from above, the hierarchical church and its present restoration. The basic Christian Communities are able to achieve all this out of the consciousness that they themselves are the church. They do not allow themselves to be maneuvered out of their being the church by those who pretend alone to be the church. The prophetic and messianic power of the Basic Communities must assert itself inside the structure of the traditional church.

Messianic Interest

The Basic Christian Community in Germany, West and East Europe, USA, Canada, Latin America and elsewhere has come into existence from below, out of the interest of its members(622). It is a community of believers, which is determined by this very interest, the interest of a messianic faith, messianic interest. These believers pray with each other and celebrate the liturgy. They share the bread and the wine and their life with each other. The Basic Christian Community knows itself as the church of Jesus the Christ, which looks through what Metz calls the unchristian bourgeois ideology of the purely religious community(623). It is no longer a feudal or bourgeois church. It is a messianic church. The Basic Christian Community constitutes a new epoch in the history of the church, after the Judeo-Christian and Greco-Roman epoch.

The Basic Christian Community is not willing to pay the price with which the bourgeois church is paid for: lack of political consciousness, fear to touch social, economic, political, historical conflicts, coldness and lack of relationships(624). Basic Christian Community tries to supersede the bourgeois apocalyptic dichotomy of life between religious and secular, faith and reason, individual and collective, work and leisure, politics and religion, public and private, producer and consumer, owner and worker, luxury and misery, rich and poor classes, nations and continents(625). For the Basic Christian Community faith is inspiration and source of energy for political action, for engagement on the side of the oppressed at home or abroad. One of the leading motives of the Basic Christian Community is resistance, the Pauline: "I have resisted into his face," the "protestant principle"(626). This leading motive includes the resistance against the Basic Community members' own apathy, against the increasing resignation of consumerism as well as against the lobbyists for nuclear power, armament and exploitation of non-renewable resources, who endanger the life of the human species for their own exaggerated profits.

Messianic Engagement

According to the political theologian Arens, in the Basic Christian Comunity the engagement for the kingdom of God, which Jesus describes in his parables, illustrations, examples and stories, is materialized and concretized(627). This messianic engagement is practiced in the communication of the members of the Basic Christian Community with each other, in search of new forms of communication, in the always to be struggled for readiness to break out of fixed role expectations and ritualized forms of interaction, in tough struggles for binding commitment and friendship. All this gives energy and encouragement again to the members of Basic Communities for new real commitment and engagement. In the Basic Community converge the becoming-subject of the members in solidarity with each other and the engagement for the being-subject of all people. No man should be treated merely as a thing or an instrument. Basic Christian Communites aim at what Habermas and Apel call personal and social identity in communicative praxis, universal solidarity and communication community(628).

Intervention

Basic Christian Communities intervene, according to the political theologian Arens, practically into the daily happenings in city, town or village, school or university, office or factory, wherever they are situated(629). They practically interfere as much as possible in the conflicts of their city block, the commune, the university and even into high politics. Basic Communities give public witness through political actions and petitions, by writing letters and making visits, in work for the Third World and in work for a district in the city, in citizens-initiative and self-help organizations, in the engagement of body and soul, physical and intellectual labor, and through sacrifice of time, energy and money for the realization of the biblical message of liberation.

Plurality of Forms

The political theologian Arens knows that Basic Christian Communities in the German Federal Republic, in Europe, in Latin

America and North America and on other continents   take many
different forms and shapes(630). They are local communities
with territorial structure. They have moved out of the non-
binding reality of a mere bourgeois Sunday—Christendom. They
are personal communities with 30-40 members. Often their
partially academic formation brings along sharp social
sensibility and an intense consciousness for social conflicts.
But those Basic Communities usually do not represent the
bottom of society and the underside of history. Other Basic
Communities are communities of emigrant and migrant workers,
who reflect their social situation in a foreign country in the
light of the biblical promise of <u>Exodus</u> and liberation from
servitude. Other Basic Communities are initiative groups,
which are not fixed toward a definite goal of action, but
simply share life with each other. Some Basic Communities are
house- and living-communities, which bring together everyday
life and action, on the one hand, and liturgy and prayer on
the other. As can easily be seen, Basic Christian Communities
are a very colorful mosaic of Christian cells in Germany,
Europe, Latin America, North America, etc. They constitute a
large plurality of social forms.

Liberation Message

In the political theologian Arens's perspective, the Basic
Christian Community is in the colorful plurality of all its
forms a socially critical, self-critical, politically active
community of Christians, which is carried by the liberation
message of the <u>Evangelium</u>(631). It exists everywhere, where
Christians stand up in public life of church or state; where
they discover the biblical message as the liberation message
for the poor and the oppressed, which breaks into the open
again on the dark backside of world history; where they put
into question in late capitalistic action systems their own
bourgeois private Christianity, which goes very well along
with politically unconscious middle class high-living-standard
consumer orientation; where they take the side of the socially
discriminated and exploited in advanced capitalistic or
bureaucratic-socialistic action systems and against worldwide
exploitation. Basic Christian Communities exist, wherever
Christians are counterfactually committed to absolute justice;
where they consistently side the the innocent victims against
the murderers, be they direct or indirect murderers, murderers
in low or high positions in late capitalistic or socialistic

action systems. Basic Christian Communities come into being wherever Christians associate themselves freely with other Christians and look for allies among other believers, e.g., Buddhists, Jews or Muslems, or among humanists and socialists, for their engagement for the church from below and a solidaristic society. Basic Christian Community comes about wherever Christians become future oriented: where they try at least to mitigate Future I – the totally administered, cyberneticized, militaristic, computerized, neo–cesaristic society; to resist with all their energy the arrival of Future II – ABC wars, the thermonuclear holocaust, and to promote passionately Future III – the reconciled society, the rational society in terms of practical, communicative brotherly– sisterly rationality, the victimless society, the universal communication community characterized by freedom in universal solidarity and by non–possessive love(632).

Abandonment and Trust

In conclusion, I would like to return once more and to refer narratively as well as reflectively to Berrigan's Uncommon Prayer, which my wife gave me for a present on Father's Day, June 18, 1978, four months before her cancer death(633). When in April 1978 I left Kalamazoo for a short time, following Margie's urgent wish, in order to direct the international course on the Future of Religion which we both had founded the year before in the Inter University Centre for Postgraduate Studies, Dubrovnik, Yugoslavia, I wrote on the cover page of the bible, which we read daily, a departure memento from the "Our Father": "ne inducas nos in tentationem, sed libera nos a malo"(634). The prayer did not reach its goal. In the coming months we were led deeper and deeper into the temptation of utter abandonment and we were not liberated from evil. To the contrary, the evil grew daily and no redemption was in sight. As Margie put it in a talk she gave to a group of students at Kanley Chapel, Western Michigan University, about her terminal illness: there was no light at the end of the tunnel! But strangely enough in this her most cruel abandonment, in the face of growing evil, Margie was never entirely without trust. Margie found both this abandonment and this trust most adequately expressed in Berrigan's equivalent of Psalm 73 and Psalm 46, published in his book, Uncommon Prayer(635).

In her dedication of Berrigan's Uncommon Prayer to me on Father's Day 1978, Margie summed up very shortly and simply

the political theology we had been committed to in theory and
praxis throughout   our   life and work together in Europe, the
USA and   Canada   and   particularly   in our   "Basic   Christian
Community"   in Kalamazoo, Michigan. Margie's loving dedication
reads: "To Rudi - who brings a fiery sword yet comes also as
reconciler   and consoler, a man who belongs to the prophets of
old and yet whose voice is new   and   fresh   in   the   twentieth
century   and   into the future. You ancient and yet new man - I
love you, your Margie." For us political theology   was   always
prophetic   and messianic theology and as such it was polemical
as well as reconciling in intent. We let ourselves   be   guided
by   such   political   theology through Inferno, Purgatorio, and
Paradisio(636).
      When one day during my teaching at   Waterloo   University,
Waterloo,   Ontario,   Canada,   I   picked up Berrigan's Uncommon
Prayer from Margie's night table, I found on   page   53,   Psalm
73:   "And Where in the World are You?" - a handwritten note by
her. Margie had written this note one day during the long hot
month   of   July, 1978, in Kitchener, Ontario, when she was very
much in pain from the expanding cancer in her liver and   right
lung   and   the   chemotherapy   and   the long range destructive
effects of radiation. She had just had prayed Psalm   73.   The
note   says: "Rudi Dear! See this picture (it is a picture of a
badly tortured man hanging head down   from   the   ceiling,   his
hands   bound   to   his   feet. The picture is connected to Psalm
73.) That's how I feel sometimes with pain. I know God is in
this   world   -   but,   really - where is he at times? If you're
still doing questioning about God in class could you use this
psalm   (if you haven't already)? I think it is very powerful."
In Berrigan's translation, Psalm 73 reads:

        I see the wicked glide by
        sleek in their velvet hearses
        rich beyond measure, egos
        puffed like an adder's

        no sons of misfortune these:
        no cares
        shadow the perfumed brows
        a wirligig of furies
        their axletree cuts;
        the innocent die.

            I sweat like a beast

for the fate of my people.
Is God ignorant, blank eyed
deaf, far distant
bought off, grown old?

They rape the fair world
they butcher, huckster
by the pound, living flesh;
their guns, their gimlets
claim us for trophy.

Why then endure
why thirst for justice?
Your kingdom come
a mirage never comes.

I sweat like a beast,
my nightmare is life long
And where in the world are you?(637)

For Margie Psalm 73 became the expression of her utter
abandonment. It signified one aspect of our political theology
which we had shared throughout our life together. We read this
psalm during Margie's funeral in St. Thomas More University
Chapel in Kalamazoo and gave a sermon on it: Margie's eulogy.

The very friendly but also very conservative bishop of
Kalamazoo had not noticed Margie's year of terminal suffering
up to the very end. But the bishop participated in Margie's
funeral. He listened to Psalm 73 and my sermon which followed
it. Afterwards the bishop told a friend, "I love this man, but
I do not understand him." The bishop could not comprehend
Psalm 73 and my sermon based on it and the suffering they
expressed. For the bishop Mary is the one through whom, as
being saved from sin, darkness will disappear, the darkness of
evil and death. But the bishop forgets that Mary, in spite of
being preserved from sin, had to live through abandoned and
helplessly the execution of her son and all the darkness of
evil surrounding it. The bishop also forgets Mary's
magnificat: "He has put down the mighty from their thrones and
has exalted the lowly. He has filled the hungry with good
things, and the rich he has sent away empty"(638). The bishop
is a pious man: he does not eat meat on Friday even after
Rome's dispensation. The bishop is a good man: he tries to
help the migrant workers. He bears bravely the sufferings of

his office. But that the catastrophe is precisely that things continue as they do and that this oppressive continuity is to be broken and that there must be the "Behold, I make all things new" - such thoughts are foreign to the bishop(639).

The bishop administers his diocese in the state of Michigan. It is the state of Henry Ford, who once said: "History is bunk." The stability of the system of Fordism and Taylorism and the totalitarianism, dictatorship and idolatry of the market(640) requires the repression of anamnesis: Christian bourgeois, Marxian or Freudian remembrance of suffering. The system demands the chronical amnesia of the innocent victims. The bishop does not know what fascism was and is. He does not know if the Vietnam war was just or unjust. The bishop does not like to remember the new martyrs of Latin America, his own prophetic and messianic brothers and sisters who have been imprisoned, tortured and slaughtered for liberation and redemption. If the stigmatized and martyred priests and sisters in Latin Amerca and elsewhere, so the bishop argues, would only not follow the "wrong theology" - liberation theology - and if they would serve their masters well, they would not have to suffer so much. The same could of course be said of Jesus of Nazareth. Memoria itself seems to have become dangerous and subversive and as such it is to be suppressed. Thus critical and progressive Christians are marginalized systematically and without end in diocese and state. For some of our conservative friends Margie's funeral was not only too theological, but most of all too political. The remembrance of the innocent victim is to be privatized! Obviously, Psalm 73 is not an establishment psalm for church or state. It is critical and revolutionary! So is the Magnificat! So is the Sermon on the Mount! So is the Apocalypse! So is the whole prophetic and messianic Christianity!

Several months after Margie's death I found another handwritten note of hers in Berrigan's Uncommon Prayer, which previously I must have overlooked. Margie put the note on page 35 of the Uncommon Prayer, to Psalm 46, The Lord is Lord, our Refuge, our Strength. Margie's note says: "Rudi Dear! How do you - how can one reconcile this psalm with psalm 73 (p. 53). Are there some dialectics involved? Probably!!!" Psalm 46 reads:

Mountains topple, streams halt in their tracks
Earth flushes and pales, storm upon calm pell mell
Time traces, retraces its steps like a sleepwalking sentry,

No matter. The Lord is Lord, our refuge, our strength.

There's a river I know of: in its arms
the city of God rests secure.
Turmoil, unrest, a fevered succession of powers?

No matter. The Lord is Lord, our refuge, our strength.

He breaks in its socket the fiery fasces of war
arrows and lances, rockets, obscene machinations
the idols we make he unmakes, false gods, cheap salvation.

Rejoice. The Lord is Lord, our refuge, our strength(641).

For Margie, Psalm 46 was an expression of her trust in
the midst of her abandonment. It signified the other aspect of
the political theology we shared: our political theology and
praxis was characterized by the dialectic of abandonment and
trust; of the closedness and the openness of history; of the
insight in the malum metaphysicum and the mala physica of
nature and history and the trust that not only world history
is world judgment, but that there will be the Last Judgment,
in which the innocent victim shall ultimately be justified.

Thursday, October 19, 1978, was a grey and cold day.
Thursday was always the day when I took Margie for chemotherapy to the cancer ward of Victoria Hospital, London, Ontario.
But on this Thursday I could not drive Margie to her treatment
since she had begun to hemorrhage. Blood was expected to flow
out of Margie's eyes, ears, nose and other openings of the
body. After I had told Margie that we could not go for chemotheraphy today, big tears ran out of her eyes down her starved
face and she said: "I am so disappointed! I am so disappointed!" Shortly afterwards Margie had a hard time getting
her breath. She felt as if tons of weight were pressing on her
chest. I held Margie in my arms until the ambulance came to
take her to Victoria Hospital for oxygen and for drugs to make
dying easier. When evening came and darkness set over the
Thames River which flows through London and right by Victoria
Hospital, Dr. White, the oncologist, came into Margie's room a
last time to check her condition. On the way out he told me
that it was utterly amazing that Margie had lived so long. She
was quite a lady! She should have died weeks ago. But now it
would take only a few hours and she would lose her
consciousness and she would die. The nurses would stand by

with the necessary drugs in case they were needed. The doctor left for home. When I returned to Margie she asked me what "White" had said. Since I did not want to repeat what the doctor had said I simply mentioned that the family had permission to stay in the hospital overnight. But Margie did not take any excuses any longer. She said quietly: "The end will come during the night." I asked Margie, "How do you know?" She anwered, "I feel it!" After a little while I asked Margie if in spite of all the horrible injustices which had happened to her during the past year, we should, nevertheless, continue to hold on in our family to faith, hope and love as we had done before throughout our life together. Margie answered with a clear and definite "Yes." This yes was Margie's final affirmation of her non-possessive love and her hope for the ultimate abolishment of death in the midst of destruction and annihilation. When Margie's end finally came between 2:00 and 3:30 a.m. on Friday morning her face turned under the strain of heavy breathing into the expression of unending silent weeping until it froze into deadly seriousness: Dies irae, dies illa!

There happened among us, the family, who surrounded protectively Margie's small dead body in the dark hospital room above the icy cold waters of the Thames River a coincidence of extreme opposites: infinite sadness, but not entirely without consolation: both united in the patient hope that the murderer shall not triumph over the innocent victim and that absolute justice will be done, ultimately. We can continue to love after the death of the innocent other, since the victim herself has done so to the bitter end. Non-possessive devotion and the liquidation of death is the highest in critical theory and political theology. In any case, the one who survives must forget nothing: neither the most cruel abandonment nor the faithful, hopeful and loving trust of the innocent victim. It is possible that the abandonment shall destroy the trust. That is nihilism! It is the great temptation of people living in the dialectic of late civil society. But there is also the possibility that the trust will conquer the abandonment: the possibility of the fulfilled life, the good state, the free humanity and the messianic redemption in God's Kingdom(642).

Notes

Chapter I: Theory of Communicative Praxis

[1]D. Horster, "Ein Marxistischer Kant" in Frankfurter Hefte, 35/2, February 1980, 58. (FH)

[2]J. Habermas, Theorie des Kommunikativen Handelns, Bd. I: Handlungsrationalitat und gesellschaftliche Rationalisierung; Bd. II: Zur Kritik der funktionalistischen Vernunft, Frankfurt: Suhrkamp, 1981. -Vorstudien und Erganzungen zur Theorie des Kommunikativen Handelns, Frankfurt: Suhrkamp, 1984. -J. B. Thompson, etc. (eds.), Habermas: Critical Debates, Cambridge, MA: MIT Press 1982, 219–283. -R. Bubner, "Rationalitat als Lebensform: Zu Jurgen Habermas 'Theorie des Kommunikativen Handelns'" in Merkur 4/36, April 1982, 341–355. -W. Abendroth, Sozialgeschichte der Europaischen Arbeiter-bewegung, Frankfurt: Suhrkamp Verlag 1969, chs. 5–7.

[3]A. Arato and E. Gebhardt, The Essential Frankfurt School Reader, New York: Continuum 1982, vii–xxi; parts I–III; 3–25, 185–224, 371–406. -M. Jay, The Dialectical Imagination: A History of the Frankfurt School and the Institute of Social Research 1923–1950, Boston: Little, Brown and Company 1973, chs. 1–8. -R. Wiggerhaus, "Die Zeitschrift fur Sozialfor-schung–eine Aufforderung zur aktualitatsbezogenen Gesell-schaftstheorie" in FH 35/10, October 1980, 49–54. -H. Scheible, "Max Horkheimer's fruhe und spate Aufzeichnungen" in FH 33/6, June 1978, 50–54. -H. Willig, "Die Aktualitat der kritischen Theorie Adorno's" in FH 35/3, March 1980, 55–64. -J. P. Scott, "Critical Social Theory: An Introduction and Critique" in British Journal of Sociology, XXIX/1, March 1978, 1–21. -Th. W. Adorno, Sociologische Schriften, Frankfurt: Suhrkamp 1972, 245–279. -L. Lowenthal and N. Guterman, Prophets of Deceit, Palo Alto, CA: Pacific Books 1970, v–xiii, xv–xvii.

[4]Horster, "Ein Marxistische Kant," op. cit., 59.

[5]M. Heidegger, Introduction to Metaphysics, New Haven: Yale University Press, 1959.

[6]G. Lukacs, History and Class Consciousness, Cambridge, MA:

MIT   Press   1976,   chs.   1,   3-5,   8.   —M. Horkheimer and
Th. W. Adorno, The Dialectics of Enlightenment, New York:
Herder and Herder 1972, 9-17. —G. Lukacs, Schriften zur
Ideologie und Politik, Neuwied: Luchterhand 1967, chs. 2-6,
9-10, 15, 19-20, 24. —Die Zerstorung der Vernunft, Darmstadt:
Hermann Luchterhand, 1974. —Deutsche Literatur in zwei
Jahrhunderten, Neuwied: Hermann Luchterhand 1964, Part III.

[7] J. Habermas,   Strukturwandel   der Offentlichkeit, Berlin:
Hermann Luchterhand 1976, 7-9, 13-41.

[8] D. Horster, "Kommunikative Ethik," in FH 37/10, October 1982,
35-41. —Ch. Jamme and H. Schneider (eds.), Mythologie der
Vernunft, Frankfurt: Suhrkamp 1984, 11-14. —G. W. F. Hegel,
Jenaer Kritische Schriften, Hamburg: Felix Meiner 1968, 58-59,
417-464, 467-485. (GW4) —R. J. Siebert, "Hegel on the
dialectic of civil society" in Procedures of the International
Hegel Society, Athens 1985.

[9] Horster,   "Ein   marxistischer   Kant,"   op. cit.   61-62.
—W. Muller, Geld und Geist. Zur Entstehungseschichte von
Identitatsbewusstsein   und   Rationalitat   seit   der   Antike,
Frankfurt/New York, 1977. —A. Sohn-Rethel, Okonomie und
Klassen-struktur des deutschen Faschismus, Frankfurt: Suhrkamp
1975, 7-38; and Geistige und Korperlich Arbeit, Frankfurt:
Suhrkamp 1973, parts I and II.

[10] J. Habermas,   Zur   Rekonstruktion   des   Historischen
Materialismus, Frankfurt: Suhrkamp 1976, chs. 1-2, esp. 6.

[11] Horster, "Ein marxistischer Kant," op. cit. 62. —Adorno,
Soziologische Schriften, op. cit. 280-353.   —J. Habermas,
"Einleitung zum Vortrag von Martin Jay" in L. von Friedeburg
and J. Habermas, Adorno-Konferenz 1983, Frankfurt: Suhrkamp
1983, 351-353. —Th. W. Adorno, et al., Der Positivismusstreit
in der deutschen Soziologie, Darmstadt: Hermann Luchterhand
1980, 7-79, 81-101, 125-143, 155-191, 235-266.

[12] J. Habermas, Legitimation Crisis, Boston: Beacon Press 1975,
parts II and III.

[13] K. Marx, Das Kapital, Berlin: Dietz 1961, 17-18. —Siebert,
"Hegel," op. cit.

[14]Marx, Kapital, op. cit., 17-18, 529, 539, 617, 634; 394, 844; 490, 492, 527. -Abendroth, Sozial-Geschichte, op. cit., chs. 5-7. -G. F. Bloom and H. R. Northrup, Economics of Labour Relations, Homewood, Ill: R. D. Irwin 1961, 418-420, 472-474. -N. W. Chamberlain, The Labor Sector, New York: McGraw-Hill Book Company 1965, 19.

[15]Habermas, Theorie, Bd. 1, I,2; II, 2,3; B2, V2,3.

[16]Habermas, D. Henrich, Zwei Reden, Frankfurt: Suhrkamp 1974, 25-75. -Habermas, Zur Rekonstruktion, op. cit., ch. 4.

[17]Habermas, Theorie, op. cit., ch. II, V, VII-VIII. -Habermas, Vorstudien, op. cit., ch. 1, 2, 7. -Horster, "Ein marxistischer Kant," op. cit., 62. -Adorno, Soziologische Schriften, op. cit., Part I.

[18]J. Habermas, Zur Logik der Sozialwissenschaften, Frankfurt: Suhrkamp 1973, parts I-IV. -Adorno, Soziologische Schriften, op. cit., 547-565.

[19]Adorno, Der Positivismusstreit, op. cit., 125-143. -B. F. Skinner, Beyond Freedom and Dignity, Toronto: Bantam Books 1980, chs. 1-4, 7-9. -Walden Two, New York: The MacMillan Co., 1962, chs. 1-12.

[20]M. Horkheimer, Notizen 1950 bis 1969 und Dammerung, Frankfurt: S. Fischer 1974, 101-104, 116-117. -Adorno, Sozialogische Schriften, op.cit., 245-279, esp. 246-247.

[21]Th. W. Adorno, "Offenbarung oder autonome Vernunft" in FH 13/6, 397. -W. Benjamin, Schriften I, Frankfurt, 1950, 494. -J. B. Metz, The Emergent Church, New York: Crossroad 1981, Ch. 1.

[22]W. Benjamin, Reflections. New York: Harcourt, Brace, Jovanovich 1978, 312-313. -Illuminations, New York: Schocken Books 1976, 253-264. -R. Wolin, Walter Benjamin, An Aesthetic of Redemption, New York: Columbia University Press 1982, ch. 4. -Metz, The Emergent Church, op. cit., ch. 1.

[23]J. Habermas and N. Luhmann, Theorie der Gesellschaft oder Sozialtechnologie, Frankfurt: Suhrkamp 1971, 142-230. -Jamme, Mythologie, op. cit., 11-14. -GW4, 58-59. -G. W. F. Hegel,

Jenaer Systementwurfe I, Hamburg: Felix Meiner 1975,   297-300,
319-326 (GW 6).   -Jenaer Systementwurfe III, Hamburg: Felix
Meiner 1976,   223-227,   243-245,   267-270,   273   (GW   8).
-Grundlinien   der   Philosophie   des   Rechts,   Stuttgart-Bad
Cannstatt: Friedrich Frommann 1964, 261-286, 310-328 (SW 7).

[24] Habermas, Theorie, op. cit. Bd.2, VII, VIII. -T. Parsons,
Societies: Evolutionary   and   Comparative   Perspectives,
Englewood Cliffs,   NJ: Prentice-Hall 1967,   ch.   I-II.
-R. J. Siebert, "Parsons' Analytical Theory of Religion as
Ultimate Reality" in G. Baum (ed.), Sociology and Human
Destiny, New York: Seabury Press 1980, 27-55.

[25] Habermas, Theorie, op. cit., BD 1, 369-452.

[26] Horster, "Ein marxistischer Kant," op. cit., 63-64. -GW 6,
265-333. -GW 8, 185-201. -Habermas, Vorstudien, op. cit., ch.
1.

[27] Habermas, Theorie, op. cit., Bd.2, 548-593, esp. 575-583.

[28] Horster,   "Ein   Marxistischer   Kant,"   op. cit.,   63-64.
-Habermas,   Vorstudien,   op. cit.,   200-214.   -Habermas,
Moralbewusstsein und Kommunikative Handeln, Frankfurt:
Suhrkamp 1983, 53-125.

[29] E. Arens, Kommunikative Handlungen, Dusseldorf: Patmos 1982,
parts I, II, IV.

[30] G. W. F. Hegel, Vorlesungen uber die Geschichte der
Philosophie, Stuttgart-Bad Cannstatt: Friedrich Frommann 1965,
Bd 2, 42-122 (SW 18).

[31] Habermas, Theorie, op. cit., Bd 2, 548-593; ch. IV.

[32] Ibid., ch. I, 3. -Habermas, Vorstudien, op. cit., 205-214.

[33] Horster,   "Ein   Marxistischer   Kant,"   op. cit.,   64-65.
-R. J. Siebert, "Communication without Domination" in
Concilium 131, 1978, 117-231.

[34] Adorno, Soziologische Schriften, op. cit., 280-353, esp.
302-309.

[35]Horkheimer/Adorno, Dialektik der Aufklarung, op. cit., ix-x, 1-7, 9-87. -Adorno, Soziologische Schriften, op. cit., 307. -R. Schmiede/E. Schudlich, "Die Entwicklung von Zeitokonomie und Lohnsystem im deutschen Kapitalismus" in Leviathan 4/1981, 9-56. -S. Kracauer, Das Ornament der Masse, Frankfurt: Suhrkamp 1977, 64-74, esp. 72-73.

[36]Adorno, Soziologische Schriften, op. cit., 280-353. -G. W. F. Hegel, Enzyklopadie der Philosophischen Wissenschaften, 1830, Hamburg: Felix Meiner 1959, 44, 73, 102-103, 184, 316 (PB 33). -Wissenschaft der Logik, Hamburg: Felix Meiner 1963, Part I, 6, 11, 20-21, 35-37, 87, 90 (PB 56).

[37]Horster, "Ein Marxistischer Kant," op. cit., 64-65.

[38]Habermas/Luhmann, Theorie der Gesellschaft, op. cit., 139.

[39]Habermas, Zur Rekonstruktion, op. cit., Ch. 4.

[40]Habermas, Theorie, op. cit., ch. VII. -Parsons, Societies, op. cit., chs. 1, 2. -Parsons, The System of Modern Societies, Englewood Cliffs, NJ: Prentice-Hall 1969, chs. 1, 2.

[41]Horster, "Ein Marxistischer Kant," op. cit., 64-65. -Habermas, Vorstudien, op. cit., chs. 1-3, 6-9, 11.

[42]Habermas, Zur Rekonstruktion, op. cit., ch. 4. -Theorie, op. cit., Bd 1, I,2; II,2-3; Bd 2, V,2.

[43]Habermas, Theorie, op. cit., ch. 8. -SW 7, 36-37. -G. W. F. Hegel, Vorlesunger uber die Philosophie der Geschichte, Stuttgart: Frommann 1961, 129, 447 (SW 11). -G. W. F. Hegel, Asthetik, Frankfurt: Europaische Verlags Anstalt 1952, II, 423.

[44]Habermas, Theorie, op. cit., ch. VIII. -Horkheimer, Die Sehnsucht nach dem ganz Anderen, Hamburg: Furche 1970, 54-56, 84-89. -Gesellschaft im Ubergang, Frankfurt: Athenaeum Fischer 1972, 162-176. -O. K. Flechtheim, Futurologie. Der Kampf um die Zukunft, Koln: Verlag fur Wissenschaft und Politik 1971, 9-10, 13--38, 309-397. -"Drei Moglichkeiten unserer Zukunft" in FH 19/7 (July 1974), 481-488. -"Widerstand gegen Abrustung" in FH 21/7 (July 1966), 455-464. -"Die Radikale Alternative-1

August 1914-1 September 1939-Wann zum letzten Mal?" in FH 17/9
(September 1962), 585-594. -"Die Menschheit am Wendepunkt" in
FH 30/3 (March 1975), 39-45. -"Humanismus und Menschenrechte"
in FH 31/9 (September 1976), 27-34. -E. Fromm, Der modern
Mensch und seine Zukunft, Frankfurt 1960, 322-323. -E. Kogon,
"Weltpolitische Zukunftsperspektiven" in FH 23/3 (March 1968),
159-170. -F. Heer, "Die Zukunft des Kommunismus" in FH 18/1
(January 1963), 41-88. -H. Marcuse, One Dimensional Man,
Boston: Beacon Press 1966, parts I-III. -E. Fromm, The
Revolution of Hope, New York: Harper and Row, Publishers 1968,
ch. 1, 3, 5, 6. -R. J. Siebert, "From Historical Materialism
to Political Theology: Two Futures," in World Futures, October
1983. -"Three Alternative Futures. Hegel's Philosophy of
Society and History" in World Futures, January 1985. -"Hegel,"
op. cit. -"The Christian Revolution: Liberation and
Transcendence" in The Ecumenist (September-October 1976),
85-91. -"Hegel's Political Theology: Liberation" in The
Ecumenist XII/3 (March-April 1974), 33-41. -W. Dirks and
E. Kogon, "Sonderheft Zukunft konkret" in FH 33/4 (April
1978), 2-13. -R. J. Siebert, Reason, Freedom and Change: A
Christian Encounter with Hegel, Washington, DC: University
Press of America 1985, ch. 3.

[45]Th. McCarthy, The Critical Theory of Jurgen Habermas,
Cambridge, MA: MIT Press 1978, ch. 1-3. -Lowenthal, Prophets,
op. cit., v-viii; xi-xiii; xv-xvii.

[46]Benjamin, Reflections, op. cit., 312-313. -Illuminations,
op. cit., 253-264. -J. Habermas, "Bewusstmachende oder
rettende Kritik-die Aktualitat Walter Benjamins" in S. Unseld
(ed.), Zur Aktualitat Walter Benjamins, Frankfurt: -Wolin,
Walter Benjamin, op. cit., ch. 5. -R. Hesse, "Ethik in der
Weltkrise" in FH 37/12 (December 1982), 20.

[47]Th. W. Adorno, Minima Moralia, Frankfurt: Suhrkamp 1980,
333-334.

[48]Habermas, "Bewusstmachende oder rettende Kritik," op. cit.,
175-223; -Theorie, op. cit., Bd 2, 383-384, 375-376, 281-282,
279-280, 147, 118-119; I, 280-281.

[49]Adorno, Minima Moralia, op. cit., 333-334. -Habermas,
Theorie, op. cit., ch. 4, 8.

Habermas, _Theorie_, op. cit., ch. 2, esp. 312-313, 330-331. -Acts 2:42-47; 4:32-37.

[51]A. Sollner, "J. Habermas und die kritische Theorie des gegenwartigen Rechtsstaates" in _Leviathan_ 1/82, 104.

[52]Q. Skinner, "Habermas's Reformation" in _New York Review of Books_, October 7, 1982,

[53]Habermas, _Theorie_, op. cit., Bd 2, 548-593, esp. 575-583.

[54]E. Jouhy, "Bedarf der Zustand des Elends der Losung oder der Erlosung" in _FH_ 37/12, December 1982, 56. -Siebert, "Hegel," op. cit.

[55]SW 7, 35-37. -Hegel, _Vorlesungen uber die Philosophie der Religion_, Stuttgart-Bad Cannstatt: Friedrich Frommann 1965, BD 1, 292-293 (SW 15).

[56]K. Marx, _Die Fruhschriften_, Stuttgart: Alfred Kroner 1953, ch. 9, esp. 509-515.

[57]Habermas, _Theorie_, op. cit., Bd 1, 7-11. Bd 2, 575-583.

[58]Habermas, _Zur Rekonstruktion_, op. cit., 101-121. -_Theorie_, op. cit., Bd 2, 577-578, 580-581.

[59]Habermas, _Theorie_, op. cit., Bd 1, 7-11, 15-24, 152-203. -R. Merkel, "Zwergenaufstand. Kontroverse um Habermas," June 1982, 51-57.

[60]Siebert, "Parsons," op. cit., 27-55.

[61]M. Horkheimer, _Die Sehnsucht_, op. cit., 54.

[62]I. Kant, _Critique of Pure Reason_, New York: St. Martin's Press 1965, 7-62. -_Critique of Practical Reason_, Chicago: University of Chicago Press 1949, 1-49. -_The Critique of Judgment_, Oxford: Clarendon Press 1957, 3-39. -Hegel, _Jenaer Kritische Schriften_, op. cit., 417-485 (GW 4). -GW 6, 235-333. -Hegel, _Jenaer Systementwurfe II_, Hamburg: Felix Meiner 1971 (GW 7). -_Jenaer Systementwurfe III_, op. cit. (GW 8). -_Wissenschaft der Logik I_, Hamburg: Felix Meiner 1978 (GW 11).

[63]A. Schmidt, "Die Zeitschrift fur Sozialforschung.' Geschichte und gegenwartige Bedeutung," in M. Horkheimer (ed.), Zeitschrift fur Sozialforschung, Munchen: Kosel 1970, 5-63. -A. Schmidt, Zur Idee der Kritischen Theorie, Frankfurt: Ullstein 1979; -Drei Studien uber Materialismus, Frankfurt: Ullstein 1979, 81-134.

[64]Habermas, Theorie, op. cit., ch. 4. -Theory and Practice, Boston: Beacon Press 1973, chs. 3-5.

[65]Th. W. Adorno, et al., Der Positivismusstreit, op. cit., 7-79; 103-123. -Adorno, Soziologische Schriften, Frankfurt: Suhrkamp 1979, 280-353.

[66]GW 6, 282-296.

[67]Habermas, Theorie, op. cit., Bd 1, ch. 4.

[68]Habermas/Luhmann, Theorie der Gesellschaft, op. cit., 7-141.

[69]Habermas, Theorie, op. cit., ch. 7. -Siebert, "Parsons," op. cit. -Parsons, Societies, op. cit., chs. 1, 2. -The System of Modern Societies, op. cit., chs. 1, 2. -A. Schutz/ T. Parsons, Zur Theorie des Sozialen Handelns, Frankfurt: Suhrkamp 1977, 127-136.

[70]Habermas, Theorie, op. cit., ch. 7.

[71]Ibid.,

[72]G. W. F. Hegel, Vorlesungen uber die Geschichte der Philosophie, Stuttgart-Bad Canstatt: Friedrich Frommann 1965, 331-367, 551-611.

[73]Jamme, Mythologie, 11-14. -GW 4, 315-414, 417-485. -GW 6, 265-326. -GW 8, 185-287.

[74]G. W. F. Hegel, Wissenschaft der Logik, Stuttgart-Bad Cannstatt: Friedrich Fromann 1964, II 36-65 (SW 5).

[75]Habermas, Theorie, op. cit., ch. 7.

[76]Ibid. -Parsons, Societies, op. cit., chs. 7, 2. -N. Luhmann, Zweck begriff und Systemrationalitat, Frankfurt: Suhrkamp

1977, 7–17; ch. 2, 4.

[77]Habermas, Theorie, op. cit., chs. 2, 4, 5, 7, 8. –Parsons, Societies, op. cit., chs. 1, 2, 7. –R. Grathoff, The Theory of Social Action, Bloomington: Indiana University Press 1978, part III. –A. Strauss (ed.), The Social Psychology of Georg Herbert Mead, Chicago: University of Chicago Press 1956, iv–vi, part I. –M. Weber, The Sociology of Religion, Boston: Beacon Press 1964, xix–Lxvii; ch. 1. – G. H. Mead, "Scientific Method and Individual Thinker" in J. Dewey and others, Creative Intelligence, New York: Octagon Books 1970; –On Social Psychology, Chicago: University of Chicago Press 1964, vii–xxv, parts I–III, VI–VII, IX. –E. Durkheim, The Elementary Forms of the Religious Life, Glencoe, Ill: Free Press 1947, 1–9; –Socialism and Saint Simon, London: Routledge and Kegan Paul, Ltd. 1959, v–xxvii, ch. 1; –The Division of Labour in Society, Glencoe, Ill: ;Free Press 1947, 1–46; –Professional Ethics and Civil Morals, Glencoe: Free Press 1958, chs. 1, 2; –Rules of Sociological Method, Glencoe: Free Press 1958, chs. 1, 2; –Durkheim, et al., Primitive Classification, Chicago: University of Chicago Press 1963, xvii–Lviii, 3–9. –M. Weber, Ancient Judaism, Glencoe, Ill: Free Press 1952, ix–xvii, part I. –G. H. Mead, Philosophy of the Present, LaSalle: Open Publishing Co., 1959, xi–xxxv; –Mind, Self and Society, Chicago: University of Chicago Press 1967, ix–xxxv; –The Philosophy of Act, Chicago: University of Chicago Press 1959, vi–Lxxiii. –H. H. Gerth and C. Wright Mills, From Max Weber: Essays in Sociology, New York: A Galaxy Book 1958, ch. 1. –M. Weber, The Protestant Ethic, and the Spirit of Capitalism, New York: Scribner's 1958, chs. 1–3; –Gesammelte Aufsatze zur Religionssoziologie, Tubingen: Mohr 1963, Vols. I–III. –W. S. F. Pickering (ed.), Durkheim on Religion, London: Routledge and Kegan Paul 1975, 1–10.

[78]Habermas, Theorie, op. cit., Bd 1, 7–11, ch. 1.

[79]Weber, Sociology of Religion, op. cit., xxxii–xxxv, xxxvii, xlii–xliii, 10, 22, 57, 336, 34, 41, 81, 216, 30; –The Religion of India, Glencoe, Ill: Free Press 1958, 3–9; –The Religion of China, Glencoe, Ill: Free Press 1951, 3–12.

[80]Jamme, Mythologie, op. cit., 11–14; –GW 4, 20–23, 58, 124–125. –GW 6, 265–281, 329. –SW 7, 19–37, esp. 33–35.

[81]GW 6, 277-300, 307-315. -J. Habermas, Theory and Praxis, op. cit., ch. 4.

[82]R. J. Siebert, "Adorno's Theory of Religion" in Telos, January 1984, 108-114.

[83]Schutz/Parsons, Zur Theorie Sozialen Handelns, op. cit., 7-18, esp. 16, 127-136, esp. 134-135.

[84]H. Scheible, "Max Horkheimer's fruhe und spate Aufzeichnungen" in FH 33/6 (June 1978), 50-54. -H. Mayer, "Nach denken uber Adorno" in FH 25/4 (April 1970), 268-280. -H. Willig, "Die Aktualitat der Kritischen Theorie Adorno's" in FH 35/3 (March 1980), 55-64.

[85]GW 6, 277-279, 282-296, 307-315. -G. W. F. Hegel, Phanemenologie des Geistes, Stuttgart-Bad Cannstatt: Friedrich Frommann 1964, 148-158 (SW 2).

[86]Habermas, Theory, op. cit., ch. 4; -Technik und Wissenschaft als Ideologie, Frankfurt: Suhrkamp 1976, 9-47; -Zwei Reden, op. cit., 25-75; -Zur Rekonstruktion, op. cit., ch. 4.

[87]GW 4, 417-485.

[88]GW 6, 282-315.

[89]Habermas, Zur Rekonstruktion, op. cit., ch. 4; -Theory, op. cit., chs. 4, 5. -L. S. Stepelvich, The Young Hegelians, New York: Cambridge University Press 1983, chs. 2, 4, 5, esp. 8, 9.

[90]GW 4, 456-460; -GW 8, 277-287; -SW 2, 517-601, esp. 571-572, 596-597. -Marx, Das Kapital, op. cit. -Siebert, "Hegel," op. cit.

[91]Habermas, Zur Rekonstruktion, op. cit., ch. 4; -Theory, op. cit., Bd 1, 15, 72-114, 122-124, 180, 183, 187-188, 193-194, 198-199, 207-208, 211-215, 222-225, 228-229, 231-264, 269, 271-313, esp. 312-313; 313-366, 369, 455-457, 462-474, 484-486, 493-494, 500-502, 505, 512-513, 518, 522-529, 531-534. Bd 2, 10, 15, 21-22, 73-75, 78-99, 107-113, 116-148, esp. 148; 149, 162-165, 17, 206-213, 218-221, 223-224, 233-239, 241-242, 244-246, 252-253, 263, 268-269, 273-274,

276,   279-293,   321-323,   325,   327,   329-331,   350,   353,   372-382,
esp.   383,   398-399,   404-405,   410-411,   esp.   411;   420-422,
424-444,   447-450,   456-457,   462,   464,   465-471,   477-491,
500-502, 513, 516-521, 533-534, 539-540, 548-589.

[92]H. Peukert,   Wissenschaftstheorie-Handlungstheorie-Fundamentale Theologie, Dusseldorf: Patmos 1976, 227-229, 278-282.

[93]J. Moltmann,   "Theologie   heute"   in   J.   Habermas   (ed.),
Stichworte zur 'Geistigen Situation der Zeit', Bd 2,   Politik
und   Kultur,   Frankfurt: 1979,   754-780.   -M. Lamb,   "The
Dialectics of Theory and Praxis within Paradigm Analysis,"
Milwaukee: Marquette   University   1983   (unpublished).
-J. B. Metz,   "Produktive   Ungleichzeitigkeit"   in   Habermas,
Stichworte,   op. cit.,   529-538.   -M. Lamb,   "Roman   Catholic
Liberation Theology   and   a   Transformative   Understanding   of
Political Life,"   Chicago   1983   (unpublished);   -"Liberation
Theology and Social Justice," Milwaukee: Marquette University
1983   (unpublished).   -D. Solle,   "Du sollst keine anderen Jeans
haben neben mir" in Habermas, Stichworte,   op. cit.,   541-553.
-Wolin,   Walter Benjamin,   op. cit.,   ch.   4-6.   -H. Brenner,
"Theodor W. Adorno als Sachwalter des Benjaminschen Werkes" in
W. F. Schoeller, Die Neue Linke nach Adorno, Munchen: Kindler
1969, 158-175. -Benjamin,   Illuminations, op. cit., 253-264;
-Reflections, op. cit., 312-313.

[94]Nicolaus   von   Cusa,   Wichtigste   Schriften,   Freiburg   im
Breisgau: Minerva 1966, 31-33. -J. Moltmann, "Theology of
Mystical Experience" in Scottish Journal of Theology, Vol. 32,
1-20.   -E. Schaefer,   Meister   Eckharts   Traktat   von
Abgeschiedenheit. Untersuchung und Textausgabe, Bonn 1956,
210-212. -H. Quint (tr.), Meister Eckhart, Deutsche Predigten
und   Schriften,   Munich   1977,   216.   -R. B. Blakney,   Meister
Eckhart, New York: Harper and Brothers 1941, 43-73, 82-91,
203-204, 227-232, 247-248.

[95]"Th. W. Adorno   an   Benjamin"   (Hornberg letter of August 2,
1935) in W. Benjamin, Briefe 2, Frankfurt: Suhrkamp 1978,
671-683, esp. 676.

[96]Habermas,   Theorie,   op. cit.,   ch.   7.   -F. Nietzsche, "The
Madman" in

[97]J. Habermas, "Tod in Jerusalem," Merkur, H4, 36 Jhrg. April

1982, 438-440; -Theorie, op. cit., Bd 2, 383.

[98]E. Hoflich, "Karl Marx fur die Kirche" in FH 24/11, November 1969, 777-785. -E. Wiesel, Four Hasidic Masters, Notre Dame: University of Notre Dame Press 1978. -E. Hoflich, "Heilsverkundigung als politische Gewissensbildung" in FH 24/12, December 1969, 843-854. -E. Wiesel, The Madness of God, New York: Random House 1974. -W. Kasper, "Politische Utopie und christliche Hoffnung" in FH 24/8, August 1969, 563-572. -E. Wiesel, The Trial of God, New York: Random House 1979.

[99]R. J. Siebert, "From Historical Materialism to Political Theology: Two Alternative Futures," op. cit.; -Peukert, Wissenschaftstheorie, op. cit., 278-280. -G. Gutierrez, A Theology of Liberation, Maryknoll, New York: Orbis Press 1973, 219-220, 216, 284, 40, 244, 31, 29, 222, 249, 187, 25, 224, 9-10, 104, 137. -J. B. Metz, Glaube in Geschichte und Gesellschaft, Mainz: Matthias-Grunewald 1978, 18, 28, 41, 50, 72, 102, 106. -J. Moltmann, Unkehr zur Zukunft, Munchen: Siebenstein Taschenbuch 1970, 15-44. -D. Solle, Revolutionary Patience, Maryknoll, New York: Orbis Press 1977, 24-26, 64, 71, 75, 79-80.

[100]Habermas, Theory, op. cit., ch. 4. -GW 6, 273-315.

[101]Habermas, Theory, op. cit., 142. -GW 4, 417-485. -Jamme, Mythologie, op. cit., 11-14.

[102]Habermas, Theory, op. cit., 142.

[103]G. Lukacs, Der Junge Hegel, Berlin 1954, chs. 1, 2, 3.

[104]SW 7, 270-272.

[105]SW 6, 265-326, 330-331. -SW 8, 185-287.

[106]SW 7, 270-286, 310-328.

[107]SW 4, 79-80. -Siebert, "Hegel," op. cit.

[108]Benjamin, Illuminations, op. cit., 254-255.

[109]G. W. F. Hegel, Vorlesungen uber die Philosophie der Religion, Stuttgart-Bad Cannstatt: Friedrich Frommann 1965, Bd

2, 286-303 (SW 16).

[110]G. W. F. Hegel, Enzyklopadie der Philosophischen Wissenschaften im Grundriss, Stuttgart: Friedrich Frommann 1956, 344
(SW 6).

[111]GW 4, 486-493, 497-500. -Dante Alighieri, The Purgatorio,
New York: New American Library 1961, ix-xxiii.

[112]GW 4, 456-464. -G. W. F. Hegel, The Phenomenology of Mind,
New York: Harper and Row 1967, 63-64. -Dante Alighieri, The
Paradiso, New York: New American Library 1970, ix-xxi.

[113]SW 7, 35-36. -SW 15, 67-68.

[114]Habermas, Zur Rekonstruktion, op. cit., ch. 4.

[115]Ibid. -GW 4, 458-459. -SW 16, 247-08, 354.

[116]GW 4, 458-459. -GW 6, 265-326. -GW 8, 185-277. -SW 2,
571-572, 596-598.

[117]GW 4, 413-414, 458-459. -GW 6, 265-326, 330-331. -GW 8,
185-287. -SW 15, 75-100.

[118]Habermas, Theory, op. cit., ch. 4. -GW 6, 265-326. -GW 8,
185-277.

[119]J. Habermas (ed.), Stichworte zur 'Geistigen Situation der
Zeit'. 1 Bd: Nation und Republik, Frankfurt: Suhrkamp 1979,
7-35.

[120]Habermas, Theory, op. cit., ch. 4. -Vorstudien, op. cit.,
chs. 1, 3, 4, 6, 8, 9, 11.

[121]Habermas, Theory, op cit., ch. 4. -GW 6, 282-326.

[122]SW 7, part III. -PB 33, 56, 343, 369-371; 323, 404-407;
175, 384, 391, 413-415, 428; 16-17, 46-47, 49, 418.

[123]Habermas, Theorie, op. cit., ch. 6. -Vorstudien, op. cit.,
35-59. -Theory, ch. 4.

[124]G. W. F. Hegel, Fruhe Schriften, Frankfurt: Suhrkamp 1971,

372-373, 197, 548-558 (TW 1). -Phanomenologie des Geistes, Frankfurt: Suhrkamp 1970, 85, 91-92, 145-147, 153-156, 170, 172-173, 175, 235-376, 378, 384, 392, 433-435, 465, 470, 478-479, 490, 508-511, 518, 521-529, 531, 586, 578 (TW 3). -Jenaer Schriften 1801-1807, Frankfurt: Suhrkamp 1970, 482, 489, 490, 547 (TW 2). -Grundlinien der Philosophie des Rechtes, Frankfurt: Suhrkamp 1970, 124, 144-145, 150, 306-339, 344-345, 349-351, 353-360, 386, 390, 394, 459, 466, 494 (TW 7). -Enzyklopadie der philosophischen Wissenschaften III, Frankfurt: Suhrkamp 1970, 219, 50, 64-67, 350 (TW 10). -Vorlesungen uber die Asthetik II, Frankfurt: Suhrkamp 1970, 182 (TW 14).

[125]D. Crittendon, "Test Results: Dealers and Dropouts," The Detroit News, Sunday, July 19, 1984, 10A.

[126]SW 5, 5-65. -Habermas, Theory, op. cit., ch. 4.

[127]Habermas, Theory, op. cit., 146-147. -Vorstudien, op. cit., 83-104, esp. 98-100.

[128]GW 4, 417-464. -GW 6, 265-326. -Habermas, Theory, ch. 2.

[129]Habermas, Theorie, op. cit., ch. 1. -Vorstudien, op. cit., 104-126, 137-149, 200-214, esp. 205. -G. W. F. Hegel, Enzyklopadie der philosophischen Wissenschaften im Grundriss, op. cit., parts B, C.

[130]Durkheim, The Division of Labour, op. cit., book I. -PB 33, 387-388.

[131]Habermas, Theory, op. cit., 147-148. -GW 6, 301-306. -GW 8, 207-213. -G. W. F. Hegel, On Christianity: Early Theological Writings, New York: Harper and Brothers 1948, 303-308. -R. J. Siebert, Hegel's Concept of Marriage and Family: The Origin of Subjective Freedom, op. cit., 23-72.

[132]GW 6, 301-306. -Siebert, Hegel's Concept of Marriage, op. cit.

[133]GW 6, 307-315. -GW 8, 214-231.

[134]GW 4, 413-414, 458-464. -SW 7, 24-25, 30-31, 33, 36. -G. W. F. Hegel, Vorlesungen uber die Philosophie der

Geschichte, Stuttgart: Frommann 1961, 37–43 (SW 11). –H. Kung, Menschwerdung Gottes, Freiburg: Herder 1970, 68–70.

[135]SW 2, 148–158.

[136]Marx, Das Kapital, op. cit., I, 18; III, 873–874.

[137]Habermas, Zur Rekonstruktion, op. cit., chs. 1, 2, 6; –Theorie, op. cit., ch. 8.

[138]Habermas, Theory, op. cit., 152–156.

[139]GW 6, 301–306.

[140]Ibid., 282–300. –Habermas, Theory, op. cit., ch. 4.

[141]GW 4, 315–414, 417–485.

[142]Habermas, Theory, op. cit., 156–158.

[143]Habermas, Zur Rekonstruktion, op. cit., ch. 4. –SW 15, 271–278. –SW 16, 308–356.

[144]Habermas, Theory, op. cit., 156–158. –SW 2, 602–620.

[145]GW 4, 417–485. –SW 2, 602–620.

[146]Habermas, Theory, op. cit., 162–163. –GW 6, 282–306. –GW 8, 185–213.

[147]SW 2, 148–158.

[148]SW 7, 261–287, 310–323. –G. W. F. Hegel, Vermischte Schriften aus der Berliner Zeit, Stuttgart: Frommann 1958, 473–518 (SW 20).

[149]Marx, Das Kapital, op. cit., 17–18, part 1.

[150]PB 33, 311–316. –GW 6, 265–279.

[151]PB 33, 314. –Nicolaus von Cusa, Wichtigste Schriften, op. cit., 517–518.

[152]G. W. F. Hegel, Wissenschaft der Logik II, op.cit., 34–65

(SW 5).

[153] SW 16, 308-356. -SW 5, 327-353. M. Horkheimer/Th. W. Adorno, Die Dialektik der Aufklarung, Frankfurt: S. Fischer 1969, 29-31.

[154] SW 16, 191-356.

[155] J. Quint (ed.), Meister Eckehart, Deutsche Predigten, op. cit., 302. -SW 15

[156] Habermas, Theory, op. cit., 163-164.

[157] GW 6, 282-296, 297-300. -GW 8, 185-201.

[158] GW 6, 297-309.

[159] Jamme, Mythologie, op. cit., 11-14. -GW 4, 417-464, esp. 458-459. -GW 8, 280-287.

[160] Habermas, Theory, op. cit., 164. -GW 6, 301-315. -GW 8, 207-231.

[161] Habermas, Theorie, op. cit., Bd 2, 548-593, esp. 581-593.

[162] Habermas, Zur Rekonstruktion, op. cit., ch. 4.

[163] K. H. Haag, Der Fortschritt in der Philosophie, Frankfurt: Suhrkamp 1983.

[164] Habermas, Vorstudien, op. cit., 35-59. -Theorie, op. cit., ch. 8.

[165] Habermas, Theory, op. cit., 164-165.

[166] GW 8, 280-283. -SW 16, 218-223. -SW 15, 227-228. -Quint, Meister Eckehart, op. cit., 302, 225, 252-253, 268-270, 292-293, 295, 298.

[167] Habermas, Theory, op. cit., 165. -GW 4, 417-485.

[168] GW 4, 458-464.

[169] Hegel, Theory, op. cit., 165. -On Christianity, op. cit.,

parts I, II. -GW 6, 315-326.

[170]Jamme, Mythologie, op. cit., 11-14. -Hegel, On Christianity, op. cit., 309-319. -GW 4, 417-485.

[171]GW 4, 417-485. -SW 5, 326-353, esp. 352-353. -G. W. F. Hegel, Wissenschaft der Logik, Stuttgart-Bad Cannstadt: Friedrich Frommann 1965, I, 36-58, esp. 45-46 (SW 4).

[172]Siebert, "Hegel," op. cit.

[173]Marx, Das Kapital, op. cit., I, 17-18; III, 873-874.

[174]Habermas, Theory, op. cit., 165-166. -GW 4, 458-459.

[175]GW 4, 458-459. -SW 15, 435-436.

[176]GW 4, 459. -GW 8, 280-286. -SW 2, 569-601. -J. Moltmann, Der Gekruzigle Gott, Munchen: Chr. Kaiser 1973, ch. 6.

[177]Quint, Meister Eckehart, op. cit., 304-305.

[178]Habermas, Theory, op. cit., 166.

[179]Benjamin, Illuminations, op. cit., 254-255.

[180]SW 7, 88-163.

[181]Hegel, On Christianity, op. cit., 309-319. -Jamme, Mythologie, op. cit., 11-14. -GW 4, 417-485, 58-59, 124-126. -SW 7, 270-272.

[182]SW 15, 24-36.

[183]GW 8, 280-286. -GW 4, 458-464.

[184]M. Horkheimer, Zur Kritik der instrumentellen Vernunft, Frankfurt: Fischer 1967, 248-268.

[185]Habermas, Theorie, op. cit., II, 352-443, esp. 383-384. -G. Scholem, Major Trends in Jewish Mysticism, New York: Schocken Books 1961, chs. 1, 3, 4, 7-9. -Habermas, "Tod in Jerusalem," op. cit., 438-440.

[186]Nicolaus von Cusa, Wichtigste Schriften, op. cit., 31–33.

[187]B. Blackney, Meister Eckehart, op. cit., 43–91, 203–206, 246–248. –Quint, Meister Eckehart, op. cit., 304–305. –Moltmann, Theology of Mysticism, op. cit.

[188]GW 4, 417–485, esp. 458–459.

[189]Th. W. Adorno, Drei Studien zu Hegel, Frankfurt: Suhrkamp 1969, 94.

[190]SW 15, 292–293.

[191]SW 7, 261–262.

[192]GW 4, 417–485. –SW 2, 24. –SW 7, 328–337. –SW 11, 125–129.

[193]SW 7, 320. –Siebert, "Hegel," op. cit.

[194]Marx, Das Kapital, op. cit., I, 17–18. – T.B. Bottomore, Karl Marx. Early Writings, New York: McGraw-Hill Book Company 1964, 195–219.

[195]SW 4, 45–46. –SW 5, 35–65. –G. W. F. Hegel, Jenaer Systementwurfe II, op. cit., 76–79, 150–154, 165–178 (GW 7). –SW 7, 261–328. –GW 4, 56, 58, 80, 81, 417, 419, 421–425, 434, 441–444, 450–462, 464, 469, 470, 476–480, 484–485. –GW 6, 265–326. –GW 8, 265–331.

[196]Marx, Das Kapital, op. cit., I, 18. – K. Marx, Die Fruhschriften, op. cit., 20–149, 207–224; ch. 6 – 9.

[197]K. Marx, Grundrisse der Kritik der politischen Okonomie, Berlin 1953, 600, 593, esp. 594.

[198]Marx, Das Kapital, op. cit., I, 17–18. –SW 15, 227–228. –Blackney, Meister Eckhart, op. cit., xiii, 60–61, 67–68, 71–72, 75–76, 85–86, 168–169, 180–181, 204–206. –Nicolaus von Cusa. Wichtigste Schriften, op. cit., 8–13, 21–22, 24–25, 27–33. –G. W. F. Hegel, Vorlesungen uber die Geschichte der Philosophie, Stuttgart-Bad Cannstatt: Friedrich Frommann 1965, III, 296–327. (SW 19) –G. G. Scholem, On the Kabbalah and its Symbolism, New York: Schocken Books 1960, 99, 132, 168; 13.

[199]H. Schnadelbach, "Dialektik als Vernunftkritik. Zur Konstruktion des Rationalen bei Adorno" in L. von Friedenburg and J. Habermas (eds.), Adorno Konferenz 1983, Frankfurt a.M.: Suhrkamp, 90.

[200]M. Horkheimer, Die Sehnsucht, op. cit., 54–55, 77.

[201]Marx, Das Kapital, op. cit., III, 873–874; I, 389; 803, 657–659. -Schnadelbach, "Dialektik," op. cit., 90. - K. Marx, Zur Kritik der politischen Okonomie, Berlin 1951, 262, 263. -Marx, Grundrisse, op. cit., 593, 600, 594, 592, 599.

[202]SW 7, 261–286, 310–328. -G. W. F. Hegel, Enzyklopadie der philosophischenn Wissenschaften im Grundriss, op. cit., 294–297. (SW 6) -G. W. F. Hegel, System der Philosophie, Stuttgart-Bad Cannstatt: Friedrich Frommann 1965, 400–403, 408, 409. (SW 10) -SW 11, 48–50, 65–69, 70, 72, 76.

[203]GW 4, 21–22, 40–41, 79–80. -P. H. D. von Holbach, Systeme de la nature ou des lois du monde physique et du monde morale, Paris 1770. -SW 15, 67–68. -G. W. F. Hegel, Jenaer Schriften 1801-1807, op. cit., 250. (GW 2) -Schmidt, Drei Studien uber Materialismus, op. cit., ch. 1 - 3.

[204]Th. Morgan, Introduction to Economics, Englewood Cliffs, NJ: Prentice-Hall, Inc. 1956, 4–5, 378–380, 534–569. -G. L. Bach, Economics, Englewood Cliffs, NJ: Prentice-Hall, Inc. 1961, 222–239, 240–242, 249–251, 274–276, 286–288. -C. R. McConnel, Economics: Principles, Problems, and Policies, New York: McGraw-Hill Book Company, Inc. 1963, 193–197, 580.

[205]SW 7, 320, 261–286, 310–328.

[206]Jamme, Mythologie, op. cit., 11–14. -Hegel, On Christianity, op. cit., 309–319. -GW 4, 417–464, 467–485. -GW 6, 265–326. -GW 8, 185–287. -SW 10, 382–445, esp. 400–409. -SW 6, 281–300, esp. 292–300. -SW 7, 262–328. -SW 11, 47–50, 69–88, 120–130, 519–568, 447. -SW 15, 24–36, 52–64, 114. -SW 16, 354–356. - G.W.F. Hegel, Asthetik, Frankfurt a.M.: Europaische Verlagsanstal 1953, II, 423. -SW 5, 35–65.

[207]SW 7, 277–278, 432–446; 237–238, 239–249, 328–337, 455–456; 35–36. -SW 11, 43–47, 125–130, 569. -SW 2, 18–20, 619–620. -SW

16, 281-282. -SW 15, 292-293. -Th. W. Adorno, Drei Studien zu Hegel, op. cit., 21-22. -Flechtheim, "Drei Moglichkeiten unserer Zukunft", op. cit., 481-488 (FH).

[208] G. W. F. Hegel, Die Vernunft in der Geschichte, Hamburg: Felix Meiner 1955, 210, 261, 262. (PB 171a)

[209] SW 11, 120-130, 447. -Adorno, Drei Studien, op. cit., 21-22. -Hegel, Asthetik, op. cit., I, 94-95, II, 423.

[210] GW 6, 330-331. -GW 8, 277-287. -SW 15, 19-64, 65-75. -SW 16, 46-95, 247-308, esp. 350-356. -Habermas, Theory, op. cit., ch. 5, esp. 189-191.

[211] E. Bloch, Subjekt-Objekt, Frankfurt a.M.: Suhrkamp 1962, chap. I, esp. 6.

[212] Th. W. Adorno, Negative Dialektik, Frankfurt a.M.: Suhrkamp 1966, 13.

[213] Marx, Die Fruhschriften, op. cit., 339-341, esp. 341. -SW 11, 43-69. -G. W. F. Hegel, Enzyklopadie der philosophischen Wissenschaften im Grundrisse, op. cit., 349-490 (SW 6). -G. W. F. Hegel, Vermischte Schriften aus der Berliner Zeit, op. cit., 473-518, 521-527.

[214] Jamme, Mythologie, op. cit., 11-12. -GW 6, 297-300, 315-326. -GW 8, 202-209, 223-227, 253-277. -SW 7, 261-262, 263, 271-272, 277-278, 328-337. -GW 4, 12-16, 20-23, 58-62, 124-128, 417-464, 467-485, 413-414.

[215] GW 4, 12-16, 50, 51, 54-55, esp. 56. -SW 7, 35, 237, 263.

[216] G. W. F. Hegel, Grundlinien der Philosophie des Rechts, op. cit., 25 (TW 7). -GW 4, 477.

[217] GW 4, 124-125. -SW 2, 19. -SW 11, 49-50, 37-43, 43-47. -SW 16, 355-356.

[218] GW 4, 12-16, 20-23, 56, 58, 124-125, 417-485. -GW 6, 269-326. -GW 8, 202-287. -SW 7, 264-286, 310-328.

[219] H. Kimmerle, "Thesen zur philosophischen Interpretation des Christentums" in FH 24/1 (January 1969), 39-47. -J. Habermas,

Philosophical-Political Profiles, Cambridge, Mass.: the MIT
Press 1983, ch. 2, 5, 7, 9, 10. -Horkheimer, Zur Kritik,
op. cit., 302-316, esp. 311-312. -S. Kracauer, Das Ornament,
op. cit., 9-119.

220E. Bloch, Das Prinzip Hoffnung, Frankfurt: Suhrkamp 1959,
1628.

221GW 4, 58, 108-109, 417-485. -SW 7, 182-183, 261-328, esp.
277-278, 286-310, 328-337. -SW 10, 400-409. -SW 6, 430-497,
297-300, 277-279, 315-326, esp. 321. -SW 11, 127-129. -PB
171a, 204-210. -GW 8, 202-209, 223-227, esp. 225, 242-245,
267-270, 228-231, 232-236, esp. 236-253, 260-265. -Hegel, On
Christianity, op. cit., 309-319.

222E. Fromm, The Anatomy of Human Destructiveness, New York:
Holt, Rinehart and Winston 1973, 6, 325-368, 436, ch. 13. -SW
7, 239-241, 432-440, 440-446, 33, 35. -GW 4, 58-62, 448,
449-450, 457, 460, 464, 467-485. -GW 6, 307-326. -SW 2,
619-620, 126-130, 447. -SW 11, 568-569. -SW 16, 281-282. -GW
8, 236-253, 272-277. - A. Sohn-Rethel, Okonomie und
Klassenstruktur des deutschen Faschismus, Frankfurt: Suhrkamp
1973, ch. 3. -R. Schmiede/E. Schudlich, "Die Entwicklung von
Zeitokonomie und Lohnsystem im deutschen Kapitalismus,"
op. cit., 57-99. -Horkheimer, Die Sehnsucht, op. cit., 80-89.
-Ch. Turcke, "Der Todestrieb der gegenwartigen Gesellschaft
und seine theologische Verklarung" in FH 37/7 (July 1982),
45-58.

223GW 4, 69, 477, 484. -SW 7, 35, 100, 265-267, 182-183. -SW
11, 568, 43-47. -PB 33. 387-388. -Horkheimer, Die Sehnsucht,
op. cit., 86-87.

224GW 4, 85-86. -SW 7, 36.

225GW 4, 430-431, 85-86. -SW 7, 35, 99-100, 182-184, 265-267.
-SW 11, 568-569, 126-130. -Hegel, Asthetik, op. cit., 423.

226GW 4, 417-493, 497-500. -Hegel, The Phenomenology of Mind,
op. cit., 63-64. -G. Lukacs, Der junge Hegel, Berlin: 1954,
ch. 1 - 3. -Habermas, Theory, op. cit., ch. 4, esp. 142.

227GW 4, 457-458. -SW 7, 88-142, 286-310, 404-432. -GW 8,
236-253.

[228]GW 4, 457–464. –GW 8, 222–287. –SW 7, 261–286, esp. 271–272, 277–286; 182–184, 99–101, 310–328, 342, esp. 435–436, 328–337, 35–37, 38–39, 39–41. –Habermas, Zur Rekonstruktion, op. cit., ch. 4. –Theory, op. cit., ch. 3, 4, 5, esp. 186–187, 190–191. –E. Fromm, To Have or To Be, New York: Harper and Row, Publishers 1976, chs. 3, 7, 9, 10, esp. 201–202.

[229]GW 4, 458–459. –Hegel, On Christianity, op. cit., 309–319.

[230]GW 4, 458–459. –SW 15, 435–436.

[231]GW 4, 458–459, 413–414. –G.W.F. Hegel, Vorlesungen uber die Philosophie der Religion, Frankfurt: Suhrkamp 1969, 286–299 (TW 17). –SW 16, 295–308. –SW 11, 409–430.

[232]Marx, Das Kapital, op. cit., III, 873–874; I, 803; II, 873–874. –GW 8, 34–100. –Haag, Der Fortschritt, op. cit., 180–201, 101–107, 107–113, 192–200. –SW 11, 47–69, esp. 49, 63.

[233]GW 6, 185–326, 329, 330–331. –GW 7, parts I, II, III. –GW 4, 417–464, 467–485. –GW 8, 185–236, 236–287. –Habermas, Theory, op. cit., ch. 4, esp. 142. –Habermas, Technik und Wissenschaft als 'Ideologie', op. cit., ch. 1, esp. 9. –G. Lukacs, Der junge Hegel, op. cit., ch. 1–4.

[234]GW 6, 297–300, 321, 323, 324. –GW 4, 50, 58, 406–408, 424, 450, 455–458. –SW 7, 273. –Marx, Das Kapital, op. cit., I, 43–44, 79–80, 99–101, 218–219, 331–333, 841–843.

[235]GW 6, 319–324, 297–300, 282–296, 307–315. –Marx, Das Kapital, op. cit., I, 53, 74–76, 92–94, 119–121; III, 873–874. –Habermas, Theorie, op. cit., Bd 2, 182–228, 229–293, 489–547, 548–593. –GW 8, 243–253, 253–277, 225, 202–207, 223–227, 242–246.

[236]SW 2, 18. –F. Wiedemann, G.W.F. Hegel, Hamburg: Rowohlt 1969, 35.

[237]SW 2, 18. –SW 11, 548–569, 125–130, 447. –E. Voegelin, From Enlightenment to Revolution, Durham, NC: Duke University Press 1975, 74. –P.A. Sorokin, The Crisis of Our Age, New York: E.P. Dutton and Co. 1941, chs. 1, 9. –Horkheimer, Die Sehnsucht, op. cit., 83–89. –E. Bloch, On Karl Marx, New York: Herder and

Herder 1971, chs. 4-9. -Bloch, A Philosophy of the Future, New York: Herder and Herder 1970, chs. 10-15. -Bloch, Man on his Own, New York: Herder and Herder 1970, chs. 6-8. -Bloch, Experimentum Mundi, Frankfurt: Suhrkamp 1975, chs. 46-49.

[238]SW 2, 18. -SW 11, 125-130, 447. -SW 16, 354-355. -SW 7, 320, 318-319, 216-217, 275-276. -GW 4,

[239]Hegel, Asthetik, op. cit., II, 423. -PB 171a, 22, 26, 29, 30, 36, 38-40, 42, 45, 46, 48, esp. 60, 77, 115, 181, 204-210, 261, 262-264, 265. -G.A. Kelly, "Hegel's America" in Philosophy and Public Affairs (Fall 1972), Vol. II, No. 1, 3-36. -SW 11,

[240]SW 11, 437-443, 569. -PB 171a, 60-61, esp. 262.

[241]Heer, "Hegel und die Jugend," op. cit. -SW 11, 37-43, 43-47, 569. -PB 171a, 26, 29, 30, 36, 38, 42, esp. 46, 60, 262.

[242]SW 2, 18-21, 618-620. -GW 4, 464, 414, 467-485. -SW 11, 569, 127-130, 447. -SW 7, 320, 310-328. -SW 15, 34, 100.

[243]SW 2, 618-620, 11-66, 67-80. -GW 4, 467-485. -GW 6, 307-326. -GW 8, 236-287. -SW 11, 149-157, 124-130, 25-120.

[244]SW 2, 620. -GW 4, 414, 444-464. -SW 16, 281-282, 296-308. -GW 6, 307-326. -GW 8, 222-287. -Revelation, 21.

[245]SW 2, 620. -GW 4, 449-464, esp. 458-459, 460-461. -SW 16, 281-282, 295-308, 354. -Quint, "Meister Eckehart," op. cit., 101-139, 143, 168, 212, 214, esp. 216, 219; 153, 316, esp. 321, 335. -Nicolaus von Cusa, Wichligste Schriften, op. cit., 533-535, 525-527, 431-449.

[246]SW 2, 620. -Hegel, Asthetik, op. cit., II, 423. -SW 11, 43-47, 47-69. -SW 7, 445-446. -D. Horster, "Kommunikative Ethik" in FH 37/10 (October 1982), 35-41. -Habermas, Theorie, op. cit., ch. 8, esp. 489-547, 548-593. -B. Pasternak, Doctor Zhivago, New York: The Modern Library 1958, 493-503.

[247]Habermas, Theory, op. cit., Bd 1, 168-169. -Stepelvich, The Young Hegelians, op. cit., chs. 3, 5, 7, 8. -Marx, Die Fruhsschriften, op. cit., parts III, VI, VIII. -Bottomore,

Karl Marx: Early Writings, op. cit., 43.

[248]Habermas, Theorie, op. cit., Bd 1, 72–114, 262–299, 299–332; Bd 2, 69–118, 351–420, 420–445.

[249]Marx, Fruhsschriften, op. cit., chs. 6, 8. –Bottomore, Karl Marx, op. cit., 63–194. –Habermas, Theory, op. cit., 168–169.

[250]Marx, Die Fruhsschriften, op. cit., chs. 6, 8. –Bottomore, Karl Marx, op. cit., ch. 3. –GW 4, 417–485. –GW 6, 297–300, 307–314. –GW 8, 202–207, 218–227. –Bloch, On Karl Marx, op. cit., ch. 7.

[251]Marx, Die Fruhsschriften, op. cit., 269. –SW 2, 602–620.

[252]Marx, Die Fruhsschriften, op. cit., 269.

[253]Habermas, Theory, op. cit., 168–169.

[254]Ibid. –Marx, Die Fruhsschriften, op. cit., 341–417.

[255]GW 6, 297–300.

[256]Benjamin, Illuminations, op. cit., 258–259. –Habermas, Theory, op. cit., 169. –Pasternak, Doctor Zhivago, op. cit., 465–503.

[257]J. Habermas, "Die Kulturkritik der Neokonservativen in den USA und in der Bundesrepublik" in Merkur, XXXVI. Jhrg., H.11, November 1982, 1059–1061.

[258]Ibid. –Habermas, Theory, op. cit., 169. –GW 6, 282–326. –GW 8, 185–287. –Habermas, Theorie, op. cit., chs. 7, 8.

[259]H. Kung, Existiert Gott?, Munchen: Piper 1978, part B, I and II.

[260]J. Habermas, Moralbewusstsein und Kommunikative Handeln, op. cit.,, 84–86, 88–264. –SW 16, 309–356. –SW 2, 517–601.

[261]SW 15, 19–36. –SW 16, 354–356.

[262]Habermas, Zur Rekonstruktion, op. cit., 100–101.

263Ibid. -SW 15, 19-36.

264SW 15, 24-26.

265Ibid., 24-36. -GW 4, 315-414. -SW 11, 42, 569. -SW 16, 355-356. -SW 15, 100.

266SW 11, 19-36, 394-409, 409-430, 519-569. -SW 16, 354-356.

267H. Kung, Menschwerdung Gottes, Freiburg: Herder 1970, 558. -Christ Sein, Munchen: Piper 1974, 74, 367, 348. -J. B. Metz, Theology of the World, New York: Seabury 1973, chs. 1, 3, 5, 6; -The Emergent Church, op. cit., chs. 1-3, 5, 6. -H. Peukert, Wissenschaftstheorie, Handlungstheorie, Fundamentale Theologie, Frankfurt: Suhrkamp 1978, part III. -J. Moltmann, Theologie der Hoffnung, Munchen 1969. -W. Pannenberg, Wissenschaftstheories und Theologie, Frankfurt: 1973. -E. Arens, Kommunikative Handlung. Die paradigmatische Bedeutung der Gleichnisse Jesu fur eine Handlungstheorie, Dusseldorf: Patmos 1982. -Horkheimer, Die Sehnsucht, op. cit., 66-69. -Kracaver, Das Ornament, op. cit., 106-119.

268Arens, Kommunikative Handlung, op. cit., part IV.

269Peukert, Wissenschaftstheorie, op. cit., part III, C.

270SW 15, 19-36. -SW 7, 19-37, 38-87. -R. J. Siebert, Reason, Freedom and Change: A Christian Encounter with Hegel, op. cit., chs. 4, 5. -GW 4, 315-414, 417-485.

271J. B. Metz, Glaube in Geschichte und Gesellschaft, Mainz: Matthias Grunewald 1977, chs. 3-7, 9, 10. -K. Bloch, et al. (eds.), Denken heisst Uberschreiten, Koln: Europaische Verlags-Anstalt 1978, 70-73. -Kracauer, Das Ornament, op. cit., 106-119, 123-156.

272Habermas, Zur Rekonstruktion, op. cit., 101-105.

273Habermas, Theorie des kommunikativen Handelns, op. cit., I, 72-113, 114-151. -SW 11, 43-47. -PB 33, 387-388.

274Habermas, Zur Rekonstruktion, op. cit., 102-105.

[275] Benjamin, Illuminations, op. cit., chs. 4-10; -Reflections, op. cit., ch. 3. -Th. W. Adorno, Introduction to the Sociology of Music, New York: Seabury 1976, chs. 5, 8, 11; -Philosophy of Modern Music, New York: Seabury 1973, chs. 2, 5-8. -H. Marcuse, The Aesthetic Dimension, Boston: Beacon Press 1977, chs. 1-5.

[276] Habermas, "Tod in Jerusalem," op. cit., 438-440. -G. G. Scholem, On the Kabbalah and its Symbolism, New York: Schocken Books 1965, chs. 1, 2.

[277] SW 7, 261-286, esp. 263. -GW 4, 417-464. -Habermas, Moralbewustsein und Kommunikative Handeln, op. cit., 127-206; -Theory, op. cit., ch. 2.

[278] GW 4, 58, 417-485. -Siebert, "Hegel," op. cit. -SW 7, 263.

[279] SW 7, 320. -Th. W. Adorno, Zur Dialektik des Engagements, Frankfurt: Suhrkamp 1973, 109, 128, 131, 134, 138, 144, 151-178.

[280] SW 7, 182-184.

[281] Habermas, Zur Rekonstruktion, op. cit., 102-103.

[282] GW 6, 265-331. -SW 15, 19.

[283] SW 4, 315-414, 417-485.

[284] Habermas, Zur Rekonstruktion, op. cit., 103-105.

[285] John Paul II, Laborem Exercens in G. Baum, The Priority of Labor, New York: Paulist Press 1982, 95-149. -The Challenge of Peace, National Conference of Catholic Bishops, May 3, 1983. -"Catholic Social Teaching and the US Economy" in Origins 14/22-23, November 15, 1984.

[286] SW 16, 354.

[287] Habermas, Zur Rekonstruktion, op. cit., 104-105.

[288] GW 4, 458-459. -GW 6, 265-331. -GW 8, 280-287. -Marx, Das Kapital, op. cit., I, 17-18.

[289] Habermas, _Zur Rekonstruktion_, op. cit., 104–105.

[290] GW 4, 458–459.

[291] Habermas, _Zur Rekonstruktion_, op. cit., 105.

[292] Horster, "Ein Marxistischer Kant," op. cit., 58.

[293] SW 7, 265–267, 182–184, 99–101. –SW 10, 365–381. –PB 33, 387–388.

[294] Marx, _Das Kapital_, op. cit., III, 873–874. –O. K. Flechtheim, _Futurologie_, op. cit., chs. 1–9.

[295] Habermas, _Theorie_, op. cit., ch. 8.

[296] GW 4, 458–459. –GW 6, 282–296, 307–314.

[297] Habermas, _Zur Rekonstruktion_, op. cit., ch. 4. –_Moralbewusstsein_, op. cit., 53–125.

[298] Haag, _Der Fortschritt_, op. cit., chs. 4, 5, 8.

[299] Habermas, _Theorie_, op. cit., ch. 8.

[300] Habermas, "Die Kulturkritik," op. cit., 1059–1061.

[301] GW 6, 301–306, 307–314. –GW 8, 211–222, 223–227.

[302] M. Horkheimer, _Critical Theory_, New York: Seabury 1972, 188–243. –_Gesellschaft im Übergang_, Frankfurt: Fischer Taschenbuch 1981, 162–175. –A. Schmidt, _Kritische Theorie, Humanismus, Aufklärung_, op. cit., 3–24, 27–51, 95–108. –_Zur Idee der kritischen Theorie_, op. cit., chs. 1–4, esp. 7–35, 36–124, 125–136. –_Drei Studien über Materialismus_, op. cit., ch. 2. –G. Brandt, "Ansichten kritischer Sozialforschung" in _Leviathan_, Sonderheft 4, 1981, 9–53.

[303] Horkheimer, _Gesellschaft_, op. cit., 152–160. –"E. Simmel und die Freudsche Philosophie" in B. Gorlich, etc. (eds.), _Der Stachel Freud_, Frankfurt: Suhrkamp 1980, 139–148. –Th. W. Adorno, "Revidierte Psychoanalyse" in Gorlich, _Stachel_, op. cit., 119–138. –H. Marcuse, "Gesellschaftliche und psychologische Repression. Die politische Aktualität

Freud's" in Gorlich, Stachel, op. cit., 186-192.
-A. Sohn-Rethel, Okonomie und Klassenstruktur des deutschen
Faschismus, op. cit., part II.

304Horkheimer and Adorno, Dialektik der Aufklarung, op. cit.,
IX-X; 1-7, 9-49, 88-127, 128-176, 177-217. -M. Horkheimer,
Eclipse of Reason, New York: Seabury 1974, ch. 1, 4. -Zur
Kritik der instrumentellen Vernunft, op. cit., 335-353.
-Habermas, Theorie, op. cit., ch. 4.

305Habermas, Theorie, op. cit., chs. 1-3.

306Horkheimer, Zur Kritik, op. cit., 63-92.

307Horkheimer, Eclipse, op. cit., chs. 1-3. -Th. W. Adorno,
Der Positivismusstreit in der deutschen Soziologie, Darmstadt:
Herman Luchterhand 1980, 7-80, 81-102, 125-144, 155-192,
235-266. -Soziologische Schriften I, op. cit., 280-353.
-Horkheimer, Gesellschaft, op. cit., 162-175. -Die Sehnsucht,
op. cit., 60-61. -Notizen 1950-1969 und Dammerung, op. cit.,
101-104, 116-117.

308Habermas, Theorie, op. cit., 504-505.

309Horkheimer, Die Sehnsucht, op. cit., 66-67. -Th. W.
Adorno/E. Kogon, "Offenbarung oder autonome Vernunft" in FH
13/6 (June 1958), 397-398. -Benjamin, Schriften I, Frankfurt:
Suhrkamp 1950, 494. -H. Marcuse, Eros and Civilization, New
York: Vintage Books 1962, 66.

310Habermas, Theory, op. cit., ch. 8, esp. 383, ch. 9.
-Politik, Kunst, Religion, Stuttgart: Phlip Reclam, June 1978,
127-142. -"Tod in Jerusalem," op. cit., 438-440.
-Gesellschaft, op. cit., 162-175. -Adorno/Kogon,
"Offenbarung," op. cit., 397-402. -R. J. Siebert, Horkheimer's
Critical Sociology of Religion: The Relative and the
Transcendent, op. cit., chs. 1-6, 8.

311Horkheimer, Die Sehnsucht, op. cit., 72-75. -Pope Paul VI's
Encyclical "Humanae Vitae," Huntington, Ind: Our Sunday
Visitor Inc 1968, esp. 13-14.

312Horkheimer, Gesellschaft, op. cit., 162-175. -Die
Sehnsucht, op. cit., 54-89. -Th. W. Adorno, Minima Moralia,

op. cit.,   333-334.   -W. Benjamin,   Reflections,   op. cit.,
312-313. -Illuminations, op. cit., 253-264.

[313]Horkheimer, Zur Kritik, op. cit., 148.

[314]Ibid., 236.

[315]Habermas,   Moralbewusstsein,   op. cit.,   chs.   3,   4.
-Horkheimer, Die Sehnsucht, op. cit., 60, 69, 78, 75, esp. 61.

[316]M. Horkheimer,   Studien   uber Autoritat und Familie, Paris:
Librairie Felix Alcan 1936. -E. Fromm, The Dogma of Christ,
New York: Holt, Rinehart and Winston 1963, 203-212. -The Art
of Loving, New York: Harper and Row 1956, 83-106. -Marcuse,
Eros, op. cit., parts 1, 2, 217-251. -Negations, Boston:
Beacon Press 1969, ch. 7. -Five Lectures, Boston: Beacon Press
1970, chs. 1-3. -W. Benjamin, Das Passagen-Werk, Frankfurt:
Suhrkamp 1983, 612-642, 997-1000. -R. J. Siebert, Hegel's
Concept of Marriage and Family: The Origin of Subjective
Freedom, op. cit., chs. 25-31.

[317]GW 6, 301-306. -GW 8, 38-242. -SW 7, 237-262, esp. 261-262.

[318]Schmidt,   Kritische   Theorie,   op. cit.,   95-108. -G. W. F.
Hegel, System der Philosophie, op. cit., II, 666-772 (SW 9).

[319]SW 9, 666-772.

[320]SW 10, II, 109.

[321]SW 7, 237-260. -Horkheimer, Notizen, op. cit., 5-8, 21-22,
41, 59, 83, 138-139, 142-144, 168-169, 181, 187-188, 203-204.
-Marcuse, Negations, op. cit., ch. 7. -Fromm, The Art,
op. cit., chs. 1-4. -Siebert, Hegel's Concept, op. cit., chs.
9-24. -SW 6, 301-306. -SW 8, 238-242.

[322]SW 7, 239-241. -GW 8, 238-242. -GW 6, 301-306. -Horkheimer,
Notizen, op. cit., 240, 292-293, 142-144, 148, 197-198,
307-308, 47-48. -Marcuse, Negations, op. cit., ch. 7.

[323]SW 7, 240-241.

[324]Ibid. -Ch. Baudelaire, Flowers of Evil, New York: Harper
and Brothers, Publishers 1936, 3-4, 7-9, 63-67, 81-84, 97-103,

143–146. –Benjamin, Das Passagen Werk, op. cit., 301–489.
–A. Strindberg, The Chamber Plays, New York: E. P. Dutton and
Co., Inc. 1962, vii–xxiv. –H. Ibsen, When We dead awaken and
three other plays, Garden City, New York: Doubleday and
Company 1960, xiii–xiv, 3–14.

[325] Horkheimer, Notizen, op. cit., 240.

[326] GW 6, 01–306, 307–315. –GW 8, 207–217, 217–231. –Habermas,
Moralbewusstsein, op. cit., 115–116. –SW 2, 148–158.

[327] GW 6, 301–306, 280–281, 297–300. –SW 7, 237–262, 276–278.

[328] Horkheimer, Notizen, op. cit., 292–293. –Strindberg, The
Chamber Plays, op. cit., 1–201.

[329] Horkheimer, Notizen, op. cit., 240. –Ibsen, When we dead
awaken, op. cit., 1–108, 109–216, 311–381.

[330] Horkheimer, Die Sehnsucht, op. cit., 73.

[331] Horkheimer, Notizen, op. cit., 148, 142–144.

[332] Ibid. –Horkheimer, Eclipse, op. cit., ch. 4.

[333] J. Habermas, Legitimation Crisis, op. cit., part III, ch.
4.

[334] Horkheimer, Die Sehnsucht, op. cit., 54–89, esp. 73–75.

[335] Horkheimer, Notizen, op. cit., 59, 296–297, 339, 43.

[336] Benjamin, Das Passagen Werk, op. cit., 997, 1000,
1054–1055. –Kracauer, Das Ornament, op. cit., 209–248, esp.
234, 236, 243, 246.

[337] Marcuse, Eros, op. cit., 44.

[338] Ibid., 44–45. –Horkheimer, Notizen, op. cit., 30, 15,
195–196.

[339] Sohn-Rethel, Okonomie, op. cit., 200–210.

[340] Benjamin, Das Passagen Werk, op. cit., 131–132.

-D. C. Johanson and M. A. Edey, Lucy The Beginnings of Humankind, New York: Warner Books 1982, ch. 6.

[341]Horkheimer, Notizen, op. cit., 195-196. -Horkheimer/ Adorno, Dialektik, op. cit., 88-127.

[342]Marcuse, Eros, op. cit., 185-196.

[343]Benjamin, Illuminations, op. cit., 261. -Nicolaus von Cusa, Wichtigste Schriften, op. cit., 563, 546, 33-535, 525-527, 511-518, 470, 466-470, 435, esp. 416-417, 414-416.

[344]E. Jones, The Life and Work of S. Freud, New York: Basic Books 1953, I, 330.

[345]R. Schmiede/E. Schudlich, "Die Entwicklung von Zeit-okonomie und Lohnsystem im deutschen Kapitalismus" in Leviathan 4/1981, 57-99. -Benjamin, Illuminations, op. cit., 253-264, esp. 261.

[346]Habermas, Theorie, op. cit., 512-513, 518, 522-525. -Kracauer, Das Ornament, op. cit., 234-237.

[347]Ibid. -Horkheimer, Notizen, op. cit., 170-171.

[348]Habermas, Theorie, op. cit., 522-523. -Theory, op. cit., ch. 4. -GW 6, 282-296, 296-300, 301-306, 307-315. -GW 8, 185-201, 202-209, 209-223, 223-236.

[349]Habermas, Theorie, op. cit., 518-523. -PB 33, 4, 9, 14, 441; 26-27, 46, 57, 85, 108, 148, 313-314, 321, 349, 30, 386-388, 398, 414-416.

[350]Th. W. Adorno, Gesammelte Schriften, Frankfurt: Suhrkamp 1973, Vol. VI, 6, 192.

[351]Habermas, Theorie, op. cit., Bd 2, ch. 4. -Th. W. Adorno, Asthetische Theorie, Frankfurt: Suhrkamp 1970, 35, 69, 86, 180, 190, 200.

[352]H. Peukert, Wissenschftstheorie, Handlungstheorie, Fundamentale Theologie, Dusseldorf: Patmos 1976, part III, esp. 289-302. -E. Arens, Kommunikative Handlungen, op. cit., part IV, esp. 374-385.

Chapter II: Critical Theory of Religion

[1] GW 6, 273–315. –GW 8, 185–287.

[2] GW 6, 3, 31, 210, 265, 315, 330. –PB 33, 53, 199, 311, 317, 389, 440, 441, 446, 450.

[3] G. W. F. Hegel, Jenaer System Entwurfe II, Hamburg: Felix Meiner 1971, 1, 179 (GW 7).

[4] GW 8, 3, 185, 222, 253, 277.

[5] R. J. Siebert, "Horkheimer's Sociology of Religion" in Telos, 127–141. –R. J. Siebert, "Adorno's Theory of Religion" in Telos 58 (Winter 1983–84), 108–114. –R. J. Siebert, "Fromm's Theory of Religion" in Telos 34 (Winter 1977–78), 111–120.

[6] Jamme, Mythologie, op. cit., 11–14. –F. Holderlin, Hyperion, New York: 1965, 7–17.

[7] GW 6, 330–331. –Quint, Meister Eckehart, op. cit., 415–424. – GW 8, 277–287. –SW 2, 517–601, 602–620. –PB 33, 440–463.

[8] GW 8, 277–286. SW 2, 517–601. –PB 33, 440–450.

[9] Hegel, On Christianity, op. cit., parts I–IV. –GW 4, 5–92, 117–173, 315–414, 417–485, 486–493. –GW 7, 150–154, 165–178. –GW 8, –G. W. F. Hegel, Phanomenologie des Geistes, Hamburg: Felix Meiner 1980, 363–443 (GW 9).

[10] G. W. F. Hegel, Wissenschaft der Logik, Stuttgart-Bad Cannstatt: Friedrich Frommann 1965, part I, 45–46 (SW 4). –Science of Logic, New York: Humanities Press 1969, 706–707. –Arens, Kommunikative Handlungen, op. cit., 277–325. –G. W. F. Hegel, Three Essays 1793–1795, Notre Dame, Ind: University of Notre Dame Press 1984, 29.

[11] F. Heer, "Hegel und die Jugend" in FH 22/5, May 1967, 324.

[12] SW 11, 569. –Hegel, Science of Logic, op. cit., 706–707.

[13] SW 7, 33, 35–36. –SW 11, 569.

[14] GW 8, 280. –G. W. F. Hegel, Asthetik, Frankfurt: Europaische

Verlagsanstalt 1950, I, 274-291.

[15]SW 16, 95-156. -SW 2, 535-569.

[16]Arens, Kommunikative Handlungen, op. cit., 265-277.
-Habermas, Moralbewusstsein, op. cit., 51, 53-54, 87-88,
90-96, 105-106, 122-124, 131, 201.

[17]Arens, Kommunikative Handlungen, op. cit., 308-325.

[18]P. Tillich, Systematic Theology, Chicago: University of
Chicago 1963, 99, 142, 190, 141-144, 219-223, 193-196,
230-236, 284. -M. Reiser, "Paul Tillich's Philosophische
Theology" in FH 15/11 (November 1960), 773-783.

[19]Habermas, Theorie, op. cit., 372-373, 374, esp. 375-377,
379, 380, 382, 383. -Parsons, Societies, op. cit., chs. 1, 2.

[20]GW 8, 280. -G. W. F. Hegel, Vorlesungen uber die Geschichte
der Philosophie, Frankfurt: Suhrkamp 1971, 525-526 (TW 19).
-Quint, Meister Eckehart, op. cit., 415-424.

[21]Benjamin, Reflections, op. cit., 312-313; -Illuminations,
op. cit., 253-265. -Bottomore, Karl Marx, op. cit., 32-34, 36,
38-39, 40. -Marx, Kapital, op. cit., III, 873-874.

[22]M. Horkheimer, Gesellschaft im Ubergang, Frankfurt: Fischer
Taschenbuch 1972, 162-175, esp. 167-168. -Horkheimer, Die
Sehnsucht, op. cit., 54-90.

[23]Th. W. Adorno, Negative Dialectics, Frankfurt: Suhrkamp
1968, part IV.

[24]Horkheimer, Gesellschaft, op. cit., 162-175. -Nicolaus von
Cusa, Wichtigste Schriften, op. cit., 31-33, 27-29.

[25]Habermas, Theorie, op. cit., ch. 7.

[26]H. Peukert, "Was ist eine praktische Wissenschaft?" in
Christen fur den Sozialismus, Munster (ed.), Zur Rettung des
Feuers. Solidaritatsschrift fur Kuno Fussel, Munster 1981,
280-294; -"Padagogik-Ethik-Politik. Normative Implikationen
padagogischer Interaktion" in Zeitschrift fur Padagogik,
Beiheft 1981, 61-69; -"Kontingenzerfahrung und

Identitatsfindung. Bemerkungen zu einer Theorie der Religion und zur Analytik religios dimensionierter Lernprozesse," in J. Blank and G. Hasenhuttle, Erfahrung, Glaube und Moral, Dusseldorf: Patmos 1982, 76–102; –"Erziehung, moralische" in D. Lenzen, Enzyklopadie. Erziehungswissenschaft, Stuttgart: Ernst Klett 1983, 394–401; –"Kritische Theorie und Padagogik" in Zeitschrift fur Padagogik 30 Jhrg. 1983, No. 2, 196–215. –M. L. Lamb, History, Method and Theology: A Dialectical Comparison of Wilhelm Dilthey's Critique of Historical Reason and Bernhard Lonergans Meta-Methodology, Missoula, Montana: Scholars Press 1978, ch. 1. –Hegel, On Christianity, op. cit., parts I, II. –Jamme, Mythologie, op. cit., 11–14. –GW 4, 315–414. –Hegel, Three Essays, op. cit., chs. 1–3. –GW 7, 154–178. –GW 8, 280–286. –Hegel, Science of Logic, op. cit., 706–707. –SW 16, 191–223.

^{27}GW 8, 281.

^{28}SW 7, 19–37. –SW 11, 37–129. –Metz, Theology, op. cit., part III. –Metz, Glaube, op. cit., 3, 4. –Kung, Menschwerdung, op. cit., 364–384, 385–407. –Siebert, Reason, op. cit., chs. 4, 5. –R. J. Siebert, "Hegel's Political Theology: Liberation" in The Ecumenist, 12/3 (March–April 1974), 33–41.

^{29}GW 8, 281. –SW 15, 19–24.

^{30}GW 4, 417–485. –SW 7, 432–446. –Nicolaus von Cusa, Wichtigste Schriften, op. cit., 530–531.

^{31}GW 8, 281. –Horkheimer, Gesellschaft, op. cit., 162–175. –Die Sehnsucht, op. cit., 54–89.

^{32}Horkheimer, Die Sehnsucht, op. cit., 54–89. –Hegel, Three Essays, op. cit., 23–24.

^{33}GW 8, 282–283.

^{34}Ibid. –SW 16, 295–308.

^{35}SW 7, 35. –SW 15, 292–293. –SW 16, 295–308. –Hegel, Three Essays, op. cit., 13, 3.

^{36}SW 11, 569. –Quint, Meister Eckehart, op. cit., 168–169.

[37] SW 15, 292-293. -SW 7, 19-37, 261-328. -Hegel, Three Essays, op. cit., 24-29. -SW 4, 458-459, 413-414.

[38] GW 8, 284. PB 33, 413-425. -SW 15, 256-267. -SW 7, 328-432.

[39] SW 16, 354. -Quint, Meister Eckehart, op. cit., 323-327.

[40] SW 7, 187-223. -SW 11, 65-69.

[41] SW 15, 24-36.

[42] SW 16, 349-356. -Hegel, Three Essays, op. cit., 1-29. -Habermas, Theory, op. cit., ch. 5.

[43] GW 4, 315-414. -GW 8, 286-287. SW 15, 19-36. -SW 16, -Benjamin, Reflections, op. cit., 312-313; -Illuminations, op. cit., 253-264.

[44] E. Bloch, Geist der Utopie, Frankfurt: Suhrkamp 1971, 345-389, 393-445. -E. Bloch, Subjekt-Objekt, Frankfurt: Suhrkamp 1962, chs. 5, 9, 13, 14, esp. 16, 20, 23, 24, 25.

[45] Benjamin, Reflections, op. cit., 312-313; -Illuminations, op. cit., 253-264.

[46] R. J. Siebert, "Dialectical Materialism and Political Theology: Two Views of the Future" in World Futures 19/142, 1983, 45-123. -Horkheimer, Gesellschaft, op. cit., 162-175. -Habermas, Theorie, op. cit., chs. 2, 7, 8. -Metz, The Emerging Church, op. cit., chs. 1, 2, 5, 7.

[47] Benjamin, Reflections, op. cit., 313.

[48] SW 7, 446-456. -SW 2, 619-620. -PB 33, 426-431. -GW 4, 413-414. -Benjamin, Reflections, op. cit., 312-313.

[49] Benjamin, Reflections, op. cit., 312-313. -SW 9, 575-722. -SW 10, 52-254.

[50] SW 7, 446-456. -PB 33, 426-431. -GW 4, 413-414. -SW 16, 295-308. 354-356. -SW 10, 400.

[51] GW 8, 286-287.

[52]SW 5, 5-65. -G. W. F. Hegel, Wissenschaft der Logik, Hamburg: Felix Meiner 1981, 11-52 (GW 12).

[53]SW 16, 300. -Horkheimer, Die Sehnsucht, op. cit., 54-89.

[54]SW 5, 34-171. -GW 12, 11-126.

[55]GW 4, 417-485. -GW 6, 265-326. -GW 8, 185-287. -SW 11, 42, 569. -SW 15, 100.

[56]GW 8, 286-287. -Nicolaus von Cusa, Wichtigste Schriften, op. cit., 533-535.

[57]Ibid. -GW 7, 3-177. -G. W. F. Hegel, Wissenschaft der Logik, Hamburg: Felix Meiner 1978, I, 5-8, 15-32, 33, 43, 60, 393 (GW 11). -Wissenschaft der Logik, Hamburg: Felix Meiner 1981, II, 179, 192, 236, 257 (GW 12).

[58]Jamme, Mythologie, op. cit., 11-14. -GW 6, 1-265. -GW 7, 179-338. -GW 8, 286-287.

[59]Jamme, Mythologie, op. cit., 11-14. -GW 8, 286-287.

[60]Benjamin, Illuminations, op. cit., 261. -Quint, Meister Eckehart, op. cit., 415-424.

[61]SW 16, 300.

[62]GW 7, 139-150.

[63]Benjamin, Illuminations, op. cit., 261.

[64]Ibid. -Quint, Meister Eckehart, op. cit., 161-162, 195, 203-204, 206, 208, 244, 358, 386, 394, 396-397.

[65]M. Reding, "Utopie, Phantasie, Prophetie-Prinzip der Hoffnung im Marxismus" in FH 16/1 (January 1961), 8-13, esp. 12.

[66]Benjamin, Illuminations, op. cit., 261.

[67]Habermas, Theorie, op. cit., I, 72-113.

[68]H. J. Birner, "Max Horkheimer" in W. Schmidt, ed., Die

Religion der Religionskritik, Munich 1972, 80–89; –W. Strolz,
"Sinnfragen nichtglaubender Juden" in FH 31/3 (March 1976),
25–34; –J. Amery, "Das Jahrhundert ohne Gott" in FH 23/3
(March 1968), 151–158.

[69]M. Horkheimer, "Foreward" in M. Jay, The Dialectical
Imagination, Boston 1973.

[70]M. Horkheimer, "Der neueste Angriff auf die Metaphysik" in
Zeitschrift fur Sozialforschung (ZfS) VI, 51. –Horkheimer, Die
Sehnsucht, op. cit., 54–89; –Aus der Pubertat: Novellen und
Tagebuchblatter, Munich 1974, 7–145.

[71]M. Horkheimer, Werk und Wirken Paul Tillichs, Stuttgart
1967, 16.

[72]G. W. F. Hegel, Lectures on the Philosophy of Religion,
trans. J. Sibree (London 1902), Vol. I, 100–212. –Horkheimer,
Critical Theory, New York 1972, 129–131; Zur Kritik der
instrumentellen Vernunft, Frankfurt 1967, 236.

[73]F. Feuerbach, The Essence of Christianity, New York 1967,
part II. –Adorno, Drei Studien zu Hegel, op. cit., 13.
–A. Schmidt, "Die 'Zeitschrift fur Sozialforschung,'
Geschichte und gegenwartige Bedeutung," in ZfS, op. cit.,
8–17. –G. Lichtheim, From Marx to Hegel, New York 1971,
vii–30. –K. Marx and F. Engels, Werke, Bern 1963, Vol. 29,
561.

[74]W. Dirks, "Am Schnittpunkt" in FH, 24 (September 1969), 613.
–E. Kogon, SS Staat, Frankfurt 1965, esp. iv–v.

[75]W. Dirks, "Die 'Frankfurter Hefte' und der Marxismus," in
FH, 7 (April 1952), 237–242; –"Bittere Frucht: Der
Bolschewismus und die Geschichte des Christentums" in FH 19
(August 1964), 533–540; –Unser Vater und das Vater unser,
Munich 1972, 120; –"Was meine ich, wenn ich sage: Ich glaube
an den Sohn Gottes" in FH 28 (April 1974), 257–260. –E. Kogon,
"Rudolf Augsteins 'Herausforderung'," in FH 28 (April 1973),
249–257 and Adorno and Kogon, "Offenbarung oder autonome
Vernunft" in FH 13 (June 1958), 392–402; 13 (July 1958),
484–498. –W. Dirks, E. Kogon, "An die Abonnenten, die Leser
und die Freunde der FH" in FH 39/10 (October 1984), 17–22.
–R. J. Siebert, Horkheimer's Critical Sociology of Religion:

The Relative and the Transcendent, op. cit., chs. 3, 6-8.

[76]M. Horkheimer and Th. W. Adorno, "Vorurteil und Charakter" in FH 7 (April 1952), 284-291. -Th. W. Adorno, "Die Soziologen und die Wirklichkeit" in FH 7 (August 1952), 585-95. -"Uber Mahler" in FH 15 (September 1960), 643-53; -"Wird Spengler rechtbehalten," FH 10 (December 1955), 841-46. -J. Habermas, "Konsumkritik eigens zum Konsumieren," in FH 12 (September 1957), 641-45. -Adorno and Horkheimer, Dialectic of the Enlightenment, New York 1972, ix-xvii; -Horkheimer, Notizen, op. cit., 54-132. -Hegel, Three Essays, op. cit., chs. 1-3. -SW 16, 207-209.

[77]Horkheimer, Die Sehnsucht, op. cit., 60-61. -SW 15, 6-18.

[78]E. Kogon and W. Dirks, "An unsere Leser" in FH 1 (April 1946), 1-2; -W. Dirks, "1903-1943-1973, Kogon zum Geburtstag," FH 28 (February 1973), 77-78. -H. Gollwitzer, "E. Kogon und die 'Frankfurter Hefte'" in FH 28 (February 1973), 125-128. -H. Rombach, "Die Religionsphanomenologie" in Theologie und Philosophie, 48 (19793), 485-93. -Adorno/Kogon, "Revelation," op. cit. -Adorno, Kierkegaard, Frankfurt 1966, ch. 7. -"On Kierkegaard's Doctrine of Love" in ZfS, VIII, 413-25. -M. Horkheimer, "Zu Theodor Haecker: Der Christ und die Geschichte" in ZfS, 372-382. -W. Dirks, "Ich glaube an Jesus Christus-Verstandigungsversuch in drei Stucken" in FH 27 (December 1973), 878-888; "Volkskirche im Ubergang Zur Krise der Kirche" (I and II) in FH 25 (February 1970), 108-116. -H. C. F. Mansilla, "Zwei Begegnungen in der Schweiz" in FH 28 (April 1973), 239-240. -H. Mayer, "Nachdenken uber Adorno" in FH 24 (April 1970), 268-280. -Dirks/Kogon, "Andre Abonnenten," op. cit., 17-22.

[79]SW 2, . -P. Tillich, Morality and Beyond, New York 1963, ch. 5. -H. Marcuse, Counterrevolution and Revolt, Boston 1972, ch. 1. -Voegelin, From Enlightenment, op. cit., 74. -Flechtheim, Futurologie, op. cit, 309-397.

[80]G. Wolff and H. Gumnior in Spiegel, January 6, 1970, "Aut das Andere hoffen," 70-84. -Hegel, Three Essays, op. cit., 24.

[81]H. C. F. Mansilla, "Zwei Begegnungen in der Schweitz" in FH 28/4, 239-240. -Adorno, Negative Dialectics, New York 1973, 3.

[82]G. W. F. Hegel, Lectures on the Philosophy of History, London 1902, 18-20. -SW 2, 685-694.

[83]Horkheimer, Notizen, op. cit., 8, 16, 18, 28-29, 92, 121-123, 127, 131-132, 148, 210-211, 218, 247, 268, 286-287, 316-320. -Hegel, Philosophy of Religion, op. cit., Vol. 3, 149.

[84]Horkheimer, Critical Theory, op. cit., 131. -K. Marx, "Contribution to Hegel's Philosophy of Right" in R. Niebuhr, Marx and Engels on Religion, New York 1949, 41.

[85]Horkheimer, Critical Theory, op. cit., 129-131.

[86]Mansilla, "Zwei Begegnungen," op. cit., 240.

[87]Horkheimer, Critical Theory, op. cit., 129. -Die Sehnsucht, op. cit., 56-57.

[88]Horkheimer, Die Sehnsucht, op. cit., 56-76. -"Zu Theodor Haecker," op. cit., 372-82.

[89]Hegel, Lectures on the History of Philosophy, Vol. 3, trans. E. S. Haldane and F. Simson, New York 1955, 61-67. Philosophy of Religion, op. cit., Vol. 1, 90-100.

[90]F. Schleiermacher, "Religion as a Faculty" in J. Bettis, Phenomenology of Religion, New York 1969, 139-168.

[91]E. Bloch, Das Prinzip Hoffnung, Frankfurt 1973, ch. 53.

[92]G. Rohrmoser, Das Elend der kritischen Theorie, Freiburg 1969, 105.

[93]Horkheimer, Die Sehnsucht, op. cit., 54-89. -SW 2, 251-267. -Marcuse, One Dimensional Man, Boston 1966, 56-83. -V. Gardavsky, Gott ist nicht ganz tot, Munchen 1969. -S. Freud, Moses and Monotheism, New York 1939, part III. -Hegel, Three Essays, op. cit., 9.

[94]Horkheimer, Aus der Pubertat, op. cit., 175-182.

[95]Blakney, Meister Eckehart, op. cit., xiv. -Hegel, The Science of Logic, op. cit., 600-622.

[96] Horkheimer, Studien uber Autoritat und Familie, op. cit., 3-76, esp. 75-76.

[97] Horkheimer, Die Sehnsucht, op. cit., 73-74. -Fromm, The Art of Loving, op. cit. -Horkheimer, Aus der Pubertat, op. cit.; -On Christianity, op. cit., 302-308. -Hegel, Three Essays, op. cit., 1-29.

[98] Mansilla, "Zwei Begegnungen," op. cit., 240.

[99] Schmidt, "Fruhe Dokumente der kritischen Theorie" in Horkheimer, Aus der Pubertat, op. cit.

[100] Hegel, The History of Philosophy, op. cit., Vol. 3, 423-478; -The Philosophy of History, op. cit., 21-37.

[101] Hegel, History of Philosophy, op. cit., Vol. 2, 1-71, 90-117. -Science of Logic, op. cit., Vol. 2, 600-622.

[102] Hegel, The Philosophy of Right, op. cit., 125; The Philosophy of History, op. cit., 203-348; The History of Philosophy, op. cit., Vol. 2, 432, Vol. 3, 25.

[103] Hegel, Philosophy of History, op. cit., 18-20; Philosophy of Right, op. cit., 126-128.

[104] Horkheimer, Notizen, op. cit.; Zur Kritik, op. cit., 124-52, 302-353.

[105] Horkheimer, Die Sehnsucht, op. cit., 83-89. Studien, op. cit., 64-76. -Flechtheim, Futurologie, op. cit., 309-397.

[106] Horkheimer and Adorno, Dialectic of Enlightenment, op. cit., 3-42. -Horkheimer, Notizen, op. cit., 25-156. -S. Kierkegaard, Fear and Trembling and the Sickness Unto Death, Princeton, NJ: 1973, 108-129.

[107] Horkheimer, Zur Kritik, op.. cit., 248-353. -Werner Post, Kritische Theorie und metaphysischer Pessimismus Zum Spatwerk Max Horkheimers, Munich 1971, 9-50.

[108] Th. Haecker, Der Christ und die Geschichte, Leipzig 1935. -Horkheimer, "Zu Theodor Haecker: Der Christ und die Geschichte," op. cit.

109Marx, Die Fruhschriften, op. cit., 339-46. -Hegel, On Christianity, op. cit., part I. -L. Feuerbach, The Essence of Christianity, New York 1957, ch. 1, part I.

110Horkheimer, "Zu Theodor Haecker," op. cit., 381-382. -Habermas, Theory, op. cit., 121-140.

111Horkheimer, Zur Kritik, op. cit., 248-64. -H. Marcuse, "On Hedonism," in Negations, Boston 1968, 159-200.

112SW 2, 74-76. -R. J. Siebert, "Three Alternative Futures" in World Futures, January 1985.

113Hegel, Philosophy of Right, Oxford 1942, 11-13, 93-103.

114Metz, Theology, op. cit., chs. 5-6. -Moltmann, Theologie der Hoffnung, op. cit., 313-334. -E. Hofflich, "Karl Marx fur die Kirche" in FH 24 (November 1969), 777-85; "Heilsverkundigung als politsche Gewissensbildung," FH 24 (December 1969), 843-854. -W. Kasper, "Politische Utopie und christliche Hoffnung" in FH 24 (August 1969), 563-572. -M. Reding, "Utopie, Phantasie, Prophetie Das Prinzip Hoffnung im Marxismus," FH 16 (January 1961), 8-13.

115E. Kogon, "Revolution und Theologie: Das Neue in unserem Zeitalter. Ein Symposium," FH 22 (September 1967), 616-630. -A. M. Greeley, Lord of the Dance, New York: Warner Books 1984. -J. Carroll, Prince of Peace, Boston: Little Brown and Co. 1984. -J. Kavanaugh, Laughing Down Lonely Canyons, San Francisco: Harper and Row Publishers 1984.

116Adorno and Kogon, "Offenbarung," op. cit., 397-398.

117Horkheimer, Die Sehnsucht, op. cit., 54-69; Critical Theory, op. cit., 129-131. -H. Kung, Christ sein, Munich 1974, 26-28, 285; Menschwerdung Gottes, Freiburg 1970, 557-558. -J. Metz, Theologie, op. cit., chs. 1-2.

118Flechtheim, Futurologie, op. cit., 311-397.

119Jay, The Dialectical Imagination, op. cit., 200. -Horkheimer, Die Sehnsucht, op. cit., 54-89; Critical Theory, op. cit., 129-131.

[120] E. Fromm, _Beyond the Chains of Illusion_, New York: 1962, 5.

[121] _Ibid._, 5-6.

[122] E. Fromm, "The Application of Humanist Psychoanalysis to Marx's Theory" in E. Fromm (ed.), _Socialist Humanism_, New York: Doubleday 1966, 228-246.

[123] SW 15, 68.

[124] Fromm, _You Shall Be As Gods_, New York: 1966, 56-62; _The Heart of Man_, New York: 1964, ch. 6.

[125] Fromm, _The Dogma of Christ and Other Essays_, New York: 1963, 11-21; "Ueber Methode und Aufgabe einer analytischen Sozialpsychologie" in _ZfS_, vol. I (1951), 28-54; -"Die psychoanalitische Characterologie und ihre Bedeutung fur die Sozialpsychologie" in _ibid._, vol. 3 (1932), 253-277; -"Review of Otto Heller, _Der Untergang des Judentums_, _ibid._, 438-439; -"Robert Briffault's Werk uber das Mutterrecht," _ibid._, (1933), 382-387; -"Die sozialpsychologische Bedeutung der Mutterrechtstheorie," _ibid._, (1934), 196-227; -"Die gesellschaftliche Bedingtheit der psychoanalytischen Therapie," _ibid._, (1935), 365-398. -"Sozialpsychologischer Teil," in Horkheimer, _Studien uber Autoritat und Familie_, op. cit., 77-135; -"Zum Gefuhl der Ohnmacht," in _ZfS_, (1937), 95-117. -"The Social Psychology of 'Will Therapy,'" _Psychiatry_ (May 1939), 229-237.

[126] Marx, "Contribution to the Critique of Hegel's 'Philosophy of Right'," in _Critique of Hegel's 'Philosophy of Right'_, Joseph O'Malley, ed. (Cambridge 1970), 131. -Feuerbach, _The Essence of Christianity_, New York: 1957, part I. -Marx, "Die deutsche Ideologie" in _Die Fruhschriften_, op. cit., 339-341.

[127] E. Fromm, _Arbeiter und Angestellte am Vorabend des Duthen Reiches_, Stuttgart: Deutsche Verlags Anstalt 1980, 7-46, 51-79.

[128] Fromm, _The Revolutionary Character_, op. cit., 148.

[129] Fromm, "The Application of Humanist Psychoanalysis to Marx's Theory" in _Socialist Humanism_, Garden City 1966, 233-234.

[130]Jay, Dialectical Imagination, op. cit., 222, 229–230. –Horkheimer, "Foreword" to Jay, Dialectical Imagination, op. cit., xii. –Marcuse, Eros and Civilization, New York: 1962, 217–251; "A Reply to Erich Fromm" in Dissent, 3:1 (Winter 1956), 79–83.

[131]Fromm, The Dogma, op. cit., 16.

[132]Ibid., 16; –Marx, "Contribution," op. cit., 131–132.

[133]Fromm, The Dogma, op. cit., 20.

[134]Ibid., 20.

[135]Ibid., 26, 37.

[136]Ibid., 39. Luke 18:18–25; Luke 16:19–31; James 5:1–11.

[137]Fromm, The Dogma, op. cit., 46–47.

[138]Ibid., 48.

[139]Ibid., 48. –Marcuse, Eros and Civilization, op. cit., 63–66.

[140]Fromm, To Have or To Be, New York: 1976, 53–65.

[141]Fromm, The Dogma, op. cit., 50–91.

[142]Ibid., 48–49. –Horkheimer, Die Sehnsucht, op. cit., 63–64.

[143]SW 16, 295–308. –SW 7, 35. –SW 15, 292–293. –Hegel, Three Essays, op. cit., 13, 3.

[144]Fromm, The Dogma, op. cit., 21–49.

[145]E. Fromm, The Sane Society, New York: 1955, chs. 1–3, 8; –Fromm, The Heart, op. cit., 116–118.

[146]E. Fromm, Marx's Concept of Man, New York: 1967, 1–83; The Heart, 116. –Nicolaus of Cusa, Wichligste Schriften, op. cit., 420–427.

[147]Horkheimer, Critical Theory, op. cit., 129.

[148] Fromm, The Heart, 118; -E. Fromm, Escape from Freedom, New York: 1970, ch. 5.

[149] E. Fromm, The Anatomy of Human Destructiveness, New York: 1973, ch. 13; The Heart, 118; Escape from Freedom, ch. 6.

[150] Fromm, The Heart, 118-119.

[151] Ibid., 119.

[152] Fromm, You Shall Be as Gods, op. cit., ch. 2.

[153] Horkheimer, Die Sehnsucht, op. cit., 57-59.

[154] Fromm, You Shall Be as Gods, op. cit., 22.

[155] Ibid., 28-32. -G. W. F. Hegel, Vorlesungen uber die Geschichte der Philosophie, Stuttgart-Bad Cannstatt: 1965, 131-132 (SW 19).

[156] Fromm, You Shall Be as Gods, op. cit., 32-33. -Nicolaus of Cusa, Wichtigste Schriften, op. cit., 31-32. -Quint, Meister Eckehart, op. cit., 213-218, 267-271, 303-310.

[157] Fromm, You Shall Be as Gods, op. cit., 41-42.

[158] Ibid., 48.

[159] Fromm, To Have or To Be, op. cit., 202. -Flechtheim, Futurologie, op. cit., 396-397. -Dante Alighieri, Inferno, Toronto: Bantam Books, Canto I, i, 112-136.

[160] W. Strolz, "Sinnragen nicht-glaubender Juden" in FH (March 1976), 25-34. -Fromm, The Heart, ch. 4; You Shall Be as Gods, chs. 2-3, pp. 53, 57, 61; To Have or To Be, 202.

[161] A. Schmidt, "Die 'Zeitschrift fur Sozialforschung' Geschichte und Gegenwartige Bedeutung" in ZfS, 9.

[162] Adorno and Kogon, "Offenbarung," op. cit., 397-402.

[163] SW 11, 43-47.

[164] SW 15, 24-36.

[165]Ibid., 23-24.

[166]Th.W. Adorno, Quasi Una Fantasia, Frankfurt: Suhrkamp 1963, 153-154, 306-338, 339-364; "Über Mahler" in FH 15/9, 643-653; –Dialektik des Engagements, Frankfurt: Suhrkamp 1973, 22-29; –Versuch das 'Endspiel' zu Verstehen, Frankfurt: Suhrkamp 1972, 167-214; "Parataxis. Zur spaten Lyrik Holderlins," in Jochen Schmidt, Über Holderlin, Frankfurt: Inselverlag 1970, 339-378.

[167]M. Horkheimer, "Foreword" in Jay, The Dialectical Imagination, op. cit., xi-xii.

[168]K. Rohring, "Theodor W. Adorno," in W. Schmidt, Die Religion der Religionskritik, Munchen: Claudius Verlag 1972, 31-32.

[169]Th. W. Adorno, Negative Dialektik, Neuwied: Luchterhand 1966, part II, 396.

[170]Adorno and Kogon, "Offenbarung," op. cit., 484-498. –SW 11, 43-47.

[171]Adorno, Negative Dialektik, op. cit., 398.

[172]Th. W. Adorno, Drei Studien zu Hegel, Frankfurt: Suhrkamp 1969, 78.

[173]Ibid., 104.

[174]Horkheimer, Die Sehnsucht, op. cit., 60.

[175]Mansilla, "Zwei Begegnungen," op. cit., 240. –SW 7, 177-178. –Horkheimer, Notizen, op. cit., 141-142; Aus der Pubertat, op. cit., 53-244; Die Sehnsucht, op. cit., 9-89.

[176]Th. W. Adorno, Kierkegaard, Frankfurt: Suhrkamp 1962, ch. 7.

[177]Horkheimer, Die Sehnsucht, op. cit., 59-62. –GW 4, 315-414. –K. H. Haag, Zur Dialektik von Glauben und Wissen, Frankfurt: Horst Heidenhoff 1971, 3-13. –Quint, Meister Eckehart, op. cit., 267-270.

[178]Horkheimer and Adorno, Dialectic of Enlightenment, New York: Seabury 1972, 23-24. -Adorno, Quasi Una Fantasia, op. cit., 312-315, 317-321.

[179]Th. W. Adorno, Minima Moralia, Frankfurt: Suhrkamp 1980, 333-334.

[180]J. B. Metz, Zur Theologie der Welt, Munchen: Chr. Kaiser 1968, ch. 5. -E. Hoflich, "Karl Marx fur die Kirche," FH, vol. 14, no. 22 (November 1966), 777-785; "Heilsverkundigung als politische Gewissensbildung," FH, vol. 24, no. 12 (December 1969), 843-854. -W. Kasper, "Politische Utopie und christliche Hoffnung" in FH, vol. 24, no. 8 (August 1969), 563-572. -F. Heer, "Hegel und die Jugend," FH, vol. 22, no. 5 (May 1967), 324. -J. B. Metz, Jenseits burgerlicher Religion, Mainz: Grunewald 1980, chs. 1-3, 5-6. -R. J. Siebert, Hegel's Philosophy of History: Theological, Humanistic and Scientific Elements, Washington DC: University Press of America 1979, chs. 1-3; Horkheimer's Critical Sociology of Religion, op. cit., chs. 1-5, 8; From Critical Theory of Society to Theology of Communicative Praxis, Washington DC: University Press of America 1979.

[181]Habermas, Theorie, op. cit., Bd 1, 15.

[182]Ibid. -G. W. F. Hegel, Vorlesungen uber die Geschichte der Philosophie, op. cit., 187-236 (SW 17).

[183]Habermas, Theorie, op. cit., ch. 4. -SW 7, 35-36, 6, 33.

[184]Feuerbach, The Essence of Christianity, op. cit., ch. 1.

[185]SW 11, 37-43. -Isaiah 1-10. -SW 17, 396-434. -Matthew 6: 25-34.

[186]GW 4, 413-414. -B. Pascal, Pensees. The Provincial Letters, New York: Modern Library 1941, chs. 2, 6-8, 11-13. -Kung, Existiert Gott?, op. cit., A, II.

[187]SW 15, 19-52. -SW 16, 351-356, 546-553.

[188]PB 33, 450-463.

[189]Horkheimer, Gesellschaft, op. cit., 162-175; Die Sehnsucht,

op. cit., 60; -and Th. W. Adorno, Dialectic of Enlightenment,
op. cit., 3-42, esp. 23-24. -Adorno and Kogon, "Offenbarung,"
op. cit., 484-498; "Offenbarung," op. cit., 397-402, esp. 402.
-W. Benjamin, Briefe 2, Frankfurt: Suhrkamp 1978, 671-683,
esp. 672, 676.

[190]H. E. Bahr, Religionsgesprache zur Gesellschaftlichen Rolle
der Religion, Darmstadt: Luchtenhand 1975, 9-30.

[191]Ibid. -J. Habermas, Stichworte zur Geistigen Situation der
Zeit, Frankfurt: Suhrkamp 1979, Bd 2: Politik und Kultur,
chs.. 19, 20, 29.

[192]Habermas, Theorie, op. cit., 7-11, 15-24; Vorstudien,
op. cit., chs. 1, 2, 4, esp. 9.

[193]Habermas, Theorie, op. cit., ch. 2.

[194]Ibid., ch. 4. -A. Schopenhauer, The World as Will and
Representation. -Th. W. Adorno, Sociologische Schriften I,
op. cit., 354-370.

[195]Horkheimer, Eclipse of Reason, New York: Seabury Press
1974, chs. 1, 3, 4.

[196]Th. W. Adorno, Asthetische Theorie, Frankfurt: Suhrkamp
1970, 9-30, 122-153, 179-04, 205-243, 296-333, 334-388.

[197]M. Weber, Sociology of Religion, Boston: Beacon Press 1972,
ix-xvii, xix-lxvii, ch. 1, 280-286; The Protestant Ethic and
the Spirit of Capitalism, New York: Scribner's 1958, ix-xi,
xiii-xvii, 1-11, 13-31. -H. H. Gerth and C. W. Mills, From Max
Weber: Essays in Sociology, New York: Oxford University Press
1958, v-vii, 3-31, 32044, 45-74, 77-128, esp. 129-156.
-Habermas, Moralbewusstsein, op. cit., 10, 20, 22, 24; 117,
120, 192, 196, 198; ch. 4.

[198]Habermas, Theorie, op. cit., chs. 4, 8.

[199]Ibid., chs. 5-8. -SW 7, 265-267, 182-184, 99-101.
-G. Lukacs, Der junge Hegel, Zurich: Europa 1967, chs. 1-4; Die
Zerstorung der Vernunft, Darmstadt: Luchterhand 1974,
chs. 5-7. Schriften zur Ideologie und Politik, Neuwied:
Luchterhand 1967, chs. 1-4, 6, 11, 13, 15, 19-22, 24, 27-28,

36; History and Class Consciousness, Cambridge: MIT Press 1976, chs. 1-8; Deutsche Literatur in zwei Jahrhundeuten, Neuwied: Luchterhand 1964, parts I-III. -I. Kant, Was ist Aufklarung?, Gottingen: Vandenhoek and Ruprecht 1975, 24-30, 40-54, 77-93, 113-122, 123-128; Die Religion inerhalb der Grenzen der blossen Vernunft, Stuttgart: Reclam 1974, 3-16, 20-68; Anthropologie in Pragmatischer Hinsicht, Stuttgart: Reclam 1983, part I; Zum Ewigen Frieden, Stuttgart: Reclam 1953, 3-12, 15-22; Kritik der Urteilskraft, Frankfurt: Suhrkamp 1974, 334-456. Schriften zur Anthropologie, Geschichtsphilosophie, Politik und Padagogik, Frankfurt: Suhrkamp 1981, 11-30, 33-61, 127-172, 175-190, 228-251. -A. Schmidt, Kritische Theorie, Humanismus, Aufklarung, Stuttgart: Reclam 1981, 3-7, 9-26, 27-51, 95-108, 110-154. -GW 6, 265-315.

[200] G. H. Mead, On Social Psychology, Chicago: University of Chicago 1964, part III; Philosophy of Art, Chicago: University of Chicago 1938, parts I, II, IV; "Scientific Method and Individual Thinker" in J. Dewey, etc., Creative Intelligence: Essays in the Pragmatic Attitude, New York: Octagon Books 1970, 176-227; Mind, Self and Society, Chicago: University of Chicago 1962, ix-xxxv, part I, III, IV.

[201] E. Durkheim, The Elementary Forms of the Religious Life, Glencoe, Ill: Free Press 1947, 1-22, book I, 415-447; Professional Ethics and Civic Morals, Glencoe, Ill: Free Press 1958, chs. 1-9; The Division of Labour in Society, Glencoe, Ill: Fre Press 1947, book I; Socialism and Saint-Simon, London: Routledge and Kegan Paul 1959, chs. 6, 9.

[202] Habermas, Theorie, op. cit., ch. 8; Moralbewusstsein, op. cit., ch. 4, esp. 174-175, 178-179, 182, 183, 188-190, 194.

[203] Habermas, Theorie, op. cit., Bd 1, 73. -Jamme, Mythologie, op. cit., 11-14. -GW 6, 269-326. -GW 8, 185-287. -L. Friedeburg and J. Habermas, Adorno-Konferenz 1983, Frankfurt: Suhrkamp 1983, 66-93.

[204] Habermas, Theorie, op. cit., ch. 8. -R. Dobert, Systemtheorie und die Entwicklung Religioser Deutungssysteme, Frankfurt: Suhrkamp 1973, 83-157.

[205] Horkheimer/Adorno, Dialektik der Aufklarung, op. cit., 9-87. -Friedeburg, Adorno Konferenz 1983, op. cit., 95-130, 138-176, 177-197. -SW 15, 19-36. -SW 16, 352-356.

[206] Habermas, Theorie, op. cit., 74-75. -L. Levy-Bruhl, La Mentalite Primitive, Paris 1922.

[207] Habermas, Theorie, op. cit. -SW 15, 179-342.

[208] Ibid.

[209] H. Pottker, "G. Dux: 'Die Logik der Weltbilder, Sinnstrukturen imWandel der Geschichte'," Frankfurt: Suhrkamp 1982, in FH 38/5 (May 1983), 68-70, esp. 70.

[210] Habermas, Moralbewusstsein, op. cit., ch. 3.

[211] Habermas, Theorie, op. cit., 76-78. -Friedeburg, Adorno Konferenz 1983, op. cit., 351-353, 226-233.

[212] Habermas, Zwei Reden, op. cit., 25-75; Zur Rekonstruktion, op. cit., 105. -Horkheimer, Die Sehnsucht, op. cit., 80-89. -Adorno, Soziologische Schriften, op. cit., 357-358, 362-363.

[213] Habermas, Theorie, op. cit., 77-78.

[214] SW 15, 100; -SW 11, 42, 48-50, 65-69. -Horkheimer, Die Sehnsucht, op. cit., 37, 56-57. -M. Weber, The Sociology of Religion, op. cit., ch. 9.

[215] Kant, Was ist Aufklarung?, op. cit., 77-93. -R. J. Siebert, "From Historical Materialism to Theology of Communicative Praxis" in Proceedings of International Hegel Society, Athens 1985.

[216] Kant, Was ist Aufklarung?, op. cit., 88-89.

[217] G. W. F. Hegel, Fruhe Schriften, Frankfurt: Suhrkamp 1971, 35-36 (TW 1); -Vorlesungen uber die Philosophie der Geschichte, Frankfurt: Suhrkamp 1970, 25-27, 35-36 (TW 12). -SW 15, 100.

[218] H. Nohl (ed.), Theologische Jugendschriften, Tubingen 1907, 22-23. -H. Kung, Menschwerdung Gottes, Frieburg: Herder 1970,

67-80.

[219] Nohl, Theologische Jugendschriften, op. cit., 3.

[220] Kung, Menschwerdung, op. cit., 41-80.

[221] SW 7, 35. -SW 11, 37-43.

[222] SW 7, 36, -Hegel, Three Essays, op. cit., 3, 13.

[223] SW 11, 42-47, 48-50, 65-69, 569. -SW 7, 35-36.

[224] SW 15, 75-100.

[225] Hegel, Asthetik, op. cit., Bd 1, 7-95. Bd 2, 7-22.
-G.W.F. Hegel, Vorlesungen uber die Geschichte der
Philosophie, Stuttgart-Bad Cannstatt: Frommann 1965, 19-135,
135-150.

[226] Hegel, On Christianity, op. cit., 69, 77, 83, 89, 179, 281,
302-308, 311-319. -GW 4, 413-414, 459-464. -SW 16, 300. -SW 2,
569-601.

[227] Peukert, Wissenschaftstheorie, op. cit., part I, C; part
III, B, C, D. -Arens, Kommunikative Handlungen, op. cit.,
parts III, IV.

[228] S. Kierkegaard, Erbauliche Reden, in Verschiedenem Geist,
Gutersloh: Gutersloher Verlagshaus 1983, 75-76, 90, 91.

[229] Hofflich, "Karl Marx," op. cit., 777-785.
-"Heilsrerkundigung," op. cit., 843-854.

[230] Peukert, Wissenschaftstheorie, op. cit., part III, D.
-Arens, Kommunikative Handlungen, op. cit., part IV.

[231] Horkheimer, Die Sehnsucht, op. cit., 37, 40-42, 54-89;
Gesellschaft, op. cit., 162-176; Sozialphilosophische Studien,
Frankfurt: Fischer 1972, 7-11, 145-156, 131-137.

[232] Weber, Sociology of Religion, op. cit., ch. 9.

[233] G. P. Maximoff (ed.), The Political Philosophy of Bakunin,
Scientific Anarchism, London: Free Press of Glencoe 1964, 62,

105,   113-115,   118,   123,   124, 130, 161. -A. Blanqui, Textes
Choisis, Paris: Editions Sociales 1955, 7-47, 71-108, 141-195;
Schriften zur Revolution, Nationalokonomie und Sozialkritik,
Hamburg: Rowohlt 1971, 40-51, 52-62; Instruktionen fur den
Aufstand, Frankfurt: Europaische 1968, 5-46, 63-68, 78-91,
92-110, 111-124, 125-153. -Marx, Early Writings, op. cit.,
43-44. -S. Freud, The Future of an Illusion, Garden City, New
York: Doubleday 1964, 18, 24, 26-30, 32-35, 37, 40-45, 47,
49-53, 55-73, 75-92; Civilization and its Discontent, New
York: Norton 1962, 21-23, 31-32, 39, 61-74. -Habermas,
Theorie, op. cit., ch. 8.

[234]M. Horkheimer, Zur Kritik der Instrumentellen Vernunft,
op. cit., 148.

[235]Horkheimer and Adorno, Dialectic, op. cit., 23-24.

[236]Horkheimer, Zur Kritik, op. cit., 227.

[237]Ibid. -Adorno/Kogon, "Offenbarung," op. cit., 397. -Haag,
Der Fortschritt, op. cit., chs. 6, 7. -Horkheimer, Die
Sehnsucht, op. cit., 54-89.

[238]Horkheimer, Zur Kritik, op. cit., 236.

[239]Horkheimer, Die Sehnsucht, op. cit., 42-53, 54-89.

[240]Habermas, Theorie, op. cit., 77-78.

[241]O. Marquard, Schwierigkeiten mit der Geschichtsphilosophie,
Frankfurt: Suhrkamp 1973, 52-66, 167-178.

[242]Habermas, Theorie, op. cit., 78-79.

[243]SW 15, 100, 279-324. -SW 16, 247-308.

[244]Habermas, Theorie, op. cit., 79.

[245]GW 6, 245-281. -GW 8, 108-222. -SW 9,, 575-722. -SW 10,
9-45. -Horkheimer/Adorno, Dialectic, op. cit., 43-80, 3-42.

[246]GW 6, 265-326. -GW 8, 285-287.

[247]SW 15, 299-324. -T. F. O'Dea, The Sociology of Religion,

Englewood Cliffs, New Jersey: Prentice-Hall 1966, chs. 3, 6.
-Parsons, Societies, op. cit., chs. 3, 4.

[248]Parsons, Societies, op. cit., chs. 5, 6. -O'Dea, The
Sociology, op. cit., 3, 4, 5.

[249]Habermas, Theorie, op. cit., 80.

[250]GW 6, 297-300, 307-315. -GW 8, 202-209, 218-231. -Marx, Die
Fruhschriften, op. cit., chs. 6-10. -Adorno, Soziologische
Schriften, op. cit., 354-370, 373-391.

[251]Habermas, Zur Rekonstruktion, op. cit., ch. 4. -Theorie,
op. cit., Bd 2, 489-547.

[252]Habermas, Theorie, op. cit., Bd 1, 80. -Parsons, System,
op. cit., chs. 1,2.

[253]Habermas, Theorie, op. cit., Bd 1, 114-151.

[254]Ibid., 80. -SW 15, 279-324, 324-342, 342-354, 355-400. -GW
6, 297-300, 307-315.

[255]Habermas, Theorie, op. cit., Bd 1, 81. -GW 6, 282-296. -GW
8, 185-201.

[256]GW 6, 282-326. -GW 8, 185-287.

[257]Habermas, Theorie, op. cit., Bd 1, 81, 76.

[258]Ibid., 81. -SW 15, 299-324, 355-400, 422-434, 434-437,
437-471. -SW 16, 95-156, 156-188.

[259]SW 15, 342-354.

[260]Parsons, System, op. cit., chs. 1, 2. -Dobert,
Systemtheorie, op. cit., 87-157.

[261]Habermas, Theorie, op. cit., Bd 1, 81-82.

[262]R. Kuhnl, "Die Ursachen des Europaischan Faschismus nach
dem Ersten Weltkrieg" in FH 38/6 (June 1983), 32-40.

[263]Habermas, Theorie, op. cit., Bd 1, 81-82.

264G. W. F. Hegel, Fruhe Schriften, Frankfurt: Suhrkamp 1971, 211–212 (TW 1). –Hegel, Jenaer Schriften 1801–1807, Frankfurt: Suhrkamp 1970, 425 (TW 2). –Marx, Die Fruhschriften, op. cit., 486–489.

265Habermas, Theorie, op. cit., Bd 1, 82.

266Horster, "Ein Marxistischer Kant," op. cit.,

267Horkheimer, Gesellschaft im Ubergang, op. cit., 167–168. Die Sehnsucht, op. cit., 64–66; Sozialphilosophische Studien, op. cit., 145–155; Critique of Instrumental Reason, New York: Seabury 1967, ch. 4. –A. Schopenhauer, Aphorismen zur Lebensweisheit, Frankfurt: Goldmann 1982, 148–172, 173–182; The World as Will and Representation, New York: Dover 1958, I, 245, 329–355, 405–406, II, 506, 507, 585, 604, 608. –L. Lutkehaus, "Der 'Fall' Reinhold Schneider" in FH 38/6 (June 1983) 41–46. –Hegel, Three Essays, op. cit., 24–27.

268A. Blanqui, Instruktionen, op. cit. Schriften, op. cit. –Maximoff, The Political Philosophy, op. cit., 9–16, 17–27, 29–48, part IV. –Marx, Die Fruhschriften, op. cit., chs. 9, 10. The 18th Brumaire of Louis Bonaparte, New York: International Publishers 1972, 118–135, 136–140. –Adorno, Soziologische Schriften, op. cit., 373–396, esp. 397–407, 408–433. Prismen, Frankfurt: Suhrkamp 1976, 283–342, 51–81, 112–143, 283–301.

269Kuhnl, "Die Ursachen," op. cit., 32–40.

270Fromm, Arbeiter, op. cit., chs. 2–4.

271PB 33, 44. –SW 7, 27–28.

272Blackney, Meister Eckehart, op. cit., 258–305. –Nicolaus of Cusa, Wichtigste Schriften, op. cit., 534–535, 491–492, 472–473, 425–427, 417–422. –Quint, Meister Eckehart, op. cit., 194–200. –Alighieri, Inferno, op. cit., I, 9; III, 21. –SW 16, 191–223. –SW 15, 227–228.

273SW 7, 19–37, 261–286. –SW 11, 47–69. –Adorno, Soziologische Schriften I, op. cit., 431–432.

274Habermas, Theorie, op. cit., 82–83.

[275]Benjamin, Reflections, op. cit., 312-313. -Lamb, "The Dialectics of Theory of Praxis," op. cit., 1-32. -Benjamin, Illuminations, op. cit., 253-264. -Lamb, "Liberation Theology and Social Justice," op. cit., 1-34. -Siebert, "Dialectical Materialism," op. cit. -Lamb, "Roman Catholic Liberation Theology," op. cit., 1-32.

[276]Nicolaus von Cusa, Wichtigste Schriften, op. cit., 533-535, 502-504, 494-495, 474-476, 300-323. -J. B. Metz, Jenseits Burgerlicher Religion, Munchen: Chr. Kaiser Verlag 1980, chs. 4, 7. -H. Kung, etc., (eds) Christentum und Weltreligionen, Munchen: R. Piper and Co. 1984.

[277]Habermas, Theorie, op. cit., Bd 1, 83-84.

[278]SW 7, 182-184, 99-101, 265-267, esp. 182. -PB 33, 387-388. -M. Horkheimer, Notizen 1950-1969 und Dammerung, Frankfurt: Fischer 1974, 86-97. -Parsons, Societies, Englewood Cliffs, NJ: Prentice-Hall 1966, chs. 5, 6.

[279]Horkheimer, Notizen, op. cit., 141-142, 187-188, 203, 316-320, 291-292, 333-334, 350-351, 26-27, 30-33, 38-39, 82-83, 88-89, 98-99, 101-104, 116-117, 139, 151-152, 168-169, 187, 203-204, 213, 230-231. Zur Kritik, op. cit., 124-152, 216-228, 229-238, 239-247, 335-354. -Habermas, The Legitimation Crisis, -Adorno, Soziologische Schriften I, op. cit., 440-456, 20-41, 42-85, 434-439. Prismen, op. cit., 144-161. Kritik, Kleine Schriften zur Gesellschaft, Frankfurt: Suhrkamp 1980, chs. 3-8, 10.

[280]Horkheimer, Notizen, op. cit., 17-18, 81, 148. -Horkheimer/Adorno, Dialectic, op. cit., 43-80, 120-167, 168-208.

[281]Habermas, Moralbewusstsein, op. cit., chs. 3, 4.

[282]Habermas, Theorie, op. cit., 85.

[283]SW 7, 19-37. -SW 11, 37-43.

[284]Habermas, Die Kulturkritik, op. cit.,

[285]Habermas, Theorie, op. cit., 93-95.

286 Ibid.,   94-95. -PB 33, 431-432, 77-79. -Kant, Die Religion, op. cit., 3-16.

287 SW 11, 42, 47-69. -SW 7, 35-36. -Horkheimer, Gesellschaft im Ubergang, op. cit., 162-176; Sozial-philosophische Studien, Frankfurt: Fischer 1981, 137-144, 145-155; Zur Kritik, op. cit., 248-268; Die Sehnsucht, op. cit., 56-57, 59-60; Notizen, op. cit., 62, 63-65, 91-92, 135-136. -Adorno, Prismen, op. cit., 315-316.

288 R. J. Siebert, From Critical Theory of Society to Theology of Communicative Praxis, Washington DC: University Press of America 1979, chs. 4, 5. "From Historical Materialism," op. cit. "Alternative Futures," op. cit. "Hegel," op. cit.

289 Siebert, "Dialectical Materialism," op. cit., 50-53. -Kung, Existiert Gott?, op. cit., part D.

290 Habermas, "Die Kultur Kritik," op. cit., 1059-1061.

291 Quint, Meister Eckehart, op. cit., Sermon 10. -Siebert, "Christian Revolution, Liberation and Transcendence," op. cit., 85-91. -Blackney, Meister Eckehart, op. cit., 43-73, 82-91. -Siebert, "Political Theology" in The Ecumenist (July-August 1971), 65-71. -Kung, Die Menschwerdung, op. cit., 68-70.

292 R. J. Siebert, Horkheimer's Critical Sociology of Religion: The Relative and the Transcendent, Washington DC: University Press of America 1979, chs. 3-6, 8; "Religion and Psychoanalysis: European Situation," op. cit., 19.

293 Peukert, Wissenschaftstheorie, op. cit., part III. -E. Arens, Kommunikative Handlungen, Dusseldorf: Patmos 1982, part IV. -Lamb, "Roman Catholic Liberation Theology," op. cit., 1-32; "Liberation Theology and Social Justice," op. cit., 1-34.

294 SW 2, 34. -S. Kierkegaard, Fear and Trembling and the Sickness unto Death, Princeton, NJ: Princeton University Press 1954, 142-213. -Th. W. Adorno, Negative Dialectics, New York: Seabury 1973, 361-365, 368-373. -W. Benjamin, Das Passagen-Werk, Frankfurt: Suhrkamp 1982, II, 997-998, 1000-1002, 1007.

[295] SW 2, 34.

[296] Hegel, Wissenschaft der Logik, Hamburg: Felix Meiner 1963, 6, 11, 20–21, 35–37, 87, 90 (PB 56). –PB 33, 44, 73, 102–103, 184, 316. –SW 16, 300–302.

[297] SW 7, 35.

[298] SW 15, 293. –Haag, Der Fortschritt, op. cit., 165–469.

[299] Habermas, Theorie, op. cit., Bd 1, 96–105. –K. Popper, The Open Society and Its Enemies; Objective Knowledge, Oxford: Clarendon Press 1972, chs. 1, 2, 8.

[300] Habermas, Theorie, op. cit., 96–97.

[301] Th. W. Adorno, etc., Der Positivismusstreit in der deutschen Soziologie, Neuwied: Luchterhand 1970, 102–124, 155–192, 235–266. –Adorno, Soziologische Schriften I, op. cit., 280–353.

[302] Habermas, Theorie, op. cit., Bd 1, 98. –Popper, Objective Knowledge, op. cit., chs. 1, 3–8.

[303] P. Picconi, etc. (eds.), "Religion and Politics," Telos (march 1984).

[304] Habermas, Theorie, op. cit., Bd 1, 98.

[305] Habermas, Zur Rekonstruktion, op. cit., chs. 1–4, 6, 10; Theorie, op. cit., ch. 8.

[306] Habermas, Theorie, op. cit., Bd 1, 99–100.

[307] Horkheimer, Notizen, op. cit., 16, 92–93, 127–128, 131–133, 158–160, 210–211, esp. 260.

[308] SW 11, 409–436, 443–465, 467–518, esp. 519–548. –SW 7,

[309] SW 11, 548–569. –SW 15, 67–68. –E. Fromm, Marx's Concept of Man, New York: Frederick Ungar 1967, v–x, 261–263; Socialist Humanism, Garden City, NY: Doubleday 1966, vii–xiii, parts I–V, esp. 228–245; To Have, op. cit.

310 Habermas, Zur Rekonstruktion, op. cit., ch. 6.

311 Habermas, Theorie, op. cit., Bd 1, 101–102. –Popper, Objective Knowledge, op. cit., chs. 1, 3–9. –Horkheimer, Notizen, op. cit., 101–104, 116–117.

312 Horkheimer, Die Sehnsucht, op. cit., 73–74.

313 Habermas, Theorie, op. cit., Bd 1, 102.

314 Popper, Objective Knowledge, op. cit., ch. 4.

315 Benjamin, Das Passagen Werk, op. cit., vol. II, 1010–1016, 1016–1025.

316 Habermas, "Die Kultur," op. cit., 1059–1061. –G. Scholem, Sabbatai Sevi: The Mythical Messiah, 1626–1676, Princeton: Princeton University Press 1973, chs. 2–6; Major Trends, op. cit., chs. 7–9; The Messianic Idea in Judaism, New York: Schocken Books 1971, chs. 1–5, 7–9, 15–16. –H. Weiner, 9 1/2 mystics. The Kabbala Today, New York: Collier Books 1969, 2–3, 5–9.

317 Habermas, Theorie, op. cit., Bd 1, 102–103.

318 Ibid., 103.

319 SW 11, 45–47. –Alighieri, Inferno, op. cit., I, 9. –Quint, Meister Eckehart, op. cit., 251–256, 262–267, 303–310, 335–340. –Nicolaus von Cusa, Wichtigste Schriften, op. cit., 507, 517.

320 Habermas, Theorie, op. cit., Bd 1, 103.

321 Ibid., 104; ch. 2. –Weber, The Sociology of Religion, op. cit., xix–lxvii, ch. 1.

322 J. Piaget, The Child's Conception of Physical Causality, London 1930; Die Entwicklung des Erkennens, Stuttgart 1973, vol. 3; Abriss der genetischen Epistemeologie, Olton 1974.

323 Habermas, Theorie, op. cit., Bd 1, 104–105. –GW 7, –SW 4.

324 Habermas, Theorie, op. cit., Bd 1, 104–105. –Dobert,

Systemtheorie, op. cit., 87–157. –Parsons, Societies, op. cit., chs. 3–6; Modern System, op. cit., 3–6.

[325]Habermas, Theorie., op. cit., chs. 6, 8, esp. 107–108.

[326]SW 15, 19–20. –Quint, Meister Eckehart, op. cit., 53–100, 101–139, esp. 213–218, 267–271, 303–310. –Hegel, Jenaer Schriften 1802–1807, Frankfurt: Suhrkamp 1970, 534–539 (TW 2); Vorlesungen uber die Philosophie der Religion, Frankfurt: Suhrkamp 1969, 209 (TW 16).

[327]SW 15, 19–20. SW 2, A, B and C.

[328]SW 15, 19–20.

[329]Nicolaus von Cusa, Wichtigste Schriften, op. cit., 385–386.

[330]SW 15, 21–23, 19, 24–36.

[331]Ibid. –SW 2, 108–138.

[332]Habermas, Zur Rekonstruktion, op. cit., ch. 4.

[333]Habermas, Theorie, op. cit., 107–108.

[334]SW 15, 75–100. –F. Heer, "Hegel und die Jugend" in FH 22/5 (May 1967), 323–332. –Habermas, Zur Rekonstruktion, op. cit., ch. 4.

[335]Habermas, Theorie, op. cit., Bd 1, 108.

[336]Ibid. –SW 15, 342–354, 355–400, 400–417, 422–437, 437–472. –SW 16, 46–95, 95–156, 156–188, 191–356.

[337]Friedeburg, Adorno-Konferenz, op. cit., 41–65. –Siebert, "Hegel," op. cit.

[338]Habermas, Theorie, op. cit., 108–109.

[339]Horkheimer, Critical Theory, op. cit., 129–131; Gesellschaft im Ubergang, op. cit., 162–175; Sozialphilosophische Studien, op. cit., 131–136, 145–155; Die Sehnsucht, op. cit., 54–89. –Benjamin, Illuminations, op. cit., 253–264; Reflections, op. cit., 312–313. –H. Marcuse, Eros and

Civilization,   New   York: Vintage   1962,   ch. 3.   -Habermas,
"Bewusstmachende oder rettende   Kritik-die   Aktualitat   Walter
Benjamin's"   in   S.   Unseld,   <u>Zur Aktualitat Walter Benjamin's</u>,
Frankfurt: Suhrkamp 1972, ch. 4.

[340]Horkheimer, <u>Gesellschaft</u>, op. cit., 162-175. -Habermas,
<u>Theorie</u>, op. cit., ch. 8. -Metz, <u>Glaube</u>, op. cit., s. 3, 4.
-Siebert, "Dialectical Materialism," op. cit., 45-81. <u>From</u>
<u>Critical Theory</u>, op. cit.

[341]Habermas, <u>Theorie</u>, op. cit., Bd 1, 109-110.

[342]<u>Ibid</u>., ch. 8.

[343]Siebert, "Hegel," op. cit. "Three Alternative Futures,"
op. cit., 231-297; "The Dialectic of European and American
Civil Society: Alternative Futures" (unpublished).

[344]Habermas, <u>Theorie</u>, op. cit., Bd 1, 109-110. -Weber, <u>The</u>
<u>Sociology of Religion</u>, op. cit., xxix-lxvii; <u>The Protestant</u>
<u>Ethic and the Spirit of Capitalism</u>, New York: Scribner's 1958,
xiii-xvii, Ia-II.

[345]Habermas, <u>Theorie</u>, op. cit., Bd 1, 109-110, chs. 2, 8.

[346]SW 11, -SW 7,

[347]Habermas, <u>Theorie</u>, op. cit., chs. 7, 8.

[348]<u>Ibid</u>., Bd 1, 109-110. -Piaget, <u>Die Entwicklung des</u>
<u>Erkennens</u>, op. cit., vol. 3, 229.

[349]Habermas, "Die Kulturkritik," op. cit., 1059-1061.

[350]SW 10, 93-109. -SW 11, 44-47, 149-157.

[351]Habermas,   <u>Theorie</u>,   op. cit.,   111-119.   -R. Dobert,
J. Habermas, etc. (eds.), <u>Entwicklung des Ichs</u>, Koln 1977,
170-172, 177-178.

[352]Habermas, <u>Theorie</u>, op. cit., 111-112. -Siebert, "Hegel,"
op. cit.

[353]<u>Ibid</u>., 112. -Horster, "Ein Marxistischer Kant," op. cit.,

58–65. –SW 7, 36.

[354]Habermas, Theorie, op. cit., 112. –Jamme, Mythologie, op. cit., 11–14. –SW 4, 417–485, 486–493. –SW 6, 111–172, 265–331. –SW 8, 108–184, 185–287.

[355]SW 15, 34.

[356]Habermas, Theorie, op. cit., 112–113.

[357]Habermas, Zur Rekonstruktion, op. cit., ch. 4. –SW 15, 75–10.

[358]Habermas, Theorie, op. cit., ch. 8. –J. Habermas/N. Luhmann, Theorie der Gesellschaft oder Sozialtechnologie, Frankfurt: Suhrkamp 1975, 101–141, 142–290. –Habermas, Technik und Wissenschaft als 'Ideologie', Frankfurt: Suhrkamp 1976, chs. 1–3, 5; Zur Logik der Sozialwissenschaften, Frankfurt: Suhrkamp 1973, chs. 2–4; Zur Rekonstruktion, op. cit., ch. 12; Theory, op. cit., chs. 2–7.

[359]Arens, Kommunikative Handlungen, op. cit., 371–373. –Metz, Glaube, op. cit., s. 1–10, 13.

[360]B. Slosser, Reagan–Inside Out, Waco, Texas: Worldbooks 1984, chs. 3, 4, 8. Luke 1:46–56. Matthew 6:25–34.

[361]Habermas, Theorie, op. cit., Bd 1, 113.

[362]Siebert, "Hegel," op. cit.; "Three Alternative Futures," op. cit.; "The Dialectic of European and American Civil Society," op. cit. –SW 4,

[363]Horkheimer, Notizen, op. cit., 106–107.

[364]SW 7, 35–36. –SW 15, 292–293. –Haag, Der Fortschritt, op. cit., 165–469. –T. deChardin, Die Zukunft des Menschen, Olten 1963, 128. –J. Moltmann, Der Gekreuzighe Gott, Munchen: Chr. Kaiser 1973, 37–39, 69–70, 86–89, 186–187, 240–241. Moralbewusstsein, op. cit., chs. 3, 4. –Kung, Menschwerdung, op. cit., 376–378. –Moltmann, Perspektives der Theologie, Munchen 1968, 212–231.

[365]Habermas, Theorie, op. cit., 231.

[366] GW 4, 417–464. –Habermas, Theory, op. cit., ch. 2.

[367] SW 4, 417–464, esp. 458–459.

[368] Habermas, Theorie, op. cit., 231–232.

[369] Ibid., 232. –L. Kohlberg, Zur Kognitiven Entwicklung des Kindes, Frankfurt: 1974.

[370] Habermas, Theorie, op. cit., 232, 312–315.

[371] E. Arens, "Schon sprosst es, gewahrt ihr es nicht?" in S. Dunde (ed.), Katholisch und rebellisch, Hamburg: Rowohlt 1984, 101–119.

[372] Habermas, Zur Rekonstruktion, op. cit., 101. Theorie, op. cit., Bd II, 312–313; Bd II 147, ch. 8.

[373] Acts 2:42–47; 4:32–35.

[374] P. Wehling, "Ars der neuesten Wissenschaft. Ein Stimmungsbild," in Diskus, H.6/1,84, 34 Jhrg. 10–13. –H. Altenhofen, "Hochdroben wo die Geister toben" in Diskus H.6/1,84, 34 Jhrg. 15–17.

[375] Habermas, Theorie, op. cit., 273. –F. H. Tenbruck, Das Werk Max Webers KZSS 27, 1975, 673–675.

[376] Habermas, Theorie, op. cit., Bd 1, 273.

[377] SW 15, 100.

[378] Habermas, Theorie, op. cit., Bd 1, 274–275. –Dobert, Systemtheorie, op. cit., 9–10, 11–12, 13–71. –Weber, Sociology, op. cit., ch. 9.

[379] Habermas, Theorie, op. cit., 275. Zur Rekonstruktion, op. cit., 134–136.

[380] Habermas, Theorie, op. cit., 275–276.

[381] Ibid. –SW 15, 42–43, 48–50, 569.

[382] Horkheimer, Die Sehnsucht, op. cit., 56–67.

[383] Habermas, "Die Kultur Kritik," op. cit., 1059-1061.

[384] Peukert, Wissenschaftstheorie, op. cit., parts II and III.
-Arens, Kommunikative Handlungen, op. cit., parts III and IV.

[385] Peukert, Wissenschaftstheorie, op. cit., part III. -Wiesel,
Four Hasidic Masters, op. cit., 1-124. -Arens, Kommunikative
Handlungen, op. cit., part IV. -Scholem, The Messianic Idea in
Judaism, op. cit., chs. 1, 2, 4-7. -Weiner, 9 1/2 Mystics,
op. cit., 2, 3, 5-9.

[386] Habermas, Theorie, op. cit., 279-280. -Weber, The Sociology
of Religion, op. cit., chs. 1-16.

[387] Habermas, Theorie, op. cit., 279. -M. Weber, The Religion
of China, Confucianismus und Taoismus, Glencoe, Ill: Free
Press 1951, parts I-III; Gesammelte Aufsatze zur
Religionssoziologie, Hinduismus und Buddhismus, Tubingen: Mohr
1966, vol. II; Gesammelte Aufsatze zur Religionssoziologie,
Das antike Judentum, Tubingen: Mohr 1966, vol. III. -SW 15,
342-417. -SW 16, 464-94.

[388] Habermas, Theorie, op. cit., Bd 1, 279-280.

[389] Ibid., Bd 1, 280.

[390] Ibid. -M. Horkheimer and Th. W. Adorno, Dialectic of
Enlightenment, New York: Seabury 1972, 43-80.

[391] Habermas, Theorie, op. cit., Bd 1, 280-281.

[392] J. De Santa Ana, Towards a Church of the Poor, Maryknoll,
New York: 1979, parts I-III. "Catholic Social Teaching" in
Origins (November 15, 1984), 338-341.

[393] Habermas, Theorie, op. cit., Bd 1, 281.

[394] Ibid., Bd 1, 281-283; ch. 8. -Habermas, Zur Rekonstruktion,
op. cit., 129-143, chs. 1, 2, 4, 6.

[395] O. Marquard, Schwierigkeiten mit der Geschichts
philosophie, Frankfurt: Suhrkamp 1973, chs. 1-5.

[396] Habermas, Theorie, op. cit., Bd 1, 281; Zur Rekonstruktion,

op. cit., chs. 4, 5, 7, 8. -Kracaver, Das Ornament, op. cit., 271-317.

[397]Habermas, Theorie, op. cit., 281. -Weber, The Sociology of Religion, op. cit., ch. 4.

[398]SW 15, 100. -Marquard, Schwierigkeiten, op. cit., 52-65. -Horkheimer, Gesellschaft, op. cit., 166-175. -Weber, The Sociology of Religion, op. cit., ch. 9. -Horkheimer, Die Sehnsucht, op. cit., 37.

[399]SW 11, 42-43, 47-69, 569. -SW 15, 100, 293. -SW 7, 33-34, 35-36, 434-435, 436, 444, 433-436.

[400]Horkheimer, Die Sehnsucht, op. cit., 37. -Weber, The Sociology of Religion, op. cit., ch. 9.

[401]Horkheimer, Die Sehnsucht, op. cit., 37. -Marx, Die Fruhschriften, op. cit., chs. 3, 6, 9, 10.

[402]H. E. Bahr (ed.), Religionsgesprache. Zur gesellschaftlichen Rolle der Religion, Darmstadt: Luchterhand 1975, ch. 1. -Habermas, Zur Rekonstruktion, op. cit., ch. 4. -Marquard, Schwiergkeiten, op. cit., parts I and II. -Weber, Sociology of Religion, op. cit., ch. 9.

[403]Horkheimer, Die Sehnsucht, op. cit., 37.

[404]Jamme, Mythologie, op. cit., 11-14. -GW 4, 58, 417-485. -GW 6, 317-326. -GW 8, 253-287. -SW 7, 19-37. -SW 15, 33-120.

[406]Marx, Fruhschriften, op. cit., chs. 6-10; Das Kapital, op. cit., I, 17-18, III, 873-879. -Siebert, "Hegel," op. cit., "The Dialectic of European and American Civil Society," op. cit.

[407]Habermas, Theorie, op. cit., Bd 1, 281-282.

[408]Ibid., 282. -SW 15, 355-400. -SW 16, 46-95. -Weber, The Sociology of Religion, op. cit., 224-228. -Nicolaus of Cusa, Wichtigste Schriften, op. cit., 420-421, 424-435, 445-449, 451-452, 474-476, 491, 492-500, 546-551. -Habermas, "Tod in Jerusalem," op. cit.

[410] Habermas, Theorie, op. cit., 282–283. Zur Rekonstruktion, op. cit., 106–107.

[411] Habermas, Theorie, op. cit., Bd 1, 282–283.

[412] O'Dea, The Sociology of Religion, op. cit., 11–13. –Weber, Gesammelte Aufsatze zur Religionssoziologie, Tubingen: Mohr 1963, vol. I, 17–206, 207–236. –Parsons, Essays in Sociological Theory, Glencoe, Ill: Free Press 1964, ch. 10. –Durkheim, The Elementary Forms of Religious Life, Glencoe, Ill: Free Press 1954, 323, 387, 416; The Division of Labor in Society, op. cit., xli–xliii, 393, xxix n, xxxii n; The Rules of Sociological Method, Glencoe, Ill: Free Press 1958, chs. 1, 2, 5.

[413] Habermas, Theorie, op. cit., 283–284. –Weber, The Sociology of Religion, op. cit., chs. 4, 9–12, 14–16.

[414] SW 15, 422–434, 434–472. –SW 16, 33–46, 46–95, 95–156. –SW 7, 82–184. –G.W.F. Hegel, Vorlesungen uber die Geschichte der Philosophie, Stuttgart–Bad Cannstatt: Frommann 1965, 551–611 (SW 19).

[415] Habermas, Theorie, op. cit., 283–284.

[416] SW 19, 551–611. –Horster, "Ein Marxistischer Kant," op. cit., 58–65. –I. Kant,

[417] Habermas, Theorie, op. cit., 284. –Weber, The Sociology of Religion, op. cit., chs. 9–12.

[418] G.W.F. Hegel, Vorlesungen uber die Geschichte der Philosophie, Stuttgart–Bad Cannstatt: Frommann 1965, 169–297 (SW 18). –SW 19, 551–611. –SW 15, 422–434.

[419] Habermas, Theorie, op. cit., 284. –Weber, Sociology of Religion, op. cit., ch. 9.

[420] Habermas, Theorie II, op. cit., 278–280, ch. 5. –Zur Rekonstruktion, op. cit., ch. 4, part III.

[421] J. Habermas, Technik und Wissenschaft als Ideologie, Frankfurt: Suhrkamp 1976, chs. 1–3; Zur Rekonstruktion, op. cit., part IV. –R.J. Siebert, "Communication without

Domination" in <u>Concilium</u>.

[422]<u>Habermas</u>, <u>Theorie</u>, op. cit., Bd 2, 279–280. –Weber, <u>Sociology of Religion</u>, op. cit., ch. 9.

[423]<u>Habermas</u>, <u>Theorie</u>, op. cit., Bd 2, 280; <u>Zur Rekonstruktion</u>, op. cit., ch. 4, parts III, IV.

[424]E. Fromm, <u>The Dogma of Christ</u>, New York: Rinehart and Winston 1963, 3–94, 95–106, 203–212. –SW 16, 286–308.

[425]<u>Habermas</u>, <u>Theorie</u>, op. cit., Bd 2, 281.

[426]R. Garaudy, <u>From Anathema to Dialogue</u>, New York: Herder and Herder 1966, ch. 3, esp. 96–98.

[427]<u>Ibid</u>., 93–100.

[428]K. Costelloe, "Pope Bans Marxism in Church" in <u>Detroit Free Press</u>, August 23, 1984. –"Pope Criticizes any Class Ideas in Theologies" in <u>National Catholic Reporter</u>, August 31, 1984. –"Retort to Rome" in <u>Time</u>, July 9, 1984. –M.R. Day, "Vatican Tempering Theology Critiques in Wake of Dialogue" in <u>National Catholic Reporter</u>, July 6, 1984. –N. Woodward, J. Lantigua and A. Nagorski, "Nicaragua's Rebel Jesuits" in <u>Newsweek</u>, September 3, 1984, 74. –P. Hebbleth Wait, "Document Wars about Liberation Theology" in <u>NCR</u>, September 7, 1984.

[429]Garaudy, <u>From Anathema</u>, op. cit., ch. 4.

[430]P. erdozain, <u>Archbishop Romero</u>, Maryknoll, NY: Orbis 1981, chs. 3–5, 89–98.

[431]SW 2,

[432]H. Marcuse, <u>Studies in Critical Philosophy</u>, Boston: Beacon Press 1972, ch. 1; <u>Kultur und Gesellschaft I</u>, Frankfurt: Suhrkamp 1980, ch. 2. –J. Mehlhausen, "'Freiheit des Glaubens' – Luther's Lehre von der Freiheit als Erbe und Auftrag" in <u>FH</u> 38/7 (July 1983), 45–54, esp. 48–49.

[433]Horkheimer, <u>Notizen</u>, op. cit., 92–93, 127, 131–132, 210–211, 286–287, 247–248, 96–97, 1212–123.

[434] Marcuse, Eros and Civilization, op. cit., 63-66. -Isaiah, 26-27. -Fromm, The Dogma, op. cit. -Luke 1:46-56; 3:1-22. -Marcuse, "Marxism and the New Humanity: An Unfinished Revolution" in J. C. Raines and Th. Dean (eds.), Marxism and Radical Religion, Philadelphia: Temple University Press 1970, 3-10, esp. 9-10. -Wiesel, The Madness of God, op. cit. -Scholem, Sabbatai Sevi, op. cit., chs. 1-6. -Quint, Meister Eckehart, op. cit., 9-50.

[435] SW 15, 256-267. -PB 33, 431-436. -Horkheimer, Notizen, op. cit., 259-260, 269, 286-287, 288-289, 293-294, 316-320. -Marx, Fruhschriften, op. cit., ch. 5. -Siebert, From Critical Theory, op. cit., ch. 3.

[436] M. Horkheimer, Critical Theory, New York: Seabury 1968, ch. 4. -R. Niebuhr, K. Marx and F. Engels on Religion, New York: 1964, 41-43. -SW 16, 223-247.

[437] Horkheimer, Die Sehnsucht, op. cit., 67-68.

[438] G.W.F. Hegel, Die Vernunft in der Geschichte, Felix Meiner 1955, 46 (PB 171a). -Nicolaus of Cusa, Wichtigste Schriften, op. cit., 569. -J. Ritter, Hegel und die Franzosische Revolution, Frankfurt: Suhrkamp 1972, 7-71.

[439] Horkheimer, Die Sehnsucht, op. cit., 68. -Metz, Theology of the World, op. cit.; The Emergent Church, op. cit., chs. 1-2, 5-7; Zeit der Orden, Frieburg: Herder 1978, chs. 1-4. -Habermas (ed.), Stichworte zur Geistigen Situation der Zeit, Frankfurt: Suhrkamp 1979, vol. 2, chs. 19-20, 29. -A. Waterman, "Theology and the Redistribution of Wealth" in The Ecumenist, vol. 22, no. 5 (July-August 1984), 75-78.

[440] J. Habermas, Legitimation Crisis, Boston: Beacon 1975, parts II, III. -Marcuse, "Marxism," op. cit., 9-10. -E. Arens, "Steh auf, Du Christ-Basisgemeinden in der Bundesrepublik" in F. Boll, et al. (eds.), Wird es denn uberhaupt gehen?, Munchen: Kaiser 1980, 23-29. -Arens, "Schon sprosstes," op. cit., 101-119. -S. Torres and J. Eagleson (eds.), The Challenge of Basic Christian Communities, Maryknoll, NY: Orbis 1980, parts I, II. -B. Paleczny and M. Cote (eds.), Becoming Followers of Jesus, Burlington, Ontario: Trinity 1983, parts II, III. -J. Eagleson (ed.), Christians and Socialism, Maryknoll: Orbis 1975, parts I-III. -J. G. Davies, Christians,

Politics and Violent Revolution, Maryknoll: Orbis 1976, chs. 2-6. -D.J. Santa Ana, Toward a Church of the Poor, Maryknoll: Orbis 1981, parts 1-3. -E. Cardenal, The Psalms of Struggle and Liberation, New York: Herder and Herder 1971. -D. Berrigan, Uncommon Prayer, New York: Seabury 1978, 53-56.

[441]Adorno/Kogon, "Offenbarung," op. cit., 484-498.

[442]Habermas, Theorie, op. cit., Bd 2, 281.

[443]Ibid. -Adorno, Soziologische Schriften, op. cit., 354-370.

[444]Metz, Theology, op. cit., 107-124.

[445]Habermas, Theorie, op. cit., Bd 2, 281.

[446]Haag, Der Fortschritt, op. cit., chs. 1-4, 6.

[447]Horkheimer, Die Sehnsucht, op. cit., 61-62. -Haag, Der Fortschritt, op. cit., chs. 4, 6-8.

[448]Habermas, Theorie, op. cit., Bd 2, 281. -SW 4, 414, 451-464. -SW 7, 35-37, 261-328. -SW 11, 37-43, 47-69. -SW 15, 19-36. -SW 16, 286-308, 354-356.

[449]Habermas, Theorie, op. cit., Bd 2, 281. -SW 16, 354-355. -Habermas, Theory, op. cit., 189-193.

[450]Habermas, Theorie, op. cit., Bd 2, 282.

[451]Ibid., 282-288. -M. Bloch, "Symbols, Song, Dance and Features of Articulation" in Archive of European Sociology 15, 1974, 55-57.

[452]SW 15, 19-36. -SW 16, 355-356. -Haag, Zur Dialektik, op. cit., VI/3-VI/13. -Habermas, Theorie, op. cit., chs. 1-2, 4, 7.

[453]Horkheimer, Critical Theory, op. cit., 129-131. -S. Schmidt, "Die Zeitschrift fur Sozialforschung. Geschichte und Gegenwartige Bedeutung" in ZfS, 8-17. -Horkheimer, Notizen, op. cit., 8, 16, 18, 96-97, 121-123, 127, 131-132; Zur Kritik der instrumentellen Vernunft, Frankfurt: Fischer 1967, 216-228, 229-238, 239-247. -Adorno/Kogon, "Offenbarung,"

op. cit., 484-498. -Adorno, Minima Moralia, op. cit., 333-334; Negative Dialectics, New York: Seabury 1973, parts 3, II, III. -Benjamin, Reflections, op. cit., 312-313; Illuminations, op. cit., 253-264. -Marcuse, Eros, op. cit., ch. 3; Studies, op. cit., 56-78; "Marxism," op. cit., 9-10. -E. Fromm, Zen Buddhism and Psychoanalysis, New York: Harper and Row 1960, vii-viii, part II; Psychoanalysis and Religion, New Haven: Yale University Press 1971, chs. 1-5; Escape from Freedom, New York: Avon Books 1968, chs. 2-4; You Shall Be as Gods, op. cit., chs. 2, 5-7. -L. Lowenthal, Mitmachen wollte ich nie. Ein autobiographisches Gesprach mit Helmut Dubiel, Frankfurt: Suhrkamp 1980, 10, 58, 60, 69, 73, 80-81, 133, 156, 158-159, 163, 166, 175-176, 191, 223; Literature and the Image of Man, Boston: Beacon 1957, chs. 1-2. -H. Dubiel, "Die Aktualitat der Gesellschaftstheorie Adorno's" in Friedeburg, Adorno Konferenz, op. cit., 293-313. -M. Theunissen, "Negativitat bei Adorno" in Frieburg, Adorno Konferenz, op. cit., 41-65. -Kracaver, Das Ornament, op. cit., 106-119, 173-186, 187-196, 249-255.

[454]Fromm, Psychoanalysis, op. cit., viii. -John Paul II, Redemptor Hominis, Washington DC: United States Catholic Conference, March 4, 1979, 45-46, 49, esp. 51.

[455]P. Tillich, On the Boundary Line, New York: Scribner's 1966, chs. 3, 5, 7-11; The Socialist Decision, New York: Harper and Row 1977, parts II, III. -T. deChardin, The Phenomenon of Man, New York: Harper and Row 1965, bk. 4. -R. Lischer, Marx and Teilhard, Maryknoll: Orbis 1979, esp. ch. 6. -Kung, Christ Sein, Munchen: Piper 1974, part D; Existiert Gott?, Munchen: 1978, parts B, F, G. -Metz, Theologie, op. cit., chs. 1-2, 5; Glaube, op. cit.; The Emergent Church, op. cit., 1, 2, 3. -W. Dirks, Der Singende Stotterer, Munchen: Kosel 1983, 11-48, 193-203. -Peukert, Wissenschaftstheorie, op. cit., part III. -Arens, Kommunikative Handlungen, op. cit., part IV.

[456]Dirks, Der Singende Stotterer, op. cit., 196.

[457]H.H. Hucking, "Christliche Basisgruppen in Ost-Europa" in FH 34/2 (February 1977), 6-8. -T. Seiferich, "Basis Gemeinden in der Bundes Republick" in FH 37/9 (September 1982), 35-42. -Arens, "Steh auf," op. cit., 23-29; "Schon sprosstes," op. cit., 101-119. -R. Bohne, "Kirche in Latein Amerka unter

Druck" in <u>FH</u> 32/2 (February 1977), 6-8.

[458]W.J.O. Malley, <u>The Voice of Blood: Five Christian Martyrs</u> <u>of our Time</u>, Maryknoll: Orbis 1979. -A. Dobrin, et al. (eds.), <u>Convictions</u>, Maryknoll: Orbis 1981, chs. 1, 3-4, 7-8. -P. Erdozain, <u>Archbishop Romero, Martyr of Salvador</u>, Maryknoll: Orbis 1981, chs. 4-5. -<u>Calendar of Martyrs</u>, Hamilton, Ontario 1983.

[459]Habermas, <u>Theorie</u>, op. cit., Bd 2, 282-283.

[460]Ibid., 290-291. -Habermas, <u>Zur Rekonstruktion</u>, op. cit., chs. 4-5.

[461]Habermas, <u>Theorie</u>, op. cit., Bd 2, 290-291. -Benjamin, <u>Illuminations</u>, op. cit., 217-251.

[462]Habermas, <u>Theorie</u>, op. cit., Bd 2, 290-291. -Adorno, <u>Asthetische Theorie</u>, op. cit., 35-36, 69-71, 86-90, 173, 179-182, 190-191.

[463]Habermas, <u>Theorie</u>, op. cit. -H. Lubbe, <u>Staat und</u> <u>Zivilreligion. Ein Aspekt politischer Legitimitat</u>, Wolfenbuttel: Lessing Akademie 1983, 5-15. -R. N. Bellah, "Civil Religion in America" in <u>Daedalus</u> 96, 1-21.

[464]Habermas, <u>Theorie</u>, op. cit., Bd 2, 291; <u>Zur Rekonstruktion</u>, op. cit., ch. 4.

[465]Horkheimer, <u>Die Sehnsucht</u>, op. cit., 61, 66-67. -Kung, <u>Die</u> <u>Menschwerdung</u>, op. cit., 369-379. -Habermas, <u>Zur</u> <u>Rekonstruktion</u>, op. cit., ch. 4.

[466]Habermas, <u>Zur Rekonstruktion</u>, op. cit., 101; <u>Theorie</u>, op. cit., Bd 2, 291.

[467]Habermas, <u>Zur Rekonstruktion</u>, op. cit., 101. -Bahr, <u>Religionsgesprache</u>, op. cit., ch. 1. -B. Bosnjak, "Was bedeutet das Dilemma: Jesus-Marx?" in I. Fetscher and M. Machovec, <u>Marxisten und die Sache Jesu</u>, Munchen: Kaiser 1974, 103-15.

[468]Habermas, <u>Stichworte</u>, op. cit., chs. 19-20, 29.

[469] Peukert, Wissenschaftstheorie, op. cit., part III. –Arens, Kommunikative Handlungen, op. cit., part 4.

[470] Habermas, Zur Rekonstruktion, op. cit., 101.

[471] Ibid. –SW 4, –SW 7.

[472] Habermas, Theorie, op. cit., Bd 2, 291.

[473] Ibid. –Horkheimer, Gesellschaft, op. cit., 162–175; Die Sehnsucht, op. cit., 66–67, 68–69, 80–81, 83–84, 86, 87, 88–89. –A. Schmidt, Zur Idee der Kritischen Theorie, Wein: Ullstein 1979, chs. 1–4; Drei Studien uber Materialismus, Wein: Ullstein 1979, ch. 2.

[474] Habermas, Theorie, op. cit., Bd 2, 292–293.

[475] Ibid.

[476] Horkheimer, Die Sehnsucht, op. cit., 88–89, 55–56.

[477] Habermas, Theorie, op. cit., Bd 2, 293, ch. 3.

[478] Adorno, Soziologische Schriften, op. cit., I, 447–449.

[479] Habermas, Theorie, op. cit., Bd 1, 312–313.

[480] Habermas, Theorie, op. cit., Bd 2, 452, 275, 581; Bd 1, 312–314, 329–331. –Horster, "Kommunikative Ethik" in FH 37/10 (October 1982), 35–41. –J. Rau, "Bruderlichkeit" in FH 37/7 (July 1982), 31–37.

[481] Habermas, Theorie, op. cit., Bd 2, 312–314, 329–331; Moralbewusstsein, op. cit., chs. 3–4. –O.K. Flechtheim, "Drei Moglichkeiten unserer Zukunft" in FH 29/7 (July 1974), 481–488; "Humanismus und Menscenrechte" in FH 31/9 (September 1976), 27–34. –Siebert, "Dialektischer Materialismus," op. cit.; "Three Alternative Futures," op. cit.

[482] Habermas, Theorie, op. cit., Bd 2, 312–314, 329–331. –F. Vilmar, "Ossip Flechtheim und der demokratische Sozialismus" in FH 34/3 (March 1979), 51–57. –Flechtheim, "Humanismus," op. cit., 27–34; "Drei Moglichkeiten," op. cit., 481–488. –"Sonderheft Zukunft Konkret" in FH 33/4 (April

1978); "Alternative Lebensformen" in FH (April 1978). -Siebert, "Communication without Domination," op. cit.

[483]Habermas, Theorie, op. cit., Bd 1, 312-313.

[484]Ibid., 312-314, 329-31, ch. 8. -Habermas, Moralbewusstsein, op. cit., chs. 3-4; Vorstudien, op. cit., 73-78. -Horster, "Kommunikative Ethik," op. cit., 35-41.

[485]Horkheimer, Die Sehnsucht, op. cit., 81. -R.J. Siebert, "Toward a Critical Catholicism: Kung and Metz I" in Anglican Theological Review, vol. LXV (January 1983), no. 1, 1-12; "Toward a Critical Catholicism II" in Anglican Theological Review, vol. LXV (April 1983), 144-163.

[486]Horkheimer, Die Sehnsucht, op. cit., 80-81, 83-89. -Habermas, Theorie, op. cit., Bd 2, ch. 8.

[487]Horkheimer, Die Sehnsucht, op. cit., 51-61. -Adorno/Kogon, "Offenbarung," op. cit.

[488]Horster, "Ein Marxistischer Kant," op. cit. -Jamme, Mythologie, op. cit., 11-14, 1256-143, 144-169. -Kung, Existiert Gott?, op. cit., parts B, C, esp. ch. 2, 3, esp. part F, ch. 1, 540-541; part G. -Habermas, Theorie, op. cit., ch. 7, 8. -Horkheimer, Die Sehnsucht, op. cit., 75-77.

[489]Horkheimer, Gesellschaft, op. cit., 162-175; Die Sehnsucht, op. cit., 69-71. -Haag, Fortschritt, op. cit., chs. 4-5, 8.

[490]Nicolaus von Cusa, Wichtigste Schriften, op. cit., 31-33. -Haag, Fortschritt, op. cit., ch. 8. -Horkheimer, Die Sehnsucht, op. cit., 118, 54-89.

[491]Habermas, Theorie, op. cit., Bd 1, 313; Zur Rekonstruktion, op. cit., ch. 4.

[492]Habermas, Theorie, op. cit., Bd 1, 313. -M. Weber, The Protestant Ethic and the Spirit of Capitalism, New York: Scribner's 1958, part II. -SW 11, 519-548.

[493]Habermas, Theorie, op. cit., BD 1, 313-314, 329-330, ch. 8. -Horkheimer, Die Sehnsucht, op. cit., 67-68.

[494] Habermas, Theorie, op. cit., Bd 1, 329-330. -Niebuhr, Marx and Engels on Religion, op. cit., 42. -SW 7, 317.

[495] Habermas, Theorie, op. cit., Bd 1, 330. -Weber, The Protestant Ethic, op. cit., chs. 4, 5. -SW 11.

[496] Habermas, Theorie, op. cit., ch. 8; Moralbewusstsein, op. cit., ch. 3-4.

[497] Habermas, Theorie, op. cit., Bd 1, 330-331. -SW 11, 548-569. -SW 7, 261-328.

[498] Habermas, Theorie, op. cit., Bd 1, 330-331.

[499] Ibid., 331. -Adorno, Asthetisch Theorie, op. cit., 7-387; -Horkheimer/Adorno, Dialectic, op. cit., chs. 1-3. -G. Lukacs, Deutsche Literatur im Zeit alter des Imperialismus, Berlin: Autbar 1950, 5-11; Essays uber Realismus, Berlin: Autbau 1948, 5-23.

[500] Habermas, Theorie, op. cit., Bd 1, 331. -SW 15, 24-36. -Kung, Die Menschwerdung Gottes, op. cit., 427-457, esp. 558; Christ Sein, op. cit., 285, 367; Existiert Gott?, op. cit., 179.

[501] Habermas, Theorie, op. cit., Bd 1, 331; Moralbewusstsein, op. cit., chs. 3, 4.

[502] Horkheimer, Die Sehnsucht, op. cit., 60-61; Gesellschaft, op. cit., 162-175.

[503] Horkheimer, Die Sehnsucht, op. cit., 60-61.

[504] Habermas, Theorie, op. cit., Bd 1, 329-331. -Horster, "Ein Marxistischer Kant," op. cit.

[505] Horkheimer, Die Sehnsucht, op. cit., 61-62.

[506] Habermas, Theorie, op. cit., Bd 1, 312-315, 329-331; Bd 2, 375-376, 379-380, 383-384; "Bewusstmachende oder Rettende Kritik," op. cit. -W. Benjamin/G. Scholem, Briefwechnel 1933-1940, Frankfurt: Suhrkamp 1980, 7-13. -G.G. Scholem, Jewish Gnosticism, Merkabah Mysticism and Talmudic Tradition, New York: Jewish Theological Seminary of America 1965,

chs. 1–5; Major Trends, op. cit., chs. 1–9. –Habermas, "Tod in Jerusalem," op. cit., 438–440. –Scholem, The Messianic Idea, op. cit., chs. 1–5; On Jews and Judaism in Crisis, New York: Schocken Books 1976, chs. 10–12; On the Kabbalah and its Symbolism, New York: Schocken Books 1965, chs. 1–5; Sabbatai Sevi, op. cit., chs. 1–8.

[507] Habermas, Theorie, op. cit., Bd 1, 312–315, 329–331; Bd 2,; "Tod in Jerusalem," op. cit.

[508] S. Freud, Civilization, War and Death, London: The Hogarth Press 1968, 1–25.

[509] Acts 1:42–47; 4:32–35. –Peukert, Wissenschaftstheorie, op. cit., part III. –Arens, Kommunikative Handlungen, op. cit., part IV.

[510] Freud, Civilization, op. cit., 1–25.

[511] Habermas, Theorie, op. cit., Bd 1, 312–331, 214–215.

[512] Habermas, "Tod in Jerusalem," op. cit., 438–440.

[513] Benjamin, Reflections, op. cit., 312–313; Illuminations, op. cit., 53–264. –Adorno, Minima Moralia, op. cit., 333–334. –Nicolaus von Cusa, Wichtigste Schriften, op. cit., 563–576, 576–582, 511–527.

[514] Habermas, Theory, op. cit., chs. 4, 7. –Siebert, From Critical Theory, op. cit., chs. 6, 12. –N. Luhmann, Funktion der Religion, Frankfurt: Suhrkamp 1977, chs. 1, 3, 4. –Habermas/Luhmann, Theorie, op. cit., 7–24, 25–100, 142–290. –N. Luhmann, Zweckbegriff und Systemrationalitat, Frankfurt: Suhrkamp 1977, 7–17, chs. 1–3.

[515] Schmidt, "Die Zeitschrift," op. cit., 5–63; Zur Idee, op. cit., chs. 1–4; Drei Studien, op. cit., ch. 2. –Horkheimer, Critical Theory, op. cit., 10–46, 188–243. –W. Strolz, "Sinnfragen nichtglaubender Juden" in FH 31/3 (March 1976), 25–34. –R. Wiggerhaus, "Die 'Zeitschrift fur Sozialforschung'–ein Aufforderung zur aktualitats–bezogener Gesellschaftstheorie" in FH 35/10 (October 1980), 49–54. –Lowith, Die Hegelsche Linke, op. cit., 7–38.

[516] Parsons, Societies, op. cit., chs. 1, 2, 115; The System of Modern Societies, op. cit., chs. 1, 2. -R.J. Siebert, "Parsons' Analytical Theory of Religion as Ultimate Reality" in G. Baum, Sociology and Human Destiny, New York: Seabury 1980, 27-55. -Lubbe, Die Hegelsche Rechte, op. cit., 7-17.

[517] SW 5, 5-65. -SW 15, 228. -W. Benjamin, Briefe 2, Frankfurt: Suhrkamp 1978, 672-676. -H. Scheible, "M. Horkheimer's fruhe und spate Aufzeichnungen" in FH 33/6 (June 1978), 50-54. -H. Willig, "Die Aktualitat der kritischen Theorie Adorno's" in FH 35/3 (March 1980), 55-64. -H. Mayer, "Nachdenken uber Adorno" in FH 25/4 (April 1970), 268-280.

[518] Bottomore, Karl Marx, op. cit., 195-219. -Bloch, On Karl Marx, op. cit., ch. 5. -Marx, Das Kapital, op. cit., I, 17-18. -E. Bloch, Subject-Object, Frankfurt: Suhrkamp 1962, chs. 9, 19. -Marx, Fruhschriften, op. cit., chs. 3, 6, 10. -H.J. Laski, The Communist Manifesto of Marx and Engels, New York: Seabury Press 1967, 109-179.

[519] Parsons, Societies, op. cit., ch. 1, 115; The System, op. cit., ch. 1.

[520] Habermas, Theorie, op. cit., ch. 7. -Siebert, From Critical Theory, op. cit., chs. 6-12.

[521] Habermas, Theorie, op. cit., chs. 4, 7.

[522] Habermas, Theory, op. cit., Bd 1, 462-463.

[523] Ibid., 462. -G.W.F. Hegel, Fruhe Schriften, Frankfurt: Suhrkamp 1971, 10, 33, 56, 76, 84, 90, 102, 103, 139, 18, 188, 195, 307 (TW 1). -SW 15, 324-342. -SW 7, 35-36. -SW 11, 568-569. -SW 19, 131-132. -Quint, Meister Eckehart, op. cit., 195-200, 237-240, 276-279.

[524] Habermas, Theorie, op. cit., Bd 1, 462. -Horkheimer, Zur Kritik der instrumentellen Vernunft, Frankfurt: Fischer 1967, 7-9, 13-14, 15-62.

[525] GW 6, 297-300, 307-315. -GW 8, 202-210, 223-231.

[526] SW 11, 33-43. -SW 7, 19-37. -SW 15, 114-220. -SW 16, 191-218.

[527]SW 11,   39-43. -TW 1, 18, 71, 101, 102, 308, 373-374, 381,
390, 394, 400, 421. -G.W.F. Hegel, Jenaer Schriften 1801-1807,
Frankfurt: Suhrkamp 1970, 411 (TW 2).   -Quint,   Meister
Eckehart, op. cit., 195-200, 274-279, 314-316, 237-240.

[528]Niebuhr, Marx, op. cit., 41-58, 69-72; S. Freud, The Future
of an Illusion, New York: Doubleday, chs. 3-6, 8; Civilization
and   its   Discontent,   New   York: Norton,   chs. 2-3, 8.
-Horkheimer, Gesellschaft, op. cit.,   162-175.   -Habermas,
Theorie, op. cit., Bd 1,   462-463. -Horkheimer, Zur Kritik,
op. cit., 15-62, esp. 16. -Horkheimer/Adorno,   Dialectic,
op. cit., 43-80.

[529]Habermas,   Theorie,   op. cit.,   Bd 1,   463. -Haag, Der
Fortschritt, op. cit., ch. 6.

[530]Horkheimer, Zur Kritik, op. cit., 15-62, esp. 22.

[531]Habermas, Theory, op. cit., 190.

[532]GW 4, 124-125.

[533]Habermas, Theorie, op. cit., Bd 1, 463-468.

[534]Ibid., 463. -Horkheimer, Zur Kritik, op. cit., 15-62,
esp. 28. -SW 15, 19-24. -SW 11, 33-47.

[535]Habermas, Theorie, op. cit., Bd 1, 463. -Horkheimer/Adorno,
Dialectic, op. cit., 81-119. -Marquis de Sade, Justine, New
York: Lancer 1964, 5-11, 14-15, 133-135, 136-144. -Horkheimer,
Zur Kritik, op. cit., part I.

[536]Horkheimer, Die Sehnsucht, op. cit.,   60-61;   Notizen,
op. cit.,   101-104, 116-117. -Haag, Der Fortschritt, op. cit.,
chs. 4-7.

[537]Horkheimer, Die Sehnsucht, op. cit., 60-61. -G. Orwell,
1984, New York: Harcourt, Brace and World 1949.

[538]Th. W. Adorno (etc.), Der Positivismus streit in du
Deutschen Soziologie, Darmstadt: Luchterhand 1980, 7-80,
chs. 1, 3, 5, 7. -Adorno, Soziologische Schriften I, op. cit.,
280-353.

[539] Habermas, Theorie, op. cit., Bd 1, 463-464. -Horkheimer, Critical Theory, op. cit., IX; Zur Kritik, op. cit., 15-62, esp. 47. -Th.W. Adorno, Zur Dialektik des Engagements, Frankfurt: Suhrkamp 1973, chs. 2-10; Versuch das "Endspiel" zu verstehen, Frankfurt: Suhrkamp 1972, chs. 2-5, 7, esp. 8; Prismen, Frankfurt: Suhrkamp 1976, chs. 6-12. -Lukacs, Deutsche Literatur, op. cit., 11-23, 24-33; Essays, op. cit., 5-23, 24-41, 42-65.

[540] Th. W. Adorno, "Zur Regression des Horens" in Horkheimer, Zeitschrift fur Sozialforschung, Munchen: Kosel 1970 (ZfS), Bd 1, 103-124, 356-378;

[541] Habermas, Theorie, op. cit., Bd 1, 462-534. -SW 15, 36-52, 52-64. -Horkheimer, Notizen, op. cit., 92, 96-97, 120-123, 127, 131-132, 268, 316-320. -L. Lowenthal and N. Guterman, Prophets of Deceit, PaloAlto, CA: Pacific Books 1970, v-viii, xi-xiii, esp. xii; ch. 1.

[542] SW 15, 279-324, 324-342.

[543] W. Benjamin, Das Passagen Werk, Frankfurt: Suhrkamp 1982, I, 45-7, 83-109, 110-132, 133-155, 156-178, 301-389, 490-510, 570-611, 612-642; II, 674-697, 971-981, 995-1038, 1041-1043, 1044-1059, 1060-1063.

[544] Habermas, Theorie, op. cit., vol. I, 464-465.

[545] Horkheimer, Zur Kritik, op. cit., 148; Eclipse of Reason, New York: Seabury 1974, ch. 6; Traditionelle und kritische Theorie, Frankfurt: Fischer Taschenbuch 1981, chs. 1, 3. -A. Schmidt, Kritische Theorie, Humanismus, Aufklarung, Stuttgart: Reclam 1981, 9-26. -Horkheimer, Gesellschaft, op. cit., 16-175; Sozialphilosophische Studien, Frankfurt: Fischer 1981, 47-58, 131-136, 145-155.

[546] Habermas, Theorie, op. cit., Bd 1, 464. -SW 7, 35-36.

[547] Habermas, Theorie, op. cit., Bd 1, 464. -SW 7, 19-37. -G.W.F. Hegel, Asthetik, Frankfurt: Europaische Verlags Anstalt 1952, I, 13-95; II, 589-624. -Adorno, Asthetische Theorie, op. cit., 491-533.

[548] Habermas, Theorie, op. cit., Bd 1, 464.   -Horkheimer,

Notizen,   op. cit.,   101–104,   116–117,   115–116.   –Adorno,
Negative Dialectics, op. cit., part I, ch. 1,   part II, part
III, chs. 1–3.

[549]Habermas, Theorie, op. cit., Bd 1, 464.

[550]Habermas, Zur Rekonstruktion, op. cit., ch. 4. –GW 4,
315–414, 417–464. –GW 6, 265–331. –GW 8, 185–287. –Schmidt,
Kritische Theorie, op. cit., 95–108.

[551]Habermas, Theorie, op. cit., Bd 1, 462–468.

[552]J. C. Flay,   "Eurocommunism and   the   Theory   of
Communication," in N. Fischer, et al. (eds.), Continuity and
Change in Marxism, New Jersey: Humanities Press 1982, 131–143.
–Benjamin, Briefe 2, op. cit., 672.

[553]Habermas, Theorie, op. cit., Bd 1, 462–468; II, ch. 8.
–Bloch, Subject-Object, op. cit., chs. 23–24; Geist der
Utopie, Frankfurt: Suhrkamp 1971, 343–389, 393–445; Man on His
Own, New York: Herder and Herder 1970, 118–141, 147–240; On
Karl Marx, op. cit., ch. 9. –Adorno, Zur Dialektik, op. cit.,
ch. 10;   Prismen,   op. cit.,   ch. 5. –Horkheimer, Notizen,
op. cit., 115–116, 196. –E. Bloch, Experimentum Mundi,
Frankfurt: Suhrkamp 1975, chs. 46–49; Tubinger Einleitung in
die Philosophie, Frankfurt: Suhrkamp 1979, chs. 11–16, 32, 33.

[554]Habermas, Theorie, op. cit., BD 1, 464–465, chs. 4, 7–8.
–Weber, Sociology of Religion, op. cit., 10, 22, 30, 57, 138,
143, 161, 170, 208, 81, 216, 224. –Horkheimer, Gesellschaft,
op. cit., 162–175.

[555]Habermas, Theorie, op. cit., Bd 1, 464–465. –Hegel, Three
Essays, op. cit., 30–49. –W. Dirks, Der Singende Stotterer,
op. cit., part IV, 11–53. –Adorno/Kogon, "Offenbarung,"
op. cit., 484–498, 392–402.

[556]"Catholics: The Pope Demands a Choice Between Marxism and
the Church" in Detroit Free Press, Sunday, September 9, 1984,
28.

[557]Habermas, Theorie, op. cit., Bd 1, 465. –GW 4, 315–414. –SW
15, 19–36.

[558] Habermas, Theorie, op. cit., BD 1, 465. –M. Horkheimer and Th. W. Adorno, Dialektik der Aufklarung, Frankfurt: Fischer 1969, 9–49. –Metz, Theologie, op. cit., ch. 5.

[559] SW 15, 24–36. –GW 4, 315–414. –Adorno/Kogon, "Offenbarung," op. cit., 392–402, 484–498. –Haag, Der Fortschritt, op. cit., VI,3–14.

[560] Habermas, Theorie, op. cit., Bd 1, 465. –Horkheimer/Adorno, Dialektik, op. cit., 9–49, 177–217. –Horkheimer, Gesellschaft, op. cit., ch. II. –E. Fromm, Escape from Freedom, New York: Hearst 1965, chs. 5–6; The Anatomy of Human Destructiveness, New York: Holt, Rinehart and Winston 1973, ch. 13; Arbeiter, op. cit., 7–38, chs. 1–4. –W. Reich, The Mass Psychology of Fascism, New York: Farrar, Straus and Groux, chs. 2, 4, 9.

[561] Lowenthal, Prophets of Deceit, op. cit., v–viii, xi–xiii, xv–xviii, chs. 1–4, 8–9. –L. Lowenthal, Mitmachen wollte ich mie, Frankfurt: Suhrkamp 1980, chs. 1–5.

[562] Habermas, Theorie, op. cit., Bd 1, 465; Zur Rekonstruktion, op. cit., 417.

[563] R.J. Siebert, Horkheimer's Critical Sociology of Religion: The Relative and the Transcendent, Washington DC: University Press of America 1979, chs. 3–4. –Scholem, Major Trends, op. cit., chs. 1–9; The Messianic Idea, op. cit., chs. 1–5. –Horkheimer, Gesellschaft, op. cit., 162–175.

[564] Habermas, Theorie, op. cit., Bd 2, ch. 8; Moralbewusstsein, op. cit., chs. 1, 3–4; Vorstudien, op. cit., chs. 2–4, 6, 8–9, 11. –Schnadelbach, Rationalitat, op. cit., 218–235.

[565] Habermas, Theorie, op./cit., Bd 1, 465. –S. Borenschen et al., Gesprache mit Herbert Marcuse, Frankfurt: Suhrkamp 1981, 16–19. –Horkheimer, Traditionelle un kritische Theorie, op. cit., chs. 1, 3; Critical Theory, op. cit., chs. 1–2, 4–6, esp. 8.

[566] Habermas, Theorie, op. cit., Bd 1, 465–466. –Horkheimer, Zur Kritik, op. cit., 15–62.

[567] Habermas, Theorie, op. cit., Bd 1, 56–57. –Horkheimer, Die Sehnsucht, op. cit., 56–57. –Haag, Der Fortschritt, op. cit.,

chs. 4-7.

[568]Habermas, Theorie, op. cit., Bd 1, 466. -Horkheimer, Zur Kritik, op. cit., 15-62; Die Sehnsucht, op. cit., 60-61; Notizen, op. cit., 101-104, 116-117.

[569]Habermas, Theorie, op. cit., Bd 1, 424. -Fromm, The Anatomy, op. cit., ch. 13.

[570]Habermas, Theorie, op. cit., Bd 1, 466. -Horkheimer/Adorno, Dialektik, op. cit., chs. 1-2, 4-6.

[571]SW 16, 298-300, 354-355. -SW 11, 404-409, 409-430. -Habermas, Theory, op. cit., 189-191. -GW 4, 417-464, 467-485.

[572]Habermas, Theorie, op. cit., Bd 1, 466.

[573]Ibid. -Habermas, Gesprache, op. cit., 49-52.

[574]M. Weber, "Wissenschaft als Beruf" in J. Winckelmann, M. Weber's Gesammelte Aufsatze zur Wissenschaftslehre, Tubingen 1968, 582-584.

[575]SW 7, 35. -SW 15, 292-293.

[576]Weber, "Wissenschaft," op. cit., 582-584.

[577]K. Popper, Die Offene Gesellschaft und ihre Feinde, Bern 1958, II, 304. -Habermas, Gesprache, op. cit., 121-141.

[578]Popper, Die Offene Gesellschaft, op. cit., 304. -Habermas, Theory, op. cit., ch. 7; Gesprache, op. cit., 121-141. -Kung, Existiert Gott?, op. cit., 128-132.

[579]Horkheimer, Die Sehnsucht, op. cit., 54-89. -R.J. Siebert, "Psychoanalysis and Religion: European Situation" in Concilium (January 1982), 18-24.

[580]Habermas, "Tod in Jerusalem," op. cit., 438-440.

[581]Habermas, Theorie, op. cit., Bd 1, 466-467; Gesprache, op. cit., 9-62, 121-141. -Horkheimer, Eclipse of Reason, op. cit., ch. 1.

[582] Horkheimer, Critique of Instrumental Reason, New York: Seabury 1974, ch. 4; Sozialphilosophische Studien, op. cit., ch. 12-13. -A. Schopenhauer, The World as Will and Representation, New York: Dover 1958, II, chs. 19-50. -Ch. Turcke, "Der Todestrieb der gegenwartigen Gesellschaft und seine theologische Verklarung" in FH 37/7 (July 1982), 45-58.

[583] Habermas, Theorie, op. cit., Bd 1, 466-467. -Horkheimer, Zur Kritik, op. cit., part I, chs. 1, 4, 6. -Schopenhauer, The World, op. cit., ch. 32.

[584] Habermas, Gesprache, op. cit., 9-62. -Marcuse, Eros and Civilization, op. cit., part II.

[585] Horkheimer, Die Sehnsucht, op. cit., 83-89. -Mayer, "Nachdenken," op. cit., 268-280. -Flechtheim, "Drei Moglichkeiten," op. cit., 481-488. -A. Huxley, Brave New World, New York: Harper and Row 1946. -G. Orwell, 1984, op. cit. -Adorno, Zur Dialektik, op. cit., ch. 8/.

[586] Habermas, Theorie, op. cit., Bd 2, 462. -Huxley, Brave New World, op. cit. -Orwell, 1984, op. cit. -B.F. Skinner, Walden Two, New York: The MacMillan Co., 1972, chs. 1, 28, 36, 26, 34, 35, 8, 10.

[587] G.W.F. Hegel, System der Philosophie, Stuttgart-Bad Cannstatt: Frommann 1965, 52-254 (SW 10). -Habermas, Gesprache, op. cit., 9-69.

[588] Habermas, Theorie, op. cit., Bd 2, 462. -Parsons, Societies, op. cit., chs. 1-2. -J. Habermas and N. Luhmann, Theorie der Gesellschaft oder Sozialtechnologie, Frankfurt: Suhrkamp 1975, 7-24, 25-100, 291-405. -K.W. Dahm, N. Luhmann and others, Religion -System and Socialization, Darmstadt: Luchterhand 1972, 11-132. -N. Luhmann, Funktion der Religion, Frankfurt: Suhrkamp 1977, chs. 1-5.

[589] Habermas, Theorie, op. cit., Bd 2, 462. -K. Gabriel, Analysen der Organisationsgesellschaft, Frankfurt: 1979, 114. -Mayer, "Nachdenken," op. cit., 268-280. -Horkheimer, Notizen, op. cit., 194, 196-197; Die Sehnsucht, op. cit., 83-89.

[590] Parsons, The System, op. cit., chs. 1, 2.

[591] Habermas, Theorie, op. cit., Bd 2, 462. -Habermas/Luhmann, Theorie der Gesellschaft, op. cit., 101-141, 142-290.

[592] Habermas, Theorie, op. cit., Bd 1, 466-467. -Horkheimer, Zur Kritik, op. cit., part I, ch. 4; Die Sehnsucht, op. cit., 54-89.

[593] Nicolaus von Cusa, Wichtigste Schriften, op. cit., 411-412. -Habermas, Gesprache, op. cit., 9-62, 121-141. -Th.W. Adorno, Versuche das 'Endspiel' zu verstehen, Frankfurt: Suhrkamp 1973, 167-214; Zur Dialektik des Engagements, Frankfurt: Suhrkamp 1973, 7-30, 151-178, 179-186. -Horkheimer, Notizen, op. cit., 8, 15, 16, 18, 27-28, 29-30, 33, 34, 38-39, 41, 45-46, 49, 54, 59, 63, 68-69, 75-76, 92, 94-95, 96-97, 195-196, 247, 316-320.

[594] Horkheimer, Zur Kritik, op. cit., 138-141.

[595] Peukert, Wissenschaftstheorie, op. cit., part III. -Arens, Kommunikative Handlungen, op. cit., IV; "Steh auf," op. cit., 23-29; "Schon sprosstes," 101-119; "Glaube und Politik. Bekennen und Viderstehen" in Public Forum 13, 29, June 1984, 29-31. -Torres, The Challenge, op. cit., parts I, II.

[596] Bottomore, Karl Marx, op. cit., 43.

[597] Habermas, Theorie, op. cit., Bd 1, 468-469.

[598] Weber, The Protestant Ethic, op. cit., chs. 3-4.

[599] Horkheimer, Zur Kritik, op. cit., ch. 4, esp. 132-134. -Benjamin, Das Passagen Werk, op. cit.; Briefe 2, op. cit., 671-683.

[600] J. Habermas, "Konventionelle oder kommunikative Ethik?" in K.O. Apel, et al. (eds.), Praktische Philosophie/Ethik I, Frankfurt: Fischer Taschenbuch 1980, 32-46. -Habermas, Moralbewusstsein, op. cit., chs. 3-4; "Legitimationsprobleme im modernen Staat" in Apel, Praktische Philosophie, op. cit., 392-401. -K.O. Apel, "Die Komflikte unserer Zeit und das Erfordernis einer ethisch-politischen Grundorientierung" in Apel, Praktische Philosophie, op. cit., 267-291.

[601] Habermas, Theorie, op. cit., Bd 1, 468-469. -Nicolaus von

Cusa, <u>Wichtigste Schriften</u>, op. cit., 411-547. -Meister Eckehart, <u>Deutsche Predigten</u>, op. cit., 53-100. -Alighieri, <u>Purgatorio</u>, op. cit., 47-291; <u>Inferno</u>, op. cit., 1/3-V/47.

[602]Weber, <u>The Protestant Ethic</u>, op. cit., parts I, II. -"Bishops Pastoral: Catholic Social Teaching and the US Economy" in <u>Origins</u> 14/22/23 (November 15, 1984). -G. Baum, "Call for Social Justice: A Comparison," in <u>The Ecumenist</u>, Vol. 23, No. 3, March-April 1985, 43-45.

[603]Habermas, <u>Theorie</u>, op. cit., Bd 1, 468-469.

[604]Horkheimer, <u>Zur Kritik</u>, op. cit., 131-133.

[605]Sw 7, 265-267, 182-184, 99-101.

[606]Horkheimer, <u>Zur Kritik</u>, op. cit., 132.

[607]<u>Ibid</u>. -R.J. Siebert, "The Frankfurt School: Enlightenment and Sexuality" in <u>Concilium</u> (June 1984), 27-37. -Marx, <u>Das Kapital</u>, op. cit., 873-874. -S. Freud, <u>Beyond the Pleasure Principle</u>, New York: Liveright 1961, 1-59; <u>Civilization and its Discontent</u>, New York: Norton 1962, 11-95; <u>The Future of an Illusion</u>, Garden City, NY: Doubleday, 1-92; <u>Leonardo da Vinci</u>, New York: Random House 1947, 3-27, chs. 1-6; <u>On Creativity and the Unconscious</u>, New York: Harper and Row 1958, part 4; <u>The Interpretation of Dreams</u>, New York: Hearst 1968, chs. 1, 3-4, 7; <u>Civilization, War and Death</u>, op. cit., chs. 1-2.

[608]SW 7, 35-36. -SW 15, 292-293. -Horkheimer, <u>Zur Kritik</u>, op. cit., chs. 1-2. -SW 16, 295-308.

[609]Blackney, <u>Meister Eckehart</u>, op. cit., 3-42. -Weber, <u>The Protestant Ethic</u>, op. cit., part II.

[610]Habermas, <u>Theorie</u>, op. cit., Bd 1, 469.

[611]<u>Ibid</u>. -Horkheimer, <u>Zur Kritik</u>, op. cit., 124-152, 335-354. -Habermas, <u>Legitimation Crisis</u>, op. cit., part III, ch. 4.

[612]Weber, <u>Protestant Ethic</u>, op. cit., part II.

[613]Horkheimer, <u>Zur Kritik</u>, op. cit., 124-152, 335-354. -Fromm, <u>Arbeiter</u>, op. cit., 7-46, 47-50; <u>Dogma of Christ</u>, op. cit.;

Man for Himself, Greenwich, Conn: Fawcett 1966, 41-42, 62-64, 232-238, 15, 200, 216-217, 227, 242.

[614]Horkheimer, Zur Kritik, op. cit., 335-354; Notizen, op. cit., 275-276, 300-301, 314, 324, 333; 15, 20-22, 25-28, esp. 29-30, 30-32, esp. 33, 38-39, 41, 44, 65, esp. 88, 117-118, 151-152, 187-188, esp. 199. -Habermas, Legitimation Crisis, op. cit., part III, ch. 4.

[615]Habermas, Theorie, op. cit., Bd 1, 473. -SW 11, 37-43. -SW 7, 35-36. -SW 16, 308-356. -Horkheimer, Die Sehnsucht, op. cit., 54-89; Gesellschaft, op. cit., 162-176.

[616]Horkheimer, Zur Kritik, op. cit., 124-152, 335-354; Eclipse, op. cit., ch. 4.

[617]Horkheimer, Zur Kritik, op. cit., 124-152, esp. 138.

[618]Ibid. -GW 4, 58, 417-485. -GW 6, 297-300, 319-326. -GW 8, 202-209, 223-227, 267-270. -SW 7, 270-286.

[619]Habermas, Theorie, op. cit., Bd 1, 473-474. -GW 6, 319-326. -GW 8, 267-270. -GW 4, 58, 417-485.

[620]Habermas, Zur Rekonstruktion, op. cit., chs. 1, 3, 4, 6, 8; "Konventionelle oder kommunikative Ethik?," op. cit., 32-45; Theorie, op. cit., Bd 1, ch. 8.

[621]Habermas, Theorie, op. cit., Bd 1, 485-486.

[622]Ibid. -L. Feuerbach, The Essence of Christianity, New York: Harper and Row 1957, ch. 1, part I. -Bottomore, Karl Marx, op. cit., 43-44. -K. Marx, Die Fruhschriften, Stuttgart: Alfred Kroner 1953, 339-340.

[623]Habermas, Zur Rekonstruktion, op. cit., 101. -SW 15, 355-400. -SW 16, 218-223.

[624]Habermas, Theorie, op. cit., Bd 1, 485-486.

[625]Marx, Die Fruhschriften, op. cit., ch. 3. -Bottomore, Karl Marx, op. cit., 43-59, 195-219.

[626]Habermas, Theorie, op. cit., Bd 1, 486.

[627] R. Bubner, "Rationalitat als Lebensform" in Merkur 4/36 (April 1982), 341-355, esp. 345. -W.J. Brazill, The Young Hegelians, New Haven: Yale University Press 1970, chs. 1, 3-7. -St. Breuer, "Die Depotenzierung der kritischen Theorie. Uber J. Habermas's 'Theorie des kommunikativen Handelns'" in Leviathan 1/82 (March 1982), 132-146. -A. Sollner, "Jurgen Habermas und die kritische Theorie des gegenwartigen Rechtsstaates-Versuch einer wissenschafts- geschichtlichen Einordnung" in Leviathan 1/82 (March 1982), 97-129.

[628] Peukert, Wissenschaftstheorie, op. cit., part III. -Arens, Kommunikative Handlungen, op. cit., part IV; Glaube, op. cit., 29-31.

[629] Habermas, Theorie, op. cit., Bd 1, 493-494.

[630] Habermas, Theorie, op. cit., Bd 2, 575-583. -SW 11, 47-50, 65-69. -SW 7, 262-286, 310-323.

[631] Habermas, Theorie, op. cit., Bd 1, 493-494. -Horkheimer, Zur Kritik, op. cit., 93-123, esp. 116-120.

[632] Horkheimer, Zur Kritik, op. cit., 118-119. -A. Sohn-Rethel, Okonomie und Klassenstruktur des deutschen Faschismus, Frankfurt: Suhrkamp 1975, chs. 3-4, 6, 8-10.

[633] Horkheimer, Notizen, op. cit., 28-29, 91-92, esp. 213, 214; Zur Kritik, op. cit., 93-123, 302-316, 317-320; Eclipse, op. cit., ch. 4. -Horkheimer/Adorno, Dialektik, op. cit., 168-208. -Sohn-Rethel, Okonomie, op. cit., ch. 3. -J.B. Metz, Jenseits burgerlicher Religion, Munchen: Kaiser 1980, ch. 2.

[634] Habermas, Theorie, op. cit., Bd 1, 500-502. -Horkheimer, Zur Kritik, op. cit., 65-92. -Nicolaus von Cusa, Wichtigste Schriften, op. cit., 413-414. -Habermas, Gesprache, op. cit., 130-133.

[635] Habermas, Theorie, op. cit., Bd 1, 500-501. -Horkheimer, Zur Kritik, op. cit., 62-92. -Haag, Der Fortschritt, op. cit., chs. 6-7.

[636] Habermas, Theorie, op. cit., Bd 1, 59, 96, 101, 115-117, 161; Bd 2, 11. -Adorno et al., Der Positivismusstreit in der deutschen Soziologie, op. cit., chs. 5, 7. -Adorno,

Soziologische Schriften, op. cit., 280-353.

[637]Y. H. Krikorian (ed.), Naturalism and Human Spirit, New York 1944. -D. Martingdale, "The Roles of Humanism and Scientism in the Evolution of Sociology," in G.K. Zollschan and W. Hirsch, Explorations in Social Change, Boston: Houghton-Mifflin 1964, 452-494. -Haag, Fortschritt, op. cit., chs. 6-7.

[638]Habermas, Theorie, op. cit., Bd 1, 501. -R.J. Siebert, From Critical Theory to Theology of Communicative Praxis, Washington DC: University Press of America 1979, ch. 4. -Haag, Der Fortschritt, op. cit., ch. 6.

[639]Horkheimer, Zur Kritik, op. cit., 63-92, esp. 66. -Adorno, Soziologische Schriften, op. cit., 354-370, 373-391, 392-396.

[640]Habermas, Zur Rekonstruktion, op. cit., 107. -J. Louber, Haushaltung Gottes, Bietigheim, Wurltemberg 1966, I, 5-7, 8-10, 11-15. -J. Dahlberg, Mensch und Gott, Frankfurt: Agnim Vertragsreihe 1980/81.

[641]Habermas, Theorie, op. cit., Bd 1, 501-592.

[642]Habermas, "Die Kulturkritik," op. cit., 1047-1061. -R. Spaemann, Zur Kritik der politischen Utopie, Stuttgart 1977. -H. Lubbe, Staat, op. cit., 5-28. -W. Scheller, "Die Neue Rechte" in FH 38/10 (October 1983), 26-32.

[643]Horkheimer, Zur Kritik, op. cit., 63-92, esp. 66.

[644]Ibid. -SW 15, 4-36. -SW 16, 344-356.

[645]Habermas, Zur Rekonstruktion, op. cit., 107. -Horkheimer, Zur Kritik, op. cit., 66. -Habermas, Theorie, op. cit., Bd 2, ch. 8.

[646]Habermas, Theorie, op. cit., Bd 2, 383; "Tod," op. cit., 438-440. -Adorno, Minima Moralia, op. cit., 333-334. -Horkheimer and Adorno, Dialektik, op. cit., 29-30. -Quint, Meister Eckehart, op. cit., 246-250.

[647]Habermas, Theorie, op. cit., Bd 1, 502. -Horkheimer, Zur Kritik, op. cit., 63-92, esp. 80-82. -Kracaver, Das Ornament,

op. cit., 106-122, 187-196, 249-255, 326-334.

[648]Horkheimer,   Notizen,   op. cit.,   101-104,   116-117.
-R.J. Siebert, "Max Horkheimer, Theology and Positivism I" in
The Ecumenist (January-February 1976), 19-23.

[649]Habermas, Theorie, op. cit., Bd 1, 502. -Horkheimer, Zur
Kritik,   op. cit.,   63-92.   -Adorno/Kogon,   "Offenbarung,"
op. cit., 397.

[650]Adorno/Kogon,   "Offenbarung," op. cit., 297-298. -Haag, Der
Fortschritt, op. cit., chs. 1-2, 6-7.

[651]W. Benjamin, Schriften I, Frankfurt 1950, 494.

[652]Adorno/Kogon, "Offenbarung," op. cit., 397-398.

[653]Habermas, Theorie, op. cit., Bd 1, 502. -Horkheimer, Zur
Kritik, op. cit., 63-92, esp. 82.

[654]Habermas, Theorie, op. cit., Bd 1, 504-505.

[655]Horkheimer, Die Sehnsucht, op. cit., 54-89; Gesellschaft,
op. cit., 162-175. -Benjamin, Briefe 2, op. cit.,   671-683.
-Haag, Der Fortschritt, op. cit., chs. 7-8.

[656]Habermas, Theorie, op. cit., Bd 1, 504-505.

[657]SW 2, 11-66. -SW 4, 36-58, 45-56. -Haag, Der Fortschritt,
op. cit., ch. 4.

[658]Habermas, Theorie, op. cit., Bd 1, 505. -Adorno, Negative
Dialectics, op. cit., 3-4. -R.J. Siebert, Reason, Freedom and
Change: A Christian Encounter with Hegel, Washington DC:
University Press of America 1985, ch. 3; "Three Alternative
Futures," op. cit.

[659]Horkheimer, Gesellschaft, op. cit.,   162-175. -Benjamin,
Briefe 2, op. cit.,   671-683. -Adorno, Negative Dialectics,
op. cit., part 3, chs. 2, 3.

[660]Habermas, Theorie, op. cit., Bd 1, 505; Bd 2,   385.
-Scholem, On the Kabbalah, op. cit., chs. 1-4; Major Trends,
op. cit., 1-9; The Messianic Idea, op. cit., chs. 1-5.

-Habermas, "Tod," op. cit., 438-440.

[661]Habermas, Theorie, op. cit., Bd 1, 512. -Adorno, Negative Dialectics, op. cit., part ii.

[662]Habermas, Theorie, op. cit., Bd 1, 512/3. -Adorno, Asthetische Theorie, op. cit., 86, 180, 190, 200. -G. Rohrmoser, Das Elend der kritischen Theorie, Freiburg 1970, 25.

[663]Habermas, Theorie, op. cit., Bd 1, 512. -Adorno, Asthetische Theorie, op. cit.

[664]SW 2, 11-66. -SW 4, 36-58. -SW 7, 35-36. -SW 10, 426-445. -M. Theunissen, "Negativitat bei Adorno" in Friedeling, Adorno Konferenz, op. cit., 41-65. -H. Altenhofen, "Hochdroben wo die Geister toben" in Discus H6/1, 84, 34. Jhrg., 15-17.

[665]SW 15, 228. -Isaiah 30. -Quint, Meister Eckehart, op. cit., 58-62, 62-63, 91-93, 104-105, 115, 117, 126-127. -G. Scholem, On Jews and Judaism in Crisis, New York: Schocken Books 1976, chs. 1, 9-12, 14. -SW 11, 41-42. -Nicolaus von Cusa, Wichtigste Schriften, op. cit., parts I-III.

[666]Habermas, Theorie, op. cit., Bd 1, 512.

[667]Ibid. -TW 2, 96-99, 111, 112, 255, 310, 371-372. -G.W.F. Hegel, Wissenschaft der Logik, Frankfurt: Suhrkamp 1969, 74, 94, 39, 40, 41, 44, 47, 75, 193, 461, 466, 467.

[668]Horkheimer, Gesellschaft, op. cit., 162-175. -Horkheimer/ Adorno, Dialektik, op. cit., 29-30. -Haag, Der Fortschritt, op. cit., chs. 4-5, 7-8. -R.J. Siebert, "Creation and Redemption," The Ecumenist, vol. 2, no. 5 (July-August 1982), 65-70.

[669]Habermas, Theorie, op. cit., Bd 1, 512, Bd 2, 383. -Benjamin, Illuminations, op. cit.; Reflections, op. cit.

[670]Habermas, Theorie, op. cit., Bd 1, 512-513. -Haag, Der Fortschritt, op. cit., ch. 5. -Marx, Die Fruhschriften, op. cit., LVII-LVIII; Das Kapital, op. cit., III, 873-874. -SW 7, 5-6, 33. -R.J. Siebert, "Hegel on the Dialectic of Civil Society: Alternative Futures," op. cit.

[671] J. Moltmann, "Theology of Mystical Experience" in Scottish Journal of Theology, Vol. 32, 1-20, esp. 12. -Quint, Meister Eckehart, op. cit., 213-217, 267-270, 303-309.

[672] Quint, Meister Eckehart, op. cit., 107, esp. 315-316.

[673] Habermas, Theorie, op. cit., Bd 1, 513. -Horkheimer/Adorno, Dialektik, op. cit., chs. 1, 4-6. -Horkheimer, Zur Kritik, op. cit., 153-174, esp. 165.

[674] Habermas, Theorie, op. cit., chs. 4-5,8; Bd 1, 522-525.

[675] Habermas, Theorie, op. cit., Bd 1, 522.

[676] R.J. Siebert, "The Frankfurt School: Enlightenment and Sexuality" in Concilium, July 1984, 27-37.

[678] Adorno, Asthetische Theorie, op. cit.

[679] Habermas, Theorie, op. cit., 523-534, chs. 2, 4, 5, 8.

[680] Peukert, Wissenschaftstheorie, op. cit., parts II, III. -Arens, Kommunikative Handlungen, op. cit., III, IV.

[681] SW 15, 114-115, 228. -SW 10, 379-445.

[682] SW 15, 228. -Quint, Meister Eckehart, op. cit.

[683] SW 7, 35-36. -SW 11, 43-47, 568-569.

[684] GW 6, 282-326. -GW 8, 185-287.

[685] Hegel, Three Essays, op. cit., chs. 1-3. -GW 6, 307-326. -GW 8, 253-287.

[686] SW 7, 35-36. PB 33, 387-388.

[687] K. Bloch (ed.), Denken heisst uberschreiten, Koln: Europaische Verlaganstalt 1978, 78-79, esp. 79.

[688] SW 7, 35-36. -SW 15, 292-293. -GW 4, 456-464. -GW 6, 315-326. -GW 8, 253-277. -Haag, Der Fortschritt, op. cit., 165-469.

689 SW 7, 35-36. -SW 11, 568-569.

690 Habermas, Zur Rekonstruktion, op. cit., ch. 4; Theory, op. cit., chs. 3-5; Gesprache, op. cit., chs. 1, 4. -Adorno, Drei Studien zu Hegel, Frankfurt: Suhrkamp 1969, chs. 1-3. -Marcuse, Reason and Revolution, op. cit., chs. 1-3. -Horkheimer, Zur Kritik, op. cit., 259-261, 311-313; Notizen, op. cit., 62, 63-65. -Adorno, Negative Dialectics, op. cit., part II. -Haag, Der Fortschritt, op. cit.

691 Habermas, Gesprache, op. cit., chs. 1, 4. -B. Piberhofer, "Zur Entegnung der politischen Subjekte und der Politisierung der unpolitischen Indindren," in Discus, op. cit., 4-9. -P. Wehling, "Aus derneuesten Wissenschaft. Ein Stimmungsbild" in Discus, op. cit., 10-13. -Altenhofen, "Hoch dreben," op. cit., 15-17; "Dialektischer Legalismus" in Discus, op. cit., 18-25. -E. Menzler, "Kritische Theorie? Obscone Kolportage im Rosselsprung-ein Dokument Verstorter Ratlosigkeit" in Discus, op. cit., 26-30. -J. Baudrillaod, "Transparenz" in Discus, op. cit., 32-35. -Siebert, "Hegel," op. cit.

692 SW 2, 34. -SW 10, 379-381, 382-384.

693 GW 4, 413-414, 458-459. -SW 2, 569-601. -SW 15, 247-308. -Scholem, On the Kabbalah, op. cit., 158-204.

694 GW 4, 413-414. -SW 2, 572-573, 596-597. -SW 16, 300-303.

695 GW 4, 413-414. -Quint, Meister Eckehart, op. cit., 229-232, esp. 361-365.

696 SW 4, 414. -SW 15, 271-278. -SW 16, 300-303

697 SW 4, 459. -SW 16, 300-303.

698 Habermas, Zur Rekonstruktion, op. cit., ch. 4, esp. 106-107. -Haag, Der Fortschritt, op. cit., ch. 4.

699 GW 4, 413-414, 458-459. -SW 2, 572-573. -SW 16, 300-303. -SW 10, 458-476. -H.H. Schrey, "Atheismus im Christentum" in FH 24/6 (June 1969), 418-428. -E. Bloch, Atheism in Christianity. -Haag, Der Fortschritt, op. cit., chs. 4-8.

[700]SW 16, 300-303. -SW 17, 23-26. -GW 4, 413-414, 458-459. -Nicolaus of Cusa, On God as Not-Other, Minneapolis: University of Minnesota Press 1979, 29-151.

[701]Baudrillard, "Transparenz," op. cit., 32-35.

[702]SW 15, 23. -Horkheimer, Die Sehnsucht, op. cit., 54-89. -Benjamin, Briefe 2, op. cit., 671-683. -Th.W. Adorno, Kierkegaard, Frankfurt: Suhrkamp 1966, chs. 5-7; Walter Benjamin, Frankfurt: Suhrkamp 1970, 9-10, 11-29, 30-32, 33-51, 52-58; Minima Moralia, op. cit., 333-334. -Benjamin, Illuminations, op. cit., 253-264; Reflections, op. cit., 312-313. -Horkheimer, Gesellschaft, op. cit., 162-175. -Habermas, Theorie, op. cit., Bd 2, 383; "Tod," op. cit., 438-440. -Kracaver, Das Ornament, op. cit.

[703]SW 15, 23. -SW 16, 295-308. -Horkheimer, Die Sehnsucht, op. cit., 54-89. -Habermas, Theorie, op. cit., Bd 2, 383; "Tod," op. cit., 438-440.

[704]S. Freud, The Psychopathy of Everyday Life, London: Hogarth 1957, 257-262, esp. 261.

[705]Ibid., 261. -Bakan, Sigmund Freud, op. cit., chs. 7-8, 17-22, 27-33; 303-320.

[706]GW 6, 297-300, 282-297, 307-15. -GW 4, 413-414, 458-459. -SW 7, 35-36. -SW 11, 568-569. -Kung, Existiert Gott?, op. cit., B.

[707]SW 11, 42, 569. -SW 15, 100.

[708]SW 11, 37-43, 43-47, 47-69. -GW 4, 413-414, 458-459. -SW 2, 2.

[709]Habermas, Zur Rekonstruktion, op. cit., ch. 4; Theorie, op. cit., Bd 1, ch. 4.

[710]Arens, Kommunikative Handlungen, op. cit., part III. -Metz, Theologie, op. cit., 98-100.

[711]SW 16, 191-218, 295-308, 52-356, 359-553.

[712]Peukert, Wissenschaftstheorie, op. cit., part III. -Arens,

Kommunikative Handlungen, op. cit., part IV. –SW 16, 118–356.
–SW 2, 34.

[713]Matthew 5–7. –Quint, Meister Eckehart, op. cit.,   303–309,
323–327. –SW 16, 286–295.

[714]K. Weill and B. Brecht, Rise and Fall of the City of
Mahagonny, New York: Columbia 1970, Act III, Scene 18 to the
end. –Peukert, Wissenschaftstheorie, op. cit., part III.

[715]SW 7, 19–37. –SW 11, 37–47. –Horkheimer, Die Sehnsucht,
op. cit., 54–89.

[716]Peukert, Wissenschaftstheorie, op. cit., part III. –Arens,
Kommunikative Handlungen, op. cit., IV. –SW 16, 359–553.
–Adorno, Negative Dialectics, op. cit., 361–364, 368–372.

[717]Habermas, Theorie, op. cit., Bd 2, ch. 7; Zur Logik der
Sozialwissenschaften, Frankfurt: Suhrkamp 1973, 163–183.
–Parsons, Essays in Sociological Theory, Glencoe: Free Press
1964, ch. 10. –Zollschan, Explorations, op. cit., ch. 8–14.
–Parsons, The Social System, Glencoe: Free Press 1964,
163–166, 367–378. –Siebert, From Critical Theory, op. cit.,
IX–XII; "Parsons' Analytical Theory of Religion as Ultimate
Reality," in G. Baum, Sociology and Human Destiny, New York:
Seabury 1980, 27–55. –Parsons, Societies, op. cit., ch. 1–2;
System of Modern Societies, op. cit., ch. 1–2. –R. Grathoff,
The Theory of Social Action, Bloomington: Indiana University
Press 1978, parts I–II. –A. Schutz/T. Parsons, Zur Theorie
sozialen Handelns, Frankfurt: Suhrkamp 1977, 7–9, 10–18,
21–24, 25–76, 79–85, 86–93, 93–107, 108–119, 119–122, 122–123,
127–136.

[718]Habermas,   Theorie,   op. cit.,   Bd 2, 372. –Parsons,
Societies, op. cit., chs. 1–2.

[719]Parsons, Societies, op. cit., 8, 9, 29.

[720]Ibid. –TW 2, 11, 17, 19, 20, 25, 57, 94, 96, 112, 113, 288,
388, 399, 409, 410, 435, 442, 456, 457, 411, 508, 537. –TW 3,
15, 20–22, 312, 416, 26–27, 62, 494, 551, 554–555. –TW 1, 18,
71, 101.

[721]Habermas,   Theorie,   op. cit.,   Bd 2,   372.   –Parsons,

Societies, op. cit., ch. 2.

722Habermas, Theorie, op. cit., Bd 2, 372. -T. Parsons, Social Systems and the Evolution of Action Theory, New York 1977, 181.

723Habermas, Theorie, op. cit., Bd 2, 372, 375. -P. Tillich, Systematic Theology, Chicago: University of Chicago Press 1963, Vol. III, 34, 36, 84, 99, 142, 190, 283, 284, 141-144, 193-196, 149-153, 219-223, 230-236, 294, 399.

724Parsons, Social Systems, op. cit., 181. -Weber, Sociology of Religion, op. cit., xlv-xlix, 27. -Siebert, "Parsons," op. cit., 27-55.

725Habermas, Theorie, op. cit., Bd 2, ch. 5,7. -E. Durkheim, Professional Ethics and Civic Morals, Glencoe, Ill: Free Press 1958, 160-161, 58, 189, 55-56, 112, 180, 153-155, 116, 55.

726Parsons, Societies, op. cit., ch. 2. -G.W.F. Hegel, Science of Logic, New York: Humanities Press 1969, 607-608, esp. 706. -SW 11, 569. -Isaiah, chs. 1-3. -Jeremiah, chs. 1-5.

727Parsons, Societies, op. cit., ch. 3. -Horkheimer, Die Sehnsucht, op. cit., 54, 61-62; Critical Theory, op. cit., 129-131, esp. 131.

728Habermas, Theorie, op. cit., Bd 2, 372-373.

729Ibid. -Habermas, Legitimation Crisis, op. cit., parts II, III, vii-xxiv.

730Habermas, Theorie, op. cit., Bd 2, 373. -Parsons, Societies, op. cit., ch. 2.

731Habermas, Theorie, op. cit., Bd 2, 373. -Parsons, Societies, op. cit., ch. 2, esp. 8-9. -T. Parsons/T.M. Platt, The American University, Cambridge, Mass.: 1973, 32.

732Hegel, Science, op. cit., 587-588, 592, 607-608, 706-708, 761-774, 782, 824-844, esp. 843-844. -SW 11, 39-43, 43-47, 569. -SW 7, 23-26, 33-36. -SW 15, 100. -SW 16, 218-356, 359-553. -H. Kung, On Being Christian, Garden City, NY: Doubleday 1976, parts C, D; Existiert Gott?, op. cit., parts

B, F, esp. G.

[733]Parsons,   Societies,   op. cit.,   ch. 2.   -Zollschan,
Explorations, op. cit., chs. 8-9, 14.

[734]Parsons, Societies, op. cit., 8, 9, 28. -G.W.F. Hegel, Die
Vernunft in der Geschichte, Hamburg: Felix Meiner 1955, 46 (PB
171a). -SW 16. -Isaiah 34-35, 43. -Jeremiah 1-14. -Matthew
3:5-7;   7.   -Lamb, "Roman Catholic Liberation Theology,"
op. cit., 1-34; "The Dialectics of Theory and Praxis,"
op. cit., 1-32.

[735]G.W.F. Hegel,   Vorlesungen uber   die   Geschichte   der
Philosophie, Stuttgart-Bad Cannstatt: Frommann 1965, Bd 1,
306-315, 343-368 (SW 17).

[736]Habermas,   Theorie,   op. cit.,   Bd   2,   373.   -Parsons,
Societies, op. cit., chs. 1-2; System, op. cit., chs. 1-2.

[737]Habermas,   Theorie,   op. cit.,   Bd   2,   373-374.   -Parsons,
Societies, op. cit., 28-29.

[738]Habermas,   Theorie,   op. cit.,   Bd   2,   373-374.   -Parsons,
Societies,   op. cit.,   28-29; Action   Theory   and   the   Human
Condition, New York: 1978, 352-354, 382; "Durkheim on Religion
Revisited.   Another Look at the Elementary Form of the
Religious Life," in Ch. Y. Glock/Ph. E. Hammond (eds.), Beyond
the Classics: Essays in the Scientific Studies of Religions,
New York: 1973.

[739]Habermas, Theorie, op. cit., Bd 2, 374-375.

[740]Habermas, Theorie, op. cit., chs. 1-2, 4-5, 7-8; Kultur und
Kritik,   Frankfurt: Suhrkamp 1973, part I; Politik, Kunst,
Religion, Stuttgart: Reclam, June 1978, 11-31, 48-89, 127-142;
Stichworte,   op. cit.,   Vol. I,   7-35;   Zur   Rekonstruktion,
op. cit., parts II-IV.

[741]Habermas,   Theorie,   op. cit.,   Bd   2,   373-376.   -Parsons,
Societies, op. cit., 114-115; System, op. cit., ch. 1; Action
Theory, op. cit., 352-354, 382.

[742]Habermas,   Theorie,   op. cit., Bd 2, 374-376; ch. 4. -SW 4,
69-70, 45-46. -SW 7, 19-36. -SW 11, 37-43.

[743]Habermas, Theorie, op. cit., Bd 2, 375-376. -Parsons, Action Theory, op. cit., 352-356.

[744]Habermas, Theorie, op. cit., Bd 2, 376-377.

[745]Ibid., 377. -F. W. Bolman, Jr., Schelling. The Ages of the World, New York: AMS Press 1967, 11-30, 31-65. -F.W.J. Schelling, The Unconditional in Human Knowledge, London: Asociated University Press 1980, 17-28, 38-149. -J. Gutmann (ed.), Schelling on Human Freedom, Chicago: Open Court 1936, xi-lii, 3-98.

[746]M. Eliade,

[747]G.W.F. Hegel, Vorlesungen uber die Geschichte der Philosophie, Stuttgart-Bad Cannstatt: Frommann 1965, Bd 3, 646-683 (SW 19). -P. Tillich, Gesammelte Werke, Stuttgart: 1959, Vol. I, Foreword; Mysticism and Guilt-Consciousness in Schelling's Philosophical Development, Lewisburg, Penn.: Bucknell University Press 1974, 9; The Construction of the History of Religion in Schelling's Positive Philosophy, Lewisburg: Bucknell University Press 1974, 11.

[748]Habermas, Theorie, op. cit., Bd 2, 377. -Parsons, Action Theory, op. cit., 355-356. -Schutz/Parsons, Zur Theorie, op. cit., 127-136.

[749]Habermas, Theorie, op. cit., Bd 2, 377. -Parsons, Action Theory, op. cit., 360-361.

[750]Habermas, Theorie, op. cit., Bd 2, 378-379. -Horster, "Ein Marxistischer Kant," op. cit. -Parsons, Action Theory, op. cit., 370-383.

[751]Habermas, Theorie, op. cit., Bd 2, 379. -Parsons, Action Theory, op. cit., 370-371. -I. Kant, Critique of Pure Reason, New York: St. Martin's Press 1965, 7-15, 17-37; Critique of Practical Reason, Chicago: University of Chicago Press 1949, 50-117; Kritik der Urteilskraft, Frankfurt: Suhrkamp 1968, 73-77, 78-109.

[752]Habermas, Theorie, op. cit., Bd 2, 379.

[753]I. Kant, Die Religion innerhalb der Grenzen der blossen

Vernunft, Stuttgart: Reclam, 1974, 3-13, 14-16.

[754] Habermas, Theorie, op. cit., Bd 2, 379-380. -Parsons, Action Theory, op. cit., 370-371.

[755] Parsons, Action Theory, op. cit., 371. -Kant, Critique of Pure Reason, op. cit., 485-570.

[756] Habermas, Theorie, op. cit., Bd 2, 380.

[757] Ibid. -W. Gouldner, The Coming Crisis in Western Sociology, New York: Hearst 1970, 138-166, part Ii, esp. 251-265, chap. 11.

[758] SW 2, 619-620. -SW 16, 281-282. -SW 11, 43-47. -Horkheimer, Die Sehnsucht, op. cit., 54-60.

[759] Habermas, Theorie, op. cit., Bd 2, 381-382; Vorstudien, op. cit., 127-174.

[760] Hegel, Science of Logic, op. cit.

[761] Habermas, Theorie, op. cit., Bd 2, 193, 382. -PB 33,

[762] Schutz/Parsons, Zur Theorie, op. cit., 7-9, 10-18, esp. 16. -Habermas, Theorie, op. cit., Bd 2, 193, 382.

[763] Habermas, Theorie, op. cit., Bd 2, 382-383; ch. 6.

[764] Ibid., 383. -Habermas, Politik, Kunst, Religion, Stuttgart: Reclam 1982, 125-142, 48-49; "Tod," op. cit., 438-440. -Scholem, The Messianic Idea, op. cit., 1-77.

[765] Habermas, Theorie, op. cit., Bd 2, 383.

[766] SW 15, 228, 114-220, 220-268, 19-24. -PB 33, 430-439. -Quint, Meister Eckehart, op. cit., 275, esp. 213-217.

[767] Habermas, Theorie, op. cit., Bd 2, 383.

[768] Quint, Meister Eckehart, op. cit., 213-217, 267-270, 303-309. -SW 16, 247-308. -PB 33, 450-463, 446-450.

[769] Habermas, Theorie, op. cit., Bd 2, 383-384.

[770] Habermas, Vorstudien, op. cit., chs. 1-3, 8-9, 11; Moralbewusstsein, op. cit., chs. 3-4. -Dunde (ed.), Katholisch, op. cit., 9-10, parts I-III. -Arens, "Bekennen," op. cit., 30-31. -"Excerpts from Vatican Statement Criticizing the Theology of Liberation" in The New York Times, Tuesday, September 4, 1984, A10-11; "Vatican Conserves Marxist Elements in New Theology" in The New York Times, Tuesday, September 4, 1984; "Vatican Denounces Radical Aspects of the Theology of Liberation in The New York Times, Tuesday, September 4, 1984.

[771] J.B. Metz, Zeit der Orden, Freiburg: Herder 1977, chs. 2-4; Jenseits burgerlicher Religion, Munchen: Kaiser, chs. 1-3, 5. -O. Poggeler, "Das Menschenwerk des Staats" in Jamme, Mythologie, op. cit., 175-225, esp. 184-188.

[772] Habermas, "Die Kulturkritik," op. cit., 1059-1061.

[773] Hegel, Three Essays, op. cit., 30-58. -Peukert, Wissenschaftstheorie, op. cit., parts II-III. -Arens, Kommunikative Handlungen, op. cit., parts III-IV.

[774] Habermas, Politik, op. cit., 127-142. -Scholem, On Jews, op. cit., chs. 9-12, 14; Die judische Mystik in ihren Hauptstromungen, Frankfurt: Suhrkamp 1967; Jewish Gnosticism, op. cit., chs. 1-10; Zur Kabala und ihrer Symbolik, Frankfurt: Suhrkamp 1973; Sabbatai Sevi, op. cit., chs. 1-6; Uber einige Grundbegriffe des Judentums, Frankfurt: Surhkamp 1976, chs. 1-3, 5; The Messianic Idea, op. cit., 1-77. -Habermas, Kultur und Kritik, Frankfurt: Suhrkamp 1973, 302-344. -D. Bakan, Sigmund Freud and the Jewish Mystical Tradition, New York: Schocken Books 1965, parts II-III, V.

[775] Habermas, Politik, op. cit., 48-49, 127-142. -Benjamin, Reflections, op. cit., 312-313; Illuminations, op. cit., 253-264. -Adorno, Prismen, op. cit., 283-301; Uber Walter Benjamin, Frankfurt: Suhrkamp 1970, 9-102.

[776] Habermas, Politik, op. cit., 131-141. -G. Scholem, Judaica III, Frankfurt: Suhrkamp 1973, 264-266.

[777] Habermas, Politik, op. cit., 132-136. -Scholem, On the Kabbalah, op. cit., ch. 4; Uber einige Grundbegriffe, op. cit., ch. 3; The Messianic Idea, op. cit., 49-77, 282-303.

[778]Scholem, Zur Kabala, op. cit., 22.

[779]Habermas,   Politik,   op. cit.,   132–133.   –Benjamin, Illuminations, op. cit., chs. 4–5. –Adorno, Versuch, op. cit., ch. 7; Prismen, op. cit., 302–342.

[780]Habermas, Politik, op. cit., 132–133. –Scholem, Uber einige Grundbegriffe, op. cit., ch. 3.

[781]Habermas, Politik, op. cit., 133–134.

[782]Ibid., 134; –Habermas, Vorstudien, op. cit., chs. 1–2, 4, 6–9, 11.

[783]Scholem, Uber einige Grundbegriffe, op. cit., ch. 3, esp. 90–92.

[784]Habermas, Politik, op. cit., 135. –Scholem, Uber einige Grundbegriffe, op. cit., ch. 3.

[785]Habermas, Politik, op. cit., 135.

[786]Ibid. –Habermas, Theorie, op. cit., Bd 1, 163, 373, 519; Bd 2, 11–12, 14. –Arens, Kommunikative Handlungen, op. cit., 175, 187. –C.S. Pierce, Schriften zum Pragmatismus, Frankfurt: Surhkamp 1976.

[787]Scholem, Uber einige Grundbegriffe, op. cit., ch. 3. –SW 2, 602–620.

[788]Habermas, Politik, op. cit., 630.

[789]Arens, Kommunikative Handlungen, op. cit., parts I, II, IV.

[790]Habermas, Politik, op. cit., 135–136. –Scholem, Uber einige Grundbegriffe, op. cit., ch. 3.

[791]Habermas, Politik, op. cit., 136–142. –Scholem, The Messianic Idea, op. cit., 1–36, 37–48; Judaica III, op. cit., 264–266; Uber einige Grundbegriffe, op. cit., chs. 1, 2, 4.

[792]Habermas, Politik, op. cit., 136. –Scholem, The Messianic Idea, op. cit., chs. 4–6; Sabbatai Sevi, op. cit., chs. 1–6; Judaica III, op. cit., 67–69, 187–189, 265–266; Major Trends,

op. cit., chs. 7-8.

[793]Habermas, Politik, op. cit., 128-129, 136-141, 11-31. -Schelling, The Ages, op. cit., 83-236. -SW 4, 13-35, 36-58, 59-66. -SW 11, 25-120. -PB 33, xli, 15-17, 468-470. -Blackney, Meister Eckehart, op. cit., xiii. -F.W. Baader, Werke, Berlin 1820, Vol. XV. -Bloch, Subjekt-Objekt, op. cit., ch. 13; A Philosophy of the Future, New York: Herder and Herder 1970, ch. 10.

[794]SW 4, 458-459. -SW 11, 37-43, 34-35. -SW 16, 223-247, 247-308, 308-356. -Hegel, Three Essays, op. cit., ch. 3. -SW 19, 26-28, 131-132, 296-327.

[795]Habermas, Politik, op. cit., 136. -Scholem, The Messianic Idea, op. cit., 37-48, esp. 44; Judaica III, op. cit., 265-267.

[796]Habermas, Politik, op. cit., 128, 136-142, 147. -Marx, Kapital, op. cit., III, 873-874. -Horkheimer, Die Sehnsucht, op. cit., 77. -W. Dirks/F. Vilmar, "Messianischer Materialismus" in FH 11/9 (September 1956), 618-626, 623-632.

[797]Habermas, Politik, op. cit., 136-142; "Tod," op. cit., 438-440; Zur Rekonstruktion, op. cit., chs. 1-2, 4, 6-7, 9-10, 12; Theorie, op. cit., ch. 8.

[798]Habermas, Politik, op. cit., 48-89, 127-142. -Scholem, On Jews, op. cit., chs. 10-12. -Benjamin, Illuminations, op. cit., 253-264.

[799]Habermas, Politik, op. cit., 136-137.

[800]Ibid. -Scholem, On the Kabbala, op. cit., ch. 4; The Messianic Idea, op. cit., 37-38; Uber einige Grundbegriffe, op. cit., ch. II. -TW 1, 234. -G.W.F. Hegel, Nurnberger und Heidelberger Schriften 1808-1817, Frankfurt: Suhrkamp 1970, 281 (TW 4); Wissenschaft der Logik, Frankfurt: Suhrkamp 1969, Bd 2, 279 (TW 6); Vorlesungen uber die Philosophie der Religion, Frankfurt: Suhrkamp 1971, 155 (TW 18).

[801]Habermas, Politik, op. cit., 136-137. -SW 11, 34-37.

[802]Habermas, Politik, op. cit., 136. -Scholem, Uber einige

Grundbegriffe, op. cit., ch. 1, esp. 53-55.

[803]Habermas, Politik, op. cit., 136-137. -J Boehme, The Way Christ, New York: McGraw-Hill 1964, 129-159. -Scholem, The Messianic Idea, op. cit., 37-48. -SW 5, -SW 11.

[804]J. Habermas, Theorie und Praxis, Frankfurt: Suhrkamp 1971, 172-227; Politik, op. cit., 11-31. -Scholem, The Messianic Idea, op. cit., 37-48.

[805]Habermas, Politik, op. cit., 137; Theorie, op. cit., chs. 2, 4, 7. -SW 11, -SW 15, 100.

[806]Habermas, Politik, op. cit., 137. -TW 3, 24, 39, 278-279, 280, 359-441.

[807]Habermas, Politik, op. cit., 137. -Scholem, Zur Kabala, op. cit., 151; Uber einige Grundbegriffe, op. cit., ch. 2; The Messianic Idea, op. cit., 37-48. -Siebert, "Hegel," op. cit.

[808]Horkheimer, Zur Kritik, op. cit., 311-312. -J. Habermas, Philosophisch-Politische Profile, Frankfurt: Suhrkamp 1973, ch. 1.

[809]Horkheimer, Zur Kritik, op. cit., 311-312. -Horkheimer/Adorno, Dialektik, op. cit., 29-30. -SW 2, 41-66. -SW 4, 36-66. -SW 5, 34-65.

[810]Marx, Kapital, op. cit., I. -Siebert, "Hegel," op. cit. -Bakan, Sigmund Freud, op. cit., parts II, III, V. -Horkheimer, Zur Kritik, op. cit.

[811]Habermas, Politik, op. cit., 137.

[812]Ibid. -SW 9, 717-722.

[813]Habermas, Politik, op. cit., 137. -Scholem, Uber einige Grundbegriffe, op. cit., ch. 2, part 84-86; Von der mystischen Gestalt der Gottheit, Frankfurt: Suhrkamp 1977, 79; Judaica III, op. cit., 189-217; Zur Kabala, op. cit., 135-137.

[814]Habermas, Politik, op. cit., 137-138.

[815]Ibid. -O. Poggeler, "Hegel der Verfasser des altesten

System programmes des deutschen Idealismus" in Jamme, Mythologie, op. cit., 126–143; –O. Poggeler, Das Menschen Werk des Staats, op. cit., 175–225. –Siebert, "Three Alternative Futures," op. cit., 231–297, esp. 236–238. –Holderlin, Hyperion, op. cit.

[816] Habermas, Politik, op. cit., 137–138.

[817] Ibid., 138. –Scholem, Uber einige Grundbegriffe, op. cit., ch. 4, esp. 135. –SW 16, 300–303.

[818] Habermas, Politik, op. cit., 138; Zur Rekonstruktion, op. cit., 106–107. –Scholem, The Messianic Idea, op. cit., 37–48.

[819] Habermas, Politik, op. cit., 138. –Scholem, Uber einige Grundbegriffe, op. cit., ch. 4; The Messianic Idea, op. cit., 37–48.

[820] Habermas, "Konventionelle oder kommunikative Ethik," op. cit., 32–45. –Scholem, The Messianic Idea, op. cit., 37–48. –Habermas, Moralbewusstsein, op. cit.; Vorstudien, op. cit., ch. 8–9, 11.

[821] Habermas, Politik, op. cit., 138. –Scholem, Zur Kabbala, op. cit., 156–158; The Messianic Idea, op. cit., 37–48.

[822] Adorno, Minima Moralia, op. cit.

[823] Habermas, Theorie, op. cit., Bd 2, 383.

[824] Habermas, Politik, op. cit., 138.

[825] Habermas, Philosophisch-Politische Profile, op. cit., chs. 1, 6, 8; Politik, op. cit., 11–31, 33–47, 48–89. –Benjamin, Illuminations, op. cit., 253–264. –E. Bloch, Tubinger Einleitung in die Philosophie, Frankfurt: Suhrkamp 1979, chs. 30–33.

[826] Habermas, Politik, op. cit., 139. –Scholem, The Messianic Idea, op. cit., 37–48, 49–77, 78–141; Uber einige Grundbegriffe, op. cit., ch. 4; Sabbatai Sevi, op. cit., chs. 1–8.

[827] Matthew 4:1-11. -Horkheimer, Notizen, op. cit., 96-97.

[828] Habermas, Politik, op. cit., 139. -Scholem, Sabbatai Sevi, op. cit., chs. 7-8.

[829] Habermas, Politik, op. cit., 139. -Benjamin, Illuminations, op. cit., 253-264; Reflections, op. cit., 312-313. -Bloch, Tubinger Einleitung, op. cit., ch. 24.

[830] Habermas, Politik, op. cit., 139. -G. Scholem, "Der Nihilismus als Religioses Phenomen" in Eranos-Jahrbuch, Leiden 1977, 1-50.

[831] Scholem, "Der Nihilismus," op. cit., 1-50.

[832] Ibid. -Jamme, Mythologie, op. cit., 11-12; -Benjamin, Reflections, op. cit.; Illuminations, op. cit.

[833] Habermas, Politik, op. cit., 139-140.

[840] Ibid. -Habermas, Theory, op. cit., ch. 3. -SW 11, 548-568.

[835] Habermas, Politik, op. cit., 139-140. -Benjamin, Reflections, op. cit., 177-192. -Adorno, Versuch, op. cit., 101-106.

[836] Habermas, Politik, op. cit., 140; Theorie, op. cit., chs. 2, 8.

[837] Habermas, Politik, op. cit., 140. -O. Rammstedt, "Die Instrumentalisierung der Baader-Meinhof Gruppe" in FH 30/3 (March 1975), 27-38. -K. Hansen, "Acht Thesen zur Gemeinrede uber den Terrorismus in der Bundesrepublik," in FH 33/5 (May 1978), 21-26.

[838] Habermas, Politik, op. cit., 140. -Adorno, Negative Dialectics, op. cit., 3.

[839] Habermas, Politik, op. cit., 141. -Scholem, On Jews, op. cit., chs. 1-15.

[840] Moltmann, Theologie, op. cit., 12-13. -R. Faber, "Atheistischer Liturgismus" in FH 38/10 (October 1983), 41-47. -Quint, Meister Eckehart, op. cit., 213-217, 267-270, 303-309,

354-355. -Adorno, Negative Dialectics, op. cit., 361-408.

[841]Habermas, "Die Kulturkritik," op. cit., 1059-1061.

[842]Habermas, "Tod," op. cit., 438-440; Politik, op. cit., 127-142. -W. Dirks, "Materialistic Messianism," op. cit., Der Singende Stotterer, Munchen: Kosel 1983, 199-201.

[843]Habermas, "Tod," op. cit., 438.

[844]Ibid. -Siebert, Hegel's Concept of Marriage and Family, op. cit., chs. 19, 31. -Poggeler, "Das Menschenwerk," op. cit., 184-188. -Pasternak, Doctor Zhivago, op./cit., 66-71.

[845]Habermas, "Tod," op. cit., 438.

[846]Ibid. -Scholem, Judaica III, op. cit., 266; Uber einige Grundbegriffe, op. cit., ch. 2; The Messianic Idea, op. cit., chs. 1-3.

[847]Quint, Meister Eckehart, op. cit., 340-341, 317-319, 315-316.

[849]Habermas, "Tod," op. cit., 438. -Scholem, The Messianic Idea, op. cit., 37-141; Zur Kabbala, op. cit., 156-157; Uber einige Grundbegriffe, op. cit., ch. 2.

[850]W. Benjamin, Briefe 1, Frankfurt: Suhrkamp 1978, 7-13, 123, 128-130, 134-139, 141-147. -Scholem, On Jews, op. cit., chs. 10-12, 14. -Benjamin, Briefe 2, op. cit., 488-494, 498-503, 505-520. -Scholem, Walter Benjamin-Gershom Scholem-Briefwechsel 1933-1940, Frankfurt: Suhrkamp 1980, 7-13.

[851]SW 15, 19-24. -SW 16, 223-247. -SW 11, 33-37. -Benjamin, Briefe 2, op. cit., 671-683, esp. 672.

[852]TW 2, 96. -SW 11, 34-35, 37-43, 369. -Haag, Der Fortschritt, op. cit., chs. 4, 5, 8. -Bakan, Sigmund Freud, op. cit., parts II, III, V.

[853]Habermas, "Tod," op. cit., 438.

854Scholem, <u>Die Judische Mystik</u>, op. cit.; <u>Sabbatai Sevi</u>,
op. cit., ix-xv, chs. 1-8; <u>Zur Kabbala</u>, op. cit.; <u>Uber einige</u>
<u>Grundbegriffe</u>,   op. cit.,   chs. 2, 4; <u>Von der mystischen</u>
<u>Gestalt</u>, op. cit.

855Habermas, "Tod," op. cit., 438-439. -Scholem, <u>Sabbatai</u>
<u>Sevi</u>, op. cit., chs. 1-8.

856Habermas, "Tod," op. cit., 439.

857Metz, <u>Glaube</u>, op. cit., 82-84, 132-133, 195-196, 203-204.
-J. Moltmann, <u>Der gekreuzigle Gott</u>, Chr. Kaiser 1973, 61, 98.

858Bloch, <u>Denken</u>, op. cit., 70-73, 78-79.

859Habermas, "Tod," op. cit., 439. -Scholem, <u>On Jews</u>,
op. cit., chs. 10-12; <u>Walter Benjamin</u>, op. cit., 7-11,
321-322, 17-320. -Benjamin, <u>Briefe 1/2</u>, Frankfurt: Suhrkamp
1978, 19-20, 463-464, 615-616, 721, 744, 767, 768, 779, 782.

860Habermas, "Tod," op. cit., 439. -Scholem, <u>Walter Benjamin</u>,
op. cit., 17. -Adorno, <u>Uber Walter Benjamin</u>, op. cit., 50-51,
73-74, 79, 89-90. -Benjamin, <u>Das Passagen Werk</u>, op. cit.,
11-41; <u>Briefe</u>, op. cit.

861Habermas, "Tod," op. cit., 439. -Scholem, <u>Uber einige</u>
<u>Grundbegriffe</u>, op. cit., chs. 2, 4; <u>Zur Kabala</u>, op. cit.

862Habermas, "Tod," op. cit., 440. -Siebert, "Hegel," op. cit.

863Habermas, "Die Kulturkritik," op. cit., 1059-1061. -Haag,
<u>Der Fortschritt</u>, op. cit., chs. 6-7.

864Habermas, "Die Kulturkritik," op. cit., 1059-1061.
-W. Scheller, "Die Neue Rechte" in <u>FH</u> 38/10 (October 1983),
26-32.

865Habermas, "Die Kulturkritik," op. cit., 1059-1061.
-Benjamin, <u>Illuminations</u>, op. cit., 256-257; <u>Das Passagen</u>
<u>Werk</u>, op. cit., part I, 45-78; part II, 991-1059.

866Habermas, "Die Kulturkritik," op. cit., 1059-1061. -Lubbe,
<u>Staat</u>, op. cit., 5-28; <u>Die Hegelsche Rechte</u>, op. cit., 7-17;
<u>Sakularisierung</u>, Munchen: Karl Alber 1975, chs. 3-7.

[867]Habermas, "Die Kulturkritik," op. cit., 1059-1061. -Adorno, Soziologsiche Schriften I, op. cit., 354-370.

[868]Freud, Civilization, op. cit., 11-12, 19, 21-24, 31-32, 39, 61; Future of an Illusion, op. cit., 24-28, 41, 47-53, 69.

[869]R.J. Siebert, "Ideology and Utopia" in Telos 58 (Winter 1983-1984), 146-148; "Adorno's Theory of Religion" in Telos 58, 108-114.

[870]Habermas, "Die Kulturkritik," op. cit., 1059-1061. -Faber, "Atheistischer Liturgismus," op. cit., 41-47. -Siebert, "Toward a Critical Catholicism I," op. cit., 1-12; "Toward a Critical Catholicism II," op. cit., 144-162. -F. Seghers, "Kirche und Streik" in Public Forum 14/15, 13, 27 (July 1984), 6-7. -H. Sibora, "Nicaragua. Dem Fischfang folgte ein Pilgergang" in Public Forum, op. cit., 12-13; "Katholikentag in Munchen" in Public Forum, op. cit., 19-38. -J. Schmetter, "Der Katholikentag von unten" in Dunde, Katholisch, op. cit., 38-63; "Durch die alternative katholische Szene" in Dunde, Katholisch, op. cit., 13-37. -W. Dirks, "Traditionen eines Linkskatholizismus" in Dunde, Katholisch, op. cit., 78-83. -H. Boll, "Verzogerter Gluckwunsch" in Dunde, Katholisch, op. cit., 318-322. -H.V. vonBrachel/N. Mette, Solidaritat und Komunikation, Frieburg: Exodus 1985.

[871]Habermas, "Die Kulturkritik," op. cit., 1059-1061.

[872]Ibid. -Habermas, Theory, op. cit., ch. 8, esp. 575-583.

[873]P. Stoop, "Niederlande: Aufgeschoben ist nicht aufgehoben" in Public Forum, op. cit., 11.

[874]Adorno, Soziologische Schriften I, op. cit., 354-370, 373-391, 392-396.

[875]PB 33, 430-439. -Hegel, Three Essays, op. cit., parts I-III.

[876]SW 15, 256-267. -PB 33, 431-436.

[877]Siebert, "Parsons' Analytical Theory," op. cit.

[878]Habermas, "Die Kulturkritik," op. cit., 1059-1061.

-Adorno/Kogon, "Offenbarung," op. cit.

[879]Horkheimer, Sozialphilosophische Studien, op. cit., 131-136, 145-155; Gesellschaft, op. cit., 162-175.

[880]Habermas, "Die Kulturkritik," op. cit., 1059-1061; Theorie, op. cit., ch. 8.

[881]R.J. Siebert, "Open Letter" in Proceedings of the Heraclitean Society, Kalamazoo: Western Michigan University 1983.

[882]Habermas, Vorstudien, op. cit., chs. 1-3, 6, 8-9, 11; Moralbewusstsein, op. cit., chs. 3-4.

[883]Benjamin, Illuminations, op. cit., 253-264; Reflections, op. cit., 312-313. -Habermas, "Tod," op. cit., 438-439.

[884]Benjamin, Briefe 2, op. cit., 671-683. -Siebert, "Hegel," op. cit.

[885]GW 4, 456-454, 413-414.

[886]Ibid. -SW 5, ch. 1.

[887]SW 16, 247-308, 308-356.

[888]GW 4, 417-485.

[889]Ibid. -Jamme, Mythologie, op. cit., 11-14. -Siebert, "Hegel," op. cit.

[890]SW 7, 261-328.

[891]Ibid., 286-310.

[892]Ibid., 320, 261-328. -SW 11, 126-130. -SW 15, 24-36.

[893]Marx, Kapital, op. cit., ch. 1, 17-18. -Siebert, "Hegel," op. cit.

[894]Marx, Early Writings, op. cit., 195-219.

[895]Marx, Die Fruhschriften, op. cit., chs. 3, 6-10.

[896] Marx, Das Kapital, op. cit., III, 873–874.

[897] Benjamin, Briefe 2, op. cit., 671–683. –Horkheimer, Gesellschaft, op. cit., 152–161, 162–175.

[898] Benjamin, Briefe 2, op. cit., 671–683; Das Passagen Werk, op. cit., 301–489, 490–510, 612–642.

[899] Horkheimer, Die Sehnsucht, op. cit., 54–89.

[900] Habermas, Vorstudien, op. cit., 273–83, 226–270.

[901] Habermas, Theorie, op. cit., ch. 8.

[902] Habermas, Gesprache, op. cit., 130–133.

[903] Benjamin, Briefe 2, op. cit., 671–683.

[904] SW 7, 35–37.

[905] GW 4, 413–414, 458–459. –SW 16, 296–308.

[906] GW 4, 5–92, 417–485. –SW 7, 261–328, esp. 320. –Habermas, Vorstudien, op. cit., 7–183.

[907] SW 7, 35. –SW 15, 292–293.

[908] R. Niebuhr, Marx and Engels on Religion, New York: Schocken Books 1967, 41–42. –Marx, Das Kapital, op. cit., I, 17–18. –SW 7, 35. –SW 15, 292–293.

[909] SW 2, 34. –Quint, Meister Eckehart, op. cit. –Nicolaus von Cusa, Wichtigste Schriften, op. cit., 593–599, 612–615, 615–617.

[910] SW 16, 296–308. –SW 7, 35. –SW 15, 292–293. –Quint, Meister Eckehart, op. cit. –Nicolaus von Cusa, Wichtigste Schriften, op. cit., 599–603, 603–611.

[911] SW 7, 35–36, 320. –Siebert, "Hegel," op. cit. –SW 16, 354, 281–282. –SW 2, 620.

[912] SW 2, 24.

913Siebert,   "Hegel,"   op. cit.;   "Christian   Revolution:
Liberation   and   Transcendence"   in   The   Ecumenist
(September/October 1976), 85-91; "Hegel and Theology," The
Ecumenist (November/December 1973) 1-6.

914SW 7,261-262, 320, 22-286, 310-323.

915"La jefatura catolica no quiere que se repita la conducta
de sus pastores en Centroamerica" in El Nuevo Diario, July 31,
1984. -D. R. Thompson, "O Cristo o Marx: los dos, no" in La
Mino Domingo, August 12, 1984. -P. Polk, "Sandinistas inician
mision en El vaticano para disminuir tensiones con la Iglesia"
in El Nuevo Diario, September 5, 1984. -P. Butturini, "El
Vaticano interrogare a teologo brasileno por predicar la
liberacion y hacer criticas" in El Nuevo Diario, September 3,
1984, 17. -"Vaticao Plantea Posicion enTeologia Liberacion" in
El Sol, August 22 1984, 4. -"Obispos aceptan criticas a
version tercermundista" in El Nuevo Diario, September 5, 1984,
16. -"Seran Procesados Publicamente" in El Nuevo Diario,
August 6, 1984, 18. -E. Rosario, "Hay una alianza Juan Pablo
II-Reagan para atacar a fondo a los liberacionistas" in El
Nuevo Diario, July 26, 1984. -E. Rosario, "La identificacion
con el Tercer Mundo, ha illevado a muchos cristianos a
cuestionar a EE,UU" in El Nuevo Diario, July 30, 1984.
-E. Rosario, "Un pequeno inconveniente para los que enfrentan
la Teologia de la liberacion: los pobres" in El Nuevo Diario,
July 27, 1984. -"Liberation Theology Criticized" in The
Detroit News, September 28, 1984. -T. Beal, "The Trials of a
Liberation Theology" in National Catholic Reporter, September
28, 1984, 20.

916Siebert, "Three Alternative Futures," op. cit.; "Historical
Materialism," op. cit.; "Communication," op. cit.

917W. Benjamin, Ausgewahlte Schriften, Frankfurt 1966, Bd II:
Angelus Novus, 55. -Unseld, Zur Aktualitat, op. cit., 221.

918Benjamin, Ausgewahlte Schriften, op. cit., 214. -Habermas,
Kultur, op./cit., 344.

919F.J. Hinkelammert, "Die Politik des 'totalen Marktes',"
Barmen, 58-70. -D. Solle, "Widerstand ist der wahre Name des
Glaubens" in Barmen, op. cit., 70- . -F. Hinkelammert, "Du
sollst keinen Gott neben ihm haben" in Entwicklungspolitik,

2/3/82, 23-28.

Chapter III: Critical Political Theology

[1]H. Peukert, Science, Action and Fundamental Theology: Toward a Theology of Communicative Action, Cambridge, Mass.: MIT Press 1984, part II. -Arens, Kommunikative Handlungen, op. cit., parts III, IV. -Metz, Glaube, op. cit., 44, 91, 99, 107, 152, 154, 171, 182-184, 114, 7, 66, 90, 117, 137, 172, 174, 208, 102, 110, 118, 139, 164, 166-167, 34, 43, 52, 206, 67, 96, 171. -O. Fuchs (ed.), Theologie und Handeln, Dusseldorf: Patmos 1984, chs. 4-5.

[2]Peukert, Science, op. cit., parts I, II. -Arens, Kommunikative Handlungen, op. cit., parts I-IV.

[3]R.J. Siebert, "Peukert's New Critical Theology I" in The Ecumenist, Vol. 16, No. 4, May-June 1978, 52-58. -R.J. Siebert, "Peukert's New Critical Theology II" in The Ecumenist, Vol. 16, No. 5, July-August 1978, 78-80.

[4]Ibid.

[5]D. Berrigan, Uncommon Prayers, New York: The Seabury Press 1978, 53-56, 35-37.

[6]The Psalms. Chicago, Illinois: Fides Publishers Association 1955, 7.

[7]Habermas, Zur Rekonstruktion, op. cit., chap. 4. -Habermas, Theorie, op. cit., Bd 1, chs. 1-3; esp. 273-275, 280-284. Bd 2, chs. 1-3; VI,2; VII,2; esp. 279-293, 375-377, 517. -Peukert, Science, op. cit., part II.

[8]Peukert, Wissenschaftstheorie, op. cit., Part II, F: part III, C,D. -Arens, Kommunikative Handlungen, op. cit., 374-385. -H. Peukert, "Padagogik-Ethik-Politik" in Zeitschrift fur Padagogik 17, Beiheft (1981) 64, 65, 67; "Was ist eine praktische Wissenschaft?", op. cit., 280, 285, 287-288, 289, 290-291, 293-294; "Kontingenzerfahrung und Identitatsfindung," in J. Blank and G. Hasenhuttl (eds) Erfahrung, Glaube und Moral, Dusseldorf: Patmos Verlag 1982, 76, 80, 83, 88, 89, 90, 91-92, 94, 95-96. -D. Benner/H. Peukert, "Erziehung-

Moralische" in D. Lenzen and K. Mollenhauser, <u>Enzyklopadie</u>
<u>Erziehungswissenschaft</u>, Stuttgart: E. Klette 1983, 395-396,
397, 398, 400, 401, 402. -H. Peukert, "Kritische Theorie und
Padagogik" in <u>Zeitschrift fur Padagogik</u>, Jahrgang 1983, Nr. 2,
205, 206, 207, 208, 213, 214; <u>Science</u>, op. cit., vii-xxii.

[9]Peukert, <u>Science</u>, op. cit., 13, 231-232, 218-227, 212,
234-235, 205-210.

[10]SW 11, 28-29.

[11]SW11, 28-29, 540.

[12]G.W.F. Hegel, <u>Vorlesungen uber die Philosophie der Religion</u>
<u>I</u>, Frankfurt: Suhrkamp 1969, 88 . -G.W.F. Hegel, <u>Vorlesungen</u>
<u>uber die Geschichte der Philosophie II</u>, Frankfurt: Suhrkamp
1971, 496-498. -G.W.F. Hegel, <u>Vorlesungen uber die Geschichte</u>
<u>der Philosophie III</u>, Frankfurt: Suhrkamp 1971, 247-249,
454-455.

[13]Habermas, <u>Zur Rekonstruktion</u>, op. cit., chap. 4, esp. 105,
101-102.

[14]S. Kierkegaard, <u>Erbauliche Reden</u>, Dusseldorf: Eugen
Diederichs 1964, 229-363.

[15]Horkheimer, <u>Die Sehnsucht</u>, op. cit., 37, 40-42, 54-63,
65-66, 67-68, 77. -Marx, <u>Das Kapital</u>, op. cit., III, 873-874.
-Horkheimer, <u>Gesellschaft</u>, op. cit., 162-175, 152-161. -Weber,
<u>Sociology</u>, op. cit., chap. 9.

[16]Benjamin, <u>Illuminations</u>, op. cit., 254; -W. Benjamin,
<u>Understanding Brecht</u>, London: NLB 1975, 43-74. -R. Wolin,
<u>Walter Benjamin. An Aesthetic of Redemption</u>, New York:
Columbia University Press 1982, chs. 5, 6.

[17]B. Brecht, <u>Seven Plays</u>, New York: Grove Press 1961, esp.
251-257. -W.F. Schoeller (ed), <u>Die Neue Linke nach Adorno</u>,
Munchen: Kindler 1969, 172-173.

[18]Horkheimer, <u>Die Sehnsucht</u>, op. cit., 6-57, 59-60.
-Horkheimer, <u>Gesellschaft</u>, op. cit., 166-169. -M. Horkheimer,
<u>Sozialphilosophische Studien</u>, Frankfurt: Fischer Taschenbuch
1981, 131-136, 145-155.

[19]Horkheimer, Die Sehnsucht, op. cit., 77.

[20]Benjamin, Reflections, op. cit., 312-313. -W. Benjamin, "Eduard Fuchs, der Sammler und der Historiker" in ZfS, Vol. VII, 346-380. -Benjamin, Das Passagen-Werk, op. cit., Vol. I, 11-41; Vol. II, 991-1059. -Benjamin, Illuminations, op. cit., 253-264. -Wolin, Walter Benjamin, op. cit., chaps. 4, 6. -R. Tiedemann, "Histor al Materialism or Political Messianism?" in The Philosophical Forum, XV, 1-2, (Fall-Winter 1983), 71-104. -Siebert, "Dialectical Materialism," op. cit., 61-98.

[21]Horkheimer, Die Sehnsucht, op. cit., 77, 56-57, 58-62, 67-68, 69, 71, 72, 75-76; Sozialphilosophische Studien, op. cit., 131-136, 145-155; Gesellschaft, op. cit., 162-176. -Adorno/Kogon, "Offenbarung" op. cit., 397-402. - M. Horkheimer, Critical Theory, New York: The Seabury Press 1972, 129-131; Notizen, op. cit., 16, 18, 92, 96-97, 121-123, 127, 131-132, 268, 286-287, 316-320. - R.J. Siebert, "Adorno's Theory," op. cit., 108-114.

[22]Adorno/Kogon, "Offenbarung," op. cit., 402.

[23]Horkheimer/Adorno, Dialektik, op. cit., 29-31. -G.W.F. Hegel, Vorlesungen uber die Geschichte der Philosophie III, Stuttgart-Bad Cannstatt: Friedrich Frommann Verlag 1965, 131-132 (SW 19). -Meister Eckehart, Deutsche Predigten und Traktate, Munchen: Diogenes Taschenbuch 1979, 242-243. -Nicolaus von Cusa, Wichtigste Schriften, op. cit., 31-33. -Benjamin, Eduard Fuchs, op. cit., 374-375; "Eduard Fuchs, Collector and Historian" in Arato, The Essential Frankfurt School, op. cit., 225-253. -Marx, Das Kapital, op. cit., III, 88-90, 428, 878. -Moltmann, "Theology," op. cit., 32, 1-20, esp. 12.

[24]L. Lutkehaus, "Der 'Fall' Reinhold Schneider" in FH 38/6, June 1983, 41-46.

[25]K. Lehmann and A. Raffelt (eds.), Rechen schaft des Glaubens, Freiburg: Herder 1979, 16-18, 58, 73, 77-78, 81-83, 83-88, 115-118, 120, 121-123, esp. 121; esp. 130, 136, 146. -K. Rahner, Grundkurs des Glaubens, Freiburg: Herder 1976, 251, 265-266, 276-277, 278-279, 297-298, 417-423, 425-426. -Nicolaus von Cusa, Wichtigste Schriften, op. cit., 362-372,

esp. 369. -SW 16, 302, 304.

[26]Schmidt,   "Die   Zeitschrift,"   op. cit.,   8-17.
-A. Schopenhauer, The World as Will and Representation, New
York: Dover 1958, I, xviii, xxi, xxiv, 223, 419, 429-437; II,
13,   34,   40-41,   65, 70, 84, 87, 192, 303, 442-443, 464, 582,
590, 616. -SW 7, 34-36. -SW 11, 41-43, 48-50, 65-69. -Kung,
Die Menschwerdung, op. cit., 364-381, esp. 377-378.

[27]H. Kung, Christentum und Weltreligionen, Frieburg: Piper
1984. -H.J. Herbort, "Zuruck zu den Ursprungen" in Die Zeit
Nr.52, December 21, 1984, 44.

[28]Horkheimer, Notizen, op. cit., 115-116.

[29]M.N. Ebertz, "Die Bergpredigt in der Jesus - und in der
Friedensbewegung-eine Auseinandersetzung mit Franz Alt" in FH
39/9 (September 1984), 15-22.

[30]E. Bloch, Thomas Muntzer, Frankfurt: Suhrkamp, parts IV-V;
Bloch, Denken, op. cit, 88.

[31]Kung, Menschwerdung, op. cit., 43, 245, 246, 15, 375,
386-397, 425; Existiert Gott?, op. cit., 397-404, 405-408,
412-413, 434-437.

[32]Revelation 21:5. -Bloch, Denken, op. cit., 80, 81.

[33]Metz, The Emergent Church, op. cit., ch. 2.

[34]SW 7, 23-26, 30-32, 32-34, 34-36. -SW 11, 42-43, 569. -SW
15, 100.

[35]W. Dirks, "Ehe/Eucharistie/Sozialismus," in FH 36/4, April
1981, 31-40; 36/5, May 1981, 48-55. -Der Singende Stotterer,
op. cit., 136-163.

[36]W. Dirks, "Wehrlos vor dem Faschismus-Das Theorie-Defizit
des Deutschen Katholizismus der Weimarer Zeit" in FH 36/12,
December   1981,   39-48.   -W. Scheller, "Das   graue
Frankreich-Paris und die Tage der Kollaboration" in FH 39/5,
May 1984, 47-52.

[37]W. Dirks, Der Singende Stotterer, op. cit., 196.

[38] A. Gide, The Return of the Prodigal Son, Logan, Utah: Utah State University Press 1960, Vol. VII, No. 4, 25-28.

[39] Dante Alighieri, The Purgatorio, New York: New American Library 1961, 112-119, 120-129, 130-138. -Inferno, Toronto: Bantam Books 1981, x, 87.

[40] Habermas, Rekonstruktion, op. cit., 101; Theorie, op. cit., Bd 1, 312-313, 330-331; Bd 2, 147. Vorstudien, op. cit., chs. 3-4, 6, 8-9, 11. -J.B. Thompson and David Held (eds.), Habermas. Critical Debates, Cambridge, Mass.: MIT Press 1982, 219-283. -G.J. Friesenhahn, "Max Horkheimer's Bedeutung fur die heutige Padagogik" in FH 39/5, May 1984, 11-12. -D. Horster, "Kommunikative Ethik" in FH 37/10, October 1982, 35-41. -J. Rau, "Bruderlichkeit" in FH 37/7, July 1982, 31-37. -B. Schoch, "Zwischen Identifikation und Solideritat-Anmerkungen zum schrieng gewerdenen Internationalismus" in FH 39/5, May 1984, 13-19. -O. Bader, "Basisorganisationen in Bolivier" in FH 39/5, May 1984, 20-26.

[41] Peukert, Wissenschaftstheorie, op. cit., 278-280; Kritische Theorie, op. cit., 214-215.

[42] M. Horkheimer, Letter of March 16, 1937 to Benjamin, in Tiedemann, Historical Materialism, op. cit., 77; Die Sehnsucht, op. cit., 61-62; Kritische Theorie, Frankfurt 1968, Vol. I, 198, 372.

[43] K. Weill and B. Brecht, Rise and Fall of the City of Mahagonny, New York: Columbia Masterworks 1970.

[44] Benjamin, Eduard Fuchs, op. cit., 354-356. -Benjamin, Letter of March 28, 1937 to Horkheimer, in Tiedemann, Historical Materialism, op. cit., 77-78; Passagen, Konvolut N.B1.8, in Tiedemann, Historical Materialism, op. cit., 78; Illuminations, op. cit., 253-264; Reflections, op. cit., 312-313.

[45] Benjamin, Eduard Fuchs, op. cit., 354-356. -Habermas, Kultur, op. cit., 302-305, 305-311, 345-351.

[46] Horkheimer, Letter of March 16, 1937 to Benjamin, op. cit.

[47]W. Benjamin, Letter of December 24, 1936 to M. Horkheimer in W. Benjamin, Briefe 2, Frankfurt a.M.: Suhrkamp Verlag 1978, 725. -Th. Haecker, Tag und Nachtbucher, Frankfurt: Suhrkamp 1975, 264-266. -R.J. Siebert, From Critical Theory of Society to Theology of Communicative Praxis, Washington D.C.: University Press of America 1979, chap. IV, V.

[48]M. Horkheimer, "Zu Theodor Haecker: Der Christ und die Geschichte" in M. Horkheimer, Zeitschrift, op. cit., V, 372-382. -Th. Haecker, Der Christ und die Geschichte, Leipzig: Hegner Verlag 1935. -Siebert, From Critical Theory, op. cit., chap. IV, esp. 26.

[49]Horkheimer, Critical Theory, op. cit., 131; Die Sehnsucht, op. cit., 54.

[50]SW 16, 546-553.

[51]Benjamin, Letter of December 24, 1936 to Horkheimer, op. cit., 725.

[52]Benjamin, Letter of March 28, 1937, op. cit.; Illuminations, op. cit., 253-264. -Tiedemann, Historical Materialism, op. cit., 71-104.

[53]Benjamin, Passagen, op. cit., Konvolut B1.8.

[54]Th.W. Adorno, Letter of August 2, 1935 to Benjamin in Benjamin, Briefe 2, op. cit., 671-683, esp. 672, 676, 682. -Benjamin, Das Passagen-Werk, op. cit., Vol. II, 991-10059.

[55]Adorno, Letter of August 2, 1935 to Benjamin, op. cit. -SW 5, 35-65.

[56]Adorno, Letter of August 2, 1935 to Benjamin, op. cit., 672. -Habermas, Kultur, op. cit., 302-305. -Schoeller, Die Neue Linke, op. cit., 171-174. -Benjamin, Reflections, op. cit., 312-313; Illuminations, op. cit., 253-264.

[57]Benjamin, Illuminations, op. cit., 253.

[58]Ibid., 261.

[59]J.B. Metz, Glaube in Geschichte und Gegenwart, Mainz:

Matthias Grunewald Verlag 1978, 170–171, 154. –Peukert,
Kritische Theorie, op. cit., 214–215. –Benjamin,
Illuminations, op. cit., 260, 261.

[60] Marx, Das Kapital, op. cit., Vol. III, 873–874.
–A.L. Blanqui, Instruktionen fur den Aufstand, Wien: Europa
Verlag 1968, 154–156, 157–163, 125–153, 48–62, 71, 74–77,
92–110, 111–124, esp. 152, 106–107, esp. 99, 91; Schriften zur
Revolution, Nationalokonomie und Sozialkritik, Hamburg:
Rowohlt Taschenbuch Verlag 1971, 39–80, 156–172, 81–97,
102–113, 112–113, 113–144, 153.

[61] G. Lukacs, Der junge Hegel, Neuwied: Hermann Luchterhand
Verlag 1967, 9–12, 13–33; Deutsche Literatur in zwei
Jahrhunderten, Neuwied: Luchterhand 1964, part III; History
and Class Consciousness, Cambridge, Massachusetts: The MIT
Press 1976, 1–2, 16–20, 27–29, 33–35, 39–40, 139–142, 144–149,
154–158, 166–173, 188–189, 206–207. –A. Schmidt, "Die
'Zeitschrift fur Sozialforschung'. Geschichte und gegenwartige
Bedeutung" in Horkheimer, Zeitschrift, op. cit., 8–17.
–H. Marcuse, Reason and Revolution, Boston: Beacon Press 1960,
part I. –W. Fuld, Walter Benjamin zwischen den Stuhlen,
Munchen: Hansler Verlag 1979, 48, 82, 163, 212, 227, 269, 285.
–Habermas, Theory, op. cit., chs. 5, 6, 7; Zur Rekonstruktion,
op. cit., chap. 4. –Th.W. Adorno, Negative Dialektik,
Frankfurt: Suhrkamp 1966, 293–351.

[62] M. Horkheimer and Th. W. Adorno, Dialektik der Aufklarung,
Frankfurt: S. Fischer 1969, 29–31. –M. Horkheimer, Zur Kritik
der instrumentellen Vernunft, Frankfurt: S. Fischer 1967,
311–312. – Schmidt, Die Zeitschrift, op. cit., 9–17.

[63] Horkheimer, Die Sehnsucht, op. cit., 55–57, 67. –Bloch,
Denken, 82.

[64] Hegel, Jenaer Systementwurfe I, op. cit., 282–296, 297–300,
307–315; Jenaer Systementwurfe III, op. cit., 185–201,
202–208, 214–222, 223–227, 228–231, 232–236. –Habermas,
Theory, op. cit., chap. 4.

[65] SW 11, 42–43. –SW 7, 35–36.

[66] SW 11, 42–43, 128–129, 447, 43–47. –Hegel, Die Vernunft in
der Geschichte, Hamburg: Felix Meiner 1955, 26, 29, 30, 36,

38-40, 42, 46, 48, 49, 60-61, 207, 262-272; Asthetik, op. cit., Bd II, 423.

[67] SW 11, 42-43. -SW 7, 5-6, 32-34. -Hegel, Die Vernunft, op. cit., 46.

[68] SW 11, 48-50, 65-69. -Horkheimer, Zur Kritik, op. cit., 259-260. -Schopenhauer, The World, op. cit., chs. 32, 38, 41, esp. 46.

[69] Benjamin, Illuminations, op. cit., 257-258. -Wolin, Walter Benjamin, op. cit., 61-63, 277 n. 9. -R.J. Siebert, "Creation and Redemption" in The Ecumenist Vol. 20, No. 5, July-August 1982, 65-70.

[70] SW 11, 48-50, 65-69. -SW 7, 35-37.

[71] SW 11, 49, 37-43, 43-47. -Hegel, Three Essays, op. cit., 89-90, 66, 50-52, 47-49; Wissenschaft der Logik, Stuttgart-Bad Cannstatt: Frommann 1965, 45-46.

[72] Hegel, Asthetik, op. cit., Bd. II, 423. -SW 11, 127-129, 447. -Adorno, Drei Studien zu Hegel, op. cit., 21-22. -SW 2, 618-620. -SW 16, 281-282.

[73] SW 11, 49-50, 37-43, 43-47. -Hegel, Reason, op. cit., 26, 29, 36, 38, 39, 40, 42, 46-60. -SW 7, 35-36.

[74] SW 7, 35-36. -SW 5, 35-171. -Nicolaus of Cusa, On God, op. cit., 45, 50-51.

[75] SW 7, 36. -SW 11, 49.

[76] SW 7, 36. -SW 11, 569.

[77] SW 7, 35. SW 15, 293.

[78] SW 16, 298-308. -SW 7, 262-286, 310-328. -Nicolaus von Cusa, Wichtigste Schriften, op. cit., 599-603, 612-615, 615-617.

[79] SW 7, 272. -SW 16, 286-308.

[80] SW 15, 227-228. -SW 16, 247-280.

[81] SW 15, 228. —Meister Eckehart, Deutsche Predigten und Traktate, Munchen: Carl Hanser 1979, 216. —Moltmann, "Theology of Mystical Experience," op. cit., 9-10.

[82] SW 2, 618-620. PB 33, 432-436. —GW 4, 413-414. —Siebert, Reason, Freedom and Change, Washington DC: University Press of America 1985, ch. VII.

[83] SW 16, 281-282. —SW 2, 618-620.

[84] SW 16, 281-282. —Meister Eckehart, Deutsche Predigten, op. cit., 194, 197, 229, 243, 246-249. —Scholem, On the Kabbalah, op. cit., 64-65, 114-117, 132-133.

[85] SW 16, 338-340, 354-356. —SW 2, 620. —SW 11, 128-129, 447. —Hegel, Asthetik, op. cit., II, 423.

[86] Bloch, Denken, op. cit., 79. —A. Schmidt, Drei Studien, op. cit., chs. 1-3, esp. 2.

[87] Hegel, Enzyklopadie der Philosophischen Wissenschaften im Grundriss, Stuttgart: Frommann 1956, 344. —Siebert, "Dialectical Materialism," op. cit., 61-98.

[88] Marx, Das Kapital, op. cit., Bd 1, 17-18. —Habermas, Zur Rekonstruktion, op. cit., 97, 101-102, esp. 105.

[89] Marx, Kapital, op. cit., vol. 1, 17-18, 533-559. —SW 7, 262-286, 310-328. —Seibert, "Hegel," op. cit.

[90] Adorno/Kogon, "Offenbarung," op. cit., 498.

[91] Peukert, Kritische Theorie, op. cit., 214-215.

[92] Ibid., 215. —Horkheimer/Adorno, Dialektik der Aufklarung, op. cit., 40.

[93] Habermas, Philosophisch-Politische Profile, op. cit., 165; "Dialektik der Rationalisierung" in Asthetik und Kommunikation 45/46, October 1981, 126-155.

[94] Peukert, "Was ist eine praktische Wissenschaft?" op. cit., 280-294; Wissenschaftstheorie, op. cit., parts I-III, esp. 289-323. —Arens, Kommunikative Handlungen, op. cit.,

338-385. -G.W.F. Hegel, Vorlesungen uber die Philosophie der Religion, Frankfurt: Suhrkamp 1969, 52-55, 218-240, 241-299 (TW 17); Vorlesunger uber die Philosophie der Religion, Frankfurt: Surhkamp 1970, 33-53, 386 (TW 12); -TW 1, 239-254, 244; -Hegel, Jenaer Schriften 1801-1807, Frankfurt: Suhrkamp 1970, 536 (TW 2). -Nicolaus of Cusa, On God, op. cit., 29-151.

[95] Peukert, "Was ist eine praktische Wissenschaft?" op. cit., 289; Wissenschaftstheorie, op. cit., 311-315. -Kierkegaard, Erbauliche Reden, op. cit., ix-xii, 9-10, 11-105. -TW 17, 205-213, 218-240, 241-299.

[96] Peukert, "Was ist eine praktische Wissenschaft?" op. cit., 289-290. -SW 11, 48-50, 65-69. -Benjamin, Illuminations, op. cit., 254-255, esp. 255, 256-257, 257-258, 260; Reflections, op. cit., 312-313. -Habermas, Vorstudien, op. cit., ch. 8.

[97] Horkheimer, Die Sehnsucht, op. cit., 61-62.

[98] Peukert, Wissenschaftstheorie, op. cit., 289-302. -Arens, Kommunikative Handlungen, op. cit., parts I, II, IV. -Isaiah 1-43. -Jeremiah 1-30. -The Lamentations of Jeremiah 1-5. -Ezekiel 1-20. -Matthew 3, 5-7.

[99] Arens, Kommunikative Handlungen, op. cit., 325-385. -Peukert, Wissenschaftstheorie, op. cit., part II.

[100] Habermas, Theorie, op. cit., chs. 7-8. -GW 6, 307-315. -GW 8, 214-222. -GW 9, 109-116. -Parsons, Societies, op. cit., chs. 1-2; The Systems, op. cit., chs. 1-2.

[101] SW 15, 47-69. -Adorno, Negative Dialectics, op. cit., 361, 368. -Horkheimer, Zur Kritik, op. cit., 248-268. -Benjamin, Illuminations, op. cit., 257-258.

[102] SW 7, 262-286, 310-38, 432-446, 446-456.

[103] SW 7, 432-456. -SW 15, 47-69. -Schopenhauer, The World, op. cit., chs. 41-42, 46, 48-49. -Kierkegaard, Erbauliche Reden, op. cit., 30-41, 42-66, 66-84, 84-128. -W. Kaufmann, Basic Writings of Nietzsche, New York: Modern Library 1968, chs. 1, 3-4, esp. ch. 6. -Blanqui, Schriften zur Revolution, op. cit., 7-38, 39-69; Instruktionen, op. cit., 5-46, 48-73.

-K. Marx, The 18th Brumaire of Louise Bonaparte, New York: International Publishers 1972, 15-26, 27-41, 42-59. -Benjamin, Illuminations, op. cit., 253-264; Reflections, op. cit., 312-313; Das Passagen Werk, Frankfurt: Suhrkamp 1982, 179-210. -Horkheimer/Adorno, Dialectic, op. cit., 81-119, 168-208, 209-258. -Horkheimer, Sozialphilosophische Studien, op. cit., 137-144, 145-155, 117-121. -E. Fromm, The Anatomy of Human Destructiveness, New York: Holt, Rinehart and Winston 1973, part III, esp. ch. 13; Arbeiter, op. cit., 7-46, 47-48; chs. 2-4. -J.B. Metz, Jenseits Burgerlicher Religion, Munchen: Kaiser 1980, 29-50. -Lamb, "Political Theology," op. cit. -Metz, Glaube, op. cit., part II. -Peukert, Wissenschaftstheorie, op. cit., 289-323. -Arens, Kommunikative Handlungen, op. cit., part IV. -Lukacs, Deutsche Literatur, op. cit., 505-509. -Th. Mann, The Magic Mountain, New York: Vintage Books 1969, ch. 5.

[104] S. Unseld (ed.), Zur Aktualitat Walter Benjamin's, Frankfurt: Suhrkamp 1972, ch. 4. -Habermas, Kultur, op. cit., 302-344, esp. 332-335, 339.

[105] Bloch, Geist der Utopie, op. cit., 391-445.

[106] Peukert, Wissenschaftstheorie, op. cit., 289-323; "Was ist eine praktische Wissenschaft?" op. cit., 289-294.

[107] Habermas, Zur Rekonstruktion, op. cit., ch. 4.

[108] Peukert, "Was ist eine praktische Wissenschaft?" op. cit., 289.

[109] Habermas, Theorie, op. cit., chs. 2-4, 7-8.

[110] N. Luhmann, Funktion der Religion, Frankfurt 1977, chs.

[111] Habermas, Theorie, op. cit., ch. 7.

[112] Peukert, "Kontingenzerfahrung und Identitatsbildung. Bemerkungen zum Religionsbegriff und zur Analytik religioser Lernprozess" in J. Blank/G. Hasenhuttle (eds.), Glaube, Erfahrung und Moral, Dusseldorf: 1982, 76-102.

[113] Ibid., 90-92.

[114] Horkheimer/Adorno, Dialectic, op. cit., ix-xvii, 3-42, 81-119, 120-167, 168-208, 209-258.

[115] SW 7, 446-456. -SW 11, 47-49.

[116] Benjamin, Illuminations, op. cit., 257-258.

[117] Peukert, "Kontingenzerfahrung," op. cit., 91. -Benjamin, Illuminations, op. cit., 253-264; Reflections, op. cit., 312-313. -Habermas, Kultur, op. cit., 302-344.

[118] Peukert, "Kontingenzerfahrung," op. cit., 91. -Habermas, Kultur, op. cit., 302-344.

[119] Peukert, "Kontingenzerfahrung," op. cit., 91. -Unseld, Zur Aktualitat, op. cit., ch. 4. -Habermas, Theorie, op. cit., ch. 8, esp. 548-554.

[120] Peukert, Wissenschaftstheorie, op. cit., 305-307; "Kontingenzerfahrung," op. cit., 91.

[121] SW 15, 47-69.

[122] Peukert, "Kontingenzerfahrung," op. cit., 92. -Benjamin, Das Passagen Werk, op. cit., 11-41, 45-49; Illuminations, op. cit., 253-264; Reflections, op. cit., 312-313. -Kierkegaard, Erbauliche Reden, op. cit., 85-105, 105-128.

[123] Peukert, "Kontingenzerfahrung," op. cit., 92. -SW 16, 46-95, 191-356.

[124] SW 15, 400-417, 422-434, 434-437.

[125] Peukert, "Was ist eine praktische Wissenschaft?" op. cit., 290. -GW 4, 417-485. -GW 6, 307-315. -GW 8, 223-253, 253-277, 277-287. -Marx, Die Fruhschriften, op. cit., chs. 3, 6-10. -Habermas, Theorie, op. cit., chs. 2, 4-5, 7-8.

[126] SW 7, 89-91, 101-102, 110-112, 129-130, 441-442. -GW 6, 301-326. -GW 8, 209-287. -Siebert, Hegel's Concept of Marriage and Family, op. cit., chs. 9, 11-13, 15, 17-18, 23-24. -Peukert, "Was ist eine praktische Wissenschaft?" op. cit., 290.

[127] Peukert, "Was ist eine praktische Wissenschaft?" op. cit., 290. –GW 6, 326–382. –GW 4, 413–414, 417–464. –SW 7, 35–36, 446–454.

[128] Peukert, "Was ist eine praktische Wissenschaft?" op. cit., 290. –SW 16, 300. –GW 4, 413–414, 458–459. –GW 6, 331. –GW 8, 280–286, esp. 282.

[129] Peukert, "Was ist eine praktische Wissenschaft?" op. cit., 290–291.

[130] Ibid. –Benjamin, Illuminations, op. cit., 255, 257–260, esp. 261.

[131] Peukert, "Was ist eine praktische Wissenschaft?" op. cit. –SW 16, 295–308. –Meister Eckehart, Deutsche Predigten, op. cit. –Kierkegaard, Erbauliche Reden, op. cit.

[132] Peukert, "Was ist eine praktische Wissenschaft?" op. cit., 291. –Kierkegaard, Erbauliche Reden, op. cit., 75–76. –SW 15, 114.

[133] GW 4, 417–485. –GW 6, 307–326. –GW 8, 214–277. –GW 9, 109–115. –Habermas, Theorie, op. cit., chs. 2–5, 7–8.

[134] Peukert, "Was ist eine praktische Wissenschaft?" op. cit., 291. –Nohl, Theologische Jugendschriften, op. cit., 3, 22–23. –Hegel, Three Essays, op. cit., 48, 50–52, 89–90. –GW 4, 414, 459. –GW 6, 307–315, 330–331. –GW 8, 214–253, 253–287. –SW 7, 6, 23–26, 30–32, 33–34, 35–37. –SW 2, 434–435, 447–448, 455–456. –SW 11, 37–43, 43–47, 47–56, 569.

[135] Peukert, "Was ist eine praktische Wissenschaft?" op. cit., 291. –PB 33, 431–439. –SW 2, 569–601.

[136] Peukert, "Was ist eine praktische Wissenschaft?" op. cit., 431–439.

[137] GW 9, 109–115, 400–421. –SW 2, 148–158, 569–601, 602–620.

[138] SW 11, 43–47. –SW 7, 262–286, 310–323, esp. 320. –GW 9, 109–115. –Marx, Das Kapital, op. cit., 18; Fruhe Schriften, op. cit., chs. 9–10. –Blanqui, Instruktionen, op. cit., 111–124, 125–153, 154–156, 157–178, 179–181.

139 Peukert,   "Kontingenzerfahrung,"   op. cit.,   92-93.
-G. Zhukov, "Victory 1941-1945" in Soviet Life, January 1985,
20-21, 26-27. -P. Balov, "Stalingrad, the Turning Point of
World War II," Soviet Life, February 1985, 45-47. -K. Simonov,
"Stalingrad Diary," Soviet Life, February 1985, 47-49.

140 Peukert, "Kontingenzerfahrung," op. cit., 92-96. -Lamb,
"Political Theology," op. cit. -Peukert, Wissenschaftstheorie,
op. cit.,   289-302.   -Arens,   Kommunikative   Handlungen,
op.'/cit., parts 1, 4. -Hegel, Three Essays, op. cit.,
104-165.

141 Peukert, "Kontingenzerfahrung," op. cit., 92-96. -Arens,
Kommunikative Handlungen, op. cit., parts 1, 4. -SW 11, 37-47.
-Matthew 5-7. -Hegel, Three Essays, op. cit., 104, 96, 89-90,
66, 50-52, 48.

142 Peukert, "Kontingenzerfahrung," op. cit., 93. -E. Arens,
"Gleichnisse als Kommunikative Handlungen Jesu," Theologie und
Philosophie 56 (1981), 47-64; Kommunikative Handlungen,
op. cit., part 4. -Matthew, 5-7.

143 Peukert, "Kontingenzerfahrung," op. cit., 93. Science,
op. cit.

144 Peukert, "Kontingenzerfahrung," op. cit., 93. -SW 19,
162-169. -SW 16, 546-553.

145 Peukert, "Kontingenzerfahrung," op. cit., 93.

146 Benjamin, Illuminations, op. cit., 253-264; Reflections,
op. cit., 312-313.

147 Habermas, "Die Kulturkritik," op. cit., 1059-1061; Kultur,
op. cit., 302-344.

148 Peukert, "Kontingenzerfahrung," op. cit., 93-94. -SW 16,
295-356.

149 Peukert, "Kontingenzerfahrung, op. cit., 93-94. -SW 16,
298-302. -Matthew 26-28. -Mark 4-16. -Luke 22-24. -John 12-21.

150 Habermas,   Theorie,   op. cit.,   ch. 8.   -Benjamin,
Illuminations, op. cit., 253-264; Reflections, op. cit.,

312-313. -Horkheimer, Die Sehnsucht, op. cit., 54-89. -Adorno, Der Positivismus Streit, op. cit., chs. 1, 3, 5, 7.

[151] Peukert, "Kontingenzerfahrung," op. cit., 94. -Matthew 26-28. -Mark 14-16. -Luke 22-24. -John 12-21.

[152] Lehmann and Raffelt, Rechenschaft op. cit., 40, 44, 48, 77, 81, 115, esp. 213-218, 218-222, 223-224, 225-228, 229-230, 434, 446, 448, 453. -Rahner, Grundkurs, op. cit., 260-278; part IX.

[153] Peukert, Wissenschaftstheorie, op. cit., parts II-III, esp. 311-313. -Arens, Kommunikative Handlungen, op. cit., part III. -H. Kung, On Being a Christian, Garden City, NY: Doubleday 1976, parts B, C, esp. D. -SW 16, 300. -SW 11, 409-430.

[154] Th. W. Adorno, Zur Dialectic des Engagement, Frankfurt: Suhrkamp 1973, 145-146, 138; Versuch das Endspiel zu Verstehen, Frankfurt: Suhrkamp 1973, 98; Minima Moralia, op. cit., 333-334.

[155] Peukert, "Kontingenzerfahrung," op. cit., 95. -SW 16, 300.

[156] Peukert, "Kontingenzerfahrung," op. cit., 95-96.

[157] Peukert, "Was ist eine praktische Wissenschaft?" op. cit., 292.

[158] PB 171a, 26, 30, 34-35, 42, 45-46, 48, 52, 60-61, 63, 72, 92, 96.

[159] SW 11, 127. -PB 171a, 46, 60-61. -Hegel, Asthetik, op. cit., II, 423. -SW 2, 18-20, 619-620. -Ritter, Hegel, op. cit., 7-72. -SW 7, 446-456, 261-286, 310-328.

[160] Peukert, "Was ist eine praktische Wissenschaft?" op. cit., 292.

[161] F. Boll, etc. (eds.), Wird es denn uberhaupt gehen?, Munchen: Kaiser 1980, 23-29, 128-133.

[162] T. Hung, "Reagan defends Covert Aid to Nicaraguan Rebels" in Kalamazoo Gazette, January 24, 1984, A1-2. -Associated

Press, "Deadly Chemical Spills Reported" in Kalamazoo Gazette, op. cit., A3. -"$525 Million to Study Routes to Safer World" in Kalamazoo Gazette, op. cit., A3. -Los Angelos Times, "Sanctuary Leaders Arraigned" in Kalamazoo Gazette, op. cit., A3.

[163]Peukert, "Was ist eine praktische Wissenschaft?" op. cit., 292.

[164]GW 8, 185-287. -SW 11, 43-47, 47-69. -Habermas, Theorie, op. cit., ch. 8.

[165]Peukert, "Was ist eine praktische Wissenschaft?" op. cit., 93.

[166]Mark 2:27. -Hegel, Three Essays, op. cit., 119. -Arens, "Gleichnisse," op. cit., 47-69; Kommunikative Handlungen, op. cit., part 4.

[167]Metz, The Emergent Church, op. cit., 119-123. -Siebert, "Toward a Critical Catholicism, I" op. cit., 1-13; "Toward a Critical Catholicism II," op. cit., 144-163.

[168]Peukert, "Was ist eine praktische Wissenschaft?" op. cit., 293-294.

[169]Peukert, "Kontingenzerfahrung," op. cit., 76-80, 96-97.

[170]Ibid. -Metz, The Emergent Church, op. cit., ch. 3.

[171]Peukert, "Kontingenzerfahrung," op. cit., 97. -SW 15, 355-400, 400-417, 422-434, 434-437, 437-471, 46-95.

[172]Peukert, "Kontingenzerfahrung," op. cit., 97-98.

[173]Weber, Sociology of Religion, op. cit., xxx-xxi, iii-iv, vi-vii, esp. ix-xvi; The Religion of India, Glencoe, Ill.: Free Press 1953, part III; Ancient Judaism, Glencoe, Ill: Free Press 1952, parts I-IV, esp. ch. 12, part V. -Durkheim, The Elementary Forms, op. cit., chs. 1-2, 8-9, 4. -S. Kracauer, Das Ornament, op. cit., 173-186, 187-196, 249-255. -Habermas, Theorie, op. cit., chs. 2, 4-5, 7-8.

[174]Parsons, Societies, op. cit., chs. 1-6; Essays in

Sociological Theory, Glencoe: Free Press 1954, ch. 10; _The Social System_, Glencoe: Free Press 1951, chs. 5, 8. —T. F. O'Dea, _The Sociology of Religion_, Englewood Cliffs, NJ: Prentice-Hall 1966, chs. 1, 2.

[175]Peukert, "Kontingenzerfahrung," op. cit., 98–99. —Luhmann, _Funktion der Religion_, op. cit. —O'Dea, _The Sociology_, op. cit., chs. 1–4, esp. 6. —Parsons, _Societies_, op. cit., chs. 1, 2. —Habermas, "Kulturkritik," op. cit.

[176]Horkheimer, _Eclipse of Reason_, op. cit., ch. 1.

[177]Horkheimer, _Notizen_, op. cit., 101–104, 116–117. —Adorno, _Der Positivismus Streit_, op. cit., chs. 2, 4, 6, 8, 10.

[178]R. Bellah, _The Broken Covenant. American Civil Religion in Time of Trial_, New York: Seabury 1975, chs. 1–6. —W. G. McLoughlin and R. N. Bellah (eds.), _Religion in America_, Boston: Houghton-Mifflin 1968, 3–23. —Hegel, _Three Essays_, op. cit., 1–29.

[179]Peukert, "Kontingenzerfahrung," op. cit., 98–99. —Lukacs, _Deutsche Literatur_, op. cit., 505–617. —Mann, _The Magic Mountain_, op. cit., chs. 1–5; _Buddenbrooks_, New York: Vintage Books 1961, chs. 1–8; _Death in Venice_, Harmondsworth, Middlesex 1957, parts I–III. —Adorno, _Zur Dialektik_, op. cit., 147–150.

[180]Peukert, "Kontingenzerfahrung," op. cit., 98–99. —Luhmann, _Funktion_, op. cit., 187. —F. Scholz, _Freiheit als Indiffernz. Alteuropaische Probleme in der Systemtheorie von N. Luhmann_, Frankfurt: 1982. —T. Rendtorff, _Gesellschaft ohne Religion?_, Munchen: 1975. —Horkheimer, _Eclipse_, op. cit., ch. 4. —Habermas, _Legitimation Crisis in Capitalism_, Boston: Beacon 1975, part III.

[181]Siebert, _From Critical Theory_, op. cit., chs. 6–12.

[182]W. Schmidt, _Die Religion der Religionskritik_, Munchen: Claudius 1972, chs. 1–9. —Luhmann, _Funktion_, op. cit., chs. 4–5.

[183]SW 15, 114.

[184] Peukert, "Kontingenzerfahrung," op. cit., 99.

[185] Habermas, Theorie, op. cit., chs. 4-8; Vorstudien, op. cit., chs. 8-11; Stichworte, op. cit., 7-35. -Horkheimer, Gesellschaft, op. cit., 162-175; Sozialphilosophische Studien, op. cit., 131-136, 145-155. -Adorno/Kogon, "Offenbarung," op. cit. -Benjamin, Illuminations, op. cit., 253-264; Reflections, op. cit., 312-313. -Siebert, "Horkheimer's Sociology of Religion" in Telos, No. 30, Winter 1976-77, 127-144.

[186] Habermas, Zur Rekonstruktion, op. cit., ch. 4; Theorie, op. cit., ch. 8.

[187] Habermas, Theorie, op. cit., chs. 7-8.

[188] Peukert, "Kontingenzerfahrung," op. cit., 99. -St. Breuer, "J. Habermas's Theorie des kommunikativen Handelns" in Leviathan 1/82, 132-146. -A. Sollner, "Jurgen Habermas und die kritische Theorie des gegenwartigan Rechtsstaates-Versuch einer wissen- schaftsgeschichtlichen Einordnung" in Leviathan 1/82, 92-129. -Habermas, Theorie, op. cit., ch. 8.

[189] Peukert, "Kontingenzerfahrung," op. cit., 99-100.

[190] Ibid. -Kierkegaard, Erbauliche Reden, op. cit., 42-128.

[191] Peukert, "Kontingenzerfahrung," op. cit., 99-100. -Scholem, The Messianic Idea, op. cit., chs. 1-5; On the Kabbala, op. cit., chs. 1-5. -Kierkegaard, Erbauliche Reden, op. cit., 84-108, 75-76. -Habermas, Theorie, op. cit., 383. -SW 15, 114.

[192] Peukert, "Kontingenzerfahrung," op. cit., 100.

[193] Ibid. -Quint, Meister Eckehart, op. cit., 174-175. -Blackney, Meister Eckehart, op. cit., 253-305, esp. 270, 288, 295, 298, 302. -Kierkegaard, Erbauliche Reden, op. cit., 75-76. -Horkheimer, Die Sehnsucht, op. cit., 54-89. -Nicolaus von Cusa, Wichtigste Schriften, op. cit., 612-615, 615-617, 617-622.

[194] Dobert, Systemtheorie, op. cit., 87-139.

[195] Horkheimer, Gesellschaft, op. cit., 162-175; Die Sehnsucht,

op. cit., 54-89.

[196]Horkheimer, <u>Notizen</u>, op. cit., 96-97, 247-248, 286, 316-321, 92-93.

[197]B. Brecht, <u>The City of Mahagonny</u>, op. cit. -Benjamin, <u>Reflections</u>, op. cit.

[198]Ebertz, "Die Berg predigt," op. cit., 15-23. -E. Kogon, "Angewemdte Bergpredigt-Eine Erwiederung" in <u>FH</u> 39/9 (September 1984), 23-24. -W. Dirks, "Politik der Christen-Eine estere Antwort" in <u>FH</u> 39/9 (September 1984), 24-27.

[199]Blanqui, <u>Schriften</u>, op. cit., 176-184. -Horkheimer, <u>Notizen</u>, op. cit., 16, 18, 92-93, 96-97, 115-116, 121-123, 127, 131-132, 210-211, 218-219, 268, 288-289, 316-320.

[200]J. B. Metz, <u>Theology of the World</u>, New York: Seabury 1973, chs. 5-6; <u>The Emergent Church</u>, op. cit., chs. 1-2, 5-6; <u>Zeit der Orden</u>, Herder: Freiburg 1978, chs. 3-4.

[201]"The Challenge of Peace: God's Promise and Our Response" in <u>The Michigan Catholic</u>, June 17, 1983, esp. 20. -Bishops Pastoral, "Catholic Social Teaching and the US Economy" in <u>Origins</u>, 14/22/23 (November 15, 1984), 334, 342-347.

[202]Peukert, "Kontingenzerfahrung," op. cit., 100-101.

[203]Ibid. -J. Piaget, <u>Das moralische Urleil beim Kinde</u>, Frankfurt: 1973. -H. Peukert, "Uber die Zukunft von Bildung" in <u>FH</u> -extra G (November-December 1984) 129-137.

[204]L. Kohlberg, <u>The Meaning and Measurement of Moral Development</u>, Worcester, Mass.: Clark University Press 1981, 1-3, 4-6, 35-52.

[205]L. Kohlberg, "Eine Neuinterpretation der Zusammenhange zwischen der Moralentwicklung in der Kindheit und im Erwachsenenalter," in R. Dobert/J. Habermas/G. Nunner-Winkler (eds.), <u>Die Entwicklung des Ich's</u>, Koln: 1977, 225-252, 249.

[206]Ibid., 250. -SW 7, 35-36. -Horkheimer, <u>Gesellschaft</u>, op. cit., 162-175; <u>Critical Theory</u>, New York: Seabury 1972, 129-131; <u>Zur Kritik</u>, op. cit., 216-228, 229-238; <u>Die</u>

Sehnsucht, op. cit., 54-89.

[207]Peukert, "Kontingenzerfahrung," op. cit., 102; "Padogogik-Ethik-Politik. Normative Implikationen padagogischer Interaction" in Zeitschrift fur Padagogik, Beiheft 17, Weinheim 1981, 61-70, esp. 66.

[208]P. Gmunder, "Entwicklung als Ziel der religiosen Erziehung" in Kat Bl. 104 (1979), 629-634, 633. -F. Oser, et al., "Stufen des religosen Urteils" in Weg zum Menschen 32 (1980), 386-398; "Zur Entwicklung kognitiver Stufen des religiosen Urteils" in G. Staches, et al., (eds.) Sozialisation, Identitatsfindung, Glaubenserfahrung, Zurich: 1979, 229-247.

[209]Peukert, Science, op. cit.

[210]Peukert, "Kontingenzerfahrung," op. cit., 102.

[211]H. Peukert, "Erziehung, moralische" in Enzyklopadie Erziehungswissenschaft, Stuttgart: E. Klett 1983, 394-395. -G.W.F. Hegel, Vorlesungen uber die Geschichte der Philosophie, Stuttgart-Bad Cannstatt: Frommann 1965, Vol. II, 169-297 (SW 18). -Plato, "Politaia" in G. Eigler, Plato's Werke, Darmstadt: 1977, vol. 4.

[212]SW 7, 265-267, 182-184, 99-101. -SW 18, 169-297.

[213]Peukert, "Erziehung," op. cit., 394-395. -SW 7, 265-267. -SW 16, 247-356. -SW 11, 409-430. -PB 33, 387-388.

[214]GW 4, 417-485. -GW 8, 223-287. -SW 7, 88-163. -Habermas, Theory, op. cit., chs. 1-2.

[215]Peukert, "Erziehung," op. cit., 395.

[216]I. Kant, Critique of Practical Reason, Chicago: University of Chicago Press 1949, 66-101.

[217]SW 7, 38-87, 164-225, 226-456.

[218]Peukert, "Erziehung," op. cit., 395.

[219]Ibid.

[220] Niebuhr, Marx, op. cit., chs. 3-4, 6-9.

[221] Nietzsche, Basic Writings, op. cit., chs. III-IV.

[222] S. Freud, Beyond the Pleasure Principle, New York: Liveright 1961. -D. Claussen (ed.), Spuren der Befreiung-Herbert Marcuse, Darmstadt: Luchterhand 1981, part II. -Marcuse, Eros, op. cit., part II; Five Lectures, Boston: Beacon Press 1970, chs. 1-3.

[223] E. Durkheim, Suicide, New York: Free Press 1951, books I, III; Professional Ethics and Civil Morals, Glencoe, Ill: Free Press 1958, chs. 1-7, 9-10.

[224] B. F. Skinner, Beyond Freedom and Dignity, Toronto: Bantam Boks 1971, chs. 1-3, 6-9; Walden Two, New York: Macmillan 1962.

[225] J. Habermas/N. Luhmann, Theorie der Gesellschaft oder Sozialtechnologie, Frankfurt: Suhrkamp 1975, 7-24, 25-100, 291-405.

[226] H. Lubbe, Sakulerisierung, Munchen: Verlag Karl Albert 1975, chs. 6-7.

[227] Siebert, "Dialectical Materialism," op. cit.; "Three Alternative Futures," op. cit.

[228] Peukert, "Erziehung," op. cit., 395.

[229] Horkheimer, Die Sehnsucht, op. cit., 60. -Horkheimer/Adorno, Dialectic, op. cit., 3-42.

[230] Horkheimer, Die Sehnsucht, op cit., 61. -Kant, "Was ist Aufklarung?" op. cit., 77-93. -Habermas, Theorie, op. cit., ch. 8; Zur Rekonstruktion, op. cit., ch. 4.

[231] Siebert, "Dialectical Materialism," op. cit.; "Three Alternative Futures," op. cit.

[232] H. Peukert, "Kritische Theorie und Padagogik," in Zeitschrift fur Padagogik, 30 Jhrg 1983, No. 2, 203. -Horkheimer, Critical Theory, op. cit., 129-131; Die Sehnsucht, op. cit., 54, 60.

[233] Benjamin,   Illuminations,   op. cit.,   253–264. –Habermas, Kultur, op. cit., 302–344.

[234] Horkheimer/Adorno,   Dialectic,   op. cit.,   ix–xvii,   3–42, 168–208.   –Habermas,   Theorie,   op. cit.,   ch. 4,   7;   "Tod," op. cit.; "Kulturkritik,"   op. cit. –Schmidt,   Die Religion, op. cit., chs. 3–4, 8–9.

[235] Horkheimer/Adorno,   Dialectic,   op. cit.,   23–24. –Siebert, "Creation," op. cit.

[236] Horkheimer/Adorno, Dialectic, op. cit., 168–208, 177–217. –Th.W. Adorno, et al., The Authoritarian Personality, New York: Norton 1969, chs. 16–19. –Horkheimer, Notizen, op. cit., 8, 28–29, 157–158, 164–165; Zur Kritik, op. cit., 302–320.

[237] SW 7, 299–301.

[238] Adorno/Kogon,   "Offenbarung,"   op. cit.,   402.   –Adorno, Negative Dialectic, op. cit., part III, chs. 2–3.

[239] Peukert, "Kritische Theorie," op. cit., 203–204.

[240] Ibid.   –Quint,   Deutsche Predigten,   op. cit.,   213–218, 267–271, 303–310. –Nicolaus von Cusa, Wichtigste Schriften, op. cit.,   31–33. –Horkheimer, Zur Kritik, op. cit., 248–268, 311–312. –SW 16, 46–95, 191–356. –SW 19, 26–28, 131–132.

[241] Peukert, "Kritische Theorie," op. cit., 204. –Adorno, The Authoritarian   Personality,   op. cit.,   chs. 16–19. –Horkheimer/Adorno, Dialectic, op. cit., 168–208. –Horkheimer, Zur Kritik, op. cit., 302–316.

[242] Peukert, "Kritische Theorie," op. cit., 204. –G. Rohrmoser, Das Elend der kritischen Theorie, Theodor W. Adorno–Herbert Marcuse–Jurgen Habermas, Frankfurt: 1970, 104.

[243] Peukert,   "Kritische Theorie," op. cit., 204. –R. Spaemann, "Die Herausforderung," in Mut Zur Erziehung. Beitrage zu einem Forum vom 9–10 Januar im Wissenschaftszentrum Bonn, Bad Godesberg, Stuttgart 1978, 16–34. –Th. W. Adorno, "Erziehung nach Auschwitz" in Adorno, Gesammelte Schriften, Frankfurt: 1977, Vol. 10/2, 674.

[244] Spaemann, "Die Herausforderung," op. cit., 24.

[245] Peukert, "Kritische Theorie," op. cit., 204. -SW 7, 35-36. -SW 11, 37-43, 43-47.

[246] SW 5, 5-65. -SW 7, 1-13, 19-37, 38-87. -SW 11, 33-47. -Benjamin, **Briefe 2**, op. cit., 671-683, esp. 672, 676, 682.

[247] Peukert, "Kritische Theorie," op. cit., 204-205. -Horkheimer/Adorno, **Dialectic**, op. cit., 23-24. -SW 2, 64-66. -Horkheimer, **Zur Kritik**, op. cit., 311-312.

[248] PB 33, 44, 73, 102-103, 184, 316. -G.W.F. Hegel, **Wissenschaft der Logik**, Hamburg: Felix Meiner 1963, 6, 11, 20-21, 35-37, 87, 90 (PB 56). -Haag, **Der Fortschritt**, op. cit., chs. 4, 8. -SW 15, 29-301. -Adorno, **Negative Dialectic**, op. cit., part 2.

[249] Peukert, "Kritische Theorie," op. cit., 204-205. -SW 7, 320.

[250] R.J. Siebert, "Communication Without Domination," in **Concilium**, 131, 1978, 117-131.

[251] J. Habermas, "Dialektik der Rationalisierung," im Gesprach mit A. Honneth, E. Knodler, et al., in **Asthetik und Kommnikation** 45/46, October 1981, 126-155.

[252] Adorno, **Minima Moralia**, op. cit., 333-334. -Adorno/Kogon, "Offenbarung," op. cit., 402.

[253] SW 5, 327-353. -SW 2, 602-620. -Horkheimer/Adorno, **Dialektik**, op. cit., 29-31.

[254] Horkheimer, **Notizen**, op. cit., 96-97.

[255] Peukert, "Kritishe Theorie," op. cit., 205.

[256] SW 11, 47-69. -A. Schopenhauer, **Aphorismen zur Lebensweisheit**, Munchen: Wilhelm Goldmann 1946, 173-182; **The World**, op. cit., chs. 26, 38, 41-42, 46-47. -A. Schmidt, "Die Zeitschrift fur Sozialforschung. Geschichte und Gegenwartige Bedeutung," in ZfS, I, 8-26. -Horkheimer, **Zur Kritik**, op. cit., 248-269.

[257]Peukert,   Wissenschaftstheorie,   op. cit.,   305–307.
-Benjamin, Das Passagen Werk, op. cit., Vol. I, 11–41, 43–300;
Illuminations,   op. cit., 253–264. -Horkheimer, Die Sehnsucht,
op. cit., 55–56.

[258]W. Benjamin, Gesammelte Schriften, Frankfurt: 1974, 1244;
Illuminations, op. cit., 253–264.

[259]H. Mayer, "Nachdenken uber Adorno" in FH 25/4 (April 1970),
268–280.

[260]Peukert, "Kritische Theorie," op. cit., 205–206.

[261]Benjamin, Gesammelte Schriften, op. cit., 1232–1233.

[262]Siebert, "Peukert's New Critical Theology, I" op. cit.;
"Peukert's New Critical Theology, II" op. cit. -Metz, The
Emergent Church, op. cit., chs. 1–3, 5–7; Faith and History.
-Peukert, Wissenschaftstheorie, op. cit., part III. -E. Arens,
"Gleichnisse als kommunikative Handlungen Jesu," in Th.Ph. 56
(1981), 47–69; "Toward a Theological Theory of Communicative
Action," in Media Development 28 (1981), No. 4,   12–16;
Kommunikative Handlungen, op. cit., part IV. -Boll, Wird es
denn uberhaupt gehen?, op. cit., 23–29, 119–123, 128–133,
166–170, 241–251, 255–262, 269–271.

[263]Peukert, "Kritische Theorie," op. cit., 213–214. -Habermas,
Theorie,   op. cit.,   ch. 8.   -Horkheimer, Die Sehnsucht,
op. cit., 55–56.

[264]Peukert, "Kritische Theorie," op. cit., 213.

[265]H. Marcuse, The Asthetic Dimension, Boston: Beacon Press
1978, chs. 1–4. -Adorno, Asthetische Theorie, op. cit.,
244–262, 296–33, 334–388; Philosophy of Modern Music, New
York: Seabury 1973, chs. 2, 4–5; Introduction to the Sociology
of Music, New York: Seabury 1976, chs. 2, 12. -Benjamin, Das
Passagen Werk, op. cit., Vol. I, 301–489; Illuminations,
op. cit., chs. 3–8; Reflections, op. cit., chs. 2–4, esp.
314–336. -C. Baudelaire, Flowers of Evil, New York: Harper and
Brothers 1936. -L. and F.E. Hyslop, Jr., Baudelaire on Poe,
State College, PA: Bald Eagle Press 1952. -C. Baudelaire, My
Heart Laid Bare, New York: Vanguard 1951.

[266] Peukert, "Kritische Theorie," op. cit., 213.

[267] Parsons, Societies, op. cit., chs. 1-2.

[268] Arens, Kommunikative Handlungen, op. cit., parts III-IV.

[269] Peukert, Wissenschaftstheorie, op. cit., 252-300. -Arens, Kommunikative Handlungen, op. cit., part III.

[270] Peukert, "Kritische Theorie," op. cit., 213-214.

[271] J. Habermas,   "Diskursethik-Notizen   zu   einem Begrundungsprogramm" in J. Habermas, Moralbewusstsein und kommunikatives Handeln, Frankfurt: 1983. -Horkheimer, Die Sehnsucht, op. cit., 54-89.

[272] Peukert, "Kritische Theorie," op. cit., 214. -Lukacs, Deutsche Literatur, op. cit., 517-534; "Uber die Zukunft," op. cit., 129-137.

[273] Peukert, "Kritische Theorie," op. cit., 214. -J. Habermas, Strukturwandel der Offentlichkeit, Neuwied: Luchterhand 1976, 7-9; chs. 2-4, 6-7; Theory and Praxis, op. cit., chs. 1-6. -SW 7, 337-440.

[274] Peukert, Padagogik, op. cit., 61-70.

[275] Peukert, "Kritische Theorie," op. cit., 214-215.

[276] SW 9, 29-69, 481-722, 400-445. -SW 10, 9-45, 46-254, 400-403, 408-409, 426-445. -SW 7, 261-286, 310-323, 432-440, 440-446, 446-452. -SW 11, 47-69.

[277] Peukert, "Kritische Theorie," op. cit., 214-215.

[278] Ibid. -Habermas, Theorie, op. cit., ch. 8.

[279] Peukert, "Kritische Theorie," op. cit., 214-215. -"Uber die Zukunft," op. cit., 129-137. -Horkheimer, Die Sehnsucht, op. cit., 55-56.

[280] Peukert, "Kritische Theorie," op. cit., 215. -Siebert, "Dialectical Materialism," op. cit.

[281]Horkheimer/Adorno, Dialektik, op. cit., 40.

[282]Peukert, "Uber die Zukunft," op. cit., 136–137. –W. Dirks, Der Singende Stotterer, Munchen: Kosel 1983, 196. –"Die alten Normen ud der neue Richtpunkt," in FH extra 6 (November–December 1984), 3–7.

[283]Peukert, Wissenschaftstheorie, op. cit., part III. –Arens, Kommunikative Handlungen, op. cit., part IV.

[284]Metz, Faith and History, op. cit. –Siebert, "Dialectical Materialism," op. cit. –Arens, Kommunikative Handlungen, op. cit., parts I, III–IV. –Matthew 13:1–58; 18:22–35; 20:1–16; 21:28–46; 22:1–14; 25:1–46. –Mark 4:1–34; 12:1–13. –Luke 5:36–39; 7:41–42; 8:4–18; 10:30–37; 11:5–13; 12:16–21; 13:6–9, 18–21; 14:16–24; 15:3–32; 16:1–13, 19–31; 18:1–14; 19:11–27; 21:29–36. –John 10:1–8.

[285]Arens, Kommunikative Handlungen, op. cit., 353–385. –Benjamin, Illuminations, op. cit., 83–110. –Metz, Faith and History, op. cit. –Siebert, "Dialectical Materialism," op. cit.

[286]Arens, Kommunikative Handlungen, op. cit., 353–356. –"Gleichnisse," op. cit., 47–69.

[287]Ibid., parts I–II, IV.

[288]Habermas, Theorie, op. cit., Bd 1, 143, 374–375, 377, 388–389, 392, 394–396, 427–429, 433–435, 449–450, 452; Bd 2, 11–68, 69–117. –Vorstudien, op. cit., chs. 1, 6–7, esp. 79, 80, 90, 91, 93.

[289]Bahr, Religionsgesprache, op. cit., ch. 1.

[290]Arens, Kommunikative Handlungen, op. cit., 353.

[291]J. Habermas, "Was heisst Universalpragmatik?" in K.O. Apel (ed.), Sprachpragmatik und Philosophie, Frankfurt: 1976, 174–272. Vorstudien, op. cit., chs. 8, 11.

[292]Arens, Kommunikative Handlungen, op. cit., 354.

[293]E. Arens, "Toward a Theological Theory of Communicative

Action," in <u>Media Development</u> 28 (1981), No. 4, 12–16.

[294] Arens, <u>Kommunikative Handlungen</u>, op. cit., 354–355.

[295] Matthew 13, 24, 32–33, 44–45, 47–48; 18, 23.

[296] Arens, <u>Kommunikative Handlungen</u>, op. cit., parts I, IV.

[297] <u>Ibid</u>., parts I, II.

[298] <u>Ibid</u>., 355–356.

[299] <u>Ibid</u>.

[300] <u>Ibid</u>., 356.

[301] SW 7, 35–36.

[302] Arens, <u>Kommunikative Handlungen</u>, op. cit., 356.

[303] <u>Ibid</u>. –Siebert, "Communication without Domination," op. cit.

[304] Arens, <u>Kommunikative Handlungen</u>, op. cit., 356–357. –SW 16, 247–308, 354. –SW 11, 409–430.

[305] Arens, <u>Kommunikative Handlungen</u>, op. cit., 357–359.

[306] <u>Ibid</u>., 357. –Peukert, <u>Wissenschaftstheorie</u>, op. cit. –Habermas, <u>Theorie</u>, op. cit., chs. 1–2; <u>Vorstudien</u>, op. cit., chs. 1–3, 6–9, 11.

[307] Arens, <u>Kommunikative Handlungen</u>, op. cit., 357–358.

[308] J. Habermas, "Wahrheitstheorien" in H. Fahrenbach (ed.), <u>Wirklichkeit und Reflexion</u>, Pfullingen 1973, 211–265; <u>Vorstudien</u>, op. cit., chs. 2–3, 5–9, 11; esp. 114–115. –Peukert, <u>Wissenschaftstheorie</u>, op. cit., 268–269.

[309] SW 11, 37–59. –Marx, <u>Die Fruhschriften</u>, op. cit., 15–19; ch. 3; 207–224, 270–316, 319–321, 321–322, 339–341, ch. 10.

[310] John 3:21; 8:32. –Galatians 1:14.

[311] Arens, _Kommunikative Handlungen_, op. cit., 357-358. -D.D. Evans, _The Logic of Self-Involvement_, London: 1963, 195; "Differences between Scientific and Religious Assertions" in I.G. Barbour (ed.), _Science and Religion_, London: 1968, 101-133. -J. Ladriere, _Rede der Wissenschaft-Wort des Glaubens_, Munchen: 1972, 131-136.

[312] Ladriere, _Rede_, op. cit., 131, 136. -Evans, _Logic_, op. cit., 195; "Differences," op. cit., 108.

[313] Arens, _Kommunikative Handlungen_, op. cit., 357/13.

[314] Ibid., 358. -Habermas, _Vorstudien_, op. cit., ch. 1, esp. 113-116; _Legitimationsprobleme in Spatkapitalismus_, Frankfurt: 1975, 148.

[315] Arens, _Kommunikative Handlungen_, op. cit., 358-359.

[316] Ibid., part II.

[317] Ibid., 358. -Siebert, "From Dialectical Materialism," op. cit. -Metz, _Glaube_, op. cit., S12.

[318] Habermas, _Legitimationsprobleme_, op. cit., 161.

[319] Arens, _Kommunikative Handlungen_, op. cit., 358-359.

[320] Ibid., 358. -SW 11, 67-68. -Adorno, _Negative Dialektik_, Frankfurt: Suhrkamp 1966, 17-18.

[321] Arens, _Kommunikative Handlungen_, op. cit., 358-359. -E. Bentley (ed.), _Seven Plays by Bertholt Brecht_, New York: Grove Press 1961, xiii-Li.

[322] Ebertz, "Die Berg predigt," op. cit., 15-23,

[323] Matthew 5-7.

[324] Arens, _Kommunikative Handlungen_, op. cit., 358-359.

[325] Ibid.

[326] Ibid.

[327] Ibid. -Habermas, Vorstudien, op. cit., ch. 1, esp. 113-116; chs. 8-9, 11.

[328] Matthew 5:22, 30; esp. 8, 12.

[329] Ibid., 4:1-11; 8:28-33; esp. 12:24-32.

[330] Schopenhauer, Aphorismen, op. cit.; The World, op. cit., chs. 1, 4, 12, 26, 29, 38, 41-42, 45-49. -Horkheimer, Zur Kritik, op. cit., 248-268.

[331] Arens, Kommunikative Handlungen, op. cit., 359/17.

[332] Ibid., 360-364. -Adorno, Soziologische Schriften, op. cit., I, 457-477. -Habermas, Vorstudien, op. cit., chs. 2, 4. -Siebert, "Communication," op. cit.

[333] Arens, Kommunikative Handlungen, op. cit., 360-364. -Siebert, "Communication," op. cit. -Bottomore, Karl Marx, op. cit., 1-40, 41-60. -Marx, Die Fruhschriften, op. cit., ch. 8-9. -Adorno, Soziologishce Schriften, op. cit., 457-477.

[334] Arens, Kommunikative Handlungen, op. cit., 360.

[35] A. v. Juchen, Die kampfgleichnisse Jesu, Munchen: 1981, 100-110.

[336] Arens, Kommunikative Handlungen, op. cit., 361. -P. Ricoeur, "Stellung und Funktion der Metaphor in der biblishen Sprache" in P. Ricoeur/E. Jungel, Metaphor. Zur Hermeneutik religioser Sprache, Munchen: 1974, 64-70.

[337] Arens, Kommunikative Handlungen, op. cit., 361. -Adorno, Soziologische Schriften, op. cit., I, 392-396, 440-456, 538-546; Minima Moralia, Frankfurt: Suhrkamp 1980, 7-12, 333-334. -Habermas, Vorstudien, op. cit., chs. 4, 8-9, 11; "Bewusstmachende oder Rettende Kritik" in S. Unseld (ed.), Zur Aktualitat Walter Benjamins, Frankfurt: Suhrkamp 1972, ch. 4.

[338] Adorno, Minima Moralia, op. cit., 333-334.

[339] Arens, Kommunikative Handlungen, op. cit., 361-362. -SW 11, 39-43. -SW 7, 33-37. -SW 16, 247-308. -Hegel, Three Essays, op. cit., 48, 50-52, 66, 89-90, 96, 104.

340 Arens, Kommunikative Handlungen, op. cit., 361-362.

341 Blanqui, Instruktionene, op. cit., 66, 17, 28-29, 66-67, 150-151, 176-184. —M. Reding, "Utopie, Phantasie, Prophetie-Das Prinzip der Hoffnung im Marxismus" in FH 16/1 (January 1961), 8-13, esp. 11. -E. Bloch, Das Prinzip der Hoffnung, Berlin: 1954, III, 200, 299, 334, 337, 343, 470, 385.

342 Arens, Kommunikative Handlungen, op. cit., 362.

343 Ibid., 362, part II.

344 Ibid., 362. -Luke 15. -Arens, "Toward a Theological Theory," op. cit., 15-16.

345 Arens, Kommunikative Handlungen, op. cit., 363.

346 Ibid., 363-364. -SW 16, 286-295. -Siebert, "Hegel's Political Theology: Liberation" in The Ecumenist, 12/3 (March-April 1974), 33-41.

347 Arens, Kommunikative Handlungen, op. cit., parts I-II, IV. -R.J. Siebert, "Jacob and Jesus: Recent Marxist Readings of the Bible." -J. Stehl, "Carl Schmitt und die Politische Theologie" in FH 17/6 (June 1972), 407-417. -Siebert, "From Dialectical Materialism," op. cit.

348 SW 16, 247-308.

349 SW 16, 295-308. -H. Meschkowski, "Nach dem Tode Gottes" in FH 25/10 (October 1970), 725-734.

350 SW 16, 247-308.

351 Ibid. -Hegel, Three Essays, op. cit., 104-165. -SW 4, 458-459, 414. -GW 8, 277-287. -SW 2, 569-601. -SW 11, 409-430. -Quint, Meister Eckehart, op. cit., 377.

352 W. Dirks, "Ich glaube an Jesus Christus-Verstandnis-versuch in drei Stucken" in 27/12 (December 1972), 878-888. -E. Kogon, "Rudolf Augstein's Herausforderung" in FH 28/4 (April 1973), 249-257. -W. Dirks, "Was meine ich, wenn ich sage: Ich glaube an den Sohn Gottes?" in FH 28/4 (April 1973), 257-260; "Warum

ich ein Christ bin–Erbe–Erfahrung–Theologie" in FH 34/5 (May 1979), 27–36. –E. Hoflich, "Karl Marx fur die Kirche" in FH 24/11 (November 1969), 777–785; "Heilsverkundigung als politische Gewissenbildung" in FH 24/12 (December 1969), 843–854. –W. Kasper, "Politische Utopie und Christliche Hoffnung" in FH 24/8 (August 1969), 563–572. –H.H. Schrey, "Atheismus im Christentum" in FH 24/6 (June 1969), 418–428. –G. Becker, "Jesus, Mensch in unserer durftigen Zeit" in FH 32/12 (December 1977), 49–60. –I. Langer, "Wallfahrt in Europa.I.Rom: Wo ist Christus?" in FH 31/8 (August 1976), 42–50. –E. Kogon, "Revolution und Theologie–Das Neue in unserem zeitalter/Ein Symposion" in FH 22/9 (September 1967), 616–630. –W. Dirks, "Ehe/Eucharistie/Sozialismus" in FH 36/4 (April 1981), 31–40; "Ehe/Eucharistie/Sozialismus II" in FH 36/5 (May 1981), 49–55. –Der Singende Stotterer, op. cit., ch. 4.

[353] Arens, Kommunikative Handlungen, op. cit., 365–373, esp. 371–373. –Habermas, Zur Rekonstruktion, op. cit., ch. 4.

[354] Arens, Kommunikative Handlungen, op. cit., 372/6.

[355] Ibid. –SW 7, 35–36.

[356] Arens, Kommunikative Handlungen, op. cit., 372/6. –SW 7, 12–13.

[357] Arens, Kommunikative Handlungen, op. cit., 372–373. –Adorno/Kogon, "Offenbarung," op. cit.

[358] Arens, Kommunikative Handlungen, op. cit., 373.

[359] Arens, "Toward a Theological Theory," op. cit., 16. –Luke 15:1–7, 8–10, 11–31; 16:1–13.

[360] Kogon, "Revolution," op. cit., 372–373. –Siebert, "Hegel's Political Theology," op. cit.

[361] Arens, "Toward a Theological Theory," op. cit., 16.

[362] E. Cardenal, Psalms of Struggle and Liberation, New York: Herder and Herder 1969, 7–8, 11–76.

[363] Ibid., 67–68.

364Ibid., 73-74.

365Arens, "Toward a Theological Theory," op. cit., 16.

366D. Berrigan, Uncommon Prayer, A Book of Psalms, New York: Seabury 1978, 53-55.

367Ibid., 53-55.

368Ibid., 35-36.

369Ibid. -Benjamin, Briefe 2, op. cit., 671-683; Das Passagen Werk, op. cit., I, 11-41, 45-59, 83-109, 156-178, 179-210, 301-489, 612-642; II, 993-1038, 1041-1043, 1044-1059. -C. Baudelaire, Flowers of Evil, New York: Harper and Brothers, 1936, v-xxxiv, 41-43, 53-61, 61-63, 63-67, 255-257, 257-259. -J. Quack, "Benjamin's Spleen-Verabschiedung oder Rettung eines modernen Hlassihers" in FH 34/9 (September 1979), 55-62.

370Berrigan, Uncommon Prayer, op. cit., 133.

371Arens, "Toward a Theological Theory," op. cit., 16.

372Ibid. -Siebert, "Dialectical Materialism," op. cit.

373Arens, "Toward a Theological Theory," op. cit., 16. -Siebert, "Dialectical Materialism," op. cit.

374Arens, "Toward a Theological Theory," op. cit., 16; "Gleichnisse," op. cit., 47-69. -SW 16, 354-355.

375Habermas, Zur Rekonstruktion, op. cit., chs. 1-2, 4, 6, 10; Vorstudien, op. cit., chs. 1, 3-4, 6-9, 11. -Horster, "Ein Marxistischer Kant," op. cit., 58-65. -Siebert, "From Dialectical Materialism," op. cit.

376Bentley, Seven Plays by Bertholt Brecht, op. cit., xiii, li, esp. 259-330. -Benjamin, Illuminations, op. cit., ch. 6. -Boll, Wird es denn uberhapt gehen?, op. cit., 29.

377Adorno, Negative Dialectic, op. cit., part II. -F.A. Scharpf, (ed.), Nicolaus von Cusa, Wichtigste Schriften, Frankfurt: Minerva 1966, 31-33.

[378] Bentley, Seven Plays, op. cit., 253–254.

[379] Ibid., 254.

[380] Ibid., 254–257.

[381] Metz, The Emergent Church, op. cit., ch. 1. –Matthew 26:66. –Mark 14:53–64. –Luke 22:66–71.

[382] Metz, The Emergent Church, op. cit., chs. 1–2, 5–7. –Adorno, Soziologische Schriften, op. cit., 578–587.

[383] B. Brecht, Selected Poems,, New York: Grove 1959, 79–81.

[384] Ibid.

[385] Brecht, Seven Plays, op. cit., 448. –SW 11, 42, 569. –SW 15, 100. –SW 7, 35–36. –Marquard, Schwierigkeiten, op. cit., 52–65. –Schmidt, "Die Zeitschrift," op. cit., 8–17. –Horkheimer, Die Sehnsucht, op. cit., 56–57, 59–60.

[386] Habermas, Theorie, op. cit., chs. 1–2, 4, 7–8; Zur Rekonstruktion, op. cit., ch. 4.

[387] Bentley, Seven Plays, op. cit., 149–248, 259–330, 331–404. –Brecht, Selected Poems, op. cit., 62–65, 78–81, 126–127, 148–159, 164–165. –Benjamin, Briefe 2, op. cit., 671–683.

[388] Adorno/Kogon, "Offenbarung," op. cit., 396–402, 484–498. –Benjamin, Briefe 2, op. cit., 671–688. –Adorno, Negative Dialectics, op. cit., part III; 300–360, 361–408; Soziologische Schriften, op. cit., 397–407, 408–433. –Horkheimer/Adorno, Dialectic of Enlightenment, op. cit., 23–24.

[389] Benjamin, Briefe 2, op. cit., 671–683, esp. 676. –SW 15, 227–228. –H. Brenner, "Theodor W. Adorno als Sachwalter des Benjaminschen Werkes" in W.F. Scholler (ed.), Die neue Linke nach Adorno, Munchen: Kindler 1962, 158–175, esp. 168–174. –Benjamin, Das Passagen Werk, op. cit., 993–1043, 1044–1059. –Bottomore, Karl Marx, Early Writings, New York: McGraw-Hill 1963, 195–219. –Marx, Kapital, op. cit., Vol. I, 17–18.

[390] Brenner, "Theodor W. Adorno," op. cit., 172. –SW 11,

33–120. –SW 10, 397–415, 446–476. –Lukacs, <u>History and Class Consciousness</u>, op. cit., chs. 1–3, 5–8. –Scholem, <u>Major Trends</u>, op. cit., chs. 3, 9; <u>Walter Benjamin</u>, op. cit., 17–18.

[391] Benjamin, <u>Briefe 2</u>, op. cit., 644. –Haag, <u>Der Fortschritt</u>, op. cit., chs. 5, 8. –Brenner, "Theodor W. Adorno," op. cit., 172.

[392] Brenner, "Theodor W. Adorno," op. cit., 172. –Scholem, <u>Sabbatai Sevi</u>, op. cit., chs. 6–8.

[393] Brenner, "Theodor W. Adorno," op. cit., 172. –<u>Benjamin Nachlass</u> im Deutschen Zentral Archiv Potsdam, Mappe 27, Blatt 39. –Haag, <u>Der Fortschritt</u>, op. cit., ch. 8.

[394] Brenner, "Theodor W. Adorno," op. cit., 173. –Benjamin, <u>Das Passagen Werk</u>, op. cit., 993–1038, 1041–1059.

[395] <u>Benjamin Nachlass</u>, op. cit., 39. –Haag, <u>Der Fortschritt</u>, op. cit., ch. 8.

[396] Arens, <u>Kommunikative Handlungen</u>, op. cit., 373. –Boll, <u>Wird es denn Uberhaupt gehen?</u>, op. cit., 29.

[397] Luke 15:1–2, 11–32. –Hegel, <u>Three Essays</u>, op. cit., 138–139.

[398] Arens, "Toward a Theological Theory," op. cit., 15–16.

[399] Adorno/Kogon, "Offenbarung," op. cit., 402.

[400] Ibid., 484.

[401] A. Gide, <u>Le retour de l'enfant prodigue</u>, Paris: Gallimard 1963; <u>La porte etroit</u>, Paris: Mercure de France 1932. –R. Mallet, <u>The Correspondence 1899–1926 between P. Claudel and A. Gide</u>, New York: Pantheon 1952. –Horkheimer, <u>Die Sehnsucht</u>, op. cit., 58–59. –Benjamin, <u>Gesammelte Schriften</u>, Frankfurt: Suhrkamp 1977, II (2), 615; IV (1) 497; Pariser Brief (1). –Hegel, <u>Three Essays</u>, op. cit., 138–139.

[402] Habermas, <u>Theorie</u>, op. cit., chs. 7–8.

[403] Adorno/Kogon, "Offenbarung," op. cit., 402. –Horkheimer,

Gesellschaft, op. cit., 162–176.

[404]Siebert, "Horkheimer's Sociology of Religion," op. cit., 127–144; "Dialectical Materialism," op. cit.; "Fromm's Theory of Religion," op. cit., 111–120. -Bahr, Religionsgesprache, op. cit., chs. 1, 68. -Schmidt, Die Religion, op. cit., chs. 1–9. -E. Fetscher/M. Machovac (eds.), Marxisten und die Sach Jesus, Munchen: Kaiser 1974, chs. 1–8. -Dobert, Systemtheorie, op. cit., part II. -Habermas, Zur Rekonstruktion, op. cit., ch. 4.

[405]Habermas, Theorie, op. cit., chs. 7–8; "Die Neo-Konservativen," op. cit.

[406]Habermas, Theorie, op. cit., ch. 8.

[407]Metz, The Emergent Church, op. cit., chs. 3–8. -Peukert, Wissenschaftstheorie, op. cit., part III. -Arens, Kommunikative Handlungen, op. cit., part IV. -Siebert, "Dialectical Materialism," op. cit.

[408]Arens, Kommunikative Handlungen, op. cit., 374.

[409]J. B. Metz, Keine Apologie des Erzahlens, Conc (D) 9 (1973), 334–341, esp. 340; Glaube, op. cit., SS 9, 11–13. -Siebert, "Dialectical Materialism," op. cit. -Benjamin, Illuminations, op. cit., chs. 1–2, esp. 3–10. -Kracauer, Das Ornament, op. cit., 249–256, 256–271.

[410]Arens, Kommunikative Handlungen, op. cit., 374.

[411]SW 11, 37–42, esp. 42. -Jamme, Mythologie, op. cit., 11–14. -Siebert, "Political Theology," op. cit.; "Hegel's Political Theology," op. cit.; "Hegel and Theology," op. cit., "Christian Revolution," op.'/cit. -Kung, Die Menschwerdung, op. cit., 364–381. -SW 16, 286–308. -SW 4, 315–414, 417–485, 486–493, 497–500. -Hegel, Three Essays, op. cit., 104, 107–109, 113, 113, 121, 144, 151, 162.

[412]SW 5, 35–64, 65–117, 118–172. -SW 15, 227–228. -Quint, Meister Eckehart, op. cit., 376–378. -Blackney, Meister Eckehart, op. cit., 288, 247–248, 231–232, 212–213, 206, 180–181, 166, 126–127, 67, 62. -Benjamin, Briefe 2, op. cit., 672. -SW 16, 286–308.

[413]SW 16, 191-223. -SW 7. -SW 11. -Kung, _Die Menschwerdung_, op. cit., 364-381, 427-457, 385-408.

[414]PB 171a, 46. -SW 16, 286-308. -Hegel, _Three Essays_, op. cit., 104-165.

[415]Ritter, _Hegel_, op. cit., 18-39. PB 33, 431-439. -Siebert, "Hegel's Political Theology," op. cit., 312; "Hegel and Theology," op. cit.; "Christian Revolution," op. cit.

[416]PB 33, 431-439. -K. Barth, _Die Protestantische Theologie, im 19 Jahrhundert_, Zurich: 1952, 10: hegel, 343-378, esp. 343. -Kung, _Menschwerdung_, op. cit., 34-37, esp. 34.

[417]Peukert, _Wissenschaftstheorie_, op. cit., part III. -Arens, _Kommunikative Handlungen_, op. cit., part IV.

[418]Benjamin, _Briefe 2_, op. cit., 672.

[419]_Ibid._ -Habermas, _Zur Rekonstruktion_, op. cit., ch. 4; _Theorie_, op. cit., Bd 1, 15-16, chs. 7-8. -Marx, _Kapital_, op. cit., I, 17-18. -Siebert, "Hegel," op. cit.

[420]E. Bloch, _Philosophy of the Future_, New York: Herder and Herder 1970, ch. 10.

[421]SW 5, 35-171. -Bloch, _Denken_, op. cit., 78-89, esp. 79. -E. Bloch, _Subjeckt-Objekt. Erlauterungen zu Hegel_, Frankfurt: Suhrkamp 1962, chs. 5, 7, esp. 9-10, 13-14, 16-20, 23, esp. 25. -Nicolaus von Cusa, _Wichtigste Schriften_, op. cit., parts I-III. -Blackney, _Meister Eckehart_, op. cit., 258-305, 43-73, 82-94, 118-124, 183-187, 203-206.

[422]SW 16, 247-308. -SW 11, 37-43, 43-47, 47-69, 568-569. -Th. A. McCarthy, _The Critical Theory of Jurgen Habermas_, Cambridge: MIT Press 1978, chs. 1-4, esp. 135, 103, 244, 32, 30, 33, 108, 18, 84-87, 110, 232-271, 354. -Berrigan, _Uncommon Prayer_, op. cit., 53-55.

[423]Bentley, _Seven Plays_, op. cit., 405-494.

[424]_Ibid._, 491-492.

[425]_Ibid._, 494.

[426]Kung, Ewiges Leben?, op. cit., ch. 2, esp. 63-64.

[427]Horkheimer, Die Sehnsucht, op. cit., 54-89. -Benjamin, Illustrations, op. cit., 253-264. -Adorno, Soziologische Schriften, op. cit., I, 9-19, 42-85, 93-121, 122-145, 147-176, 217-237, 280-353, 373-391, 392-396, 397-407, 408-433, 434-439, 440-456, 457-477, 569-573, 578-587.

[428]SW 7, 35-36. -SW 16, 147-308. -SW 15, 292-293. -SW 5, 35-65. -Hegel, Three Essays, op. cit., 3, 13, 57, 104, 109.

[429]SW 7, 35-36.

[430]Arens, Kommunikative Handlungen, op. cit., 374. -Matthew 6:25-34. -Kung, Die Menschwerdung, op. cit., 68-70.

[431]Arens, Kommunikative Handlungen, op. cit., 374. -GW 6, 265-326. -GW 8, 185-287. -Hegel, Three Essays, op. cit., 104-165. -John 1:18.

[432]Arens, Kommunikative Handlungen, op. cit., 374-375. -Hegel, Three Essays, op. cit., 143-165.

[433]Blanqui, Instruktionen, op. cit., 66. -Matthew 27:15-25. -Luke 23: 13-27. -Mark 15:6-15. -John 19:1-16.

[434]Arens, Kommunikative Handlungen, op. cit., 375.

[435]Ibid., 375. -Peukert, Wissenschaftstheorie, op. cit., 299. -Hegel, Three Essays, op. cit., 104-165. -SW 16, 247-308.

[436]Arens, Kommunikative Handlungen, op. cit., 375/4.

[437]D. Bonhoeffer, Letters and Papers from Prison, New York: MacMillan 1967, chs. 7-8.

[438]Peukert, Wissenschaftstheorie, op. cit., 300. -Arens, Kommunikative Handlungen, op. cit., 375.

[439]Arens, Kommunikative Handlungen, op. cit., 375-376. -Hegel, Three Essays, op. cit., 104-165.

[440]Peukert, Wissenschaftstheorie, op. cit., 300. -Kierkegaard, Erbauliche Reden, op. cit., 163-224, 225-356.

[441]J.B. Metz, Jenseits burgerlicher Religion, Mainz: Grunewald 1980, chs. 1-3. -Arens, Kommunikative Handlungen, op. cit., 375-376. -H. Peukert, Wissenschaftstheorie, Handlungstheorie, Fundamentale Theologie, Frankfurt: Suhrkamp 1978, 329-331.

[442]SW 16, 295-300. -Hegel, Three Essays, op. cit., 153-165. -SW 2, 569-601.

[443]SW 16, 298-300. -SW 2, 569-601. -SW 11, 409-430.

[444]SW 16, 300.

[445]J. Moltmann, Der Gekreuzigte Gott, Munchen: Kaiser 1973, chs. 2-3, esp. 6. -SW 4, 414, 458-485.

[446]SW 15, 300.

[447]Moltmann, Der Gekreuzigte Gott, op. cit., chs. 5-8.

[448]Arens, Kommunikative Handlungen, op. cit., 375-376. -Peukert, Wissenschaftstheorie, op. cit., 299-300. -Kessler, Die theologische Bedeutung des Todes Jesu, Dusseldorf: 1970, 335-337.

[449]Arens, Kommunikative Handlungen, op. cit., 375/5. -J. Becker, "Das Gottesbild Jesu und die alteste Auslegung von Ostern," in Jesus Christus in Historie und Theologie, Tubingen: Conzelman 1975, 105-126, esp. 106.

[450]Arens, Kommunikative Handlungen, op. cit., 375/6. -E. Jungel, Gott als Geheimnis der Welt, Tubingen: 1978, 497. -W. Kasper, Jesus der Christus, Mainz: 1974, 162-164. -Rahner, Grundkurs, op. cit., 300-302. -Peukert, Wissenschaftstheorie, op. cit., 300-302.

[451]Arens, Kommunikative Handlungen, op. cit., 375. -J.D. Crossan, The Dark Interval: Towards a Theology of Story, Niles, Ill: 1975, 124. -Hegel, Three Essays, op. cit., 121, 130, 132, 138, 142, 144, 147.

[452]Arens, Kommunikative Handlungen, op. cit., 376. -SW 7, 35. -SW 15, 292-293. -Kierkegaard, Erbauliche Reden, op. cit., 229-355.

[453] Arens, Kommunikative Handlungen, op. cit., 376.

[454] Adorno/Kogon, "Offenbarung," op. cit., 392–402, 484–498.

[455] J. Quint (ed.), Meister Eckehart, Deutsche Pradigten und Traktate, Munchen: Carl Hanser 1979, 195–200. –Hegel, Three Essays, op. cit., 105, 3, 5, 13, 48, 50–52, 57, 66, 89–90, 96, 107–109, 113–114. –TW 12, 20–22, 24–26, 28–29, 40, 49, 53. –Habermas, Theorie, op. cit., chs. 1–2, 7–8.

[456] Habermas, Zur Rekonstruktion, op. cit., ch. 4; Theorie, op. cit., chs. 7–8.

[457] Arens, Kommunikative Handlungen, op. cit., 376–377.

[458] Peukert, Wissenschaftstheorie, op. cit., part III, esp. 306.

[459] Metz, Theology of the World, New York: Seabury 1973, part III; Glaube, op. cit., 44–57.

[460] Arens, Kommunikative Handlungen, op. cit., 377. –SW 7, 35. –SW 15, 292–293.

[461] Metz, Glaube, op. cit., 44–57, esp. 51.

[462] Arens, Kommunikative Handlungen, op. cit., 377.

[463] Ibid. –Metz, Glaube, op. cit., 52.

[464] Arens, Kommunikative Handlungen, op. cit., part III.

[465] SW 15, 24–36. –Habermas, Zur Rekonstruktion, op. cit., ch. 4. –SW 16, 308–356. –Metz, The Emergent Church, op. cit., chs. 1, 4–7.

[466] Arens, Kommunikative Handlungen, op. cit., 378. –Metz, Glaube, op. cit., 7, 106–108, 172, esp. 208. –GW 8, 243–253, 253–287. –SW 7, 130–141, 262–328. –Adorno, Soziologische Schriften I, op. cit., 464–467.

[467] SW 7, 320.

[468] Peukert, Wissenschaftstheorie, op. cit., 273–82, esp. 273.

469Metz, Glaube, op. cit., 7/7. -Habermas, Zur Rekonstruktion, op. cit., chs. 1-2, 4, esp. 5-8.

470Metz, Glaube, op. cit., 7/7. -SW 11, 43-47. -Marx, Die Fruhschriften, op. cit., chs. 9-10. -Benjamin, Illuminations, op. cit., 253-264. -Haag, Der Fortschritt, op. cit., chs. 4-5.

471Metz, Glaube, op. cit., 106-107. -GW 6, 265-315. -GW 8, 185-231.

472Metz, Glaube, op. cit., 106-107.

473Ibid., 207-208. -SW 7, 130-142, 262-286. -GW 8, 185-231.

474Metz, Glaube, op. cit., 207-208.

475SW 11, 43-69. -GW 6, 307-314. -SW 2, 148-158. -Horkheimer, Zur Kritik, op. cit., 248-268. -Siebert, From Critical Theory, op. cit., chs. 2, 16.

476SW 11, 43-47. -SW 2, 620. -SW 16, 281-282.

477Siebert, "Dialectical Materialism," op. cit. -Benjamin, Illuminations, op. cit., 254. -Marx, Kapital, op. cit., 17-18.

478SW 7, 261-286, 310-323. -SW 11, 536-568. -GW 8, 232-287. -Jamme, Mythologie, op. cit., 11-14. -GW 4, 58, 417-485. -Siebert, "Hegel," op. cit. -Marx, Die Fruschriften, op. cit., chs. 7-10; Kapital, op. cit., I, 17-18; III, 873-874. -Benjamin, Reflections, op. cit., chs. 1-3, 6-10, 12-14, 16; Illuminations, op. cit., 253-264. -Adorno, Soziologische Schriften, op. cit., chs. 1-3, 5-8, 10, 13-14.

479Arens, Kommunikative Handlungen, op. cit., 379-380.

480Habermas, Zur Rekonstruktion, op. cit., 154-155.

481Ibid., 181.

482Arens, Kommunikative Handlungen, op. cit., 379/21. -Benjamin, Illuminations, op. cit., 253-264; Reflections, op. cit., 277-301. -Unseld, Zur Aktualitat, op. cit., 175-221. -Habermas, Politik, op. cit., 127-143.

[483] Arens, Kommunikative Handlungen, op. cit., 379/21.

[484] Siebert, "Dialectical Materialism," op. cit. -SW 11, 42-43, 48-50, 65-69. -SW 7, 261-286, 311-323.

[485] Habermas, Theorie, op. cit., ch. 8. -GW 8, 185-287. -GW 7, 265-326.

[486] SW 11, 43-47. -Hegel, Asthetik, op. cit., I, 106-107, 209.

[487] SW 11, 33-43.

[488] Arens, Kommunikative Handlungen, op. cit., 380. -GW 6, 297-30, 307-315.

[489] Arens, Kommunikative Handlungen, op. cit., 380. -Metz, Glaube, op. cit., 106.

[490] Arens, Kommunikative Handlungen, op. cit., 380. -Metz, Glaube, op. cit., 108-119.

[491] SW 11, 43-47, 47-69, 129-130. -SW 2, 619-620. -SW 7, 36. -SW 15, 292-293. -SW 16, 282.

[492] SW 11, 42, 46-47, 48-50. -SW 15, 100.

[493] Benjamin, Illuminations, op. cit., 253-264; Reflections, op. cit., 312-313.

[494] Arens, Kommunikative Handlungen, op. cit., 380. -Peukert, Wissenschaftstheorie, op. cit., 280-282.

[495] Arens, Kommunikative Handlungen, op. cit., 308. -Habermas, Theorie, op. cit., chs. 2-3, 5-8. -GW 6, 265-326. -Habermas, Theory, op. cit., chs. 2-5. -Schnadelbach, Rationalitat, op. cit., 15-31, 218-235. -Habermas, Vorstudien, op. cit., chs. 1-4, 6, 8-9, 11. -Peukert, Wissenschaftstheorie, op. cit., part III.

[496] SW 11, 361-409. -SW 16, 156-188.

[497] SW 7, 261-286, 310-323. -SW 15, 24-36, 44-52, 52-64.

[498] Arens, Kommunikative Handlungen, op. cit., 380.

[499]Horkheimer, Die Sehnsucht, op. cit., 63. -Hegel, Three Essays, op. cit., 131. -Luke 10:27.

[500]Arens, Kommunikative Handlungen, op. cit., 380.

[501]R.J. Siebert, "Ernesto Cardenal and the Nicaraguan Revolution: From Theological Theory to Revolutionary Praxis," in Cross Currents, Vol. XXX, No. 3, 241-251.

[502]Arens, Kommunikative Handlungen, op. cit., 382-383. -Peukert, Wissenschaftstheorie, op. cit., 280-282. -Siebert, "Peukert's New Critical Theology I," op. cit., 52-58; "Peukert's New Critical Theology II," op. cit., 78-80.

[503]Peukert, Wissenschaftstheorie, op. cit., 283. -Siebert, "Peukert's New Critical Theology I," op. cit., 52-58; "Peukert's New Critical Theology II," op. cit., 78-80.

[504]Arens, Kommunikative Handlungen, op. cit., 382/37.

[505]Ibid., 383-384. -Habermas, Vorstudien, op. cit., chs. 3-4, 8-9, esp. 11.

[506]Ibid. -Peukert, Wissenschaftstheorie, op. cit., 286-287. -SW 11, 33-47, 568-569. -SW 7, 35. PB 33, 387-388. -SW 16, 191-218, esp. 206-208.

[507]K. Lowith, Die Hegelsche Linke, Stuttgart-Bad Cannstatt: Frommann 1962, 7-38. -Haag, Der Fortschritt, op. cit., chs. 4-5, 8.

[508]H. Lubbe, Die Hegelsche Rechte, Stuttgart-Bad Cannstatt: Frommann 1962, 7-17. -Haag, Der Fortschritt, op. cit., chs. 6, 8.

[509]Arens, Kommunikative Handlungen, op. cit., 383-384. -Peukert, Wissenschaftstheorie, op. cit., 286-287.

[510]Peukert, Wissenschaftstheorie, op. cit., 287.

[511]Arens, Kommunikative Handlungen, op. cit., 383-384.

[512]Horkheimer, Die Sehnsucht, op. cit., 55-56.

[513]Arens, Kommunikative Handlungen, op. cit., 384; part III.
-Peukert, Wissenschaftstheorie, op. cit., part IV.

[514]Arens, Kommunikative Handlungen, op. cit., parts I, IV.
-Habermas, Vorstudien, op. cit., ch. 8.

[515]Arens, Kommunikative Handlungen, op. cit., 384. -Peukert,
Wissenschaftstheorie, op. cit., parts II, III.

[516]Peukert, Wissenschaftstheorie, op. cit., 288. -SW 16,
46-95, 191-356.

[517]SW 15, 400-417.

[518]Peukert, Wissenschaftstheorie, op. cit., 288.

[519]S. Kierkegaard, Fear and Trembling and the Sickness Unto
Death, Princeton, NJ: Princeton University Press 1954, 30-37,
38-64.

[520]SW 15, 19-36, 100. -SW 4, 315-414. -SW 16, 340-356.

[521]Arens, Kommunikative Handlungen, op. cit., 384-385.
-Peukert, Wissenschaftstheorie, op. cit., part III.

[522]SW 16, 212-218, 359-553. -Kung, Menschwerdung, op. cit.,
499-500.

[523]Arens, Kommunikative Handlungen, op. cit., 384.

[524]G.A. Lindbeck, "Theologische Methode und
Wissenschaftstheorie", in Theological Review, 74 (1978),
265-280, esp. 273.

[525]SW 16, 213-214, 546-553. -Kant, Critique of Pure Reason,
New York: St. Martin's Press 1929, 500-507.

[526]SW 16, 355-356.

[527]Ibid., 295-308.

[528]Arens, Kommunikative Handlungen, op. cit., 384-385. -Metz,
Theology, op. cit., chs. 1,3; The Emergent Church, op. cit.,
chs. 1, 3.

[529] Arens, Kommunikative Handlungen, op. cit., 384-385. -Peukert, Wissenschaftstheorie, op. cit., 306.

[530] Arens, Kommunikative Handlungen, op. cit., 385, 277-324; part IV.

[531] Ibid., 385. -Hegel, Three Essays, op. cit., 104-165. -SW 7, 35-36. -SW 15, 292-293. -John 3:21, 8:32.

[532] J.B. Metz, "Dom Paulo Evaristo Arms-Kardinal der Dritten Welt," (unpublished), 1-11, esp. 8-11. -R.J. Siebert, "Towards a Critical Catholicism: Kung and Metz (I)," in Anglican Theological Review, Vol. LXV, No. 1 (January 1983), 1-13; "Towards a Critical Catholicism: Kung and Metz (II)," Anglican Theological Review, Vol. LXV, No. 2 (April 1983), 144-1163; "Dialectical Materialism," op. cit. -Benjamin, Illuminations, op. cit., 253-264; Das Passagen Werk, op. cit., parts I-II. -Horkheimer, Die Sehnsucht, op. cit., 54-89; Notizen, op. cit., 316-320. -Lowenthal, Mitmachen wollte ich nie. Ein autobiographisches Gesprach mit Helmut Dubiel, Frankfurt: Suhrkamp 1980, chs. 1-2, 4; Notizen zur Literatur Soziologie, Stuttgart: Ferdinand Enke 1975, V-VI, chs. 1-3; Literature and the Image of Man, Boston: Beacon Press 1957, chs. 1-2, 4, esp. 5-7. -Th.W. Adorno, Jargon der Eigentlichkeit, Frankfurt: Suhrkamp 1980, 7-139; Versuch, das Endspiel zu verstehen, Frankfurt: Suhrkamp 1973, chs. 2-3, 5, 7-8; Prismen, Frankfurt: Suhrkamp 1976, chs. 1-3, 5, 7-8, 10-12; Kritik, Kleine Schriften zur Gesellschaft, Frankfurt: Suhrkamp 1980, chs. 2-4, 6-10; Soziologische Schriften I, op. cit., 397-408, 408-434, 478-494, 500-532. -Habermas, Theorie, op. cit., chs. 1-2, 4, 7. -Rahner, Grundkurs, op. cit., 5-9, 13-34. -Lehmann, Rosenschaft, op. cit., 5-6, 13-49.

[533] Metz, "Dom Paulo," op. cit., 8-11; Theology, op. cit., ch. 1; Kirche im Prozess der Aufklarung, Munchen: Kaiser 1970, 53-90.

[534] Metz, The Emergent Church, chs. 4, 8.

[535] Schmidt, Die Religion, op. cit., chs. 1-9.

[536] E. Fromm, Psychoanalysis and Religion, New Haven: Yale University Press 1970, vi-viii.

[537] Metz, "Dom Paulo," op. cit., 8-11.

[538] Horkheimer/Adorno, Dialectic, op. cit., ix-xvii, ch. 1.
-Habermas, Vorstudien, op. cit., ch. 4.

[539] Metz, The Emergent Church, op. cit., ch. 1.

[540] G.M. Osthathios, Theology of a Classless Society,
Maryknoll, NY: Orbis 1980, chs. 1-2, 4-5, 9-10. -M. Hope and
J. Young, The Struggle for Humanity, Maryknoll, NY: Orbis
1977, chs. 1, 4-5, 7.   -A. Perez-Esclarin, Atheism and
Liberation,   Maryknoll,   NY: Orbis   1974,   part   II.
-T. Balasuriya, The Eucharist and Human Liberation, Maryknoll,
NY: Orbis 1979, chs. 3, 5, 7, 10, 12. -L. Boff, Jesus Christ
Liberator,   Maryknoll,   NY: Orbis   1981,   chs. 3-4,   7,
pp. 264-295. -A. Paoli, Freedom to be Free, Maryknoll, NY:
Orbis 1973, chs. 1-6, 9-12, 14-16, 18. -J. Eagleson and
P. Scharper (eds.), Puebla and Beyond, Maryknoll, NY: Orbis
1980, parts I-III.

[541] M. Hope and J. Young, The South African Churches in a
Revolutionary   Situation,   Maryknoll,   NY: Orbis   1981,
chs. 17-20.   -W.R. Duggen   and J.R. Civille, Tanzania and
Nyerere, Maryknoll: Orbis 1976, chs. 10-14. -J. deSantaAna,
Towards   a   Church   of   the Poor, Maryknoll: Orbis 1979, parts
1-3.   -J.G. Davies,   Christians,   Politics   and   Violent
Revolution,   Maryknoll: Orbis 1976, chs. 2-6. -J. Comblin, The
Church and the National Security State, Maryknoll: Orbis 1979,
chs. 2-8, 225-228.

[542] P. Ballard, et al., Calendar of Martyrs, Dundas, Ontario:
1983. -W.J. O'Malley, S.J., The Voice of Blood, Five Christian
Martyrs of Our Time, Maryknoll: Orbis 1980. -P. Erdozain,
Archbishop Romero, op. cit., chs. 3-5, 89-98. -A. Dobrin, et
al., Convictions, Maryknoll: Orbis 1981, chs. 1, 3-4, 7-9.

[543] Metz, "Dom Paulo," op. cit., 8-11. -P. Bascio, Building a
Just   Society,   Maryknoll: Orbis   1981,   chs. 2-4,   6.
-J. Eagleson, (ed.) Christians and Socialism, Maryknoll: Orbis
1975, parts I, III-VI. -J. deSantaAna, Separation without
Hope: The Church and the Poor During the Industrial Revolution
and Colonial Expansion, Maryknoll: Orbis 1978, chs. 1-10.
-D.H. Camera, The Desert is Fertile, Maryknoll: Orbis 1974,
part III. -J.M. Gonzales-Ruiz, The New Creation: Marxist and

Christian?, Maryknoll: Orbis 1976, chs. 3-8. -J. Miranda, Marx and the Bible, Maryknoll: Orbis 1974, chs. 2-5; Marx against the Marxists, Maryknoll: Orbis 1980, chs. 1-3, 5-10. -R. Turner, The Eye of the Needle, Maryknoll: Orbis 1978, chs. 1-2, 4-8. -F. Belo, A Materialist Reading of the Gospel of Mark, Maryknoll: Orbis 1981, parts III-IV. -W. Buhlmann, The Missions on Trial, Maryknoll: Orbis 1979, parts I-II; The Coming of the Third Church, Maryknoll: Orbis 1976, chs. 5, 7-8, 10, 13, 23. -J. Amstutz, Kirche der Volker, Frieburg: Herder 1972, part III.

[544]Metz, The Emergent Church, op. cit., ch. 6. -E. Arens, "Steh auf, du Christ-Basisgemeinden in der Bundesrepublik" in Boll, Wird es denn uberhaupt gehen? op. cit., 23-29. -J.B. Metz, "Nicaragua-Eindrucke aus einem Biblischen Land" in Boll, Wird, op. cit., 128-133. -J. Storres and J. Eagleson (eds.), The Challenge of Basic Christian Communities, Maryknoll: Orbis 1980, parts I-III, V. -H.H. Hucking, "Christliche basisgruppen in Osteuropa" in FH 34/2 (February 1979), 43-51. -R. Bohne, "Kirche in Lateinamerika unter Druck" in FH 32/2 (February 1977), 6-8. -H.V.Gizycki, "Die Christliche Kommunitat der koinonia-Partner in Georgia" in FH 31/3 (March 1976), 35-42. -W. Dirks, "Volkskirche im Ubergang-Zur Krise der Kirche (1)" in FH 25/2 (February 1976), 108-116. -K. Walf, "Eine andere Kirche-Hollands Katholiken auf Konfliktkurs," in FH 35/7 (July 1980), 24-30. -W. Strolz, "Dem grosseren Gott entgegen-Gedanken zur universalen Okumene," in FH 36/1 (January 1981), 59-66. -T. Seiferich, "Basisgemeinden in der Bundesrepublik" in FH 37/9 (September 1982), 35-42. -R. Bohne, "'Im Untergrund der Geschichte'-Die katholische Kirche und Lateinamerika" in FH 38/4 (April 1983), 20-31.

[545]H.D. Zimmerman, "San Gimiguano-Zu Aufsatzen von Reinhold Schneider und Walter Benjamin" in FH 36/11 (November 1981), 55-62. -W. Dirks, "Wehrlos vor dem Fashismus-Das Theorie Defizit des Deutschen Katholizismus der Weimarer Zeit" in FH 36/12 (December 1981), 39-48.

[546]E. Jouhy, "Bedarf der Zustand des Elends der Losung oder der Erlosung," in FH 37/12 (December 1982), 48-66. -Siebert, "Toward a Critical Catholicism: Kung and Metz," op. cit.

[547]W. Weymann-Weyhe, "Die Rede von Gott-Der Konflikt zwischen Wort und Erfahrung" in FH 38/4 (April 1983), 59-66.

548 W. Strolz, "Sinnfragen nicht-glaubender Juden" in FH 31/3 (March 1976), 25-34. -H. Willig, "Die Aktualitat der kritischen Theorie Adornos" in FH 35/3 (March 1980) 55-64. -W. Strolz, "Denker der gepruften Hoffnung-Ernst Bloch und Paul Schutz" in FH 35/3 (May 1978), 49-62. -H. Mayer, "Nachdenken uber Adorno" in FH 25/4 (April 1970), 268-280. -H. Scheible, "Max Horkheimer's fruhe und spate Aufzeichnungen" in FH 33/6 (June 1978), 50-54. -R. Wiggerhaus, "Die 'Zeitschrift fur Sozialforschung'-eine Aufforderung zu Aktualitats-bezogener Gesellschaftstheorie" in FH 35/10 (October 1980), 49-54. -E. Fromm, To Have or To Be, New York: Harper and Row 1976, 201-202. -H.J. Brandt, "Benjamin und kein Ende/Zur Filmtheorie Walter Benjamin," in FH 38/3 (March 1983), 48-53. -Marcuse, Eros and Civilization, op. cit., 63-66. -E. Bornemann, "Sigmund Freud und sein Heimatland," in FH 36/11 (November 1981), 37-44. -J. Quack, "Benjamin's Spleen," op. cit., 55-62.

549 H. Meschkowski, "Nach dem Tode Gottes" in FH 38/2 (February 1983), 47-56. -P. Eicher, "Besinnung auf den Gott der Gottlosen heute" in FH 34/9 (September 1979), 47-54. -G.R. Lys, "Ein Gott fur die Verdammten?-Zine Anfrage" in FH 34/11 (November 1979), 47-52.

550 I. Langer, "Jesus und das Kreuz," in FH 38/2 (February 1983), 47-56. -R. Bohne, "Der Kirchen Christus und das Evangelium" in FH 35/5 (May 1980), 35-44.

551 J. Nolte, "Nichts fur sich allein-Zur Frage einer 'metadogmatischen' Vertretbarkeit des Christlichen" in FH 30/6 (June 1975), 35-40.

552 R. Hesse, "Ethik in der Weltkrise" in FH 37/12 (December 1982), 15-20. -D. Horster, "Kommunikative Ethik" in FH 37/10 (October 1982), 35-41. -J. Rau, "Bruderlichkeit" in FH 37/7 (July 1982), 31-37. -Acts 2:43-47; 4:32-35.

553 Metz, Theology of the World, op. cit., 137-140. -C. Turcke, "Der Todestrieb der gegenwartigen Gesellschaft und seine theologische Yerklarung" in FH 37/7 (July 1982), 45-58.

554 Metz, "Dom Paulo," op. cit., 8-11. -Habermas, "Bewusstmachende oder rettende Kritik," op. cit., 175-221. -N.W. Bolz, "Politische-Kritik-Zum Streit um Walter Benjamin,"

FH 35/8 (August 1980), 59–65.

555Metz, "Dom Paulo," op. cit., 10–11.

556Benjamin, Illuminations, op. cit., 255.

557Matthew 14:5; 16:21; 21:35–39; 27:20. –Mark 8:31. –Luke 13:31.

558John 15:18–20.

5592 Corinthians 4:8–10.

560Metz, "Dom Paulo," op. cit., 10–11.

561Horkheimer, Die Sehnsucht, op. cit., 61–62. –Daniel 2.

562Matthew 5–7.

563Benjamin, Reflections, op. cit., 312–313.

564Metz, "Dom Paulo," op. cit., 10–11.

565SW 15, 34–36, 100. –GW 4, 315–414, 417–485. –GW 6, 330–331. –GW 8, 277–287. –Siebert, "Parsons' Analytical Theory of Religion," op. cit., 27–53; Reason, Freedom and Change: A Christian Ecounter with Hegel, Washington: University Press of America 1985, chs. 4–5.

566SW 15, 24–36. –Kung, Menschwerdung Gottes, op. cit., 558; Christ Sein, Munchen: Piper 1974, 285, 367; Existiert Gott?, Munchen: Piper 1978, B, I–II; 179, 733–734. –Siebert, Reason, op. cit.

567Habermas, Zur Rekonstruktion, op. cit., ch. 4. –Metz, Theologie der Welt, op. cit., 11–50.

568Hegel, On Christianity, New York: Harper and Brothers 1961, parts I–IV; Three Essays, op. cit., chs. 1–3.

569GW 6, 315–414. –GW 8, 277–287. –SW 7, 23–26, 33, 35–36. –SW 11, 33–47, 47–69, 568–569. –SW 15, 19–64, 100. –SW 16, 344–356.

[570] GW 4, 486–493, 497–500. –G.W.F. Hegel, The Phenomenology of Mind, New York: Harper and Row 1967, 63–64. –GW 6, 297–300. –GW 8, 202–209, 223–227, 243–246, 269–270, 273. –Habermas, Theory and Practice, op. cit., ch. 4.

[571] GW 8, 280–287.

[572] Ibid. –SW 16, 192–356.

[573] W 8, 280–287.

[574] Habermas, Zur Rekonstruktion, op. cit., ch. 4; Theory, op. cit., chs. 2–7; Theorie, op. cit., chs. 1–2, 7–8.

[575] Habermas, Zur Rekonstruktion, op. cit., ch. 4; Theorie, op. cit., ch. 8' Sozialphilosophishe Studien, op. cit., 131–136, 145–155. –Horkheimer, Gesellschaft, op. cit., 397–402, 484–498. –Adorno/Kogon, "Offenbarung," op. cit., 397–402, 484–498.

[576] Benjamin, Briefe 2, op. cit., 671–673, 676, 682. –Siebert, "Dialectical Materialism," op. cit., 45–83.

[577] Habermas, Zur Rekonstruktion, op. cit., ch. 4.

[578] Habermas, Theorie, op. cit., ch. 4.

[579] Ibid., chs. 2, 4–5, 7. –Habermas/Luhmann, Theorie der Gesellschaft oder Sozialtechnologie, Frankfurt: Suhrkamp 1975, 101–141, 142–290. –Siebert, From Critical Theory, op. cit., chs. 6–12.

[580] J. Habermas (ed.), Stichworte zur "Geistigen Situation der Zeit", Frankfurt: Suhrkamp 1979, 115–133, 529–539, 754–781. –Arens, Kommunikative Handlungen, op. cit., parts II, IV. –Peukert, Wissenschaftstheorie, op. cit., parts II–III. –Siebert, From Critical Theory, op. cit., chs. 6–12.

[581] Acts 2:45–46; 4:32. –Arens, Kommunikative Handlungen, op. cit., 277–324, part IV. –Peukert, Wissenschaftstheorie, op. cit., part III. –Habermas, Theorie, op. cit., chs. 4–8. –Siebert, From Critical Theory, op. cit., chs. 6–12.

[582] Marx, Das Kapital, op. cit., 873–874. –GW 6, 297–300,

307-315. -GW 8, 202-209, 214-222. -Haag, Der Fortschritt, op. cit., ch. 5.

583Habermas, Theory and Praxis, op. cit., ch. 4; Zur Rekonstruktion, op. cit., chs. 1-4, 6; Theorie, op. cit., Bd 1, 489-547.

584Habermas, Zur Rekonstruktion, op. cit., ch. 4; Vorstudien, op. cit., 8, 11.

585SW 15, 24-36. -Habermas, Zur Rekonstruktion, op. cit., ch. 4. -Metz, "Dom Paulo," op. cit., 8-11. -Peukert, Wissenschaftstheorie, op. cit., part III. -Arens, Kommunikative Handlungen, op. cit., part IV.

586Habermas, Theorie, op. cit., ch. 8, esp. 575-583. -R.J. Siebert, Horkheimer's Critical Sociology of Religion, Washington DC: University Press of America 1979, chs. 1-7. -R. Hoffmann, "Probleme und Aufgaben der Bugerinitiativen" in FH 33/1 (January 1978), 21-29. -Adorno/Kogon, "Offenbarung," op. cit. -M. Gronemeyer, "Anders leben, anders lernen, anders leisten. Impressionen zu einem Kongress uber 'alternative leben'" in FH 35/8 (August 1980), 37-43. -Horster, "Kommunikative Ethik," op. cit., 35-41. -Rau, "Bruderlichkeit," op. cit., 31-131. -H.V. Gizycki, "Aufbruch aus dem Neandertal/Entwurfskizzen fur eine neue Kommune" in FH 16/12 (December 1971), 913-924.

587Habermas, Theorie, op. cit., ch. 8.

588Metz, The Emergent Church, op. cit., ch. 6, -Hucking, "Christliche Basisgruppen in Osteuropa," op. cit., 42-51. -D. Solle, "Theologie der Befreiung, Theologie des Widerstandes" in FH 34/4 (April 1979), 149-155. -W. Dirks, "Alternative Christliche Lebensformen" in FH Extra 1 (April 1978), 133-136. -Seiterich, "Basisgemeinden in der Bundes-Republik" op. cit., 35-42. -Gizycki, "Die Christliche Kommunitat," op. cit., 35-42. -Bohne, "Im Untergrund der Geschichte" op. cit., 20-31; "Die Entdeckung der Gerechtigkeit-Kirche und Repression in Brasilien" in FH 29/9 (September 1974), 647-655. -Torres, The Challenge, op. cit., parts I-III.

589Metz, Theology, op. cit., chs. 5-6; Glaube, op. cit.,

SS2-4. -Seiterich, "Basisgemeinden" op. cit., 35-42. -Hucking, "Chrislich Basisgruppen in Osteuropa" op. cit., 43-51. -Siebert, "Toward a Critical Catholicism," op. cit., 1-12, 144-162.

[590] Arens, "Steh auf," op. cit., 23-29; "Schon sprosst es, gewahrt ihr es nicht" in Dunde, Katholische und rebellisch, Hamburg: Rowohlt 1984, 101-119. -Brachel/Mette, Kommunikation und Solidaritat, op. cit.

[591] Arens, "Steh auf," op. cit., 23. -Seiterich, "Basisgemeinden," op. cit., 35-42. -Habermas, Zur Rekonstruktion, op. ct., ch. 4; Theorie, op. cit., ch. 8.

[592] Arens, "Steh auf," op. cit., 23. -Seiterich, "Basisgemeinden," op. cit., 35-42.

[593] Arens, "Steh auf," op. cit., 23-24. -Torres, The Challenge, op. cit., chs. 10, 15-16. -F. Peggeler, "Christliches Zeugnis in der sakularisierten Gesellschaft" in FH 31/5 (May 1976), 15-20. -Seiterich, "Basisgemeinden," op. cit., 35-42.

[594] Arens, Kommunikative Handlungen, op. cit., parts I, IV. -Peukert, Wissenschaftstheorie, op. cit., part III. -SW 7, 35. -SW 15, 292-293. -SW 16, 281-282, 295-308.

[595] Arens, "Steh auf," op. cit., 23-24. -Kierkegaard, Erbauliche Reden, op. cit., 225-355.

[596] Arens, "Steh auf," op. cit., 24.

[597] Torres, The Challenge, op. cit., parts II-IV. -De Santa Ana, Toward a Church of the Poor, op./cit, parts 1-3; Separation without Hope, op. cit., chs. 1, 4-5, 8-9. -A.J.van der Bent, God so Loves the World, Maryknoll: Orbis 1977, chs. 2, 4-7. -Duggan, Tanzania, op. cit., chs. 5, 9-11, 14. -R. Gibellini, Frontiers of Theology in Latin America, Maryknoll: Orbis 1979, chs. 1, 5-6, 8-9, 11-13.

[598] Arens, "Steh auf," op. cit., 24. -Metz, The Emergent Church, op. cit., chs. 1-5.

[599] Arens, "Steh auf," op. cit., 24. -SW 7, 35. -TW 12, 25-28.

600Arens, "Steh auf," op. cit., 24.

601Habermas, Theory and Praxis, op. cit., ch. 4; Theorie, op. cit., 575-583.

602Arens, "Steh auf," op. cit., 23-29. -Luke 1:52-53. -PB 171a, 46. -Hucking, "Christliche Basisgruppen," op. cit., 43-51. -Torres, The Challenge, op. cit., parts I-II. -P. Lupide, "Kann man die Bibel ubersetzen" in FH 28/11 (November 1973), 812-819.

603Seiterich, "Basisgemeinden," op. cit., 35-42. -Torres, The Challenge, op. cit., parts I, II. -J. Eagleson (ed.), Christians and Socialism, Maryknoll: Orbis 1975, parts I-VI. -Miranda, "Marx and the Bible," op. cit., chs. 2-3, 5. -Belo, A Materialist Reading, op. cit., parts III, IV. -A.F. McGovern, Marxism: An American Christian Perspective, Maryknoll: Orbis 1981, chs. 3-5. -Gonzales-Ruiz, The New Creation, op. cit., chs. 3-8.

604Hucking, "Christliche Basisgruppen," op. cit., 43-51. -Miranda, Marx against the Marxists, op. cit., chs. 8-10. -W. Sawatsky, Soviet Evangelicals Since World War II, Kitchener, Ontario: Herald Press 1981, chs. 1-16.

605Arens, "Steh auf," op. cit., 24-25.

606Acts 2:42-47, 4:32-35.

607Arens, "Steh auf," op. cit., 25. -Seiterich, "Basisgemeinden," op. cit., 40.

608Arens, "Steh auf," op. cit., 25. -Eagleson, Puebla and Beyond, op. cit., 11-13, 17, 24, 28, 289-292, parts I-III.

609Arens, "Steh auf," op. cit., 25. -Bohne, "Die Entdeckung der Gerechigkeit," op. cit., 647-655. -Camara, The Desert, op. cit., part III. -Comblin, The Church, op. cit., chs. 1, 4. -Hope, The Struggle, op. cit., chs. 1, 4. -Boff, Jesus, op. cit., chs. 4, 6-7, 9-13; 264-295. -Comblin, The Meaning of Mission, Maryknoll: Orbis 1977, parts II-III. -Siebert, "Ernesto Cardenal," op. cit., 241-251.

610PB 171a, 46. -SW 16, 247-308, esp. 286-302, 308-342.

[611]PB 33, 431–439.

[612]Arens, "Steh auf," op. cit., 25. –Seiterich, "Basisgemeinden," op. cit., 35–42. –Siebert, "Toward a Critical Catholicism," op. cit., 1–12, 144–162.

[613]Arens, "Steh auf," op. cit., 25. –Torres, The Challenge, op. cit., parts I–III. –Comblin, The Church, op. cit., chs. 2, 5–8. –Davies, Christians, op. cit., chs. 2–6. –Eagleson, Christians, op. cit., part IV. –Dobrin, Convictions, op. cit., chs. i, ix. –Erdozain, Archbishop Romero, op. cit., chs. 3–5. –Gibellini, Frontiers, op. cit., chs. 1–2, 4–13.

[614]R. Kuhnl, "Die Ursachen des eropischen Faschismus nach dem Ersten Weltkrieg" in FH 38/6 (June 1983), 32–40. –L. Lutkehaus, "Der 'Fall' Reinhold Schneider" in FH 38/6 (June 1978), 41–46. –D.S. Lutz, "Zur Rechtswidrigkeit atomarer Massenvernichtungs– mittel," FH 38/6 (June 1983), 15–22. –Hucking, "Christliche Basisgruppen," op. cit., 43–51. –Seiterich, "Basisgemeinden," op. cit., 35–42.

[615]Arens, "Steh auf," op. cit., 25. –Seiterich, "Basisgemeinden," op. cit., 41.

[616]Arens, "Steh auf," op. cit., 25. –Habermas, Theorie, op. cit., chs. 7–8, esp. 489–547.

[617]Arens, "Steh auf," op. cit., 25–26. –Seiterich, "Basisgemeinden" op. cit., 35–42.

[618]Arens, "Steh auf," op. cit., 26–27. –Seiterich, "Basisgemeinden," op. cit. –Hucking, "Christliche Basisgruppen," op. cit., 43–51.

[619]Arens, "Steh auf," op. cit., 27.

[620]Siebert, "Toward a Critical Catholicism," op. cit., 1–12, 144–162.

[621]Arens, "Steh auf," op. cit., 27.

[622]Ibid., 27–28. –Seiterich, "Basisgemeinden," op. cit., 35–42. –Hucking, "Christliche Basisgruppen," op. cit., 43–51. –Torres, The Challenge, op. cit., 4–7, 10–11, 15–16, 18,

20-22.

623Metz, The Emergent Church, op. cit., chs. 1, 2, 4.

624Ibid., chs. 5, 6, 7.

625Arens, "Steh auf," op. cit., 27. -Metz, Theology of the World, op. cit., parts I, III; The Emergent Church, op. cit., chs. 2, 4-7; Zeit der Orden, Freiburg: Herder 1978, chs. II-IV. -SW 15, 19-36. -SW 7, 261-286, 310-328.

626SW 7, 35-36.

627Arens, "Steh auf," op. cit., 28.

628Arens, Kommunikative Handlungen, op. cit., 265-324. -Peukert, Wissenschaftstheorie, op. cit., part III. -Habermas, Theorie, op. cit., ch. 9.

629Arens, "Steh auf," op. cit., 28. -Seiterich, "Basisgemeinden," op. cit., 35-42. -Hucking, "Christliche Basisgruppen," op. cit., 43-51.

630Arens, "Steh auf," op. cit., 28.

631Ibid., 28-29.

632Siebert, "Dialectical materialism," op. cit., 45-83, 113-123; "Three Alternative Futures," op. cit. -O.K. Flechtheim, "Drei Moglichkeiten unserer Zukunft" in FH 29/7 (July 1974), 481-488; "Humanismus und Menschenrechte" in FH 31/9 (September 1976), 27-34; "Die Menschheit am Wendepunkt" in FH 30/3 (March 1975), 39-45. -F. Vilmar, "O. K. Flechtheim und der Demokratische Sozialismus" in FH 34/3 (March 1979), 51-57. -C.F. von Weizsacker, "Entsetzen als Anfang eines Bewusstseins wandels" in C.F. von Weizsacker et al. (eds.), Bilder einer Welt von Morgen-Modelle bis 2009, Stuttgart: Horst Poller 1984. -Adorno, Soziologische Schriften, op. cit., I, chs. 1, 6, 10, 13-14, 16-21, 28, 30. -Nicolaus von Cusa, Wichtigste Schriften, op. cit., 538. -M.J. Farrell, "Elie Wiesel in Search for Questions," in National Catholic Reporter, December 14, 1984, 21/8, 9-11.

633Berrigan, Uncommon Prayer, op. cit., ix-xii.

[634]Nicolaus von Cusa, Wichtigste Schriften, op. cit., 504-527, esp. 524-527.

[635]Berrigan, Uncommon Prayer, op. cit., 35-37, 53-56.

[636]GW 4, 486-493, 497-500. -G.W.F. Hegel, The Phenomenology of Mind, New York: :Harper and Row 1967, 63-64. -Alighieri, Inferno, op. cit., Cantos I-IV; Purgatorio, op. cit., Cantos I-V; Paradisio, op. cit., Cantos I-IV.

[637]Berrigan, Uncommon Prayer, op. cit., 53-55.

[638]Luke 1:52-53.

[639]Apocalypse 21,5.

[640]Bishops Pastoral, Catholic Social Teaching, op. cit., 343-349, 358-362, 362-367. -Hinkelammert, "Die Politik," op. cit., 58-70; "Du sollst keinen Gott neben ihm haben," op. cit., 23-28.

[641]Berrigan, Uncommon Prayer, op. cit., 35-36.

[642]Nicolaus von Cusa, Wichtigste Schriften, op. cit., 462-470. -Quint, Meister Eckehart, op. cit., 213-217, 267-270, 303-309. -SW 16, 354-356, 282. -SW 2, 620. -SW 15, 292-293. -GW 4, 413-414, 417-464, 467-485, 486-493, 497-500. -Benjamin, Reflections, op. cit., 312-313; Illuminations, op. cit., 253-264. -Adorno, Minima Moralia, op. cit., 333-334; Negative Dialectics, op. cit., 368-372, 373-375, 390-392, 399-401, 402-404; Asthetische Theorie, op. cit., 69-70, 86-89, 173-175, 180-18, 190, esp. 200-202, 510-512, 523. -Kung, Ewiges Leben, op. cit., chs. 7-9; 283-296, esp. 63-64. -H. Kung, Art and the Question of Meaning, New York: Crossroad 1981, 59-60, 61-63, 64-69, 70-71; Menschwerdung, op. cit., 76, 68-70, 364-381, esp. 370-379; Existiert Gott?, op. cit., B, I-II; 740-743. -J. Moltmann, Das Reich Gottes und die Treue zur Erde, Wuppertal-Barmen: Jugenddienst 1963, 3-23; Der Gekreuzigte Gott, op. cit., chs. 5-8; Umkehr zur Zukunft, Munchen: Siebenstern 1970, 148-167, 168-187; Political Theology, Montgomery, Ala.: Huntington College 1970, 1-19. -Metz, Theology, op. cit., chs. 5-6; Glaube, op. cit., SS6-7, 10, 13. -Bloch, Denken, op. cit., 70-73, 78-89. -Dirks, Der Singende Stotterer, op. cit., 196; Politik der Christen, op. cit.,

24-27. -W. Dirks, "Verbundung fur eine andere Republik" in Die Neue Gesellschaft. Frankfurte Hefte 1, 32 (January 1985), 4-6. -B. Haunhorst, "Katholizismus und Sozialismus" in Die Neue Gesellschaft, op. cit., 80-86. -Kogon, "Angewandte Bergpredigt," op. cit., 23-24. -Hinkelammert, "Die Politik," op. cit., 58-70; "Du sollst keinen Gott neben ihm haben," op. cit., 23-28. -Solle, "Widerstand," op. cit., 70-86. -E. Cardenal, Zero Hour, New York: New Directions 1980, ix-xxii; The Psalms, op. cit., Psalms 1, 4-5, 7, 11, 15-16, 21, 25-93, 130, 136, 150. -Berrigan, Uncommon Prayer, op. cit., psalms 4, 10, 19, 2, 31-32, 46, 61, 63-64, 73-74, 76, 78, 82, 85, 88, 94, 102, 114-115, 119, 121, 123, 125-127, 130-131, 133, 139, 146. -Horkheimer/Adorno, Dialectic, op. cit., 29-31. -Horkheimer, Zur Kritik, op. cit., 311-312. -Adorno, Negative Dialectic, op. cit., 392-395, 395-398. -Haag, Der Fortschritt, op. cit., chs. 7-8. -Peukert, "Uber die Zukunft," op. cit., 136-137; "Fundamentaltheologie" in P. Eicher (ed.), Neues Handbuch Theologischer Grundbegriffe, Munchen 1984, 16-25. -Th. E. Quigley, "Oscaro Romero Remembered" in National Catholic Reporter 21/21 (March 22, 1985), 1, 7, 8. -E. McAlister, "Don't Let Reason Kid You - 'Whoever has faith in me will not die'" in National Catholic Reporter, op. cit., 17. S. Wiesenthal, Sunflower, New York: Schocken Books 1976, 3-5, 9-99, 125-129, 129-130, 169-170.

Index of Authors

A

Adorno, Th. W., v, 2, 4, 6, 9, 13, 15–17, 20, 21, 23, 25, 33,
44, 49, 51, 53, 58, 85, 92, 93, 94, 99, 105–107, 109,
115, 116, 123, 127–131, 156, 157, 158, 159, 160–168, 179,
180, 183, 194, 197, 198, 201, 213, 240, 244, 245, 252,
254, 255, 259, 262, 263, 264, 274–279, 281, 286, 292,
310, 313, 321, 327, 329, 330, 331, 332, 347, 349, 360,
361, 369, 371, 372, 373, 375, 382, 401, 402, 403, 404,
405, 406, 407, 410, 427, 442, 443, 447, 449, 451, 465,
466, 467, 469, 480, 483, 484
Aeschylos, 351.
Alighieri, Dante, 25, 62, 226.
Amery, 128, 158.
Anselm of Canterbury, 472.
Apel, K. O., 104, 115, 463, 464, 465, 469, 470, 473.
Aquinas, T., 226.
Arens, E., iii, 238, 336, 344, 382, 407, 411, 412, 413, 414,
415, 416, 417, 418, 420, 422, 423, 424, 425, 426, 427,
428, 429, 430, 431, 432, 433, 434, 439, 444, 446, 449,
455, 456, 459, 461, 462, 465, 466, 467, 469, 470, 471,
473, 474, 477, 487, 488, 489, 490, 491, 493, 495, 496.
Aristotle, 54.
Arns, P.E., 482.
Augustine, 226, 328.

B

Baader, F., 257, 305.
Bakunin, 127, 179, 361.
Baudelaire, 98, 329.
Baum, G., iv, 353, 354.
Becker, J., 438.
Bell, D., 273, 322.
Bellah, R., 390.
Benjamin, W., v, 5, 6, 12, 13, 15, 22, 23, 24, 85, 94, 102,
103, 107, 109, 116, 123, 124, 127, 128, 158, 164, 165,
194, 197, 202, 222, 238, 276, 310, 312, 317, 318, 319,
321, 322, 326, 327, 329, 331, 334, 355, 356, 357, 358,
359, 360, 361, 362, 363, 364, 370, 371, 372, 374, 375,
377, 391, 405, 406, 407, 411, 412, 427, 438, 443, 449,

I

J

Bibliography

A

Abendroth, W.
1969   Sozialgeschichte der Europaischen Arbeiterbewegung,
        Frankfurt: Suhrkamp Verlag.

Adorno, Th.W.
1952   "Die Soziologen und die Wirklichkeit" in Frankfurter
        Hefte, 7/8, August.
1955   "Wird Spengler rechtbehalten" in Frankfurter Hefte,
        10/12, December.
1960   "Uber Mahler" in Frankfurter Hefte, 15/9, September.
1963   Quasi Una Fantasia, Frankfurt: Suhrkamp.
1966   Kierkegaard, Frankfurt.
1966   Negative Dialektik, Neuwied: Luchterhand.
1966   Negative Dialektik, Frankfurt a.M.: Suhrkamp.
1968   Negative Dialektik, Frankfurt: Suhrkamp.
1969   Drei Studien zu Hegel, Frankfurt: Suhrkamp.
1970   Asthetische Theorie, Frankfurt: Suhrkamp.
1970   Uber Walter Benjamin, Frankfurt: Suhrkamp.
1970   "Parataxis. Zur Spaten Lyrik Holderlins," in
        J.Schmidt, Uber Holderlin, Frankfurt: Inselverlag.
1970   "Zur Regression des Horens" in Horkheimer, Zeitschrift
        fur Sozialforschung, Munchen: Kosel.
1972   Socialogische Schriften, Frankfurt: Suhrkamp.
1972   Versuch das 'Endspiel' zu Verstehen, Frankfurt:
        Suhrkamp.
1973   Philosophy of Modern Music, New York: Seabury.
1973   Zur Dialektik des Engagements, Frankfurt: Suhrkamp.
1973   Gesammelte Schriften, Frankfurt: Suhrkamp.
1973   Negative Dialectics, New York: Seabury.
1976   Introduction to the Sociology of Music, New York:
        Seabury.
1976   Prismen, Frankfurt: Suhrkamp.
1977   "Erziehung nach Auschwitz" in Adorno, Gesammelte
        Schriften, Vol. 10/2, Frankfurt.
1978   Letter of August 2, 1935 to Benjamin, in Benjamin,
        Briefe 2, Frankfurt: Suhrkamp.
1979   Soziologische Schriften, I, Frankfurt: Suhrkamp.
1980   Kritik, Kleine Schriften zur Gesellschaft, Frank-
        furt: Suhrkamp.
1980   Minima Moralia, Frankfurt: Suhrkamp.

1980   "Revidierte Psychoanalyse" in Gorlich, Der Stachel
        Freud, Frankfurt: Suhrkamp.
1980   Jargen der Eigentlichkeit, Frankfurt: Suhrkamp.
        "On Kierkegaard's Doctrine of Love" in Zeitschrift fur
        Sozialforschung, VIII.

Adorno, Th.W., and Kogon, E.
1958   "Offenbarung oder autonome Vernunft" in Frankfurter
        Hefte, 13/6, June.

Adorno, Th.W., et al.
1969   The Authoritarian Personality, New York: Norton.
1980   Der Postivismusstriet in der deutshen Soziologie,
        Darmstadt: Hermann Luchterhand.

Alighiere, D.
1961   The Purgatorio, New York: New American Library.
1967   The Paradisio, New York: New American Library.
1981   Inferno, Toronto: Bantam Books.

Altenhofen, H.
1984   "Hochdroben wo die Geister toben" in Diskus,
        H.6/1.34Jhrg.
1984   "Dialektischer Legalismus" in Diskus, H.6/1.34Jhrg.

Amery, J.
1968   "Das Jahrhundert ohne Gott" in Frankfurter Hefte,
        23/3, March.

Amstutz, J.
1972   Kirche der Volker, Freiburg: Herder.

Apel, K.O.
1980   "Die Komflikte unserer Zeit und das Erfordernis einer
        ethisch-politischen Grundorientierung" in K.O. Apel,
        et al. (eds) Praktische Philosophie/Ethik I,
        Frankfurt: Fischer Taschenbuch.

Apel, K.O., et al., (eds.)
1980   Praktische Philosophie/Ethik I, Frankfurt: Fischer
        Taschenbuch.

Arato, A., and Gebhardt, E.
1982   The Essential Frankfurt School Reader, New York:

Continuum.

Arens, E.
1980   "Steh   auf,   Du   Christ-Basisgemeinden   in   der
        Bundesrepublik" in F.Boll, et al. (eds.), Wird es denn
        uberhaupt gehen? Munchen: Kaiser.
1981   "Gleichnisse als kommunikative Handlungen Jesu" in
        Theologie und Philosophie, 56.
1981   "Toward a Theological theory of Communicative Action"
        in Media Development, 28, No. 4.
1982   Kommunikative   Handlungen.   Die   paradigmatische
        Bedeutung   der   Gleichnisse   Jesu   fur   eine
        Handlungstheorie, Dusseldorf: Patmos.
1984   "Schon sprosst es, gewahrt ihr es nicht?" in S.Dunde
        (ed.) Katholisch und Rebellisch, Hamburg: Rowohlt.
1984   "Glaube und Politik. Bekennen und Viderstehen" in
        Public Forum, June.

B
Baader, F.W.
1820   Werke, Vol. XV, Berlin.

Bach,   G.L.
1961   Economics, Englewood Cliffs, NJ: Prentice-Hall, Inc.

Bader, O.
1984   "Basisorganisationen in Bolivien" in Frankfurter
        Hefte, 39/5, May.

Bahr,   H.E.
1975   Religionsgesprache zur Gesellschaftlichen Rolle der
        Religion, Darmstadt: Luchtenhand.

Bakan, D.
1965   Sigmund Freud and the Jewish Mystical Tradition, New
        York: Schocken Books.

Balasuriya, T.
1979   The Eucharist and Human Liberation, Maryknoll, NY:
        Orbis.

Ballard, P. et al.
1983   Calendar of Martyrs, Dundas, Ontario.

Balov, P.
1985   "Stalingrad, The Turning Point of World War II," in
        Soviet Life, February.

Barth, K.
1952   Die Protestantische Theologie, im 19 Jahrhundert,
        Zurich.

Bascio, P.
1981   Building a Just Society, Maryknoll, NY: Orbis.

Baudelaire, Ch.
1936   Flowers of Evil, New York: Harper and Brothers,
        Publishers.
1951   My Heart Laid Bare, New York: Vanguard.

Baudrillaod, J.
1984   "Transparenz" in Diskus, H.6/1.34Jhrg.

Baum,   G.
1985   "Call   for Social Justice: A Comparison" in The
        Ecumenist, Vol. 23, No. 3, March–April.

Beal,   T.
1984   "The Trials of a Liberation Theology" in National
        Catholic Reporter, September 28.

Becker, J.
1975   "Das Gottesbild Jesu und die alteste Auslegung von
        Ostern" in Jesus Christus in Historie und Theologie,
        Tubinghen: Conzelmann.

Bellah, R.N.
1975   The Broken Covenant. American Civil Religion in time
        of Trial, New York: Seabury.
        "Civil Religion in America" in Daedalus, 96.

Belo,   F.
1981   A Materialist Reading of the Gospel of Mark,
        Maryknoll: Orbis.

Benjamin, W.
1950   Schriften I, Frankfurt.
1966   Ausgewahlte Schriften, Bd. II: Angelus Novus,

Frankfurt.
1975   Understanding Brecht, London: NLB.
1976   Illuminations, New York: Schocken Books.
1977   Gesammelte Schriften, Frankfurt: Suhrkamp.
1978   Reflections, New York: Harcourt, Brace, Jovanovich.
1978   "Th.W.Adorno on Benjamin" (Hornberg Letter of August
         2, 1935) in W. Benjamin, Briefe II, Frankfurt:
         Suhrkamp.
1978   Briefe I, Frankfurt: Suhrkamp.
1978   Briefe II, Frankfurt: Suhrkamp.
1978   Letter of December 24, 1936 to Horkheimer in Benjamin,
         Briefe II, Frankfurt a.M.: Suhrkamp Verlag.
1982   "Eduard Fuchs, Collector and Historian" in Aroto, The
         Essential Frankfurt School Reader, New York:
         Continuum.
1982   Das Passagen-Werk, I, II, Frankfurt: Suhrkamp.
1983   Das Passagen-Werk, Frankfurt: Suhrkamp.
1983   Letter of March 28, 1937 to Horkheimer, in Tiedemann,
         "Historical Materialism or Political Messianism?" in
         The Philosophical Forum, XV, 1-2, Fall-Winter.
1983   Passagen, Konvulut N.B1.8, in Tiedemann, "Historical
         Materialism or Political Messianism?" in The
         Philosophical Forum, XV, 1-2, Fall-Winter.
         "Eduard Fuchs, der Sammler und der Historiker" in
         Zeitschrift fur Sozialforschung, Vol. VII.
         Benjamin Nachlass im Deutschen Zentral Archiv Potsdam,
         Mappe 27, Blatt 39.

Benjamin, W. and Scholem, G.
1980   Briefwechnel 1933-1940, Frankfurt: Suhrkamp.

Benner, D. and Peukert, H.
1983   "Erziehung-Moralische" in D. Lenzen and K.
         Mollenhauser, Enzyklopadie Erziehungswissenschaft,
         Stuttgart: E. Klette.

Bentley, E. (ed.)
1961   Seven Plays by Bertholt Brecht, New York: Grove Press.

Berrigan, D.
1978   Uncommon Prayer, New York: Seabury.

Bettis, J.
1969   Phenomenology of Religion, New York.

Birner, J.
1972   "Max Horkheimer" in W.Schmidt (ed.), Die Religion der
        Religionskritik, Munich.

Bishop's Pastoral Letter
1984   "Bishop's Pastoral: Catholic Social Teaching and the
        US Economy" in Origins, November.

Blakney, R.B.
1941   Meister Eckhart, New York: Harper and Brothers.

Blanqui, A.
1955   Textes Choisis, Paris: Editions Sociales.
1968   Instruktionen   fur   den   Aufstand,   Frankfurt:
        Europaische.
1968   Instruktionen fur den Aufstand, Wien: Europa Verlag.
1971   Schriften   zur   Revolution,   Nationalokonomie   und
        Sozialkritik, Hamburg: Rowohlt.

Bloch, E.
1954   Das Prinzip der Hoffnung, Berlin.
1959   Das Prinzip Hoffnung, Frankfurt: Suhrkamp.
1962   Subjekt–Objekt. Erlauterungen zu Hegel, Frankfurt:
        Suhrkamp.
1970   A Philosophy of the Future, New York: Herder and
        Herder.
1970   Man On His Own, New York: Herder and Herder.
1971   On Karl Marx, New York: Herder and Herder.
1971   Geist der Utopie, Frankfurt: Suhrkamp.
1972   Atheism in Christianity, New York: Herder and Herder.
1975   Experimentum Mundi, Frankfurt: Suhrkamp.
1979   Tubinger   Einleitung   in   die   Philosophie, Frankfurt:
        Suhrkamp.
        Thomas Muntzer, Frankfurt: Suhrkamp.

Bloch, K., et al (eds.)
1978   Denken heisst Uberschreiten, Koln: Europaische Verlags
        Anstalt.

Bloch, M.
1974   "Symbols, Song, Dance and Features of Articulation" in
        Archive of European Sociology, 15.

Bloom, G.F., and Northrup, H.R.

1961   Economics   of   Labour   Relations,   Homewood,   Ill:
            R.D. Irwin.

Boehme, J.
1964   The Way of Christ, New York: McGraw-Hill.

Boff,   L.
1981   Jesus Christ Liberator, Maryknoll, NY: Orbis.

Bohne,   R.
1974   "Die   Entdeckung   der   Gerechtigkeit-Kirche   und
            Repression in Brasilien" in Frankfurter   Hefte,   29/9,
            September.
1977   "Kirche in Latein Amerika unter Druck" in Frankfurter
            Hefte, 32/2, February.
1980   "Der   Kirchen   Christus   und   das   Evangelium"   in
            Frankfurter Hefte, 35/5, May.
1983   "'Im Untergrund der Geschichte'-Die katholische Kirche
            und Lateinamerika" in Frankfurter Hefte, 38/4, April.

Boll,   F., et al (eds.)
1980   Wird es denn uberhaupt gehen? Munchen: Kaiser.

Boll,   H.
1984   "Vezogerter   Gluckwunsch"   in   Dunde,   Katholisch und
            Rebellisch, Hamburg: Rowohlt.

Bolman, F.W., Jr.
1967   Schelling. The Ages of the World, New York: AMS Press.

Bolz,   N.W.
1980   "Politische-Kritik-Zum Streit um Walter Benjamin," in
            Frankfurter Hefte, 35/8, August.

Bonhoeffer, D.
1967   Letters and Papers from Prison, New York: MacMillan.

Borenschen, S., et al.
1981   Gesprache mit Herbert Marcuse, Frankfurt: Suhrkamp.

Bornemann, E.
1981   "Sigmund Freud und sein Heimatland" in Frankfurter
            Hefte, 36/11, November.

Bosnjak, B.
1974   "Was bedeutet das Dilemma: Jesus-Marx?" in I.Fetscher
        and M.Machovec, Marxisten und die Sach Jesu, Munchen:
        Kaiser.

Bottomore, T.B.
1964   Karl Marx. Early Writings, New York: McGraw-Hill Book
        Co.

von   Brachel, H.V. and Mette, N.
1985   Solidaritat und Kommunikation, Freiburg: Exodus.

Brandt, G.
1981   "Ansichten kritischer Sozialforschung" in Leviathan,
        Sonderheft 4.

Brandt, H.J.
1983   "Benjamin und kein Ende/Zur Filmtheorie   Walter
        Benjamin" in Frankfurter Hefte, 38/3, March.

Brazill, W.J.
1970   The Young Hegelians, New Haven: Yale University Press.

Brecht, B.
1959   Selected Poems, New York: Grove.
1961   Seven Plays, New York: Grove Press.
        The City of Mahagonny.

Brenner, H.
1969   "Theodor W. Adorno als Sachwalter des Benjaminschen
        Werkes" in W.F.Schoeller, Die Neue Linke nach Adorno,
        Munchen: Kindler.

Breuer, St.
1982   "Die Depotenzierung der kritischen Theorie. Uber
        J.Habermas' Theorie des kommunikativen Handelns" in
        Leviathan, 1/82, March.
1982   "J.Habermas' Theorie des kommunikativen Handelns" in
        Leviathan, 1/82.

Bubner, R.
1982   "Rationalitat als Lebensform: Zu Jurgen Habermas'
        Theorie des Kommunikativen Handelns" in Merkur, 4/36.

Buhlmann, W.
1976   The Coming of the third Church, Maryknoll: Orbis.
1979   The Missions on Trial, Maryknoll: Orbis.

Butturini, P.
1984   "Seran Procesados Publicamente" in El Nueva Diario,
        August 6.
1984   "Vaticao Plantea Posicion en Teologia Liberacion" in
        El Sol, August 22.
1984   "El Vaticano interrogare a teologo brasileno
        porpredicar la liberacion y hacer criticas" in El
        Nueva Diario, September 3.
1984   "Obispos aceptan criticas a version tercermundista" in
        El Nueva Diario, September 5.

C
Camera, D.H.
1974   The Desert is Fertile, Maryknoll: Orbis.

Cardenal, E.
1971   The Psalms of Struggle and Liberation, New York:
        Herder and Herder.
1980   Zero Hour, New York: New Directions.

Carroll, J.
1984   Prince of Peace, Boston: Little Brown and Co.

Chamberlain, N.W.
1965   The Labor Sector, New York: McGraw-Hill Book Co.

Claussen, D. (ed.)
1981   Spuren der Refreiung-Herbert Marcuse, Darmstadt:
        Luchterhand.

Comblin, J.
1979   The Church and the National Security State, Maryknoll,
        NY: Orbis.

Costelloe, K.
1984   "Retort to Rome" in Time, July 9.
1984   "Pope Bans Marxism in Church" in Detroit Free Press,
        August 23.
1984   "Pope Criticizes any Class Ideas in theologies" in
        National Catholic Reporter, August 31.

Crittendon, D.
1984   "Test Results: Dealers and Dropouts," The Detroit
        News, Sunday, July 19.

Crossan, J.D.
1975   The Dark Interval: Towards a Theology of Story, Niles,
        Ill.

D
Dahlberg, J.
1980/81 Mensch und Gott, Frankfurt: Agnim Vertragsreihe.

Dahm,   K.W., Luhmann, N., et al.
1972   Religion-System and Socialization, Darmstadt:
        Luchterhand.

Davies, J.G.
1976   Christians, Politics and Violent Revolution,
        Maryknoll: Orbis.

Day,   M.R.
1984   "Vatican Tempering Theology Critiques in the Wake of
        Dialogue" in National Catholic Reporter, July 6.

de   Chardin, T.
1963   Die Zukunft des Menschen, Olten.
1965   The Phenomenon of Man, New York: Harper and Row.

de   Sade, M.
1964   Justine, New York: Lancer.

De   Santa Ana, J.
1978   Separation without Hope: The Church and the Poor
        During the Industrial Revolution and Colonial
        Expansion, Maryknoll: Orbis.
1979   Towards a Church of the Poor, Maryknoll, New York.
1984   "Catholic Social Teaching" in Origins, November 15.

Dirks, W.
1952   "Die 'Frankfurter Hefte' und der Marxismus" in
        Frankfurter Hefte, 7/4, April.
1964   "Bittere Frucht: Der Bolschewismus und die Geschichte
        des Christentums," Frankfurter Hefte, 19/8, August.

1969   "Am   Schnittpunkt"   in   Frankfurter   Hefte,   24/9,
         September.
1970   "Volkskirche im Ubergang Zur Krise der Kirche" (I and
         II) in Frankfurter Hefte, 25/2, February.
1972   Unser Vater und das Vater unser, Munich.
1972   "Ich   glaube   an Jesus Christus-Verstandnes-Versuch in
         drei Stucken" in Frankfurter Hefte, 27/12, December.
1973   "1903-1943-1973, Kogon zum Beburtstag," in Frankfurter
         Hefte, 28/2, February.
1973   "Ich glaube an Jesus Christus-Verstandigungsversuch in
         drei Stucken" in Frankfurter Hefte, 27/12, December.
1974   "Was meine ich, wenn ich sage: Ich glaube an den Sohn
         Gottes" in Frankfurter Hefte, 28/4, April.
1976   "Volkskirche im Ubergang-Zur Krise der Kirche (1)" in
         Frankfurter Hefte, 25/2, February.
1978   "Alternative Christliche Lebensformen" in Frankfurter
         Hefte, Extra 1, April.
1979   "Warum ich ein Christ bin-Erbe-Erfahrung-Theologie" in
         Frankfurter Hefte, 34/5, May.
1981   "Ehe/Eucharistie/Sozialismus"   in   Frankfurter   Hefte,
         36/4, April.
1981   "Ehe/Eucharistie/Sozialismus II" in Frankfurter Hefte,
         36/5, May.
1981   "Wehrlos vor dem Faschismus-Das Theorie-Defizit des
         Deutschen   Katholizismus   der   Weimarer   Zeit"   in
         Frankfurter Hefte, 36/12, December.
1983   Der Singende Stotterer, Munchen: Kosel.
1984   "Traditionen eines Linkskatholizismus" in   Dunde,
         Katholische und Rebellisch, Hamburg: Rowohlt.
1984   "Politik   der   Christen-Eine   estere   Antwort"   in
         Frankfurter Hefte, 39/9, September.
1984   "Die alten Normen und der neue Richtpunkt"   in
         Frankfurter Hefte, extra 6, November-December.
1985   "Verbundung fur eine andere Republik" in Die Neue
         Gesellschaft, Frankfurter Hefte, 1/32, January.

Dirks,   W., and Kogon, E.
1978   "Sonderheft Zukunft konkret" in Frankfurter Hefte,
         33/4, April.
1984   "An die Abonnenten, die Leser und die Freunde der FH"
         in Frankfurter Hefte, 39/10, October.

Dirks,   W., and Vilmar, F.
1956   "Messianischer Materialismus" in Frankfurter Hefte,

11/9, September.

Dobert, R.
1973   Systemtheorie und die Entwicklung Religioser Deutungssysteme, Frankfurt: Suhrkamp.

Dobert, R., and Habermas, J., etc. (eds.)
1977   Entwicklung des Ichs, Koln.

Dobrin, A., et al (eds.)
1981   Convictions, Maryknoll: Orbis.

Dubiel, H.
1983   "Die Aktualitat der Gesellschaftstheorie Adorno's" in Friedeburg, Adorno-Konferenz, Frankfurt: Suhrkamp.

Duggen, W.R. and Civille, J.R.
1976   Tanzania and Nyerere, Maryknoll, NY: Orbis.

Dunde, S. (ed.)
1984   Katholisch und rebellisch, Hamburg: Rowohlt.

Durkheim, E.
1947   The Elementary Forms of the Religious Life, Glencoe, Ill: Free Press.
1947   The Division of Labour in Society, Glencoe, Ill: Free Press.
1951   Suicide, New York: Free Press.
1954   The Elementary Forms of Religious Life, Glencoe, Ill: Free Press.
1958   Professional Ethics and Civil Morals, Glencoe: Free Press.
1958   Rules of Sociological Method, Glencoe: Free Press.
1959   Socialism and Saint Simon, London: Routledge and Kegan Paul, Ltd.

Durkheim, E., et al.
1963   Primitive Classification, Chicago: University of Chicago Press.

E
Eagleson, J. (ed.)
1975   Christians and Socialism, Maryknoll: Orbis.

Eagleson, J., and Scharper, P. (eds.)
1980   Puebla and Beyond, Maryknoll, NY: Orbis.

Ebertz, M.N.
1984   "Die Bergpredigt in der Jesus-und in der
        Friedensbewegung- eine Auseinandersetzung mit Franz
        Alt" in Frankfurter Hefte, 39/9, September.

Eckehart, M.
1979   Deutsche Predigten und Traktate, Munchen: Diogenes
        Taschenbuch.
1979   Deutsche Predigten und Traktate, Munchen: Carl Hanser.

Eicher, P.
1979   "Besinnung auf den Gott der Gottlosen heute" in
        Frankfurter Hefte, 34/9, September.

Erdozain, P.
1981   Archbishop Romero, Martyr of Salvador, Maryknoll, NY:
        Orbis.
1983   Calendar of Martyrs, Hamilton, Ontario.

Evans, D.D.
1963   The Logic of Self-Involvement, London.
1968   "Differences between Scientific and Religious
        Assertions" in I.G.Barbour, (ed.), Science and
        Religion, London.

F
Faber, R.
1983   "Atheistischer Liturgismus" in Frankfurter Hefte,
        38/10, October.

Farrell, M.J.
1984   "Elie Wiesel in Search for Questions" in National
        Catholic Reporter, December 14.

Fetscher, E. and Machovac, M. (eds.)
1974   Marxisten und die Sach Jesus, Munchen: Kaiser.

Feuerbach, F.
1967   The Essence of Christianity, New York.

Flay, C.

1982   "Eurocommunism and the Theory of Communication" in N. Fischer, et al. (eds.), Continuity and Change in Marxism, NJ: Humanities Press.

Flechtheim, O.K.

1962   "Die Radikale Alternative – 1 August 1914 – 1 September 1939– Wann zum letzten Mal?" in Frankfurter Hefte, 17/9, September.

1966   "Widerstand gegen Abrustung" in Frankfurter Hefte, 21/7, July.

1971   Futurologie. Der Kampt um die Zukunft, Koln: Verlag fur Wissenschaft und Politik.

1974   "Drei Moglichkeiten unserer Zukunft" in Frankfurter Hefte, 19/7, July.

1975   "Die Menschheit am Wendepunkt" in Frankfurter Hefte, 30/3, March.

1976   "Humanismus und Menschenrechte" in Frankfurter Hefte, 31/9, September.

1978   "Sonderheft Zukunft Konkret" in Frankfurter Hefte, 33/4, April.

1978   "Alternative Lebensformen" in Frankfurter Hefte, 33/4, April.

Freud, S.

1939   Moses and Monotheism, New York.

1947   Leonardo da Vinci, New York: Random House.

1957   The Psychopathy of Everyday Life, London: Hogarth Press.

1958   On Creativity and the Unconsciousness, New York: Harper and Row.

1961   Beyond the Pleasure Principle, New York: Liveright.

1962   Civilization and its Discontent, New York: Norton.

1964   The Future of an Illusion, Garden City, New York: Doubleday.

1968   Civilization, War and Death, London: The Hogarth Press.

1968   The Interpretation of Dreams, New York: Hearst.

Friedeburg, L. and Habermas, J.

1983   Adorno–Konferenz, Frankfurt: Suhrkamp.

Friesenhahn, G.J.

1984   "Max Horkheimer's Bedeutung fur die heutige Padagogik" in Frankfurter Hefte, 39/5, May.

Fromm,   E.
1932   "Die   psychoanalitische   Characterologie   und   ihre
        Bedeutung fur die Sozialpsychologie" in Zeitschrift
        fur Sozialforschung, Vol. 3.
1932   "Review of Otto Heller, Der Untergang des Judentums"
        in Zeitschrift fur Sozialforschung, Vol. 3.
1933   "Robert Briffault's Werk uber das Mutterrecht" in
        Zeitschrift fur Sozialforschung.
1934   "Die   sozialpsychologische   Bedeutung   der
        Mutterrechtstheorie"   in   Zeitschrift   fur
        Sozialforschung.
1935   "Die   gesellschaftliche   Bedingtheit   der
        psychoanalytischen Therapie"   in   Zeitschrift   fur
        Sozialforschung.
1936   "Sozialpsychologischer Teil" in Horkheimer, Studien
        uber Autoritat und Familie, Paris: Libraire Felix
        Alcan.
1937   "Zu   Gefuhl   der   Ohnmacht"   in   Zeitschrift fur
        Sozialforschung.
1939   "The Social Psychology of 'Will Therapy'"   in
        Psychiatry, May.
1951   "Uber   Methode   und   Aufgabe   einer   analytischen
        Sozialpsychologie" in Zeitschrift fur Sozialforschung,
        Vol. 1.
1955   The Sane Society, New York.
1956   The Art of Loving, New York: Harper and Row.
1960   Der modern Mensch und seine Zukunft, Frankfurt.
1960   Zen Buddhism and Psychoanalysis, New York: Harper and
        Row.
1962   Beyond the Chains of Illusion, New York.
1963   The Dogma of Christ, New York: Holt, Rinehart and
        Winston.
1964   The Heart of Man, New York.
1965   Escape from Freedom, New York: Hearst.
1966   Socialist Humanism, Garden City, NY: Doubleday.
1966   "The Application of Humanist Psychoanalysis to Marx's
        Theory" in E. Fromm 'ed.), Socialist Humanism, New
        York: Doubleday.
1966   You Shall Be As Gods, New York.
1966   Man for Himself, Greenwich, Conn: Fawcett.
1967   Marx's Concept of Man, New York: Frederick Ungar.
1968   The Revolution of Hope, New York: Harper and Row.
1970   Escape From Freedom, New York.
1971   Psychoanalysis   and   Religion,   New   Haven: Yale

University Press.
1973   The Anatomy of Human Destructiveness, New York: Holt, Rinehart and Winston.
1976   To Have or To Be, New York: Harper and Row Publishers.
1980   Arbeiter und Angestellte am Vorabend des Deutschen Reiches, Stuttgart: Deutsche Verlags Anstalt.

Fuchs, O. (ed.)
1984   Theologie und Handeln, Dusseldorf: Patmos.

Fuld,   W.
1979   Walter Benjamin zwischen den Stuhlen, Munchen: Hansler Verlag.

G
Gabriel, K.
1979   Analysen der Organisationsgesellschaft, Frankfurt.

Garaudy, R.
1966   From Anathema to Dialogue, New York: Herder and Herder.

Gardavsky, V.
1969   Gott ist nicht gans tot, Munchen.

Gerth, H.H. and Mills, C.W.
1958   From Max Weber: Essays in Sociology, New York: A Galaxy Book.

Gibellini, R.
1979   Frontiers of Theology in Latin America, Maryknoll: Orbis.

Gide,   A.
1932   La porte etroit, Paris: Mercure de France.
1960   The Return of the Prodigal Son, Vol. VII, No. 4, Logan, Utah: Utah State University Press.
1963   Le retour de l'enfant prodigue, Paris: Gallimard.

Gizycki, H.V.
1971   "Aufbruch aus dem Neandertal/Entwurfskizzen fur eine neue Kommune" in Frankfurter Hefte, 16/12, December.
1976   "Die Christliche Kommunitat der koinonia-Partner in

Georgia" in <u>Frankfurter Hefte</u>, 31/3, March.

Gmunder, P.
1979   "Entwicklung als Ziel der religiosen Erziehung" in
        Kat.Bl.104.

Gollwitzer, H.
1973   "E.Kogon und die 'Frankfurter Hefte'" in <u>Frankfurter
        Hefte</u>, 28/2, February.

Gonzales-Ruiz, J.M.
1976   <u>The New Creation: Marxist and Christian?</u>, Maryknoll:
        Orbis.

Gouldner, W.
1970   <u>The Coming Crisis in Western Sociology</u>, New York:
        Hearst.

Grathoff, R.
1978   <u>The Theory of Social Action</u>, Bloomington: Indiana
        University Press.

Greeley, A.M.
1984   <u>Lord of the Dance</u>, New York: Warner Books.

Gronemeyer, M.
1980   "Anders leben, anders lernen, anders leisten.
        Impressionen zu einem Kongress uber 'alternative
        leben'" in <u>Frankfurter Hefte</u>, 35/8, August.

Gutierrez, G.
1973   <u>A Theology of Liberation</u>, Maryknoll, New York: Orbis
        Press.

Gutmann, J. (ed.)
1936   <u>Schelling on Human Freedom</u>, Chicago: Open Court.

H
Haag,   K.H.
1971   <u>Zur Dialektik von Glauben and Wissen</u>, Frankfurt: Horst
        Heidenhoff.
1983   <u>Der Fortschritt in der Philosophie</u>, Frankfurt:
        Suhrkamp.

Habermas, J.

1957   "Konsumkritik eigens zum Konsumieren" in Frankfurter Hefte, 12/9, September.

1971   Theorie und Praxis, Frankfurt: Suhrkamp.

1972   "Bewusstmachende oder rettende Kritik—die Aktualitat Walter Benjamins" in S.Unseld (ed.), Zur Aktualitat Walter Benjamins, Frankfurt: Suhrkamp.

1973   Theory and Practice, Boston: Beacon Press.

1973   Zur Logik der Sozialwissenschaften, Frankfurt: Suhrkamp.

1973   Kultur und Kritik, Frankfurt: Suhrkamp.

1973   "Wahrheitstheorien" in H. Fahrenbach (ed.), Wirklichkit und Reflexion, Pfullingen.

1975   Legitimationsprobleme in Spatkapitalismus, Frankfurt.

1975   Legitimation Crisis, Boston: Beacon Press.

1976   Strukturwander der Offentlichkeit, Berlin: Hermann Luchterhand.

1976   Strukturwander der Offentlichkeit, Neuwied: Luchterhand.

1976   Zur Rekonstruktion des Historischen Materialismus, Frankfurt: Suhrkamp.

1976   Technik und Wissenschaft als Ideologie, Frankfurt: Suhrkamp.

1976   "Was heisst Universalpragmatik?" in K.O.Apel (ed.), Sprachpragmatik und Philosophie, Frankfurt.

1978   Politik, Kunst, Religion, Stuttgart: Philip Reclam.

1979   Stichworte zur 'Geistigen Situation der Zeit', Bd.I: Nation und Republik, Bd.II: Politik und Kultur, Frankfurt: Suhrkamp.

1980   "Konventionelle oder kommunikative Ethik?" in K.O.Apel, et al. (eds.) Praktische Philosophie/Ethik I, Frankfurt: Fischer Taschenbuch.

1980   "Legitimationasprobleme im modernen Staat" in K.O.Apel, et al. (eds.), Praktische Philosophie/Ethik I, Frankfurt: Fischer Taschenbuch.

1981   Theorie des Kommunikativen Handelns, Bd.I: Handlungsrationalitat und gesellschaftliche Rationalisierung; Bd.II: Zur Kritik der funktionalistischen Vernunft, Frankfurt: Suhrkamp.

1981   "Dialektik der Rationalisierung" im Gesprach mit A. Honneth, E. Knodler, et al., in Asthetik und Kommunikation, 45/46, October.

1982   "Tod in Jerusalem" in Merkur, XXXVI.Jhrg., H.4, November.

1982   "Die Kulturkritik der Neokonservativen in den USA und
        in der Bundesrepublik" in <u>Merkur</u>, XXXVI.Jhrg., H.11,
        November.
1983   <u>Moralbewusstsein und kommunikative Handeln</u>, Frankfurt:
        Suhrkamp.
1983   "Diskursethik-Notizen zu einem Begrundungsprogramm" in
        J. Habermas, <u>Moralbewusstsein und kommunikative
        Handeln</u>, Frankfurt: Suhrkamp.
1983   "Einleitung zum Vortrag von Martin Jay" in L. von
        Friedeburg and J. Habermas, <u>Adorno-Konferenz 1983</u>,
        Frankfurt: Suhrkamp.
1983   <u>Philosophical-Political Profiles</u>, Cambridge, Mass.:
        MIT Press.
1984   <u>Vorstudien und Erganzungen zur Theorie des
        Kommunikativen Handelns</u>, Frankfurt: Suhrkamp.

Habermas, J., and Henrich, D.
1974   <u>Zwei Reden</u>, Frankfurt: Suhrkamp.

Habermas, J., and Luhmann, N.
1971   <u>Theorie der Gesellschaft oder Sozialtechnologie</u>,
        Frankfurt: Suhrkamp.

Haecker, Th.
1935   <u>Der Christ und die Geschichte</u>, Leipzig: Hegner Verlag.
1975   <u>Tag und Nachtbucher</u>, Frankfurt: Suhrkamp.

Hansen, K.
1978   "Acht thesen zur Gemeinrede uber den Terrorismus in
        der Bundesrepublik" in <u>Frankfurter Hefte</u>, 33/5, May.

Haunhorst, B.
1985   "Katholizismus und Sozialismus" in <u>Die Neue
        Gesellschaft. Frankfurter Hefte</u>, 1/32, January.

Hegglethwait, P.
1984   "Document Wars about Liberation Theology" in <u>National
        Catholic Reporter</u>, September 7.

Heer,   F.
1963   "Die Zukunft des Kommunismus" in <u>Frankfurter Hefte</u>,
        18/1, January.
1967   "Hegel und die Jugend" in <u>Frankfurter Hefte</u>, 22/5,
        May.

Hegel,   G.W.F.
1902   Lectures on the Philosophy of History, London.
1902   Lectures on the Philosophy of Religion, I, trans. J.Sibree, London.
1942   Philosophy of Right, Oxford.
1948   On Christianity: Early Theological Writings, New York: Harper and Brothers.
1950   Asthetik, I, Frankfurt: Europaische Verlags Anstalt.
1952   Asthetik, II, Frankfurt: Europaische Verlags Anstalt.
1953   Asthetik, II, Frankfurt a.M.: Europaische Verlags Anstalt.
1955   Die Vernunft in der Geschichte, Hamburg: Felix Meiner.
1955   Lectures on the History of Philosophy, Vol. 3, trans., E.S. Haldane and F. Simson, New York.
1956   Enzyklopadie der Philosophischen Wissenschaften im Grundriss, Stuttgart: Friedrich Frommann.
1959   Vermischte Schriften aus der Berliner Zeit, Stuttgart: Frommann.
1959   Enzyklopadie der Philosophischen Wissenschaften, 1830, Hamburg: Felix Meiner.
1961   Vorlesungen uber die Philosophie der Geschichte, Stuttgart: Frommann.
1963   Wissenschaft der Logik, Hamburg: Felix Meiner.
1964   Grundlinien der Philosophie des Rechts, Stuttgard-Bad Cannstatt: Friedrich Frommann.
1964   Wissenschaft der Logik, II, Stuttgart-Bad Cannstatt: Friedrich Frommann.
1964   Phanomenologie des Geistes, Stuttgart-Bad Cannstatt: Friedrich Frommann.
1965   Vorlesungen uber die Geschichte der Philosophie, I, II, III, Stuttgart-Bad Cannstatt: Friedrich Frommann.
1965   Vorlesungen uber die Philosophie der Religion, I, II, III, Stuttgart-Bad Cannstatt: Friedrich Frommann.
1965   System der Philosophie, Stuttgart-Bad Cannstatt: Friedrich Frommann.
1965   Wissenschaft der Logik, Stuttgart-Bad Cannstatt: Friedrich Frommann.
1967   The Phenomenology of Mind, New York: Harper and Row.
1968   Jenaer Kritische Schriften, Hamburg: Felix Meiner.
1969   Vorlesungen uber die Philosophie der Religion, I, Frankfurt: Suhrkamp.
1969   Science of Logic, New York: Humanities Press.
1969   Wissenschaft der Logik, Frankfurt: Suhrkamp.
1970   Phanomenologie des Geistes, Frankfurt: Suhrkamp.

1970   Jenaer Schriften 1801-1807, Frankfurt: Suhrkamp.
1970   Nurnberger und Heidelberger Schriften 1808-1817, Frankfurt: Suhrkamp.
1970   Grundlinien der Philosophie des Rechtes, Frankfurt: Suhrkamp.
1970   Enzyklopdie der philosophischen Wissenschaften III, Frankfurt: Suhrkamp.
1970   Vorlesungen uber die Asthetik II, Frankfurt: Suhrkamp.
1970   Vorlesungen uber die Philosophie der Geschichte, Frankfurt: Suhrkamp.
1971   Fruhe Schriften, Frankfurt: Suhrkamp.
1971   Vorlesunge uber die Geschichte der Philosophie, II, III, Frankfurt: Suhrkamp.
1971   Vorlesungen uber die Philosophie der Religion, Frankfurt: Suhrkamp.
1971   Jenaer Systementwurfe II, Hamburg: Felix Meiner.
1976   Jenaer Systementwurfe I, Hamburg: Felix Meiner.
1976   Jenaer Systementwurfe III, Hamburg: Felix Meiner.
1978   Wissenchaft der Logik, I, II, Hamburg: Felix Meiner.
1980   Phanomenologie des Geistes, Hamburg: Felix Meiner.
1981   Wissenschaft der Logik, Hamburg: Felix Meiner.
1984   Three Essays, 1793-1795, Notre Dame, Ind.: University of Notre Dame Press.

Heidegger, M.
1959   Introduction to Metaphysics, New Haven: Yale University Press.

Herbort, H.J.
1984   "Zuruck zu den Ursprungen" in Die Zeit, Nr.52, December 21.

Hesse, R.
1982   "Ethik in der Weltkrise" in Frankfurter Hefte, 37/12, December.

Hinkelammert, F.J.
1982   "Du solst keinen Gott neben ihm haben" in Entwicklungspolitik, 2/3.
        "Die Politik des 'totalen Marktes'" in Barmen.

Hoffmann, R.
1978   "Probleme und Aufgaben der Bugerinitiativen" in Frankfurter Hefte, 33/1, January.

Hoflich, E.
1969   "Karl Marx fur die Kirche" in Frankfurter Hefte,
        24/11, November.
1969   "Heilsverkundigung als politishe Gewissensbildung" in
        Frankfurter Hefte, 24/12, December.

von   Holbach, P.H.D.
1770   Systeme de la nature ou des lois du monde physique et
        du monde morale, Paris.

Holderlin, F.
1965   Hyperion, New York.

Hope,   M. and Young, J.
1977   The Struggle for Humanity, Maryknoll, NY: Orbis.
1981   The South African Churches in a Revolutionary
        Situation, Maryknoll, NY: Orbis.

Horkheimer, M.
1936   Studien uber Autoritat und Familie, Paris: Libraire
        Felix Alcan.
1967   Zur Kritik der instrumentellen Vernunft, Frankfurt:
        Fischer.
1967   Werk und Wirken Paul Tillichs, Stuttgart.
1967   Critique of Instrumental Reason, New York: Seabury.
1970   Die Sehnsucht nach dem ganz Anderen, Hamburg: Furche.
1972   Gesellschaft im Ubergang, Frankfurt: Athenaeum
        Fischer.
1972   Critical Theory, New York: Seabury.
1972   Sozialphilosophische Studien, Frankfurt: Fischer.
1973   "Foreword" in M.Jay, The Dialectical Imagination,
        Boston.
1974   Notizen 1950 bis 1969 und Dammerung, Frankfurt: S.
        Fischer.
1974   Eclipse of Reason, New York: Seabury.
1974   Aus der Pubertat: Novellen und Tagebuchblatter,
        Munich.
1980   "E.Simmel und die Freudsche Philosophie" in B.Gorlich,
        etc. (eds.), Der Stachel Freud, Frankfurt: Suhrkamp.
1981   Gesellschaft im Ubergang, Frankfurt: Fischer
        Taschenbuch.
1981   Sozialphilosophische Studien, Frankfurt: Fischer
        Taschenbuch.
1981   Traditionelle und kritische Theorie, Frankfurt:

Fischer Taschenbuch.
"Der neueste Angriff auf die Metaphysik" in Zeitschrift fur Sozialforschung, VI.

1983   Letter of March 16, 1937 to Benjamin, in Tiedemann, "Historical Materialism or Political Messianism?" in The Philosophical Forum, XV, 1-2, Fall-Winter.
"Zu Theodor Haecker: Der Christ und die Geschichte" in Zeitschrift fur Sozialforschung, V.

Horkheimer, M. and Adorno, Th.W.
1952   "Vorurteil und Charakter" in Frankfurter Hefte, 7/4, April.
1969   Die Dialektik der Aufklarung, Frankfurt: S.Fischer.
1972   The Dialectics of Enlightenment, New York: Herder and Herder.

Horster, D.
1980   "Ein marxistischer Kant" in Frankfurter Hefte, 35/2, February.
1982   "Kommunikative Ethik" in Frankfurter Hefte, 37/10, October.

Hucking, H.H.
1977   "Christliche Basisgruppen in Ost-Europa" in Frankfurter Hefte, 34/2, February.

Hung, T.
1984   "Reagan defends Covert Aid to Nicaraguan Rebels" in Kalamazoo Gazette, January 24.

Huxley, A.
1946   Brave New World, New York: Harper and Row.

Hyslop, L. and F.E., Jr.
1952   Baudelaire on Poe, State College, PA: Bald Eagle Press.

I
Ibsen, H.
1960   When We Dead Awaken and Three Other Plays, Garden City, New York: Doubleday and Co.

J
Jamme, Ch., and Schneider, H. (eds.)

1984   Mythologie der Vernunft, Frankfurt: Suhrkamp.

Jay,   M.
1973   The Dialectical Imagination: A History of the Frankfurt School and the Institute of Social Research 1923-1950, Boston: Little, Brown and Co.

Johanson, D.C., and Edey, M.A.
1982   Lucy. The Beginnings of Humankind, New York: Warner Books.

John   Paul II
1979   Redemptor Hominis, Washington DC: United States Catholic Conference, March 4.
1982   Laborem Exercens in G.Baum, The Priority of Labor, New York: Paulist Press.

Jones,   E.
1953   The Life and Work of S. Freud, New York: Basic Books.

Jouhy,   E.
1982   "Bedarf der Zustand des Elends der Losung oder der Erlosung" in Frankfurter Hefte, 37/12, December.

von   Juchen, A.
1981   Die kampfgleichnisse Jesu, Munchen.

Jungel,   E.
1978   Gott als Geheimnis der Welt, Tubingen.

K
Kant,   I.
1929   Critique of Pure Reason, New York: St. Martin's Press.
1949   Critique of Practical Reason, Chicago: University of Chicago Press.
1953   Zum Ewigen Frieden, Stuttgart: Reclam.
1957   The Critique of Judgment, Oxford: Clarendon Press.
1965   Critique of Pure Reason, New York: St. Martin's Press.
1968   Kritik der Urteilskraft, Frankfurt: Suhrkamp.
1974   Die Religion inerhalb der Grenzen der blossen Vernunft, Stuttgart: Reclam.
1974   Kritik der Urteilskraft, Frankfurt: Suhrkamp.
1975   Wo ist Aufklarung?, Gottingen: Vandenhoek and Ruprecht.

1981   Schriften zur Anthropologie, Geschichtsphilosophie,
        Politik und Padagogik, Frankfurt: Suhrkamp.
1983   Anthropologie in Pragmatischer Hinsicht, Stuttgart:
        Reclam.

Kasper, W.
1969   "Politische   Utopie   und christliche   Hoffnung" in
        Frankfurter Hefte, 24/8, August.
1974   Jesus der Christus, Mainz.

Kaufmann, W.
1968   Basic Writings of Nietzsche, New York: Modern Library.

Kavanaugh, J.
1984   Laughing Down Lonely Canyons, San Francisco: Harper
        and Row Pub.

Kelley, G.A.
1972   "Hegel's America" in Philosophy and Public Affairs,
        Vol. II, No. 1.

Kessler,
1970   Die theologische Bedeutung des Todes Jesu, Dusseldorf.

Kierkegaard, S.
1973   Fear and Trembling and the Sickness Unto Death,
        Princeton, NJ.
1983   Erbauliche Reden, in Verschiedenem Geist, Gutersloh:
        Gutersloher Verlagshaus.

Kimmerle, H.
1969   "Thesen zur philosophischen Interpretation des
        Christentums" in Frankfurter Hefte, 24/1, January.

Kogon, E.
1965   SS Staat, Frankfurt.
1967   "Revolution and Theologie: Das Neue in unserem
        Zeitalter. Ein Symposium" in Frankfurter Hefte, 22/9,
        September.
1968   "Weltpolitische Zukunftsperspektiven" in Frankfurter
        Hefte, 23/3, March.
1973   "Rudolf Augsteins 'Herausforderung'" in Frankfurter
        Hefte, 28/4, April.
1984   "Angewemdte   Bergpredigt-Eine   Eriederung"   in

Frankfurter Hefte, 39/9, September.

Kogon,   E., and Dirks, W.
1946   "An unsere Leser" in Frankfurter Hefte, 1/4, April.

Kohlberg, L.
1974   Zur Kognitiven Entwicklung des Kindes, Frankfurt.
1977   "Eine neuinterpretation der Zusammenhange zwischen der
         Moralentwicklung   in   der   Kindheit   und   im
         Erwachsenenalter"   in
         R.Dobert/J.Habermas/G.Nunner-Winkler   (eds.),   Die
         Entwicklung des Ich's, Koln.
1981   The Meaning and Measurement of Moral Development,
         Worcester, Mass.: Clark University Press.

Kracauer, S.
1977   Das Ornament der Masse, Frankfurt: Suhrkamp.

Krikorian, H. (ed.)
1944   Naturalism and Human Spirit, New York.

Kuhnl,   R.
1983   "Die Ursachen des Europaischan Faschismus nach dem
         Ersten Weltkrieg" in Frankfurter Hefte, 38/6, June.

Kung,   H.
1970   Menschwerdung Gottes, Freiburg: Herder.
1974   Christ Sein, Munchen: Piper.
1976   On Being Christian, Garden City, NY: Doubleday.
1978   Existiert Gott?, Munchen: Piper.
1981   Art and the Question of Meaning, New York: Crossroad.
         Ewiges Leben,

Kung,   H., et al. (eds.)
1984   Christentum und Weltreligionen, Munchen: R. Piper.

L
Ladriere, J.
1972   Rede der Wissenschaft-Wort des Glaubes, Munchen.

Lamb,   M.
1978   History, Method and Theology: A Dialectical Comparison
         of Wilhelm Dilthey's Critique of Historical Reason and
         Bernhard   Lonergans   Meta-Methodology,   Missoula,

Montana: Scholars Press.
1983   "The Dialectics of a Theory and Praxis within Paradigm
        Analysis,"   Milwaukee: Marquette   University.
        (unpublished)
1983   "Roman   Catholic   Liberation   Theology   and   a
        Transformative Understanding of Political Life,"
        Chicago. (unpublished)
1983   "Liberation Theology and Social Justice," Milwaukee:
        Marquette University. (unpublished)

Langer, I.
1976   "Wallfahrt in Europa.I.Rom: Wo is Christus?" in
        Frankfurter Hefte, 31/8, August.
1983   "Jesus und das Kreuz" in Frankfurter Hefte, 38/2,
        February.

Laski, H.J.
1967   The Communist Manifesto of Marx and Engles, New York:
        Seabury Press.

Lehmann, K. and Raffelt, A. (eds.)
1979   Rechenschaft des Glaubens, Freiburg: Herder.

Levy-Bruhl, L.
1922   La Mentalite Primitive, Paris.

Lichtheim, G.
1971   From Marx to Hegel, New York.

Lindbeck, G.A.
1978   "Theologische Methode und Wissenschaftstheorie" in
        Theological Review, 74.

Lischer, R.
1979   Marx and Teilhard, Maryknoll: Orbis.

Louber, J.
1966   Haushaltung Gottes, Bietigheim, Wurltemberg.

Lowenthal, L.
1957   Literature and the Image of Man, Boston: Beacon Press.
1975   Notizen zur Literatur Soziologie, Stuttgart: Ferdinand
        Enke.
1980   Mitmachen wollte ich nie. Ein autobiographisches

Gesprach mit Helmut Dubiel, Frankfurt: Suhrkamp.

Lowenthal, L. and Guterman, N.
1970   Prophets of Deceit, Palo Alto, CA: Pacific Books.

Lowith, K.
1962   Die   Hegelsche   Linke,   Stuttgart-Bad   Cannstatt:
        Frommann.

Lubbe,   H.
1962   Die   Hegelsche   Rechte,   Stuttgart-Bad   Cannstatt:
        Frommann.
1975   Sakularisierung, Munchen: Karl Alber.
1983   Staat   und   Zivilreligion. Ein   Aspekt   politischer
        Legitimitat, Wolfenbuttel: Lessing Akademie.

Luhmann, N.
1977   Zweck   begriff   und   Systemrationalitat,   Frankfurt:
        Suhrkamp.
1977   Funktion der Religion, Frankfurt: Suhrkamp.

Lukacs,   G.
1948   Essays uber Realismus, Berlin: Autbau.
1950   Deutsche   Literatur   im   Zeit alter des Imperialismus,
        Berlin: Autbau.
1954   Der junge Hegel, Berlin.
1964   Deutsche Literatur   in   zwei   Jahrhunderten,   Neuwied:
        Hermann Luchterhand.
1967   Schriften   zur   Ideologie   und   Politik,   Neuwied:
        Luchterhand.
1974   Die Zerstorung   der   Vernunft,   Darmstadt: Hermann
        Luchterhand.
1975   History   and   Class   Consciousness, Cambridge, MA: MIT
        Press.

Lupide,   P.
1973   "Kann man die Bibel ubersetzen" in Frankfurter   Hefte,
        28/11, November.

Lutkehaus, L.
1983   "Der   'Fall' Reinhold Schneider" in Frankfurter Hefte,
        38/6, June.

Lutz,   D.S.

1983   "Zur   Rechtswidrigkeit   atomarer
        Massenvernichtungsmittel" in Frankfurter Hefte, 38/6,
        June.

Lys,   G.R.
1979   "Ein Gott fur die Verdammten?-Zine   Anfrage"   in
        Frankfurter Hefte, 34/11, November.

M
Mallet, R.
1952   The Correspondence 1899-1926 between P. Claudel and A.
        Gide, New York: Pantheon.

Mann,   Th.
1957   Death in Venice, Harmondsworth, Middlesex.
1961   Buddenbrooks, New York: Vintage Books.
1969   The Magic Mountain, New York: Vintage Books.

Mansilla, H.C.F.
1973   "Zwei Begegnungen in der Schweiz" in Frankfurter
        Hefte, 28/4, April.

Marcuse, H.
1956   "A Reply to Erich Fromm" in Dissent, 3:1, Winter.
1960   Reason and Revolution, Boston: Beacon Press.
1962   Eros and Civilization, New York: Vintage Books.
1966   One Dimensional Man, Boston: Beacon Press.
1968   "On Hedonism" in Negations, Boston.
1969   Negations, Boston: Beacon Press.
1970   Five Lectures, Boston: Beacon Press.
1970   "Marxism and the New Humanity: An Unfinished
        Revolution" in J.C. Raines and Th. Dean (eds.),
        Marxism and Radical Religion, Philadelphia: Temple
        University Press.
1972   Counter Revolution and Revolt, Boston.
1972   Studies in Critical Philosophy, Boston: Beacon Press.
1977   The Aesthetic Dimension, Boston: Beacon Press.
1980   "Gesellschaftliche und psychologische Repression. Die
        politische Aktualitat Freud's" in Gorlich, Der Stachel
        Freud, Frankfurt: Suhrkamp.
1980   Kultur und Gesellschaft, Frankfurt: Suhrkamp.

Marquard, O.
1973   Schwierigkeiten mit der Geschichtsphilosophie,

Frankfurt: Suhrkamp.

Martingdale, D.
1964   "The Roles of Humanism and Scientism in the Evolution
        of Sociology" in G.K. Zollschan and W. Hirsch,
        Explorations in Social Change, Boston:
        Houghton-Mifflin.

Marx,   K.
1949   "Contribution to Hegel's Philosophy of Right" in R.
        Niebuhr, Marx and Engels on Religion, New York.
1951   Zur Kritik der politischen Okonomie, Berlin.
1953   Die Fruhschriften, Stuttgart: Alfred Kroner.
1953   "Die deutsche Ideologie" in Die Fruhschriften,
        Stuttgart: Alfred Kroner.
1953   Grundrisse der Kritik der politischen Okonomie,
        Berlin.
1961   Das Kapital, Berlin: Dietz.
1970   "Contribution to the Critique of Hegel's 'Philosophy
        of Right'" in Critique of Hegel's 'Philosophy of
        Right', Joseph O'Malley (ed.), Cambridge.
1972   The 18th Brumaire of Louis Bonaparte, New York:
        International Publishers.

Marx,   K., and Engels, F.
1963   Werke, Vol. 29, Bern.

Maximoff, P. (ed.)
1964   The Political Philosophy of Bakunin, Scientific
        Anarchism, London: Free Press of Glencoe.

Mayer, H.
1970   "Nach denken uber Adorno" in Frankfurter Hefte, 25/4,
        April.

McAlister,
1985   "Don't Let Reason Kid You—'Whoever has faith in me
        will not die'" in National Catholic Reporter, 21/21,
        March.

McCarthy, Th.
1978   The Critical Theory of Jurgen Habermas, Cambridge, MA:
        MIT Press.

McConnel, C.R.
1963   Economics: Principles, Problems, and Policies, New
        York: McGraw-Hill Book Co.

McGovern, A.F.
1981   Marxism: An American Christian Perspective, Maryknoll:
        Orbis.

McLoughlin, W.G. and Bellah, R.N. (eds.)
1968   Religion in America, Boston: Houghton-Mifflin.

Mead,   G.H.
1938   Philosophy of Art, Chicago: University of Chicago
        Press.
1959   Philosophy of the Present, LaSalle: Open Court
        Publishing Co.
1959   The Philosophy of Art, Chicago: University of Chicago
        Press.
1962   Mind, Self and Society, Chicago: University of Chicago
        Press.
1964   On Social Psychology, Chicago: University of Chicago
        Press.
1967   Mind, Self and Society, Chicago: University of Chicago
        Press.
1970   "Scientific Method and Individual Thinker" in J. Dewey
        and others, Creative Intelligence, New York: Octagon
        Books.

Mehlhausen, J.
1983   "'Freiheit des Glaubens'-Luther's Lehre von der
        Freiheit als Erbe und Auftrag" in Frankfurter Hefte,
        38/7, July.

Menzler, E.
1984   "Kritische Theorie? Obscone Kolportage im
        Rosselsprung-ein Dokument Verstorter Ratlosigkeit" in
        Diskus, H.6/1.34 Jhrg.

Merkel, R.
1982   "Zwergenaufstand. Kontroverse um Habermas," June.

Meschkowski, H.
1970   "Nach dem Tode Gottes" in Frankfurter Hefte, 25/10,
        October.

Metz,   J.B.
1968   Zur Theologie der Welt, Munchen: Chr.Kaiser.
1970   Kirche im Prozess der Aufklarung, Munchen: Kaiser.
1973   Theology of the World, New York: Seabury.
1973   Keine Apologie des Erzahlens, Conc D.9.
1978   Zeit der Orden, Freiburg: Herder.
1978   Glaube in Geschichte und Gesellschaft, Mainz: Matthias
        Grunewald.
1978   Glaube in Geschichte und Gegenwart, Mainz: Matthias
        Grunewald.
1979   "Produktive Ungleichzeitigkeit" in J. Habermas (ed.),
        Stichworte zur 'Geistigen Situation der Zeit', Bd.2,
        Politik und Kultur, Frankfurt.
1980   Jenseits burgerlicher Religion, Mainz: Grunewald.
1980   Jenseits burgerlicher Religion, Munchen: Chr. Kaiser
        Verlag.
1980   "Nicaragua-Eindrucke aus einem Biblischen Land" in
        Boll, Wird es denn uberhaupt gehen?, Munchen: Kaiser.
1981   The Emergent Church, New York: Crossroad.
        "Dom Paulo Evaristo Arms-Kardinal der Dritten Welt,"
        (unpublished).

Miranda, J.
1974   Marx and the Bible, Maryknoll: Orbis.
1980   Marx against the Marxists, Maryknoll: Orbis.

Moltmann, J.
1963   Das Reich Gottes und die Treue zur Erde,
        Wuppertal-Barmen: Jugenddienst.
1968   Perspektives der Theologie, Munchen.
1969   Theologie der Hoffnung, Munchen.
1970   Umkehr zur Zukunft, Munchen: Siebenstein Taschenbuch.
1970   Political Theology, Montgomery, Ala.: Huntington
        College.
1973   Der gekruzigte Gott, Munchen: Chr. Kaiser.
1979   "Theologie heute" in J. Habermas (ed.), Stichworte zur
        'Geistigen Situation der Zeit', Bd. 2, Politik und
        Kultur, Frankfurt.
        "Theology of Mystical Experience" in Scottish Journal
        of Theology, Vol. 32.

Morgan, Th.
1956   Introduction to Economics, Englewood Cliffs, NJ:
        Prentice-Hall, Inc.

Muller, W.
1977   Geld und Geist. Zur Entstehungsegeschichte von
        Identitatsbewusstsein und Rationalitat siet der
        Antike, Frankfurt/New York.

N
Nicolaus von Cusa
1966   Wichtigste Schriften, Freiburg im Breisgau: Minerva.
1979   On God as Not-other, Minneapolis; University of
        Minnesota Press.

Niebuhr, R.
1964   K.Marx and F.Engels on Religion, New York.

Nietzsche, F.
1968   "The Madman" in Kaufmann, Basic Writings of Nietzsche,
        New York: Modern Library.

Nohl, H. (ed.)
1907   Theologische Jugendschriften, Tubingen.

Nolte, J.
1975   "Nichts fur sich allein-Zur Frage einer
        'metadogmatischen' Vertretbarkeit des Christlichen" in
        Frankfurter Hefte, 30/6, June.

O
O'Dea, T.F.
1966   The Sociology of Religion, Englewood Cliffs, NJ:
        Prentice- Hall.

O'Malley, W.J.
1979   The Voice of Blood: Five Christian Martyrs of Our
        Time, Maryknoll: Orbis.

Orwell, G.
1949   1984, New York: Harcourt, Brace and World.

Oser, F., et al.
1979   "Zur Entwicklung kognitiver Stufen des religiosen
        Urteils" in G.Staches, et al. (eds.), Sozialisation,
        Identitatsfindung, Glaubenserfahrung, Zurich.
1980   "Stufen des religosen Urteils" in Weg zum Menschen,
        32.

Osthathios, G.M.
1980   Theology of a Classless Society, Maryknoll, NY: Orbis.

P
Paleczny, B., and Cote, M. (eds.)
1983   Becoming Followers of Jesus, Burlington, Ontario:
        Trinity.

Pannenberg, W.
1973   Wissenschaftstheorie und Theologie, Frankfurt.

Paoli, A.
1973   Freedom to be Free, Maryknoll, NY: Orbis.

Parsons, T.
1951   The Social System, Glencoe: Free Press.
1954   Essays in Sociological Theory, Glencoe: Free Press.
1964   Essays in Sociological Theory, Glencoe: Free Press.
1964   The Social System, Glencoe: Free Press.
1967   Societies: Evolutionary and Commparative Perspective,
        Englewood Cliffs, NJ: Prentice-Hall.
1969   The System of Modern Societies, Englewood Cliffs, NJ:
        Prentice-Hall.
1973   "Durkheim on Religion Revisited. Another Look at the
        elementary Form of the Religious Life" in Ch.Y.
        Glock/Ph.E. Hammond (eds.), Beyond the Classics:
        Essays in the Scientific Studies of Religions, New
        York.
1977   Social Systems and the Evolution of Action Theory, New
        York.
1978   Action Theory and the Human Condition, New York.

Parsons, T., and Platt, T.M.
1973   The American University, Cambridge, Mass.

Pascal, B.
1941   Pensees. the Provincial Letters, New York: Modern
        Library.

Pasternak, B.
1958   Doctor Zhivago, New York: The Modern Library.

Paul   VI
1968   "Humanae Vitae," Huntington, Ind: Our Sunday Visitor,

Inc.

Peggeler, F.
1976   "Christliches   Zeugnes   in   der   sakularisierten
        Gesellschaft" in Frankfurter Hefte, 31/5, May.

Perez-Esclarin, A.
1974   Atheism and Liberation, Maryknoll, NY: Orbis.

Peukert, H.
1976   Wissenschaftstheorie-Handlungstheorie-Fundamentale
        Theologie, Dusseldorf: Patmos.
1978   Wissenschaftstheorie, Handlungstheorie, Fundamentale
        Theologie, Frankfurt: Suhrkamp.
1981   "Was ist eine praktische Wissenschaft?" in Christen
        fur den Sozialismus, Munster (ed.), Zur Rettung des
        Feuers. Solidaritatsschrift fur Kuno Fussel, Munster.
1981   "Padagogik-Ethik-Politik.   Normative   Implikationen
        padagogischer   Interaktion"   in   Zeitschrift   fur
        Padagogik, Beiheft 17, Weinheim.
1982   "Kontingenzerfahrung   und   Identitatsfindung.
        Bemerkungen zu einer Theorie der Religion und zur
        Analytik religios dimensionierter Lernprozesse" in
        J.Blank and G. Hasenhuttle, Erfahrung, Glaube und
        Moral, Dusseldorf: Patmos.
1983   "Erziehung, Moralische" in D. Lenzen, Enzyklopadie
        Erziehungswissenschaft, Stuttgart: Ernst Klett.
1983   "Kritische Theorie und Padagogik" in Zeitschrift fur
        Padagogik, 30 Jhrg., No. 2.
1984   Science, Action and Fundamental Theology: Toward a
        Theology of Communicative Action, Cambridge, Mass.:
        MIT Press.
1984   "Uber die Zukunft von Bildung" in Frankfurter Hefte,
        extra G, November-December.
1984   "Fundamentaltheologie" in P. Eicher (ed.), Neues
        Handbuch Theologischer Grundbegriffe, Munich.

Piaget, J.
1930   The Child's Conception of Physical Causality, London.
1973   Die Entwicklung des Erkennens, Stuttgart.
1973   Das moralische Urteil beim Kinds, Frankfurt.
1974   Abriss der genetischen Epistemeologie, Olton.

Piberhofer, B.

1984   "Zur   Entegnung   der   politischen   Subjekte   und   der
        Politisierung der unpolitischen Indindren" in Discus,
        H.6/1, 34 Jhrg.

Picconi, P., et al. (eds.)
1984   "Religion and Politics" in Telos, March.

Pickering, W.s.F. (ed.)
1975   Durkheim   on   Religion,   London: Routledge   and
        Kegan-Paul.

Pierce, C.S.
1976   Schriften zum Pragmatismus, Frankfurt: Suhrkamp.

Plato,
1977   "Politaia" in G. Eigler, Plato's Werke, Darmstadt.

Poggeler, O.
1984   "Das Menschenwerk des Staats" in Jamme, Mythologie der
        Vernunft, Frankfurt: Suhrkamp.
1984   "Hegel der Verfasser des altesten Systemprogrammes des
        deutschen   Idealismus"   in   Mythologie   der   Vernunft,
        Frankfurt: Suhrkamp.

Popper, K.
1958   Die Offene Gesellschft und ihre Feinde, Bern.
1972   The Open Society and Its Enemies: Objective Knowledge,
        Oxford: Clarendon Press.

Post, W.
1971   Kritische   Theorie und metaphysischer Pessimismus. Zum
        Spatwerk Max Horkheimers, Munich.

Pottker, H.
1983   "G.Dux: 'Die Logik der Weltbilder, Sinnstrukturen im
        Wandl der Geschichte" in Frankfurter Hefte, 38/5, May.

Q
Quigley, Th.E.
1985   "Oscar   Romero   Remembered"   in   National   Catholic
        Reporter, 21/21, March.

Quint, H. (tr.)
1977   Meister Eckhart, Deutsche Predigten und Schriften,

Munich.

R
Rahner, K.
1976   Grundkurs des Glaubens, Freiburg: Herder.

Rau,   J.
1982   "Bruderlichkeit" in Frankfurter Hefte, 37/7, July.

Rammstedt, O.
1975   "Die Instrumentalisierung der Baader-Meinhof Gruppe"
        in Frankfurter Hefte, 30/3, March.

Reding, M.
1961   "Utopie, Phantasie, Prophetie-Prinzip der Hoffnung im
        Marxismus" in Frankfurter Hefte, 16/1, January.

Reich, W.
1970   The Mass Psychology of Fascism, New York: Farrar,
        Straus and Groux.

Reiser, M.
1960   "Paul Tillich's Philosophische Theologie" in
        Frankfurter Hefte, 15/11, November.

Rendtorff, T.
1975   Gesellschaft ohne Religion?, Munchen.

Ricouer, P.
1974   "Stellung und Funktion der Metaphor in der biblishen
        Sprache" in P. Ricouer/E. Jungel, Metaphor. Zur
        Hermeneutik religioser Sprache, Munchen.

Ritter, J.
1972   Hegel und die Franzosische Revolution, Frankfurt:
        Suhrkamp.

Rohring, K.
1972   "Theodor W. Adorno" in W. Schmidt, Die Religion der
        Religionskritik, Munchen: Claudius Verlag.

Rohrmoser, G.
1969   Das Elend der kritischen Theorie, Freiburg.
1970   Das Elend der kritischen Theorie, Theodor W.

<u>Adorno-Herbert Marcuse-Jurgen Habermas</u>, Frankfurt.

Rombach, H.
1979   "Die   Religionsphanomenologie"   in   <u>Theologie   und
        Philosophie</u>, 48.

Rosario, E.
1984   "Hay   una   alianza   Juan   Pablo   II-Reagan   para   atacar   a
        fondo   a   los   liberacionistas"   in   <u>El   Nuevo   Diario</u>,   July
        26.
1984   "Un   pequeno   inconveniente   para   los   que   enfrentan   la
        Teologia   de   la   liberacion: los   pobres"   in   <u>El   Nuevo
        Diario</u>, July 27.
1984   "La   identificacion con el Tercer Mundo, ha illevado a
        muchos christianos a cuestionar a EE,UU" in <u>El   Nuevo
        Diaro</u>, July 30.

S
Santa   Ana, D.J.
1981   <u>Toward   a   Church   of   the   Poor</u>, Maryknoll, New York:
        Orbis Books.

Sawatsky, W.
1981   <u>Soviet Evangelicals Since   World   War   II</u>,   Kitchener,
        Ontario: Herald Press.

Schaefer, E.
1956   <u>Meister   Eckhart's   Traktat   von   Abgeschiedenheit
        Untersuchungund Textausgabe</u>, Bonn.

Scharpff, F.W. (ed.)
1966   <u>Nicolaus von Cusa</u>, Frankfurt a.M.: Minerva G.M.B.H.

Scheible, H.
1978   "Max Horkheimer's fruhe und spate   Aufzeichnungen"   in
        <u>Frankfurter Hefte</u>, 33/6, June.

Scheller, W.
1983   "Die   Neue   Rechte"   in   <u>Frankfurter   Hefte</u>,   38/10,
        October.
1984   "'Das   grave   Frankreich'   Pans   und   die   Tage   der
        Kollaboration" in <u>Frankfurter Hefte</u>, 39/5, May.

Schelling, F.W.J.

1980   The   Unconditional   in   Human   Knowledge,   London:
        Associated University Press.

Schleiermacher, F.
1969   "Religion as a Faculty" in J. Bettis, Phenomenology of
        Religion, New York.

Schmetter, J.
        "Der Katholikentag von unten" in Dunde, Katholisch
        "Durch die alternative Katholische Szene" in Dunde,
        Katholisch.

Schmidt, A.
1970   "'Die Zeitschrift fur Sozialforschung.' Geschichte und
        Gegenwartige   Bedeutung"   in   M. Horkheimer   (ed.),
        Zeitschrift   fur   Sozialforschung,   Munchen: Kosel
        Verlag.
1979   Zur   Idee   der   Kritischen   Theorie,   Frankfurt   a.M.:
        Ullstein.
1979   Drei   Studien   uber   Materialismus,   Frankfurt   a.M.:
        Ullstein.

Schmidt, W.
1972   Die Religion der Religionskritik, Munchen: Claudius.

Schmiede, R., and Schudlich, E.
1981   "Die Entwicklung von Zeitokonomie und Lohnsystem im
        deutschen Kapitalismus" in Leviathan, 4.

Schnadelbach, H.
1983   "Dialektik als Vernunftkritik. Zur Konstruktion des
        Rationalen bei Adorno" in L.von Friedenburg and J.
        Habermas (eds.), Adorno-Konferenz 1983, Frankfurt
        a.M.: Suhrkamp.

Schoch, B.
1984   "Zwischen Identifikation und Solideritat-Anmerkungen
        zum   schrieng   gewerdenen   Internationalismus"   in
        Frankfurter Hefte, 39/5, May.

Schoeller, W.F. (ed.)
1969   Die Neue Linke nach Adorno, Munchen: Kindler.

Scholz, F.

1982   Freiheit als Indiffernz. Alteuropaische Probleme in der Systemtheorie von N. Luhmann, Frankfurt.

Schopenhauer, A.
1946   Aphorismen zur Lebensweisheit, Munchen: Wilhelm Goldmann.
1958   The World as Will and Representation, New York: Dover Publications, Vol. I, II.
1982   Aphorismen zur Lebensweisheit, Frankfurt a.M.: Wilhelm Goldman Verlag.

Schrey, H.H.
1969   "Atheismus im Christentum" in Frankfurter Hefte, 24/6, June.

Schultz, A., and Parsons, T.
1977   Zur Theorie des sozialen Handelns, Frankfurt: Suhrkamp.

Scott, J. P.
1978   "Critical Social Theory: An Introduction and Critique" in The British Journal of Sociology, XXIX/1, March.

Seghers, F.
1984   "Kirche und Streik" in Public Forum, 14/15, July.

Seiferich, T.
1982   "Basis Gemeinden in der Bundesrepublik" in Frankfurter Hefte, 32/2, February.

Sholem, G.
1961   Major Trends in Jewish Mysticism, New York: Schocken Books.
1965   Jewish Gnosticism, Merkabah Mysticism and Talmudic Tradition, New York: Jewish Theological Seminary of America.
1965   On the Kabbalah and its Symbolism, New York: Schocken Books.
1967   Die judische Mystik in ihren Hauptstromungen, Frankfurt: Suhrkamp.
1971   The Messianic Idea in Judaism, New York: Schocken Books.
1973   Zur Kabbala und ihrer Symbolik, Frankfurt: Suhrkamp.
1973   Sabbatai Sevi: The Mystical Messiah, New York:

Schocken Books.
1973   Judaica III, Frankfurt: Suhrkamp.
1976   On Jews and Judaism in Crisis, New York: Schocken
        Books.
1977   Uber einige Grundbegriffe des Judentums, Frankfurt:
        Suhrkamp.
1977   "Der Nihilismus als Religioses Phenomen" in
        Eranos-Jahrbuch, Leiden.
1980   Walter Benjamin-Gershom Scholem Briefwechsel,
        1933-1940, Frankfurt: Suhrkamp.

Sibora, H.
1984   "Nicaragua. Dem Fischfang folgte ein Pilgergang" in
        Public Forum, 14/15, July.
1984   "Katholikentag in Munchen" in Public Forum, 14/15,
        July.

Siebert, R.J.
1971   "Political Theology" in The Ecumenist, July-August.
1973   "Hegel and Theology" in The Ecumenist,,
        November-December.
1974   "Hegel's Political Theology: Liberation" in The
        Ecumenist, XIII/3, March-April.
1976   "The Christian Revolution: Liberation and
        Transcendence" in The Ecumenist, January-February.
1976   "Max Horkheimer, Theology and Positivism I" in The
        Ecumenist, January-February.
1977   "Horkheimer's Sociology of Religion" in Telos, No. 30,
        Winter.
1978   "Communication Without Domination" in Concilium, #131.
1978   "Fromm's Theory of Religion" in Telos, 34.
1978   "Peukert's New Critical Theology I" in The Ecumenist,
        Vol. 16, No. 4, May-June.
1978   "Peukert's New Critical Theology II" in The Ecumenist,
        Vol. 16, No. 5, July-August.
1979   Horkheimer's Critical Sociology of Religion: The
        Relative and the Transcendent, Washington, DC:
        University Press of America.
1979   "Horkheimer's Sociology of Religion" in Telos.
1979   Hegel's Concept of Marriage and Family: The Origin of
        Subjective Freedom, Washington, DC: University Press
        of America.
1979   Hegel's Philosophy of History: Theological, Humanistic
        and Scientific Elements, Washington, DC: University

716   Bibliography

Press of America.
1979   From Critical Theory of Society to Theology of
        Communicative Praxis, Washington, DC: University Press
        of America.
1980   "Parsons' Analytical Theory of Religion as Ultimate
        Reality" in G.Baum, Sociology and Human Destiny, New
        York: Seabury Press.
1982   "Religion and Psychoanalysis: European Situation" in
        Concilium, New York: Seabury Press, June, #156.
1982   "Creation and Redemption" in The Ecumenist, Vol. 2,
        No. 5, July–August.
1983   "Dialectical Materialism and Political Theology: Two
        Views of the Future" in World Futures, 19/142.
1983   "Toward a Critical Catholicism I: Kung and Metz" in
        Anglican Theological Review, Vol. LXV, January.
1983   "Toward a Critical Catholicism II" in Anglican
        Theological Review, Vol. LXV, April.
1983   "From Historical Materialism to Political Theology:
        Two Futures" in World Futures, October.
1983   "Open Letter" in Proceedings of the Heraclitean
        Society, Kalamazoo: Western Michigan University.
1984   "Adorno's Theory of Religion" in Telos, 58, January.
1984   "Ideology and Utopia" in Telos, 58, January.
1984   "The Frankfurt School: Enlightenment and Sexuality" in
        Concilium, June.
1985   "Hegel on the Dialectic of Civil Society" in
        Procedures of the International Hegel Society, Athens.
1985   "Three Alternative Futures. Hegel's Philosophy of
        Society and History" in World Futures, January.
1985   Reason, Freedom and Change: A Christian Encounter with
        Hegel, Washington DC: University Press of America.
1985   "From Historical Materialism to Theology of
        Communicative Praxis" in Proceedings of the
        International Hegel Society, Athens.
        "The Dialectic of European and American Civil Society:
        Alternative Futures" (unpublished).
        "Jacob and Jesus: Recent Marxist Readings of the
        Bible."
        "Ernesto Cardenal and the Nicaraguan Revolution: From
        Theological Theory to Revolutionary Praxis" in Cross
        Currents, Vol. XXX, No. 3.

Simonov, K.
1985   "Stalingrad Diary" in Soviet Life, February.

Skinner, B.F.
1962   Walden Two, New York: The MacMillan Co.
1980   Beyond Freedom and Dignity, Toronto: Bantam Books.

Skinner, Q.
1982   "Habermas' Reformation" in New York Review of Books,
        October 7.

Slosser, B.
1984   Reagan - Inside Out, Waco, Texas: Worldbooks.

Sohn-Rethel, A.
1973   Geistige und Korperlich Arbeit, Frankfurt   a.M.:
        Suhrkamp Verlag.
1975   Okonomie und Klassenstruktur des deutschen Faschismus,
        Frankfurt a.M.: Suhrkamp Verlag.

Solle, D.
1977   Revolutionary Patience, Maryknoll, New York: Orbis
        Press.
1979   "Du sollst keine anderen Jeans haben neben mir" in J.
        Habermas (ed.), Stichworte zur 'Geistigen Situation
        der Zeit', 2 Bd. Politik und Kultur, Frankfurt:
1979   "Theologie der Befreiung, Theologie des Widerstandes"
        in Frankfurter Hefte, 34/4, April.
        "Widerstand ist der wahre Name des Glaubens" in
        Barmen.

Sollner, A.
1982   "Jurgen Habermas und die kritische Theorie des
        gegenwartigen   Rechtsstaates-Versuch   einer
        wissenschaftsgeschichtlichen Einordnung" in Leviathan,
        1/82, March.

Sorokin, P.A.
1941   The Crisis of Our Age, New York: E.P.Dutton and Co.

Spaemann, R.
1977   Zur Kritik der politischen Utopie, Stuttgart.
1978   "Die Herausforderung" in Mut Zur Erziehung. Beitrage
        zu   einem   Forum   vom   9-10   Januar   im
        Wissenschaftszentrum, Bonn, Bad Godesberg, Stuttgart.

Stehl, J.

1972   "Carl Schmitt un die Politische Theologie" in
        Frankfurter Hefte, 17/6, June.

Stepelevich, L.S.
1983   The Young Hegelians, New York: Cambridge University
        Press.

Stoop, P.
1984   "Niederlande: Aufgeschoben ist nicht aufgehoben" in
        Public Forum, 14/15, July.

Storres, J., and Eagleson, J. (eds.)
1980   The Challenge of Basic Christian Communities,
        Maryknoll: Orbis.

Strauss, A. (ed.)
1956   The Social Psychology of Georg Herbert Mead, Chicago:
        The University of Chicago Press.

Strindbergg, A.
1962   The Chamber Plays, New York: E.P.Dutton and Co., Inc.

Strolz, W.
1976   "Sinnfragen nichtglaubender Juden" in Frankfurter
        Hefte, 31/3, March.
1978   "Denker der gepruften Hoffnung-Ernst Bloch und Paul
        Schutz" in Frankfurter Hefte, 35/3, March.
1981   "Dem grosseren Gott entgegen-Gedanken zur universalen
        okumene" in Frankfurter Hefte, 36/1, January.

T
Tenbruck, F.H.
1975   Das Werk Max Webers, KZSS 27.

Theunissen, M.
1983   "Negativitat bei Adorno" in Adorno Konferenz 1983,
        Frankfurt: Suhrkamp.

Thompson, D.R.
1984   "O Cristo o Marx: los dos, no" in La Mino Domingo,
        August 12.

Thompson, J.B., etc. (eds.)
1982   Habermas: Critical Debates, Cambridge, MA: The MIT

Press.

Tiedemann, R.
1983   "Historical Materialism or Political Messianism?" in
        The Philosophical Forum, XV, 1-2, Fall-Winter.

Tillich, P.
1959   Gesammelte Werke, Vol. I, Stuttgart.
1963   Systematic Theology, Chicago: University of Chicago
        Press.
1963   Morality and Beyond, New York.
1966   On the Boundary Line, New York: Charles Scribner's
        Sons.
1974   Mysticism and Guilt-Consciousness in Schelling's
        Philosophical Development, Lewisburg: Penn.: Bucknell
        University Press.
1974   The Construction of the History of Religion in
        Schelling's Positive Philosophy, Lewisburg: Bucknell
        University Press.
1977   The Socialist Decision, New York: Harper and Row.

Torres, S., and Eagleson, J. (eds.)
1980   The Challenge of Basic Christian Communities,
        Maryknoll, New York: Orbis Press.

Turcke, Ch.
1982   "Der Todestrieb der gegenwartigen Gesellschaft und
        seine theologische Verklarung" in Frankfurter Hefte,
        37/7, July.

Turner, R.
1978   The Eye of the Needle, Maryknoll, New York: Orbis
        Press.

U
Unseld, S., (ed.)
1972   Zur Aktualitat Walter Benjamin's, Frankfurt: Suhrkamp.

V
van   der Bent, A.J.
1977   God So Loves the World, Maryknoll, New York: Orbis
        Press.

Vilmar, F.

1979   "Ossip Flechtheim und der demokratische Sozialismus"
        in Frankfurter Hefte, 34/3, March.

Voegelin, E.
1975   From Enlightenment to Revolution, Durham, NC: Duke
        University Press.

W
Walf, K.
1980   "Eine   andere   Kirche-Hollands   Katholiken   auf
        Konfliktkurs" in Frankfurter Hefte, 35/7, July.

Waterman, A.
1984   "Theology and the Redistribution of Wealth" in The
        Ecumenist, Vol. 22, No. 5, July-August.

Weber, M.
1951   The Religion of China, Confucianismus und Taoismus,
        Glencoe, Ill: The Free Press.
1952   Ancient Judaism, Glencoe, Ill: Free Press.
1953   The Religion of India, Glencoe, Ill: Free Press.
1958   The Religion of India, Glencoe, Ill: Free Press.
1959   The Protestant Ethic and the Spirit of Capitalism, New
        York: Charles Scribner's Sons.
1959   Ancient Judaism, Glencoe, Ill: The Free Press.
1963   Gesammelte Aufsatze zur Religionssoziologie, Tubingen:
        J.C.B. Mohr, Vol. I.
1964   The Sociology of Religion, Boston: Beacon Press.
1966   Gesammelte   Aufsatze   zur   Religionssoziologie,
        Hinduismus und Buddhismus, Tubingen: J.C.B. Mohr, Vol.
        II.
1966   Gesammelte   Aufsatze   zur   Religionssoziologie, Das
        antike Judentum, Tubingen: J.C.B. Mohr, Vol. III.
1968   "Wissenschaft als Befur" in J. Winkelmann, M.Weber's
        Gesammelte Aufsatze zur Wissenschaftslehre, Tubingen.
1972   Sociology of Religion, Boston: Beacon Press.

Wehling, P.
1984   "Ars der neuesten Wissenschaft. Ein Stinnungsbild" in
        Diskus, H.6/1.34 Jhrg. 10-13.

Weill, K., and Brecht, B.
1970   Rise and Fall of the City of Mahagonny, New York:
        Columbia.

Weiner, H.
1969   9 1/2 Mystics. The Kabbalah Today, New York: Collier
        Books.

von   Weizsacker, C.F., et al. (eds.)
1984   Bilder einer Welt von Morgen-Model bis 2009,
         Stuttgart: Horst Poller.

Weymann-Weyhe, W.
1983   "Die rede von Gott-Der Konflikt zwishen Wort un
        Erfahrung" in Frankfurter Hefte, 38/4, April.

Wiedemann, F.
1969   G.W.F. Hegel, Hamburg: Rowohlt.

Wiesel, E.
1974   The Madness of God, New York: Random House.
1978   Four Hasidic Masters, Notre Dame: University of Notre
        Dame Press.
1979   The Trial of God, New York: Random House.

Wiesenthal, S.
1976   The Sunflower, New York: Schocken Books.

Wiggerhaus, R.
1980   "Die Zeitschrift fur Sozialforschung-eine Auforderrung
        zur aktualitats-bezogener Gesellschaftstheorie" in
        Frankfurter Hefte, 35/10, October.

Willig, H.
1980   "Die Aktualitat der kritischen Theorie Adorno's" in
        Frankfurter Hefte, 35/3, March.

Wolff   and Gumnior, H.
1970   "Aut das Andere hoffen" in Spiegel, January, 6.

Wollin, R.
1982   Walter Benjamin, An Aesthetic of Redemption, New York:
        Columbia University Press.

Woodward, N., Lantigua, J., and Nagorski, A.
1984   "Nicaragua's Rebel Jesuits" in Newsweek, September 3.

Z
Zhukov, G.
1985   "Victory 1941-1945" in Soviet Life, January.

Zimmerman, H.D.
1981   "San Gimiguano-Zu Aufsatzen von Reinhold Schneider und
       Walter Benjamin" in Frankfurter Hefte, 36/11,
       November.

Zollschan, G.K., and Hirsch, W.
1963   Explorations in Social Change, Boston:
       Houghton-Mifflin Company.